The Canadian Spelling Program 2.1

Teacher's Edition

Ruth Scott
Sharon Siamon

gage EDUCATIONAL PUBLISHING COMPANY
A DIVISION OF CANADA PUBLISHING CORPORATION
Vancouver · Calgary · Toronto · London · Halifax

Acknowledgments:

The authors and publisher gratefully acknowledge the contributions of the following educators to The Canadian Spelling Program 2.1:

Carol Chandler
Halifax, Nova Scotia

Jean Hoeft
Calgary, Alberta

Bill Nimigon
North York, Ontario

Every reasonable effort has been made to trace ownership of copyrighted material. Information that would enable the publisher to correct any reference or credit in future editions would be appreciated.

Barton, 201. ©1991 Bob Barton "A Storyteller Comments: Highway Relish" in David Booth, ed. *Spelling Links* (Pembroke Publishers Limited); Bear, et al., 33, 75, 173. WORDS THEIR WAY by Bear/Templeton/Invernizzi/ Johnston, ©1996. Reprinted by permission of Prentice-Hall Inc., Upper Saddle River, NJ; Bradley, 82. "Organizing Sound and Letter Patterns for Spelling" by Lynette Bradley, in *Handbook of Spelling: Theory, Process and Intervention* by Gordon Brown and Nick Ellis. Copyright ©1994 John Wiley & Sons, Ltd. Reprinted by permission of John Wiley & Sons, Ltd.; Calkins, 47. *The Art of Teaching Writing* by Lucy Calkins. Copyright ©1986 Heinemann; Cunningham, 26, 117, 208. Paticia Cunningham, *Classrooms That Work: They Can All Read & Write*. Copyright ©1994. Reprinted by permission of Addison-Wesley Educational Publishers Inc.; Funk, 236. Wilfred Funk, *Word Origins: An Explanation and History of Words and Language* (New York: Wings Book/Random House Value Publishing Inc.). ©1950 by Wilfred Funk, Inc.; Gentry/Gillet, 152. *Teaching Kids to Spell* by Richard Gentry and Jean Wallace Gillet. Copyright ©1993 Heinemann; Henderson, 19, 103, 145, 250. Edmund Henderson, *Teaching Spelling*. Copyright ©1985 by Houghton Mifflin Company; Lederer, 159, 215. Reprinted with the permission of Pocket Books, a Division of Simon & Schuster from ADVENTURES OF A VERBIVORE by Richard Lederer. Copyright ©1994 by Richard Lederer; Lederer, 229. Reprinted with the permission of Pocket Books, a Division of Simon & Schuster from THE MIRACLE OF LANGUAGE by Richard Lederer. Copyright ©1991 by Richard Lederer; Lederer, 40. Reprinted with the permission of Pocket Books, a Division of Simon & Schuster from THE PLAY OF WORDS by Richard Lederer. Copyright ©1990 by Richard Lederer; Rosenbloom, 70. Used with permission of Sterling Publishing Co., Inc., 387 Park Ave. S., NY, NY 10016 from WORLD'S TOUGHEST TONGUE TWISTERS by Joseph Rosenbloom, ©1986 by Joseph Rosenbloom; Scott, 110, 131, 194; Tarasoff, 68, 89, 124. *Spelling Strategies You Can Teach* by Mary Tarasoff (Victoria, BC, Active Learning Institute Inc., 1990). Reprinted with permission; Templeton, 166. "Synthesis of Research on the Learning and Teaching of Spelling," by Shane Templeton in *Educational Leadership*, 43, 6 (March, 1986): 73, 78; Wilde, 61, 187, 243. *You Kan Red This: Spelling and Punctuation for Whole Language Classrooms, K-6* by Sandra Wilde. Copyright ©1992 Heinemann.

Cover Design: Gord Pronk, Pronk&Associates

Text Design: Christine Dandurand

Illustration: Christine Dandurand, Jane Whitney

ISBN 0-7715-**1583-9**

4 5 TRI 00 99

Written, printed, and bound in Canada.

CONTENTS

Introduction

The Canadian Spelling Program 2.1 is designed to provide students and teachers with a resource that is based on the most current research in the field. The program is carefully structured to support the developmental stages through which children progress, yet is flexible enough to accommodate a wide variety of individual differences. Most importantly, *The Canadian Spelling Program 2.1* seeks to stimulate interest in all areas of language, and to promote a confident, positive attitude toward writing as a means of self-expression.

Spelling Development in Grades 4 through 6

Students in grades 4 through 6 continue to make significant progress toward spelling maturity. When supported by a well-balanced spelling program, most will increase their understanding of spelling patterns, and develop a variety of strategies for learning to spell irregular words.

Spelling Patterns

Sound Patterns

Students in the middle grades continue to internalize the spelling generalizations they experimented with in the early years. Some grade 5 students have developed competence in utilizing the sound level of spelling, including consonant blends, short and long vowel patterns, and vowel combinations. Many students at this level, however, still require reinforcement and review of the basic sound-symbol patterns.

While a firm grasp of the sound level of spelling is important in the development of spelling competence, it is crucial that students in grades 4 through 6 move beyond the strategy of simply matching letters and sounds, a practice characteristic of earlier stages of invented spelling. A knowledge of within-word patterns, such as **fought** and **light**, will help students select the spelling patterns appropriate to specific words, and to relate them to word families.

Structural Patterns

Students in the middle grades also begin to internalize generalizations about the syntactic or structural level of the English spelling system. They require opportunities to observe the patterns inherent in the formation of plurals, compound words, contractions, possessives, and the addition of endings such as **–ed** and **–ing**. These patterns often require alterations to the base word, as in, **cherry / cherries** and **hope / hoping**.

Meaning Patterns

The deepest and most complex layer of the spelling system is the semantic or meaning level. As students increase their spoken and written vocabularies, they become more sensitive to the range of meanings of a given word. Spelling instruction at this level should encourage an exploration of word origins, multiple meanings, connotations of words, and idiomatic expressions.

It is also crucial that students begin to understand a key principle under-lying our language: *words which are related in meaning are usually spelled in a similar fashion.* Thus, by moving from base words to derivatives, students are able to spell such word pairs as **sign / signal**; **muscle / muscular**; and **compete / competition**.

Word building becomes an important skill in the middle grades, as students encounter increasingly complex words in their reading, and wish to use these words in their writing. They need to be aware of the function of simple prefixes and suffixes, and learn to add these systematically to base words.

Spelling Strategies

In addition to an understanding of spelling patterns on a variety of levels, students in grades 4 through 6 need to expand their repertoire of spelling strategies for words which do not have predictable spellings. These strategies will reflect both the student's preferred learning style and the characteristics of the specific words. A multisensory approach integrating visual, auditory, and tactile skills helps the student to approach the spelling of words from a variety of perspectives.

The development of these strategies can often be accomplished most effectively through discussions in a co-operative group format. Students need to reflect on which features of a word are challenging, and design useful strategies for recalling these parts. By sharing these insights with classmates and the teacher, a metacognitive awareness of spelling strategies is fostered.

Connections

Although many skills need to be addressed in a comprehensive spelling program for grades 4 through 6, spelling should never be viewed as an isolated area of study. The movement toward conventional spelling is essentially a complex thinking skill which is vitally linked with all aspects of the curriculum.

Students should be encouraged to view spelling in the context of the composing process. The ability to spell correctly is an important skill in today's world, but more important are the thoughts and ideas which underlie a piece of writing. Many students continue to confine their written output to words which they can spell, often limiting their creativity in the process. A comprehensive spelling program can expand the students' abilities to make useful generalizations about the spelling system, and thus free them to focus more fully on the ideas and feelings they may wish to convey.

ESL

Students from many language groups learn to spell English in Canadian schools. This book describes some of these languages, and highlights areas where children may experience interference from their own languages. For example, some languages do not have as many consonant blends (br, pl, etc.) as English, or they may not have capital letters, or an alphabetical writing system. With this information, it is easier to predict what may be difficult for the learner, and to practise what is important.

At the same time you can never assume that all students from a certain culture or language group will experience the same difficulties learning English. Factors such as prior education, home background, and exposure to English will have an impact on the child's learning.

Program Outcomes

The Canadian Spelling Program 2.1 provides opportunities for students to demonstrate learning in the following areas:

Knowledge

Students will:
- spell the words they need in their everyday writing as well as the words they are most likely to write as adults
- demonstrate knowledge of common spelling patterns by applying them to known words and unfamiliar words

Skills

Students will:
- develop personal strategies for learning and retaining the spelling of words
- apply spelling skills in a variety of writing contexts, and transfer these skills to writing needs in other subject areas
- apply self-analysis and self-correction skills as evidence of a spelling consciousness

Attitudes

Students will:
- demonstrate a positive attitude toward spelling and a sense of achievement in their own spelling growth

Scope and Sequence

The chart on pages 4 and 5 lists the phoneme-grapheme patterns, word structures, grammar skills, and other spelling skills that are treated in the grade 5 level of this program.

Scope and Sequence Chart

Lesson Focus ■ Review X Applications ●

Phoneme-Grapheme Relationships	Units																																		
	1	2	3	4	5	6	7	8	9	10	11	12	13	14	15	16	17	18	19	20	21	22	23	24	25	26	27	28	29	30	31	32	33	34	35
/a/ a	■					X																													
/e/ e		■				X																													
/ē/ ee, ea		■				X																													
/ī/ i_e, i			■			X																													
/ō/ o_e, oa, ow				■		X																													
/ü/ /ÿu/ u_e, ew, ue					■	X																													
/är/ ar							■					X																							
/er/ ir, ur, er, ear							■					X																							
/ôr/ or								■				X																							
/e/ ea									■			X																							
/ē/ e_e, ey, y									■			X																							
/ī/ i, y, igh										■		X																							
/ėr/ er, ur, or											■	X																							
/ō/ ow, ey, y													■				X																		
schwa /ə/																■	X																		
schwa vowels																		■						X							■				X
/ē/ ie, ea																							■	X											
/o/ ought																																		■	X
Word Structure																																			
Plurals														■				X																	
Irregular Plurals															■			X																	
Syllables and Stress																■	X	X																	X
Capitals																	■	X														■			X
Homophones																			■				X								X				
Base Words and Endings																				■	■		X												
Number Words																						■	X												X

Scope and Sequence Chart

Lesson Focus ■ **Review** X **Applications** •

Word Structure (Units)	1	2	3	4	5	6	7	8	9	10	11	12	13	14	15	16	17	18	19	20	21	22	23	24	25	26	27	28	29	30	31	32	33	34	35
Prefixes																							■	X									X		
Possessives																									■	■				X					
Contractions																											■			X					
Suffixes																												■		X				X	
Compounds																					•								■	X					
Related Words																																	■		X
Writing Skills																																			
Proofreading						•								•			•	•	•	•		•		•		•		•		•					•
Dictation	•	•	•	•	•	•	•	•	•	•	•	•	•	•	•	•	•	•	•	•	•	•	•	•	•	•	•	•	•	•	•	•	•	•	•
Personal Writing	•	•	•	•	•	•	•	•	•	•	•	•	•	•	•	•	•	•	•	•	•	•	•	•	•	•	•	•	•	•	•	•	•	•	•
Grammar Skills																																			
Nouns: Common, Proper, Abstract						•																													
Nouns: Collective																								•											
Adjectives												•																							•
Verbs: Past, Present, Future																								•											
Helping Verbs																														•					•
Special Verbs																																			•
Adverbs																		•						•											
Joining Sentences																			•																
Subject and Verb Agreement																								•											
Unbiassed Language																								•											
Quotation Marks																														•					
Paragraphs																																			•

Program Structure – Student's Edition

Regular Unit

The thirty-five units in the Student's Edition of *The Canadian Spelling Program 2.1* are organized into groups of five regular units, each followed by a Looking Back unit. Regular units focus on common spelling patterns. Looking Back units provide an opportunity for students to review the patterns addressed in that block of units and also words that are commonly misspelled, or with which they have had difficulty.

A **Precheck** serves as a diagnostic tool to determine which list words the individual student needs to learn.

understand
tracked
female
chase
stayed
anyway
display
remain
fail
male
trai

Word lists are based on a nation-wide research study of words used by Canadian children and adults. This list has been revised to reflect increased current usage.

- Word lists have a specific focus such as sound-symbol relationships, word structure patterns, or spelling generalizations.

- Word lists are presented in an easily identifiable vertical design, to help students focus on features of individual words.

- A multisensory study format uses visual, auditory, cognitive, and kinesthetic strategies to appeal to varied learning styles.

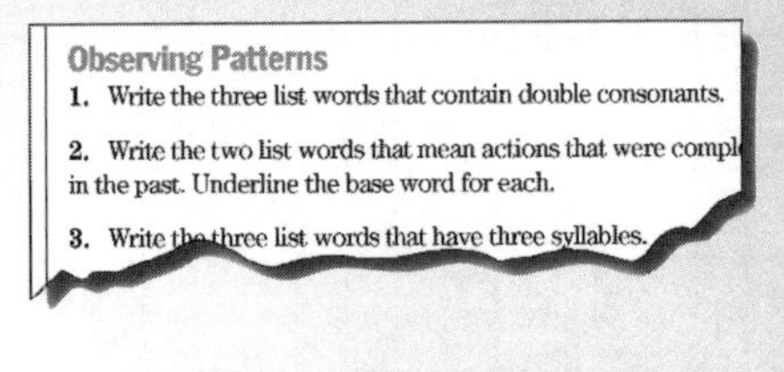

Observing Patterns

1. Write the three list words that contain double consonants.
2. Write the two list words that mean actions that were compl in the past. Underline the base word for each.
3. Write the three list words that have three syllables.

The **Powerbooster** draws attention to spelling generalizations in a concise form.

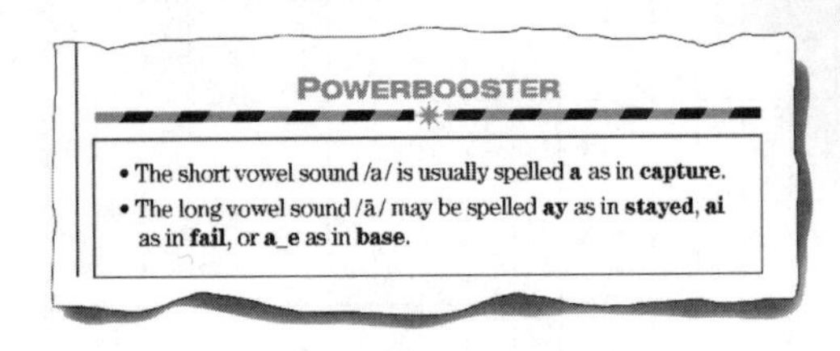

POWERBOOSTER

- The short vowel sound /a/ is usually spelled **a** as in **capture**.
- The long vowel sound /ā/ may be spelled **ay** as in **stayed**, **ai** as in **fail**, or **a_e** as in **base**.

List words are presented in the context of a selection to reinforce meaning.

Exploring the World of a Shy Giant

The rare mountain gorilla lives on the slopes of the Virungu Volcanoes in East Africa. From a base camp at the foot of the mountains, the gorilla bands are tracked by guides who understand their habits. The gorillas leave a trail of broken plants up the steep-sided valleys. At some points leaves and

and attack any intruder who gives a display of anger. If a visitor can remain quiet and still, gorillas are quite tame and shy. Some people have tried to capture baby gorillas for zoos. But gorillas will fight to the de... defend their you...

Exercises are written in clear, predictable, instructional language so that students can complete appropriate exercises independently.

- A balance of teacher-directed, independent, small group, and paired exercises are suggested.

- Word-building exercises focus on rhymes, visual patterns, and spelling generalizations.

Exploring Patterns

1. Write the word in each set which has the sound /ü/ as in **crew**, **glue**, and **rule** or /yü/ as in **mule**, **few**, and **cue**. Circle the first letter of each answer. Then copy down the circled letters to find the answer to this question.

What was the sound that Captain Hook feared the most in the story *Peter Pan*? _ _ _k _ _ _k

a) crust

- Spelling is placed within the context of the composing process, with provision for the transfer of spelling skills to meaningful writing experiences.

5. Imagine you are in this spacecraft, orbiting Earth. You're having a problem with something on board and you want help from Earth. Write the message you might send to your control centre. Use some of these list words in your message.

temperature electric melt metal heat sending

Challenges with Words: There is provision within each unit for both basic and enrichment exercises.

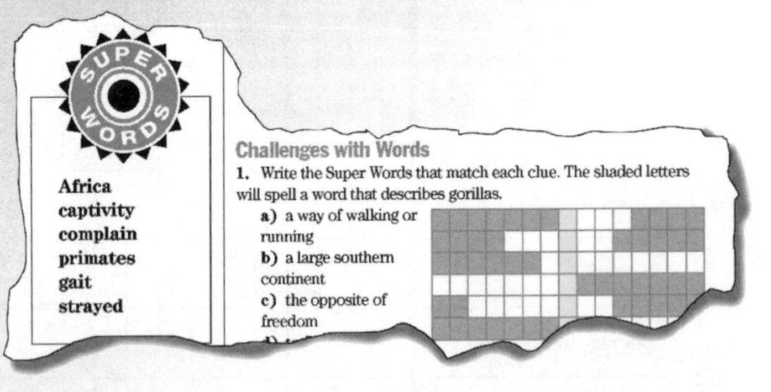

Africa
captivity
complain
primates
gait
strayed

Challenges with Words

1. Write the Super Words that match each clue. The shaded letters will spell a word that describes gorillas.
   a) a way of walking or running
   b) a large southern continent
   c) the opposite of freedom

New Words: Many units contain a list of words that are new to English. Some of these words are new creations, while others are familiar words that have taken on new meanings. Both categories reflect recent advances in technology, clothing, food, and entertainment.

NEW WORDS

air miles
talking book
air bags

Looking Back Unit

Words on the **review list** are selected from the five preceding units. Selection is based on irregular sound-symbol relationships, homonyms, or the presence on the list of frequently misspelled words.

6 Looking Back

STUDY STEPS

LOOK at each word.
SAY each word clearly.

Here is a list of words that may have been hard for you in Units 1–5. You and your teacher may add other words to the list.

accident	difficult	temperature	thumb
equipment	disease	guide	knew
gorilla	electric	whole	wrote
capture	fifth	jewels	argue

1. Use the Study Steps for each word. Your teacher will dictate the words.

Study Steps is a systematic procedure for word study which combines visual, auditory, and motor responses.

2. Complete each sentence with words from the Study List that match the shape and suit the meaning. Write the sentences in your notebook.

a) The doctor [ ] the boy's illness would be [ ] to treat. The boy had a high [ ] and his [ ]

Looking Back exercises are designed to review and reinforce all sound-symbol relationships and concepts introduced in the previous five units.

Personal Review List: Students establish their own lists from a variety of sources including errors on Unit Tests, previous review lists, words drawn from other subject areas, and so forth.

Dictionary Skills: These exercises serve to make students aware that **dictionary skills** are an important part of developing spelling abilities. Some skills, such as the use of guide words, are practised in regular units, but it is here they are emphasized.

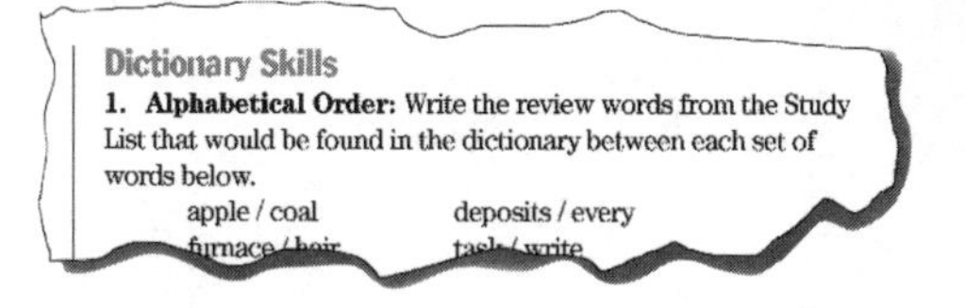
Dictionary Skills

1. Alphabetical Order: Write the review words from the Study List that would be found in the dictionary between each set of words below.

apple / coal   deposits / every

A **Mini-Dictionary** is included at the back of the student's text.

Each **writing page** focusses on a different aspect of exploration. Several forms of writing are required for each exercise (e.g., classification charts, open-ended stories, personal expression, descriptive writing).

Exploring the World of Inventions

1. Brainstorm with your group to list as many important recent inventions as you can. Sort your inventions into categories. For example:

Communications	Electronics	Medicine
the Internet	CD player	ultrasound

2. Imagine you have perfected an amazing new invention which will change the world. Write a description of your invention.

• Specific **grammatical principles** such as parts of speech, verb tenses, and correct sentence structure are systematically introduced. These principles are outlined in the Scope and Sequence Chart, pages 4 and 5.

Grammar Power

1. Writing with common and proper nouns: We use a **noun** to name a **person**, **place**, or **thing**.

A **common noun** names a person, place, or thing. A **proper noun** is a special name, place, or thing.

	Common Nouns	Proper Nouns
Person	man	Bruno
Place	country	Mexico
Thing	magazine	

Proofing Power: These passages contain errors in words from the review list. Misspellings may also be drawn from concepts studied in the previous block of units.

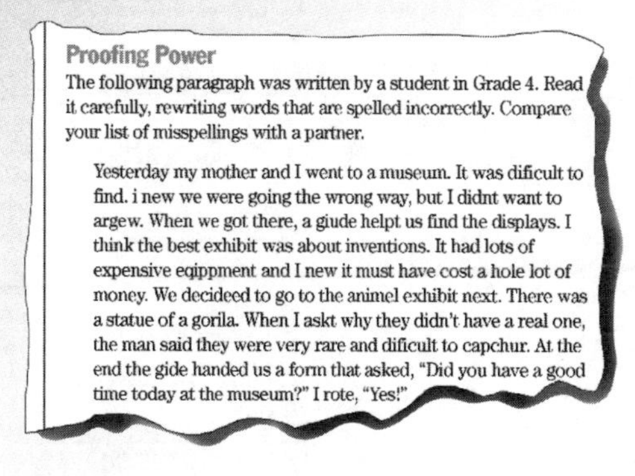
Proofing Power

The following paragraph was written by a student in Grade 4. Read it carefully, rewriting words that are spelled incorrectly. Compare your list of misspellings with a partner.

Yesterday my mother and I went to a museum. It was dificult to find. i new we were going the wrong way, but I didnt want to argew. When we got there, a giude helpt us find the displays. I think the best exhibit was about inventions. It had lots of expensive eqippment and I new it must have cost a hole lot of money. We decideed to go to the animel exhibit next. There was a statue of a gorila. When I askt why they didn't have a real one, the man said they were very rare and dificult to capchur. At the end the gide handed us a form that asked, "Did you have a good time today at the museum?" I rote, "Yes!"

Program Structure – Teacher's Edition

The Teacher's Edition of *The Canadian Spelling Program 2.1* is designed to facilitate the use of the program and to help teachers incorporate spelling effectively into their total language program. While an emphasis has been placed on concrete suggestions for each component, the classroom teacher's judgment should prevail.

Each unit in the Teacher's Edition has an introductory page that gives information on patterns to be examined, a list of important 'Preknowledge' concepts, additional patterns that can be explored, 'Sharing the Secrets with Kids' tips, and a 'Professional Notebook' with ideas, research findings, and advice.

Following the unit introduction are the reduced and annotated pages from the student text.

- The top part of each of these pages gives 'nuts and bolts' suggestions for working with the program and with students.
- The bottom part of the same page gives options, such as ESL, Writing, and Co-operative Learning, for adapting the spelling program to the special needs of the classroom and students.

Concluding pages include strategies for assessment and assessment follow-up, home and curriculum connections.

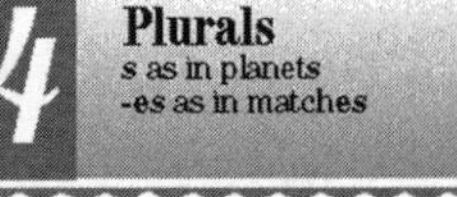

14
Plurals
s as in planets
-es as in matches

Patterns
Forming plurals is one of the first structural principles students attempt as they move from a sound-based approach to spelling to one focussed on structure, meaning, and other elements. By grade 5, many students will spell dogs rather than dogz, signalling they understand that s added to the end of a word means more than one, even though the final sound is /z/.

Preknowledge
Help students understand the following concepts as they work with the patterns in this unit.
- Base words and adding to them. A base word is the 'root' to which plurals, tense markers, suffixes, and prefixes are added. In the case of plurals, the base word is the singular form (**wave/waves**; **bunch/bunches**).
- Singular refers to one, plural refers to more than one.

More Patterns
Other patterns you might wish to review or

Professional Notebook
What we have not widely been aware of is that children quite naturally approach spelling through the techniques of problem-solving. There is a large body of research which suggests that learning to spell involves problem-solving on a variety of levels. Children observe language patterns, formulate hypotheses about the spelling system, and test these hypotheses in their own writing.
(Scott, Spelling: Sharing the Secrets 14)

Sharing the Secrets with Kids
Suggest students try to say words such as **houses** and **glasses** without the second vowel sound—as if they were written **houz**, or **glassz**. Have them

This shade of brown **matches** your eyes.
There are three **states** of matter: animal, vegetable, mineral.
The tree had many **branches**.
My **arms** were tired after carrying the groceries.
We have two **coaches** for our hockey team.
She bought three **bunches** of flowers.
The huge **waves** sank the ship.
There are three separate **classes** in grade 5 this year.
Several **objects** fell out of her knapsack.
The students worked in **groups** of four.
Can you give me **directions** from Edmonton to Calgary?
Do you know the names of all the **planets**?

Words in Context
Have students read the paragraph, noting all the plural forms. Then ask them to identify the two list words that are not included in the paragraph and write their own sentences for these words (**coaches**, **directions**).

Observing Patterns
1. The visual features of these words may be further enhanced by circling or underlining the difficult parts, or using configuration boxes and lines. Have students suggest strategies for remembering the double d and s in **addresses** ("add two Ds and two Ss to my **address**").
2. Students will likely know that a **telescope** is an instrument for viewing or observing the stars. Point out that the prefix **tele-** comes from the Greek word meaning 'far off'. Therefore, a **telescope** is an instrument for viewing objects that are far away. Have them brainstorm other common words that begin with **tele-** (**television, telephone, telephoto, telegram, telemarketing**).

Precheck
When presenting the words to the class after the Precheck, point out difficult parts of words and spelling patterns by underlining, boxing parts, or using a different colour of chalk or marker. You may want to keep your list visible in the room throughout the unit until the Unit Test is given.

Dictation
Corkscrews are shaped like **spirals**.
I have two different e-mail **addresses**.
A pirate captain always carried a **telescope**.
Canada is more than 3000 **kilometres** from east to west.

Writing
- Students could research a topic about the universe, using reference books or a CD-ROM source. Have them write a short paragraph and give it a snappy title. They might like to illustrate their work and display it in the classroom.

Unit 14 111

Home Connection
Many people make errors with the plural forms. Have students become 'spelling detectives' watching for signs in store windows, and for flyers or advertisements where errors in spelling are made. Have them bring samples they have found to begin a class list of 'Great Spelling Goofs'.

Sail of the Century! 20% off all watchez in the store

Diarys on special for this week only at ...

Add a few luxurys to your life! For the holiday of a lifetime, call...

Teacher's Notes

Assessment
- Emphasis should be placed on developing a positive attitude toward spelling through self-correction and self-diagnosis of errors. Provide as much support as possible.
- When students make errors on plural forms, either on the Unit Test or in their everyday writing, ask them to explain why they spelled the word as they did. This may reveal that the student is using primarily a visual or phonetic strategy rather than understanding the patterns for forming plurals, or that he/she is encountering interference from a first language. (See ESL p. 114.)

Follow-up
- Check that the concept of 'more than one' is clearly understood.
- Provide further support for the various plural forms, using the activities found in *Sharing the Secrets: Teach Your Child to Spell*, Units 27 and 28. Exercises and activities in this resource can be shared with parents for reinforcement at home.

116 Unit 14

Special Features

The following features in the Teacher's Edition are designed to help you adapt and individualize *The Canadian Spelling Program 2.1* to meet varied learning styles.

ESL: For students for whom English is their second language, suggestions identify structural, phonetic, and other spelling difficulties not common to English-speaking students. Each Looking Back unit includes an ESL feature called Language Snapshot. This snapshot provides background information on the language and its features that may create areas of difficulty for many students. Each Teacher's Edition in *The Canadian Spelling 2.1* program will profile different languages.

> **ESL**
>
> The /s/ and /z/ sound at the ends of words may be difficult for many ESL students to hear and thus spell or pronounce.
> • Have students practise the plural forms in sentences.

Special Needs: For students needing extra practice with patterns or alternative approaches, suggestions are provided for a variety of learning styles. These suggestions may also be used with ESL students.

> **Special Needs**
>
> • Use word wheels to help children build patterns. When students have finished generating the words with the word wheels, have them copy the words on cards. These can be used for word sorts at a later date.

Writing: Suggestions and activities for making connections with personal and classroom writing are suggested in this feature.

> **Editing Conferences**
> • Many spelling errors by students in the middle grades involve schwa vowels. In editing conferences note if the student is having difficult with spelling unstressed vowels. Encourage students to work at these words in a positive w by showing them how much of the word they

Oral Language and Literature: Spelling relates closely to patterns of oral language such as rhyme and rhythm. Tongue twisters, oral word games, poems, and stories that include the patterns being studied help link spelling to oral and written language.

> **Oral Language and Literature**
>
> • Bees seem to fascinate people. Maybe that's why we have several idioms based on bees and their beehaviour! Students can work on their own or with a partner to illustrate and present their image of each of the idioms given here.

Co-operative Learning: The co-operative learning model is ideally suited to spelling instruction. Groups work best when students with a variety of skills and abilities work together to achieve results and reflect on their strategies. The most important ingredient for the success of co-operative learning groups is that all members feel responsibility for a common goal.

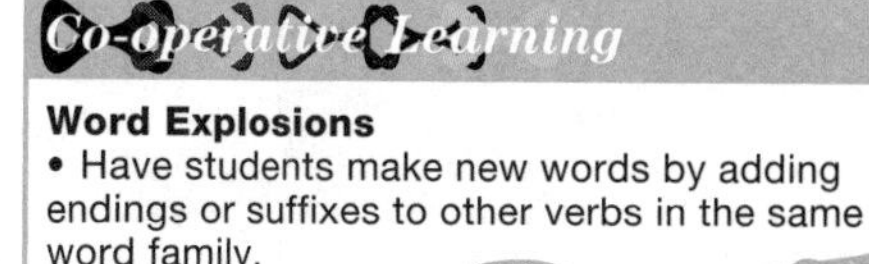

Co-operative Learning
Word Explosions
• Have students make new words by adding endings or suffixes to other verbs in the same word family.

Critical Thinking: Critical thinking skills are fostered through activities that involve students in classifying words on the basis of a variety of patterns, using graphic organizers such as Venn diagrams, cross-classification charts, or word webs. Each suggestion is linked with the focus of the unit, and helps to consolidate and extend the pattern.

> **Critical Thinking**
>
> • As a follow-up to the code activity in Challenges with Words 3, have students invent their own codes to send messages, or have them
>
> A B C D E F G H I
> . ? z y x w v u t
>
> Riddle
> what was

Multiple Intelligences: The work of Howard Gardner on multiple intelligences has great potential for the teaching of spelling. This theory acknowledges the special strengths of each child and advocates a multisensory approach in the classroom. Specific intelligences include: verbal/ linguistic; bodily/ kinesthetic; logical/mathematical; musical; visual/spatial; interpersonal and intrapersonal.

> **Multiple Intelligences**
>
> • Spelling strategies for stress patterns can be designed to appeal to a variety of intelligences.
>
> **Visual/Spatial:** Highlight stressed syllables using highlighter pens. Underline stressed syllables with coloured markers. Print syllables on different cards, with the stressed syllable

Curriculum Connection: Where applicable, connections are suggested to help integrate the spelling lists and topics with themes and subjects from across the curriculum. Students are encouraged to apply spelling strategies and generalizations in all areas of the curriculum.

> **Curriculum Connection**
>
> • Students may enjoy finding out more about grizzlies. Picture files, filmstrips, and magazines such as *Owl*, *World*, and *Canadian Geographic*, or CD-ROMs on animals or mammals may provide pictures as well as information.

Home Connection: In some units, suggestions are given to help involve parents in spelling instruction, helping to take spelling beyond the school context into the community as a whole. These suggestions can be part of an ongoing communication with parents concerning their child's progress.

> **Home Connection**
>
> Alert parents to the fact that the students will be studying vowels with r patterns in three of the next five units. You could provide a chart listing the various patterns and encourage each family to add to each list as they meet such words in their everyday lives.

Using *The Canadian Spelling Program 2.1*

Introductory Page (Teacher's Edition only)

Patterns

This section elaborates on the focus for the unit. It explains the importance of the spelling patterns to be taught and puts them in the context of the overall spelling program.

Preknowledge

There is a logical sequence to the learning of spelling patterns. In *The Canadian Spelling Program 2.1*, concepts are introduced, developed, and reviewed throughout the grades. The Preknowledge section lists concepts students need to feel comfortable with in order to access the new knowledge of the unit.

More Patterns

Each unit word list reviews patterns studied earlier, or patterns, such as homophones and plurals that are important at this level. As well, words that are commonly misspelled are included and footnoted.

Sharing the Secrets with Kids

A special box listing tips or features of English spelling for sharing with students is often included on this or subsequent pages.

Professional Notebook

Ideas, research findings, and advice are provided for teachers from leading educators.

Lesson Page 1

Exercises on this page are intended to be done by all students. Teacher involvement is suggested as students examine the visual and auditory features of the list words.

Precheck

The Precheck introduces each regular unit of the program. A list of sentences is provided in the Teacher's Edition for dictating the list words in context. You may wish to personalize these sentences to reflect the students' interests, themes, events, seasons, stories read in class, etc.

Students write the list words in Column A of their Student Record Sheet. By correcting their own Prechecks, and writing the words correctly beside their misspellings, students can begin to develop a sense of personal responsibility toward the spelling task.

Word List

Following the Precheck, students turn to the word list in their texts. Each list has a specific focus such as a sound-symbol relationship, a word structure pattern, or spelling generalization. Some words in the list exemplify this pattern, while others are selected to review and reinforce a pattern introduced in a previous unit. In grade 5, unit word lists are organized so there is a gradual introduction and review of words with irregular patterns.

A Note on...

Spelling Variation

For a number of words used in this program, common spelling variations exist. Only one variant and its pattern are consistently used throughout this program. The choice of spelling is based on frequency of usage across Canada as a whole, but it is not to be considered prescriptive. If you wish to use with your students a variant such as **color** rather than **colour**, or **gray** rather than **grey**, for example, feel free to do so. Such variation continues to be a fact of Canadian spelling.

Word Lists

Word lists in *The Canadian Spelling Program 2.1* have been carefully selected and ordered to reflect a variety of features. These words are:

- examples of spelling patterns on the levels of sound, structure, and meaning
- sequenced to match the developmental stages of learning to spell
- used in the writing of Canadian children (based on the research of Dr. Ves Thomas)
- sensitive to the need for inclusive language
- new words that have entered the vocabulary
- words that are identified as most frequently misspelled words in English
- challenging enrichment words for more advanced spellers

Research by Darrell Morris has indicated that children should be able to spell at least half the list words before beginning a unit in order for effective learning to take place. Otherwise, the concepts will likely be too advanced for the child, and frustration will interfere with learning.

This research also recommends flexible programming for students based on the results of the Precheck. *The Canadian Spelling Program 2.1* is designed to meet the needs of a wide range of abilities, from careful practice for students who experienced problems with the Precheck to special Challenge Words and enrichment activities in *every unit* for more able spellers. (See page 14.)

List Words in Context

The word list is presented in the context of an informative article. This feature provides an opportunity for shared reading and serves to ensure that students have a clear understanding of the list words.

Lesson Page 2

Observing Patterns

Students look at the patterns revealed by the list words: the difficult letter combinations, syllables that are sometimes dropped in speech, visual features, variations in pronunciations, or any auditory features that may promote learning. You may want to have students point out any useful features of shape, endings, or base words. Instructions are clear and brief so that most students will be able to complete this section on their own.

Lesson Page 3

Discovering Patterns

These teacher-directed activities draw attention to the patterns used in spelling specific groups of the list words and should involve all students, even those who did well on the Precheck. The list words are presented a second time in cursive writing. Here students will see an alternative representation of the written form, one that more closely reflects what they will see when they write the words. If the students copy the words in their own handwriting, then they will aid the learning of spelling through the kinesthetic stimulus. Students are then led through a series of questions which help them to verbalize the patterns and to formulate spelling generalizations.

The Powerbooster draws attention to these spelling generalizations in concise form at the end of the section.

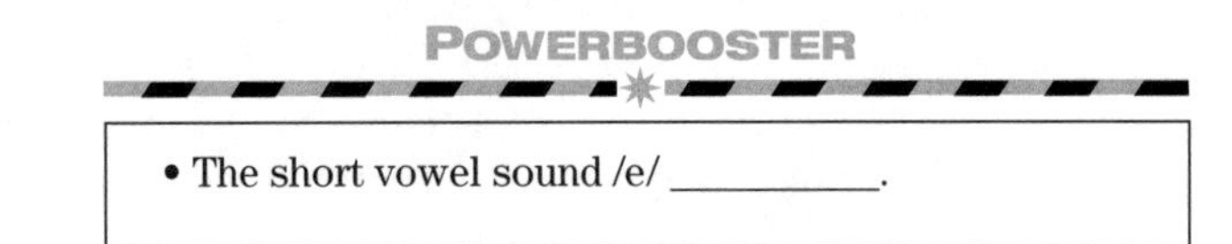

Lesson Page 4

Exploring Patterns

Spelling generalizations and word patterns are extended to other familiar words. Some exercises reinforce knowledge of spelling by cuing recall and writing of list words through sound or meaning. Some explore the meaning of words through the use of word connotations, word origins, and multiple meanings. Other exercises give students the chance to use the spelling patterns presented in the Powerbooster to write new words that follow the same pattern. Each *Exploring Patterns* section concludes with an open-ended exercise that encourages students to transfer some of their spelling skills to their personal writing and ties in with the unit theme.

Challenges with Words

This enrichment section is intended for students who have had little or no difficulty with the Precheck. Six Super Words give additional examples of the spelling patterns of the unit, or build compound and derived forms of the list words. Students may wish to use the five Study Steps (Look, Say, Cover, Write, Check) to study the Super Words.

The exercises are intended to be primarily independent, or done in pairs or small groups. Some Challenges with Words exercises reflect the spelling generalizations of the unit or provide further study of the Super Words. Others deal with classifying, exploring meaning and associations, word building, solving codes and riddles, and writing.

Lesson Page 5

New Words

Many units contain a list of new words that are entering the language from the worlds of technology, electronics, recreation, and other cultures. Some new words reflect changes in usage of familiar words, or changes in language to avoid gender bias. Activity suggestions invite students to explore new words they are familiar with, alternate spellings for new words (inline skates, in-line skates), or how words are created.

Concluding Page

On the final page of each unit in the Teacher's Edition, resources and suggestions for assessment, assessment follow-up, and connections to the home and curriculum are outlined. There is also a space for teachers to record their own notes on the unit, with ideas and resources that have worked for them.

Assessment

At the end of each unit, students write a test consisting of the list words for the unit. It is left to your discretion whether or not to include the Super Words and New Words for those students who have been working in the Challenges with Words section. Students can mark their own tests, as in the Precheck, and rewrite their misspelled words correctly in column D of the Student Record Sheet. You may wish to monitor the self-correction to observe whether students understand the unit focus and which students may need further help.

Spelling assessment should, however, go beyond the Unit Test. Assessment is an ongoing process that can provide information to guide further instruction. Focus your assessment on the positive—what strategies students are using to spell words correctly—as well as patterns of difficulty. For example, some students at the grade 5 level experience difficulty moving from strategies focussed on sound to strategies that emphasize meaning and structure.

Assessment Follow-up

What do you do when assessment tools tell you that the student is not transferring spelling skills and strategies to his or her everyday writing? The assessment follow-up suggestions in the Teacher's Edition are focussed on creating links between spelling and writing and reinforcing the patterns taught in the unit. Many of the suggestions refer to strategies and activities from *Sharing the Secrets: Teach Your Child to Spell* by Ruth Scott and Sharon Siamon and *Spelling: Sharing the Secrets* by Ruth Scott.

Individualizing the Units to Meet Varied Learning Levels

The Canadian Spelling Program 2.1 recognizes that students will perform at a variety of levels in the Precheck. The program is structured to provide support for students who experience difficulty on the Precheck and enrichment opportunities for those who have few errors.

All students are expected to participate with the teacher in the first page of each unit. The remaining activities can be assigned according to individual needs. The chart that follows recommends a typical breakdown of exercises for three levels of performance on the Precheck.

Student Profile

Monday	Tuesday	Wednesday	Thursday	Friday
Sample A: For students with difficulties on the Precheck, including the spelling patterns which are the focus of the unit.				
Precheck Self-checking. Rewriting misspelled words correctly. ***Reading the list words in story context.***	***Observing Patterns*** Exercises.	***Discovering Patterns*** Exercises. ***Exploring Patterns*** (as many exercises as time permits).	***Exploring Patterns*** Exercises if time permits.	***Unit Test*** Self-checking. Rewriting misspelled words correctly on Student Record Sheet. Adding words to Personal Word list.
Sample B: For students with few problems on the Precheck but not with the spelling patterns which are the focus of the unit.				
Precheck Self-checking. Rewriting misspelled words correctly. ***Reading the list words in story context.***	***Observing Patterns*** Exercises. ***Discovering Patterns*** Exercises.	***Exploring Patterns*** Exercises (if completed begin Challenges with Words).	***Challenges with Words*** Study Super Words, begin exercises.	***Unit Test*** Self-checking. Rewriting misspelled words correctly on Student Record Sheet. Adding words to Personal Word List.
Sample C: For students with no problems with the Precheck.				
Precheck Self-checking.	***Discovering Patterns*** Exercises.	***Challenges with Words*** Study Super Words, begin exercises.	***Challenges with Words*** Supplementary suggestions in Teacher's Edition.	***Unit Test*** Self-checking (may include Super Words). Rewriting words correctly on Student Record Sheet. Adding Words to Personal Word List.

Student Record Sheets

- reproducible as blackline masters
- provide a new sheet to each student for every unit

Column A

This is where you may wish to have students write their Precheck. Students may mark their own Precheck under your supervision.

Column B

Words spelled incorrectly on the Precheck may be rewritten correctly in the space beside the misspelling. This column isolates the list words which need special attention on the part of individual students.

Column C

This is a column for writing the Unit Test. Super Words and New Words may be dictated on the same sheet. It is at the discretion of the teacher whether students doing Challenges with Words should include the Super Words on the Unit Test.

Column D

Correct spellings for errors which persist in the Unit Test may be recorded here for inclusion in students' Personal Word Lists. You may wish to have students use the Study Steps to learn each word which appears in Column D. Completed Student Record Sheets may be kept in a spelling folder.

Student Record Sheet

Name: ____________________

Unit: ____________________

A	B
Precheck	**Words I Need to Study**
1	
2	
3	
4	
5	
6	
7	
8	
9	
10	
11	
12	
13	
14	
15	
16	

Student Record Sheet

Name: ____________________

Unit: ____________________

C D

	List Word	Words I Need to Study		
		Mistake in first part of word	Mistake in middle of word	Mistake in last part of word
1				
2				
3				
4				
5				
6				
7				
8				
9				
10				
11				
12				
13				
14				
15				
16				

References

Cunningham, P. *Phonics They Use.* New York: Harper Collins, 1995.

Frank, M. *If You're Trying to Teach Kids How to Write, You've Gotta Have this Book!* Nashville: Incentive Publications, 1979.

Gardner, H. *Frames of Mind: The Theory of Multiple Intelligences.* New York: Basic Books, 1983.

Gentry, Richard, and Jean Wallace Gillet. *Teaching Kids to Spell.* Portsmouth, New Hampshire: Heinemann Educational Books, Inc., 1993.

Henderson, E. *Teaching Spelling.* Boston: Houghton Mifflin, 1985.

Lazear. *Seven Ways of Teaching: The Artistry of Teaching With Multiple Intelligences.* Illinois: Skylight, 1991.

Lederer, R. *Adventures of a Verbivore.* New York: Pocket Books, 1994.

----. *Crazy English: The Ultimate Joy Ride Through Our Language.* New York: Pocket Books, 1989.

Morris, D. "Exploring the concept of 'spelling instructional level' through the analysis of error-types." *The Elementary School Journal.* (87, 2), 181–200.

Scott, R. *The Student Editor's Guide to Words.* Toronto: Gage Educational Publishing Company, 1991.

----. *Spelling: Sharing the Secrets.* Toronto: Gage Educational Publishing Company, 1993.

Scott, R. and S. Siamon *Sharing the Secrets: Teach Your Child to Spell.* Toronto: Macmillan, 1994.

Tarasoff, Mary. *Spelling Strategies You Can Teach.* Winnipeg, Manitoba: Active Learning Institute Inc., 1990.

Templeton, S. "Using the spelling/meaning connection to develop word knowledge in older students." *Journal of Reading,* October 1983: 9.

----. "Synthesis of research on the learning and teaching of spelling." *Educational Leadership,* March 1986: 73–78.

Uhry, J. "Segmentation/spelling instruction as part of a first-grade reading program: Effects on several measures of reading." *Reading Research Quarterly,* July-August-September 1993: 219–233.

Willows, D. and R. Scott "Spelling processes of the reading disabled." *Handbook of normal and disturbed spelling development: theory, processes and interventions,* ed. G. Brown & N. Ellis. Chichester: John Wiley & Sons Ltd, 1994.

Wilde, S. *You Kan Red This!: Spelling and Punctuation for Whole Language Classrooms, K–6.* Portsmouth: Heinemann Educational Books Inc., 1992.

Long a

a __ e as in base
ay as in display
ai as in trail

Patterns

By grade 5 students should be aware there can be many ways of spelling the same sound in English. It is important at this level that they move beyond sound/symbol relationships to explore structural and meaning patterns in words. However, it is useful to review and consolidate students' strategies for spelling vowel sounds in longer words that they will increasingly use as their vocabularies develop (**nineteen**, **battery**).

Preknowledge

Students should have an understanding of the following concepts as they work with the patterns in this unit.

- Many words are derived from others. Base words and derived forms are common in everyday English (**track/tracked**; **stay/stayed**).
- The vowel sound /a/ can be long or short (h**a**t/h**a**t**e**).
- Syllables are word parts that contain a vowel sound (**un**/**der**/**stand**).
- Homophones present special problems in spelling because they sound alike but have different spellings and meanings (**bough/bow**; **pale/pail**).

More Patterns

Other patterns you may wish to review or introduce in this unit include the following.

- The **-ed** form of a verb indicates past tense (**tracked**, **stayed**).
- Compound words are made up of two words related in meaning (**anyway**, **classroom**).
- Homophones (**male/mail**; **tracked/tract**).
- The plural **s**. Some students might have difficulty recognizing that the plural **s** can have the sound /s/ or /z/ (book**s**; valley**s**).

Professional Notebook

English spelling is not learned all at once but over the school years. Each step forward depends upon the firmness of the foundation that has been built to that point. That is why spelling needs the guiding hand of a teacher who knows what the basics are and how to maintain them.

(Henderson 151)

Sharing the Secrets with Kids

The old rhyme "If two vowels go walking, the first one does the talking" works for ***ay*** *in* ***display*** *and* ***ai*** *in* ***trail****.*

Precheck

General information about the Precheck is given on page 10 of the Introduction. You might wish to have students use the record forms on pages 16–17.

Students should understand that the Precheck is not a graded test, but is meant to help them recognize which words they know how to spell and those they must study carefully.

Dictation

I **understand** the problem.
They **tracked** the tiger for days.
The **female** bird flew away.
The **chase** ended quickly.
He **stayed** home from school.
He did his homework **anyway**.
Is your project on **display**?
Please **remain** standing.
Don't **fail** to bring the ice cream for the party!
The **male** gorilla is enormous.
This mountain-bike **trail** is terrific!
A frightened animal can **attack**.
She ran to first **base**.
Did you **capture** the spider?
We searched in all the **valleys**.
That **gorilla** looks hungry.

Read the section *How to Study Your Words* with students. Encourage students to use the five-step study method opposite p. 1 in the text. This process is multisensory—requiring visual, auditory, and tactile responses.

Words in Context

Use the paragraph that introduces the unit to present the list words in context. Discuss the meanings of the words with students, and invite them to suggest synonyms. (See Writing, p. 21.)

You may wish to have students brainstorm ideas about the concept of exploring, which is used in the title of all the context paragraphs in the student text. Encourage them to include all types of exploration, from discovering new lands, to research by scientists, to talking about and sharing ideas with their own classmates and friends.

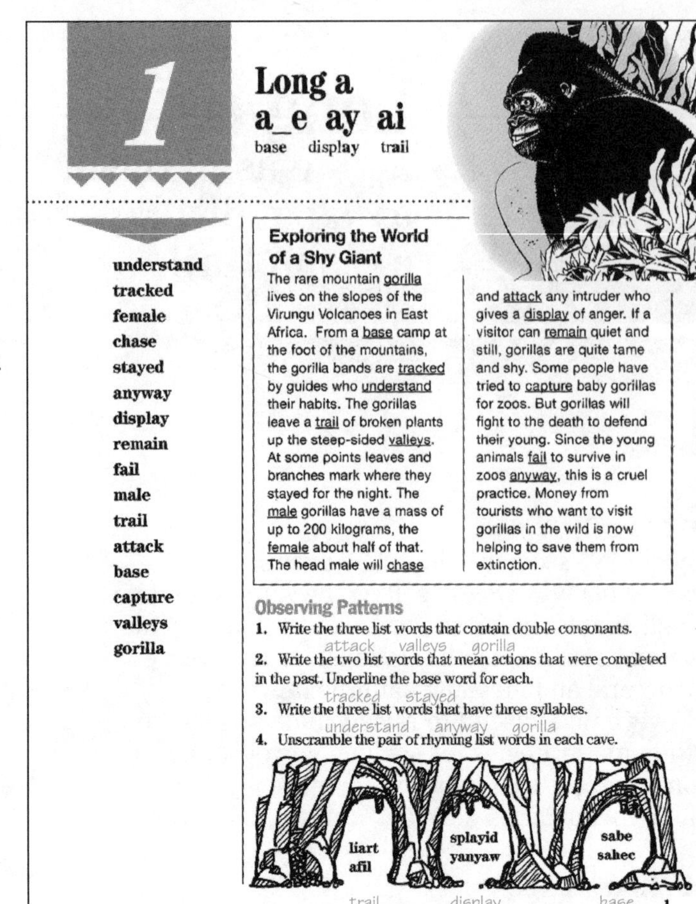

1

Long a
a_e ay ai
base display trail

understand
tracked
female
chase
stayed
anyway
display
remain
fail
male
trail
attack
base
capture
valleys
gorilla

Exploring the World of a Shy Giant

The rare mountain gorilla lives on the slopes of the Virungu Volcanoes in East Africa. From a base camp at the foot of the mountains, the gorilla bands are tracked by guides who understand their habits. The gorillas leave a trail of broken plants up the steep-sided valleys. At some points leaves and branches mark where they stayed for the night. The male gorillas have a mass of up to 200 kilograms, the female about half of that. The head male will chase and attack any intruder who gives a display of anger. If a visitor can remain quiet and still, gorillas are quite tame and shy. Some people have tried to capture baby gorillas for zoos. But gorillas will fight to the death to defend their young. Since the young animals fail to survive in zoos anyway, this is a cruel practice. Money from tourists who want to visit gorillas in the wild is now helping to save them from extinction.

Observing Patterns

1. Write the three list words that contain double consonants.
attack valleys gorilla
2. Write the two list words that mean actions that were completed in the past. Underline the base word for each.
tracked stayed
3. Write the three list words that have three syllables.
understand anyway gorilla
4. Unscramble the pair of rhyming list words in each cave.

trail fail display anyway base chase

1

Observing Patterns

1. Have students note that the double consonants in **attack**, **valley**, and **gorilla** occur in the middle of the words. Suggest ways for students to highlight the doubling to help remember it.

attack valley gorilla

2. Review with students that **track** and **stay** are verbs, and that the **-ed** ending indicates the action occurred in the past. Have them note the pronunciation (trackt, stayd) and reinforce the idea that in English regular verbs form the past tense by adding **-ed**, although the pronunciation can be **t**, **d**, or **ed** (**passed**, **played**, **wanted**).

3. Review the concept of syllables, reminding students that each syllable in English contains one vowel sound.

Students can put one hand under their chin and feel how their jaw drops as vowels are spoken.

4. Unscrambling list words helps students focus on the sequence of letters. They may enjoy using other list words to write scrambled messages for a partner to decipher.

5. Write the list word that means the opposite of each word below.

succeed male release leave

fail female capture stay

Words with opposite meanings are called **antonyms**.

Discovering Patterns

understand tracked female chase stayed anyway display remain fail male trail attack base capture valleys gorilla

1. Write the list words that have the short sound /a/ as in **tack**. Circle the letter that makes this sound.

understand tracked attack capture valleys gorilla

2. Make a chart in your notebook like the one below. Write the following list words under the correct headings.

female chase stayed remain display fail male trail base

long a spelled **ay** as in **day**	long a spelled **ai** as in **sail**	long a spelled **a_e** as in **name**
stayed display	remain fail trail	female base chase male

POWERBOOSTER

- The short vowel sound /a/ is usually spelled **a** as in **capture**.
- The long vowel sound /ā/ may be spelled **ay** as in **stayed**, **ai** as in **fail**, or **a_e** as in **base**.

2

5. Students might point out that the opposite of 'leave' is 'stay' and not 'stayed' as appears in the word list. You could use this opportunity to review the **-ed** verb ending indicating past tense.

Discovering Patterns

1. Contrast the long and short sounds of **a** as in **fat** (short) and **fate** (long). Remind students that the symbol / / will always represent sounds, not spellings. The sound /a/ is heard most clearly in the second syllable of **attack**.

Some students may suggest the final **a** in gorilla is a short **a**. Accept this answer, but point out that it is actually pronounced slightly differently, since it is an unstressed vowel.

2. Have students look for other words to add to each category in the chart. Encourage them to check the spelling of any words they are unsure of. (See Critical Thinking, below.)

long a spelled		
ay	**ai**	**a_e**
play	mail	bale
crayon	drain	became
delay	painful	migrate
daylight	brain	stage
highway	raining	scale

Writing

- Synonyms are a great help in writing both fiction and non-fiction. Often, a writer needs to say the same thing in several different ways. How many synonyms can students discover for the list words in this unit? Encourage them to use a thesaurus whenever they have problems finding a particular synonym.

Critical Thinking

- Students should be aware that longer words contain the same short and long vowel spelling patterns as smaller words do. To give them practice sorting words with long and short **a** hand out packs of cards that have one of the words given here written on each card. Students will also need two large hoops. Have them discover ways to sort the words according to whether they contain a long or short **a**, and to explain their choices. Some words contain both sounds, and they will need to overlap the hoops to form a third category.

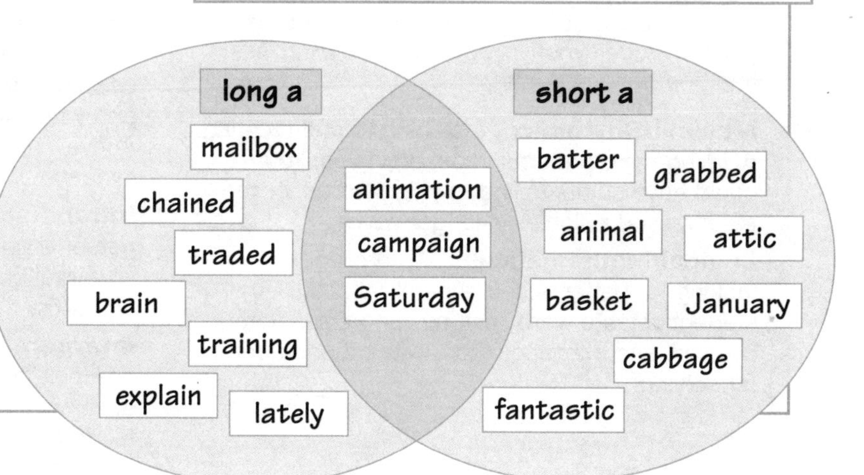

Exploring Patterns

1. The words **mail**, **tail**, **sail**, **pail** all have homophones in which the long **a** is spelled **a_e**. Ask students to develop sentences that show the difference in meaning between each homophone 'pair'.

I bought a new **sail** for my boat at the **sale**.

2. You may wish to point out other ways to spell the sound at the end of **capture** (pit**cher**, but**cher**; sol**dier**).

Students could write clues for other words ending in **-ture**.

–ture words	clue
creature	another name for an animal
puncture	a tire that's flat has one of these
fracture	a break in a bone
caricature	a cartoon drawing

3. This exercise helps students discriminate between long and short **a** in longer words. If students experience difficulty with this, try easier pairs such as **fat/fate**, **hat/hate**, **flat/fate**.

4. You might point out to students that the word **base** has a homograph—**base** meaning low, or humble.

In some dictionaries, students will find homographs listed as separate entries.

Exploring Patterns

1. Climb the mountain! As you meet each letter, make a word that rhymes with **fail**. The answers all contain /ā/ spelled **ai**.

mail, jail, tail, nail, sail, rail, pail

2. Write the words that fit these clues! The answers are all words that end in **-ture**, as in **capture**.

a) p i c ture — a drawing or photograph
b) a d v e n ture — an exciting or dangerous experience
c) v u l ture — a bird that eats dead animals
d) n a ture — the world not made by humans

3. Follow the trail of gorilla tracks. Write the word from each pair of prints that has the /a/ sound as in **valley**.

a) bakery / back — back
b) castle / claim — castle
c) maybe / magic — magic

4. The dictionary gives a number of meanings for the word **base**. Read the entry below.

base (bās) **1** the part of a thing on which it rests; bottom **2** in certain games, a station or goal **3** a starting place **4** a permanent camp or other place where units of the armed forces are stationed.

Write the number of the definition that fits the meaning of **base** in each of the sentences below.

a) The player slid into third base. (2)
b) There is an armed forces base at Gagetown. (4)
c) The machine rests on a steel base. (1)
d) The base of our hiking trip was beside a brook. (3)

3

Multiple Intelligences

- Spelling strategies for long vowel combinations can be designed to appeal to a variety of intelligences.

Verbal/Linguistic: Word play, computer games, talking about words—such an approach might include synonym and antonym exercises, and homophone riddles.

Musical/Rhythmic: Listening to and creating rhyming word patterns, raps, or jingles. You could have students find rhyming words, or tap the stressed syllables in longer words.

Logical/Mathematical: Word puzzles, looking for patterns and generalizations. Have students create word searches and crossword puzzles, and exchange them with other students for solving.

Visual/Spatial: Students could use colour-coding systems for difficult letters, highlighter pens, word cards, letter tiles, and other forms of visualization.

Bodily/Kinesthetic: Have students undertake hands-on work with words—let them use various writing instruments or a keyboard, and write words in the air or on a partner's back. Active involvement of students is the key in this instance.

Intrapersonal: Challenge students to set personal goals. Encourage them to use the visualization activities described in visual/spatial, and allow them independent working time.

Interpersonal: Have students work in co-operative learning groups to study words and develop strategies. Be sure to give positive feedback about improvement and how much the student knows.

5. a) Imagine you and your guide have just come upon a family of mountain gorillas. Brainstorm with a partner and list six adjectives that describe your feelings. Then list six verbs that describe what you will do in the next sixty seconds.

b) Using the word lists you made in a), write a short paragraph about your meeting with the mountain gorillas.

SUPER WORDS

Africa
captivity
complain
primates
gait
strayed

Challenges with Words

1. Write the Super Words that match each clue. The shaded letters will spell a word that describes gorillas.

a) a way of walking or running
b) a large southern continent
c) the opposite of freedom
d) to find fault with
e) the highest order of mammals
f) wandered, roamed

gait
Africa
captivity
complain
primates
strayed

2. Make four columns in your notebook like this.

one syllable	two syllables	three syllables	four syllables
gait	complain	Africa	captivity
strayed	primates		

Write each Super Word in the correct column. Mark the syllable we stress in each word.

In words with two or more syllables, one syllable is spoken with more force or stress. cap'ture

4

5. In most units, writing exercises encourage students to use the words they are studying in their own writing. If there are two exercises, the first is usually focussed on word-building or is linked directly to the list words, or both. The second exercise is more open-ended, providing a support for the students' own writing. Be sure to encourage students to write freely, using the prompt if they need it, and going off in their own directions if they wish.

Ask students to work in small groups and brainstorm a list of adjectives and verbs that describe feelings and actions. If necessary, review what each part of speech does in a sentence. Have students share their lists with other groups.

feelings	actions
wonder, fear, amazement, awe, interest, fascination, amusement, disbelief	run, watch, hide, sit, stare, follow, photograph, draw

Challenges with Words

The Super Words and Challenges with Words are intended for students who have experienced little or no difficulty with the Precheck.

1. Have students pronounce each word, listening for the long and short sounds of **a**, and noting how they are spelled. Ask them to underline the letters that spell the long **a** sound in compl**ai**n, prim**a**t**e**s, g**ai**t, and str**ay**ed.

2. Have students clap or tap the syllables as they say the words if they have difficulty hearing the number of syllables. It is important that students hear and are aware of the syllables in longer words if they are to spell them correctly.

ESL

- The long vowel **a** is common in many languages. In English, it appears in a complex variety of spellings. Reinforce spelling patterns with the long vowel **a** by having students build word circles with the more common patterns. Provide them with a circle in which you have the pattern in the centre and the beginning consonants around the outside.
- Ask students to write the words, then say each one. Have them note that the words rhyme, and that sometimes rhyming words have different spelling patterns in English (ch**ase**/f**ace**).

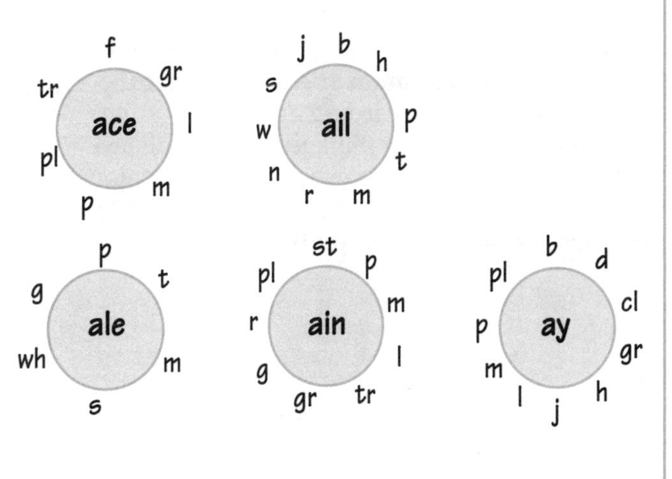

3. Ask students to work with partners or in groups of three to brainstorm a list of homophone pairs that have long vowel sounds. Then have each team write a homophone error paragraph similar to the one in this exercise. One team can challenge another to solve its puzzle paragraph.

homophone pairs		
pain/pane great/grate	know/no sew/so	led/lead week/weak

4. Students may wish to design a word search or crossword puzzle with the **ay** words they find.

■	■	T 1	R 2	A	Y
■	C 4	■	A		
D 5	R	A	Y		
■	A	■	■		
	Y				

ACROSS
1. Used to carry things on
5. Pulled by horses

DOWN
2. A ____ of sunshine
4. Like a small lobster

3. Many homophones have the spelling pattern **ai** or **a_e**.

Example: The gorilla, with its shuffling ***gait****, went through the* ***gate*** *of its cage.*

Gait and **gate** sound the same but have different spellings. When we write a homophone we must think about its meaning as well as its sound to spell the correct word.

Rewrite the paragraph below, using the correct homophones.

The unfriendly dog was not wagging its <u>tale</u> [tail] when I delivered [mail] <u>male</u> to the house. As the dog leaped at me I turned <u>pail</u>, [pale] and [made] <u>maid</u> a flying leap through the gate—just like a <u>plain</u> taking off! [plane]

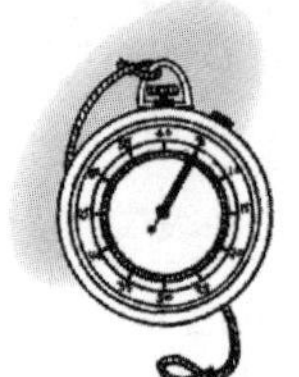

4. One–Two–Three–GO! Find as many words as you can with the **ay** pattern as in **stayed**. Give yourself five minutes.

5. The Super Word **primates** comes from the word **prime**, which means 'first in rank or order'. Find three words in the dictionary that have the base word **prime**. Write your own definitions for these words.

6. Finish this story with Super Words and your own words.

Far away, in the continent of ______, there lived a small band of ______. One day a young male ______ from the band and was captured and kept in ______. The poor animal.....

air miles
talking book
air bags

7. These new words are all created by combining two simple words. Write the words that fit the sentences below.

a) When you travel some airlines give you __air__ __miles__ toward a free flight.

b) __Air__ __bags__ may save lives in a car crash.

c) Listening to a __talking__ __book__ helps pass the time on a long car trip.

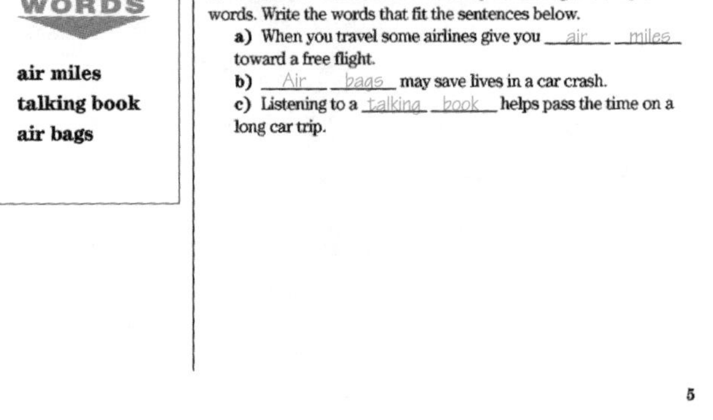

5

5. and **6.** Filling in cloze passages is a good way to practise writing words in context. Students could extend the exercise by writing their own sentences with 'prime' words. For example: primary, primer, prime minister, primeval, primitive, and priming.

New Words

7. New words are included in every other unit. The purpose is to help students realize that language is always changing and new words are being added. As you study the words:

• talk about the way new words are made (for example, combining two simple words like air and **bags**).
• ask students to suggest synonyms for the new words in the list (**air miles**/travel rewards; **talking book**/taped book; **air bags**/restraint system)
• discuss how long they think the words will last in the language. Do words ever go 'out of fashion'?
• ask if other spellings for the same terms have been spotted (**airbags** or **air bags**).

Special Needs

• Some students might need extra help distinguishing between the sound of long and short **a**. You can identify these students by dictating word pairs such as the following.

short	long
plan	plane
Stan	stain
man	main
ran	rain
can	cane
van	vain

• Once you know which students are having difficulty hearing and spelling the sound, take some time to review long and short vowel patterns, using *The Canadian Spelling Program 2.1*, Book 4, Units 1-10. (See ESL, p. 23.)

Curriculum Connection

An important sanctuary for mountain gorillas is located in strife-torn Rwanda, in East Africa. Students may wish to find Rwanda on a map, and discuss the effects the fighting in that country might be having on the gorilla population.

Students could compile a list of fascinating gorilla facts from reference books and CD-ROMs as a reference for further study.

Home Connection

Alert parents to the fact that the students will be studying long vowel spelling patterns in this and the next four units. You may wish to provide a chart showing the various spelling patterns, and encourage the students' families to add to each list as they encounter such words in their everyday lives.

Dear Parent,

We have been studying words with the long **a** sound, such as **plain**, **display**, and **base**. Please help us by making lists with your children of objects and activities around your home that have this sound. For example, outside you may have a **driveway** or a **lane**. Each window will have a **pane** of glass in it.

Assessment

Help students identify their errors on the unit test. Did they make the same errors on the Precheck? Have these errors persisted because they are not hearing the sequence of sounds clearly? Or are they uncertain of which pattern to use to spell the specific vowel sound?

Follow-up

Use a variety of strategies to work with students still experiencing difficulty. (See Multiple Intelligences, p. 22.)

Monitor the spelling of long **a** and the **-ed** ending in students' everyday writing. Encourage them to proofread for long **a** errors, especially homophone errors, such as **plane/plain**, that a computer spell check will not pick up.

Teacher's Notes

2 Long and short e

e as in lens
ee as in speed
ea as in heat

Patterns

This unit reviews common spellings of the long **e** sound. Students need to learn to use visual as well as sound strategies to decide which spelling of the long **e** is correct. Is it balance b**ea**m or b**ee**m? Both are logical and fit spelling patterns, but students need tactics—visual strategies—to remember what the word looks like.

Preknowledge

Students should have an understanding of the following concepts as they work through this unit.

- Long vowels say the letter names (h**a**te, b**ea**t, qu**i**te, r**o**pe).
- The same sound can have different spellings in English (t**ai**l/t**a**l**e**; m**ee**t/m**ea**t; b**ite**/b**ight**).
- Many words are composed of base words and endings (**mountain/eer**, **locat/ion**, **hope/ful**).

More Patterns

Other patterns you might wish to introduce or review in this unit include the following.

- The sound /z/ spelled **s** as in la**s**er.
- Words that end in **-ing** and **-ed** (**sitting**, **seated**).

Professional Notebook

English is an alphabetic language. Once you get past the most frequent words, there is a great deal of predictability in the letter-sound patterns. This predictability is not based on a one-letter, one-sound relationship, however. Rather, it is based on the pattern of letters that follow the vowel. The vowel and following letters have been given a variety of labels. Some teachers call them word families, others call them phonograms. Linguists refer to them as rimes.

(Cunningham 150)

Sharing the Secrets with Kids

*The **ea** spelling of the long **e** sound is tricky because it also spells short **e** as in w**ea**ther, and long **a** as in st**ea**k. Reassure students that **ea** spells long **e** more often than not, and help them group words with other sounds.*

spelled ea		
long /a/	short /e/	long /e/
steak break bear	weather bread head	lead leash beat

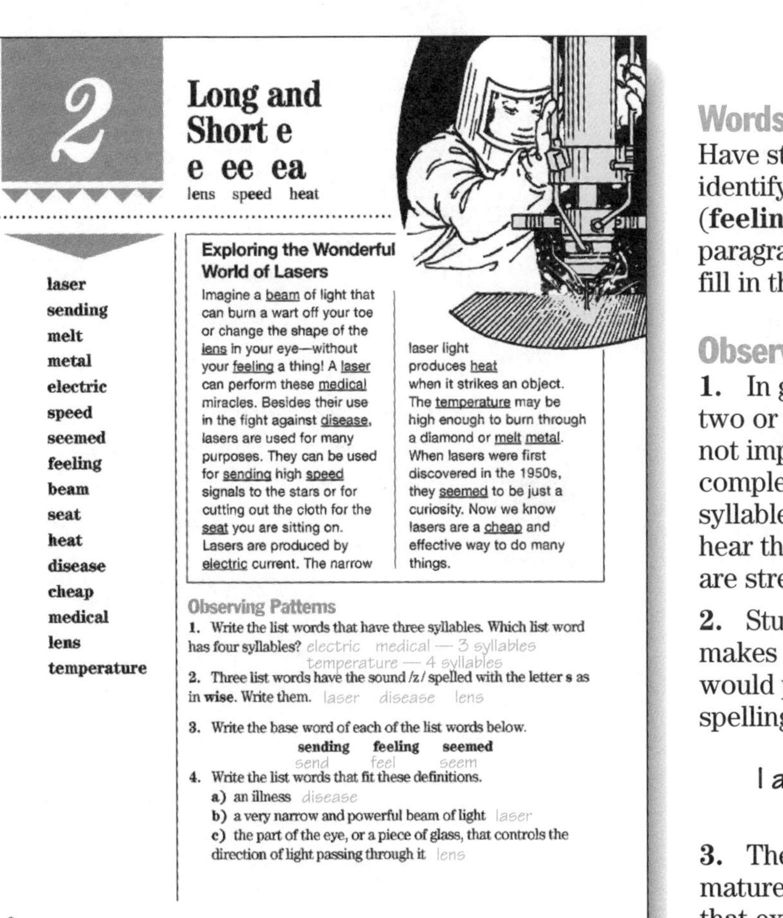

2 Long and Short e

e ee ea

lens speed heat

laser
sending
melt
metal
electric
speed
seemed
feeling
beam
seat
heat
disease
cheap
medical
lens
temperature

Exploring the Wonderful World of Lasers

Imagine a beam of light that can burn a wart off your toe or change the shape of the lens in your eye—without your feeling a thing! A laser can perform these medical miracles. Besides their use in the fight against disease, lasers are used for many purposes. They can be used for sending high speed signals to the stars or for cutting out the cloth for the seat you are sitting on. Lasers are produced by electric current. The narrow laser light produces heat when it strikes an object. The temperature may be high enough to burn through a diamond or melt metal. When lasers were first discovered in the 1950s, they seemed to be just a curiosity. Now we know lasers are a cheap and effective way to do many things.

Observing Patterns

1. Write the list words that have three syllables. Which list word has four syllables? electric medical — 3 syllables temperature — 4 syllables
2. Three list words have the sound /z/ spelled with the letter **s** as in **wise**. Write them. laser disease lens
3. Write the base word of each of the list words below.
   sending send **feeling** feel **seemed** seem
4. Write the list words that fit these definitions.
   a) an illness disease
   b) a very narrow and powerful beam of light laser
   c) the part of the eye, or a piece of glass, that controls the direction of light passing through it lens

6

Precheck

Emphasize that the Precheck is not a test. Stress the importance of listening for letter sounds in the list words. As an aid to correct spelling, encourage students to say the word to themselves before writing it.

Dictation

A **laser** is often used in medicine.
Sending messages is fast with e-mail.
Ice-cream will **melt** very quickly.
The **metal** chain rusted badly.
Electric cars would save gas.
My 10-**speed** bike was stolen.
He **seemed** to be sad.
She was **feeling** sick.
The balance **beam** broke.
That **seat** is very hard!
Heat up that pizza.
It was an infectious **disease**.
Cheap CDs sound OK.
My sister is a **medical** doctor.
The camera **lens** is dusty.
The **temperature** was -30 degrees.

Words in Context

Have students read the paragraph and then identify the list words with the long **e** sound (**feeling**, **beam**). You may wish to reproduce the paragraph as a cloze passage and have students fill in the list words.

Observing Patterns

1. In grade 5, you will often find words with two or more syllables in students' writing. It is not important that they be able to apply the complex rules for dividing the words into syllables. Students should, however, be able to hear the distinct syllables and the fact that some are stressed.

2. Students could circle the letter **s** which makes the /z/ sound in each word. This practice would provide a visual reinforcement for the spelling of **laser**, **disease**, and **lens**.

l a (s) e r   d i (s) e a (s) e   l e n (s)

3. The concept of base words is crucial to a mature understanding of the spelling system that extends beyond the level of sound. Further practice in isolating the base words may be necessary for some students who have difficulty separating them from prefixes and suffixes. If you use the term root word in your class, remind students that base word means essentially the same thing.

word	prefix	base	suffix
unreasonable	un-	reason	-able
bicycle	bi-	cycle	—
refreshment	re-	fresh	-ment
unacceptable	un-	accept	-able
illogical	il-	logic	-al
international	inter-	nation	-al

4. Students could work in pairs to write definitions for other list words, then challenge a partner to guess the words.

What ice begins to do when the temperature rises	*Melt*
The opposite of expensive	*Cheap*
The rate at which something travels	*Speed*

5. Ask students to explain the relationship between their chosen list word and the other words in the set. For example, gold, copper, and tin are all types of metal.

6. Many of the vowels omitted in the exercise are schwa vowels /ə/, the short vowels in unstressed syllables that are pronounced "uh" (medi**ca**l). We will focus on schwa vowels in units 17 and 31. To demonstrate the difference, you may wish to provide students with a derivative of such words in which the unstressed syllable is now stressed, and the vowel is clearly pronounced.

unstressed:	metal	medical
stressed:	metallic	medicinal

7. Configuration boxes provide a visual prompt to the spelling of words. Another method involves the use of lines to represent the shape of words.

f e e l i n g | | | | | | |

Discovering Patterns

1. For some students, it may be useful to contrast short **e** with long **e** using word pairs.

short e:	met	set	step	pep	wed
long e:	meet	seat	steep	peep	weed

Can you think of other words that fit each set?

5. Write a list word that goes with each set.
a) gold copper tin metal
b) boiling lukewarm freezing heat
c) camera glasses microscope lens

6. Sometimes it is difficult to hear the vowel sounds in words. Complete each list word with the correct vowel and write the words in your notebook.

met _ l **temp _ rat _ re** **med _ c _ l** **d _ sease**

7. Write the list words that fit these boxes.

e l e c t r i c t e m p e r a t u r e

Discovering Patterns

laser sending melt metal electric
speed seemed feeling beam seat heat
disease cheap medical lens temperature

1. Write the list words that have the short vowel sound /e/ as in **lens**. Circle the letter that makes this sound. sending melt electric medical lens temperature

2. Many of the list words have the long vowel sound /ē/ as in **seat**. The /ē/ sound can be spelled in more than one way. Write the /ē/ list words under two headings.

/ē/ spelled **ea** as in **meat**	/ē/ spelled **ee** as in **feet**
beam disease seat cheap heat	speed feeling seemed

POWERBOOSTER

- The short vowel sound /e/ is usually spelled **e** as in **lens**.
- The long vowel sound /ē/ may be spelled **ea** as in **meat** or **ee** as in **feet**.

7

2. Create a large classroom chart for students to fill in words with the **ee** or **ea** spelling of long **e**. Students may find words in their own writing, or might encounter them in other content areas.

street	agree	squeeze	wheel	peel	heel
east	eagle	please	weak	beak	teak

ESL

- Develop rhyming word families with the long **e** spelled **ea** and **ee**. The long vowel sound /ē/ is common in many languages, but is spelled in a variety of ways in English. Organizing words into patterns helps with recall for many students.

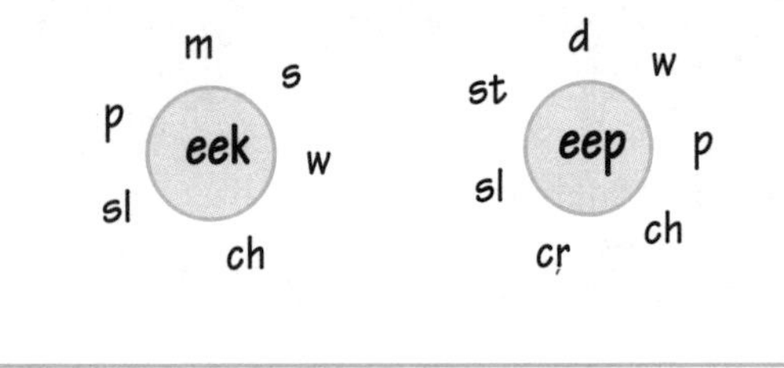

- Students from other language backgrounds may be confused by the different forms of common words such as **electric**, **metal**, and **medical**. Work with a small group and practise using these words in spoken sentences.

noun	adjective
My watch is made of metal.	It has a metallic shine.
Electricity is expensive.	The electric kettle is boiling.
She is studying medicine.	They are medical doctors.

Exploring Patterns

1. Transform the word **seat** into **read** using seven steps. For each step change only one letter at a time. Read these clues to help you.

seat

a) drums and hearts do this ______ beat
b) a laser ______ beam
c) people working as a unit ______ team
d) saltwater drop from the eye ______ tear
e) the feeling of being afraid ______ fear
f) opposite of front ______ rear

read

2. Do you feel hungry? Here are some things for you to eat! Write the name of each **ee** or **ea** word in the picture.

meat cheese beans peanuts seeds

3. The words below have the same bases as the list words **electric**, **metal**, and **medical**. Complete each sentence with one of the words. Write the sentence.

electricity medicine
electrician metallic

a) Don't forget to take your ______ at bedtime. medicine
b) Our cabin in the woods has no ______. electricity
c) The spaceship had a strange ______ glow. metallic
d) We called an ______ to repair the stove. electrician

4. Make a word pole with the word **temperature**. Add one weather word for each letter. The pole has been started for you.

Answers will vary

T hermometer
sunshin E
H U M I D
P ressure
c E lsius
R A I N I N G
w A rm
ho T
clo U dy
deg R ees
fre E zing

Make up a personal list of interesting weather words.

8

Exploring Patterns

1. Puzzles such as this word transformation are fun for students and help them focus on the sequence of letters in a word. Suggest to students that they work with a partner if they experience difficulty.

2. Encourage students to watch out for homophones (**meat/meet**; **been/bean**; **hare/hair**).

3. Suggest that students say the sentences quietly to themselves. ESL students might need extra help in recognizing that **electric** is the adjective, while **electricity** is the noun. (See ESL, p. 28.)

Ask students for other words sharing the same bases as **electric** and **medical**. Encourage students to use a dictionary to help them in their search.

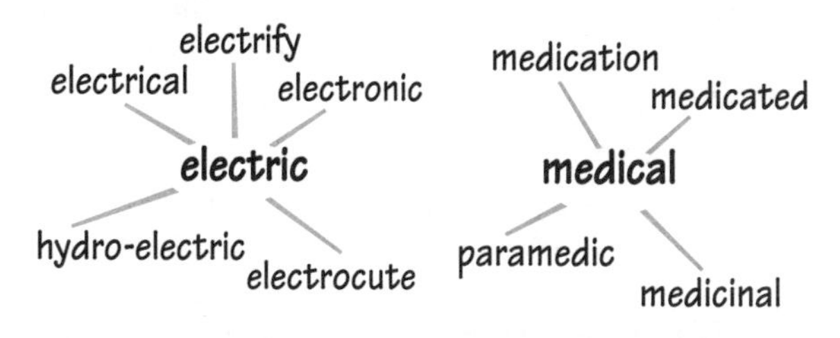

4. Word poles also help students focus on the sequence of letters in a longer word such as **temperature**. Have students share their contributions to the word pole and create a master word pole for the class.

Co-operative Learning

Several activities in this unit can be adapted to work with co-operative groups.

- In Exploring Patterns 2 you might wish to have students work with a partner and brainstorm to create a list of other long **e** food words, using supermarket ads as a resource.

long e	
seafood	wheat
greens	beef
tea	peach
beets	leeks
soybeans	meat

- You could also plan a discrimination exercise in which students isolate food words with the long vowel sound /ē/ (b**ea**ns, t**ea**, m**ea**t, p**ea**ches) from other food words that contain the spelling pattern **ea** but not the /ē/ sound (st**ea**k, br**ea**d).
- In Exploring Patterns 5, divide the whole group into smaller groups for discussions about what to include in the message. Students might find it helpful to make point-form notes as they work together. Have them share their finished messages with the whole group.

From Spaceship Galaxy 1. Near Mars.
Temperature in electric systems rising.
Heat making metal wires melt...

5. Some students may prefer to plan the message as a group. (See Co-operative Learning, p. 29.) Have them discuss the problem their spacecraft is having and the help that might be needed. What should they include in the message? You might find it useful to discuss the style of emergency messages—brief, unemotional, and clear.

Challenges with Words

1. Have students create their own sentences using the Super Words. They may select a different topic from among the list words.

2. Emphasize to students that their answers will be synonyms that are close to, but not exactly the same as, the meaning of the Super Word. Encourage them to develop sentences that illustrate shades of meaning. (A **battery** is a source of electrical power. It takes a lot of **energy** to ride up a steep hill.)

3. As an alternative, students may wish to create acronyms or initials for classroom or recreational activities.

activity	acronym	
recess	SORT	student on release time
lunch	SACT	student at chow time
bedtime	LON	lights out now
reading	CAB	cruising a book

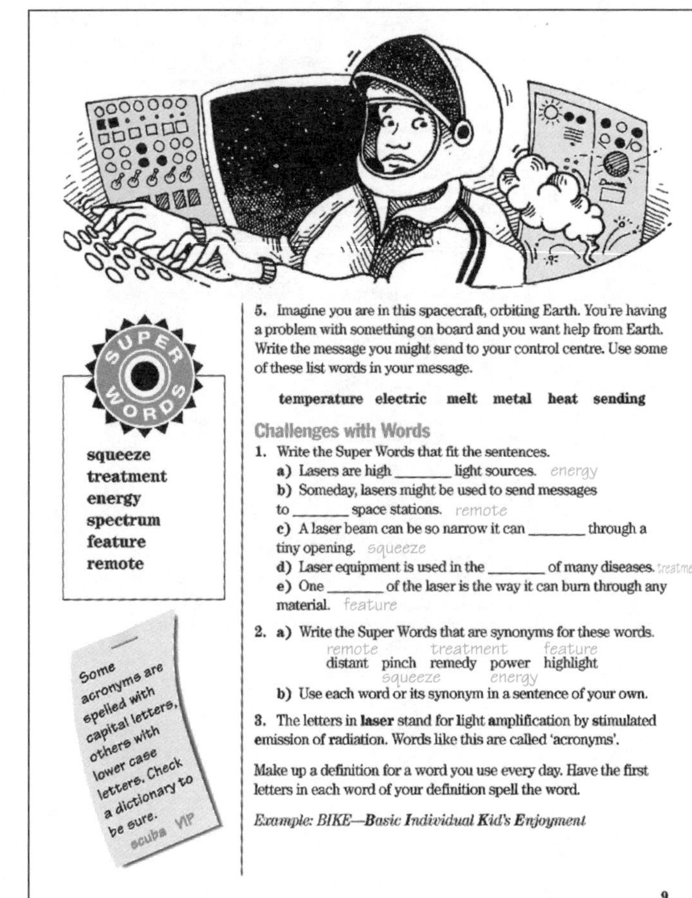

SUPER WORDS

squeeze
treatment
energy
spectrum
feature
remote

Some acronyms are spelled with capital letters, others with lower case letters. Check a dictionary to be sure. scuba VIP

5. Imagine you are in this spacecraft, orbiting Earth. You're having a problem with something on board and you want help from Earth. Write the message you might send to your control centre. Use some of these list words in your message.

temperature electric melt metal heat sending

Challenges with Words

1. Write the Super Words that fit the sentences.

a) Lasers are high _______ light sources. energy

b) Someday, lasers might be used to send messages to _______ space stations. remote

c) A laser beam can be so narrow it can _______ through a tiny opening. squeeze

d) Laser equipment is used in the _______ of many diseases. treatment

e) One _______ of the laser is the way it can burn through any material. feature

2. a) Write the Super Words that are synonyms for these words.

distant (remote) pinch (squeeze) remedy (treatment) power (energy) highlight (feature)

b) Use each word or its synonym in a sentence of your own.

3. The letters in **laser** stand for light amplification by stimulated emission of radiation. Words like this are called 'acronyms'.

Make up a definition for a word you use every day. Have the first letters in each word of your definition spell the word.

Example: BIKE—Basic Individual Kid's Enjoyment

9

Special Needs

• Some students may need more practice visually sorting long **e** words spelled **ee** and **ea**. Provide them with word cards and have them sort words in boxes, circles, or hoops.

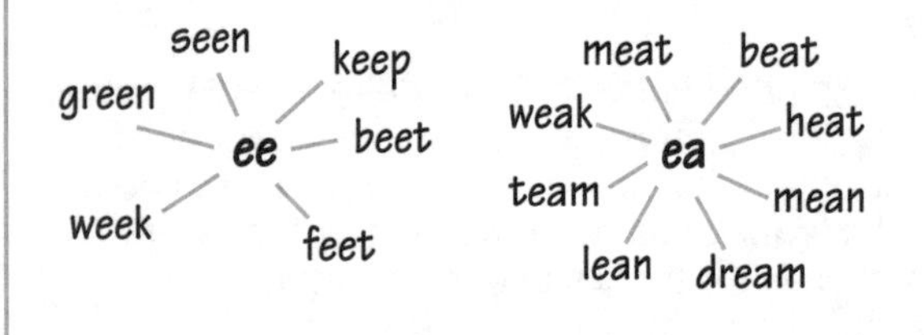

• Students might also enjoy filling in homophone frames to reinforce word meaning. Provide them with frames such as the following.

He can't chew the m______t. His teeth are too w______k.

Next w______k, she will m______t them at the park.

I can't s______m to sew the s______m on this shirt.

• Creating word wheels with rhyming words that follow the same spelling patterns is a useful visual, auditory, and tactile strategy for learning long **e** words. Here are three examples.

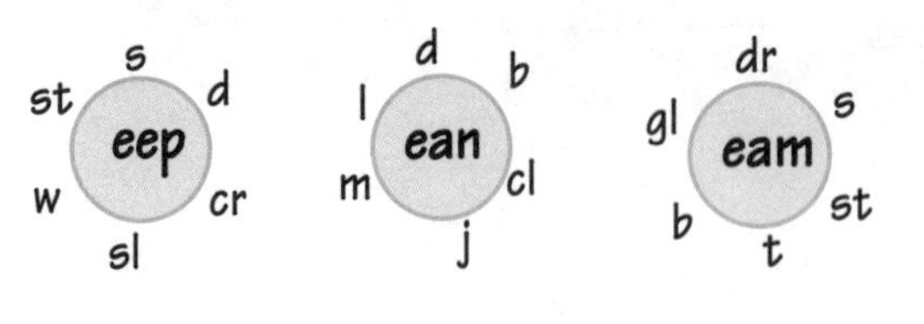

4. Write a word with the long vowel sound /ē/ that fits these patterns.

a) It was (ee) freezing cold as the wind howled through the (ee) trees in the forest.

b) Don't (ea) leave your little brother alone!

c) The goalie dropped to her (ee). knees

d) For years, the ship had sailed the high (ea). seas

5. Use the Super Words and your own words to finish this story.

The young scientist was proud of his invention. It was a water treatment method that would provide clean water for the city and conserve energy at the same time. No longer would water be piped from a remote lake high in the mountains. Water from deep wells would be used for most of the city's needs. Another special feature of his invention was....

10

4. Students' answers will vary in this exercise. Students should be encouraged to be creative but to use words that fit the context of the sentence. Have students share their answers with the group.

5. Have students brainstorm as a group to gather ideas and vocabulary to expand the story. Encourage students to choose words that make the story interesting.

Proofreading Strategies

- Encourage students to become good proofreaders as well as good writers. Proofreading is a definite skill that needs to be practised on a regular basis. Good writers always proofread their work before 'going public'.

  1. Read your writing out loud to a partner.

  2. Switch writing with a partner. You may catch each other's mistakes.

  3. The first time you check a draft, put a mark around words that 'look wrong'.

  4. Use a dictionary to help you proofread.

- Suggest students work with a partner to proofread their writing. They can develop personal proofreading checklists such as the following.

Proofreading Checklist

This piece of writing has been checked for:

Capitals and periods................. ☐

Spelling mistakes................... ☐

New paragraph for each new speaker..................... ☐

Quotation marks..................... ☐

Other errors......................... ☐

____

____

____

Curriculum Connection

Invite students to brainstorm 'laser' words. Develop a word web on the chalkboard as students supply responses. Have one group find information about lasers from the encyclopedia and other library media. Then, in a class discussion, have students share their research. During the discussion, add other laser words to the word web that students have researched. Students might like to make a personal record of words they discover, word extensions, or words with difficult spellings as an ongoing project.

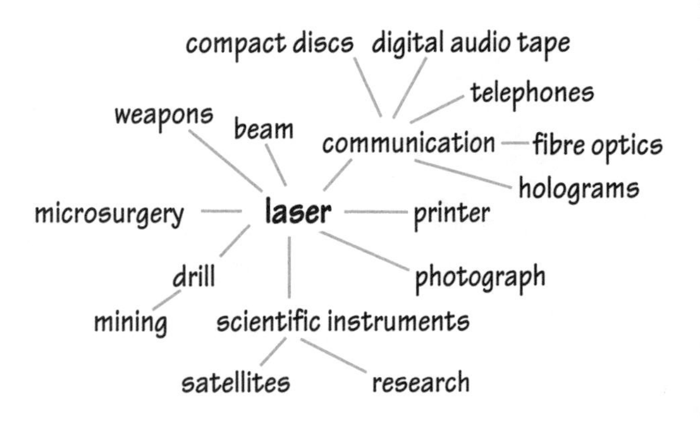

Assessment

Remind students to listen carefully and to say the list words to themselves as they write. After the test and self-correction, have students compare results with the Precheck. Do they notice an improvement? Can they see a pattern to their errors? Encourage students to write words they misspelled with spaces for the specific letters they need to focus on. Then, fill in the letters.

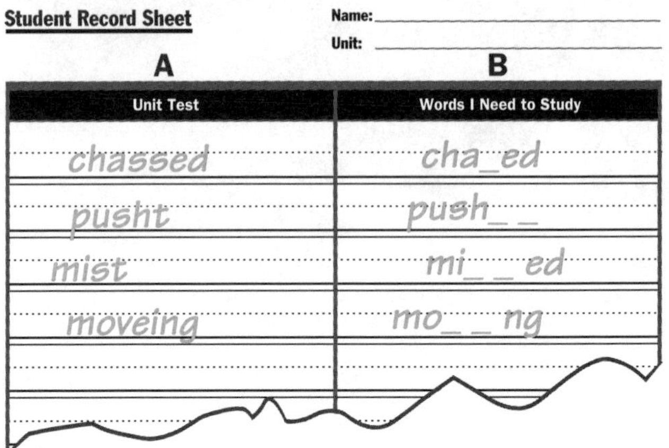

Student Record Sheet

Name:

Unit:

A Unit Test	B Words I Need to Study
chassed	cha_ed
pusht	push__
mist	mi__ed
moveing	mo__ng

Follow-up

Students can begin a Personal Review List comprised of words that contained errors on the unit tests, words that give them particular problems (**because**, **surprise**), and words from content areas that they are studying. Suggest that they add to this list on an on-going basis and strike off words as they master the spelling of them.

Teacher's Notes

3 Long and short i

i_e as in slide
i as in cliff

Patterns

This unit reviews the long and short **i** sound. Students can contrast the sounds in such words as b**i**t and b**i**te, and discuss how a final silent **e** changes the sound from short to long. The one-syllable patterns reviewed here form the basis for multisyllabic list words that students will encounter in speaking and writing (**difficult**, **organized**).

Preknowledge

Students should have an understanding of the following concepts as they work with the patterns in this unit.

- English vowel sounds can be long or short (b**a**t/b**ai**t; qu**i**ck/qu**i**t**e**).
- A silent **e** at the end of a word usually means the vowel is long (m**a**t/m**a**t**e**).
- Adding **-ed** to a verb indicates past tense (**walk/walked**).
- Adding **-ly** to the end of a word usually turns it into an adverb (**quick/quickly**).
- Consonant blends such as **pr**, **gr**, **cl**, **sl**, **sp** occur often at the beginning of words (**pr**etend/**gr**eat/**cl**ear/**sl**ip/**sp**ell).

More Patterns

Other patterns you might wish to review or introduce in this unit include the following.

- The **-ed** ending usually signals the past tense of a verb (**organize/organized**). If a verb ends in **e**, that **e** is dropped when **-ed** is added (**guide/guided**).
- Some words contain the double consonants **ff**, **ll**, **cc** (gira**ff**e, pi**ll**ar, a**cc**ent). In such words the vowel sound is usually short (b**i**tter/b**i**ter).

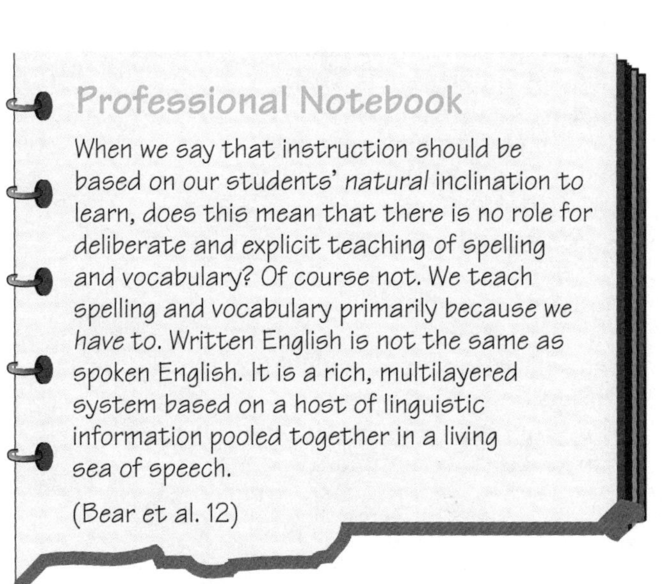

Professional Notebook

When we say that instruction should be based on our students' *natural* inclination to learn, does this mean that there is no role for deliberate and explicit teaching of spelling and vocabulary? Of course not. We teach spelling and vocabulary primarily because we *have* to. Written English is not the same as spoken English. It is a rich, multilayered system based on a host of linguistic information pooled together in a living sea of speech.

(Bear et al. 12)

Sharing the Secrets with Kids

Syllable juncture—the place where two syllables divide—is an important spelling principle in grades 4–6. If students understand that a word such as ***e /quip /ment*** *can be divided into three syllables, it is much easier to spell.*

Some students might find it helpful to 'clap' the syllables of a word as they say it. Have them practise, using their own names or the list words. It might also be useful to provide visual reinforcement. You could write each syllable of a word on a separate card and have students reassemble the scrambled cards in the correct order.

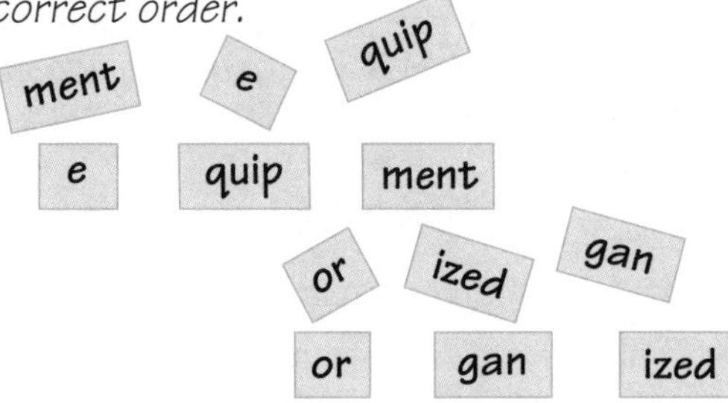

Precheck

Make sure that students understand the Precheck has two purposes. It will help them recognize words they already know how to spell as well as those they need to study. Try to create a positive, self-confident attitude toward spelling by emphasizing what students know as well as what they need to learn.

Dictation

My mom **fixed** the brakes on my bike.
Volleyball **practice** is at 4 p.m.
The paint spilled by **accident**.
I got a good **grip** on the bat.
That was a **difficult** word.
It takes **skill** to play the piano.
The **fifth** of March is a holiday.
The **cliff** is 200 metres high.
Sports **equipment** can be expensive.
She **quit** her job.
Walk **quickly** please.
It's fun to **slide** on ice.
The safety **line** broke suddenly.
Our **guide** got lost.
Keep your notebook **organized**.
The **spike** is 30 centimetres long.

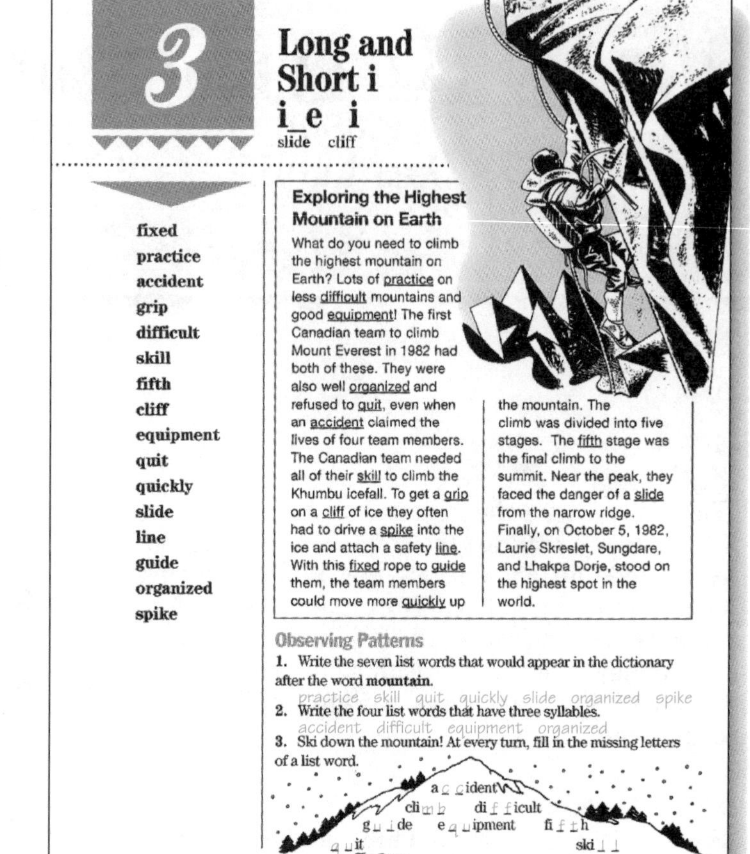

3

Long and Short i

i_e i

slide cliff

fixed
practice
accident
grip
difficult
skill
fifth
cliff
equipment
quit
quickly
slide
line
guide
organized
spike

Exploring the Highest Mountain on Earth

What do you need to climb the highest mountain on Earth? Lots of practice on less difficult mountains and good equipment! The first Canadian team to climb Mount Everest in 1982 had both of these. They were also well organized and refused to quit, even when an accident claimed the lives of four team members. The Canadian team needed all of their skill to climb the Khumbu icefall. To get a grip on a cliff of ice they often had to drive a spike into the ice and attach a safety line. With this fixed rope to guide them, the team members could move more quickly up the mountain. The climb was divided into five stages. The fifth stage was the final climb to the summit. Near the peak, they faced the danger of a slide from the narrow ridge. Finally, on October 5, 1982, Laurie Skreslet, Sungdare, and Lhakpa Dorje, stood on the highest spot in the world.

Observing Patterns

1. Write the seven list words that would appear in the dictionary after the word **mountain**.
practice skill quit quickly slide organized spike
2. Write the four list words that have three syllables.
accident difficult equipment organized
3. Ski down the mountain! At every turn, fill in the missing letters of a list word.

11

Words in Context

Read the passage with students, and point out that it is a true story. Make sure students understand all of the words, and discuss any they are unsure of. Ask students to suggest synonyms for words such as **fixed**, **organized**, **quickly**.

Observing Patterns

1. Activities like this help students become familiar with the dictionary and confident in using it to look up words for spellings or meanings.

2. If students have difficulty identifying syllables, encourage them to say the words aloud. Ask them to identify the stressed syllable in each word. Have them rewrite the words showing the syllables and marking which is stressed.

3. Students could also underline or circle or highlight these letters to reinforce them in their memories.

- Students need to recognize that the silent **e** at the end of words usually signals a long vowel. This is increasingly important as words become longer and more complex (**organize**, **define**). Have students make new words by adding **e** to the words given here, listening for the change in sound as they say each word.

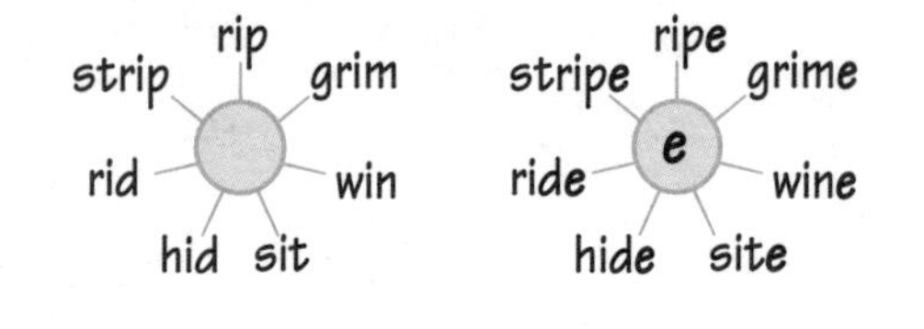

- Develop **i-consonant-e** word wheels with students and display them in the classroom for practice.

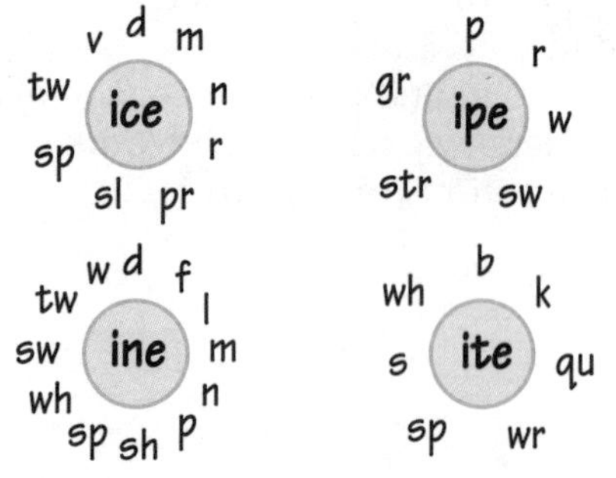

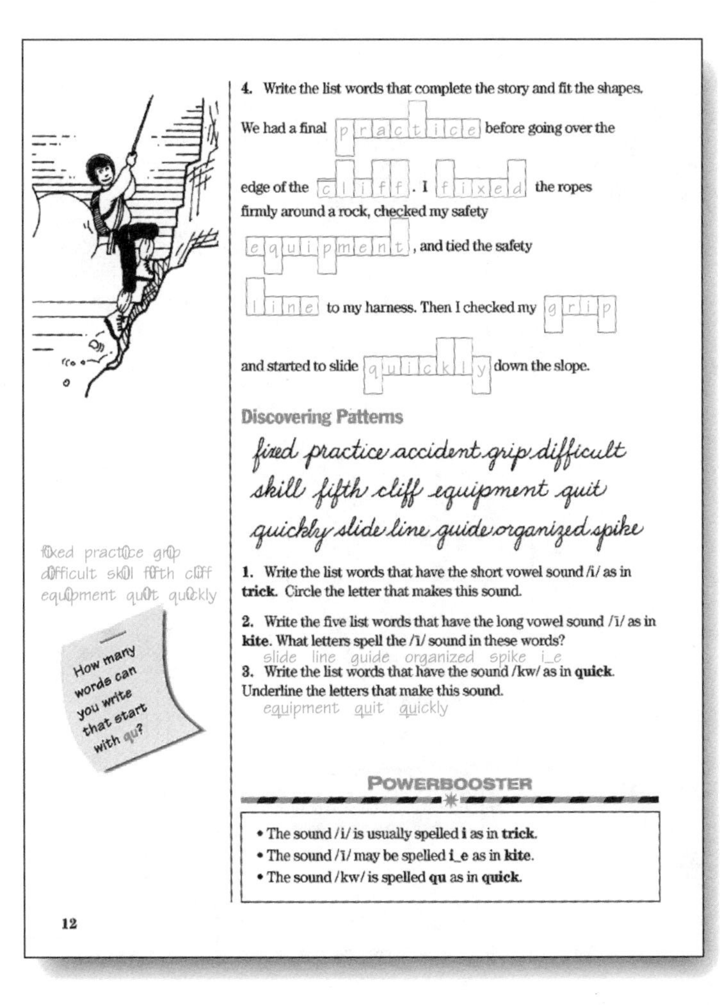
4. Write the list words that complete the story and fit the shapes.

We had a final practice before going over the edge of the cliff. I fixed the ropes firmly around a rock, checked my safety equipment, and tied the safety line to my harness. Then I checked my grip and started to slide quickly down the slope.

Discovering Patterns

fixed practice accident grip difficult skill fifth cliff equipment quit quickly slide line guide organized spike

1. Write the list words that have the short vowel sound /i/ as in **trick**. Circle the letter that makes this sound.

fixed practice grip difficult skill fifth cliff equipment quit quickly

2. Write the five list words that have the long vowel sound /ī/ as in **kite**. What letters spell the /ī/ sound in these words?

slide line guide organized spike i_e

3. Write the list words that have the sound /kw/ as in **quick**. Underline the letters that make this sound.

equipment quit quickly

How many words can you write that start with qu?

POWERBOOSTER

- The sound /i/ is usually spelled **i** as in **trick**.
- The sound /ī/ may be spelled **i_e** as in **kite**.
- The sound /kw/ is spelled **qu** as in **quick**.

12

4. Students will find it helpful to read the passage aloud, either on their own or to a partner. Configuration is another visual strategy that helps students remember the 'look' of words.

Discovering Patterns

1. The short **i** in unstressed syllables is pronounced as a schwa vowel ("uh"). This occurs in the words pract**i**ce, diff**i**cult, and acc**i**dent. Because they will be exaggerating the pronunciation as they sort the words, students might identify these as having a short **i**. This is acceptable, and may help them remember the letter **i** as they write the word.

2. Ask students to brainstorm and list as many variations as possible of the **i_e** pattern of the **i** sound.

-ite	-ime	-ipe	-ile
bite	mime	pipe	file
quite	lime	ripe	mile
site	grime	stripe	smile
excite	dime	wipe	while

3. Point out that in English, the letter **q** is always followed by the letter **u**. Contrast the spelling of the sound /kw/ as in **quick** with the spelling of the sound /g/ as in **guide**. Develop a list of words that reflect each pattern.

qu	gu
quiet	guardroom
quite	guarantee
quick	guard
quickly	guardian
quote	guardrail

ESL

- Discriminating between short and long **i** sounds may present problems to students whose first language is not English. Give them practice with word cards that have short vowels on one side and long on the other. Have students flip the cards and say each word, noting the changes in pronunciation and spelling.

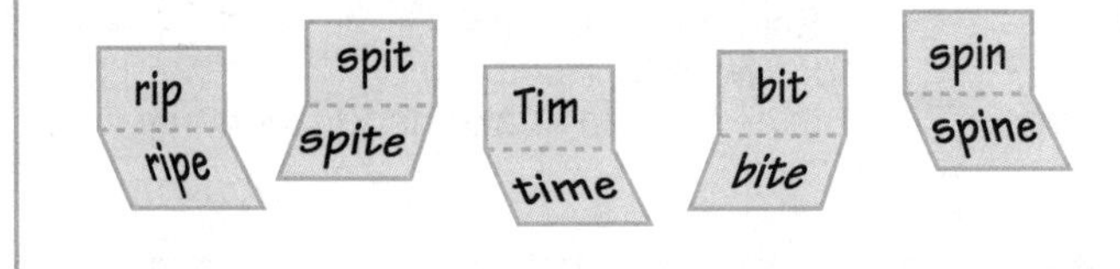

- Have all students look in telephone books for names beginning with **Q**. Note names such as **Qadar** and **Qin** that do not follow the **qu** pattern.
- Discuss how new languages bring new words and spellings of sounds into English. Ask students if there are any words in their first language that are spelled with a **q** at the beginning or end. (In English, **q** rarely occurs at the ends of words.)

Exploring Patterns

1. Remind students of the rhyme scheme of a limerick. Lines 1, 2, and 5 rhyme; lines 3 and 4 rhyme. It might help them to remember it as 'aabba'. Students might enjoy creating limericks using other list words or words from in their Personal Review Lists. (See Oral Language and Literature, below.)

2. It may be necessary to explain the terms verb, past tense, and present tense to some students. Note with students that when **-ed** is added to words ending in silent **e**, the silent **e** is dropped (**guide/guided**).

Another pattern to note is the addition of **-ed** to a single-syllable base word containing a short vowel and ending with a consonant (**grip/gripped**). You might wish to have students practise this pattern using other examples (**bat/batted**; **hop/hopped**). Have students contrast the /o/ sound in **hopped** with that in **hoped**.

Students should also note the irregular verb form **slid**.

3. Students may use a dictionary to help them solve the word ladder puzzle. Reinforce the **qu** pattern in each word.

4. Discuss the margin note with students. Ask them to suggest other analogies. You might offer examples such as the following.

bark is to **dog** as **meow** is to ________

grass is to **lawn** as **trees** are to ________

sun is to **day** as **moon** is to ________

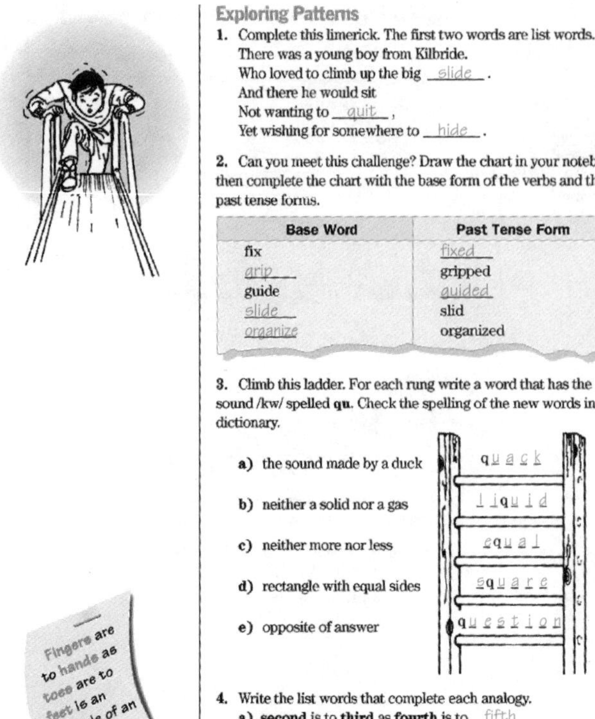

Exploring Patterns

1. Complete this limerick. The first two words are list words.
There was a young boy from Kilbride.
Who loved to climb up the big slide.
And there he would sit
Not wanting to quit,
Yet wishing for somewhere to hide.

2. Can you meet this challenge? Draw the chart in your notebook, then complete the chart with the base form of the verbs and their past tense forms.

Base Word	Past Tense Form
fix	fixed
grip	gripped
guide	guided
slide	slid
organize	organized

3. Climb this ladder. For each rung write a word that has the sound /kw/ spelled **qu**. Check the spelling of the new words in a dictionary.

a) the sound made by a duck — quack
b) neither a solid nor a gas — liquid
c) neither more nor less — equal
d) rectangle with equal sides — square
e) opposite of answer — question

Fingers are to hands as toes are to feet is an example of an analogy.

4. Write the list words that complete each analogy.
a) second is to **third** as **fourth** is to fifth
b) injured is to **healed** as **broken** is to fixed
c) quietly is to **loudly** as **slowly** is to quickly

13

Oral Language and Literature

A limerick is a form of poetry that is often recited aloud, or told as a joke. Some limericks you might share with students follow.

There was a young man from Vancouver
Whose favourite toy was a hoover
He vacuumed all day
'Twas all he could play
And now he's a shaker and mover.

There was an old man in Peru
Who dreamed he was eating his shoe.
He woke in the night
In a terrible fright
And found it was perfectly true.

There was an old lady of Kent
Whose nose was remarkably bent
One day, they suppose,
She followed her nose,
And no one knows which way she went.

There was a young student of Crete
Who stood on his head in the street.
Said he, "It is clear
If I want to stay here
I will have to shake hands with my feet."

Anonymous

5. What thoughts are going through the mind of this mountaineer? Write a few sentences that put her thoughts into words. Use some of the list words below.

difficult quickly grip cliff slide

6. a) Many things you do require skill, practice, and good equipment, just as mountaineering does. Choose a physical activity you like and list in a chart the things you need to do it well. When you are finished you will have notes about your favourite activity.

Example: soccer

Skills	Practice	Equipment
kicking, running	every day	soccer ball, shoes

b) Now write a paragraph about your favourite activity.

Challenges with Words

1. Use the Super Words to complete the story. Then match the letters in each word to the numbered spaces below to name the two men who first climbed Mount Everest.

The Conquerors of Everest

Mount Everest has a _ 1 _ _ _ _ 8 _ rise of 8848 metres. Many mountain _ 7 _ 3 _ _ _ _ have tried to reach its summit. The first _ _ _ 12 10 for the top was in 1922, but that _ _ _ _ 2 _ _ _ 11 _ was unsuccessful. It wasn't until 1953 that two men, neither of them a _ 4 _ _ _ _ 9, finally conquered the mountain. Imagine the _ _ _ 6 _ _ _ _ 5 _ of being the first to reach the top!

vertical, climbers, quest, expedition, quitter, excitment

Sir Edmund HillarY
12 6 9   1 2 3 4 5 2   6 7 7 8 9

TenZ inG NorGaY
10 1 5   6 5   5 11 9 8

14

5. In most units, the first writing exercise asks students to use the list words in context. The second is more open-ended, and often focusses on a particular writing skill or type of writing. Have students use the illustration as a prompt for writing sentences with the list words.

6. Encourage students to jot notes about their favourite sport or activity, and then to organize their information under the headings given. Suggest that they use categories to help organize their non-fiction paragraphs. (See Writing, p. 38.)

Challenges with Words

1. Ask students to identify the base words of the Super Words **quitter**, **excitement**, **expedition**, **climbers**. They may need to use a dictionary to find **expedite**. Have them note the endings **-er**, **-ment**, **-ion**, and changes made to the base words when endings are added.

word	base word	changes
quitter	quit	double the **t** and add **-er**
excitement	excite	add **-ment**
expedition	expedite	drop the **e** and add **-ion**
climbers	climb	add **-ers**

Students might have fun creating their own puzzle paragraphs leaving blanks for the challenge words, and sharing their work with a partner.

Co-operative Learning

Word Explosions

- Have students make new words by adding endings or suffixes to other verbs in the same word family.

You may wish to have students use each of the new words in a sentence. Have them share their words and sentences in small groups.

- In Challenges with Words 4a), students could brainstorm as a group to gather synonyms for the 'exciting' words. This will help them to create more interesting stories to share with classmates once they have been completed and proofread.

word	add **-ed**	add **-ment**	add **-ing**	add **er**	add **s**
engage	engaged	engagement	engaging	—	engages
stage	staged	—	staging	—	stages
advise	advised	—	advising	adviser	advises
revise	revised	—	revising	—	revises

2. Discuss the margin note with students. A synonym rarely has exactly the same meaning as the word to which it relates. Have students use a thesaurus to help them create word webs of synonyms for the four mountaineering words in their list.

3. Suggest students start with verbs, then add either **-or** or **-er**. Encourage students to use a dictionary if they are uncertain of any meanings. Have them share their words with a group.

If you have ready access to a computer with appropriate software, such as most word processing programs, have students perform word searches for words that end in **-or** and **-er**. Many dictionaries are now available on CD-ROM, and are another useful resource for this type of activity.

4. a) Have students watch for the change in the base word **excite** as suffixes are added.

A group paragraph which uses all of the 'exciting' words could be quite amusing.

> The excitable mountaineer gazed in excitement at the excitingly sheer drop.

You might wish to extend this activity by using other words to 'explode'.

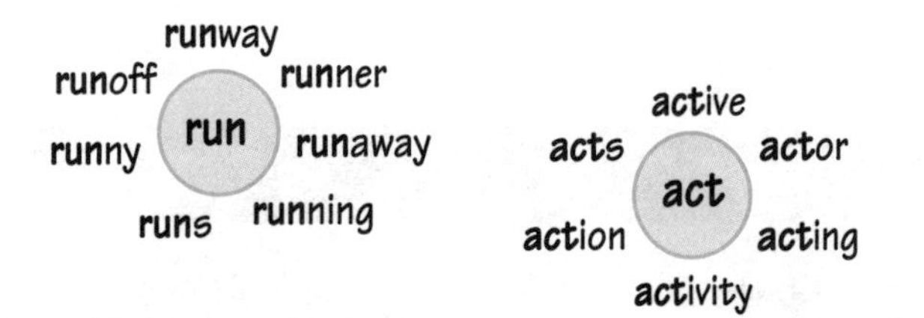

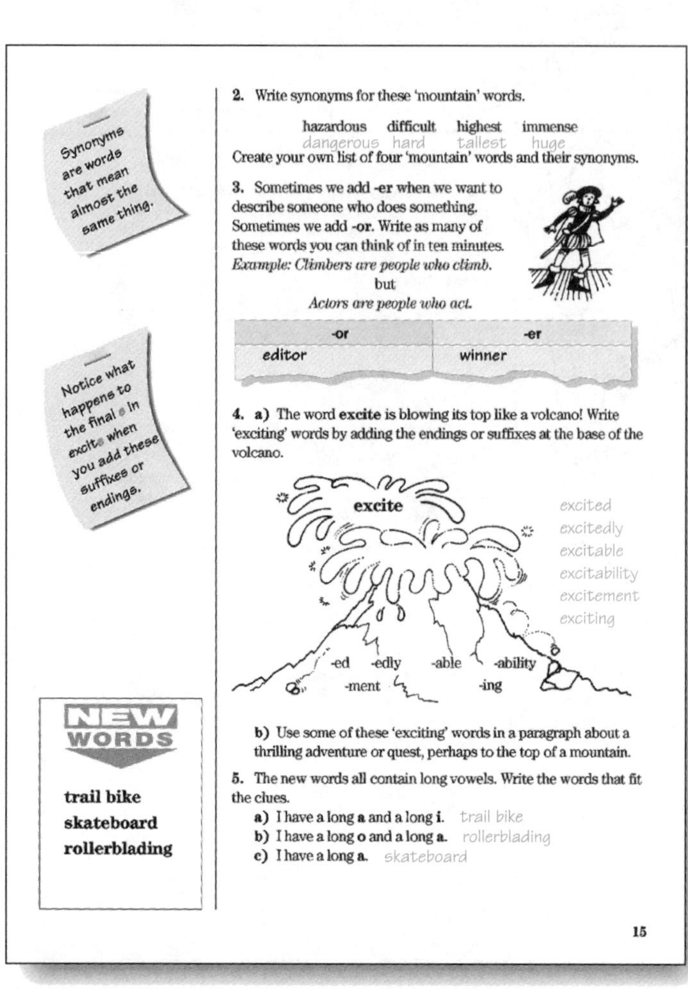

Synonyms are words that mean almost the same thing.

2. Write synonyms for these 'mountain' words.

hazardous — dangerous; difficult — hard; highest — tallest; immense — huge

Create your own list of four 'mountain' words and their synonyms.

3. Sometimes we add **-er** when we want to describe someone who does something. Sometimes we add **-or.** Write as many of these words you can think of in ten minutes.

Example: Climbers are people who climb.
but
Actors are people who act.

-or	-er
editor	winner

Notice what happens to the final e in excite when you add these suffixes or endings.

4. a) The word **excite** is blowing its top like a volcano! Write 'exciting' words by adding the endings or suffixes at the base of the volcano.

excite

-ed -edly -able -ability -ment -ing

excited
excitedly
excitable
excitability
excitement
exciting

b) Use some of these 'exciting' words in a paragraph about a thrilling adventure or quest, perhaps to the top of a mountain.

NEW WORDS

trail bike
skateboard
rollerblading

5. The new words all contain long vowels. Write the words that fit the clues.

a) I have a long **a** and a long **i**. trail bike
b) I have a long **o** and a long **a**. rollerblading
c) I have a long **a**. skateboard

15

New Words

5. Have students investigate new words associated with their favourite recreational activities. Catalogues from sports or department stores, as well as newspaper and magazine ads are useful resources. Ask students to identify alternative terms and spellings for the same items and discuss which words they think will last. For example: **inline** skates, **in line** skates, or **in-line** skates.

- Encourage students to choose their own topics for writing whenever possible. The directed writing exercises suggested are intended to be brief, collaborative 'warm-ups' for more meaningful, personal writing. In this unit, students are encouraged to write and organize notes about a physical activity. Similar pre-writing activities will help them write on virtually any topic.

- Some teachers suggest quick 'jot notes' to capture the main ideas of a written or oral passage. For example, if students were describing baseball, as they talked or thought about the game they might jot: ball and bat; bases; pitcher, catcher, hitter; running; home run.

Later, they can arrange their quick notes using graphic organizers such as flowcharts.

Curriculum Connection

Ask students to imagine how they would feel if they were making a climb up Mount Everest. Afraid? Excited? Have them locate Mount Everest on a map of Asia.

Some students might wish to research Canadian mountain-climbing achievements, including Mount Everest. Students could create a personal diary account of the climb, using as many 'mountain' words as they can. Other students could research the first expedition to make a successful ascent of Everest. Students might present their findings in a variety of ways, such as in a diary, or in a role-play interview.

Assessment

After dictation and self-correction, have students check which errors were the same on the Precheck and the Unit Test. You might wish to arrange one-on-one conferences with students to identify the reason(s) for continued errors and help them develop strategies for dealing with problem words.

Follow-up

Monitor students' spelling of long and short vowels **a**, **e**, and **i** in their everyday writing. Do they have a firm grasp of the spelling patterns? Can they extend these patterns into longer words such as **equipment** and **organized**?

If more practice with long vowel patterns is needed, see *Sharing the Secrets*, *Teach Your Child to Spell*, Units 8–14, and *The Student Editor's Guide to Words*, pp. 138–139.

long a	long e	long i
escape	compete	combine
female	complete	decide
repair	repeat	fried
despair	meat	tried
crayon	agree	bright
sleigh	eagle	sigh

Teacher's Notes

4 Long o

o_e as in smoke
oa as in goal

Patterns

There are several ways to spell the long vowel sound /ō/ in English. This unit reviews the **o-consonant-e** and **oa** patterns. The basic one-syllable patterns of spelling long **o** are expanded in longer words such as **bulldozer** and **loaded**.

Preknowledge

Students should have an understanding of the following concepts as they work through this unit.

- The spelling patterns of long and short **o** in short words (**hop/ hope**).
- Compound words that are formed of two base words (**waterfall**).
- Words consisting of one or more syllables (**ex/ped/i/tion**).
- Consonant blends such as **pr**, **sm**.
- The consonant digraph **wh**.
- The **wr** spelling of **r** (**wrote**).

More Patterns

Other patterns you might wish to review or introduce during the unit include the following.

- The long /ō/ sound spelled **o** at the end of words (**Mexico**, **potato**).
- The sound /ks/ spelled **ex** (**explodes**, **Mexico**).
- The past tense of verbs (**loaded**, **wrote**).

Professional Notebook

Words and people have a lot in common. Like people, words are born, grow up, get married, have children, and even die. And, like people, words come in families—big and beautiful families. A word family is a cluster of words that are related because they contain the same root; a root is a basic building block of language from which a variety of related words are formed. You can expand your vocabulary by digging down to the roots of an unfamiliar word and identifying the meanings of those roots.

(Lederer 248)

Sharing the Secrets with Kids

*The old rhyme 'when two vowels go walking, the first one does the talking' may help some students remember which letter comes first in words such as **road** and **load**.*

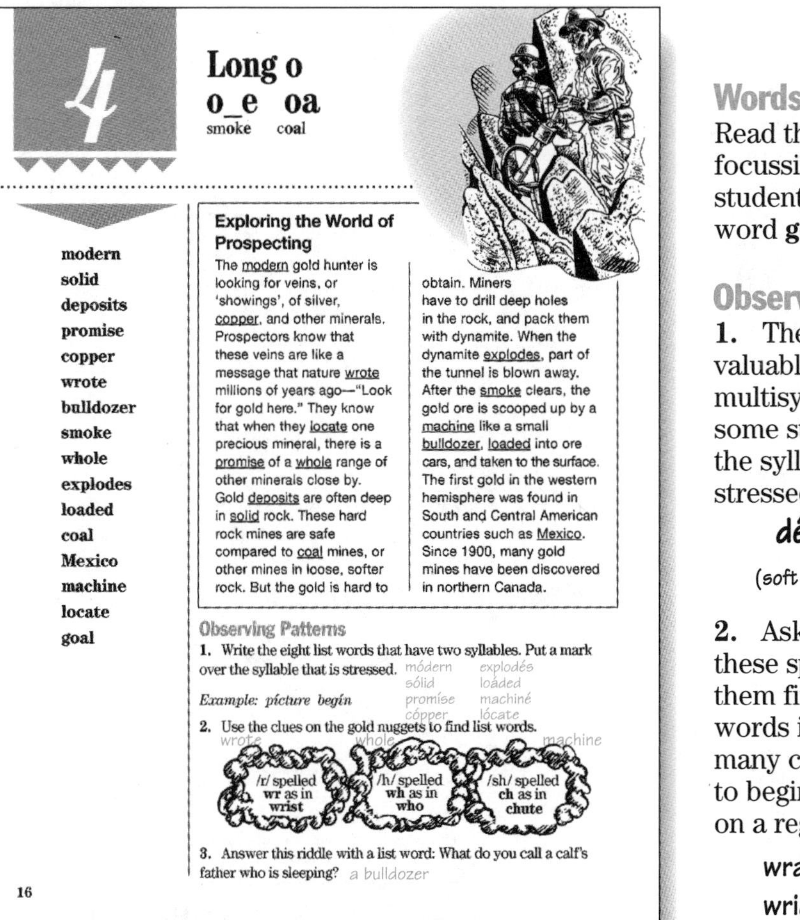

4

Long o

o_e oa

smoke coal

modern
solid
deposits
promise
copper
wrote
bulldozer
smoke
whole
explodes
loaded
coal
Mexico
machine
locate
goal

Exploring the World of Prospecting

The modern gold hunter is looking for veins, or 'showings', of silver, copper, and other minerals. Prospectors know that these veins are like a message that nature wrote millions of years ago—"Look for gold here." They know that when they locate one precious mineral, there is a promise of a whole range of other minerals close by. Gold deposits are often deep in solid rock. These hard rock mines are safe compared to coal mines, or other mines in loose, softer rock. But the gold is hard to obtain. Miners have to drill deep holes in the rock, and pack them with dynamite. When the dynamite explodes, part of the tunnel is blown away. After the smoke clears, the gold ore is scooped up by a machine like a small bulldozer, loaded into ore cars, and taken to the surface. The first gold in the western hemisphere was found in South and Central American countries such as Mexico. Since 1900, many gold mines have been discovered in northern Canada.

Observing Patterns

1. Write the eight list words that have two syllables. Put a mark over the syllable that is stressed. *módern, sólid, prómise, cópper, explodés, loáded, machiné, lócate*

Example: pícture begín

2. Use the clues on the gold nuggets to find list words. *wrote, whole, machine*

/r/ spelled **wr** as in **wrist**
/h/ spelled **wh** as in **who**
/sh/ spelled **ch** as in **chute**

3. Answer this riddle with a list word: What do you call a calf's father who is sleeping? *a bulldozer*

16

Precheck

Remind students to listen while you say the word, use it in a sentence, and then say the word again before they write. This establishes the word meaning.

Dictation

Rollerblades are a **modern** invention.
The cake was **solid** as a rock.
Gold **deposits** are mined.
Promise you'll do it!
That roof is made of **copper**.
I **wrote** the letter.
The **bulldozer** shifted the dirt.
Do you smell **smoke**?
I ate the **whole** pie!
Dynamite **explodes**.
Is the car **loaded** yet?
Coal is a fossil fuel.
Mexico is a beautiful country.
The **machine** broke down.
Did you **locate** him?
He scored a **goal**.

Words in Context

Read the context paragraph aloud with students, focussing on words with the long /ō/ sound. Have students write their own sentences using the list word **goal** and share their work with a partner.

Observing Patterns

1. The ability to identify stressed syllables is a valuable skill for students as they encounter multisyllabic words. It may be necessary for some students to read the words aloud or to 'tap' the syllables of the word in order to hear the stressed syllable(s).

dé	pos´	its´
(soft clap)	(loud clap)	(soft clap)

2. Ask students to find other words that follow these spelling patterns. The dictionary will help them find some of the words. The family of **wr** words is particularly important, as it includes many commonly used words. Students might like to begin a class list to be displayed and added to on a regular basis.

wrap, write, wreck, wrinkle,
wriggle, wrong, wrestle

3. Students might need help to answer this riddle. Remind them that a compound word is made up of two base words that are somehow related in meaning, so that **carpet** is not a compound. Ask students to decide whether they think **bulldozer** is a true compound, and give reasons for their answer.

4. Draw students' attention to the margin note. Matching configuration boxes and words also helps students focus on the sequence of letters. It is a strategy that will help students who learn visually.

5. This activity also helps students focus on letter sequence. Ask students to share their contributions to the word pole. A master word pole could be created with the class.

Discovering Patterns

1. Have students say the words in the chart and listen for the short /o/ sound. Ask them to circle the **o** or highlight it with colour.

> **modern, solid, deposits, promise, copper**

You might wish to have students pay special attention to the final **i** in **promise** and **machine**, as these are difficult words to spell.

2. Since only one list word fits the /ō/ spelled **o** pattern, ask students to contribute other words they know to this category.

/o/ spelled o	patio, piano, radio, potato, tomato

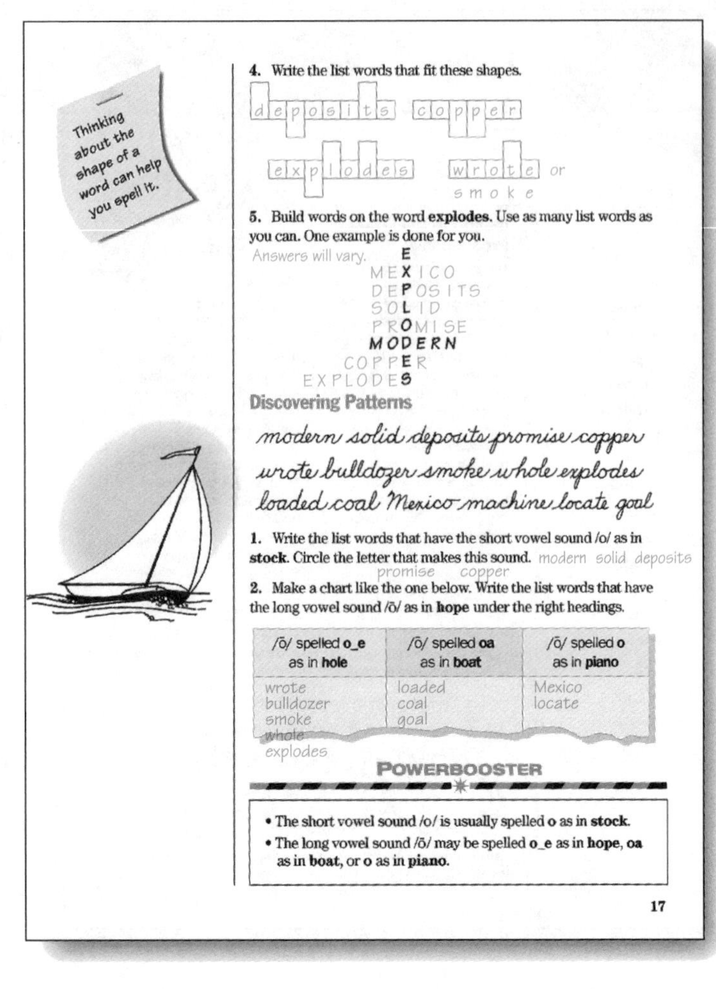

Thinking about the shape of a word can help you spell it.

4. Write the list words that fit these shapes.

deposits copper

explodes wrote or smoke

5. Build words on the word **explodes**. Use as many list words as you can. One example is done for you.

Answers will vary.

E
MEXICO
DEPOSITS
SOLID
PROMISE
MODERN
COPPER
EXPLODES

Discovering Patterns

modern solid deposits promise copper wrote bulldozer smoke whole explodes loaded coal Mexico machine locate goal

1. Write the list words that have the short vowel sound /o/ as in **stock**. Circle the letter that makes this sound. modern solid deposits promise copper

2. Make a chart like the one below. Write the list words that have the long vowel sound /ō/ as in **hope** under the right headings.

/ō/ spelled **o_e** as in **hole**	/ō/ spelled **oa** as in **boat**	/ō/ spelled **o** as in **piano**
wrote bulldozer smoke whole explodes	loaded coal goal	Mexico locate

POWERBOOSTER

- The short vowel sound /o/ is usually spelled **o** as in **stock**.
- The long vowel sound /ō/ may be spelled **o_e** as in **hope**, **oa** as in **boat**, or **o** as in **piano**.

17

Critical Thinking

- Creating word webs around list words as in Exploring Patterns 2, helps students build vocabulary and develop classifying and sorting skills. Have students work in groups to make their word webs, using a large piece of paper or space on the chalkboard.

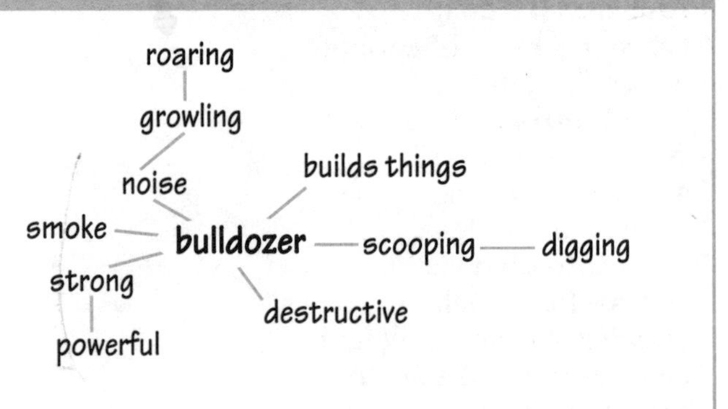

Watch out! Words like **some** and **come** do not have the long **o** sound.

Answers will vary.
boat
coat
goat
toe

Exploring Patterns

1. Combine the letters on the pennies with the long /ō/ patterns on the gold coins to make words with the long **o** sound.

o_e | c | l | s | b

oa | m | k | g | r

2. A word web contains words and phrases that go with the word at the centre. Make a word web for these list words: **bulldozer modern.**

Example: machine — saves work, repairs, industry, car, motor

3. Many words can be 'exploded' to form new words. These words are all related to the list word **locate**.

dislocated relocate local location

A prefix is attached to the beginning of the word and a suffix is attached to the end.

Complete each sentence below with the correct word. You will find this word by adding suffixes or prefixes to the base word **locate**.

a) We decided this was the perfect _______ to look for gold. location
b) The _______ people told us there was no gold in the area. local
c) We then decided to _______ our base in another area. relocate
d) While I was digging for gold I _______ my back. dislocated

4. Sometimes the meaning of a word suggests a shape. Write these list words in shapes that suggest their meaning.

smoke **explode**

Example: dome

18

Exploring Patterns

1. Discuss the margin note with students. Other words that break the pattern are **love**, **above**, **glove**. Advise students that they may use as many letters as they wish to create new /ō/ words (b**oa**st). You might wish to have students compile a group list or have them share their lists with a partner. (See Co-operative Learning, p. 45.)

coke	lore	sore	bore	more	gore
loam	roam	boar	cloak	soak	soar

2. Ask students to share their additions to each word web. Discuss ways to group or classify the sets of words or phrases. (See Critical Thinking Skills, p. 42.)

3. Direct students' attention to the margin note about prefixes and suffixes. Students might be interested to know the word 'local' comes from the Latin word *localis*, meaning 'place'. Relate each derived form to the concept of 'place'.

4. Ask students to share their 'word shapes' with one another. Students might like to create other word portrayals using list words and make a classroom display of their work.

Special Needs

- Help students build on words with similar patterns.

derived forms	silent letters
write wrote written speak spoke spoken	wrap wrist write wrote whole who whose

- Configuration or cloze strategies may help students remember silent letters of vowel combinations.

whole ma_ _ine

ESL

- The long **o** sound can be spelled many different ways in English. Help students recognize that the sound does not change even though the spelling is different. Grouping words according to spelling patterns is a useful strategy to use.

Long o		
at the beginning	in the middle	at the end
open	pole	radio
over	rope	piano
ocean	soap	tomato
obey	load	toe
okay	mole	hoe

5. Use the illustration to introduce the writing activity. Students might enjoy contrasting an old-fashioned telegram which was as short as possible, with a modern e-mail message or fax sent to the prospector's friends or family.

Don't forget to proofread your message.

SUPER WORDS

underground
explosion
prospector
propose
loaves
discovery

5. This prospector is in for a surprise. The fire that he lit last night is melting down through the snow to solid rock. When he scrapes back the ashes in the morning to make a new fire, he'll see something gleaming through the black soot. Gold! Write the message this prospector might send back to his family or friends.

Challenges with Words

1. Looking for gold, or what? Use the clues below to help you find your way through the shafts to the mother lode.

1. a large blast explosion
2. subterranean underground
3. someone who looks for precious metals prospector
4. suggest propose
5. large masses of bread loaves
6. something discovered discovery

19

Challenges with Words

1. Have students look for the long and short **o** spelling patterns in the Super Words, then identify base words and what has been added to them. Note that in **discovery** the **o** has the sound of short /u/ (as it does in **cover**).

word	pattern	base	add
prospector	short o	prospect	-or
explosion	long o	explode	-ion
propose	short o	—	—
loaves	long o	loaf	-ves

Ask students to write a cloze paragraph using the Super Words, and share their work with a partner.

2. Make sure students are aware of the change in pronunciation when **-es** is added. Have them focus on the /**ves**/ sound as opposed to /**fs**/ sound (loaves/loa**fs**). Ask for exceptions to the rule (Toronto Maple Leafs; chiefs).

Oral Language and Literature

- Students might enjoy creating riddles based on list words, words of personal interest, or words from other subject areas.

- A classroom joke book could be compiled and updated regularly. Activities that encourage students to play with language help them develop sensitivity to language patterns on a variety of levels.

What's a greasy insect?

A butterfly.

What's a sleepy earthmover?

z z z

A bulldozer.

What kind of company is a country?

Mexi-Co.

What's an entire vacancy?

A whole hole.

2. Some words that end in **f** make their plurals by changing the **f** to **v** and adding **-es**. Write plurals that end in **ves** to fit the sentences below.

a) Armand cut the pie into two _______. halves
b) The gang of _______ robbed the bank. thieves
c) One of the bookcase _______ was empty. shelves
d) The whole wheat _______ were half price. loaves
e) Handle the sharp _______ with care. knives

3. Write sentences of your own with the plural forms of these words. selves wolves leaves lives calves
self wolf leaf life calf

4. Add prefixes and suffixes to the word **cover** to make as many words as you can. How many did you discover? (19)

re- -s -ed dis- cover -ing un- -ies -y

WORDS IN HISTORY

Discovery is made from the base word **cover**. According to the general rule, the **v** should be doubled to keep the sound of the **o** short. In Old English the doubled **v** looked the same as a **w**. To keep the word from looking like **cower**, the **v** was kept single.

5. You found this map in the burned-out remains of Jim's cabin. Use the Super Words and your own words to tell how you discovered the Crazy Moose Mine.

CRAZY MOOSE MINE
JIM'S CABIN
trail to crossing
CRAZY MOOSE RIVER
abandoned dog sled
about 800 m
about 1.5 km
three rocks
trail
pine
1000 paces
Entrance covered With brush
N W E S

I followed the trail from the cabin door to the Crazy Moose River. There I...

20

3. Have students exchange sentences with a partner for proofreading.

4. Students can make up to 18 different words with the base word **cover**. Have them note that, in this case, the base word does not change when suffixes are added. Ask students to share their words in small groups. You may wish to have students create more words by adding the prefixes and suffixes to another base word such as **charge.** (See Co-operative Learning, this page.)

base word 'cover'		
covers	covered	covering
recover	discover	uncover
recovery	discovery	recoveries
uncovered	discovered	recovered
discovering	recovering	uncovering
discoveries	uncovers	recovers

Words in History

Students may want to research word histories for other Super Words. They may also like to keep a 'Words in History' notebook, where they can record interesting etymologies.

5. Students can use the map as a prompt for their own writing. They may also want to write about what happened to 'Jim', and how the narrator solved the mystery.

Co-operative Learning

- Have students work with partners or in small groups to make as many words as possible using the letters on the coins in Exploring Patterns 1. When they are finished, ask them to combine their lists and see how many overlapping words there are.

o_e	lobe	sole	Coke	mole	
oa	moat	coat	goat	boat	soak

- In Challenges with Words 4 have students, as a group, share their words with other classmates. You may wish to have students create more words by adding the prefixes and suffixes to another base word such as **charge**.

base word 'charge'		
recharge	discharge	charges
charged	charging	recharges
recharged	recharging	discharges
discharged	discharging	uncharged

Curriculum Connection

• Social Studies: a CD-ROM or encyclopedia would yield useful information to students studying Canadian geography and interested in researching mining or prospecting. A useful mapping activity would be to identify and then highlight gold-producing areas on a map of Canada. Students might want to take the activity further and research similar areas worldwide.

• Science: some students might want to research mining technology, particularly as it is used in gold mining.

Home Connection

Send home spelling tips in your classroom newsletters or homework sheets. Enlist the support of parents in reinforcing spelling strategies such as highlighting silent letters in words that begin with **wr** or **wh** (**w** is silent if it's in **whale**, but not in **where**), or looking at the shapes of words.

Assessment

Dictate words in a different order from the Precheck dictation. You could use the same sentences or make up your own. Have students compare the results of their Precheck and Unit Test on the student record sheet. They may want to add some words to their Personal Review List of challenging words.

Follow-up

Have students monitor their own writing for errors with vowel combinations. For more practice with longer words where the long vowel /ō/ is spelled **o_e** see *The Student Editor's Guide to Words*, pp. 138 and 196-197. For the **oa** spelling, see p. 140.

o_e	oa
compose	coach
dispose	coast
quote	railroad
telephone	toast
alone	roast
note	foal
stroke	roach
stone	broach

Teacher's Notes

Long u

ew	as in cr**ew**
ue	as in bl**ue**
u _ e	as in h**u**g**e**

Patterns

The long **u** sound can be spelled several ways in English. To add to this confusion it is pronounced both as /ü/ and /yü/ and in some words can be pronounced either way (**dew**). In other words, the sound is invariably /ü/ (**drew**, **blew**). Sometimes, the long **u** is always pronounced as /yü/ (**huge**, **continue**). Let the students' natural pronunciation be your guide, while being aware that the long **u** may present a challenge for many ESL students.

Preknowledge

Students should have an understanding of the following concepts as they work with the patterns in this unit.

• One sound in English can have many spellings (**drew**, **blue**, **include**).
• Homophones are words that sound alike but have different meanings and spellings (**blew**, **blue**).
• Some words are spelled with a silent letter at the beginning or the end (**knew**, **dumb**). A few have a silent letter in both places (**knuckle**, **wriggle**, **write**, **wrote**, **wrinkle**).
• Most words can be made plural by adding **s**.
• Longer words can be broken into syllables (**con/tin/ue**).

More Patterns

Other patterns you might wish to review or introduce in this unit include the following:

• The silent final **b** (**thumb**, **dumb**).
• Plurals made with s (**rules**, **jewels**).
• The consonant blends **dr**, **cr**, **gl**, **bl**, **sk** (**drew**, **crew**, **glue**, **blue**, **skull**).
• The consonant digraph **th** (**thumb**).
• Two- and three-syllable words (**ar/gue**, **con/tin/ue**).

Professional Notebook

Our first priority must be to encourage our students to regard themselves as people who have important reasons not only to write well, but also to spell and punctuate well and use precise, graceful language. Then we can encourage them to notice and explore and borrow and reflect on the conventions of written language they see around them.

(Calkins 289)

Sharing the Secrets with Kids

*The family of words with a silent **b** at the end is a small one. Students can learn these as a group of words, and think of interesting ways to join them.*

*The monkey hangs from the **limb** of the tree by one **thumb**.*

***Comb** the wool from the **lamb**.*

Or, have them learn the words as a rhyme.

words with silent b		
bomb	tomb	plumber
climb	lamb	dumb
comb	limb	thumb
crumb	numb	plumb

Precheck

The purpose of the Precheck is to help students identify the words they need to study, as well as to demonstrate what they already know. Follow the same procedures for the Precheck in each unit to establish a routine for this learning strategy. After the self-correction exercise, encourage students to observe from their own work the type of errors they are making.

Dictation

He was struck **dumb** with fear.
The pirate flag has a **skull** on it.
Her **luck** was good.
The monster was **huge**.
Did you **include** my name?
What are the **rules** of the game?
Continue writing please.
Try to **reduce** the number we need.
She **knew** the way there.
The ship has a **crew** of forty.
The pirate **drew** her sword.
Glue the pieces together.
Never **argue** with a tiger!
I broke my **thumb**.
The lost **jewels** were found.
Blue is my favourite colour.

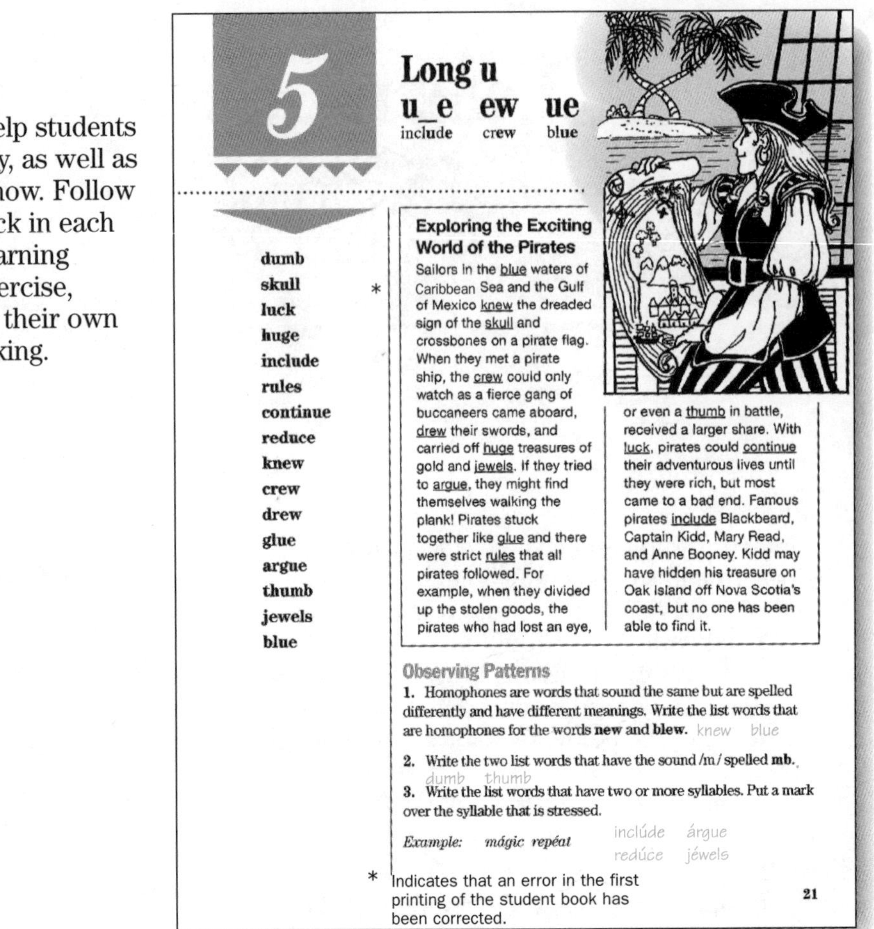

5

Long u

u_e include **ew** crew **ue** blue

dumb
skull
luck
huge
include
rules
continue
reduce
knew
crew
drew
glue
argue
thumb
jewels
blue

Exploring the Exciting World of the Pirates

Sailors in the blue waters of Caribbean Sea and the Gulf of Mexico knew the dreaded sign of the skull and crossbones on a pirate flag. When they met a pirate ship, the crew could only watch as a fierce gang of buccaneers came aboard, drew their swords, and carried off huge treasures of gold and jewels. If they tried to argue, they might find themselves walking the plank! Pirates stuck together like glue and there were strict rules that all pirates followed. For example, when they divided up the stolen goods, the pirates who had lost an eye, or even a thumb in battle, received a larger share. With luck, pirates could continue their adventurous lives until they were rich, but most came to a bad end. Famous pirates include Blackbeard, Captain Kidd, Mary Read, and Anne Booney. Kidd may have hidden his treasure on Oak Island off Nova Scotia's coast, but no one has been able to find it.

Observing Patterns

1. Homophones are words that sound the same but are spelled differently and have different meanings. Write the list words that are homophones for the words **new** and **blew**. knew blue

2. Write the two list words that have the sound /m/ spelled **mb**. dumb thumb

3. Write the list words that have two or more syllables. Put a mark over the syllable that is stressed.

Example: mágic repéat includ́e árgue redúce jéwels

* Indicates that an error in the first printing of the student book has been corrected.

21

Words in Context

The paragraph presents the list words in context to help students grasp their meanings. Suggest that students read the paragraph aloud to a partner, noting list words that may not already be part of their written vocabulary (**continue**, **include**). Have students write their own sentence for the list word **reduce**.

Observing Patterns

1. It may be helpful to ask students for other homophone pairs (**here/hear**; **through/threw**). Each student could begin a personal homophone list, or add to a class homophone list.

2. Tell students that the list of words ending in silent **b** is a short one, and that these words can be learned as a group. (See Sharing the Secrets With Kids, p. 47.)

3. If students have difficulty hearing the stressed syllable, have them try saying alternate syllables with more force, and decide which pronunciation sounds more natural (**magic**/magic).

Special Needs

- Some students may need practice discriminating between the long and short sounds of **u**. Use cards such as are shown here, with a short **u** word on one side, and a long **u** word on the other. Or, have the silent **e** on a fold-out tab so that students can at once see the influence of the added letter.

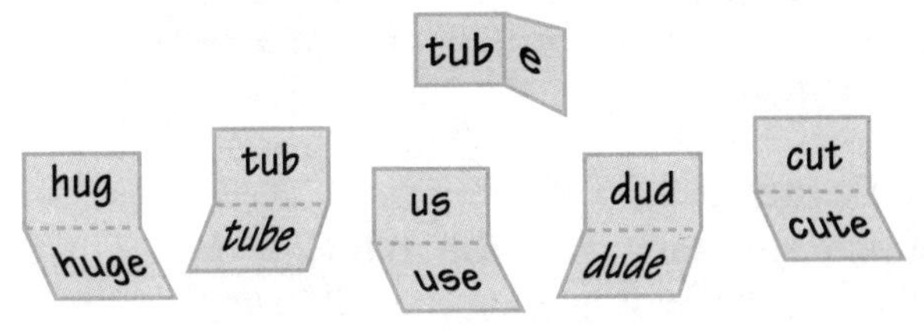

- For additional practice with the spelling patterns of long **u**, have students work with partners completing word wheels.

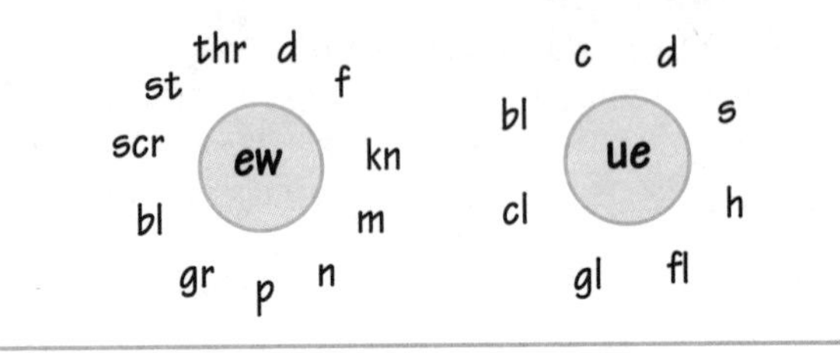

4. Complete these sets with list words. Write the list word that goes with the words in each treasure chest.

gigantic enormous	cement paste	collarbone shoulder
huge	glue	skull

Discovering Patterns

dumb skull luck huge include rules continue reduce knew crew drew glue argue thumb jewels blue

1. Write the four list words that have the short vowel sound /u/ as in **truck**. Circle the letter that makes this sound.

dumb
skull
luck
thumb

2. Make two charts like the ones below in your notebook. Add to your first chart the list words that have the long vowel sound /ü/ as in **spoon**. Add to your second chart the list words that have the sound /yü/ as in **huge**.

/ü/ spelled **u_e** as in **salute**	/ü/ spelled **ew** as in **flew**	/ü/ spelled **ue** as in **true**
include rules reduce	knew drew crew	glue blue

/yü/ spelled **u_e** as in **mule**	/yü/ spelled **ew** as in **few**	/yü/ spelled **ue** as in **cue**
huge reduce	knew	continue argue

The word knew can be pronounced nyü or nü. How do you pronounce it?

POWERBOOSTER

- The short vowel sound /u/ is usually spelled **u** as in **truck**.
- The long vowel sound /ü/ may be spelled **u_e** as in **rule**, **ew** as in **flew**, or **ue** as in **blue**.
- The long vowel sound /yü/ may be spelled **u_e** as in **mule**, **ew** as in **few**, or **ue** as in **cue**.

22

4. Two of the word sets contain synonyms (**gigantic/enormous/huge**; **cement/paste/glue**). The third set names parts of the body (**collarbone/shoulder/skull**). Help students see the classification system for each set and suggest other words that would fit in each chest.

synonyms		body parts
big	epoxy	arm
vast	adhesive	elbow
large	super glue	toe
giant	gum	ear

Discovering Patterns

1. Discovering Patterns exercises are ideally done with the whole class examining the patterns and 'discovering' the Powerbooster rule inductively. Use exercise 1 to review the short **u**, and contrast it with long **u** (**hug/huge**).

2. Point out to students that some words may be pronounced either /ü/ or /yü/ (**knew**: **noo/nyu**; **reduce**: **redooce/redyuce**). Have students say the list words aloud to determine which pronunciation is natural for them. Explain that the spelling remains the same.

Ask students to brainstorm long **u** words for each category from a variety of sources such as theme words and other subject areas.

long u	
pronounced ü	pronounced yü
brew	cue
chew	hue
screw	pew
drew	cute
clue	mute
lute	newt
chute	

ESL

- The consonant blends in English are difficult for speakers of many different languages. Students whose first language is, for example, Chinese, may have trouble hearing and spelling sounds such as **bl**, **br**, **cr**, **dr**, **gr**, **cl**. In spelling words with these sounds, they may add an extra syllable (g**a**lue, b**u**rew).
- Practise with pairs such as the following. Have students say each pair, listening for the difference in sound, then write the words.

consonant blends		
goo	grew	glue
coo	crew	clue
boo	brew	blue

Exploring Patterns

1. Have students read the instructions carefully. Some may not be familiar with the story of 'Peter Pan', in which Captain Hook is afraid of the sound of the alarm clock inside his enemy, the crocodile. In this case the answer to the puzzle will require some explanation.

2. Writing the complete passage gives students experience in using the words in a meaningful context. The activity also provides practice in writing correct sentence structure and paragraph formation.

3. Students may enjoy using the code to write other messages to one another, or to compose a reply to those who removed the treasure from the chest (see Critical Thinking, this page).

Exploring Patterns

1. Write the word in each set which has the sound /ü/ as in **crew**, **glue**, and **rule** or /yü/ as in **mule**, **few**, and **cue.** Circle the first letter of each answer. Then copy down the circled letters to find the answer to this question.

What was the sound that Captain Hook feared the most in the story *Peter Pan*? tick tock

a)	crust	true	shoulder	true
b)	trouble	clumsy	include	include
c)	clue	outside	rumble	clue
d)	would	rusty	threw	threw
e)	overdue	shook	buckle	overdue
f)	should	cute	doubt	cute

2. Complete this pirate story with list words. Write the story in your notebook.

The captain _drew_ an X over a tree on the treasure map. He and his _crew_ of pirates _knew_ they would find a chest of precious _jewels_ buried near that tree. With any _luck_, they would soon be rich! They found the tree and dug up a _huge_ box. But instead of _jewels_, they found only a note with a drawing of a human _skull_ on it. The note was written in code.

3. Decode the message in the treasure chest using the code below.

27	26	25	24	23	22	21	20	19	18	17	16	15	
A	B	C	D	E	F	G	H	I	J	K	L	M	
14	13	12	11	10	9	8	7	6	5	4	3	2	1
N	O	P	Q	R	S	T	U	V	W	X	Y	Z	!

3 13 7   16 19 23   27 14 24   3 13 7
Y O U   L I E   A N D   Y O U

25 20 23 27 8   27 14 24   26 10 23 27 17   27 16 16
C H E A T   A N D   B R E A K   A L L

8 20 23   10 7 16 23 9   14 13 5
T H E   R U L E S   N O W

9 13 15 23 26 13 24 3   23 16 9 23   20 27 9
S O M E B O D Y   E L S E   H A S

8 27 17 23 14   8 20 23   18 23 5 23 16 9 1
T A K E N   T H E   J E W E L S !

23

Writing

- Students may enjoy using reference books to find more visual information about pirates. Extend their vocabulary with names for parts of a pirate's gear.

  plume, sword, cutlass,
  telescope, scabbard, parrot,
  gauntlet, eye patch

- Have students think about a variety of classroom objects and tell the order in which they would describe them. Use the objects as a prompt for description.

Critical Thinking

- Codes are excellent for developing problem-solving skills. They also help students focus on the sequence of letters in words, a valuable strategy for both spelling and reading. Students can develop codes of their own and try them out on a partner. The simplest codes are based on the alphabet, with numbers standing for letters. Other codes use symbols such as combinations of geometric shapes. If students have access to a computer, they could use it to help them create their codes.

A	B	C	D	E	F	G	H	I	J	K	L	M
20	30	40	50	60	70	80	90	21	31	41	51	61
N	**O**	**P**	**Q**	**R**	**S**	**T**	**U**	**V**	**W**	**X**	**Y**	**Z**
71	81	91	22	32	42	52	62	72	82	92	23	33

A	B	C	D	E	F	G	H	I	J	K	L	M
▽	✸	▲	□	◎	●	✲	⬢	◎	▲	▼	■	◎
N	**O**	**P**	**Q**	**R**	**S**	**T**	**U**	**V**	**W**	**X**	**Y**	**Z**
▼	⬢	✹	✕	△	■	✶	●	⬡	✕	◎	□	✷

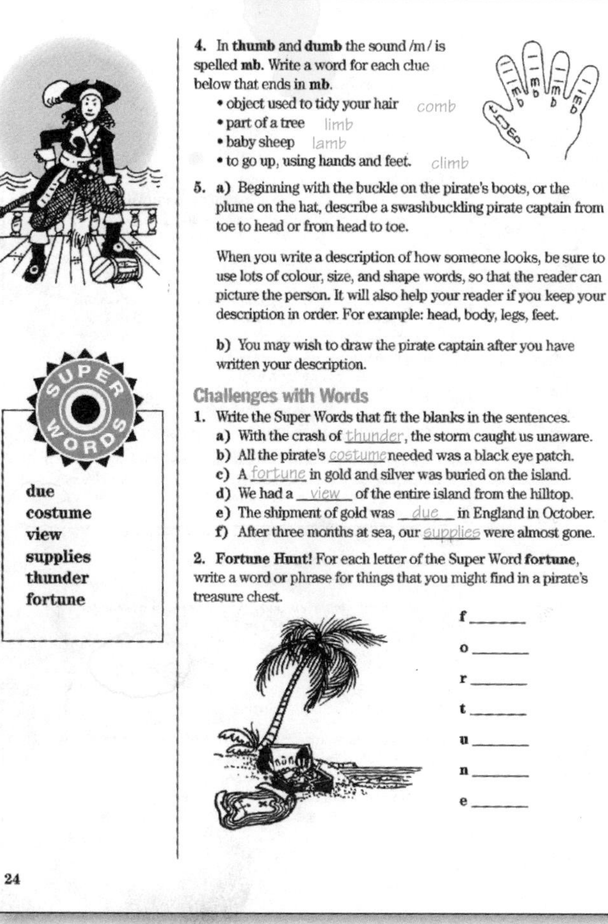

4. In **thumb** and **dumb** the sound /m/ is spelled **mb.** Write a word for each clue below that ends in **mb.**

- object used to tidy your hair comb
- part of a tree limb
- baby sheep lamb
- to go up, using hands and feet. climb

5. a) Beginning with the buckle on the pirate's boots, or the plume on the hat, describe a swashbuckling pirate captain from toe to head or from head to toe.

When you write a description of how someone looks, be sure to use lots of colour, size, and shape words, so that the reader can picture the person. It will also help your reader if you keep your description in order. For example: head, body, legs, feet.

b) You may wish to draw the pirate captain after you have written your description.

SUPER WORDS

due
costume
view
supplies
thunder
fortune

Challenges with Words

1. Write the Super Words that fit the blanks in the sentences.
   a) With the crash of thunder, the storm caught us unaware.
   b) All the pirate's costume needed was a black eye patch.
   c) A fortune in gold and silver was buried on the island.
   d) We had a view of the entire island from the hilltop.
   e) The shipment of gold was due in England in October.
   f) After three months at sea, our supplies were almost gone.

2. Fortune Hunt! For each letter of the Super Word **fortune**, write a word or phrase for things that you might find in a pirate's treasure chest.

f ______
o ______
r ______
t ______
u ______
n ______
e ______

24

4. Ask students to add other items that have the same spelling of /m/ and suggest the clues for these (**crumb**, **numb**). (See Sharing the Secrets With Kids, p. 47.)

5. Writing descriptions of clothing, machinery, landscapes, and people is easier for students if they determine an order or direction for the description before starting to organize details. An airplane, for example, could be described from nose to tail, a stereo from left to right, a lamp from top to bottom, and a peach from outside to inside. (See Writing p. 50.)

Students may also wish to describe other well-known figures such as rock stars and sports heroes who wear colourful and distinctive costumes.

Challenges with Words

1. Have students group the Super Words in two categories according to whether they contain a long or short **u** sound. Challenge students to find other words with the /yü/ sound as in **view**.

long u	short u	/yü/ words
due	supplies	few
view	thunder	cue
costume		overdue
fortune		curfew
chew		new

Ask students to write their own sentences or a paragraph using the Super Words.

2. The fortune hunt is a variation on the word pole. Encourage students to use their imaginations in suggesting objects found in a treasure chest.

fax machine
old socks
red pen
ten thousand dollars
umbrella
notebook
eggs

Oral Language and Literature

- Have students listen for the long **u** sounds in this nonsense poem. You may wish to copy it as a cloze exercise, having them fill in the words. If necessary, explain that a flue is a kind of chimney, or smokestack.

A Fly and a Flea in a Flue

A fly and a flea in a flue
Were imprisoned so what could they do?
Said the fly, "Let us flee!"
"Let us fly!" said the flea,
So they flew through a flaw in the flue.

Anon.

A fly and a flea in a fl_ _
Were imprisoned so what could they d_ ?
Said the fly, "Let us flee!"
"Let us fly!" said the flea,
So they fl_ _ through a flaw in the fl_ _.

3. Have students brainstorm as a group to compile a list of pirate words. (See Writing, p. 50). To create a crossword, have them use graph paper, or a computer crossword puzzle program. Many word and crossword puzzle programs are available as shareware. If you have Internet access, a good source of such software is website: http://www.puzzledepot.com/software.shtml

4. Some of the homophones in the box are short, but unusual (**hue/hew**). Have students check the meanings in a dictionary and write their own sentences for each homophone pair.

5. Remind students that a log is a type of diary in which information is recorded in brief, point form. Ask them to complete the log until the ship sinks. Students should be encouraged to be creative but cautioned to use the Super Words correctly. Have them share their passages, filling in the missing words.

Students may wish to write a log of a trip, either imaginary or real, that they have taken.

New Words

6. Have students create a word web with the prefix 'micro', meaning very small. Many of these words are recent additions to the English language, although some are older (**microphone**, **microscope**).

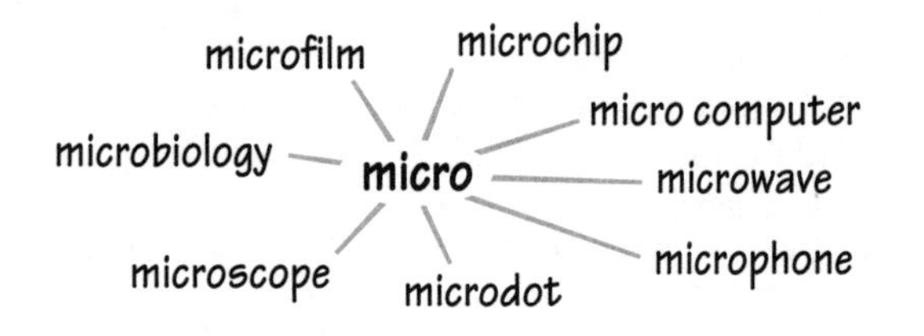

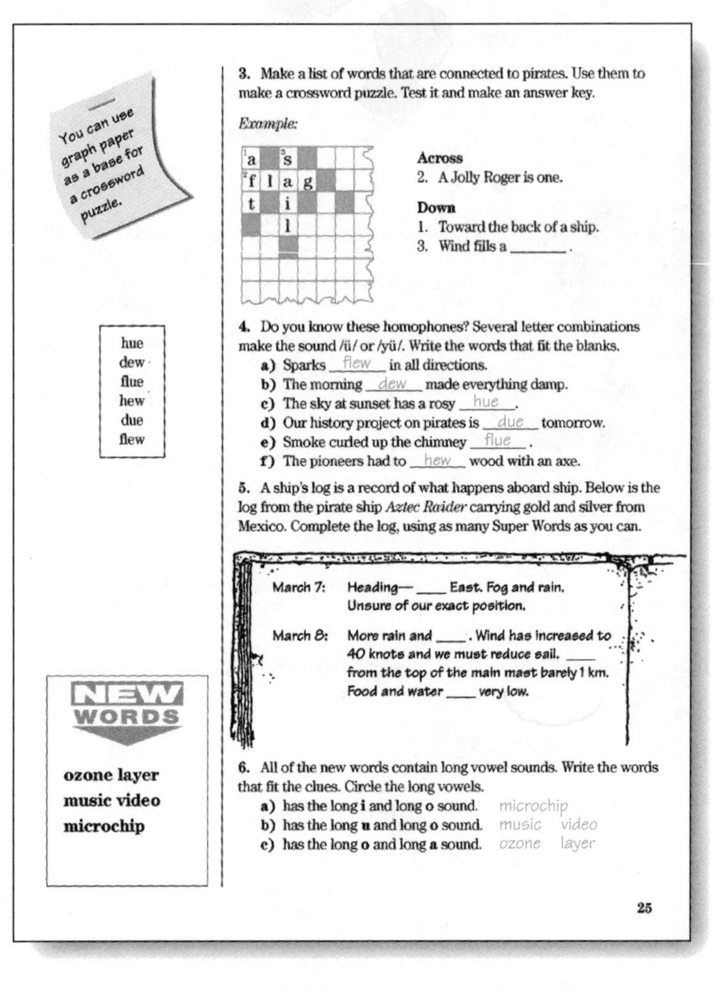

You can use graph paper as a base for a crossword puzzle.

3. Make a list of words that are connected to pirates. Use them to make a crossword puzzle. Test it and make an answer key.

Example:

Across
2. A Jolly Roger is one.

Down
1. Toward the back of a ship.
3. Wind fills a ______.

hue
dew
flue
hew
due
flew

4. Do you know these homophones? Several letter combinations make the sound /ü/ or /yü/. Write the words that fit the blanks.

a) Sparks flew in all directions.
b) The morning dew made everything damp.
c) The sky at sunset has a rosy hue.
d) Our history project on pirates is due tomorrow.
e) Smoke curled up the chimney flue.
f) The pioneers had to hew wood with an axe.

5. A ship's log is a record of what happens aboard ship. Below is the log from the pirate ship *Aztec Raider* carrying gold and silver from Mexico. Complete the log, using as many Super Words as you can.

March 7: Heading— ____ East. Fog and rain. Unsure of our exact position.

March 8: More rain and ____. Wind has increased to 40 knots and we must reduce sail. ____ from the top of the main mast barely 1 km. Food and water ____ very low.

NEW WORDS

ozone layer
music video
microchip

6. All of the new words contain long vowel sounds. Write the words that fit the clues. Circle the long vowels.

a) has the long **i** and long **o** sound. microchip
b) has the long **u** and long **o** sound. music video
c) has the long **o** and long **a** sound. ozone layer

25

Curriculum Connection

Have a small group of students research information about famous pirates, then share their findings with the class.

Students might want to read about Oak Island, off the coast of Nova Scotia, where people have been searching for pirate treasure for over 200 years. (For reference see *Oak Island Gold* by William S. Crooker, Nimbus Publishing, 1993.)

Assessment

Dictate the list words following the same procedure as in the Precheck, and have students self-correct, or correct their test with a partner. Following this Unit Test, use words from Column D, 'Words I Need to Study', on the Student Record Sheet to identify which students need special help.

Follow-up

Students who are having difficulties with the spelling of long **u** may require additional practice with the various spelling patterns. Keep a box of cloze cards that have words with the **u_e**, **ew**, and **ue** spellings, and have students use them to write the completed words, then turn over the cards to check the spelling.

thr_w   bl_e   perf_m_

ch_w   gl_e

Teacher's Notes

6 Looking Back
Units 1–5

Patterns to Review

Review the following sound-symbol relationships:

- Long **a** spelled **a_e**, **ay**, or **ai** as in **page**, **play**, **paid**
- Short **e** as in **spell**
- Long **e** spelled **ee** or **ea** as in **cheek**, **cheat**
- Long **i** spelled **i_e** as in **pride**
- Short **i** as in **pick**
- Long **o** spelled **o_e** or **oa** as in **rope**, **road**
- Long **u** spelled **u_e**, **ew**, or **ue** as in **rule**, **drew**, **clue**
- **yü** spelled **u_e**, **ew**, or **ue** as in **mule**, **few**, **cue**

The list of words for review is a selection from the preceding units. It includes words known to be commonly misspelled and others representative of the spelling patterns that have been presented.

Previous Spelling Instruction

Some students in your class may have experienced an informal spelling program. Others will have participated in a formal approach to spelling involving the use of spelling texts and regular dictations. It is important to be aware of these factors, since students who appear to be lagging behind in spelling skills may simply lack the experience of looking at spelling patterns and utilizing spelling strategies when faced with unfamiliar words. Another possibility is that previous instructional strategies for spelling may have been inappropriate for the needs of a particular student. A heavy focus on phonics, for example, would be ineffective for a student who is having difficulty recalling the visual features of words.

Creating a Personal Review List

Looking Back units should also provide an opportunity for students to review words and concepts which gave them particular difficulty in the preceding units. These personal study lists could involve words from a variety of sources, as suggested below:

- words misspelled in the students' Unit Tests and everyday writing (writing folders, note-books, tests)
- words used throughout the day: current themes, content areas, current events, media, holidays
- lists such as "The 200 Words Most Frequently Misspelled" and "The 200 Words Most Frequently Written" (See Appendix.)

Transfer of Spelling Knowledge

The following suggestions will help students to retain the knowledge and skills they acquire through word study and apply them in their everyday writing:

- Do not treat words on study lists as single entities, but as examples of larger spelling patterns. Build on word patterns to maximize the benefit of word study.
- Reintroduce frequently misspelled words on subsequent lists.
- When errors reoccur in student writing, ask students to recall the strategies they had used for studying these words.
- Discuss the use of spelling strategies for new words as they occur in a variety of classroom contexts.

6 Looking Back

STUDY STEPS

LOOK at each word.
SAY each word clearly.
COVER each word.
WRITE each word.
CHECK each word carefully.

Here is a list of words that may have been hard for you in Units 1–5. You and your teacher may add other words to the list.

accident	difficult	temperature	thumb
equipment	disease	guide	knew
gorilla	electric	whole	wrote
capture	fifth	jewels	argue

1. Use the Study Steps for each word. Your teacher will dictate the words.

2. Complete each sentence with words from the Study List that match the shape and suit the meaning. Write the sentences in your notebook.

a) The doctor knew the boy's illness would be difficult to treat. The boy had a high temperature and his whole body shook with chills.

b) "You can avoid having an accident at work by using proper equipment," wrote the manager.

c) The zookeeper wanted to capture the gorilla to treat its sore thumb.

3. Write the study words that have three or more syllables. Put a mark over the syllable that is stressed.

* *Example:* con tin´ ue   áccident équipment gorílla dif´ficult eléctric témperature

* correction

26

Looking Back

1. As well as using the Study Steps, have students focus on those letters of each word that may give them difficulty. This might be double consonants (a**cc**ident, gori**ll**a, di**ff**icult), silent letters (thum**b**, **w**rote, **k**new, **w**hole), or letters not clearly pronounced (fi**f**th, temp**er**ature, acci**d**ent, diffic**u**lt).

Dictation

The car **accident** happened suddenly.
Do you have any baseball **equipment**?
A **gorilla** is a huge animal.
Did they **capture** the escaped tiger?
That was a **difficult** problem to solve.
The **disease** made her skin itchy.
An **electric** car is very quiet.
Our apartment is on the **fifth** floor.
The **temperature** today is 20 degrees.
Follow the **guide** or you may get lost.
The **whole** class roared with laughter.
The **jewels** were stolen in the robbery.
The carpenter hit her **thumb** with the hammer.
He **knew** the answer to my question.
I **wrote** two letters yesterday.
Please don't **argue** with me!

2. Once the students have completed the sentences, have them brainstorm synonyms for some of the words.

list word	synonym
accident	mishap
equipment	tools
gorilla	ape
capture	catch
hard	whole

3. To help reinforce the number and sequence of syllables, write the syllables of all the longer review words at random on a large sheet of paper. Have students cut out the syllables and rearrange them to form the review words.

ac ture dif e go
quip e per dent la
fi ci tric a tem
ment ril cult lec

Record Keeping:

You may wish to use the following chart to help students analyse their own errors. By reflecting on their spelling strategies and error patterns students will often become more conscious of these factors as they write every day.

review list word	my misspelling	mistake at beginning	mistake in middle	mistake at end
fifth	fith		✓	
whole	hole	✓		
thumb	thum			✓

4. You might wish to have students complete this activity as a word sort. Provide students with a deck of cards that has one word written on each card, and have them sort the cards into the appropriate columns.

Co-operative groups could brainstorm additional long **a**, **e**, and **o** words and then sort these further into the appropriate spelling patterns for the sound.

a_e	ay	ai	ee	ea
bale	say	bait	green	beat
rate	play	pair	agree	easel
escape	crayon	drain	between	eastern

o_e	oa	o
pole	boat	patio
hopeful	coast	hero
lonely	road	echo

5. Students may enjoy creating their own word puzzles similar to this one, using other review words, or words from a current classroom theme. Have them make up a riddle, then write the clues for each letter of the answer.

6. Have students add words to each pattern.

/ü/			/yü/		
_ue	_ew	u_e	_ue	_ew	u_e
true	brew	chute	revue	curfew	dispute
issue	chew	conclude	barbecue	knew	perfume
bluejay	threw	consume			useful

4. a) Make a chart like this in your notebook.

/ā/ spelled as in **base, stay,** or **fail**	/ē/ spelled as in **beam** or **speed**	/ō/ spelled as in **smoke, coat,** or **Mexico**
remain display basement trailer	dream seemed feeling disease	bulldozer explode goalie piano

b) Put the words below into the correct column on your chart.

bulldozer	**display**	**piano**	**seemed**
remain	**goalie**	**disease**	**explode**
dream	**feeling**	**basement**	**trailer**

5. Use each clue to find a letter. Then use the letters and the code to find the answer to the riddle below.

This letter is in **goal** but not in **log.** 1 a
This letter is in **dumb** but not in **drum.** 2 b
This letter is in **line** but not in **file.** 3 n
This letter is in **whole** but not in **lower.** 4 h
This letter is in **glue** but not in **leg.** 5 u
This letter is in **metal** but not in **trailer.** 6 m
This letter is in **quit** but not in **quickly.** 7 t

Question: What do you get when there's a hole in your mitten?
Answers: a n u m b t h u m b
1 3 5 6 2 7 4 5 6 2

6. Each picture word contains the sound /ü/ as in **blue** and **drew**, or /yü/ as in **huge** and **few**. Write the words.

glue
flute
jewels
ruler
screw

7. Write the word in each set that has the sound /ī/ as in **spike**.

a) linen line skinny line
b) quit quickly guide guide
c) slide slippery slither slide

27

7. Note with students that the spelling pattern for /ī/ in each example is **i-consonant-e**.

From Short-term to Long-term Memory

Effective spelling instruction supports the process of taking sight, sound, and other cues and storing them in memory through four main stages:

1. Focussing Attention: Focussing attention on words as specific bits of information to be learned is the student's first task. Each word has a sound, a shape, and features that are the same as other words. Focussing on these helps put the word in the student's short-term or 'working' memory.

2. Encoding: To move words into long-term memory, students need to have a visual image of the word, relate it to other words with the same pattern, or develop a personal mnemonic to remember it. (Did you ever see '**a bun dance**'?)

3. Practising: Many short practice sessions spread over time are more effective than one long learning session. Practice should come as close to real use as possible—truly interactive use of words is better than simple rote learning.

4. Retrieving: Once words are stored in long-term memory they can be retrieved at any time for use. We retrieve information the way it was stored. For example, to remember the **ie** sequence in **retrieve**, many people remember the rhyme, '**i** before **e**, except after **c**.'

Dictionary Skills

1. Alphabetical Order: Write the review words from the Study List that would be found in the dictionary between each set of words below.

apple / coal — argue, capture
deposits / every — difficult, electric, equipment
furnace / hair — gorilla, guide
task / write — temperature, thumb, whole

captive 80 cave

2. Guide Words: Every page in a dictionary has a set of guide words at the top of it. The guide word **captive** on the left is the first entry on that page. The guide word **cave** on the right is the last entry on the page.

For each picture in the left column, write the correct set of guide words.

a) janitor / jacket; (jeans / jigsaw;) joker / junk

b) slide / solid; seemed / skill; (sending / smoke)

c) violin / volcano; (vacuum / vampire;) vanish / victim

3. Word Meaning: A dictionary gives the meanings or definitions of the entry words. Most entry words have more than one meaning. The different meanings for an entry word help us to understand the word better and tell us how it can be used in different ways.

Read the entry for the word **beam**.

beam (bēm) **1** a radio signal used to guide aircraft, ships, etc. **2** a ray of light or heat **3** look or smile brightly **4** the main horizontal support of a building or ship

Write the definition of **beam** used in each of these sentences.

a) The child's face beamed with delight. (3)
b) Laser beams are used to treat some diseases. (2)
c) They walked along the beams in the attic. (4)
d) The captain used the beams to change course. (1)

28

1. Students may find this task quite challenging, since they have to consider four sets of guide words. There are several strategies that might help them:

- suggest that they first of all arrange the review words in alphabetical order
- write each guide word on a card and arrange the four sets in order, spaced well apart
- provide students with a deck of cards containing the review words, and have them place each card under the appropriate guide words; keep a separate pile for those words that do not fit in any of the categories (**accident**, **fifth**, **jewels**, **knew**).

(apple/coal) argue capture

2. Be sure that students agree on what each picture represents (jewels, skull, valley). This exercise requires students to alphabetize to the third letter, and to eliminate choices systematically.

Point out that a dictionary is not the only reference book that depends on the use of guide words—phone directories, encyclopedias, and almanacs all use guide words. Provide practice in using these sources to locate information.

3. Note that when the various meanings of a word are grouped under a single entry, they usually come from the same word origin and have some similarity in meaning. Words that are distinctly different in meaning and word origin, but which are spelled alike, are given separate entries, and are known as homographs (mail [letters]/mail [armour]).

You might point out to students that the first meaning given for a word is not always the most common definition; different dictionaries organize definitions in different ways.

mail[1] (māl) n., v.
— n. 1 letters, postcards, papers, parcels, etc. sent or to be sent by post. 2 the system by which such mail is sent, managed by the Post Office. 3 all that comes by one post or delivery. 4 a train, boat, etc. that carries mail.
— v. post; send by mail; put in a mailbox: *He mailed the letter for his mother.*
[ME < OF *male* wallet < Gmc.]
Hom. male.

mail[2] (māl) n., v.
— n. 1 flexible armour made of metal rings, loops of chain, or small plates linked together. 2 the hard, protective covering of some animals, such as turtles.
— v. cover or protect with mail.
[ME < OF *maille* < L *macula* a mesh in network]
Hom. male.

(*Gage Canadian Dictionary*)

Exploring the World of Inventions

1. Invite students to research information about current scientific inventions, using both print and electronic media such as CD-ROMs, and the World Wide Web, as well as other sources such as local businesses. You may wish to have a group discussion for students to share their findings with classmates. Have students make a list of new words that have been added to our language as a result of these inventions.

information highway, fax, cell phone, woofer, tweeter, airbus, photoradar, robotics, biodegradable, modem, web site

2. To help students develop ideas for their inventions suggest they jot down thoughts under headings such as the following.

problem	solution	description
icy roads in winter	heated car tires	electric wires inside tire switch on dash etc.

3. Have students conference with a partner before editing their writing. Emphasize to students that they should be helpful and encouraging when commenting on their partner's work.

Exploring the World of Inventions

1. Brainstorm with your group to list as many important recent inventions as you can. Sort your inventions into categories. For example:

Communications	Electronics	Medicine
the Internet	CD player	ultrasound

2. Imagine you have perfected an amazing new invention which will change the world. Write a description of your invention. Describe it from top to bottom or left to right. You will probably want to include a diagram of your invention.

3. Edit your description carefully to make sure your sentences are clear and interesting.

29

ESL

Language Snapshot — Arabic

Arabic is an old and beautiful tongue, the language of the Koran, the holy book of Islam. The main difficulty in writing and spelling Arabic stems from the fact that Arabic script is written from right to left, rather than from left to right as in English. This means that students may misread and spell letters within words (**form** for **from**; **twon** for **town**).

Language Features

- Arabic depends on consonant sounds and long vowels to express meaning. There are eight vowel sounds and 32 consonants, compared to 22 vowel sounds and 24 consonant sounds in English.
- Short vowels sound similar and are glossed over.
- The consonants **p** and **b** sound alike, as do **v** and **f**.
- Initial consonant clusters **pr**, **pl**, **gr**, **gl**, **sp**, **spr**, **skr**, **str**, **spl** do not exist. Students may attempt to say and write an extra syllable (**ispring** or **sipring** for **spring**).
- Some students may reverse letters that have 'mirror shapes' (**p**/**q**; **b**/**d**).
- Stress in Arabic is more predictable and regular than in English. Students may have trouble with the concept that stress changes meaning in words such as **pre** 'sent and pre**sent** '.
- There are no capital letters in Arabic, and these may be omitted.
- There is no indefinite article (**a**, **an**).

Grammar Power

1. Writing with common and proper nouns: We use a **noun** to name a **person, place,** or **thing**.

A **common noun** names a person, place, or thing. A **proper noun** is a special name, place, or thing.

	Common Nouns	Proper Nouns
Person	man	Bruno
Place	country	Mexico
Thing	magazine	National Geographic

Make two columns in your notebook and sort the nouns below into the correct column.

Common Nouns	Proper Nouns
gorilla thumb hospital island sister	John Vancouver Uncle Elvis Alberta Simi Stanley Cup Glenbow Museum

John	Alberta	sister	hospital
gorilla	thumb	Simi	Stanley Cup
island	Vancouver	Uncle Elvis	Glenbow Museum

When you use a common noun like boy, car, or horse, you often need to use another word, such as the, a, or my.

2. Complete these sentences by adding either a common or a proper noun. These nouns will be the **subject** of the sentence, or what the sentence is about.

a) _______ jumped over the fence.
b) _______ zoomed down the highway.
c) _______ ate fried worms.
d) _______ wore a ridiculous hat.

29a

Grammar Power

1. The old rule that a noun is the **name** of a **person**, **place**, or **thing** is one way for students to remember what nouns do. We use capital letters for proper nouns—the names of specific people, places, and things. Have students examine the first chart on page 29a and discuss how the proper nouns are different from the common nouns.

You may wish to extend the word sorting activity by providing other common and proper nouns, all without capitals. Have students write them in the correct column, with a capital letter as appropriate.

common	holiday weekend month prime minister teacher continent
proper	Saturday Ms. Donato Lake Huron January Africa

2. Direct students to the note in the margin. When they use a common noun, such as **elephant**, they will need to add an article (**a**, **an**, **the**), or another modifier (**this**, **that**, **my**, **his**). If they use a proper noun, no modifiers are need.

An elephant jumped over the fence.
Jumbo jumped over the fence.
The race car zoomed down the highway.
Mario Andretti zoomed down the highway.
Those boys ate fried worms. **Mike and Ali** ate fried worms.
That clown wore a ridiculous hat. **Darcy** wore a ridiculous hat.

POWERBOOSTERS

1 The short vowel sound /a/ is usually spelled **a** as in **capture**.
The long vowel sound /ā/ may be spelled **ay** as in **stayed**, **ai** as in **fail**, or **a_e** as in **base**.

2 The short vowel sound /e/ is usually spelled **e** as in **lens**.
The long vowel sound /ē/may be spelled **ea** as in **meat** or **ee** as in **feet**.

3 The sound /i/ is usually spelled **i** as in **trick**.
The sound /ī/ may be spelled **i_e** as in **kite**.
The sound /kw/ is spelled **qu** as in **quick**.

4 The short vowel sound /o/ is usually spelled **o** as in **stock**.
The long vowel sound /ō/ may be spelled **o_e** as in **hope**, **oa** as in **boat**, or **o** as in **piano**.

5 The short vowel sound /u/ is usually spelled **u** as in **truck**.
The long vowel sound /ü/ may be spelled **u_e** as in **rule**, **ew** as in **flew**, or **ue** as in **blue**.
The long vowel sound /yü/ may be spelled **u_e** as in **mule**, **ew** as in **few**, or **ue** as in **cue**.

3. Abstract nouns name ideas, concepts, and other things we cannot touch, taste, or see. Brainstorm with the group a list of abstract nouns that name feelings or ideas. Use a thesaurus to expand the list.

Suggest that students write their own sentences using three of the abstract nouns.

4. Abstract nouns ending in **-ness** are dealt with in greater detail in Unit 28.

When students have written their own definitions of happiness, suggest that they try to imagine happiness from other points of view: their little brother or sister, a dog, a computer games enthusiast, an inline skater, etc.

Proofing Power

Students may wish to do this proofreading with a partner. It may be useful to prepare a cloze version of the passage, in which the correct letters are given, but a space is left blank for incorrect portions of the word.

> It was dif_icult to find. _ _ new we were going the wrong way, but I didn_t want to arg_ _.

---

3. Using Abstract Nouns: Some nouns name things such as courage, or happiness, that we can't touch, smell, see, hear, or taste. These are called abstract nouns. In Units 1 – 6 you studied the following abstract nouns:

luck promise skill practice

Unscramble the words in the sentences below.

a) This computer game requires **lslik** and **clku** to win! skill luck

b) I **miserop** you will have time to attend the next **rcatcpie**. promise practice

4. Write your own definition for the abstract noun **happiness**. Here are some sample definitions.

Happiness is a warm puppy. (Charlie Brown)

Happiness is getting everything you want for your birthday.

Happiness is ________________. (your own definition)

Proofing Power

The following paragraph was written by a student in Grade 4. Read it carefully, rewriting words that are spelled incorrectly. Compare your list of misspellings with a partner.

Yesterday my mother and I went to a museum. It was dificult to find. i new we were going the wrong way, but I didnt want to argew. When we got there, a giude helpt us find the displays. I think the best exhibit was about inventions. It had lots of expensive eqippment and I new it must have cost a hole lot of money. We decideed to go to the animel exhibit next. There was a statue of a gorila. When I askt why they didn't have a real one, the man said they were very rare and dificult to capehur. At the end the gide handed us a form that asked, "Did you have a good time today at the museum?" I rote, "Yes!"

difficult / I/knew / didn't / argue / guide/helped / equipment/knew / whole / decided/animal / gorilla/asked / difficult/capture / guide / wrote

29b

Teacher's Notes

Vowels with r

ar as in ap**ar**t
ir as in c**ir**cle
ur as in s**ur**face
er as in larg**er**
ear as in s**ear**ch

Patterns

The many ways of spelling the /är/ and /ėr/ sounds pose spelling challenges, especially for students who rely too heavily on sounding words out. Students will need to develop strategies for remembering which pattern fits a given word.

Preknowledge

Students should have an understanding of the following concepts as they work with the patterns in this unit.

- Base words and derived forms (**remark/ remarkable**; **east/eastern**).
- The sound /s/ can be spelled **s** as in **s**earch, or **c** as in **c**ircle.

More Patterns

Other patterns you may wish to review or introduce in this unit include the following.

- Proper nouns require a capital letter (**Earth**).
- Homophones are words that sound alike but have different spellings and meanings (**desert/dessert**).
- Comparative and superlative forms of adjectives (**large/larger/largest**).
- Some words contain silent letters (**often**).

Professional Notebook

There is a definite role for instruction in learning to spell. Although children will pick up a good deal of knowledge on their own, teachers have a very important role in getting children to think about spelling. If spelling instruction takes a discovery approach and builds on the teachable moment, it's valuable not just as a means to the end of producing better spellers but as an intellectual pursuit that's worthwhile for its own sake.

(Wilde 72)

Sharing the Secrets with Kids

*A mnemonic can help distinguish between the homophones **desert** and **dessert**. Just remember that you like **s**trawberry **s**hortcake for de**ss**ert, or that you wish to have two de**ss**erts.*

Precheck

Encourage students to become their own 'word detectives'. Immediately following the Precheck, allow time for them to proofread their lists before you present the words visually for self-correction.

Dictation

The book has fallen **apart**.
Lean **against** me!
Which piece is **larger**?
I'm **certain** it was the correct answer.
Perhaps it was.
Which are the **eastern** provinces?
Wipe the **dirt** off your shoes.
A **circle** is round.
The **surface** was very rough.
Search for him!
She likes to be **earliest** in class.
What a **remarkable** dog.
Soil is another name for **earth**.
The **desert** is hot and dry.
It was a **surprise** party.
She's **often** there.

Words in Context

Read the passage aloud with students. You might wish to use it as a cloze exercise and have students fill in the list words. Ask students to suggest synonyms for the list words, so that the sentences still make sense. Discuss why it is difficult to find synonyms for some words, such as **eastern** and **desert**.

list word	synonym(s)	list word	synonym(s)
apart	distant, isolated	against	opposite
larger	bigger	certain	sure, positive
perhaps	maybe, possibly	eastern	—
dirt	soil, earth	circle	ring, circuit
surface	top, face	search	seek, sift
earliest	first	remarkable	amazing, astonishing
Earth	the world	desert	wilderness
surprise	unexpected	often	frequently

7

Vowels with r
ar ir ur er ear
art circle surface
larger search

apart
against
larger
certain
perhaps
eastern
dirt
circle
surface
search
earliest
remarkable
earth
desert
surprise
often

Exploring the Fossil Record of Early Human Beings

In Africa, scientists have discovered skeletons of perhaps the earliest human beings on Earth. No one is certain, but it seems these remarkable fossil bones found on the eastern plains of Africa are more than a million years old. This is a surprise. Until recently, many scientists believed that human history only went back about 10 000 years. Sometimes these bones are found near the surface of the ground, sometimes deep in caves. Although a few larger pieces, such as lower jawbones, are uncovered intact, usually the skeletons have been broken into tiny pieces and these are found far apart. Workers must search through layers of dirt and desert sand in an ever-widening circle to recover each piece, then fit them together like a jigsaw puzzle. Often, they must race against time to save valuable fossil records from bulldozers and building crews.

Observing Patterns

1. Write the five list words that have the stress on the second syllable. Place a stress mark over the second syllable.
apárt agáinst perháps remárkable surpríse
2. Write the list words that begin with the sound /s/. Circle the letter that makes the /s/ sound in each word.
ⓒertain ⓒircle ⓢurface ⓢearch ⓢurprise
3. Write the list word that means the opposite of the underlined word or phrase in each sentence.
a) Their latest discovery was quite remarkable. earliest
b) Some people think that the mythical lost city of Atlantis lies on the floor of the ocean. surface
c) We are not sure what caused the destruction of the Inca civilization. certain

30

Observing Patterns

1. Read aloud the list words that have the stress on the first syllable. Do the same with those that have the stress on the second syllable. This will reinforce the concept of stress in words.

2. Remind students that the symbol /s/ refers to the sound /s/, not the letter **s**. Have students divide the words beginning with /s/ into two columns, /s/ spelled **c** and /s/ spelled **s**. Add to the list throughout the unit.

/s/ spelled c	/s/ spelled s
certain circle	surface search surprise

3. Students should not be asked to rewrite the sentences after substituting the correct word, since the new constructions would no longer make sense in b) and c). Instead, students could be asked to use the list words in sentences that show their meaning.

Think of your own words to add to each set.

4. Write the list word that belongs in each set.
a) taller heavier younger — larger
b) sand cactus heat — desert
c) triangle oval square — circle
d) mud sand clay — dirt
e) always regularly frequently — often

5. Complete each list word below.

de_s_ert s_u_r_pri_s_e ag_a_i_nst _c_ert_a_i_n o_f_t_en

Discovering Patterns

apart against larger certain perhaps eastern dirt circle surface search earliest remarkable earth desert surprise often

1. Write the list words that have the sound /är/ as in **farm**. Circle the letters that make this sound. apart larger remarkable

2. Many of the list words have the sound /ėr/ as in **bird**. The /ėr/ sound can be spelled in more than one way. Write the /ėr/ list words under the following headings.

/ėr/ spelled **er** as in **term**	/ėr/ spelled **ir** as in **bird**	/ėr/ spelled **ur** as in **burn**	/ėr/ spelled **ear** as in **earth**
larger	dirt	surface	search
certain	circle	surprise	earliest
perhaps			earth
eastern			
desert			

POWERBOOSTER

- The sound /är/ is usually spelled **ar** as in **chart**.
- The sound /ėr/ may be spelled **er** as in **term**, **ir** as in **bird**, **ur** as in **burn**, or **ear** as in **earth**.

31

4. Ask students to give a reason for their choice. Encourage them to add additional words to each set.

a) older, lighter, thinner, fatter
b) sunshine, dryness, barren, snake
c) rectangle, quadrangle, block, cube
d) soil, silt, loam, gravel, grit
e) consistently, continually, generally

5. Students could circle the letters they have supplied, or write them in a different colour as a further aid to memory.

Discovering Patterns

1. Ask students to brainstorm with a partner and list as many words as possible containing the sound /är/ spelled **ar**. Compile a master list with the class.

bar car bark dark hark
afar carpet parted scarper supermarket
hard yard far tarp
spark darken marker parking

2. You might wish to have students work in small groups to generate lists of other words fitting the various /ėr/ patterns.

er	alert persuade shopper camera observe verse
ir	shirt third circus birthday skirt thirst
ur	hurt curt burden murder curve urgent
ear	early heard earn learn search earnest

Multiple Intelligences

- A variety of approaches can be used to help students remember which spelling pattern for /ėr/ fits a specific word.

Visual/spatial: Exaggerate the size of letters; colour code the letters spelling /ėr/.

Bodily/kinesthetic: Physically arrange words in common spelling patterns, as described in Critical Thinking; use letter tiles to form words.

Musical: Create songs or chants for words in a given pattern.

Verbal/Linguistic and Logical/ Mathematical: Discuss the sorting of words and try to add words to each category.

ESL

- Students from some language backgrounds have difficulty distinguishing /är/ and /ėr/ from other vowel sounds. To add to the problem, there are many ways of spelling /ėr/. Give students who are experiencing such difficulties practice with pairs of words that point up the contrasts.

short a	/är/	short e	/ėr/	/är/	/ėr/
cap	carp	pet	pert	barn	burn
tap	tarp	ten	turn	hard	herd
shack	shark	Ben	burn	Bart	Bert
lack	lark	wed	word		
back	bark	bed	bird		
ban	barn				

1. Advise students that only two of the answers are list words. Part c) has more than one possible answer (fearful, nervous).

2. Some students might need further practice with words ending in **y**.

heavy	heavier	heaviest
busy	busier	busiest
funny	funnier	funniest
lucky	luckier	luckiest
silly	sillier	silliest
happy	happier	happiest

3. You may wish to have students recall any visits they might have made to a circus, or circus shows that they have seen on television. How are circles used in a circus? Why is the area where all the action takes place called the 'ring'?

4. Be certain that students drop the **e** in **love** before adding **-able**. Encourage them to think of other words ending in the suffix **-able**, and to identify the base word of each. Distinguish between these words and other words containing **able** (**table**, **fable**, **stable**).

acceptable	available	believable
comfortable	considerable	inflammable
dependable	fashionable	memorable

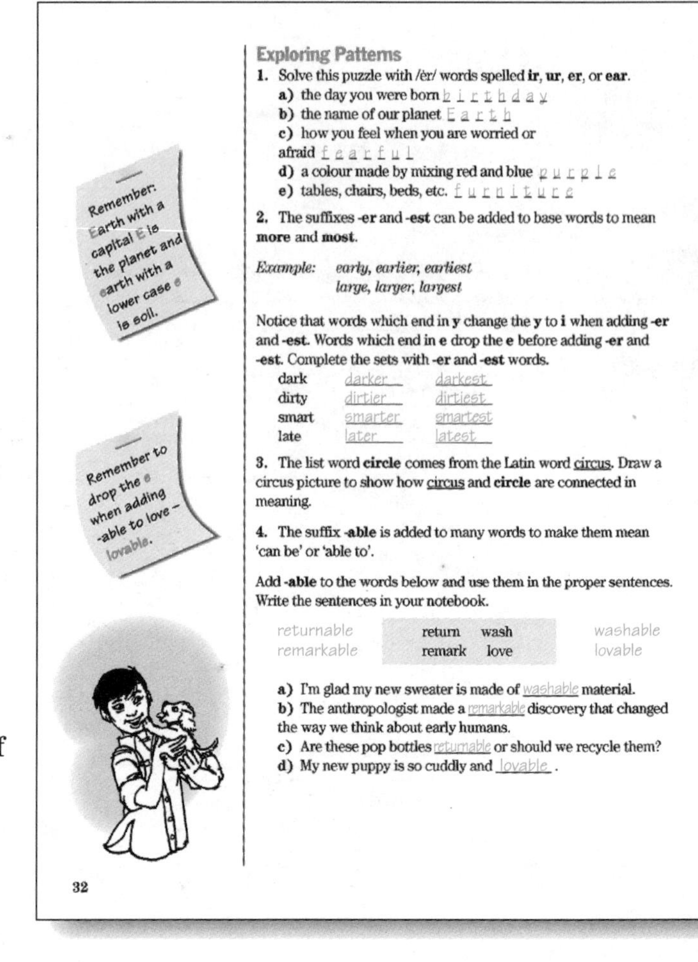

Remember: Earth with a capital E is the planet and earth with a lower case e is soil.
Remember to drop the e when adding -able to love – lovable.

Exploring Patterns

1. Solve this puzzle with /ėr/ words spelled **ir**, **ur**, **er**, or **ear**.

a) the day you were born b i r t h d a y

b) the name of our planet E a r t h

c) how you feel when you are worried or afraid f e a r f u l

d) a colour made by mixing red and blue p u r p l e

e) tables, chairs, beds, etc. f u r n i t u r e

2. The suffixes **-er** and **-est** can be added to base words to mean **more** and **most**.

Example: *early, earlier, earliest*
large, larger, largest

Notice that words which end in **y** change the **y** to **i** when adding **-er** and **-est**. Words which end in **e** drop the **e** before adding **-er** and **-est**. Complete the sets with **-er** and **-est** words.

dark	darker	darkest
dirty	dirtier	dirtiest
smart	smarter	smartest
late	later	latest

3. The list word **circle** comes from the Latin word circus. Draw a circus picture to show how circus and **circle** are connected in meaning.

4. The suffix **-able** is added to many words to make them mean 'can be' or 'able to'.

Add **-able** to the words below and use them in the proper sentences. Write the sentences in your notebook.

returnable
remarkable

return wash
remark love

washable
lovable

a) I'm glad my new sweater is made of washable material.

b) The anthropologist made a remarkable discovery that changed the way we think about early humans.

c) Are these pop bottles returnable or should we recycle them?

d) My new puppy is so cuddly and lovable.

32

Critical Thinking

- Word sorts for the /ėr/ and /är/ sounds can be built systematically through Units 7, 8, and 11. In this unit, provide each group with a deck of word cards containing each list word that has either the sound /är/ or /ėr/. The students' first task is to sort the deck into three piles: words with the sound /är/; the sound /ėr/; both /är/ and /ėr/ (**larger**). The next step is to focus on the /ėr/ pile, and sort these words into the various patterns for spelling /ėr/: **er**, **ir**, **ur**, **ear**.

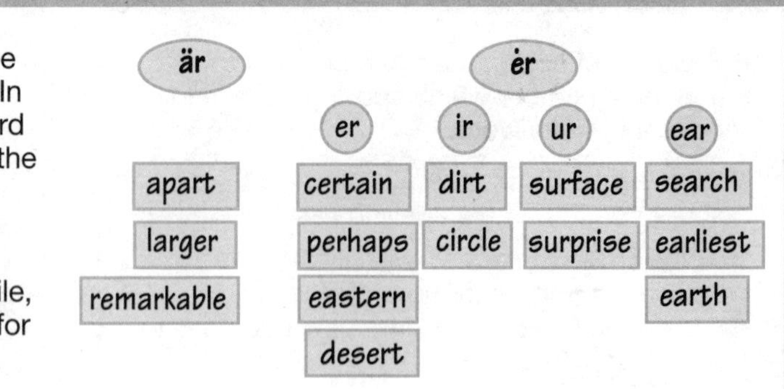

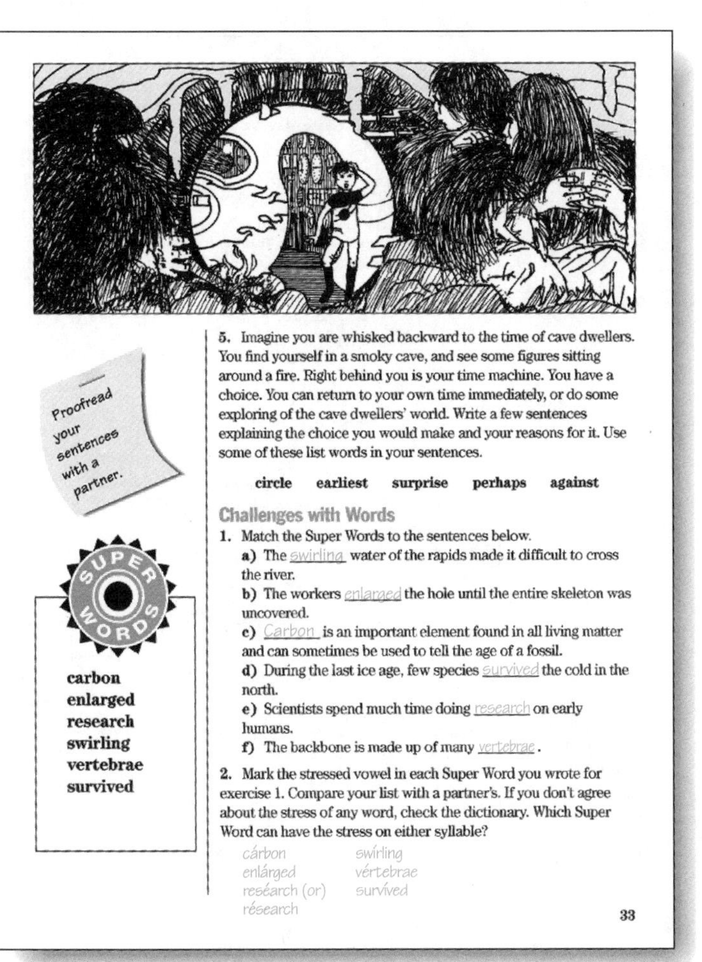

5. Imagine you are whisked backward to the time of cave dwellers. You find yourself in a smoky cave, and see some figures sitting around a fire. Right behind you is your time machine. You have a choice. You can return to your own time immediately, or do some exploring of the cave dwellers' world. Write a few sentences explaining the choice you would make and your reasons for it. Use some of these list words in your sentences.

circle earliest surprise perhaps against

Proofread your sentences with a partner.

SUPER WORDS

carbon
enlarged
research
swirling
vertebrae
survived

Challenges with Words

1. Match the Super Words to the sentences below.
   a) The swirling water of the rapids made it difficult to cross the river.
   b) The workers enlarged the hole until the entire skeleton was uncovered.
   c) Carbon is an important element found in all living matter and can sometimes be used to tell the age of a fossil.
   d) During the last ice age, few species survived the cold in the north.
   e) Scientists spend much time doing research on early humans.
   f) The backbone is made up of many vertebrae.

2. Mark the stressed vowel in each Super Word you wrote for exercise 1. Compare your list with a partner's. If you don't agree about the stress of any word, check the dictionary. Which Super Word can have the stress on either syllable?

cárbon swírling
enlárged vértebrae
reséarch (or) survíved
résearch

33

5. Suggest to students that this exercise is similar to a 'choose your own ending' story. Divide the group in two and have each half select either of the choices offered. Have students share their completed stories.

If your students are familiar with hypermedia software such as 'Hypercard' they may compose their stories including the various options and endings.

Challenges with Words

1. Have students identify which Super Words contain the sound /är/ or /ėr/ then underline the letters that spell these sounds in each word.

/är/	/ėr/
carbon enlarged	research swirling vertebrae survived

2. The Super Word research is pronounced re**search**´ or **re**´search. Students may be interested to note that a shift in stress usually indicates a change in meaning (**con**´tent/con**tent**´; **pre**´sent/pre**sent**´). In the case of **research**, when the stress is on the first syllable the word is a noun; when the last syllable is stressed, it is a verb.

Special Needs

• Less able spellers often rely too heavily on sounding words out as a spelling strategy. Such students will find words with /ėr/ very challenging, since there are so many patterns for spelling the same sound. Encourage students to group the list words into their respective patterns (**er**, **ear**, **ir**). It may help if they highlight or use a different size to write the letters that spell **er** in each case.

certain dirt

surface earth

• The silent **t** in **often** could be recalled by purposely sounding the **t** or by drawing the configuration of the word.

often

3. Have students brainstorm to find other unusual plurals. Ask them to suggest why strange plurals are particularly common in scientific words. You might wish to point out that many of these words originate from Latin and their plurals are formed according to the rules of that language rather than English.

singular	plural
agendum	agenda
analysis	analyses
crisis	crises
criterion	criteria
medium	media
larva	larvae

4. A word search could also be made using Super Words from previous units. Rather than creating a word search on graph paper, students may choose to use a software program such as 'Crossword Magic' that creates these and other word puzzles. Many such useful programs are available via the Internet.

Fossil search

dig	sand	sun	heat	sunburn
sift	gravel	ancient	primitive	early
dry	water	spade	sunstroke	sunhat
relic	care	time	research	science

5. Encourage students to look for information in library reference books as well as CD-ROMs if they can. Suggest that they organize their information according to the animal's category. Have students share their research with a classmate.

whales — mammals — sheep

whales: biggest mammal, endangered species, various types

sheep: produces wool, food source, many breeds, New Zealand–major producer, 'black sheep', sheep dogs

3. Plurals are interesting. **Vertebrae** is the plural of **vertebra**, a word we seldom use in its singular form. Write the words below. Circle the one you think is the plural form in each pair. Then check it in your dictionary.

bacteria, bacterium   data, datum   alga, algae
fungus, fungi   hippopotamus, hippopotami

4. Brainstorm with a partner to think of twenty words that have to do with searching for fossil bones. Then make a word search for another set of partners to solve. Give them a time limit to find all the words.

f			
o			
s	a	n	d
s			i
i			g
l			

5. **Research** is an investigation of a subject. Using classroom or library reference materials, research these topics.

Subject: Animal classification
Find two animals for each of the following categories:

- mammals
- reptiles
- amphibians
- birds
- insects

NEW WORDS

hardware
hacker
desktop

6. New words from the computer world are added to our language all the time. Match the new words to their original meaning. Then write a brief definition of each word as you use it to refer to computers or people who use them.

a) the top of a desk   desktop
b) nuts, bolts, nails, etc.   hardware
c) a person who chops things in pieces   hacker

34

6. Students could be challenged to create sentences that contain a number of computer words. They would then have to 'decipher' the sentences for someone who knew little about computers.

My computer crashed and its RAM was destroyed.
I've got an 800 meg hard drive, a 28.8 modem, and a 16-bit sound card.
Surfing the Net from one web site to another is cool.

Curriculum Connection

The sound /ėr/ is often found at the ends of words, and may indicate the name of a profession. Have students generate a list of words that mean 'someone who ...' Sort these words into **er** and **or** endings.

or	actor	sculptor	doctor	director
er	lawyer	teacher	designer	producer

Home Connection

Alert parents to the fact that the students will be studying vowels with **r** patterns in three of the next five units. You could provide a chart listing the various patterns and encourage each family to add to each list as they meet such words in their everyday lives.

Dear Parent,
In three of the next five spelling units, we're going to be studying vowels with **r** patterns. You can help your child with these by adding words to the chart as you come across them together.

ar	ir	ur	er	ear	or	or
art	circle	surface	larger	search	shore	worst
smart	bird	hurt	prefer	learn	more	work

Assessment

Help students understand the nature of any errors they are still making.

- Are they confusing /ėr/ and /är/ sounds?
- Are they missing silent letters (of**t**en) or letters that are not clearly pronounced (**sur**prised, ag**ai**nst)?
- Is it a schwa vowel that is causing difficulty (cert**ai**n)?
- Are students remembering to change **y** to **i** (earl**y**/earl**i**est)?
- Are homophones a problem (**desert**/**dessert**)?

Follow-up

Have frequent reviews of words with /ėr/ sounds. These words could be reinforced through word searches produced on computer software. Students could also add words to the lists of patterns as they are encountered throughout the day.

Teacher's Notes

8 Vowels with r
or as in shore
ar as in darkness
our as in four

Patterns

As with the /ėr/ patterns in Unit 7, the many ways of spelling the sound /ôr/ pose spelling difficulties. Students need to develop strategies for remembering the spelling of this sound in specific words and practise them often. It is also important for students to distinguish between the common (**or**, **ore**) and the irregular (**ar**, **our**, **oar**, **oor**) patterns for spelling /ôr/.

Preknowledge

Students should have an understanding of the following concepts as they work with the patterns in this unit.

- Proper nouns are capitalized (**Arctic**).
- Homophones are words that sound the same but have different spellings and meanings (**four/fore**).

More Patterns

Other patterns you may wish to introduce or review in this unit include the following.

- Adding an ending to a base word creates a new word (**dark/ness**, **warm/est**).
- Compound words usually consist of two distinct words (**ice/berg**).

Professional Notebook

'Expert' spellers effectively use a visualization strategy; that is, they use visual imagery to encode the spelling and visualization to retrieve it from memory. Kinesthetic feedback provides the cue that the spelling is correct ("It looks right" or "It feels good," they might comment). This proofreading (monitoring) step is an essential part of an effective spelling process.

(Tarasoff 29)

Sharing the Secrets with Kids

Compound words are not simply little words inside a big word. There is usually a logical connection between the parts of a compound word.

Vowels with r

or shore **ar** darkness **our** four

Arctic
darkness
shore
force
order *
before
explore
support
forever
north
warmest
four
aboard
outdoors
iceberg
quarter

* correction

Exploring the Arctic World

Inside the Arctic Circle the sun never rises on December 21st. There is darkness for twenty-four hours. Further north, toward the North Pole, this polar night may last a quarter of the year or longer. Instead of four seasons, in the Arctic world there are two—a winter that seems to last forever and a short, cool summer. But even though the summer is only two months long, the Arctic can support a wide variety of plant and animal life, such as wildflowers, foxes, lemmings, and caribou. The children who live along the shore of the Arctic Ocean enjoy being outdoors during this warmest part of the year. They can jump aboard boats to go fishing, watch an iceberg more than a kilometre long float by, or explore the tundra. They know that before long winter storms will sweep across the Arctic with terrible force as the sun sinks close to the horizon once more. Long winters followed by short summers—this order, or pattern, is something people in the Arctic know well.

Observing Patterns

1. Write the list words that have the sound /är/ as in **parka**.
   Arctic darkness
2. Which list word was borrowed from the Dutch word ijsberg and means 'mountain of ice'? iceberg
3. Write the list words that would be found in the dictionary between the words below.

express / freeze	nature / question
force	order
forever	outdoors
four	north
	quarter

35

Precheck

Remind students to practise their word lists at home, not just at school. Encourage them to create a home-study sheet that includes all the list words and highlights those that gave them problems in the Precheck.

Dictation

The North Pole is in the **Arctic**.
Darkness fell quickly that night.
The sea **shore** was covered in oil.
Don't **force** me to go!
The list is in alphabetical **order**.
Be home **before** dark.
Let's **explore** that cave.
Which team do you **support**?
It took **forever** to get there.
Go **north** on Brick Road.
Which sweater is **warmest**?
I bought **four** apples today.
Climb **aboard** the bus.
Let's go **outdoors** now.
An **iceberg** sank the *Titanic*.
She ate a **quarter** of the cake.

Words in Context

Ask students to imagine what it would be like growing up in the Arctic. How might their lives be different? Read the passage aloud with students and challenge them to use list words in sentences that describe the changes they would likely experience.

Observing Patterns

1. Students could suggest other words that conform to the same pattern.

parka	part
dark	park
lark	mark
darn	yarn

2. Students might enjoy discovering other English words that have been borrowed from Dutch.

English	waffle	yacht	coleslaw	knuckle
Dutch	wafel	jacht	koolsla	kneukel

3. Some students might incorrectly include the list word **explore** in their answer. Remind them that their choices must come after the first guide word and before the last.

Special Needs

- Some students may struggle to remember which spelling of /ôr/ is correct. They should be aware that most /ôr/ words are spelled either **ore** or **or**. Other spellings of the sound will need to be memorized using a variety of strategies. Since sounding the word out will not always identify the correct spelling pattern, visual strategies may often be the most effective.
- In addition to suggestions given in Unit 7, chapters 11–16 in *Spelling: Sharing the Secrets* focus on a wide range of spelling strategies.

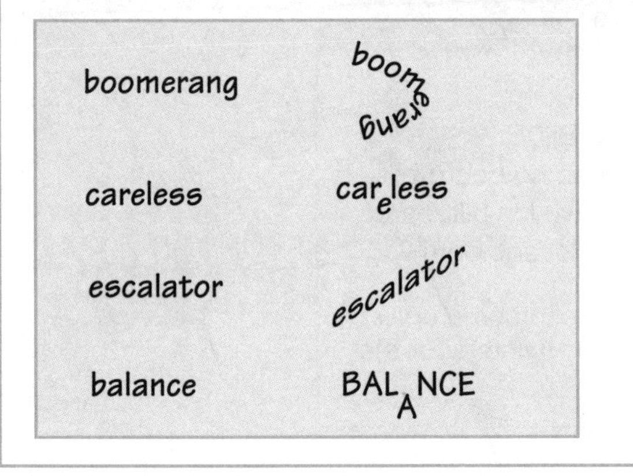

4. Students could highlight aspects of these words by circling or underlining to help them remember the patterns.

Discovering Patterns

1. If students tend to place **forever** under the **ore** pattern, remind them that this is a compound word (**for/ever**). Encourage students to think of other words they know that fit these patterns.

ore: more bore core lore pore

or: report import storm form norm

2. and **3.** Encourage students to add more words that share the patterns **ar** and **our**.

ar: swarm warm war wart ward

our: pour your downpour outpour

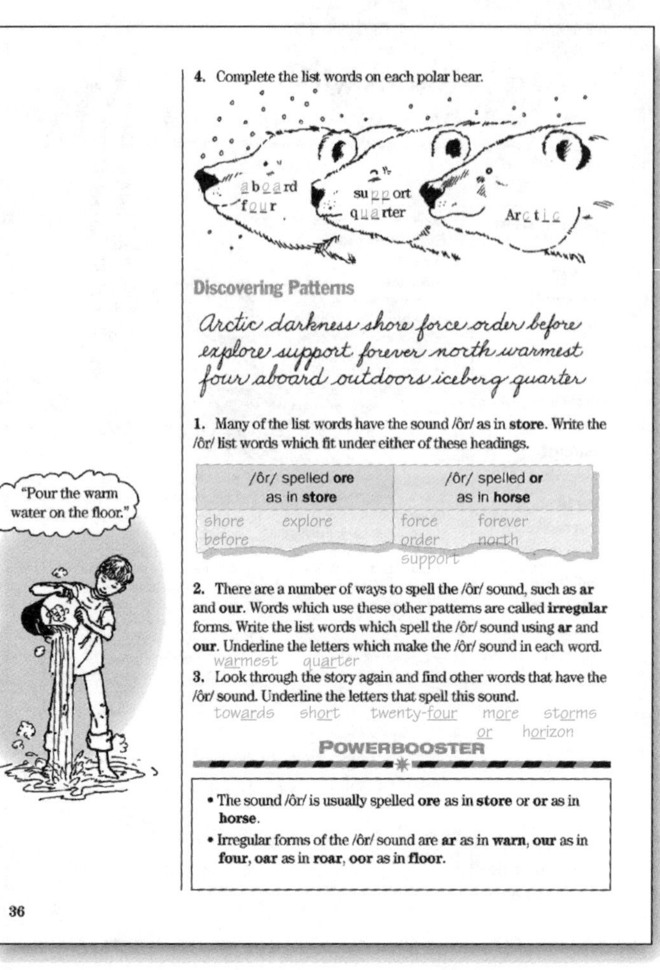

4. Complete the list words on each polar bear.

"Pour the warm water on the floor."

Discovering Patterns

Arctic darkness shore force order before explore support forever north warmest four aboard outdoors iceberg quarter

1. Many of the list words have the sound /ôr/ as in **store**. Write the /ôr/ list words which fit under either of these headings.

/ôr/ spelled **ore** as in **store**	/ôr/ spelled **or** as in **horse**
shore explore before	force forever order north support

2. There are a number of ways to spell the /ôr/ sound, such as **ar** and **our**. Words which use these other patterns are called **irregular** forms. Write the list words which spell the /ôr/ sound using **ar** and **our**. Underline the letters which make the /ôr/ sound in each word.

warmest quarter

3. Look through the story again and find other words that have the /ôr/ sound. Underline the letters that spell this sound.

towards short twenty-four more storms or horizon

POWERBOOSTER

- The sound /ôr/ is usually spelled **ore** as in **store** or **or** as in **horse**.
- Irregular forms of the /ôr/ sound are **ar** as in **warn**, **our** as in **four**, **oar** as in **roar**, **oor** as in **floor**.

36

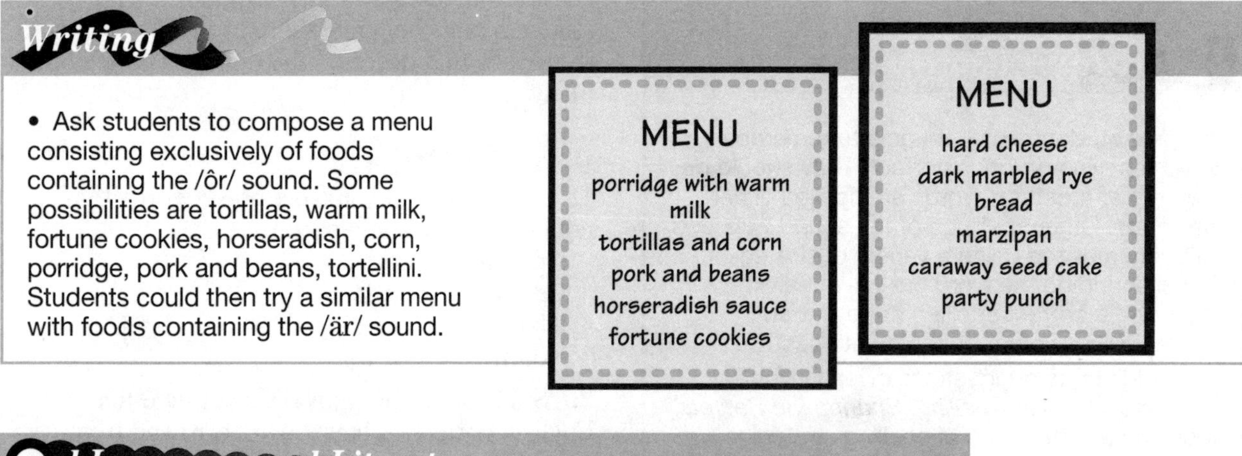

Writing

- Ask students to compose a menu consisting exclusively of foods containing the /ôr/ sound. Some possibilities are tortillas, warm milk, fortune cookies, horseradish, corn, porridge, pork and beans, tortellini. Students could then try a similar menu with foods containing the /är/ sound.

MENU
porridge with warm milk
tortillas and corn
pork and beans
horseradish sauce
fortune cookies
MENU
hard cheese
dark marbled rye bread
marzipan
caraway seed cake
party punch

Oral Language and Literature

- Tongue twisters are a fun way to reinforce the /ôr/ sound.

Bill had a billboard.
Bill also had a board bill.
The board bill bored Bill,
So Bill sold his billboard
And paid his board bill.
Then the board bill
No longer bored Bill,
But though he had no board bill,
Neither did he have his billboard!
(Rosenbloom 21)

- Challenge students to come up with their own tongue twisters for the /ôr/ sound.

more store tore
shore storing torch
shores storm torn
short sore
north sort
nor
pore pores
porch poring

Think of other analogies with list words.

Exploring Patterns

1. It's just the tip of the iceberg! Combine the letters below the surface of the ocean with the /ôr/ patterns on the tip of the iceberg to create more words with the /ôr/ sound.

ore
or
t th st sh ing ch m s p n

2. Write the list word that completes each analogy.
   a) **Four** is to **two** as **half** is to _______. quarter
   b) **Grass** is to **lawn** as **sand** is to _______. shore
   c) **Light** is to **darkness** as **after** is to _______. before

3. The prefix **ex-** usually means 'out' or 'out of'. The list word **explore**, for example, means 'to search beyond'. Replace the underlined words or phrases in each sentence with a word from below. Write the sentences.

exit	exhale
extinguish	explode
exceed	exterior

   a) We plan to paint the outside of our house. exterior
   b) Do you know where the way out is? exit
   c) The mass of your suitcase must not go beyond twenty kilograms. exceed
   d) The firefighters worked quickly to put out the blaze. extinguish
   e) Take a deep breath, and then let the air out. exhale
   f) If you throw that spray can in the fire, it could blow apart. explode

4. Make a word web for the list words **darkness**, **Arctic**, and **outdoors**. Sometimes you can make smaller webs with the words you add.

Example:

rain forests, explore, danger, books, movies, excitement, space, Venus, Mars

37

Exploring Patterns

1. Explain to students that letters can be combined in any order. Develop a comprehensive list of words based on the words generated by individuals or groups.

2. Ask students to suggest the common elements of each analogy.

- **two** is half of **four**, **quarter** is half of **half**
- **grass** covers a **lawn**, **sand** covers a **beach**
- **light** is the opposite of **darkness**, **after** is the opposite of **before**

3. If students do not know the meaning of some of the words in the box and are unsuccessful in using contextual cues, suggest that they use a dictionary to clarify the meaning.

4. Word webs are an excellent device for stimulating descriptive writing. The smaller webs that develop as offshoots of the central concept are a good way for students to organize different aspects of the topic.

This exercise would lend itself well to co-operative groups. Emphasize that any word may be added to the word web as long as it bears some connection to the central word.

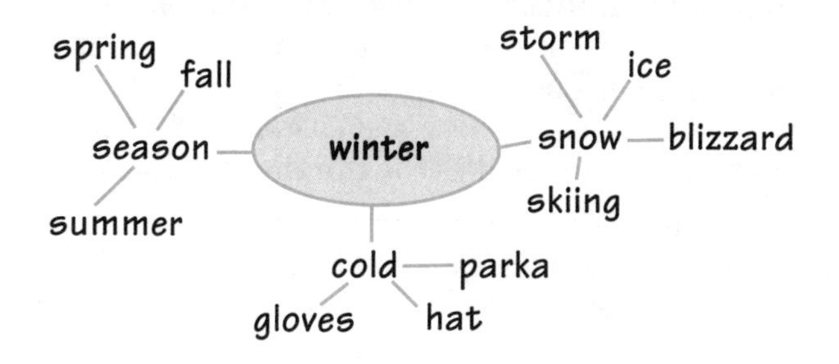

- The tree diagram suggested in Critical Thinking could be generated through co-operative groups. Additional words gleaned from a variety of sources could be added to each category. The relatively few words for each of the minor patterns will confirm that most /ôr/ words are spelled either **or** or **ore**.

5. Encourage students to plan together for this exercise. For example, one person could carry playing cards for the whole group. Ask students to rank the objects from the most to least important. Have them share their rankings with other groups and justify their choices.

things I'd like to take	things I could carry
sleeping bag	sleeping bag
spare clothes	two spare t-shirts/ jeans/socks/underwear
stereo	Walkman
all my CDs and tapes	four CDs
computer	my mom's laptop
my own bed	two or three books
lots of books	extra sweater
my TV	extra hat/gloves
playing cards	playing cards
board games	one board game

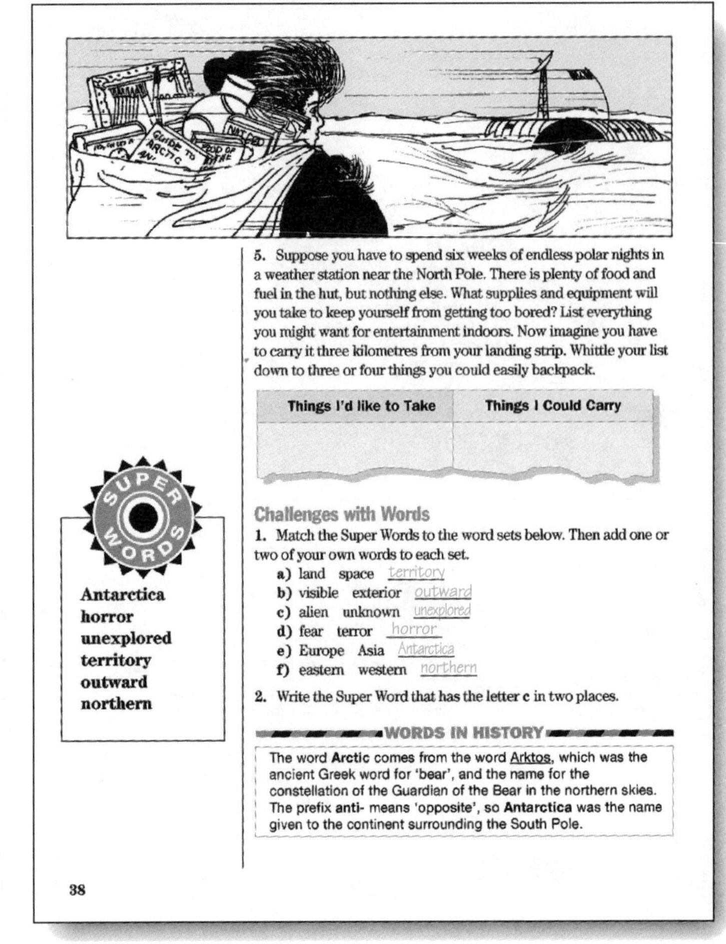

5. Suppose you have to spend six weeks of endless polar nights in a weather station near the North Pole. There is plenty of food and fuel in the hut, but nothing else. What supplies and equipment will you take to keep yourself from getting too bored? List everything you might want for entertainment indoors. Now imagine you have to carry it three kilometres from your landing strip. Whittle your list down to three or four things you could easily backpack.

Things I'd like to Take	Things I Could Carry

SUPER WORDS

Antarctica
horror
unexplored
territory
outward
northern

Challenges with Words

1. Match the Super Words to the word sets below. Then add one or two of your own words to each set.

a) land space territory
b) visible exterior outward
c) alien unknown unexplored
d) fear terror horror
e) Europe Asia Antarctica
f) eastern western northern

2. Write the Super Word that has the letter **c** in two places.

WORDS IN HISTORY

The word **Arctic** comes from the word Arktos, which was the ancient Greek word for 'bear', and the name for the constellation of the Guardian of the Bear in the northern skies. The prefix **anti-** means 'opposite', so **Antarctica** was the name given to the continent surrounding the South Pole.

38

Challenges with Words

1. Have the students write each of the Super Words and underline the letters that spell the /ôr/, /är/, or /ėr/ sound in each. Encourage students to use mnemonic devices to help remember difficult spellings. For example, there are two 'seas' in **Antarctica**. You might find it helpful to discuss the use of capitals with words such as northern and eastern ('**Western** Hemisphere'; She likes the **northern** climate).

2. It may help students to remember the two c's in **Antarctica** if you isolate the base word, **arctic**. Exaggerate the sound of the first **c**, since students often fail to articulate this sound in the word.

Critical Thinking

- Have students construct a tree diagram similar to the one shown to represent the various patterns for spelling the /ôr/ sound. Add List Words and Super Words to each category.

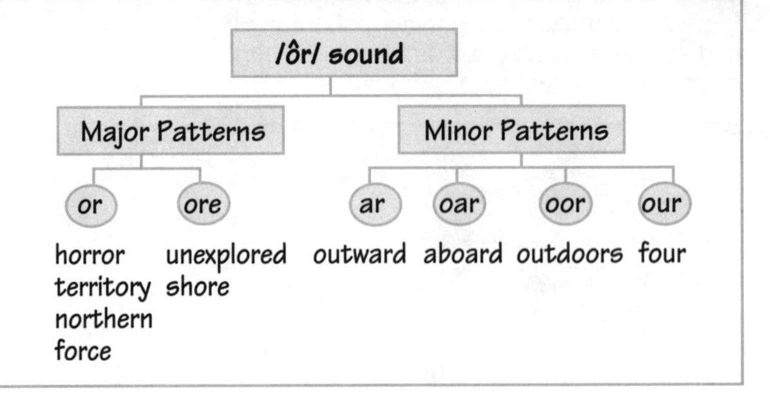

3. The sound /ôr/ can be spelled in many ways. Find words that are **opposites** of the words below. Each one will contain the /ôr/ sound.

a) excited or interested — b ored
b) ceiling — f loor
c) fall or descend — s oar
d) the outside layer — c ore
e) pay attention — i gnore
f) cool — w arm

4. For each letter of the word ANTARCTICA write the name of a country or continent. Answers will vary.

A frica
N orway
T urkey
A ustralia
R ussia
C anada
T rinidad
I celand
C uba
A sia

5. What other words do you think of when you hear the Super Word **northern**. Write the words, then make a triangle poem by organizing some of your words into the shape of a triangle.

Example:

Northern

_____ _____

_____ _____ _____

_____ _____ _____ _____

6. Use the Super Words to finish this story about an expedition to reach the South Pole by crossing Antarctica.

All night the wind howled across the frozen wasteland of Antarctica. By morning, there was no sign of our tents and vehicles. We were lost in the vast territory of this unexplored continent. We only had enough supplies to....

39

3. Remind students that words opposite in meaning are called antonyms.

4. Have students share their answers with classmates. Encourage them to use an atlas to locate these places.

A Africa, Australia
N Norway, Nepal
T Tanzania, Thailand
A Aruba, America
R Russia, Romania
C Chad, China
T Tonga, Tobago
I Ireland, Iceland
C Cameroon, Cambodia
A Andalusia, Afghanistan

5. Words may be generated initially through brainstorming or by creating a word web, then you might ask students to use specific parts of speech for a given line.

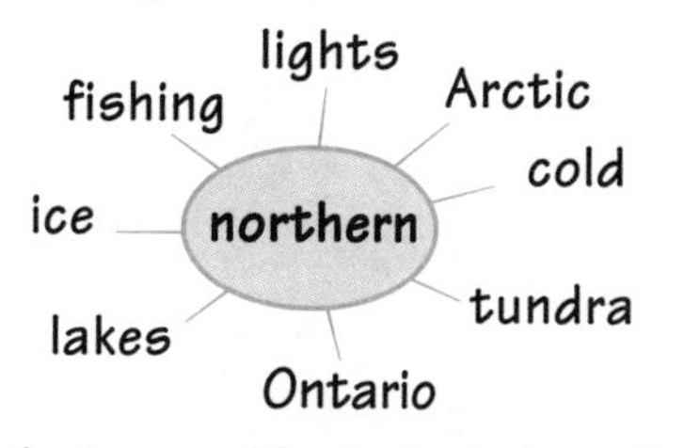

6. Brainstorm with students to gather ideas and words for completing the story. You may wish to provide students with illustrations, photographs, or slides from Antarctica, have them search electronic media for information, or refer them to accounts of expeditions to Antarctica. (See *Handshakings*, Expressways II, Gage Educational Publishing Company, 1988, p.164.)

ESL

- The /ôr/ sound may be difficult for some ESL students to hear and pronounce. As well, there are many spellings of the same sound—this may be confusing for those students whose first language uses phonetic spelling. Give students practice with contrasting the short **o** (**hot**) and /ôr/ (**storm**).

short o	pot	shot	cod
/ôr/	port	short	cord

- Give students word cards with various spellings of /**ôr**/ and have them sort the words into the appropriate spelling patterns.

our	oor	ore	oar
four pour court	floor door	more sore store shore	roar soar

Curriculum Connection

You might wish to include work on the /ôr/ and /är/ patterns in an activity centre during theme work or in words from current events. Survey content area subjects for words with these patterns.

Home Connection

Let parents know that vowels with **r** are being studied. Encourage them to watch for such words in their daily encounters and comment upon the various spelling patterns.

Assessment

Help students monitor any persistent errors related to the spelling of the /ôr/ sound. Discuss spelling strategies that have helped them improve their scores from the Precheck to the Unit Test.

Follow-up

Keep an ongoing chart of words with the /ôr/ sound. Add to the chart as new words are encountered.

Teacher's Notes

9 Long and short e

e_e as in suprem**e**   **y** as in carr**y**
ey as in journ**ey**   **ea** as in ah**ea**d

Patterns

Unit 2 presented the short **e** pattern spelled **e** and long **e** spelled **ee** and **ea** (**bed**, **beet**, **bead**). This unit extends these patterns to include short **e** spelled **ea** and long **e** spelled **y**, **ey**, and **e-consonant-e**. For many students in grade 5, short and long vowel patterns will already be in place and will simply need to be reviewed and applied to the list words. Other students, however, may need more focussed attention on the concept of short and long vowels and the choices involved in spelling these sounds.

Preknowledge

Students should have an understanding of the following concepts as they work with the patterns in this unit.

- The theory of short and long vowels (**car/care**; **mitt/might**).
- Adding suffixes to a base word creates another word that is related in meaning (**light/lighter**).
- Words can contain a number of syllables.

More Patterns

Other patterns you might wish to introduce or review in this unit include the following.

- Adding the suffix **-ly** to a base word turns that word into an adverb (**quick/quickly**).
- Double consonants usually indicate the preceding vowel sound is a short one (b**ea**ter/be**tt**er).

Professional Notebook

Teaching is not telling. In word study, students examine, manipulate, and categorize words. Teachers stack the deck, so to speak, to focus students on a particular contrast and to create a task which forces them to do so. Stacking the deck for a discovery approach to word study is not the absence of directed instruction. To the contrary, a systematic program of word study, guided by an informed interpretation of spelling errors and other literacy behaviors, is a teacher-directed, child-centred approach to vocabulary growth and spelling development.

(Bear et al 77)

Precheck

Remind students to listen as you say the word, repeat it in a sentence, then say it once more before they write it down.

Dictation

He ran **ahead** of his friends.
You've finished **already**?
His pet's **death** upset him.
You're **wearing** my sweater!
Have salad **instead** of fries.
Complete your work quickly.
She's the **supreme** champion.
She's a super **athlete**!
The **journey** seemed endless.
Hockey is my favourite sport.
Please **carry** my bag.
Did you look **everywhere**?
This is an **especially** cold day.
I **finally** got there!
It happened **suddenly**.
His **body** was sunburned.

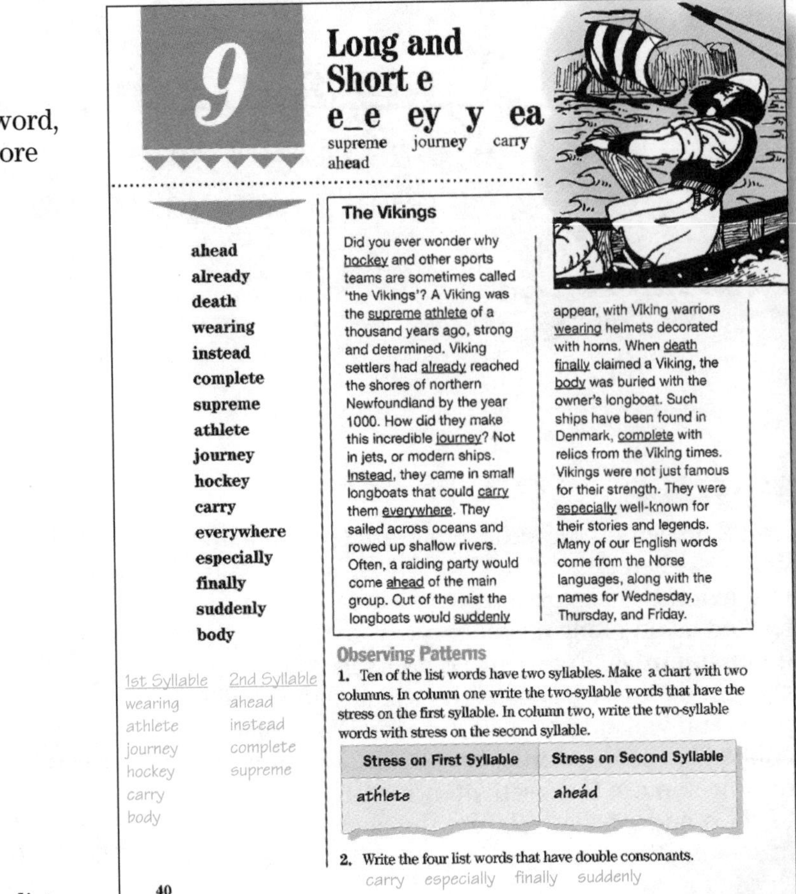

9 Long and Short e

e_e ey y ea
supreme journey carry ahead

ahead
already
death
wearing
instead
complete
supreme
athlete
journey
hockey
carry
everywhere
especially
finally
suddenly
body

The Vikings

Did you ever wonder why hockey and other sports teams are sometimes called 'the Vikings'? A Viking was the supreme athlete of a thousand years ago, strong and determined. Viking settlers had already reached the shores of northern Newfoundland by the year 1000. How did they make this incredible journey? Not in jets, or modern ships. Instead, they came in small longboats that could carry them everywhere. They sailed across oceans and rowed up shallow rivers. Often, a raiding party would come ahead of the main group. Out of the mist the longboats would suddenly appear, with Viking warriors wearing helmets decorated with horns. When death finally claimed a Viking, the body was buried with the owner's longboat. Such ships have been found in Denmark, complete with relics from the Viking times. Vikings were not just famous for their strength. They were especially well-known for their stories and legends. Many of our English words come from the Norse languages, along with the names for Wednesday, Thursday, and Friday.

Observing Patterns

1. Ten of the list words have two syllables. Make a chart with two columns. In column one write the two-syllable words that have the stress on the first syllable. In column two, write the two-syllable words with stress on the second syllable.

Stress on First Syllable	Stress on Second Syllable
athlete	ahead

1st Syllable	2nd Syllable
wearing	ahead
athlete	instead
journey	complete
hockey	supreme
carry	
body	

2. Write the four list words that have double consonants.

carry especially finally suddenly

40

Words in Context

You may wish to have students read the passage aloud, paying special attention to list words containing the /ē/ sound.

Invite students to share what they know about the Vikings. Students could use their dictionaries to find the origins of Wednesday, Thursday, and Friday. Read a Viking legend to the class about Thor, Woden, or Frey. Students might enjoy finding other Viking legends or researching for more information about the Vikings and the words they have added to our language.

Observing Patterns

1. It may help to have students copy the ten words with two syllables first, then sort them according to the stress pattern.

2. When double consonants are letters that are ascenders or descenders, the use of configuration boxes or lines can reinforce the image of the word.

Point out that the double consonants in **carry** and **suddenly** are part of the base word and must simply be memorized. In **finally** and **especially**, however, they result from the suffix **-ly** being added to a base word. (See Exploring Patterns 3.)

Critical Thinking

This word sort requires students to arrange 20 words on the basis of sound rather than sight. Each word contains the vowel combination **ea**. In ten of them, the **ea** spells the long **e** sound (/ē/); in the other ten it spells the short **e** (/e/). The students' task is to sort the pile of cards according to the vowel pattern.

short e	ahead wealth already death stealth measure breath dread leather feather
long e	appeal weak appearance deals weary meaning breathe dream beaches feast

3. A comparison that shows differences is called a **contrast**. Complete each contrast below by writing a list word.

a) At first the small ship was behind the rest, but later it sailed ahead.

b) I was missing two stamps from my collection, but now it is complete.

c) The Vikings looked everywhere, but land was nowhere to be found.

We use the word *but* to signal a contrast in a sentence.

4. Write the four list words that would be found in the dictionary between the words below.

dream / icicle

hockey everywhere especially finally

Discovering Patterns

ahead already death wearing instead complete supreme athlete journey hockey carry everywhere especially finally suddenly body

1. Write the five list words that have the short vowel sound /e/ as in **heaven**. Circle the letters that make this sound.

ahead already death instead wearing

2. Many of the list words have the long vowel sound /ē/ as in **me**. The /ē/ sound can be spelled in more than one way. Write the /ē/ list words under three headings.

/ē/ spelled **e_e** as in **these**	/ē/ spelled **ey** as in **money**	/ē/ spelled **y** as in **happy**
complete supreme athlete	journey hockey	carry everywhere especially finally suddenly body

POWERBOOSTER

- The short vowel sound /e/ is sometimes spelled **ea** as in **heaven**.
- The long vowel sound /ē/ may be spelled **e_e**, **ey**, or **y**.

41

Remind them that **dream** would be the first entry on the page and **icicle** the last.

Note that while **death** and **instead** each begin with the same letter as one of the guide words, they do not fall between the guide words alphabetically.

Discovering Patterns

1. Note that the list words **everywhere** and **especially** also have the /e/ sound, but spell it with the letter **e**.

2. Since there are seven list words to be added to the /ē/ spelled **y** category, challenge students to add enough words from other sources to total seven entries under the **e_e** and **ey** patterns.

e_e	eve here mere fever lever meter renew repel reset severe
ey	key galley attorney alley chimney monkey honey jersey money phoney tourney storey turkey volley

3. Students could write sentences that develop contrasts based on other list words such as **already**, **instead**, **finally**.

4. If students have difficulty with this activity they could write each list word on a card, then sort them on a blank dictionary page with **dream** in the upper left corner and **icicle** in the right.

Oral Language and Literature

- Shel Silverstein's poem, "IMPORTNT?", in *A Light in the Attic* (p. 54) relates to both the long and short **e** sounds. This intriguing poem shows the importance of vowels in determining meaning, but also reveals that we use contextual clues to substitute for vowels that are missing. Students could try to rewrite the poem from the point of view of **G** and discuss whether vowels or consonants are more important in conveying meaning.

Special Needs

- Students who have difficulty recalling the correct spelling for the long and short **e** sounds or in distinguishing between long and short vowels may benefit from the word sort outlined in Critical Thinking.
- Encourage students to add to the columns in the chart in Discovering Patterns 2.

long e		
spelled e_e	**spelled ey**	**spelled y**
compete extreme these	donkey monkey honey	funny runny family

- Assist students in understanding the logic behind the double consonants in **especially** and **finally** by providing the base word for each in one colour and using a second colour to add the suffix **-ly**. In similar fashion, show the f... tion of the compound word **everywhere** ... **every** in a different colour from wh... the two parts on separate cards.

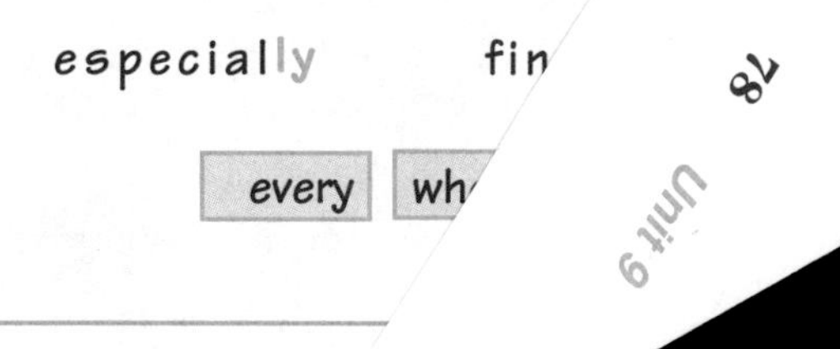

Exploring Patterns

1. This exercise will help to identify students who are unable to discriminate between long and short vowels as well as among various long vowels (/ē/, /ā/, /ī/). It may help such students to read the words aloud so that the sound patterns become more obvious.

2. Ask students to share their lists and compile a master list for the class. Note that **no one** must be spelled as two separate words.

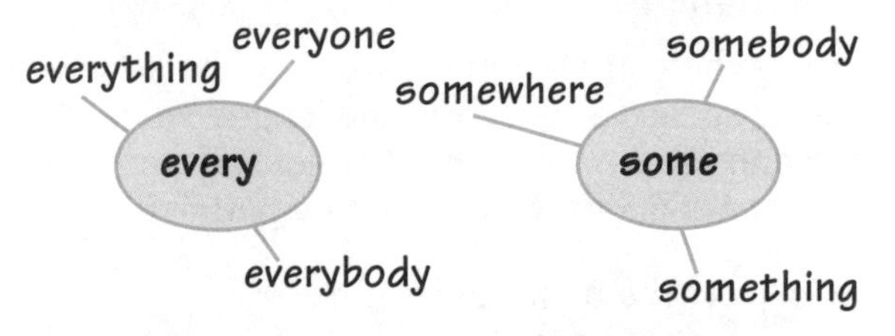

3. You might wish to have students use each adverb in the chart in a sentence.

Brainstorm for other adverbs ending in **-ly**. Write the base word beside each and note any changes in the spelling of the base word.

adverb	base word	changes
angrily	angry	y to i
busily	busy	y to i
heavily	heavy	y to i
hungrily	hungry	y to i
merrily	merry	y to i
absolutely	absolute	none
bravely	brave	none
carefully	careful	none
closely	close	none
severely	severe	none

4. Encourage students to write their own limericks. Be sure they understand the rhyme scheme of this poetic form. (See p. 36.)

Exploring Patterns

1. In each set of words below, one word contains the long vowel sound /ē/. Write the /ē/ words, but remember that /ē/ can be spelled several ways. Copy the circled letters. When they are unscrambled, they will tell how it might feel to meet a ship of Viking sailors.

a) leather cream heaven — cream
b) hey away key — key
c) January May July — January
d) they these away — these
e) spade spread speaker — speaker

Unscrambled word: scary

2. Combine the base words below to form as many compound words as possible.

some thing any body
every one no where

something, somebody, someone, somewhere, nothing, anything, anybody, anyone, anywhere, nobody, everything, everybody, everyone, everywhere, noone, nowhere

3. Many adverbs are formed by adding **-ly** to base words.

Example: *final* + **ly** = *finally*; *late* + **ly** = *lately*
Notice what happens when the base word ends in **y**.

Example: *happy* + **ly** = *happily*

Copy the chart into your notebook and fill in all the spaces.

Base Word	Adverb
complete	completely
sudden	suddenly
easy	easily
secret	secretly
greed	greedily

4. Complete this limerick with list words that fit the shapes.

There once was a great hockey team
They'd carry the puck like a dream
Then suddenly score
And go back for more.
As athletes they all were supreme.

- Exploring Patterns 5, and Challenges with Words 4, offer opportunities for peer editing and proofreading. Have students pay particular attention to the spelling of list words in their stories.
- Remind students of the rules for proofreading. You might want to have them use a proofreading checklist similar to that shown here.

Proofreading Checklist

	Yes	No
First reading for meaning		
Any words left out?	☐	☐
Is there repetition?	☐	☐
Are the ideas clear?	☐	☐
Second reading for sentence errors		
Any incomplete sentences?	☐	☐
Do subjects and verbs agree?	☐	☐
Too many 'ands' or 'thens'?	☐	☐
Final reading for spelling and punctuation		
Capitals, periods, and question marks correct?	☐	☐
Any homophone errors?	☐	☐
Any spelling errors?	☐	☐

SUPER WORDS

voyage
survey
fierce
robbery
weapons
completion

5. Describe how these Viking children like being in your class. For example, how do they like playing baseball at recess or using a computer to do their work?

Challenges with Words

1. Write the Super Word that fits each blank below.

a) The Vikings were fierce sailors and pirates.

b) By the completion of the Viking era, their armies had travelled across Europe.

c) A survey of English towns would show that many were first Viking settlements.

d) The sword, axe, and longbow were Viking weapons.

e) On a voyage across the Atlantic, Viking sailors navigated by the stars and sun.

f) The Vikings are not only remembered for their robbery and plunder, but for their strength and skill.

WORDS IN HISTORY

Some Viking words have come down to us almost unchanged. These words — **egg**, **tree**, **band**, **leg**, **race**, **take**, and **thrust** — are the same words in modern English.

2. Many English words that begin with **sk** or **sc** come from the Vikings. Write the English words for these Old Norse words.

Old Norse	English
skyrta, a long shirt	skirt
skrap, something scraped off	scrape
skith, a slab of wood or a snowshoe	ski
skraema, to cry out	scream

43

ESL

• The long **e** as in **beat** is spelled many different ways in English and, in addition, can be difficult for some ESL students to distinguish from the short **e** as in **bet**. Give students practice in listening to the difference between the two sounds.

short e	bed	fed	led	wed	Ned
long e	bead	feed	lead	weed	need

• Have students listen for the long **e** in longer words.

hockey   monkey
money   journey
especially   suddenly

5. It might help to have students discuss possible formats for this exercise. For example, they could write a paragraph, an interview, a dialogue, or a journal entry. Have them spend some time reflecting on how a young person transported from an earlier time might feel in a modern classroom.

I am sitting behind something they call a 'desk' and it is full of strange things I have never seen before...

Challenges with Words

1. Note that some of the unit patterns are repeated in the Super Words. The Super Word **robbery** contains the long /ē/ sound spelled **y**, and **weapons** contains a short /e/ spelled **ea**.

Students should also be aware of the double consonant in ro**bb**ery and the **ie** in f**ie**rce. You might remind them about "i before e except after c." Relate **completion** to its base word **complete**.

Words in History

Students could try to find the origin of the following English words that have been borrowed from other languages.

English	borrowed from
fiord	Norwegian
lemming	Norwegian
ski	Norwegian
slalom	Norwegian
rutabaga	Swedish
smorgasbord	Swedish
tungsten	Swedish
geyser	Icelandic
saga	Icelandic

2. Encourage students to collect other **sc** or **sk** words.

sc: scalp scale scanty scar scene school scoff

sk: skin skip skipper skit skulk skunk

3. The word sort activity in Critical Thinking would reinforce the concepts in this exercise. The words generated could be included in a word search using appropriate software if you have access to it.

4. Have students brainstorm to gather words and ideas to complete the story. You may wish to have them research the Viking settlement of L'Anse aux Meadows, in Newfoundland, which is believed to be the site of the first colonization of North America more than 1000 years ago.

New Words

5. Ask students to consider the meanings of the following words and phrases that have been created in recent times: **cashless society**; **sugarless**; **homeless**; **cineplex**; **duplex**.

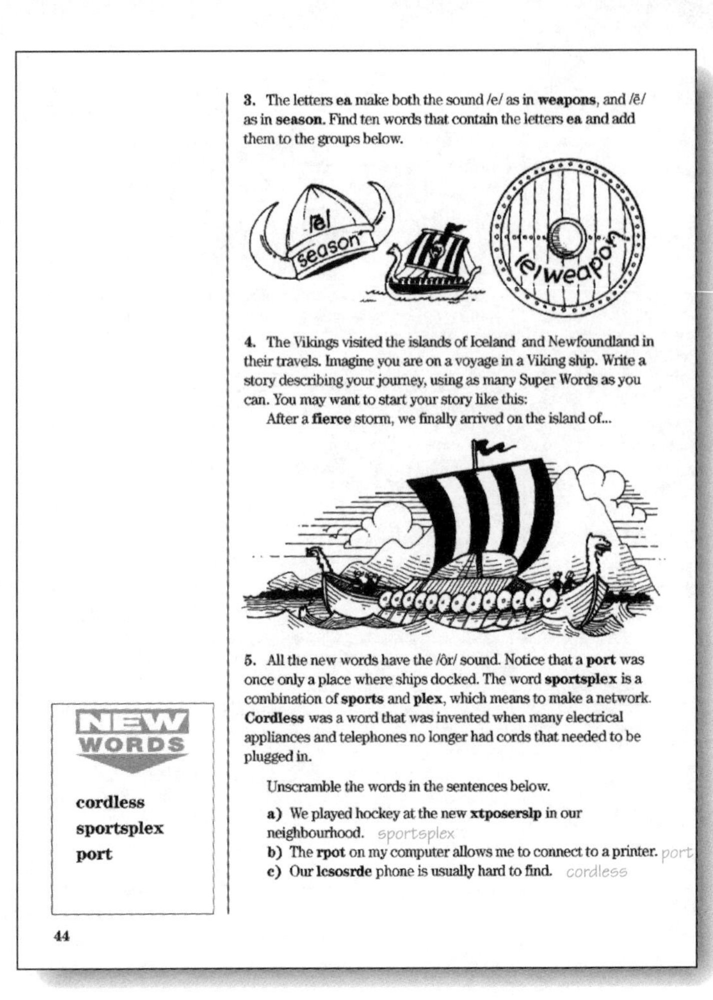

3. The letters **ea** make both the sound /e/ as in **weapons**, and /ē/ as in **season.** Find ten words that contain the letters **ea** and add them to the groups below.

4. The Vikings visited the islands of Iceland and Newfoundland in their travels. Imagine you are on a voyage in a Viking ship. Write a story describing your journey, using as many Super Words as you can. You may want to start your story like this:

After a **fierce** storm, we finally arrived on the island of...

NEW WORDS

cordless
sportsplex
port

5. All the new words have the /ōr/ sound. Notice that a **port** was once only a place where ships docked. The word **sportsplex** is a combination of **sports** and **plex**, which means to make a network. **Cordless** was a word that was invented when many electrical appliances and telephones no longer had cords that needed to be plugged in.

Unscramble the words in the sentences below.

a) We played hockey at the new **xtposerslp** in our neighbourhood. sportsplex
b) The **rpot** on my computer allows me to connect to a printer. port
c) Our **lcsosrde** phone is usually hard to find. cordless

44

Co-operative Learning

There are many opportunities for using co-operative groups in this unit, including the following:

- Creating word puzzles (Exploring Patterns 1, Challenges with Words 3).
- The word sort activity described in Critical Thinking.
- Searching for word origins (Words in History).
- Brainstorming ideas for story writing (Exploring Patterns 5, Challenges with Words 4).

Curriculum Connection

The writing suggestions related to Vikings in this unit link language arts, geography, and history. Students should also be encouraged to use current software in the form of atlases, encyclopedias, databases, word processors, and word games to maximize the effectiveness of these activities.

Assessment

Note the nature of spelling errors on the Unit Test.

- Are students confusing **y** and **ey** endings?
- Is the **a** omitted from the **ea** spelling in words such as **death**?
- Is the double **l** omitted from especi**ll**y or fina**ll**y?

Follow-up

Suggestions given in Special Needs include a variety of strategies for helping students with list words that continue to present difficulties.

Teacher's Notes

Long i

i as in pilot
y as in style
igh t as in flashlight

Patterns

It is important for students to recognize the major patterns for spelling the long vowel **i**. Unit 3 dealt with the **i-consonant-e** pattern. Unit 10 extends this to include **i**, **y**, and **igh**. The fact that there are several ways of spelling a given sound means that students must develop visual strategies for recognizing patterns rather than simply relying on sounding out the word. They need to remember which spelling pattern applies to a particular word.

Preknowledge

Students should have an understanding of the following concepts as they work with the patterns in this unit.

- Vowel sounds can be long or short. Students should be able to distinguish between the two (**bite/bit**).
- Words can contain a number of syllables (**sur/pris/ing**).
- Analogies can help show the meaning of a word (**snow** is to **cold** as **rain** is to **wet**).
- Some words are derived from base words (**fright/fright**en/**fright**ful).

More Patterns

Other patterns you may wish to introduce or review in this unit include the following.

- Compound words (**playground**, **railway**).
- The prefix **bi-** (**biannual**).
- Adding **-ed** and **-ing** to base words.
- The suffix **-ed** is a marker that signifies past tense in a verb (**play/played**).

Professional Notebook

Rhymes are particularly important for organizing memory for spelling. They are the key to our filing system for the spelling patterns of hundreds of words that we will never have to learn individually... Moreover, by having their memory for spelling organized on this basis, children are more likely to have memory capacity available to remember orthographic patterns which cannot be categorized in this way, such as **yacht** and **people**, and to be able to distinguish between homonyms such as **there** and **their**, **so**, **sew**, and **sow**, and **steak** and **stake**, which must also be remembered orthographically.

(Bradley 433)

Sharing the Secrets with Kids

To make word searches easy:

- *Use graph paper.*
- *Outline an area approximately 30 x 30 squares.*
- *Fill in the words you want searched—vertically, horizontally, diagonally, frontward, backward.*
- *Fill in the rest of the letters at random It helps to go through the alphabet in order as you fill in the blanks. This make sure the same letter is not used too often.*
- *Write the words you want searched at the side of the puzzle.*

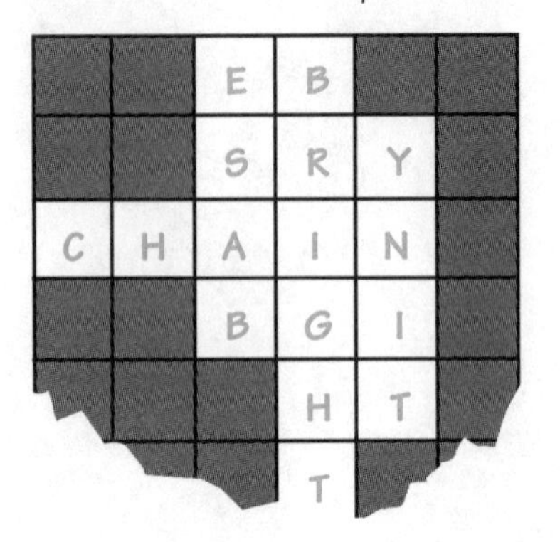

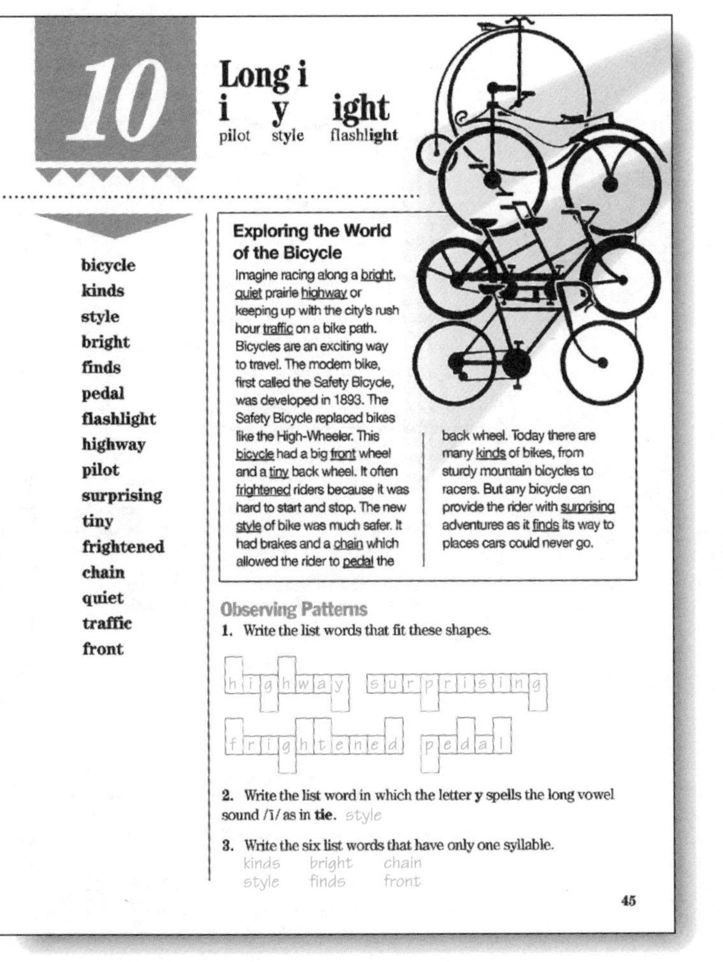

10 Long i

i y ight

pilot style flashl**ight**

- bicycle
- kinds
- style
- bright
- finds
- pedal
- flashlight
- highway
- pilot
- surprising
- tiny
- frightened
- chain
- quiet
- traffic
- front

Exploring the World of the Bicycle

Imagine racing along a bright, quiet prairie highway or keeping up with the city's rush hour traffic on a bike path. Bicycles are an exciting way to travel. The modern bike, first called the Safety Bicycle, was developed in 1893. The Safety Bicycle replaced bikes like the High-Wheeler. This bicycle had a big front wheel and a tiny back wheel. It often frightened riders because it was hard to start and stop. The new style of bike was much safer. It had brakes and a chain which allowed the rider to pedal the back wheel. Today there are many kinds of bikes, from sturdy mountain bicycles to racers. But any bicycle can provide the rider with surprising adventures as it finds its way to places cars could never go.

Observing Patterns

1. Write the list words that fit these shapes.

highway surprising

frightened pedal

2. Write the list word in which the letter **y** spells the long vowel sound /ī/ as in **tie**. style

3. Write the six list words that have only one syllable.

kinds bright chain
style finds front

45

Precheck

After the self-correcting of this Precheck, survey the class to find which words were difficult for most students. Highlight this list for the week and encourage students to study these words very carefully. The class can be challenged to eliminate these errors on the Unit Test.

Dictation

Can you ride a **bicycle**?
There were seven **kinds** of ice cream available.
What **style** of jacket do you like?
What a **bright** sunny day it is!
He **finds** the way every time.
It's hard to **pedal** uphill.
Your **flashlight** gives a good light.
The **highway** was long and wide.
The **pilot** landed the plane safely.
You're always **surprising** me!
One **tiny** snowflake floated by.
Are you **frightened** of dogs?
He wore a gold **chain** round his neck.
The room was **quiet** and still.
The **traffic** moved slowly but steadily.
Stand in **front** of me please.

Words in Context

Students could read the passage and then write their own paragraphs about the bicycle, using as many of the list words as they can.

Observing Patterns

1. The shape of these words could also be reinforced through the use of line patterns or letter tiles.

Pilot and **pedal** both contain a schwa vowel (a vowel in an unstressed syllable: pil ə t, ped ə l). The **l** sound can also be spelled **le** as in **kettle**, **el** as in **camel**, **ol** as in **capitol**, or **il** as in **pupil**. Using a visual strategy such as highlighting the letters **o** and **a** in a different colour may help students to consolidate the spelling of these two words.

2. Note with students that if the prefix **bi-** is removed from **bicycle**, the base word follows the same pattern as **style**. Even though the vowel sound changes from a long **i** in **cycle** to a short **i** in **bicycle**, the spelling does not change. This is an example of the 'meaning principle' in English—words that are related in meaning tend to be spelled alike even if the pronunciation changes.

Students could brainstorm other words with the long **i** spelled **y**.

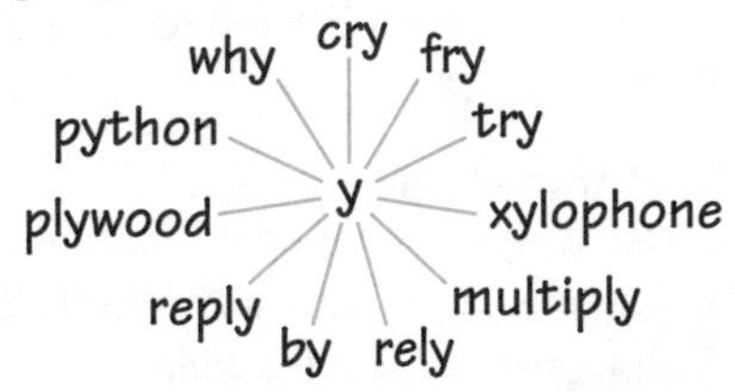

3. If a student includes the word **quiet** in the list of single syllable words it may be that the word is being confused with **quite**. Ask the student to read the word **quiet** aloud.

Writing

- Students could be challenged to write humorous poems using the words created in Exploring Patterns 1.
- A handy classroom reference is a rhyming dictionary. Its use requires knowledge of phonetic symbols, but it is a wonderful source of words for word families and poetry.

5. If students have difficulty unscrambling the letters it may help to use letter tiles, available in many commercial games, or squares of paper for each letter.

6. Ask students to consider how the word **highway** received its name. Contrast **highway** with **subway**, in which **sub** means 'below'.

Discovering Patterns

1. The **i_e** pattern for spelling the long **i** sound was the focus for Unit 3. The Powerbooster for that unit could be reviewed if necessary.

2. Remind students that **-ed** signifies the past tense of a verb. Some students may still be tempted to spell the word as it sounds, and add only **d** to the base word.

3. You might wish to have students brainstorm for other words to add to each column.

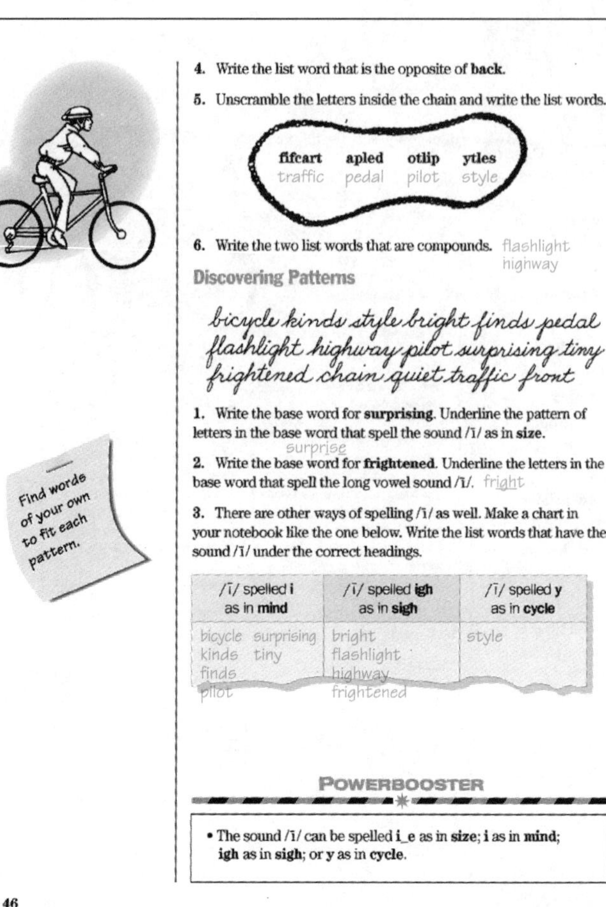

4. Write the list word that is the opposite of **back**.

5. Unscramble the letters inside the chain and write the list words.

ffcart traffic **apled** pedal **otlip** pilot **ytles** style

6. Write the two list words that are compounds. flashlight highway

Discovering Patterns

bicycle kinds style bright finds pedal flashlight highway pilot surprising tiny frightened chain quiet traffic front

1. Write the base word for **surprising**. Underline the pattern of letters in the base word that spell the sound /ī/ as in **size**. surprise

2. Write the base word for **frightened**. Underline the letters in the base word that spell the long vowel sound /ī/. fright

3. There are other ways of spelling /ī/ as well. Make a chart in your notebook like the one below. Write the list words that have the sound /ī/ under the correct headings.

/ī/ spelled **i** as in **mind**	/ī/ spelled **igh** as in **sigh**	/ī/ spelled **y** as in **cycle**
bicycle surprising kinds tiny finds pilot	bright flashlight highway frightened	style

Find words of your own to fit each pattern.

POWERBOOSTER

• The sound /ī/ can be spelled **i_e** as in **size**; **i** as in **mind**; **igh** as in **sigh**; or **y** as in **cycle**.

46

Multiple Intelligences

• The activities in the unit combine with those suggested in the Teacher's Edition to appeal to a variety of intelligences.

Logical/Mathematical
- word puzzles (see Co-operative Learning).
- word games (see Challenges with Words 2, 5).
- meaning relationships (see Exploring Patterns 2).

Visual/Spatial
- manipulatives such as letter tiles and commercial word games.
- word cards and word sorts (see Critical Thinking).
- charts, posters, diagrams (see Challenges with Words 4 and 5).
- word pictures (see Exploring Patterns 4).
- configuration (see Observing Patterns 1).

Verbal/Linguistic
- games (see Co-operative Learning, and Challenges with Words 5).
- classification and discussion of language patterns (see Discovering Patterns).

Musical/Rhythmic
- rhyming activities (see Exploring Patterns 1, and Writing).

Co-operative Learning

• Divide the class into four groups (or eight smaller groups). Each group has the task of brainstorming as many words as possible to fit one of the four patterns for spelling the long **i** sound: **i**, **y**, **igh**, **i-consonant-e**. In larger classes, two groups could be assigned each pattern and then combine their lists. Wall charts could be created and added to throughout the week.

i	y	igh	i-consonant-e
bind	by	high	bite
wind	dry	sigh	kite
kind	flying	light	bike
remind	lying	frighten	admire
humankind	crying	fighter	decide

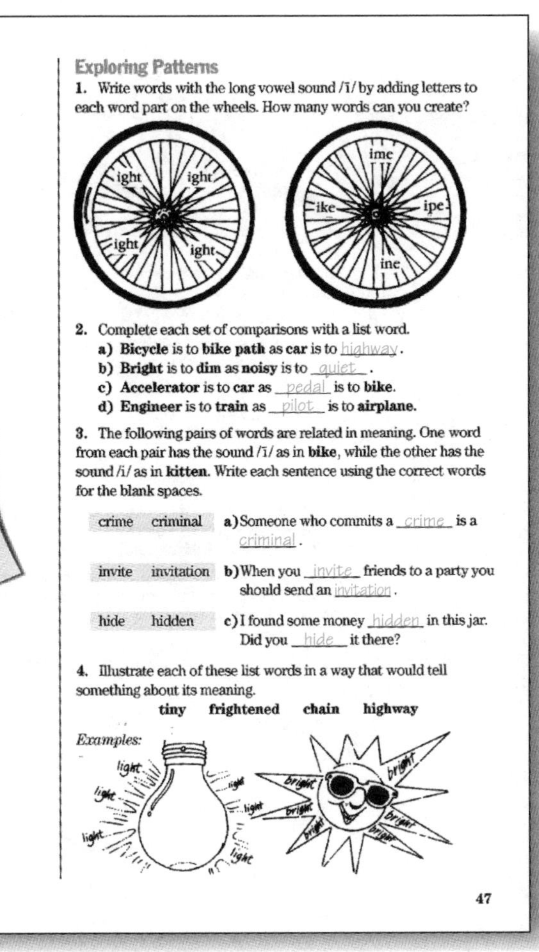

Exploring Patterns

1. Write words with the long vowel sound /ī/ by adding letters to each word part on the wheels. How many words can you create?

2. Complete each set of comparisons with a list word.

a) Bicycle is to **bike path** as **car** is to highway.
b) Bright is to **dim** as **noisy** is to quiet.
c) Accelerator is to **car** as pedal is to **bike**.
d) Engineer is to **train** as pilot is to **airplane**.

3. The following pairs of words are related in meaning. One word from each pair has the sound /ī/ as in **bike**, while the other has the sound /i/ as in **kitten**. Write each sentence using the correct words for the blank spaces.

crime criminal **a)** Someone who commits a crime is a criminal.

invite invitation **b)** When you invite friends to a party you should send an invitation.

hide hidden **c)** I found some money hidden in this jar. Did you hide it there?

4. Illustrate each of these list words in a way that would tell something about its meaning.

tiny frightened chain highway

Examples:

Knowing how to spell invite and crime helps you spell invitation and criminal.

47

Exploring Patterns

1. Ask students to share their lists with one another. They should use a dictionary when they are unsure of any words.

ight	ime	ipe	ine	ike
bright/ly	crime	gripe	dine	bike
fight/ing	dime	pipe	fine	hike
fright	lime	ripe	line	like
frightening	mime	swipe	mine	dislike

2. In addition to completing each comparison, students should be prepared to discuss the basis of their choice. For example, "You press the accelerator to make a car go, and you push a pedal to make a bike go."

3. Understanding the relationship between base word and derivative is particularly significant with **invite/invitation**, since the /ī/ in the base becomes a schwa vowel in **invətation**. Schwa vowels present problems for spellers because they are not clearly articulated. If a student can relate **invitation** to **invite**, it will be much easier to recall the letter **i** in the derived form.

4. Give students an opportunity to share their results with the class and to display them appropriately.

Tiny tiny frightened

c h a i n

highway

Special Needs

A variety of strategies may be needed to help students focus on aspects of list words that are not clearly pronounced. The suggestions in Multiple Intelligences can help students deal with such spelling challenges as:

- The schwa vowels in ped**a**l and pil**o**t (see Observing Patterns 1).
- Possible confusion of **quiet** and **quite**.
- The double consonant in tra**ff**ic.
- The sequence of letters in the **igh** pattern.
- The **bi-** prefix in **bicycle** (students often confuse the order and spell the word as **bycicle**).
- /ėr/ spelled **ur** in **surprising**.

ESL

- Students whose first language is spelled phonetically, with one sound represented by one letter, may have difficulty with the variety of ways to spell the long **i** sound. Have them develop rhyming word families with the basic word patterns before going on to longer words such as **frightened** and **surprising**.
- Have students note that **wind** can be pronounced **wind** or **wind** and has two separate meanings.

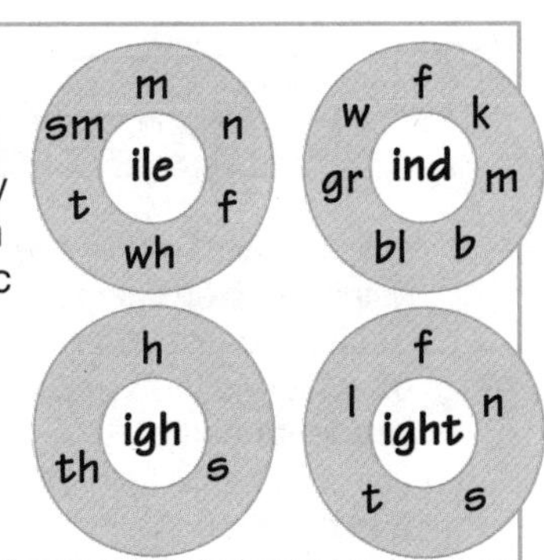

5. Encourage the students to write the rules in a positive manner. For example, "Always keep both hands on the handlebar" rather than "Never ride hands-free."

6. An alternative approach would be to make a list of words with the prefix **bi-**, meaning two or twice. For each word, show how the prefix **bi-** conveys the meaning 'two'.

bicentennial	*occurring every 200 years*
biceps	*muscle with two points of origin*
biannual	*occurring twice a year*
biennial	*occurring every two years*
bilingual	*able to speak two languages*

5. Cyclists must obey the law, just like motorists. Use the picture to write the rules for the cyclists. Use some of these list words in your rules.

bicycle **highway** **travel** **traffic**

6. Make your own list of bike words. Study this list and have a partner dictate it to you. Your list might include useful words such as **spokes** or **reflectors**.

SUPER WORDS

tighten
cyclists
vehicle
reflector
gearshift
repair

Challenges with Words

1. Write the Super Words that fit these clues.
   - **a)** You might need this when going up hills. gearshift
   - **b)** Don't forget to tighten your spokes.
   - **c)** Any type of land transportation is a vehicle.
   - **d)** This is how you fix a broken part. repair
   - **e)** You will need this on the rear of your bike. reflector
   - **f)** The athletes in this race are cyclists.

2. Use the letters of the word **gearshift** to make other words. Score two points for every word you make with two letters, three points for every three-letter word, and so on. How far can you get on the race track?

START 50 points 75 points FINISH 100 points 125 points 150 points

48

Challenges with Words

1. Students could create another set of clues for the Super Words, but instead of meaning clues these should deal with spelling features. For example:

- Two words with a silent **h** (**tighten**, **vehicle**).
- A word that is plural (**cyclists**).
- A word that contains the /ėr/ sound spelled **or** (**reflector**).
- Words that have two syllables (**tighten**, **cyclists**, **gearshift**, **repair**).

2. Letter tiles for each letter in **gearshift** may help students to form other words.

Students may be interested in making a 'word graph' with their words. Have students construct a bar graph of their words putting the two letter words in one vertical column, the three letter words in another, and so on. Students may prefer to work in a group to complete the graph.

		hare	
		hire	
		rise	raise
	are	tear	share
	sat	fear	tries
is	rag	sage	fries
it	sit	fist	arise
if	fig	gist	grist
as	fit	rage	shift
at	hit	gear	shear

Critical Thinking

- Play a version of the game Concentration, using list words and variations. Provide a 'double deck' of cards that contains two copies of a card on which is written each of the following words. Students can play with a partner or a small group. Cards are laid face down and the player turns up two cards. If they match, the player keeps the cards and turns up two more. When all cards are matched, the player with the most cards wins.
- This game can be adapted for most list words. Students are required to examine words carefully, since most word pairs have another which is very similar in spelling (**pedal/petal**). Concentration is a good game for building visual memory.

pedal	petal	quiet	quite	quit	chain	claim
pilot	pillow	tiny	shiny	skinny	bright	fright

3. Keep your 'i's on this thrilling race! Use words with the long vowel sound /ī/ to fill in the blanks. Then finish the story with your own words. Use as many 'i' words as you can.

It was a terrifying (igh) sight to see my brother Kevin (i_e) drive into the wall on the turn. Luckily, he suffered only a (igh) slight scrape on his leg, but his glasses were broken in his fall. We all gave a huge (igh) sigh of relief when he rode over the finish (i_e) line. He was not (i_e) quite last—just (i) ninth out of ten riders. I was just glad to see him (i_e) alive!....

WORDS IN HISTORY

The word **cycle** probably came from the word kyklos, which meant a 'ring' or 'circle' in ancient Greek. It was later used to mean anything which moved in a circle—like the wheel of a bicycle.

4. How many parts of a bicycle can you name? Draw a picture of a bicycle and label its parts with the names you know. Then check an encyclopedia or picture dictionary for more part names and correct spellings.

5. Make your own **vehicle** crossword. With a partner, list all the types of vehicles you know. Then write definitions for each one and make a crossword puzzle to try on your friends.

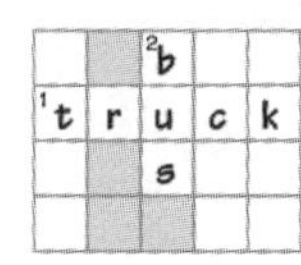

49

Oral Language and Literature

• Play a word game with the class involving long /ī/ words. The first player offers a word containing the long /ī/ sound, and spells it. The next person must think of a long /ī/ word beginning with the last letter of the previous answer. For example, if player 1 said "sight," an acceptable answer for player 2 might be "tire." If a player cannot think of a suitable answer or misspells the word, that student must drop out. This game can also be played with teams.

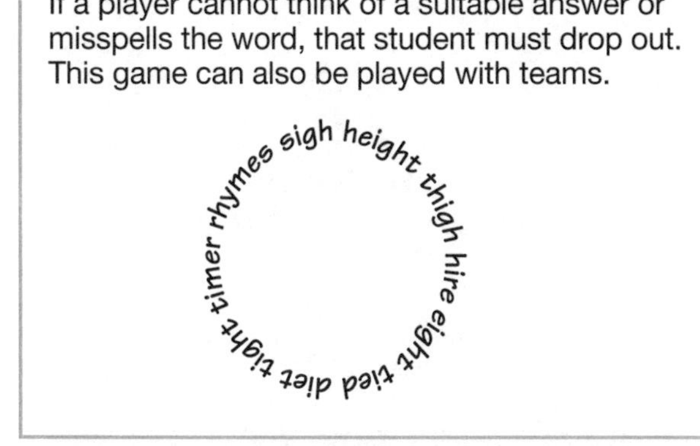

3. Remind students that the clues in brackets refer to the spelling pattern, and that letters can come before and after the pattern. The answers are not List or Super Words. Some students may find it easier to work with a partner.

Words in History

Students might try making a web of word extensions of the base word **cycle**. They may wish to use a dictionary to help them in making their web.

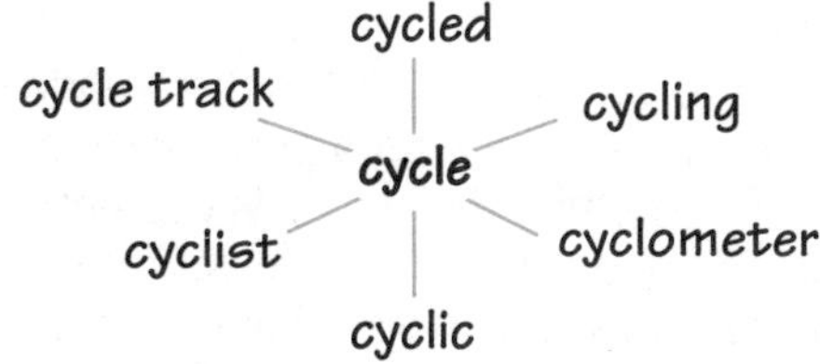

4. Students may wish to make a word search or crossword puzzle using these words. Many software packages, such as 'Crossword Magic', make the design of such puzzles easy and attractive. Many similar programs are available as shareware via the Internet, so that you have the chance to try them out before purchase.

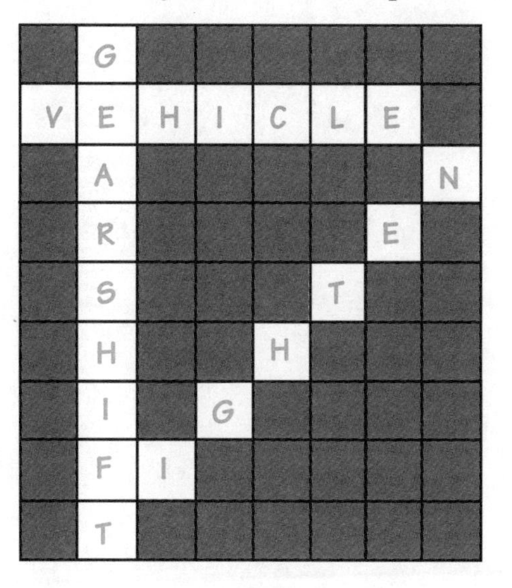

5. Have students brainstorm classes of vehicles. Ask them to classify various vehicles in these categories: two-wheel, three-wheel, four-wheel, and commercial.

Curriculum Connection

Exploring Patterns 5 and 6, and Challenges with Words 4 and 5, offer interesting connections with design and technology as well as safety awareness.

Assessment

Note the spelling challenges described in Special Needs. Do students' errors on the Unit Test reflect these difficulties?

Follow-up

Have students correct the errors they made on the Unit Test and work with a partner to design strategies for spelling these words correctly. The following day partners dictate the study words. Repeat the process for words that continue to present problems. It may also help to switch partners so that a new range of strategies can be tried.

Teacher's Notes

11 Vowels with r

er as in serve
ur as in fur
or as in worked

Patterns

This unit reinforces the patterns for spelling /ėr/ that were introduced in Unit 7, and adds the **or** spelling (**worst**). Studies have shown that difficulties with the spelling of vowels with **r** (/ėr/, /är/, /ôr/) persist throughout the grades, unlike some patterns which are characteristic only of young spellers. Students in the early grades will begin by spelling /ėr/ with only the letter **r**. As they move beyond this stage they include a vowel letter with the **r**, but are often unsure of which vowel to use. Such recall often requires a visual strategy rather than simply sounding out the word.

Preknowledge

Students should have an understanding of the following concepts as they work with the patterns in this unit.

• Base words (**silent/silently**; **purr/purring**).
• Silent letters present spelling challenges (**muscle**). Students should develop a variety of strategies to help them remember patterns that are particularly challenging. Some might find it useful to highlight the silent letter in a word; others will benefit from remembering a mnemonic "See what strong muscles he has."
• Double consonants. As with silent letters, double consonants need strategies to help with their recall (**furry**; **purring**).

More Patterns

Other patterns you might wish to introduce or review in this unit include the following.

• Adding the suffix **-ly** to base words creates an adverb (**silently**, **swiftly**, **greatly**, **quietly**).
• **-le** endings (**handle**, **people**, **muscle**, **gentle**, **example**).

Professional Notebook

An individual writing conference is a way of meeting each child's specific needs. The conference should be constructive, treating errors as opportunities to learn. Ask the child to locate errors and to try to self-correct them. Choose an appropriate number of errors to discuss. Ask how he/she identifies errors and knows when spelling is standard. Discuss, choose, and model strategies. Relate the focus of instruction to other knowledge known by the student and to other language activities in the classroom. Provide feedback on progress. Review how and what has been learned and how it was learned.

(Tarasoff 91)

Precheck

By now, students should have a positive attitude toward the Precheck because of your encouragement in promoting it. After self-correction exercises, have them underline or circle parts of words misspelled, then go back through other Prechecks and Unit Tests (Columns B and D on the Student Record Sheet) to notice any pattern to their errors.

Dictation

How many **people** were there?
He pulled a **muscle** in his leg.
Cats are usually **gentle** pets.
Here's an **example** of good handwriting.
The waiter went to **serve** at the table.
The cat was **purring**.
There was no **handle** on the door.
She sat by **herself**.
The **furry** animal rolled over.
We **worked** all morning.
They were **greatly** amused by the joke.
Rajiv ran **swiftly**.
We sat **silently** and listened.
The dog's w**hiskers** were turning grey.
Sit here **quietly**.
It was the **worst** thing to happen.

Words in Context

Students could pursue the origin of the term 'domesticate'. What other animals have humans domesticated? How does this word relate in meaning to 'domestic' and 'domicile'? How is it connected with the terms 'domestic affairs' or 'domestic news'? (Note: **domesticate** comes from *domus* the Latin for house.)

Observing Patterns

1. Make students aware that, while the words ending in the /l/ sound in the word list are spelled **le**, the same sound combination is sometimes spelled **el**, **al**, and, occasionally, **ol**.

el	al	ol
angel bagel jewel	normal final animal	carol symbol pistol

2. The letters needing special attention could be reinforced by underlining, circling, exaggerating the print (fuRRy), or exaggerating the pronunciation (sounding the **c** in **muscle**).

Vowels with r

serve fur worked

people
muscle
gentle
example
serve
purring
handle
herself
furry
worked
greatly
swiftly
silently
whiskers
quietly
worst

Exploring the History of Cats

One day, more than 5000 years ago, a small striped animal with whiskers walked silently into the fields of an Egyptian farmer. It was the African wildcat, and the farmer let it stay to catch mice and rats. The arrangement worked well, for rodents were one of the worst problems facing farmers in Egypt, and the cat could kill them swiftly and quietly. After a thousand years the wildcat became gentle and easy to handle. It was greatly loved by the people of Egypt and even thought of as a god. This Egyptian cat was the first example of the present-day house cat. Today's cats serve us more as pets than rodent catchers. What could be more peaceful than a furry ball, purring herself to sleep in your lap? With every muscle relaxed, it is hard to imagine that this cat was once a fierce wildcat of Africa.

Observing Patterns

1. Write the five list words that end in the letters **le**.
   people muscle gentle example handle
2. Complete the list words on each paw.

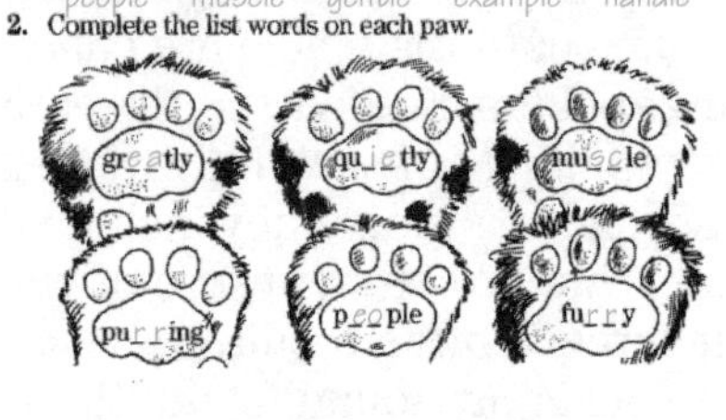

50

Special Needs

- Students should be encouraged to group the list words into similar patterns for study purposes. By chunking words into categories, suitable word study strategies can be applied to each group. Note that not all students will pronounce whiskers with a silent **h**.

ly ending	le ending	double consonant	silent letters
greatly swiftly silently quietly	people muscle gentle example handle	purring furry	muscle people whiskers

3. Write the list words that mean the opposite of these words.

rough best slowly himself

gentle worst swiftly herself

4. Write the six list words that would be found in the dictionary between the words shown below. Hint! You need to look at the third letter in the word **would**.

sample / would

serve silently worked whiskers swiftly worst

5. Unscramble the list words. The circled letters should tell you what clouds are:

ferselh herself
legent gentle
rupginr purring
rufry furry
ylfiwst swiftly
lqieuyt quietly
Unscrambled word: fluffy

Discovering Patterns

people muscle gentle example serve purring handle herself furry worked greatly swiftly silently whiskers quietly worst

1. Seven of the list words have the sound /ėr/ as in **dirt**. Make a chart like the one below in your notebook. Write the list words that have the sound /ėr/ under the correct headings.

/ėr/ spelled **er** as in **under**	/ėr/ spelled **ur** as in **curly**	/ėr/ spelled **or** as in **worm**
serve	purring	worked
herself	furry	worst
whiskers		

2. Write the list words that end in **-ly**. Underline the base word for each. greatly swiftly silently quietly

POWERBOOSTER

- The sound /ėr/ is sometimes spelled **er** as in **her**, **ur** as in **curly**, or **or** as in **worm**.
- The suffix **-ly** may be added to many base words.

51

3. Remind students that words opposite in meaning are known as **antonyms**.

4. Note that in the case of **worked** and **worst**, it is necessary to alphabetize to the third letter, since the guide word also begins with **wo**.

5. Some students may find it easier to unscramble letters using letter tiles such as those found in many commercial word games. This activity helps students to sequence letters correctly, especially vowel combinations such as **uie** in **quietly**.

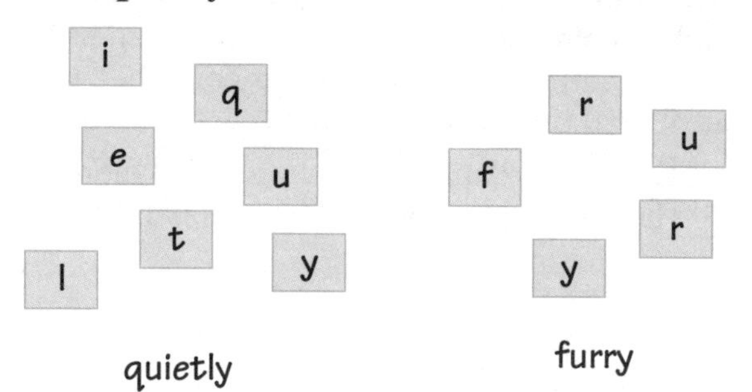

Discovering Patterns

1. Words which spell /ėr/ with either **ur** (**curly**) or **urr** (**purr**) should be classified under the middle column.

Build on each pattern by adding from a variety of sources such as the students' Personal Review Lists, other subject areas, general knowledge, and themes.

	/ėr/	
spelled er	**spelled ur**	**spelled or**
allergy	burden	world
battery	disturb	worship
observe	furnish	worth
reverse	urge	worthy
camera	burst	word
person	curve	worse
stern	turtle	world

2. Students could brainstorm other words ending in the suffix **-ly**. Note when such derived forms involve a change to the spelling of the base word (**happily**, **gentle**) or result in double consonants (**beautifully**, **normally**).

luckily gladly beautifully largely correctly
happily sadly wonderfully wrongly quickly

Writing

- In editing conferences with individual students look for patterns of errors related to /ėr/, /ôr/, or /är/ sounds. Discuss effective strategies for recalling the correct spelling of these sounds in specific words. (See Professional Notebook.)

Exploring Patterns

1. This activity encourages students to examine list words carefully and to focus on the specific letters in each word.

2. Ask students to look in the Mini Dictionary to determine which other list words have several meanings. They could then focus on one of the words, such as **handle**, and write a sentence that shows each meaning.

3. Invite students to work in pairs to produce other 'Tom Swifties'. A 'Tom Swifty Joke Book' could be compiled for the class and placed in a reading centre. Additional entries could be contributed throughout the year.

"That dog is dangerous," she snarled bitingly.
"The flashlight went out," he said darkly.

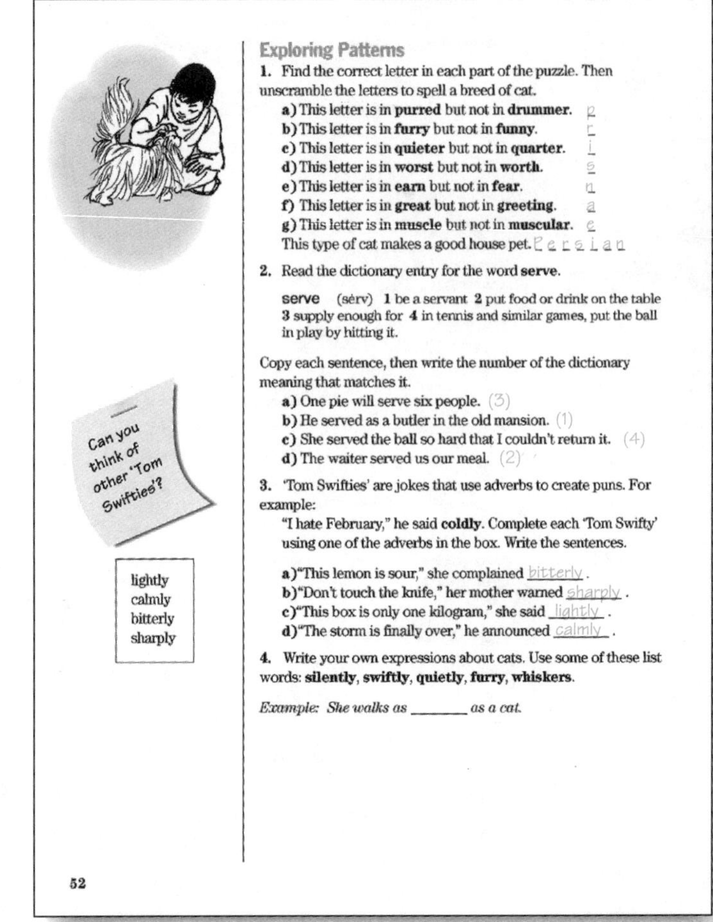

Can you think of other 'Tom Swifties'?
lightly
calmly
bitterly
sharply

Exploring Patterns

1. Find the correct letter in each part of the puzzle. Then unscramble the letters to spell a breed of cat.

a) This letter is in **purred** but not in **drummer**. p
b) This letter is in **furry** but not in **funny**. r
c) This letter is in **quieter** but not in **quarter**. i
d) This letter is in **worst** but not in **worth**. s
e) This letter is in **earn** but not in **fear**. n
f) This letter is in **great** but not in **greeting**. a
g) This letter is in **muscle** but not in **muscular**. e

This type of cat makes a good house pet. Persian

2. Read the dictionary entry for the word **serve**.

serve (sėrv) **1** be a servant **2** put food or drink on the table **3** supply enough for **4** in tennis and similar games, put the ball in play by hitting it.

Copy each sentence, then write the number of the dictionary meaning that matches it.

a) One pie will serve six people. (3)
b) He served as a butler in the old mansion. (1)
c) She served the ball so hard that I couldn't return it. (4)
d) The waiter served us our meal. (2)

3. 'Tom Swifties' are jokes that use adverbs to create puns. For example:

"I hate February," he said **coldly**. Complete each 'Tom Swifty' using one of the adverbs in the box. Write the sentences.

a) "This lemon is sour," she complained bitterly.
b) "Don't touch the knife," her mother warned sharply.
c) "This box is only one kilogram," she said lightly.
d) "The storm is finally over," he announced calmly.

4. Write your own expressions about cats. Use some of these list words: **silently**, **swiftly**, **quietly**, **furry**, **whiskers**.

Example: She walks as _______ as a cat.

52

Co-operative Learning

- Students may enjoy working in small co-operative groups to create word puzzles similar to those in Exploring Patterns 1. They could choose a different breed of cat or link the puzzle with a current theme or holiday. Groups could exchange their completed puzzles.

Oral Language and Literature

- In Richard Lederer's book *The Play of Words*, a chapter entitled 'Dog My Cats!' (pp. 49-53) provides riddles of words that contain the word cat. ('This cat is a disaster' — **cat**astrophe.)
- Ask students to work in pairs and brainstorm lists of words containing the word **cat**, then create riddles with some of them. A **cat**alogue of cat riddles could be compiled.

cat words	
catamaran	catwalk
catfish	catacomb
catalyst	catapult
cataract	cat call

5. There are lots of expressions or **idioms** about cats. Use each of these idioms in a sentence or two that explains what you think they mean.

a) raining cats and dogs
b) looks like something the cat dragged in
c) curiosity killed the cat
d) let the cat out of the bag
e) cat-nap

SUPER WORDS

intelligent
gracefully
gobble
wrestle
lazily
pounce

Challenges with Words

1. Write the Super Words that are synonyms for the underlined words below.

The night wind howled through the thick forest. The jaguar moved smoothly from tree to tree in search of food. It was a clever and skilful hunter. Its quivering muscles were ready to dive on anything moving on the jungle floor. Suddenly it spied two small, glowing eyes. It plunged down into the darkness, ready to grapple with its surprised prey. Quickly the jaguar would eat up its meal, then sluggishly steal off to a sheltered tree for a rest.

gracefully
intelligent
pounce
wrestle
gobble/
lazily

2. How many different words can you find that are synonyms for **gobble**? Use the chart below to match syllables and make three such words. Then think of three more of your own.

swal	vour	swallow
con	low	consume
de	sume	devour

53

5. See Oral Language and Literature.

Challenges with Words

1. Draw attention to challenging features of the Super Words:

- silent letters in **wr**es**t**le
- double consonants in go**bb**le and inte**ll**igent
- adding **-ly** to **lazy** (lazy/lazily), and **graceful** (graceful/gracefully)

Have students create their own sentences using the Super Words. This would be a good opportunity to encourage the use of a thesaurus to generate synonyms for the Super Words.

super word	synonyms
intelligent	bright, sharp, smart
gracefully	easily, flowingly, gently
gobble	devour, gulp, swallow
wrestle	tangle, scuffle, tussle
lazily	idly, slowly, slothfully
pounce	leap, jump, bound

2. Have students brainstorm other words that describe how a person eats.

messily rudely politely quickly
sloppily neatly quietly slowly

Students might want to make a synonym word web with another Super Word.

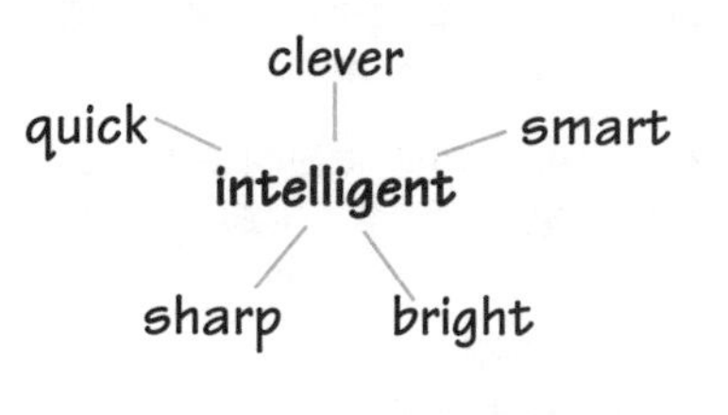

Critical Thinking

- A word sorting task could be designed as a review and consolidation of the patterns for spelling /ėr/ in Units 7 and 11.
- Have students sort the following words into the various patterns for spelling /ėr/. This sort requires that they use a visual approach to features of the words.

spelling of /ėr/ sound				
er	**or**	**ir**	**ear**	**ur**
serve herself whiskers iceberg	worst worked	dirt circle	earliest earth	purring furry surprise surface

3. Remind students that **-lē** has the sound of /ə l/ and **-ly** the sound of /lē/ when these letter combinations occur at the end of words.

4. It may help to use letter tiles or a separate card for each letter. Manually resorting the letters may provide additional words.

let tig ten gin tin get net nit gel
gent lent tent gill till tell lint ting tinge

5. Students will enjoy sharing their stories and perhaps drawing a picture of Mortimer in his transformed state.

New Words

6. Students could try to explain these terms to someone who was not familiar with the latest technology. Some students may be particularly knowledgeable about the Internet; others may be more familiar with current options related to telephones.

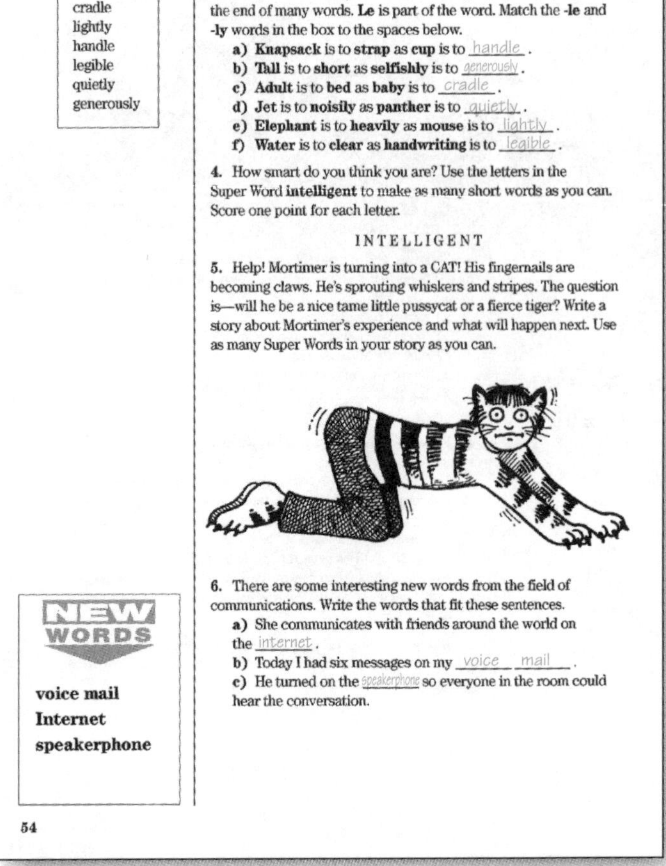

cradle
lightly
handle
legible
quietly
generously

3. Many words in English end in **-le** or **-ly**. **Ly** is a suffix we add to the end of many words. **Le** is part of the word. Match the **-le** and **-ly** words in the box to the spaces below.

a) **Knapsack** is to **strap** as **cup** is to handle.
b) **Tall** is to **short** as **selfishly** is to generously.
c) **Adult** is to **bed** as **baby** is to cradle.
d) **Jet** is to **noisily** as **panther** is to quietly.
e) **Elephant** is to **heavily** as **mouse** is to lightly.
f) **Water** is to **clear** as **handwriting** is to legible.

4. How smart do you think you are? Use the letters in the Super Word **intelligent** to make as many short words as you can. Score one point for each letter.

INTELLIGENT

5. Help! Mortimer is turning into a CAT! His fingernails are becoming claws. He's sprouting whiskers and stripes. The question is—will he be a nice tame little pussycat or a fierce tiger? Write a story about Mortimer's experience and what will happen next. Use as many Super Words in your story as you can.

NEW WORDS

voice mail
Internet
speakerphone

6. There are some interesting new words from the field of communications. Write the words that fit these sentences.

a) She communicates with friends around the world on the internet.
b) Today I had six messages on my voice mail.
c) He turned on the speakerphone so everyone in the room could hear the conversation.

54

Multiple Intelligences

- A variety of approaches should be used to deal with the challenges of /ėr/ patterns.

Visual/Spatial: Highlight the spelling of /ėr/, silent letters, and double consonants through colour, shape, size, or configuration.

Bodily/Kinesthetic;Logical/ Mathematical: Use word sorts and letter tiles to manipulate words physically.

serve musCle

Verbal/Linguistic; Interpersonal: Brain-storm effective spelling strategies in co-operative groups and use a pre/post test measure to show the effectiveness of the techniques.

Discuss the strategies used and reflect on those which were most effective.

- Help students practise forming the adverb from the adjective by adding **-ly**. Using word cards, have students join the adjective with the ending, then write a sentence containing the adverb.

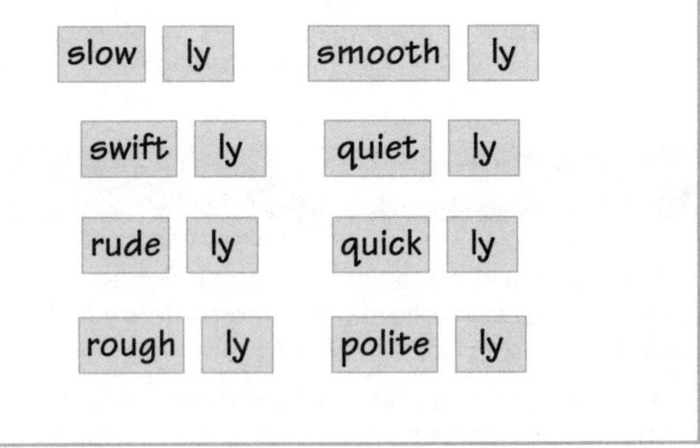

Curriculum Connection

To emphasize how frequently the /ėr/ sound appears in English have students examine a page or two of text from other subject areas, newspapers, or literature and record all the words they discover containing the /ėr/ sound. Classify the words according to spelling patterns for /er/.

Home Connection

Note the suggestion under Follow-up for compiling a list of words from Units 7, 8, and 11 containing the sounds /ėr/, /ôr/, and /är/. Send this list home to parents as an aid to studying these words. Have students star any words they misspelled on unit tests.

Assessment

Ask students to examine the words they misspelled on the unit test. Where did they make their errors? Have them work with a partner to develop strategies for remembering these problem words. Partners could repeat the dictation to one another or simply focus on the misspelled words.

Follow-up

Since Units 7, 8, and 11 all deal with r-influenced vowels, a master list of the words from these units containing the sounds /ėr/, /ôr/, and /är/ could be dictated. Special attention could be placed on any words still presenting difficulties.

Teacher's Notes

/ėr/				/ôr/						/är/
er	ir	ur	ear	or	ore	ar	oar	oor	our	ar
certain perhaps eastern desert serve herself whiskers iceberg	dirt circle	surface surprise purring furry	search earliest Earth	horror territory northern force worst worked support forever north	unexplored shore before explore	outward	aboard	outdoors	four	apart larger remarkable Arctic darkness

Looking Back Units 7–11

Patterns to Review

Review the following sound-symbol relationships:

• Vowels with **r** spelled **ar**, **ir**, **ur**, **er**, or **ear** as in **part**, **circle**, **surface**, **larger**, **search**
• Vowels with **r** spelled **or**, **ar**, or **our** as in **for**, **darkness**, **four**
• Long **e** spelled **e_e**, **ey**, or **y** as in **supreme**, **journey**, **carry**
• Short **e** as in **bread**
• Long **i** spelled **i**, **y**, or **ight** as in **pilot**, **style**, **flashlight**

The following words in the review list are found on the list of "The 200 Words Most Frequently Misspelled."

especially	finally	quiet

Creating a Personal Review List

Looking Back units should also provide an opportunity for students to review words and concepts which gave them particular difficulty in the preceding units. These personal study lists could involve words from a variety of sources, as suggested below:

• words misspelled in the students' Unit Tests and everyday writing (writing folders, notebooks, tests)
• words used throughout the day: current themes, content areas, current events, media, holidays
• lists such as "The 200 Words Most Frequently Misspelled" and "The 200 Words Most Frequently Written" (See Appendix.)

Transfer of Spelling Knowledge

The following suggestions will help students to retain the knowledge and skills they acquire through word study and apply them in their everyday writing:

• Do not treat words on study lists as single entities, but as examples of larger spelling patterns. Build on word patterns to maximize the benefit of word study.
• Reintroduce frequently misspelled words on subsequent lists.
• When errors reoccur in student writing, ask students to recall the strategies they had used for studying these words.
• Discuss the use of spelling strategies for new words as they occur in a variety of classroom contexts.

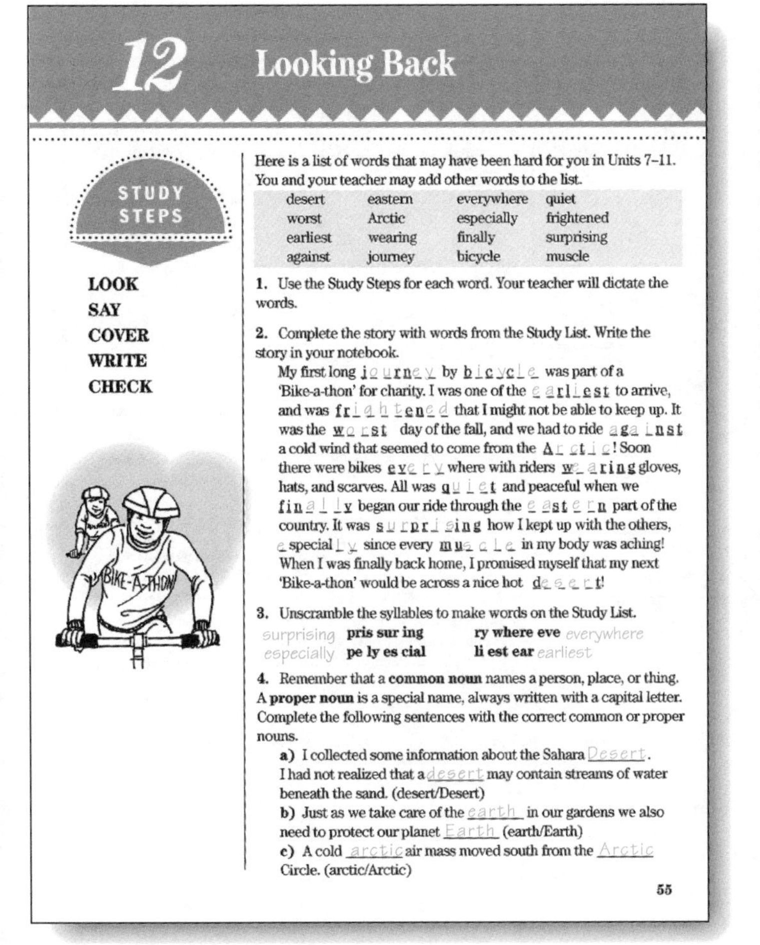

12 Looking Back

STUDY STEPS

LOOK
SAY
COVER
WRITE
CHECK

Here is a list of words that may have been hard for you in Units 7–11. You and your teacher may add other words to the list.

desert	eastern	everywhere	quiet
worst	Arctic	especially	frightened
earliest	wearing	finally	surprising
against	journey	bicycle	muscle

1. Use the Study Steps for each word. Your teacher will dictate the words.

2. Complete the story with words from the Study List. Write the story in your notebook.

My first long journey by bicycle was part of a 'Bike-a-thon' for charity. I was one of the earliest to arrive, and was frightened that I might not be able to keep up. It was the worst day of the fall, and we had to ride against a cold wind that seemed to come from the Arctic! Soon there were bikes everywhere with riders wearing gloves, hats, and scarves. All was quiet and peaceful when we finally began our ride through the eastern part of the country. It was surprising how I kept up with the others, especially since every muscle in my body was aching! When I was finally back home, I promised myself that my next 'Bike-a-thon' would be across a nice hot desert!

3. Unscramble the syllables to make words on the Study List.

surprising **pris sur ing** **ry where eve** everywhere
especially **pe ly es cial** **li est ear** earliest

4. Remember that a **common noun** names a person, place, or thing. A **proper noun** is a special name, always written with a capital letter. Complete the following sentences with the correct common or proper nouns.

a) I collected some information about the Sahara Desert. I had not realized that a desert may contain streams of water beneath the sand. (desert/Desert)
b) Just as we take care of the earth in our gardens we also need to protect our planet Earth (earth/Earth)
c) A cold arctic air mass moved south from the Arctic Circle. (arctic/Arctic)

55

Looking Back

1. Ask students to consider why each word has been included on the Review List. What features of these words make them difficult to spell? What strategies could be used in studying these features?

Students could work in co-operative groups to discuss the words and share the strategies they identify with classmates.

Dictation

There was a sandstorm in the **desert**.
It was the **worst** storm in fifty years.
Who arrived **earliest**?
Prop the picture **against** the wall.
The **eastern** part of the city is the oldest.
It can be very cold in the **Arctic**.
Why are you **wearing** my coat?
The **journey** down the river took four days.
In fall there are leaves **everywhere**!
We **especially** liked the desserts Dad made.
I **finally** finished my project last night.
My **bicycle** has a flat tire.
You need to find a **quiet** place to study.
Are you **frightened** of dogs?
Snow in winter is not **surprising**.
I pulled a **muscle** during the race.

2. Students are asked to write the complete passage so that they see the words in the context of both a sentence and a paragraph. It may help to have students underline the words from the list.

3. This exercise is intended to reinforce the concept of syllables, without the need to learn the sometimes confusing rules for dividing words . To help students who have difficulty sequencing multisyllabic words, prepare a deck of cards that has one syllable on each card. Encourage students to unscramble the syllables as quickly as possible. You might wish to have them repeat the task and try to improve their times.

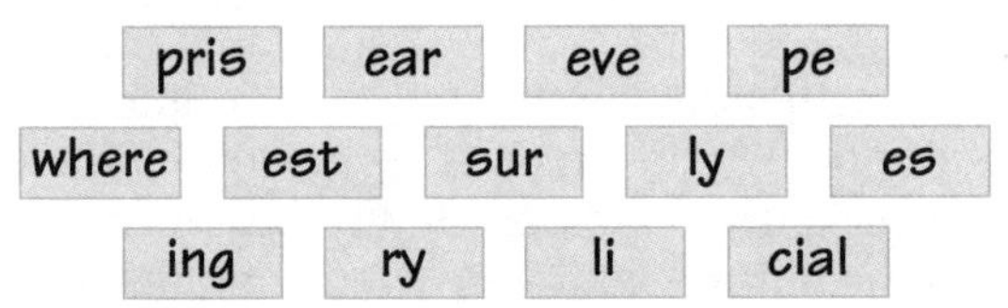

4. Students could write similar sentences containing both the common and proper forms of a noun with pairs such as north/North, ocean/Ocean, street/Street, doctor/Doctor.

Special Needs

- For more practice with comparative and superlative forms, you may wish to have students complete a chart, such as the following.

adjective	-er	-est
smooth		
fast		
happy		
pretty		
green		
blue		
red		

5. Some students may need guidance in setting up charts or headings to reflect each sound/spelling pattern.

It may help students to sort the words in the chart in a tangible way using word cards. Then have them locate words from units 7–11 that fit one of the patterns for the /ėr/ sound.

er (her)	ir (dirt)	ur (turn)	ear (early)	or (work)
certain	birthday	purple	search	worth
service	circle	surface	earth	world
herself	third	surname	earliest	worst

6. Ask students to justify their choice of words in each sentence. They will need to take the full context into account to explain, for instance, why **swiftly** is more appropriate than **quietly** in **b)**.

7. Students could play a game in which one person begins with a straightforward sentence such as 'Yesterday I went to visit my cousin'. The next player then adds a word ending in **-ly**, such as 'unfortunately'. The following player must continue the story, adding another sentence, and so on. Other **-ly** choices could include: **happily**, **unexpectedly**, **gladly**, **apparently**, **luckily**, **eventually**, **foolishly**, **wisely**.

8. Note with students that both the sound and the spelling pattern must be present in the answer. In a), for example, all three choices contain the letter **y**, and **tiny** even contains the sound /ī/. It is only the word **style**, however, that uses the letter **y** to spell the sound /ī/.

5. Sort the words below into the following categories.

a) /ėr/ spelled **er** as in **her** certain service herself
b) /ėr/ spelled **ir** as in **dirt** birthday circle third
c) /ėr/ spelled **ur** as in **turn** purple surface surname
d) /ėr/ spelled **ear** as in **early** search earth earliest
e) /ėr/ spelled **or** as in **work** worth world worst

search	certain	world	circle	surname
worth	birthday	earth	worst	herself
purple	service	surface	earliest	third

6. Complete the following sentences with one of the words below. Sometimes more than one word will fit.

greatly quietly swiftly silently

a) The parents talked quietly because the baby was asleep.
b) The river flowed swiftly as it neared the rapids.
c) The cat waited _______ for the mouse to appear. silently/quietly
d) Your skating has improved greatly since you began taking lessons.

Make your own review list, and use the five study steps.

7. Write sentences using these **-ly** words.

suddenly finally brightly gently

8. Write the word from each set that fits the clues in the brackets.

a) journey style tiny (/ī/ spelled **y** as in **cycle**) style
b) death hear better (/e/ spelled **ea** as in **heaven**) death
c) horse worth north (/ėr/ spelled **or** as in **work**) worth
d) warm barely darkness (/är/ pelled **ar** as in **large**) darkness

9. The following words contain letters which are not clearly sounded. Write each word and highlight these letters in some way. For example, print them in large letters, use a different colour ink, or underline them.

Example: *SeasOn*

Arctic **muscle** **surprising** **everywhere** **frightened**

56

9. Clarify with students the letters in each word which are not clearly sounded. Discuss the advantages of various ways of highlighting the features. More than one strategy may work with a given word. For example, in **muscle**, many students may choose to exaggerate the pronunciation so that the silent **c** is sounded (mus**k**el). Other students might best remember the pattern by relating **muscle** to the derived form **muscular**, in which the **c** is sounded.

ESL

Language Snapshot — Greek

Many English words have Greek roots or contain prefixes and suffixes that have come to us from that language (**television**, **crisis**, **catastrophe**).

Language Features

- Greek spelling has a close match between sound and graphic symbol. Students may try the same one-to-one matching in English, resulting in misspellings such as **Inglish** or **sistem**.
- Because of the sound-symbol correspondence, students may omit silent letters, such as the **l** in **talk**.
- Most letters in the Greek alphabet are different from those in English. When they learn the English letters, some students may try to use one English letter for one sound.
- There are fewer distinctions between vowels: Students may confuse **sit** and **seat**, **bad** and **bed**, and **hat** and **hut**.
- The consonant sound /sh/ may be pronounced as /s/.
- Greek punctuation differs from English.
- Some uncountable English nouns can be counted in Greek (**informations**, **luggages**, **works**).
- Adjectives agree with the nouns they modify (I have three **blacks** dogs).

Dictionary Skills

1. Using a Spelling Chart: A spelling chart in a dictionary gives the common spellings of English sounds. It can help you spell words you do not know.

Study the part of the spelling chart shown below.

Common Spelling of English Sounds	
Sound	**Spelling**
/ī/	aisle, either, eye, ice, high
/g/	go, ghost, guess
/h/	he, who
/m/	me, climbing, solemn
/n/	gnaw, knife, nut
/r/	run, rhythm, wrong
/s/	cent, psalm, say, science, sword

a) In what ways can the consonant sound /s/ be spelled at the beginning of words? c, ps, s, sc, sw
b) In what ways is /ī/ spelled at the beginning of words? ai, ei, eye, i
c) In what ways is the /n/ sound spelled at the beginning of words? gn, kn, n
d) In what ways is the /h/ sound spelled at the beginning of words? h, wh

2. Look at the words below. If you did not know how to spell them, how would you use the chart to help find them in a dictionary? Write the word from the spelling chart that would help you find the correct spelling in the dictionary.

science	wrong	cent	high
scene	write	circle	bright
guide	whole	knew	thumb
guess	who	knife	climbing

57

Dictionary Skills

1. Using a spelling chart may be a new experience for many students, and they will need guidance in interpreting the initial questions. Note that the word **either** is meant in this case to be pronounced with an /ī/ sound, not an /ē/ sound.

Students could work in co-operative groups to take one of the sound patterns in the chart and brainstorm as many words as possible that fit each spelling of that sound. They should be warned that some categories may have very few examples.

/h/ spelled		/n/ spelled		
h	wh	gn	kn	n
her help hope high hail	whose whom	gnat gnu gnarl gnash gnome	know knot knack knee knit	not name note number night

2. Stress with students how useful a tool the spelling chart can be when they must find a word in the dictionary, but are unsure of the first letters in the word.

Common Spellings of English Sounds

When the beginning letters of a word are not known, it is more difficult to locate the word in a dictionary. Try these strategies:

1. Make an educated guess about the likely spelling of the word. Try all possible ways of spelling the sound/letter combination.

2. Use the Spelling Chart which is found in most dictionaries. This chart outlines the many ways in which particular sounds in the language can be spelled at the **beginning**, **middle**, or **end** of words. Suppose you want to locate the word science in the dictionary, but are not sure of the beginning letters. By looking up the sound /s/ on the chart, you would know that this sound can be spelled in five ways when it comes at the beginning of words: **c**, **ps**, **s**, **sc**, and **sw**. By searching the dictionary for each possible beginning letter combination, you would eventually find the correct spelling of **science**.

	beginning	middle	end
r	run, rhyme, wrong	parent, hurry	bear, burr
s	cent, psalm, say science, sword	decent, mason muscle massive, extra	nice, bogus miss, lax
th	thin	toothpaste	bath

Exploring Ways to Travel

1. Students could add other categories to the chart, including different modes of transportation, such as a car, and another features such as fastest speed or passenger capacity.

2. Encourage students to include walking, running, skateboarding, and rollerblading as methods of travel. Students could conduct a survey in the class to determine the favourite method of transportation.

favourite method of travel	reason	student name
bicycle canoe plane walking running car boat		

3. There are many excellent stories for children about time travel. Encourage students to follow up their writing about time travel with some exploration of this story genre. For example, *The Root Cellar*, by Janet Lunn, and *The Other Elizabeth*, by Karleen Bradford.

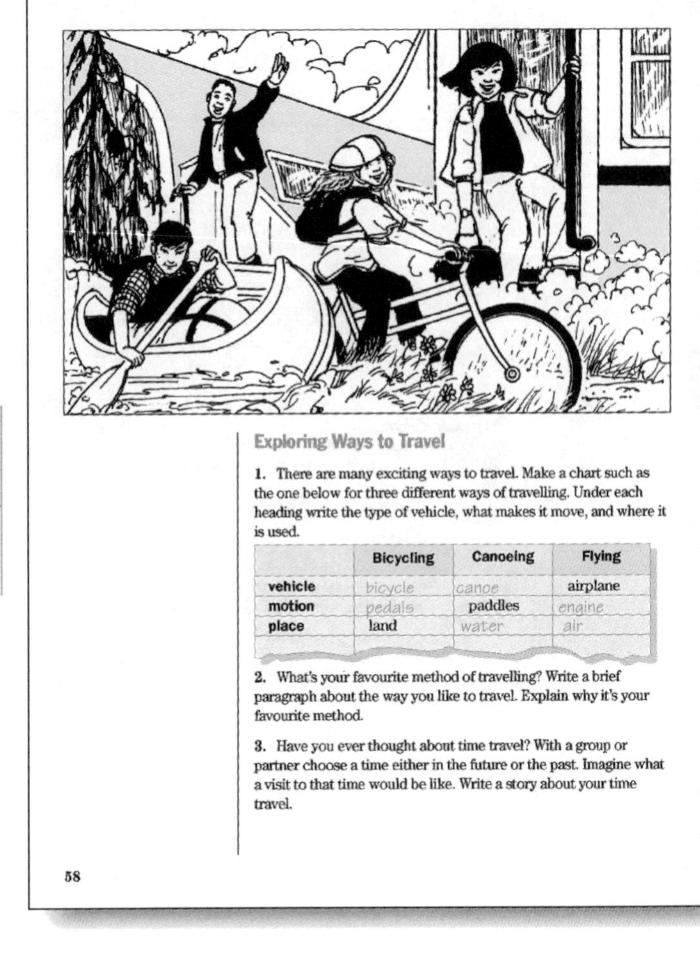

Exploring Ways to Travel

1. There are many exciting ways to travel. Make a chart such as the one below for three different ways of travelling. Under each heading write the type of vehicle, what makes it move, and where it is used.

	Bicycling	Canoeing	Flying
vehicle	bicycle	canoe	airplane
motion	pedals	paddles	engine
place	land	water	air

2. What's your favourite method of travelling? Write a brief paragraph about the way you like to travel. Explain why it's your favourite method.

3. Have you ever thought about time travel? With a group or partner choose a time either in the future or the past. Imagine what a visit to that time would be like. Write a story about your time travel.

58

POWERBOOSTERS

7 The sound /är/ is usually spelled **ar** as in **chart**.
The sound /ėr/ may be spelled **er** as in **term**, **ir** as in **bird**, **ur** as in **burn**, or **ear** as in **earth**.

8 The sound /ôr/ is usually spelled **ore** as in **store** or **or** as in **horse**.
Irregular forms of the /ôr/ sound are **ar** as in **warn**, **our** as in **four**, **oar** as in **roar**, **oor** as in **floor**.

9 The short vowel sound /e/ is sometimes spelled **ea** as in **heaven**.
The long vowel sound /ē/ may be spelled **e_e**, **ey**, or **y**.

10 The sound /ī/ can be spelled **i_e** as in **size**; **i** as in **mind**; **igh** as in **sigh**; or **y** as in **cycle**.

11 The sound /ėr/ is sometimes spelled **er** as in **her**, or **ur** as in **curly**, or **or** as in **worm**.
The suffix **-ly** may be added to many base words.

Grammar Power

1. Writing with Adjectives: Adjectives describe, or modify, nouns. A dog isn't just a dog. It can be big and hairy, or thin and yappy. Here are some adjectives from Units 1–12.

difficult **huge** **cheap** **solid** **blue**
bright **tiny** **quiet** **gentle** **furry**

Find a noun to go with each adjective above. Write a phrase.

Example: *a solid chocolate*

2. Making Comparisons: You can use adjectives to compare two persons or things. For example, suppose you want to compare an elephant to a mouse. If the adjective is a short word like big, add **-er**. If it is a long word like lovable, then use **more** before the adjective.

Example: *The elephant is* ***bigger*** *than a mouse.*

Complete these comparisons:
a) An elephant is **quieter** than ______ .
b) An elephant is **smaller** than ______ .
c) An elephant is **more lovable** than ______ .
d) An elephant is **more expensive** than ______ .

3. Using Superlatives: You can also use adjectives to compare more than two persons or things. If the adjective is a short word like fast, add **-est**. If it is a long word like experienced, then use **most** before the adjective.

Example: *You are the* ***fastest*** *swimmer of the six team members.*
She is the ***most experienced*** *player in the class.*

Complete these superlatives with your own ideas.
a) I think the **greatest** baseball player in the world is ______ .
b) I think the **tallest** building in the world is ______ .
c) I think the **most beautiful** view in the world is ______ .
d) I think the **most delicious** food in the world is ______ .

"Why are an elephant's ankles more wrinkled than a giraffe's? Because elephants wear their running shoes too tight."

58a

Grammar Power

1. Using precise adjectives can help students become better writers. Write the following sentences on chart paper or the board. Have students underline the adjectives and compare the two sentences. Discuss how adjectives can change the meaning, mood, and tone in a piece of writing.

It was a **cold**, **damp**, **miserable** morning.
It was a **bright**, **sunny**, **spring** morning.

You might wish to have students work with a partner to choose nouns to go with each adjective, trying them orally before writing down their choice.

difficult	huge	cheap	solid	blue
problem job question	dog building grin	watch person ticket	rock gold sense	mood moon cloth

2. Discuss the comparative forms of adjectives with students. We can use adjectives to compare two objects or people. When making such comparisons, a general rule of thumb is that if the adjective is one or two syllables, add **-er** to the end; if it is longer than two syllables, add **more** before the adjective (**big**/**bigger**; **enormous**/**more enormous**).

Have students note that some base words will change when **-er** is added. Give examples such as the following and see if they can formulate generalizations for adding the ending. Have them compare these generalizations to those for adding **-ed**.

large/larger shiny/shinier tall/taller
fat/fatter easy/easier thin/thinner
hot/hotter cold/colder brave/braver

Suggest that students add **more** to longer words and use each in a sentence:

mysterious furious beautiful
exciting wonderful

3. We also use adjectives to compare more than two objects or people. The same general rule applies to using the superlative: one- or two-syllable words usually add **-est**; longer adjectives are preceded by **most**.

Students could work in small groups to write their own ideas of 'the greatest baseball player ...' etc., then present their sentences to the group.

You may wish to have students make a chart in their notebooks and sort adjectives according to how the base word is changed when **-est** is added.

no change	drop final e	double final letter	change y to i
rich quiet long	close rude huge	dim wet fat	busy noisy tiny

4. a) Many adjectives have synonyms which mean almost the same thing. As students fill in the synonym chart, ask them to think about or discuss the subtle shades of meaning of the various words. For example, do **huge**, **enormous**, and **gigantic** mean exactly the same thing? How are they different? Which nouns might each word describe?

Adjectives describe things we see, feel, taste, smell, and hear. You may wish to have students work in groups to brainstorm adjectives around each of the five senses.

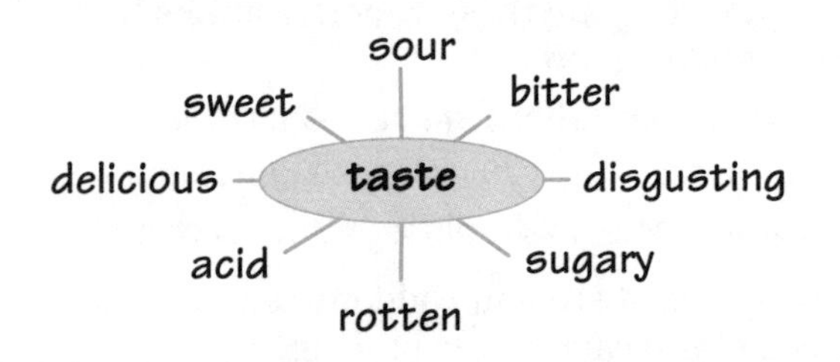

b) Antonyms are opposites. Some students may relate the prefix **anti-**, meaning 'against', to remember this word. You may wish to explore synonyms and antonyms in a thesaurus for this activity.

Proofing Power

Encourage students to share their edited version. Be sure that they do not 'correct' words which are already correctly spelled.

Once an error has been identified, have students brainstorm strategies for remembering the difficult features.

Look in a thesaurus to find lots of synonyms. Sometimes antonyms are listed too.

4. Synonyms are words that mean the same or almost the same thing. **Antonyms** mean the opposite.

a) Find two synonyms for each adjective in the chart below.

Adjective	Synonym
huge	
gentle	
bright	

b) Find antonyms for the adjectives in the chart below.

Adjective	Antonym
cheap	
difficult	
quiet	

Proofing Power

Read the following paragraph, looking for errors. List the words you think are misspelled, giving their correct spelling.

Last night I had a dream that I was riding around the world on my bicicle. I was ridding agianst the wind, and everything else was quite. I was waring my favourite pair of overalls that were perfect for the jerney. I rode everywere: in the dessert, in the artic, in the mountains. It is surprising how much mussle it takes to ride a bike! Sometimes, esecially in the most earlyest morning hours, I was frigtened that I might not make it home. But I kept going. When I was in easturn Canada, they had the wesrt storm I had ever seen. Finaly, I made it home. Was I exhausted!

bicycle/riding/against
quiet/wearing
journey/everwhere
desert
Arctic
muscle
especially/earliest
frightened
eastern
worst
Finally

58b

Proofreading Strategies

1. Try not to proofread your piece of writing immediately after you have written it. Your attention will still be focussed on the meaning rather than the spelling. Wait until the next day.

2. Read your work out loud. You will notice many errors when you read your words to another person.

3. Use a ruler beneath the line you are proofreading to keep track of each line.

4. Proofread from the bottom of the page to the top, or from right to left.

5. Switch papers with a friend. It is often easier to proofread someone else's work.

Long o
o as in hold
ow as in slowly

Patterns

The long **o** sound is found often in English speech. Unit 4 looked at the **o_e** and **oa** spellings of the sound; in this unit we examine the **o** and **ow** spellings, which are less common. The **ow** pattern may confuse students who think of it as spelling the sound in **how** and **cow**. Other spellings of long **o** include **oe** and **ough** (**toe**, **though**).

Preknowledge

Students should have an understanding of the following concepts as they work with the patterns in this unit.

• Base words and endings. Different endings can be added to base words to form other words related in meaning (**happy/happily**).
• Words that contain silent letters present special spelling challenges (**k**nown). Students need to develop strategies for dealing with such words.
• Syllables. A syllable contains a vowel, and words can contain one or more syllables (**hope**; h**o**pe/**ful**/l**y**).

More Patterns

Other patterns you might wish to review or introduce from the list words in this unit include the following.

• Compound words. Two words can be joined to form another word (**space/ship**). You might wish to remind students that not all words containing smaller words are in fact compounds. **Carpet**, for example, contains the words **car** and **pet**, but is not a compound word.
• Adding **-ing** to base words usually indicates actions that are taking place now (**growing**).
• /chər/ spelled **-ture** at the end of words (**furniture**, **adventures**, **future**, **picture**).

Professional Notebook

There are simply thousands of interesting and useful things to explore in words: structure, pronunciation, meaning, derivation, usage, big words that mean one thing, little words that mean all kinds of things, nice words, naughty words, kind words, and mean words. One short period a week seems little to spend on a playground so rich.

(Henderson 158)

Sharing the Secrets with Kids

The spelling of irregular verbs can often be remembered by comparing them with other words that fit the same pattern.

know	knew	known
grow	grew	grown
blow	blew	blown
fly	flew	flown

Precheck

Remind students to listen, then write their words in a list. Writing in a list helps students focus on the visual features of words.

Dictation

Please **hold** this book while I tie my shoe.
The boat's **motor** broke down.
Did you **notice** what time it is?
I'd like to have a **robot** to do my homework.
Follow your nose and you'll find the bakery.
You are continually **growing** and changing.
I've **known** her for seven years.
The rocket lifted **slowly** off the launch pad.
Throw the ball to me!
Move the **furniture** before cleaning the carpet.
Many exciting **adventures** are found in books.
Draw a **picture** of your family.
We don't know what the **future** will bring.
Perhaps we'll travel by **spaceship** some day.
I'd like to **travel** to Mars and beyond.
It started to rain **during** the night.

Words in Context

You might wish to use the context paragraph as a cloze passage by reproducing it (with blanks for the list words) on an overhead. Use it a second time and have students supply as many synonyms as they can for the list words.

Observing Patterns

1. Have students say the list words aloud, listening for the syllables in each. Remind them that each syllable has one vowel sound. Since all of the two-syllable list words place the stress on the first syllable, it may be useful to contrast these with other two-syllable words in which the second syllable is stressed.

words with stress on second syllable	
report	recline
balloon	explain
apart	complain
report	
extinct	
distinct	

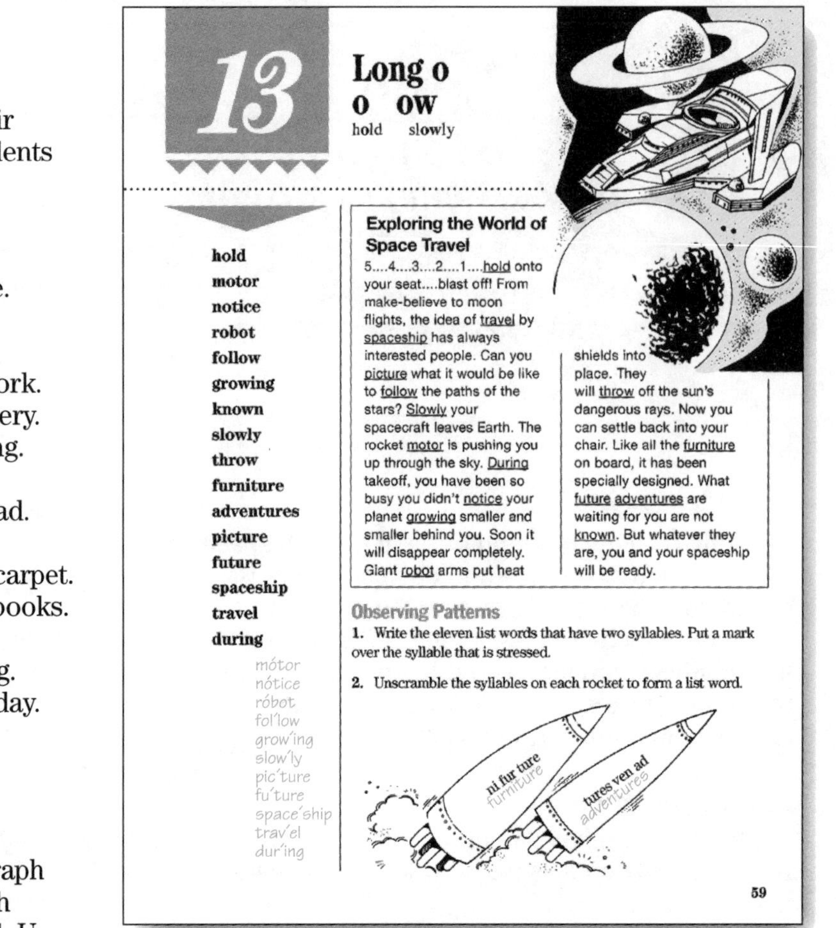

13 Long o

o ow
hold slowly

hold
motor
notice
robot
follow
growing
known
slowly
throw
furniture
adventures
picture
future
spaceship
travel
during

mótor
nótice
róbot
fol'low
grow'ing
slow'ly
pic'ture
fu'ture
space'ship
trav'el
dur'ing

Exploring the World of Space Travel

5....4....3....2....1....hold onto your seat....blast off! From make-believe to moon flights, the idea of travel by spaceship has always interested people. Can you picture what it would be like to follow the paths of the stars? Slowly your spacecraft leaves Earth. The rocket motor is pushing you up through the sky. During takeoff, you have been so busy you didn't notice your planet growing smaller and smaller behind you. Soon it will disappear completely. Giant robot arms put heat shields into place. They will throw off the sun's dangerous rays. Now you can settle back into your chair. Like all the furniture on board, it has been specially designed. What future adventures are waiting for you are not known. But whatever they are, you and your spaceship will be ready.

Observing Patterns

1. Write the eleven list words that have two syllables. Put a mark over the syllable that is stressed.

2. Unscramble the syllables on each rocket to form a list word.

59

2. Unscrambling words in this way helps students focus on the sequence of syllables, and on syllables they may miss in pronunciation, such as the **i** in **furniture**.

Special Needs

• Use word wheels to help children build patterns. When students have finished generating the words with the word wheels, have them copy the words on cards. These can be used for word sorts at a later date.

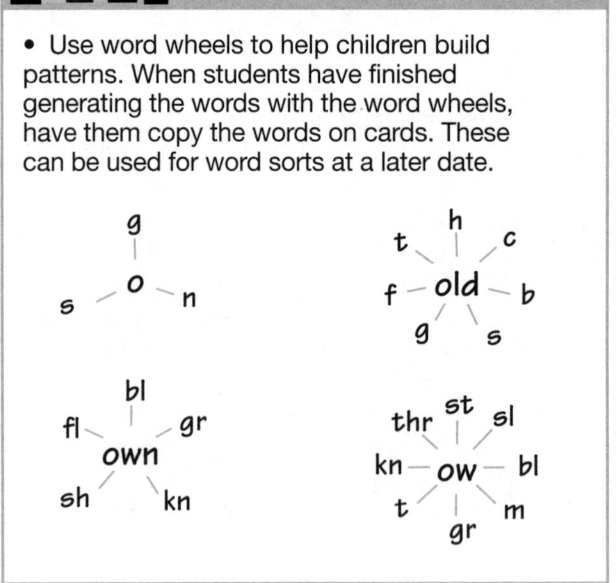

3. Write the list words that mean almost the same as the words below.

hold motor travel
grasp engine journey

4. Write the list words that mean the opposite of these words.

shrinking catch past lead
growing throw future follow

5. Write the two list words that begin with the sound /n/. Underline the letter or letters that spell the /n/ sound in each word.

notice known

6. Write the two list words that would be found in the dictionary between the words below.

snowball / told
throw spaceship

Synonyms mean the same. Antonyms mean the opposite.

Discovering Patterns

hold motor notice robot follow growing known slowly throw furniture adventures picture future spaceship travel during

1. Write the list words that have the sound /ch/ as in **nature**. Underline the parts of these words that are the same.

furniture adventures picture future

2. Many of the list words have the long **o** sound as in **old** and **blow**. Write the /ō/ list words under two headings.

/ō/ spelled **o** as in **old**	/ō/ spelled **ow** as in **blow**
hold robot motor notice	follow slowly growing throw known

POWERBOOSTER

- The long vowel sound /ō/ may be spelled **o** as in **old** or **ow** as in **blow**.
- In some words the /cher/ sound follows the pattern **-ture** as in **nature**.

60

3. If students are unfamiliar with the terms synonym and antonym, refer them to the margin note, and have them suggest synonyms and antonyms for simple words such as **big**, **sad**, and **poor**. Students could use a thesaurus to locate more synonyms for these and other list words.

list word	antonym	synonym
slowly	quickly	sluggishly
growing	shrinking	increasing
follow	lead	tag along
throw	catch	pitch
known	unknown	familiar

4. In this exercise, the list word **follow** is the opposite of **lead**. Point out that the word **lead** was not used in the context paragraph. Have students discuss the two pronunciations and meanings of the word.

Please **lead** (long *e*) your dog away from my flowers!

That monitor is as heavy as **lead.** (short *e*)

Students may note that the word **read** has the same spelling pattern and also has two pronunciations and meanings.

5. Ask students to make a list of other words which begin with the sound /n/ spelled **kn**. They may wish to begin with words in their current vocabulary, then consult a dictionary for additional words. Have them circle the words such as **knapsack** that are important for them.

knapsack knee kneel knew knife
knock knot know knowledge
known knuckle

6. It may help if students write the alphabet across the top of their notebook for reference. Students must consider each word carefully, since only two of the words would be found on a dictionary page with the given guide words. Although **slowly** and **travel** begin with appropriate letters, their second letter places them on different dictionary pages.

Discovering Patterns

1. Compile a list of words in which the /chər/ sound follows the pattern **-ture** (**mature**, **nature**, **fracture**, **gesture**, **capture**). Many word-processing programs have the ability to search for words with specific endings.

2. Read the list words carefully with students, noting the spelling patterns of the long **o** sound. Give students a pile of word cards to sort under the headings in their notebook or on a large sheet of chart paper. (See Special Needs , p.104.)

Exploring Patterns

1. Help students think of words in which the long **o** is spelled **ow** by drawing a circle with the /ow/ sound in the centre, and consonants (and consonant combinations) around the outside. Suggest that they write the words they make in two columns: **ow** as in **blow**; **ow** as in **cow**.

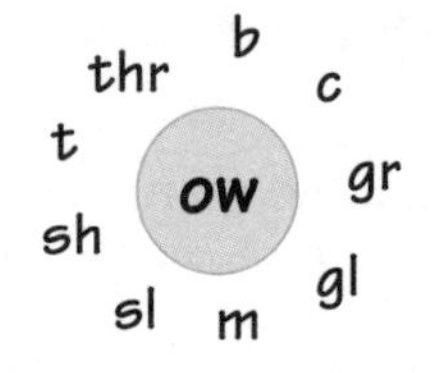

2. Some students may need help in completing the cloze passage, particularly the third sentence. This is an excellent activity for students to do in pairs or small groups. They may want to copy the word list on a sheet of chart paper and cross off words as they use them in the passage.

3. Examine the sample word web with the students and discuss the sub-categories indicating location, materials, and country of origin. Ask students to try using subdivisions to organize the word webs they create. Provide time for sharing and comparing the various products.

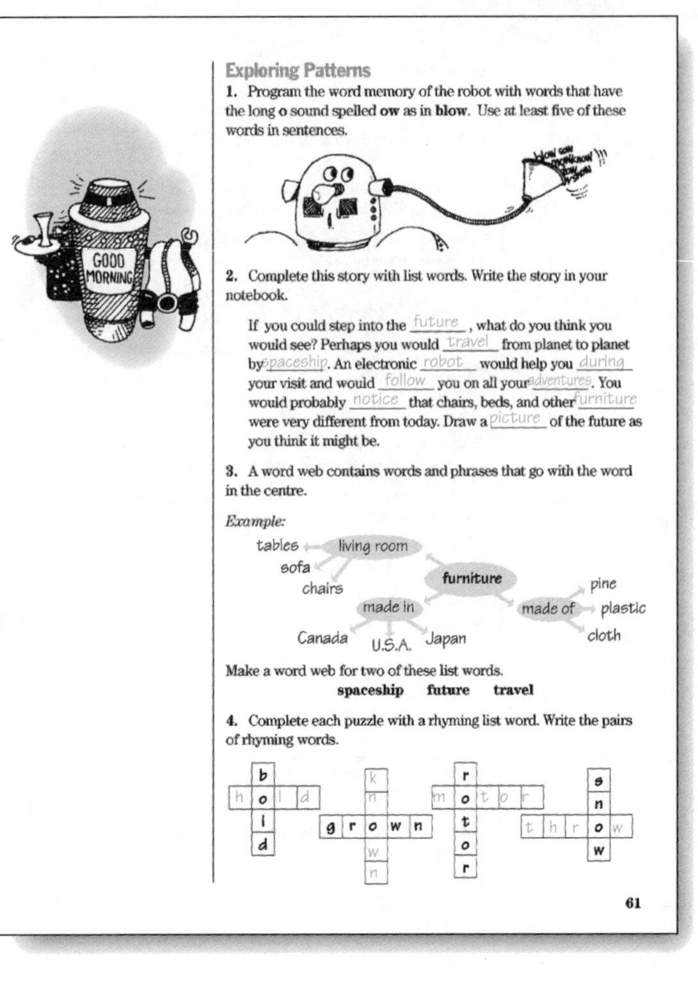

Exploring Patterns

1. Program the word memory of the robot with words that have the long **o** sound spelled **ow** as in **blow**. Use at least five of these words in sentences.

2. Complete this story with list words. Write the story in your notebook.

If you could step into the future, what do you think you would see? Perhaps you would travel from planet to planet by spaceship. An electronic robot would help you during your visit and would follow you on all your adventures. You would probably notice that chairs, beds, and other furniture were very different from today. Draw a picture of the future as you think it might be.

3. A word web contains words and phrases that go with the word in the centre.

Example:

Make a word web for two of these list words.

spaceship **future** **travel**

4. Complete each puzzle with a rhyming list word. Write the pairs of rhyming words.

61

Critical Thinking

- Students need practice in expanding word webs as in Exploring Patterns 3. Suggest several words from the list that they could web to develop the idea of categories. For example, sensory categories: shape, size, feel, appearance; categories of time and place; purpose or direction.

other countries
in Canada
to
Spring Summer Fall Winter
when
travel
method of
reason for
car train ship plane bicycle
fun holiday business

5. Your travel agency is selling seats on a tour of the planets. Design a poster to attract customers for this exciting trip to Mars, Jupiter, Saturn, Mercury, Pluto, Venus, Uranus, and Neptune. Use some of these list words on your poster.

travel **adventures** **future** **spaceship**

Check your poster carefully to make sure you've included all the important information about the tour.

SUPER WORDS

lunar
motion
exposed
cosmic
departure
noticeable

Challenges with Words

1. Use the Super Words to complete the radio message below.

Radio Log. Moon City. April 25, 2145
From: Landing Module, Captain Isaacs
Message: Completed our lunar landing at 1500 hours. Two crew members suffered slight motion sickness but since landing there have been no noticeable health problems. Just before landing, spacecraft was exposed to high levels of cosmic radiation. Expect our departure date to be May 3 or 4.

2. a) The following words all have something to do with space travel. Write an antonym or opposite for each word.

launch (land) enormous (tiny) motion (still) freezing (melting) survive (die)
automatic (manual) distant (near) breathable (suffocating) approach (leave) known (unknown)

b) Write five more words that describe space travel, then write antonyms for your words.

62

5. Have students quickly jot down all the information a poster should include. Encourage them to make a rough sketch of their poster so that they can determine how to arrange the information in the overall design.

Challenges with Words

1. Have students note the spelling of long **o** in **motion**, **exposed**, and **noticeable** and the **-ture** ending in **departure**. You may wish to suggest that they write a cloze passage of their own for the Super Words after they have completed Challenges 1.

2. Discuss how there may be several antonyms for one word, depending on how it is used, just as there are often many synonyms for a word. There is no one right answer.

word	antonyms	synonyms
launch	crash, bring back	send forth, fire off, propel
enormous	tiny, small, little	huge, gigantic, big
motion	motionless, still, immobile	movement, action
freezing	boiling, hot	icy, cold
survive	die, perish	remain, exist
automatic	manual	mechanical, motorized
dis[illegible]		[illegible]

Writing

- Students may wish to take Exploring Patterns 5 further and design bumper stickers or buttons for travellers who have been passengers on the space flight.

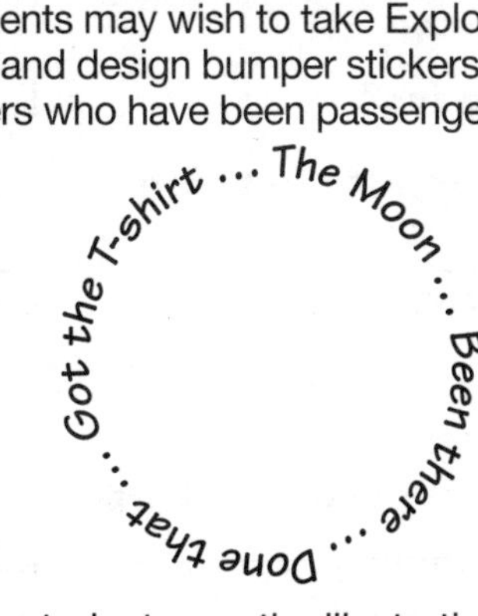

- Have students use the illustrations of posters on page 62 to design and create a poster for a class, school, or community event. Suggest that besides being eye-catching and appealing, posters need to be proofread and checked carefully to make sure all the information is clear and accurate. A poster should tell where and when an event will occur, how much it will cost (if anything), and what the purpose of the event is.

Biggest Barbecue on Earth!
Saturday, September 27
Priory Park
6 p.m.
$2.00 per person
All proceeds to
Green Space
See You There!

Words in History

Students might want to make a word web of the word **lunar**, writing all the words which are forms of this base word. Encourage students to use the dictionary for help with these words.

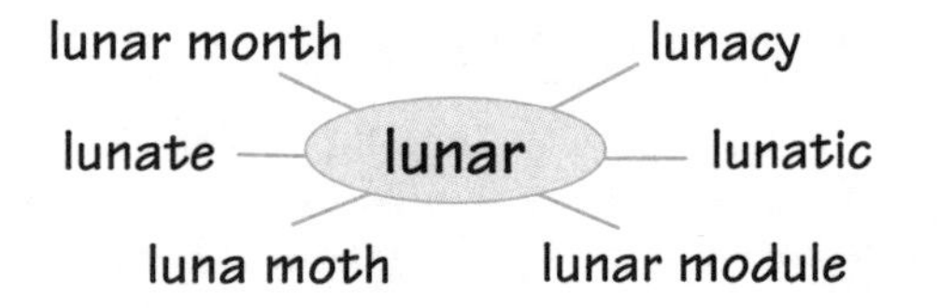

3. Students could create a word search for a partner with their cosmic words, as well as adding some of these words to their Personal Review Lists.

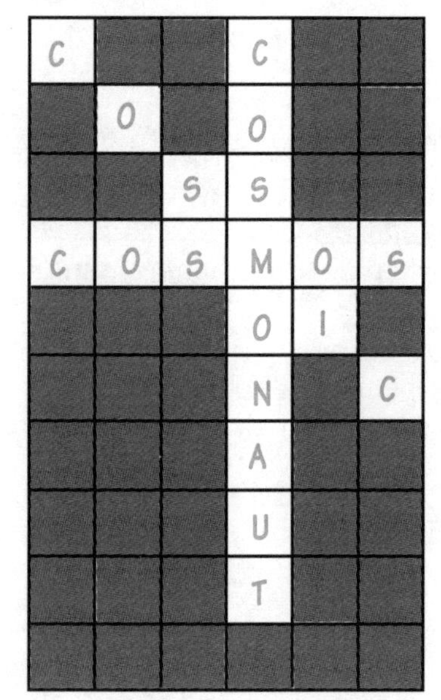

4. Ask students to brainstorm a rule for keeping the **e** on the ends of words when adding **-able**. You might have students look at the incorrect spelling of the word **noticable**. Ask them how they would pronounce the word. Which vowels, following a **c**, give it the sound /s/? (**i**, **e**) Which give it the sound /k/? (**a**, **o**, **u**)

5. Have students note the **-ture** ending is not a suffix. Challenge them to get as many of the words as they can into one sentence. Have them proofread the sentences before sharing them with a partner.

6. Students may wish to work in a group to complete this dialogue. They also may wish to do some research into space flights to the moon.

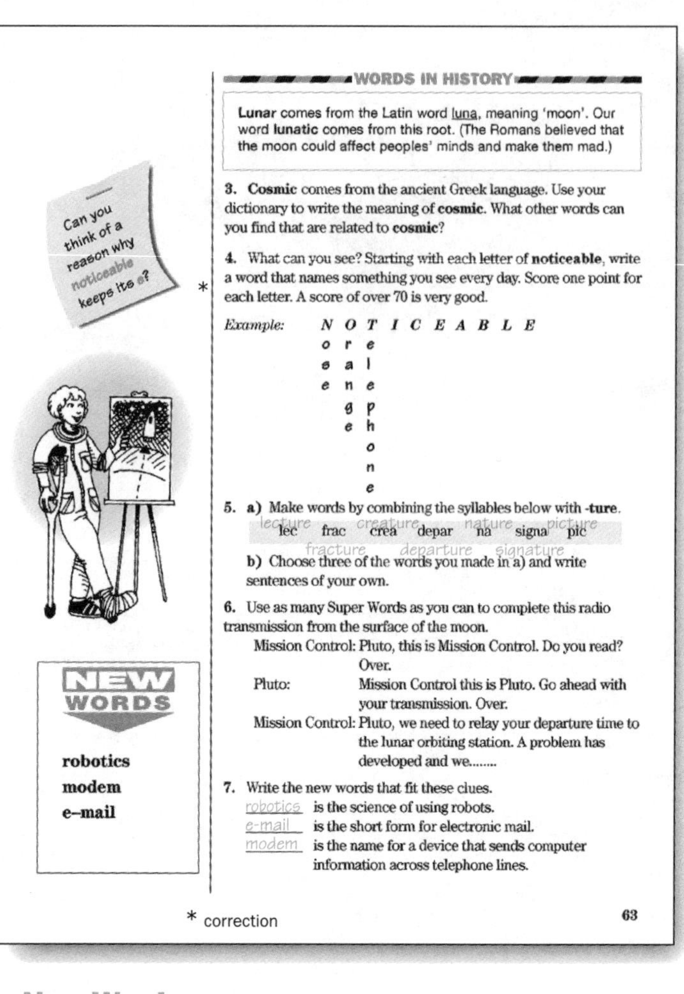

WORDS IN HISTORY

Lunar comes from the Latin word luna, meaning 'moon'. Our word **lunatic** comes from this root. (The Romans believed that the moon could affect peoples' minds and make them mad.)

3. Cosmic comes from the ancient Greek language. Use your dictionary to write the meaning of **cosmic**. What other words can you find that are related to **cosmic**?

Can you think of a reason why noticeable keeps its e?

* **4.** What can you see? Starting with each letter of **noticeable**, write a word that names something you see every day. Score one point for each letter. A score of over 70 is very good.

Example: N O T I C E A B L E

o r e
e a l
e n e
g p
e h
o
n
e

5. a) Make words by combining the syllables below with **-ture**.

lec frac crea depar na signa pic

lecture fracture creature departure nature signature picture

b) Choose three of the words you made in a) and write sentences of your own.

6. Use as many Super Words as you can to complete this radio transmission from the surface of the moon.

Mission Control: Pluto, this is Mission Control. Do you read? Over.

Pluto: Mission Control this is Pluto. Go ahead with your transmission. Over.

Mission Control: Pluto, we need to relay your departure time to the lunar orbiting station. A problem has developed and we........

NEW WORDS

robotics
modem
e-mail

7. Write the new words that fit these clues.

robotics is the science of using robots.
e-mail is the short form for electronic mail.
modem is the name for a device that sends computer information across telephone lines.

* correction

63

New Words

7. Have students share their background knowledge of the three new words. If your school is connected to the Internet, perhaps they could experiment with sending e-mail messages.

Proofreading Checklist	Yes	No
Have you watched for homophones **toe/tow; know/no?**	☐	☐
Have you dropped the **e** before adding **-ing**? com~~e~~ing; bak~~e~~ing	☐	☐
Have you doubled final consonants before adding **-ing** if the vowel is short? sho**pp**ing; swi**mm**ing	☐	☐
Did you write compound words correctly?	☐	☐

Curriculum Connection

Have students design a list of questions they would like to ask about space travel. They can then research the topic to find answers to their questions.

> How long would it take to travel to the nearest star?
>
> How far is it to the moon?
>
> Who was the first woman in space?

Assessment

Review with students the procedures for the Unit Test that you feel best suit your class. Encourage them to record their results and compare them to the Precheck and tests on other units. Can they see steady progress? Are they keeping a Personal Review List of difficult words? Schedule conferences with individual students to discuss their progress and the strategies they are discovering to help them be better spellers.

Follow-up

If more practice is needed, you may wish to work on the spelling patterns for long **o** suggested in *Sharing the Secrets: Teach your Child to Spell*, pp. 47–50.

Teacher's Notes

14 Plurals

s as in planets
-es as in matches

Patterns

Forming plurals is one of the first structural principles students attempt as they move from a sound-based approach to spelling to one focussed on structure, meaning, and other elements. By grade 5, many students will spell **dogs** rather than **dogz**, signalling they understand that **s** added to the end of a word means more than one, even though the final sound is /z/.

Preknowledge

Help students understand the following concepts as they work with the patterns in this unit.

- Base words and adding to them. A base word is the 'root' to which plurals, tense markers, suffixes, and prefixes are added. In the case of plurals, the base word is the singular form (**wave/waves**; **bunch/bunches**).
- Singular refers to one, plural refers to more than one.

More Patterns

Other patterns you might wish to review or introduce in this unit include the following.

- The use of **kilo** as a prefix (**kilogram**, **kilometre**).
- The consonant digraph **ch**. It is important that students are able to recognize when two letters together form a single sound (**branches**).
- The consonant blends **sp**, **st**, **br**, **cl**, **gr**, **pl**.

Professional Notebook

What we have not widely been aware of is that children quite naturally approach spelling through the techniques of problem-solving. There is a large body of research which suggests that learning to spell involves problem-solving on a variety of levels. Children observe language patterns, formulate hypotheses about the spelling system, and test these hypotheses in their own writing.

(Scott, *Spelling: Sharing the Secrets* 14)

Sharing the Secrets with Kids

*Suggest students try to say words such as **houses** and **classes** without the second vowel sound—as if they were written **houzs**, or **classz**. Have them listen to the way that another vowel creeps in. This becomes the **-es** in plural forms where the base word ends in **ss**, **x**, **z**, **sh**, or **ch**.*

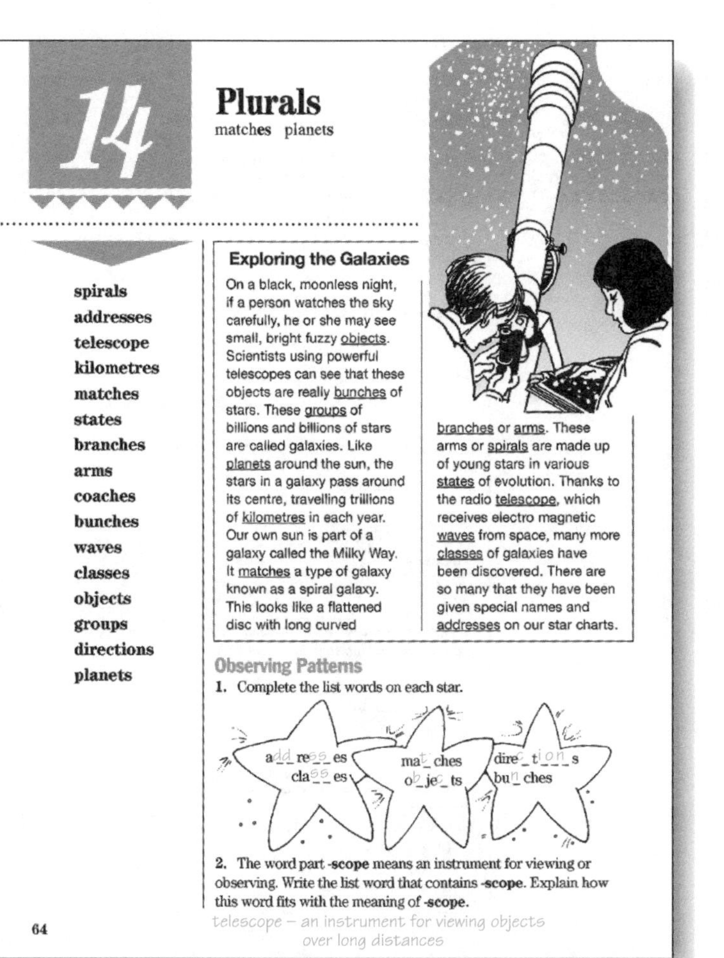

14 Plurals

matches planets

spirals
addresses
telescope
kilometres
matches
states
branches
arms
coaches
bunches
waves
classes
objects
groups
directions
planets

Exploring the Galaxies

On a black, moonless night, if a person watches the sky carefully, he or she may see small, bright fuzzy objects. Scientists using powerful telescopes can see that these objects are really bunches of stars. These groups of billions and billions of stars are called galaxies. Like planets around the sun, the stars in a galaxy pass around its centre, travelling trillions of kilometres in each year. Our own sun is part of a galaxy called the Milky Way. It matches a type of galaxy known as a spiral galaxy. This looks like a flattened disc with long curved branches or arms. These arms or spirals are made up of young stars in various states of evolution. Thanks to the radio telescope, which receives electro magnetic waves from space, many more classes of galaxies have been discovered. There are so many that they have been given special names and addresses on our star charts.

Observing Patterns

1. Complete the list words on each star.

2. The word part **-scope** means an instrument for viewing or observing. Write the list word that contains **-scope**. Explain how this word fits with the meaning of **-scope**.

telescope – an instrument for viewing objects over long distances

64

Precheck

When presenting the words to the class after the Precheck, point out difficult parts of words and spelling patterns by underlining, boxing parts, or using a different colour of chalk or marker. You may want to keep your list visible in the room throughout the unit until the Unit Test is given.

Dictation

Corkscrews are shaped like **spirals**.
I have two different e-mail **addresses**.
A pirate captain always carried a **telescope**.
Canada is more than 3000 **kilometres** from east to west.
This shade of brown **matches** your eyes.
There are three **states** of matter: animal, vegetable, mineral.
The tree had many **branches**.
My **arms** were tired after carrying the groceries.
We have two **coaches** for our hockey team.
She bought three **bunches** of flowers.
The huge **waves** sank the ship.
There are three separate **classes** in grade 5 this year.
Several o**bjects** fell out of her knapsack.
The students worked in **groups** of four.
Can you give me **directions** from Edmonton to Calgary?
Do you know the names of all the **planets**?

Words in Context

Have students read the paragraph, noting all the plural forms. Then ask them to identify the two list words that are not included in the paragraph and write their own sentences for these words (**coaches**, **directions**).

Observing Patterns

1. The visual features of these words may be further enhanced by circling or underlining the difficult parts, or using configuration boxes and lines. Have students suggest strategies for remembering the double **d** and **s** in **addresses** ("add two **D**s and two **S**s to my **address**").

2. Students will likely know that a **telescope** is an instrument for viewing or observing the stars. Point out that the prefix **tele-** comes from the Greek word meaning 'far off'. Therefore, a **telescope** is an instrument for viewing objects that are far away. Have them brainstorm other common words that begin with **tele-** (**television**, **telephone**, **telephoto**, **telegram**, **telemarketing**).

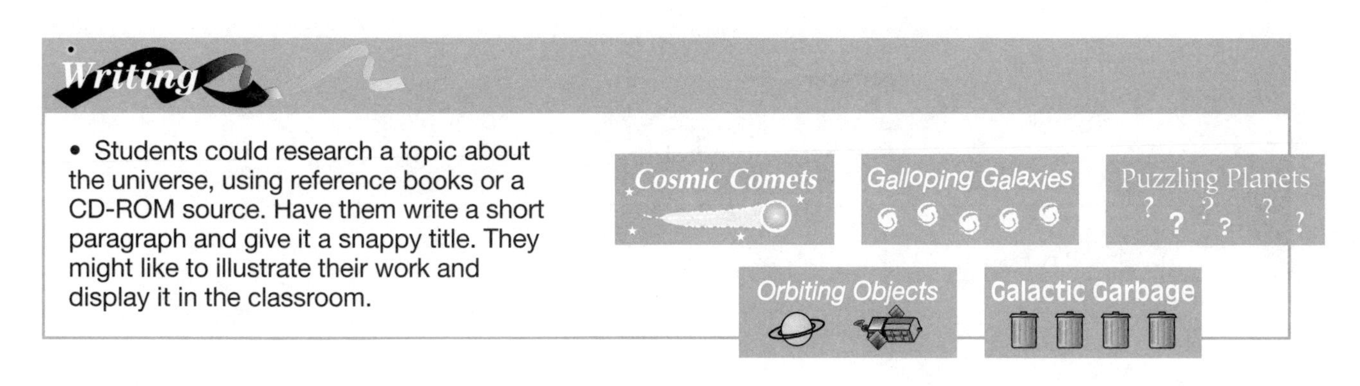

- Students could research a topic about the universe, using reference books or a CD-ROM source. Have them write a short paragraph and give it a snappy title. They might like to illustrate their work and display it in the classroom.

3. Writing words as part of a set helps with understanding word meaning as well as building vocabulary. Ask students to state the common link within each set and to justify their choice of list words in each case. ("All the words in **b)** are parts of the body.")

4. Remind students that words which rhyme need not have identical spelling patterns for the rhyming sounds (**waits/states**).

Have students add other words which fit the pattern in each sound.

waits	alarms	behaves	stoops
states plates grates hates slates	arms farms harms	waves graves slaves raves saves	groups soups dupes troops

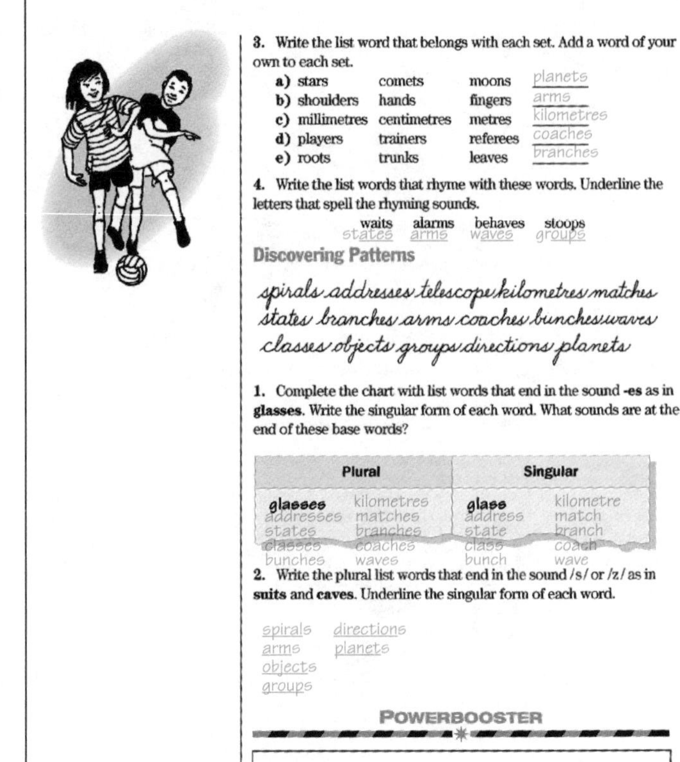

3. Write the list word that belongs with each set. Add a word of your own to each set.

a) stars comets moons planets
b) shoulders hands fingers arms
c) millimetres centimetres metres kilometres
d) players trainers referees coaches
e) roots trunks leaves branches

4. Write the list words that rhyme with these words. Underline the letters that spell the rhyming sounds.

waits alarms behaves stoops
states arms waves groups

Discovering Patterns

spirals addresses telescope kilometres matches states branches arms coaches bunches waves classes objects groups directions planets

1. Complete the chart with list words that end in the sound **-es** as in **glasses**. Write the singular form of each word. What sounds are at the end of these base words?

Plural		Singular	
glasses	kilometres	glass	kilometre
addresses	matches	address	match
states	branches	state	branch
classes	coaches	class	coach
bunches	waves	bunch	wave

2. Write the plural list words that end in the sound /s/ or /z/ as in **suits** and **caves**. Underline the singular form of each word.

spirals directions
arms planets
objects
groups

POWERBOOSTER

- In many words the plural is formed by adding **-s** to the singular form.
- Singular words that end in the sound /ch/ or /s/ form the plural by adding **-es**.

65

Discovering Patterns

1. It may be helpful for some students to read the list words aloud so that the final sound can be distinguished more easily.

2. Remind students that words ending in the sound /z/ often are spelled with an **s** if the word means 'more than one' (**dogs**, **waves**).

Critical Thinking

- As a follow-up to the code activity in Challenges with Words 3, have students invent their own codes to send messages, or have them use the code given here to solve a space riddle.

A	B	C	D	E	F	G	H	I	J	K	L	M	N	O	P	Q	R	S	T	U	V	W	X	Y	Z	?	.
.	?	z	y	x	w	v	u	t	s	r	q	p	o	n	m	l	k	j	i	h	g	f	e	d	c	b	a

Riddle

what was the alien's favourite snack?

f u . i f . j i u x . q t x o a j w . g n h k t i x j o . z r b

Answer

p . k j ? . k j

Exploring Patterns

1. Make a list of the objects in outer space that you might see with a powerful telescope. In one column, write the singular form of the word, then in the second column write the plural.

Example: ***Singular*** *planet* ***Plural*** *planets*

2. Many of the list words can be used as either nouns or verbs.

Example: *That plant has many tiny branches.*
This road branches off in three directions.

Use each of these list words in two sentences—first as a noun, then as a verb.

waves **coaches**

3. Complete this story with the list words that fit the shapes below. Write the story in your notebook.

For our scavenger hunt, the [c l a s s e s] were broken into five [g r o u p s]. We were given [d i r e c t i o n s] for finding several [a d d r e s s e s], and at each place we had to locate certain [o b j e c t s]. We ended up walking about five [k i l o m e t r e s] but we found everything on the list!

4. Write these list words so that their shape tells something about their meaning.

waves **directions** **planets** **spirals**

Example:

growing

66

Exploring Patterns

1. This activity works well with small groups. Make sure that students have spelled the singular and plural forms correctly, particularly in words ending with **y** (**galaxy/galaxies**). Compile a master list with the class.

singular	plural
planet	planets
galaxy	galaxies
spaceship	spaceships
satellite	satellites
star	stars
UFO	UFOs

2. Some students may need further help in distinguishing between nouns and verbs. Have students give oral examples of each. ("The waves were six metres high." "He waves to the crowd.") The list words **addresses**, **matches**, and **states** could be used as other examples of words that can be either nouns or verbs.

There were two **addresses** on the envelope.

She always **addresses** him as "sir."

Both hockey **matches** are today.

This colour **matches** my shirt.

How many **states** are there in the U.S.?

The letter **states** the time we're to be there.

3. Cloze exercises help students see and write the list words in context. Extend the activity by having students write their own 'shape sentences' for a partner to complete.

4. Challenge students to use their imaginations to think of an image that represents the meaning of the words. Similar drawings could be done for other list words such as **telescope** and **matches**. Students may want to display their work on a poster.

Co-operative Learning

- Students can work with a partner or in small groups to create lists of plural words from everyday objects in the classroom and outside it.

What's ...			
in your desk?	on the wall?	on the floor?	outside the window?
pens	charts	desks	trees
pencils	displays	tiles	leaves
notebooks	chalkboards	chairs	clouds
books	pictures	scraps	buildings

5. Encourage students to add other parts to the message, including sound effects or music, or favourite jokes. The collected messages could be combined in a class book or tape. Have students suggest titles for their collection.

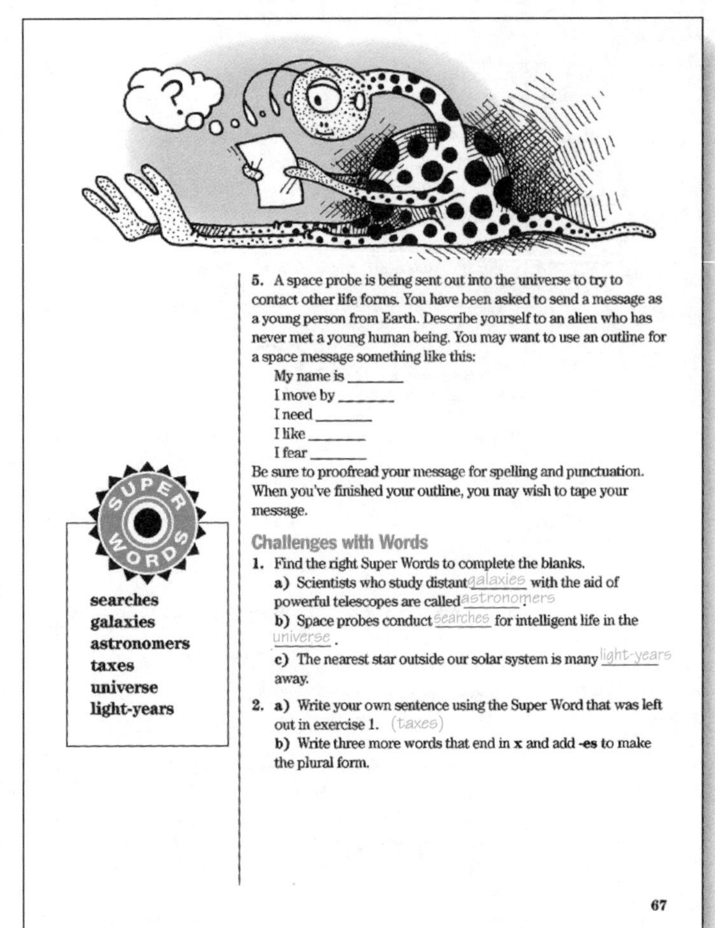

5. A space probe is being sent out into the universe to try to contact other life forms. You have been asked to send a message as a young person from Earth. Describe yourself to an alien who has never met a young human being. You may want to use an outline for a space message something like this:

My name is ______
I move by ______
I need ______
I like ______
I fear ______

Be sure to proofread your message for spelling and punctuation. When you've finished your outline, you may wish to tape your message.

SUPER WORDS

searches
galaxies
astronomers
taxes
universe
light-years

Challenges with Words

1. Find the right Super Words to complete the blanks.
   a) Scientists who study distant galaxies with the aid of powerful telescopes are called astronomers.
   b) Space probes conduct searches for intelligent life in the universe.
   c) The nearest star outside our solar system is many light-years away.
2. a) Write your own sentence using the Super Word that was left out in exercise 1. (taxes)
   b) Write three more words that end in **x** and add **-es** to make the plural form.

67

Challenges with Words

1. Ask students to state the rule for making each Super Word plural. (They may want to discuss whether universe can ever be made plural!) Have them note other features of each word, such as the number of syllables, and whether it is hyphenated (**light-years**).

super word	base word	rule
searches	search	add **-es**
galaxies	galaxy	change y to i and add **-es**
astronomers	astronomer	add **-s**
taxes	tax	add **-es**
light-years	light-year	add **-s**

2. You might want to remind students that **cks** and **cts** make the sound /x/ at the end of words such as **facts** and **packs**. In this case the plurals are formed with **s**.

ESL

The /s/ and /z/ sound at the ends of words may be difficult for many ESL students to hear and thus spell or pronounce.

- Have students practise the plural forms in sentences.

  I have two hats. The glasses are on the desk.

- Include lots of practice with pronunciation and spelling of the final **-s** and **-es**.

one boat	two boats
one watch	two watches
one car	five cars
one house	two houses

WORDS IN HISTORY

The Ancient Greek word for **star** was aster or astron. From this word comes our word **astronomer**.

3. Use the code below to discover other words that come from the Greek roots aster and astron. Be careful. Extra letters have been added at the beginning and end of some words.

z y x w t q m l k j i h g f d c b s u p e r n o v a
A B C D E F G H I J K L M N O P Q R S T U V W X Y Z

a) ozupsdfzepz *ASTRONAUT* **b)** zszupsdhdmv **ASTROLOGY **c)** zuptskuihg ASTERISK**
d) pzzuptsdkwb **ASTEROID* **e)** zupsdfdgv ASTRONOMY **f)** lkzupsdfdgkxzh **ASTRONOMICAL

4. Write the plural forms of these words. Some are tricky, so check your dictionary for irregular plurals.

a) blush blushes **b)** hostess hostesses **c)** zoo zoos
d) galaxy galaxies **e)** chief chiefs **f)** hero heroes
g) shelf shelves **h)** waltz waltzes **i)** wretch wretches

5. Verbs that end in **ch**, **sh**, **ss**, **zz**, and **z** also add **-es**.

*Example: The light **flashes** on and off.*

Use a verb that ends in **-es** to complete these sentences.

a) She leashes her dog. **b)** He wishes on a star.
c) The bee buzzes. **d)** The runner finishes 100 metres.

6. Write your own sentences with these verbs.

crunches crushes tosses fizzes

7. A **light year** is the distance light travels in one year. That's about 9 500 000 000 000 (9.5 trillion) kilometres! Use a book or a CD-ROM to research astronomy and complete the space chart below. You may want to add other planets, galaxies, nebulas, or quasars to the list.

OBJECTS IN SPACE		
Name	**Type**	**Distance from Earth**
Mars	planet	78 000 000 km
Andromeda	galaxy	
Neptune		
Venus		
Milky Way		

68

Words in History

Encourage students to look for other 'astro' words in the dictionary. They may also want to look up the word history of other Super Words.

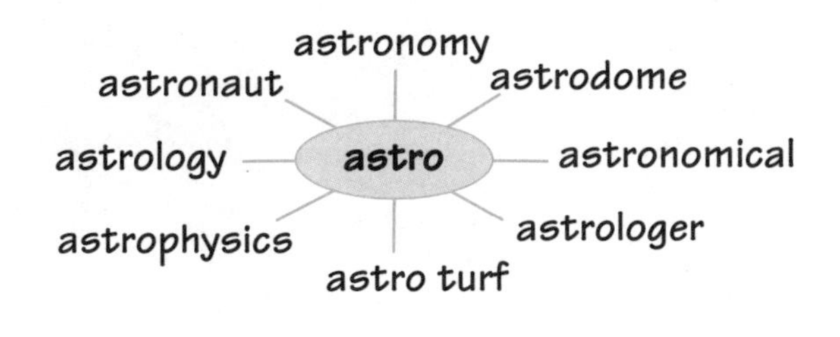

3. After solving the code word puzzle, suggest students write sentences with some or all of these words. Encourage them to choose one of their sentences and develop it into a story.

4. Have students sort the words under the headings given here and formulate rules for each pattern.

tricky plural endings				
add -s	**add -es**	**change y to i and add -es**	**change f to v and add -es**	**irregular**
zoos	blushes wretches waltzes heroes hostesses	galaxies	shelves	chiefs

5. Have students look for examples of words ending in **zz**, **ss**, **ch**, and **sh** and form plurals with these words. Some word-processing programs will enable them to search for groups of words with special endings.

6. Encourage students to write a story using as many **-es** words as they can. They may be interested to note the onomatopoeia of words such as **crunch**, **scrunch**, **munch**, **punch**.

7. Students might want to investigate other constant measurement terms such as **mach number**, **nautical mile**, **sidereal day/month**, and the **speed of light**. They might add these terms to their Personal Review List.

Special Needs

- Have students examine newspaper ads and stories, flyers, magazine pages, and so on, and underline words that mean 'more than one' and end in **-s** or **-es**. Talk about how the plurals were formed. Then have the students find singular nouns, write them in a list, and discuss how to make them plural. Encourage them to rely on the way they pronounce the word as a guide. For example, if they say aloud "one batch, two batches," they will hear the **-es**.

Home Connection

Many people make errors with the plural forms. Have students become 'spelling detectives' watching for signs in store windows, and for flyers or advertisements where errors in spelling are made. Have them bring samples they have found to begin a class list of 'Great Spelling Goofs'.

Sail of the Century!
20% off all watchez in the store

Diarys on special for this week only at ...

Add a few luxurys to your life!
For the holiday of a lifetime, call...

Assessment

• Emphasis should be placed on developing a positive attitude toward spelling through self-correction and self-diagnosis of errors. Provide as much support as possible.

• When students make errors on plural forms, either on the Unit Test or in their everyday writing, ask them to explain why they spelled the word as they did. This may reveal that the student is using primarily a visual or phonetic strategy rather than understanding the patterns for forming plurals, or that he/she is encountering interference from a first language. (See ESL p. 114.)

Follow-up

• Check that the concept of 'more than one' is clearly understood.

• Provide further support for the various plural forms, using the activities found in *Sharing the Secrets: Teach Your Child to Spell*, Units 27 and 28. Exercises and activities in this resource can be shared with parents for reinforcement at home.

Teacher's Notes

Irregular plurals
ies as in berries
ves as in knives

Patterns

Patterns for making nouns plural are fairly simple in English. We add **-s** in most cases, or add an **-es** when the pronunciation indicates it (**matches**, **churches**, **foxes**). This unit looks at the changes that take place in the base word when the plural is added:

- when a word ends in **y**, change the **y** to **i** and add **-es**
- when a word ends in **f**, change the **f** to **v** and add **-es**.

Preknowledge

Students should have an understanding of the following concepts as they work with the patterns in this unit.

- Most plural words end in **s**.
- Plural means 'more than one'.
- Some nouns are collective, or uncountable, and are rarely made plural (**furniture**).
- We add **-er** and **-est** to adjectives to make the comparative and superlative forms (**high**/high**er**/high**est**).
- Names of specific places are capitalized in English (**Canada**, **London**, **Timbuktu**).

More Patterns

Other patterns you might wish to review or introduce from the list words in this unit include the following.

- Some words have no plural form (**deer**).
- Proper nouns are capitalized (**America**).
- The superlative form of adjectives (**largest**).

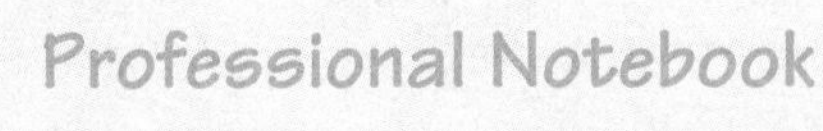

Professional Notebook

When you consider that the most frequently occurring words are usually meaningless, abstract words that may be irregular in their spelling/pronunciation and which children use but don't even realize are separate words, it is a wonder that any children learn to recognize and spell them! In order to read and write fluently, however, children must learn to instantly recognize and automatically spell these words.

(Cunningham 125)

Sharing the Secrets with Kids

*'Change the **y** to **i** and add **-es**' is one of the few rules that holds true in most cases in English (**century/centuries; city/cities**). It also applies to verbs that end in **y** when they add **-s** in the third person (I marry, you marry, she/he marries).*

Precheck

Pronounce the words clearly but naturally as you dictate. Encourage students to say the word softly to themselves before writing. When self-correcting the Precheck, have students rewrite the words they misspelled, leaving out the difficult letters as a cloze activity (**gri_ _lies**, **usu_ _ly**).

Dictation

I use ripe **berries** to make pies.
I **usually** do my homework before supper.
The **enemies** fought a battle.
The **mountain** is 4000 metres high.
Grizzlies can be dangerous bears.
Are you **digging** for treasure?
I'll take the **largest** apple!
Those **knives** are very sharp.
Deer are very graceful animals.
Canada is part of North **America**.
Most dogs like to chew **bones**.
Many husbands and **wives** attended the party.
Our **camper** van can sleep six people.
Bees sting when they're angry.
Do cats have nine **lives**?
Little puppies can **become** big dogs.

Words in Context

Have students read the paragraph themselves, or use it as a cloze passage. Ask them to identify the list word that does not appear (**wives**) and challenge them to think of a sentence that uses the word and fits into the paragraph.

Observing Patterns

1. It may be helpful to have students think of other words that fit the doubled letter pattern. Learning words in groups is an efficient practice.

double consonant			double vowel	
berries	usually	grizzlies	deer	bees
cherries	casually	sizzle	steer	knees
ferries	visually	fizzle	beer	fees
			leer	sprees
			peer	trees

2. Ask students to explain the relationships present in each analogy and to justify their choice of list word to complete each comparison.

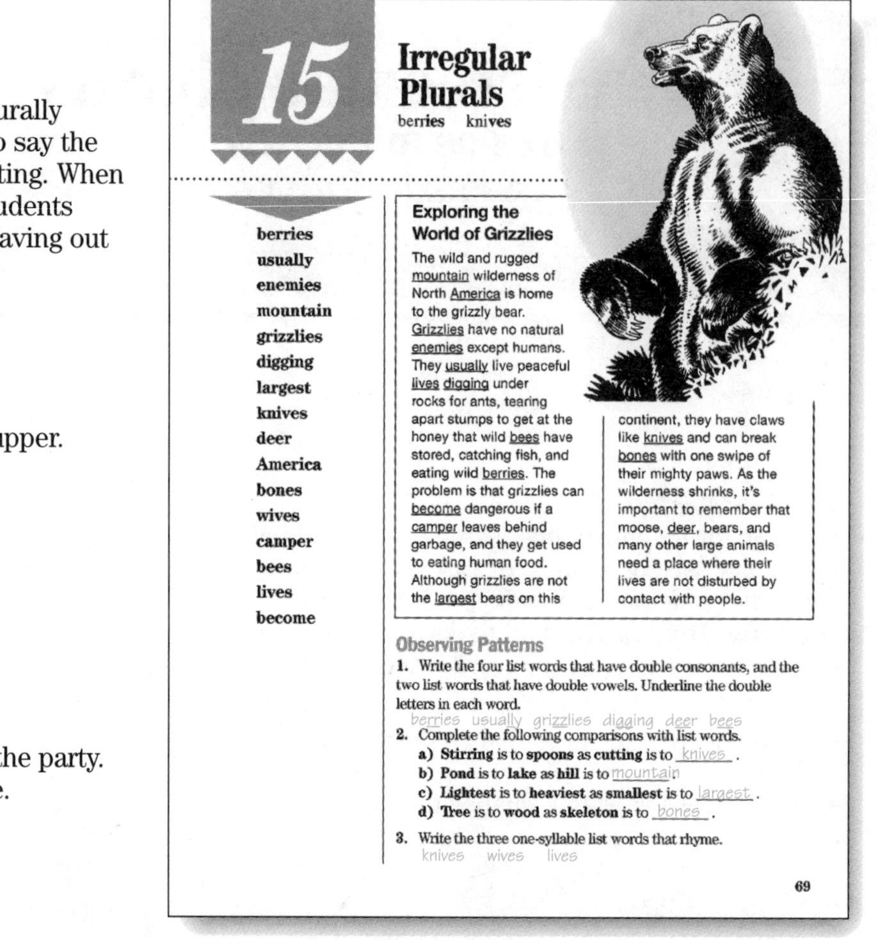

15

Irregular Plurals

berries knives

berries
usually
enemies
mountain
grizzlies
digging
largest
knives
deer
America
bones
wives
camper
bees
lives
become

Exploring the World of Grizzlies

The wild and rugged mountain wilderness of North America is home to the grizzly bear. Grizzlies have no natural enemies except humans. They usually live peaceful lives digging under rocks for ants, tearing apart stumps to get at the honey that wild bees have stored, catching fish, and eating wild berries. The problem is that grizzlies can become dangerous if a camper leaves behind garbage, and they get used to eating human food. Although grizzlies are not the largest bears on this continent, they have claws like knives and can break bones with one swipe of their mighty paws. As the wilderness shrinks, it's important to remember that moose, deer, bears, and many other large animals need a place where their lives are not disturbed by contact with people.

Observing Patterns

1. Write the four list words that have double consonants, and the two list words that have double vowels. Underline the double letters in each word.
berries usually grizzlies digging deer bees
2. Complete the following comparisons with list words.
a) **Stirring** is to **spoons** as **cutting** is to knives.
b) **Pond** is to **lake** as **hill** is to mountain
c) **Lightest** is to **heaviest** as **smallest** is to largest.
d) **Tree** is to **wood** as **skeleton** is to bones.
3. Write the three one-syllable list words that rhyme.
knives wives lives

69

3. Some students may find it difficult to rhyme **knives** and **wives** with **lives** if they pronounce it with a short **i** as in **gives**. Remind them of how the word is used in the context paragraph. (...their lives are not disturbed by contact with people.)

Critical Thinking *

- You may want to give students some simple examples to help them complete the analogies in Observing Patterns 2.

  finger is to **hand** as **toe** is to _ _ _ _.

  scissors are to **paper** as **saw** is to _ _ _ _.

- Demonstrate strategies for completing analogies by classifying words.

  a **pond** is like a small **lake**, so a **hill** is like a small _ _ _ _ _ _ _ _.

  lightest is the opposite of **heaviest**, so **smallest** is the opposite of _ _ _ _ _ _ _.

4. Write list words by unscrambling the syllables on the caves.

u us ly al — usually
mies en e — enemies
mer i ca A — America

5. Complete the sets with a list word that has the same spelling pattern.

a) cheer	steer	deer
b) damper	hamper	camper
c) stones	telephones	bones
d) captain	fountain	mountain
e) trees	knees	bees
f) welcome	handsome	become

Hint! Look for the rhyming pattern at the ends of the words.

Discovering Patterns

berries usually enemies mountain grizzlies digging largest knives deer America bones wives camper bees lives become

1. Write the singular forms of these plural list words.
knives **wives** **lives** knife wife life
What change is made to the singular when the plural is formed?
change the f to v and add s
2. Write the singular forms of these plural words.
berry **berries** **grizzlies** **enemies** grizzly enemy
What change is made to the word when the plural is formed?
change the y to i and add es
3. Which list word is spelled the same in the singular and the plural form? deer

POWERBOOSTER

- Words that have the pattern **ife** as in **life** form the plural by changing the **f** to v and adding **-s**.
- Words that end in a consonant plus **y** such as **story** form the plural by changing y to **i** and adding **-es**.

70

Discovering Patterns

1. Note with students that in each case the word ends in **-fe**. Have them try to pronounce **knifes** several times quickly and note what happens to the /f/. How do they think the spelling change happened?

2. Note with students that in each case the base word ends in a **consonant** + **y.** Words ending in a **vowel** + **y** simply add **-s** when forming the plural.

vowel + y	consonant + y
monkeys	berries
bluejays	galaxies
trays	cities
bays	groceries
toys	dairies
chimneys	memories
valleys	lilies

3. Talk about other words in English which do not usually have a plural form (**deer**, **moose**, **sheep**, **salmon**). Discuss how these words are different from collective nouns, where the noun refers to something that is not usually counted. (See ESL, p. 120.)

4. Although for spelling purposes it is important to hear and pronounce each of the four syllables in the word **usually**, remind students that it is **usually** pronounced with three syllables.

5. Students can underline the parts of each word which contain the same spelling pattern (cap**tain**, foun**tain**, moun**tain**.)

Oral Language and Literature

- Bees seem to fascinate people. Maybe that's why we have several idioms based on bees and their **bee**haviour! Students can work on their own or with a partner to illustrate and present their image of each of the idioms given here.

busy as a bee
a bee in one's bonnet
as happy as a bee in clover
make a bee line

- Alternatively, you could ask students to match the idioms with their meanings.
  - proceed in a straight line (as a bee does on its way home)
  - having some particular idea, usually slightly crazy
  - very, very busy, or active
  - happy and satisfied (as a bee when it finds lots of flowers).

Exploring Patterns

1. Encourage the students to write sentences that sound interesting even if they make little sense. Have the students read their sentences to a partner. Students can make 'bear tracks' with their sentences written on each one, and decorate the classroom.

> The babies and the bullies love the candies on the shelves.
>
> Thieves stole the leaves for their hobbies from the families.

2. You many wish to have students invent their own sentences with the three words. For ESL students, it may be helpful to give some examples of how the word **usually** is used in a sentence to tell how often an action occurs.

Usually, I go to bed at nine. (but sometimes I stay up till ten)
I **usually** go to bed at nine. (and that's when I'll go tonight)
I go to bed at nine, **usually**. (but just for tonight I'm staying up till eleven)

3. Remind students that when the underlined words are changed from singular to plural, other words in the sentence will likely need to be altered as well. It may be helpful to complete the first sentence with the class, and to note the additional changes required. (The **campers** took **knives** with **them** when **they** went camping in the mountains.)

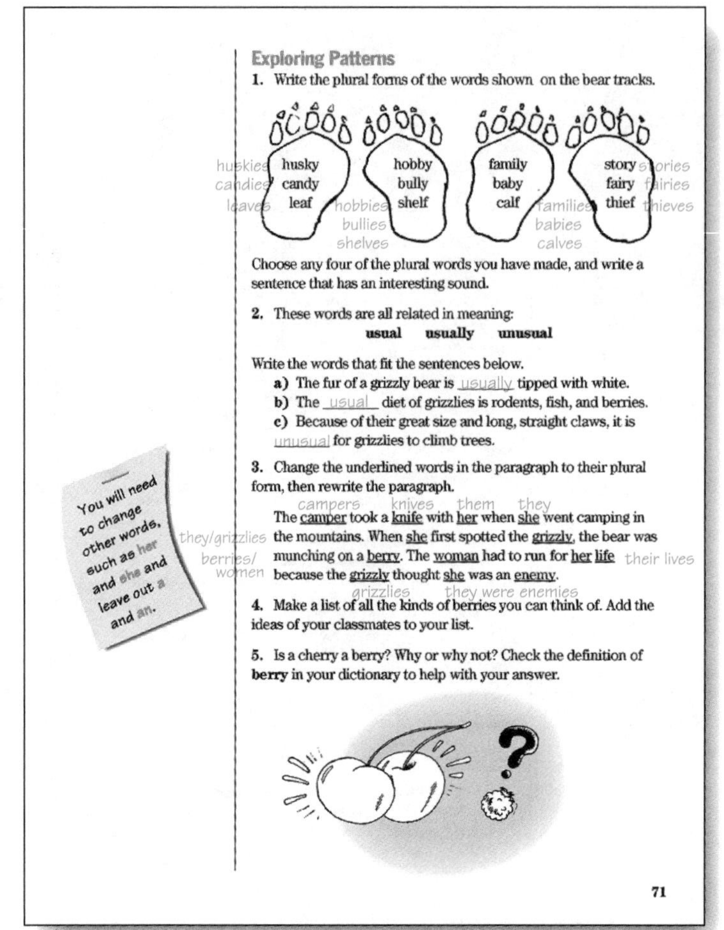

Exploring Patterns

1. Write the plural forms of the words shown on the bear tracks.

Choose any four of the plural words you have made, and write a sentence that has an interesting sound.

2. These words are all related in meaning:

usual **usually** **unusual**

Write the words that fit the sentences below.

a) The fur of a grizzly bear is usually tipped with white.
b) The usual diet of grizzlies is rodents, fish, and berries.
c) Because of their great size and long, straight claws, it is unusual for grizzlies to climb trees.

3. Change the underlined words in the paragraph to their plural form, then rewrite the paragraph.

The camper (campers) took a knife (knives) with her (them) when she (they) went camping in the mountains. When she (they/grizzlies) first spotted the grizzly, the bear was munching on a berry (berries/). The woman (women) had to run for her life (their lives) because the grizzly (grizzlies) thought she was an enemy (they were enemies).

You will need to change other words, such as her and she and leave out a and an.
?

4. Make a list of all the kinds of berries you can think of. Add the ideas of your classmates to your list.

5. Is a cherry a berry? Why or why not? Check the definition of **berry** in your dictionary to help with your answer.

71

5. Many of the berries are compound words (**blue/berries**, **cran/berries**, **black/berries**). Students are required to read the definition of **berry** carefully in order to answer the question. A cherry is a small, juicy fruit; it is not a berry since it contains a pit rather than many small seeds.

ESL

• The English use of collective nouns is often especially difficult for ESL students. The concept should be introduced carefully, and practised often. Words such as **weather**, **information**, **luggage**, and **furniture** are collective nouns in English. In some other languages, these nouns can be counted. ("The **works** are hard.")

• Teach collective nouns as words that do not usually require a plural ending. Display lists of collective nouns in the classroom, and add to them as words arise in everyday speech and writing.

> work furniture money weather rain
> snow hail fog milk water sugar
> salt flour sand

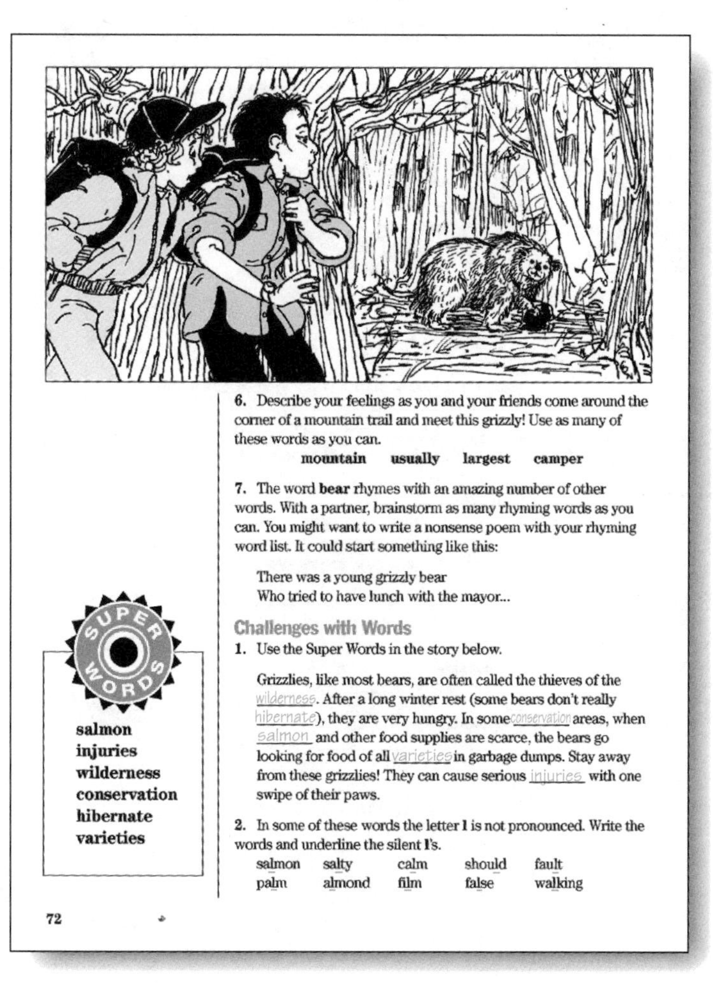

6. Describe your feelings as you and your friends come around the corner of a mountain trail and meet this grizzly! Use as many of these words as you can.

mountain **usually** **largest** **camper**

7. The word **bear** rhymes with an amazing number of other words. With a partner, brainstorm as many rhyming words as you can. You might want to write a nonsense poem with your rhyming word list. It could start something like this:

There was a young grizzly bear
Who tried to have lunch with the mayor...

SUPER WORDS

salmon
injuries
wilderness
conservation
hibernate
varieties

Challenges with Words

1. Use the Super Words in the story below.

Grizzlies, like most bears, are often called the thieves of the wilderness. After a long winter rest (some bears don't really hibernate), they are very hungry. In some conservation areas, when salmon and other food supplies are scarce, the bears go looking for food of all varieties in garbage dumps. Stay away from these grizzlies! They can cause serious injuries with one swipe of their paws.

2. In some of these words the letter **l** is not pronounced. Write the words and underline the silent **l**'s.

salmon	salty	calm	should	fault
palm	almond	film	false	walking

72

6. Some students may prefer to write their description in the form of a dialogue between two hikers who come upon a bear.

"That's the largest bear I've ever seen!"

"Is it going to attack? I'm scared!"

"We better run down the mountain."

"No! Don't run. That usually makes them angry."

"How will we get back to our camper then?"

"Help!"

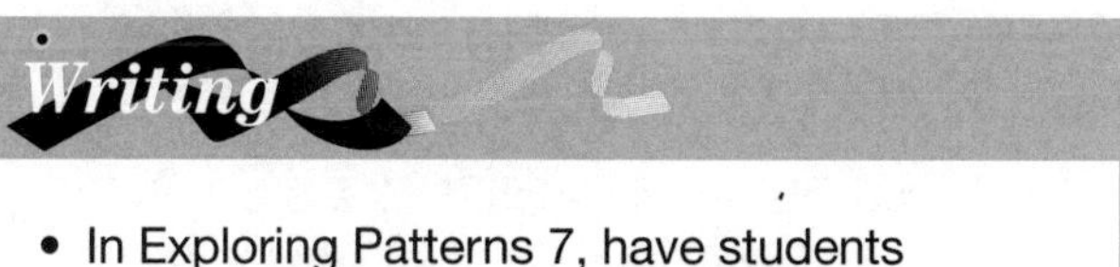

- In Exploring Patterns 7, have students brainstorm words rhyming with **bear** in the whole group. List the words on a large sheet of chart paper or the chalkboard for reference as they write their nonsense poems. Then encourage them to work with a partner or in a small group to do the writing and share with another pair or group.

7. When students have brainstormed as many words as possible they might sort them into pairs for rhyming couplets. You may wish to supply sample couplets to help them. (Did you see the biggest bear?/It was standing over there.)

Discuss all the patterns for spelling /air/ — **air**, **are**, **ear**.

Challenges with Words

1. Discuss the patterns for adding plural endings to the Super Words **injury** and **variety**. You might also want students to list words, such as **conservation**, **salmon**, and **wilderness**, which have no plural forms. Students may want to add these words to their Personal Review Lists.

2. Have students brainstorm other words with a silent **l**. Note that **l** is usually pronounced when it occurs before **t**. The final /lt/ may be difficult for some students to hear.

silent l	l before t
would, talking, almond, calm, could, stalking, psalm	halt, malt, quilt, gilt, welt, bolted, salt, fault, guilt, melting, pelt, moulted

3. Students can sort the words in groups according to whether they are: irregular plurals, change the **y** to **i**, add **-es**, and so on.

You might have students try to write a forest story using as many of these plurals as they can.

4. Have students choose one of these words and develop a word web for it. Encourage them to explore all the meanings for a particular word.

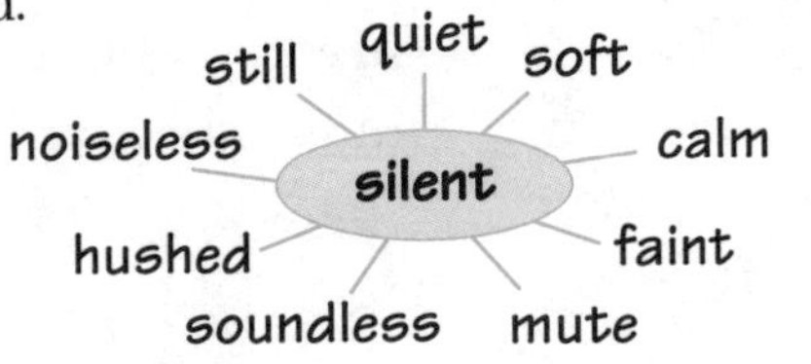

5. Students may want to write sentences or a short paragraph about bears with some of these words.

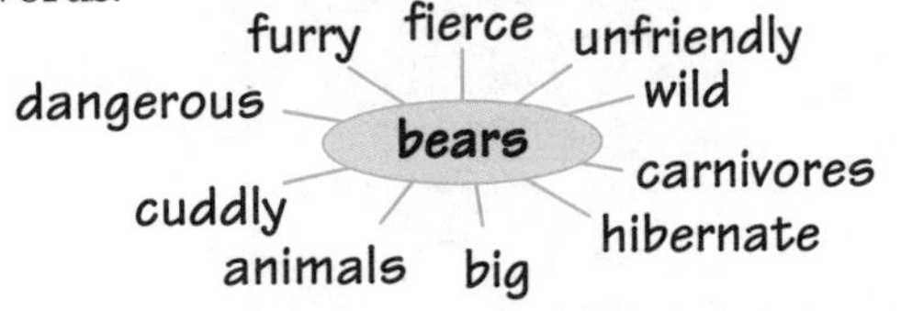

6. Suggest that conservation can also take place in urban environments. Have students talk about conserving water, as well as clean air and soil, before writing their paragraphs.

New Words

7. Make a 'New Words Menu' for a totally New Food Restaurant. Have students think of as many 'new' foods as they can. These can be new packaging ideas (pizza pockets), or foods from other countries that are new in Canada (patties, burritos).

salmon
moose
caribou
deer

women

geese
mice

grasses
patches
bunches

factories
varieties
injuries
lilies

wives
calves
wolves

3. Write the plural forms for all the words in the forest. Then sort them into groups and say how the plural for each group is formed.

variety
salmon
factory
injury
caribou
woman
goose
patch
moose
wife
bunch
mouse
wolf
grass
lily
calf
deer

4. Here are six words that describe the wilderness. Write a synonym for each word.

silent untamed vacant lovely hazardous deserted

5. List six of your own words to describe bears. Write synonyms for your words.

6. One meaning for the Super Word **conservation** is 'the protection and management of forests, rivers, and wildlife'. Write a paragraph about what conservation means to you. Choose one of the topics below or make up your own. Look at the Super Words to help you get ideas.

- Animals need wilderness areas untouched by people.
- Wilderness areas are important for people as well as animals.

NEW WORDS

granola bars
freeze-dried
trail mix

7. The new words are all things that are handy to eat on a trip to the woods. Write the words that fit each sentence.

a) Packets of freeze-dried food are handy on a camping trip.
b) She carried granola bars in her pocket as emergency snacks.
c) Our trail mix spilled all over the inside of my knapsack.

73

The New Food Restaurant

Menu

Lunch

Burritos
Enchiladas
Pizza Pockets
Tacos
Hottie Patties
Gyros
Pita Bread
Pasties

Special Needs

- The use of word sorts is an effective means of reinforcing the patterns for spelling plurals. Supply each group with a stack of cards, with a plural noun written on each card. One quarter of the words used add **-s** to form a plural, one quarter add **-es**, one quarter change the **y** to **i**, one quarter change the **f** to **-ves**.

Have students shuffle each deck thoroughly. Challenge the group to sort the cards into the four patterns for plurals, as shown. They could also give the singular form of each word.

add -s	add -es	y to i	f to v
shoes	wishes	activities	wolves
cars	bushes	candies	calves
books	boxes	ponies	halves
computers	potatoes	fries	shelves

Curriculum Connection

• Students may enjoy finding out more about grizzlies. Picture files, filmstrips, and magazines such as *Owl*, *World*, and *Canadian Geographic*, or CD-ROMs on animals or mammals may provide pictures as well as information.

• Have students proofread the following paragraph on bears and indicate misspelled words.

> I would love to own a campper and travel evywhere in it. I'd visit campsites across North Amerika, especially the ones in mountin areas. Camping can be dangarus, and lifes have been lost, usully because of carelessness. Don't eat strange berrys, because they may be poisonous. Clean up your campsite, because grizzlys are in some parts of Canada and they think humans are emenies. Also be careful if you camp during dear hunting season, since you could be mistaken for a deer. Knifes are important camping tools, but acidents can happen if you leave the blade open. As long as you are careful, camping can be great fun!

Assessment

It is important to help students identify the cause(s) of their errors. Can they see a consistent pattern, such as not changing the **y** to **i** (**candy/candies**)? Discuss strategies for learning to spell plurals. Stress that learning to spell is a life-long process, and that many adults still need to check the dictionary for plurals such as **potatoes** and **tomatoes**.

Follow-up

• Provide individual or small-group mini-lessons to reinforce the patterns for forming plurals.

• Monitor the students' everyday writing for the spelling of plurals. If problems persist, review the unit or refer to the activities in Unit 27 of *Sharing the Secrets: Teach Your Child to Spell* pp. 93-98 or *The Student Editor's Guide to Words*.

Teacher's Notes

Syllables and stress

dív/er
ín/stru/ments
in/form/á/tion

Patterns

In English, one syllable in each word is given major stress when we speak, and the other syllables are often 'swallowed' or pronounced very quickly and without emphasis. This can cause spelling difficulties with words such as **ínterested**, particularly for ESL students. Breaking words into smaller units such as syllables can help students spell the longer words they encounter in the middle years of elementary school. For example, if students split the word **dangerous** into three parts (**dáng/er/ous**) they can use different strategies to focus on the difficult parts.

Although many longer words have a secondary stress in addition to the primary stress, this concept is too complex for many students at this level.

Preknowledge

Help students understand the following concepts as they work with the patterns in this unit.

- A syllable is a word part that contains one vowel sound.
- One syllable in each word is pronounced with more stress than the others.

More Patterns

Other patterns you might wish to review or introduce in this unit include the following.

- The **-ed** ending indicates the past tense in a verb (**discovered**, **locked**).
- Base words change when **-ing** is added (**beginning**, **exploring**).
- Plural words most often end in **s** (**instruments**, **treasures**).
- The suffixes **-tion** and **-ous** can be added to base words (**dangerous**, **information**). Adding **-ous** changes a noun to an adjective, while adding **-tion** changes a verb to a noun.

Professional Notebook

Some intermediate students have difficulty spelling multisyllabic words because they are not clearly enunciating the words and syllables. They need to be taught the strategy of saying words clearly and in syllables to help the spelling process. Teach students to use syllables to make smaller, more manageable units for using other strategies (e.g., visualization).

(Tarasoff 51)

Sharing the Secrets with Kids

The way to count the syllables in a longer word is to put your hand under your chin and feel when your jaw drops as you say a word. Pronouncing a vowel causes the lower jaw to 'drop'.

Syllables and Stress

spécial discóvered

discovered
instruments
carefully
interested
special
beginning
science
information
dangerous
exploring
geography
pollution
diver
least
locked
treasures

Exploring Under the Sea

People have always been interested in the treasures which lie under the sea. Some search for gold or silver locked in a sunken ship. Others look for valuable mineral deposits and oil. The beginning of serious deep-sea exploration was 100 years ago when telegraph cables were first laid across the Atlantic Ocean. Recently, underwater science has been devoted to carefully exploring and mapping the geography of the ocean floor. Scientists have discovered underwater mountain ranges, deep trenches, and information about the least known forms of life—bottom feeding fish. While it is dangerous for a diver to descend too deeply, special diving compartments and instruments have been invented to make exploration safer. Unfortunately, in recent years scientists have discovered that pollution is a problem in the oceans.

Observing Patterns

1. Write the list words that have **-ed** and **-ing** endings. Underline the base word in each.
   (explore)
   discovered interested beginning exploring locked
2. Write the list words that mean the opposite of these words.
   ordinary carelessly safe most
   special carefully dangerous least
3. Write the three list words that would be found in the dictionary between these words.
   region / universe
   special science treasures

74

Precheck

It would be useful to conduct a class survey to find those list words that caused the most difficulty. How many of them contained unstressed syllables as in **ínterested**? This could be done following the self-correction of the Precheck. Highlight the study of the more difficult words and stress the use of the five Study Steps.

Dictation

I **discovered** a loonie in my pocket.
Telescopes are **instruments** for studying the stars.
Look **carefully** before crossing the road.
Are you **interested** in playing video games?
He's a **special** friend of mine.
I'm **beginning** to learn about computers.
My favourite subject is **science**.
Research is about gathering **information**.
Grizzly bears can be **dangerous**.
We got lost **exploring** the forest.
Geography is about places and people.
Pollution makes the air dirty.
The **diver** swam thirty metres under water.
The **least** known creatures live near the ocean floor.
My dad **locked** his keys in the car!
Her **treasures** were kept locked up safely.

Words in Context

The paragraph that opens each unit provides an opportunity for shared reading and helps students gain a clear understanding of the list words. Ask students to look for words of three or four syllables in the paragraph, other than the underlined list words (**míneral**, **compártment**, **unfórtunately**). You may wish to have them indicate orally which syllable in each is usually given the greatest stress.

Observing Patterns

1. Examine the word **exploring** with students. Notice that when **-ing** is added to a word ending in silent **e**, the **e** is dropped. Reinforce this pattern with similar words. Have students supply other words that fit the pattern (**hope/hoping**; **come/coming**; **love/loving**; **stare/staring**; **give/giving**; **bore/boring**).

Another pattern for adding **-ing** or **-ed** is seen in **begin/beginning**. Notice that **begin** ends in a **vowel** + **consonant** and that the final syllable is stressed. In such words, the final consonant is usually doubled when adding **-ed** or **-ing**. The doubling also often occurs in one-syllable words ending in a **vowel** + **a single consonant**.

adding -ing or -ed to vowel + consonant		
occúr	occúrring	occúrred
forgét	forgétting	—
slíp	slípping	slípped
swím	swímming	—
ríp	rípping	rípped
sláp	slápping	slápped

2. Remind students that opposites are called antonyms and that one word can have more than one antonym. For example, the antonyms of **ordinary** include: **different**, **special**, **curious**, **strange**, **uncommon**, **incredible**, and **amazing**.

3. Dictionary exercises help students become comfortable with and skilled at finding words listed alphabetically. A quick jotting of the alphabet across the top of the notebook can help provide reference points. Note that there are no list words beginning with **r** or **u**, so that students are looking for words beginning with **s** and **t**.

4. Unscrambling exercises help students focus on the sequence of syllables. Remind students that the syllables are divided as they would be in a dictionary (though obviously not in the correct order here), but not necessarily as they are divided in normal speech. A more natural division for **pollútion**, for example would be **poll/ú/tion**.

Discovering Patterns

1. Depending on regional variations, **ínterested** and **geógraphy** may be placed in the three- or four-syllable category.

If students are experiencing difficulty identifying the syllables in the longer words, have them say the words aloud while tapping for each vowel sound.

2. If students are having trouble finding where the stress is placed, try pronouncing the word for them with the stress on a different syllable so they can hear the difference (**in/strúm/ents** instead of **ín/strum/ents**). It may be effective for some students to do this exercise orally with a partner.

4. Unscramble the syllables on the shipwreck to make four list words.

phy ra og ge — geography
tion in for ma — information
stru in ments — instruments
lu pol tion — pollution

5. Write the list words that have double consonants.

carefully beginning pollution

Discovering Patterns

discovered instruments carefully interested
special beginning science information
dangerous exploring geography pollution
diver least locked treasures

1. Draw four columns in your notebook, add the headings below, then write the list words under the correct heading.

one syllable	two syllables	three syllables	four syllables
least locked	special science diver treasures	discovered instruments carefully beginning dangerous exploring pollution	interested information geography

2. a) Listen to where the stress is placed in the words with three syllables. Write the three-syllable words that have the stress placed on the first syllable. Put a stress mark over the first syllable.

Example: *súddenly*

ínstruments
cárefully
dángerous

b) Write the three-syllable words that have the stress placed on the second syllable. Put a stress mark over the second syllable.

Example: *recóver*

discóvered exploríng
begínning pollútion

POWERBOOSTER

- In words of more than one syllable, stress is placed on only one of the syllables.

75

Special Needs

- Some students may need more practice in seeing and hearing the sequence of syllables. They may hear and write the first and last syllables in a word but omit those in the middle. Or, they may write the stressed syllables, but be unclear about the unstressed, as in **interested**.
- Make a deck of cards on which a single syllable is written for each list word of two or more syllables (a total of 41 cards). Give two groups of students half the deck each, making sure both halves contain the syllable cards to form complete words.Have them shuffle the deck, then unscramble it to match the list words.

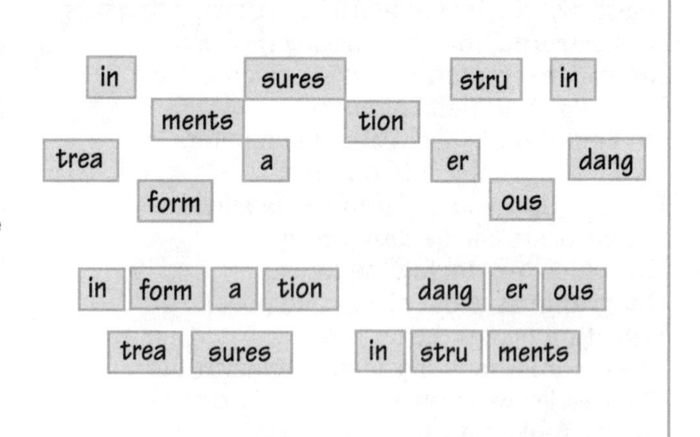

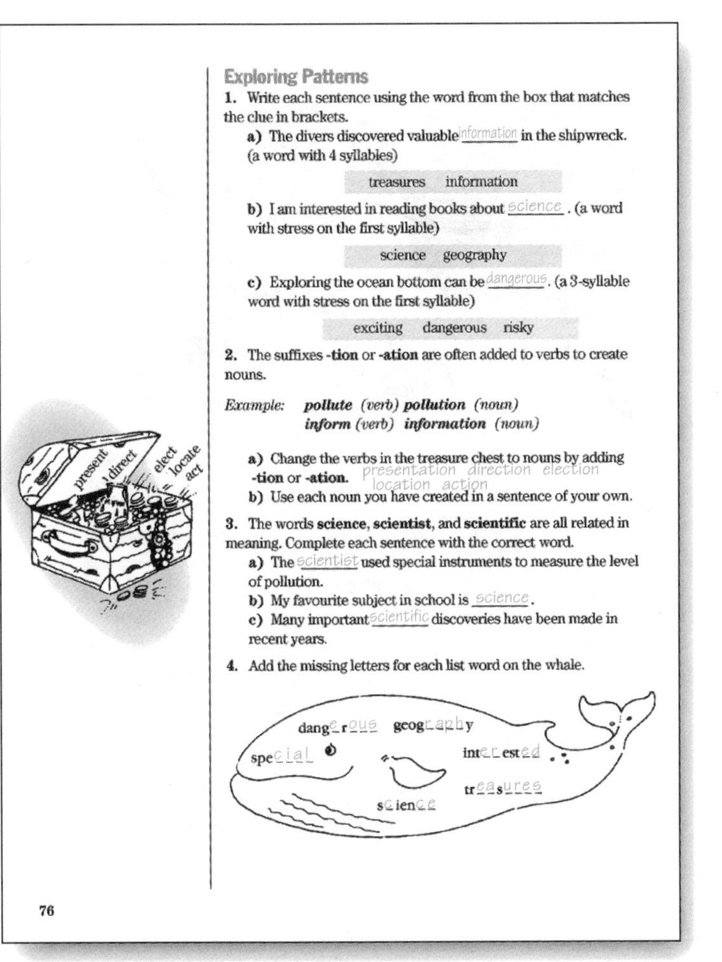

Exploring Patterns

1. Write each sentence using the word from the box that matches the clue in brackets.

a) The divers discovered valuable information in the shipwreck. (a word with 4 syllables)

treasures information

b) I am interested in reading books about science . (a word with stress on the first syllable)

science geography

c) Exploring the ocean bottom can be dangerous. (a 3-syllable word with stress on the first syllable)

exciting dangerous risky

2. The suffixes **-tion** or **-ation** are often added to verbs to create nouns.

Example: ***pollute*** *(verb)* ***pollution*** *(noun)*
inform *(verb)* ***information*** *(noun)*

a) Change the verbs in the treasure chest to nouns by adding **-tion** or **-ation.**
presentation direction election location action

b) Use each noun you have created in a sentence of your own.

3. The words **science, scientist,** and **scientific** are all related in meaning. Complete each sentence with the correct word.

a) The scientist used special instruments to measure the level of pollution.

b) My favourite subject in school is science.

c) Many important scientific discoveries have been made in recent years.

4. Add the missing letters for each list word on the whale.

76

Exploring Patterns

1. It is important for students to realize that while all the choices fit the blanks in terms of meaning, the correct answer must contain the number of syllables and/or stress indicated in brackets.

2. Students may also find it helpful to use the verb and noun forms in separate sentences and to examine the function of these words in the sentences.

Point out to students that the **e** is dropped when **-tion** is added to **locate**. Have them examine words such as **pollúte**, **admíre**, **cálculate**, **accúse**, **élevate**, and see if they can find a pattern.

3. Have students note how the stress shifts in **scientífic**. Students can be encouraged to find the forms of other list words and then use each word in a sentence.

Ask students to consult the spelling chart shown here and find other words which match the spelling of the initial /s/ in **science**. Have students extend the chart by adding the /f/ as in **geography** and the /sh/ as in **special**.

sound	spelling
/i/	aisle, either, eye, ice, high
/g/	go, ghost, guess
/h/	he, who
/m/	me, climbing, solemn
/n/	gnaw, knife, nut
/r/	run, rhythm, wrong
/s/	cent, psalm, say, science, sword, scissors, scenic, scenery, ascend, scent

4. Students can highlight the missing letters by writing them in a different colour, printing them in capitals, or with a darker pen. The cloze procedure helps students focus on the parts of words that are difficult to spell, such as the **ea** in **treasures**.

ESL

- Stress patterns in English may cause difficulties for ESL students when syllables in their first language are spoken with approximately equal stress. English speakers hurry over our unstressed syllables, making them difficult to hear and write. For example, in **informátion**, we hear mainly the stressed vowel **á**.
- Have students note that some base words change stress when suffixes are added, while others keep the same stress.
- Use activities such as those suggested in Special Needs (p. 126) and Multiple Intelligences (p.129) to help students recognize and work with stress patterns.

Stress	
changes	**stays the same**
infórm/ informátion	cáreful/cárefully
geógraphy/geográphic	explóre/explóring
scíence/scientífic	begín/begínning
	pollúte/pollútion
	discóver/discóvered
	ínterest/ínterested

5. The first writing exercise in each unit focusses on the list words. Talk about **submersibles** with students, and have them look up the word in a dictionary or encyclopedia if it is unfamiliar. You may want to use questions such as the following as a scaffold for their writing:

- What kind of ship is a submersible?
- Why do scientists want to explore the bottom of the sea?
- What do you think they might find there?

6. Students may wish to research the topic of underwater life before writing. Encourage the group to make this a collaborative effort, sharing magazine articles, photos, encyclopedia or CD-ROM information that may be of use. Encourage them to draw, paint, or model their deep sea creature.

Challenges with Words

1. Have students count the number of syllables and locate the stress in each list word. Ask them to note what happened to the base words **occur** and **submerge** when endings were added. Encourage them to explore the word histories of **marine** and **ecology** and to look for other words from the same roots. Students might consult an etymological dictionary for this activity.

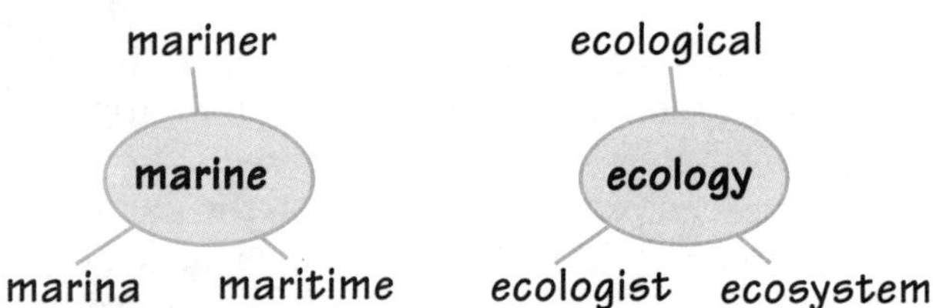

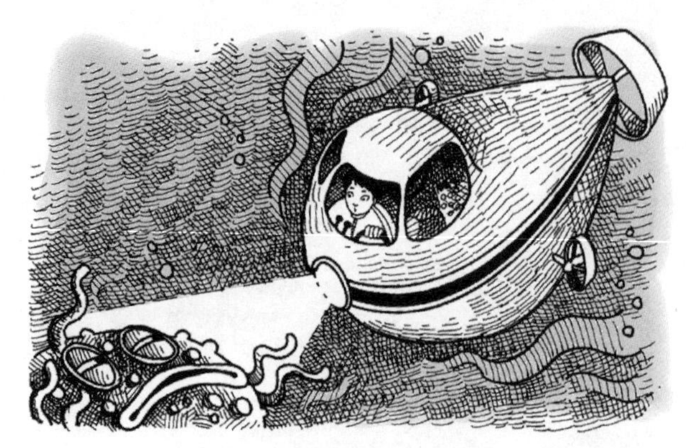

5. Check your instruments! You're going down 3000 metres to the bottom of the sea. Write a few sentences about what is going on in your submersible vessel. Use some of these list words in your sentences.

diver **instruments** **carefully** **interested**

6. Imagine that you have discovered a new kind of sea creature at the bottom of an ocean trench. Describe your imaginary creature. Remember, it lives in total darkness and under the enormous pressure of the sea water.

SUPER WORDS

marine
occurring
currents
ecology
submersible
trenches

Challenges with Words

1. Use the Super Words in the following sentences.
   - **a)** It is important to study ecology in order to understand how animals survive in the wild.
   - **b)** Salmon is both a marine and a freshwater fish.
   - **c)** During springtime river currents often wash away soil from river banks.
   - **d)** A submarine is a submersible boat or ship.
   - **e)** Deep sea trenches have been found in parts of the ocean.
   - **f)** Petroleum is a naturally occurring form of oil.

77

Multiple Intelligences

- Spelling strategies for stress patterns can be designed to appeal to a variety of intelligences.

Visual/Spatial: Highlight stressed syllables using highlighter pens. Underline stressed syllables with coloured markers. Print syllables on different cards, with the stressed syllable on a vivid neon background.

Verbal/Linguistic: Practise words orally, moving the stress from one syllable to another to hear the difference in sound.

Musical/Rhythmic: Listen to the rhythmic sounds of stressed and unstressed syllables. Clap or tap the syllables giving the stressed syllable extra force. Use rhyme to emphasize rhythm patterns in the language.

Ínformátion
For the nátion

A solútion
For pollútion

Bodily/Kinesthetic: Use hands-on work with syllable cards, putting word parts together.

Logical/Mathematical: Have students classify words according to which syllable is stressed and look for patterns.

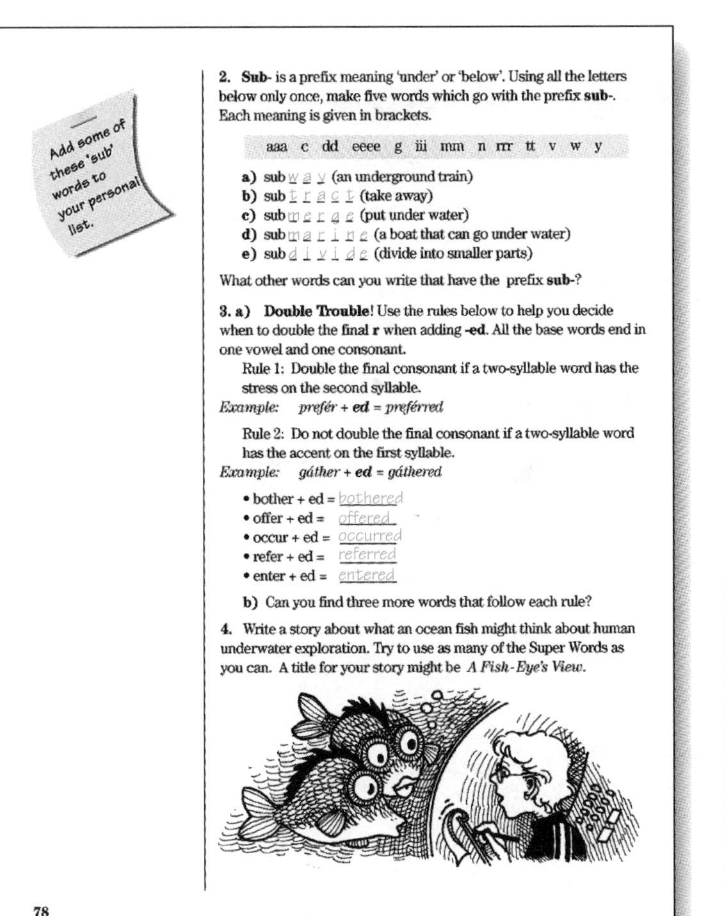

Add some of these 'sub' words to your personal list.

2. Sub- is a prefix meaning 'under' or 'below'. Using all the letters below only once, make five words which go with the prefix **sub-**. Each meaning is given in brackets.

aaa c dd eeee g iii mm n rrr tt v w y

a) sub w a y (an underground train)
b) sub t r a c t (take away)
c) sub m e r g e (put under water)
d) sub m a r i n e (a boat that can go under water)
e) sub d i v i d e (divide into smaller parts)

What other words can you write that have the prefix **sub-**?

3. a) Double Trouble! Use the rules below to help you decide when to double the final **r** when adding **-ed**. All the base words end in one vowel and one consonant.

Rule 1: Double the final consonant if a two-syllable word has the stress on the second syllable.
Example: prefér + **ed** = *preférred*

Rule 2: Do not double the final consonant if a two-syllable word has the accent on the first syllable.
Example: gáther + **ed** = *gáthered*

- bother + ed = bothered
- offer + ed = offered
- occur + ed = occurred
- refer + ed = referred
- enter + ed = entered

b) Can you find three more words that follow each rule?

4. Write a story about what an ocean fish might think about human underwater exploration. Try to use as many of the Super Words as you can. A title for your story might be *A Fish-Eye's View*.

78

2. Have students consult their dictionary to find more words that begin with **sub-**. They might also note that a 'sub' is a type of sandwich shaped like a submarine.

Students might like to work in groups and make up their own prefix exercise similar to this one. Groups can exchange and complete each other's exercises.

3. This rule for doubling or not doubling the final consonant when adding **-ed** or **-ing** is quite complex, and will require a lot of practice and reinforcement. At this stage it is merely introduced, and students can work with partners to say the words aloud, listen to the stress, and decide whether to double the letter.

Double			Don't double	
word	-ing	-ed	-ing	-ed
begin	beginning	—		
happen			happening	happened
forget	forgetting	—		
listen			listening	listened
equip	equipping	equipped		
limit			limiting	limited

4. The human explorer in an underwater world is a stranger. How would she or he seem to the everyday inhabitants of that environment? Have students try to visualize the experience and brainstorm words to use before they begin to write. Encourage them to use peer editors to proofread their work.

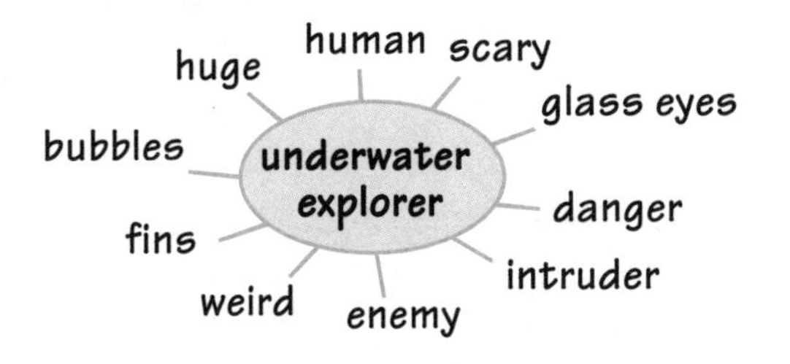

Oral Language and Literature

- Use poems such as "Eletelephony" by Laura E. Richards to practise stress and rhythm with the language. Have students say the poem aloud, noticing where the stress falls. Point out that one syllable in **however** has to be reduced to keep the rhythm (**howe'er**).

Curriculum Connection

- Students will encounter many multisyllabic words in subjects such as science and mathematics. When these long words occur it may be helpful to have students divide the word into syllables, or into base words, suffixes, and prefixes to help remember the spelling and pronunciation.
- Students might wish to do further research on marine life and ecology. Have them brainstorm topics on marine ecology, then choose one particular topic to research. They could present their research information in a variety of interesting ways, such as interview, poster, and so on. Students may want to work in small groups rather than individually.
- Remind students that they may wish to add interesting marine words to their Personal Review List.

Assessment

Following the Unit Test take another survey to find out if the special study list was eliminated. Make sure students make corrections on Column D of the Student Record Sheet.

Follow-up
Monitor students' everyday writing for spelling errors on missed syllables in words such as **interesting**, **vegetable**, **Wednesday**, **library**. Encourage them to say the words with exaggerated syllables and stress as they write them to help remember the unstressed syllables.

Teacher's Notes

Unstressed Vowel Capital Letters
Manitoba

Patterns

Unstressed (schwa) vowel

A schwa (shown phonetically as an upside down e, /ə/) is the name given to the vowel sound in unstressed syllables. Schwa vowels sound something like "uh", and can be spelled with any vowel (d**i**rection; c**o**nnection; **a**ffection; d**e**tection). Students trying to use sounding out strategies will therefore have problems spelling these words. They need visual and other strategies to help them remember the correct spelling of words with schwa vowels.

Capital letters

Students at the grade 5 level may still be uncertain whether a noun should begin with an upper- or lower-case letter. They may have trouble distinguishing between common nouns such as **province** or **country** and proper nouns which name specific places, such as **Alberta** or **Canada**. This will be particularly difficult for students coming from language backgrounds where proper nouns are not capitalized.

Preknowledge

Students should have an understanding of the following concepts as they work with the patterns in this unit.

- Proper nouns in English are the names of specific places, people, and things (**Canada**; **Doctor Kaminski**; **World War II**).
- The /ə/ (schwa) sound occurs only in unstressed syllables (syll**a**bles; sp**e**cific).

More Patterns

Other patterns you might wish to review or introduce from the list words in this unit include the following.

- The sound /f/ spelled **ph** (**photograph**).

Professional Notebook

One of the great 'secrets' about learning to spell is that it can and should be fun! When you approach the teaching of spelling with enthusiasm and view yourself as a fellow learner, you will engage your students in an ongoing exploration of the spelling system and its connection with language in general.

(Scott, *Spelling: Sharing the Secrets* 33)

Sharing the Secrets with Kids

*Learning which vowel spells a schwa sound is a lifelong process in English. People use memory tricks such as 'Did you ever see **a bun dance**?' to remember the **a** in words such as **abundant** and **abundance**. In fact, most adults make spelling mistakes with schwa vowels. It's a good idea to start a list of words that are especially difficult to spell because of a schwa sound.*

Precheck

Dictate the words in sentences that make the meaning of each list word clear. You can use the sentences below, or invent your own. Following the Precheck, have the students self-correct their lists. Observe Student Record Sheets to check that words are spelled correctly in Column B. Encourage those students who require extra study time to make a home-study sheet. You may want to include the five study steps: look, say, cover, write, check.

Dictation

That **photograph** is a good likeness of you.
How many **possible** answers are there?
Who's the most **famous** woman in Canada?
Calgary is a prairie city.
Winnipeg is the capital of **Manitoba**.
Our bus left the **station** at noon.
What **amount** of money do you have?
Oil spills harm the environment.
Put a saucer **beneath** your cup!
Which **area** of town do you live in?
Canada is the world's second largest country.
Is there any **reason** that he's late?
Alberta is one of the prairie provinces.
Canada is part of the North American **continent**.
A rich person has **millions** of dollars.
Would you like to live in the **country** or the city?

Words in Context

Have students read the passage, watching for capital letters on proper nouns. You may want to explain that 'seismological waves' are movements of the rock formation that are caused by earthquakes or produced artificially by prospectors using explosives to help them in their search for oil.

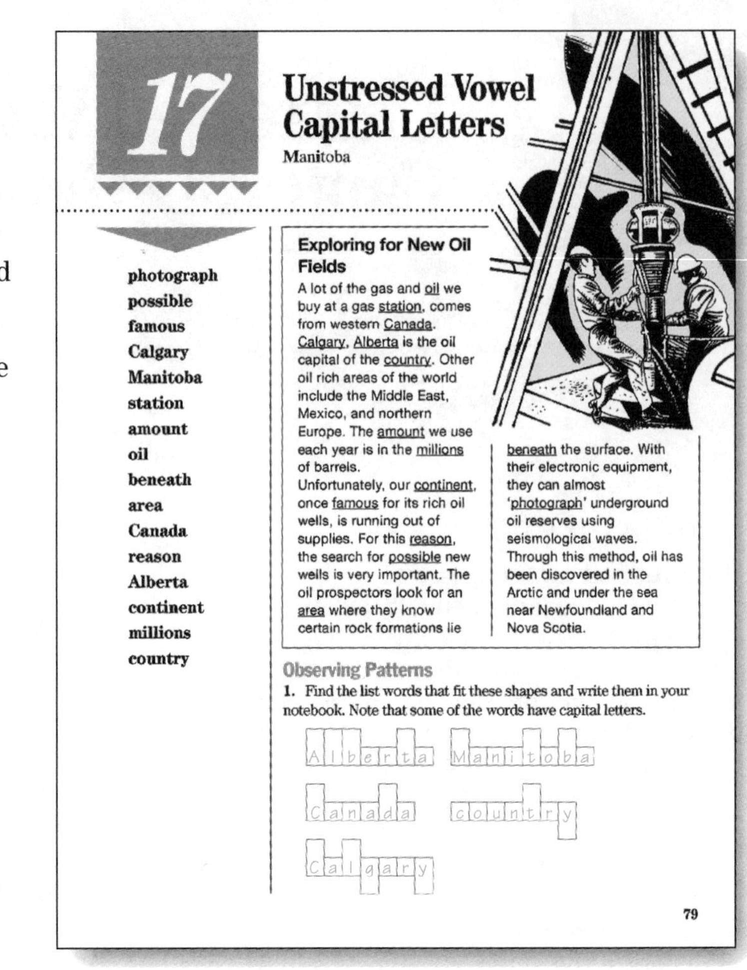

17

Unstressed Vowel
Capital Letters
Manitoba

photograph
possible
famous
Calgary
Manitoba
station
amount
oil
beneath
area
Canada
reason
Alberta
continent
millions
country

Exploring for New Oil Fields

A lot of the gas and oil we buy at a gas station, comes from western Canada. Calgary, Alberta is the oil capital of the country. Other oil rich areas of the world include the Middle East, Mexico, and northern Europe. The amount we use each year is in the millions of barrels. Unfortunately, our continent, once famous for its rich oil wells, is running out of supplies. For this reason, the search for possible new wells is very important. The oil prospectors look for an area where they know certain rock formations lie beneath the surface. With their electronic equipment, they can almost 'photograph' underground oil reserves using seismological waves. Through this method, oil has been discovered in the Arctic and under the sea near Newfoundland and Nova Scotia.

Observing Patterns

1. Find the list words that fit these shapes and write them in your notebook. Note that some of the words have capital letters.

Alberta Manitoba
Canada country
Calgary

79

Ask students to identify the list word that is not used in the paragraph and suggest why the author did not include it (**Manitoba**). Students could write a sentence of their own using the word.

Observing Patterns

1. Students could reinforce their memories of the shapes by drawing a line configuration beside each word.

Super Strategies

- Gather a list of words that are frequently misspelled by your students. Use writing folders, personal word lists, unit tests, and lists on page 264 of this book. Provide each group with seven words. Have them think of strategies for learning each of the words and record those strategies on chart paper. Then have the group meet as a whole and share strategies.

word	strategy
friend	Remember! A friend to the end
Tuesday	Say **Tu-es-day** when you write this word.
surprise	Surprise! There is an extra **r** in surprise.
then	Then answers the question **when?**
weren't	Write the words **were not** together, and kick out the **o** — weren t.
too	**Too** has too many Os
excitement	Write the word with the hard parts missing e_cit_ment.

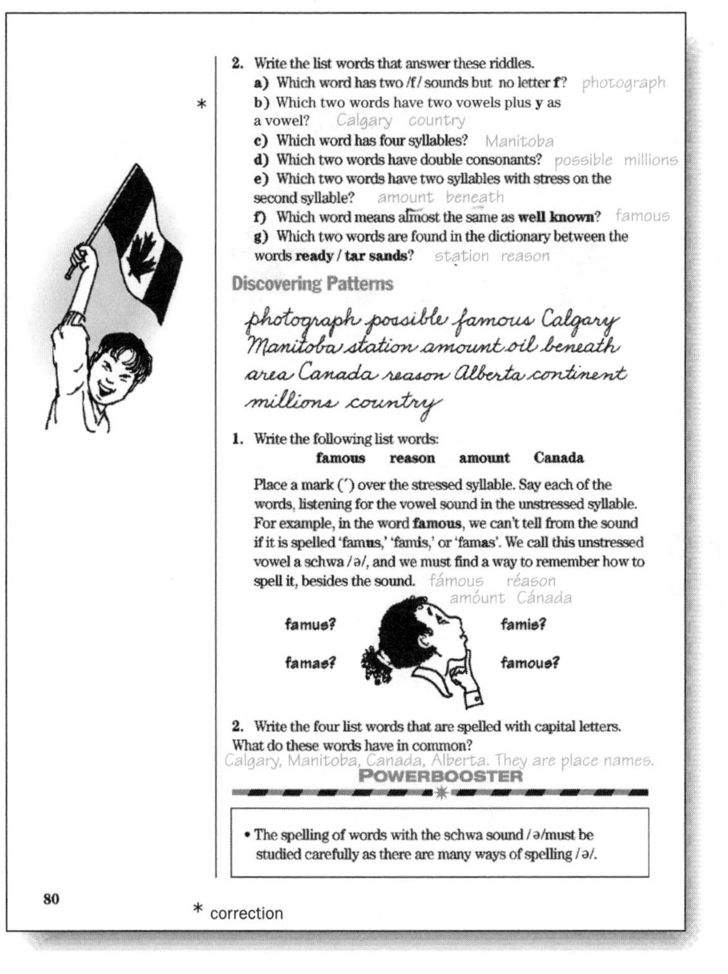
2. Write the list words that answer these riddles.
a) Which word has two /f/ sounds but no letter **f**? photograph
* b) Which two words have two vowels plus **y** as a vowel? Calgary country
c) Which word has four syllables? Manitoba
d) Which two words have double consonants? possible millions
e) Which two words have two syllables with stress on the second syllable? amount beneath
f) Which word means almost the same as **well known**? famous
g) Which two words are found in the dictionary between the words **ready** / **tar sands**? station reason

Discovering Patterns

photograph possible famous Calgary Manitoba station amount oil beneath area Canada reason Alberta continent millions country

1. Write the following list words:
famous **reason** **amount** **Canada**

Place a mark (´) over the stressed syllable. Say each of the words, listening for the vowel sound in the unstressed syllable. For example, in the word **famous**, we can't tell from the sound if it is spelled 'famus,' 'famis,' or 'famas'. We call this unstressed vowel a schwa /ə/, and we must find a way to remember how to spell it, besides the sound. fámous réason amóunt Cánada

2. Write the four list words that are spelled with capital letters. What do these words have in common?
Calgary, Manitoba, Canada, Alberta. They are place names.

POWERBOOSTER

• The spelling of words with the schwa sound /ə/must be studied carefully as there are many ways of spelling /ə/.

80

* correction

2. This activity requires students to examine the list words carefully and match the clues. Suggest that they discuss their answers with a partner.

Discovering Patterns

1. The schwa vowel creates spelling difficulties for many students. Those who rely too heavily on the sounds of words for clues to spelling are particularly challenged because the schwa sound is not clearly articulated in everyday speech.

Students must develop a set of strategies, such as finding rhyming words with the same pattern, for remembering the spelling of schwa vowels. For example, many words, such as **famous**, **dangerous**, **nervous**, and **jealous** end in the suffix **-ous**, meaning 'full of'. Some words, such as **reason**, **cotton**, **carbon**, **apron**, and **bacon** end in **-on**. Students can also use memory tricks to help them remember difficult spellings (**Alberta** starts and ends with **a**).

2. Discuss the use of place names that are proper nouns. Not all place names are proper nouns (we drove through the **city**). Proper nouns name specific places and are capitalized (We drove through **Toronto**).

Have students recognize the difference between the following.

common noun	proper noun
city	Calgary
province	Manitoba, Alberta
country	Canada

ESL

The schwa sound presents problems for many ESL students. In some cases, the unstressed syllable may not be heard. In many languages the stress patterns are predictable and students may have difficulties with the way stress 'wanders' in English (ph**ó**tograph/phot**ó**graphy). It is impossible to tell by sound alone which vowel is used to spell the schwa sound in unstressed syllables.

Use activities such as those suggested in Special Needs (p. 136), as well as the following:

• examine word structure for common patterns. For example, the endings **-ible**, **-tion**, and **-ous** are seldom stressed in English.

possible station famous

• group words season reason

• look for meaning connections. For example, look for place names that end in **a**.

Alberta Canada
Manitoba India
Nova Scotia China
British Columbia

Exploring Patterns

1. This activity provides students with a strategy for recalling schwa vowels: linking the target word with a corresponding rhyming word. These then become small 'families' of words related by sound and spelling (**millions/billions/trillions**).

2. Another strategy for focussing on the schwa vowel is through cloze activities. These vowels could be circled, underlined, or exaggerated in appearance or pronunciation.

3. Ask students to explain the relationships involved in each set of comparisons, and give additional examples: "Calgary is a city and Alberta is a province." (Note that the city is not necessarily the capital of the province.) See if students can name each province and a major city in it. Have them note the capital letters on the names of cities and provinces. (See Critical Thinking, this page.)

4. Related words often provide an excellent strategy for remembering the spelling of schwa vowels. Students need to become aware of a vital principle underlying the spelling system of English: words which are related in meaning usually are spelled alike. The letter **o** in **phóto** is easy to remember because it is sounded. When this letter becomes a schwa vowel, as in phótography, it is not clearly articulated. Encourage students to think of **photo** when spelling **photograph**.

Note how the stress shifts in the words related to **photograph**.

phótograph, photógraphy,
photógrapher, photográphic

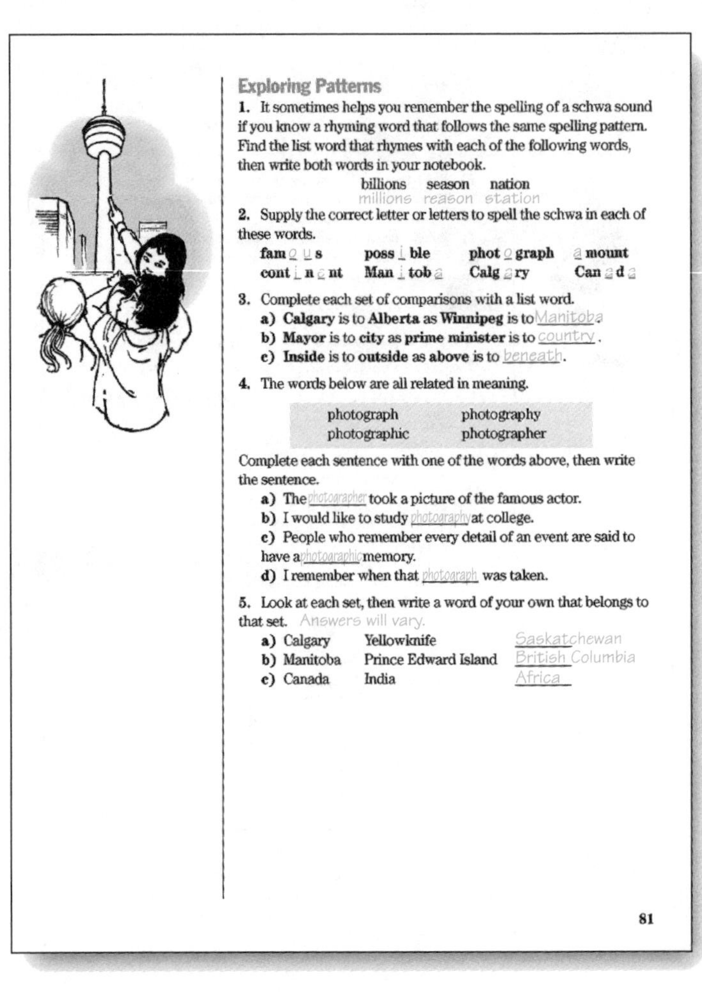

Exploring Patterns

1. It sometimes helps you remember the spelling of a schwa sound if you know a rhyming word that follows the same spelling pattern. Find the list word that rhymes with each of the following words, then write both words in your notebook.

billions season nation
millions reason station

2. Supply the correct letter or letters to spell the schwa in each of these words.

fam o u s	**poss i ble**	**phot o graph**	**a mount**
cont i n e nt	**Man i tob a**	**Calg a ry**	**Can a d a**

3. Complete each set of comparisons with a list word.

a) **Calgary** is to **Alberta** as **Winnipeg** is to Manitoba.
b) **Mayor** is to **city** as **prime minister** is to country.
c) **Inside** is to **outside** as **above** is to beneath.

4. The words below are all related in meaning.

photograph photography
photographic photographer

Complete each sentence with one of the words above, then write the sentence.

a) The photographer took a picture of the famous actor.
b) I would like to study photography at college.
c) People who remember every detail of an event are said to have a photographic memory.
d) I remember when that photograph was taken.

5. Look at each set, then write a word of your own that belongs to that set. Answers will vary.

a) Calgary Yellowknife Saskatchewan
b) Manitoba Prince Edward Island British Columbia
c) Canada India Africa

81

5. Brainstorm words in sets to ensure students have an understanding of the concept. Be sure students have understood the idea linking the first two words in each set.

breakfast foods	pets	sports
cereal	dog	hockey
waffles	cat	basketball
pancakes	budgie	soccer
toast	fish	baseball

Critical Thinking

- Exploring Patterns 3 and 5 ask students to think about analogies and the relationships among words. Using a map of Canada or their previous knowledge, have them work with a partner to write similar analogies to those in # 3, using other Canadian cities and provinces. Then, have partners switch with another pair to solve their analogies.

  Toronto is to **Ontario** as **Halifax** is to _ _ _ _ _ _ _ _ _ _.

- Encourage students to create and solve similar analogy puzzles using prepositions.

  Above is to **below** as **over** is to _ _ _ _ _.

  Before is to **after** as **early** is to _ _ _ _.

- Have students discuss the categories of words they brainstormed in Exploring Patterns 5. Would all members of these word sets begin with capital letters? Why or why not?

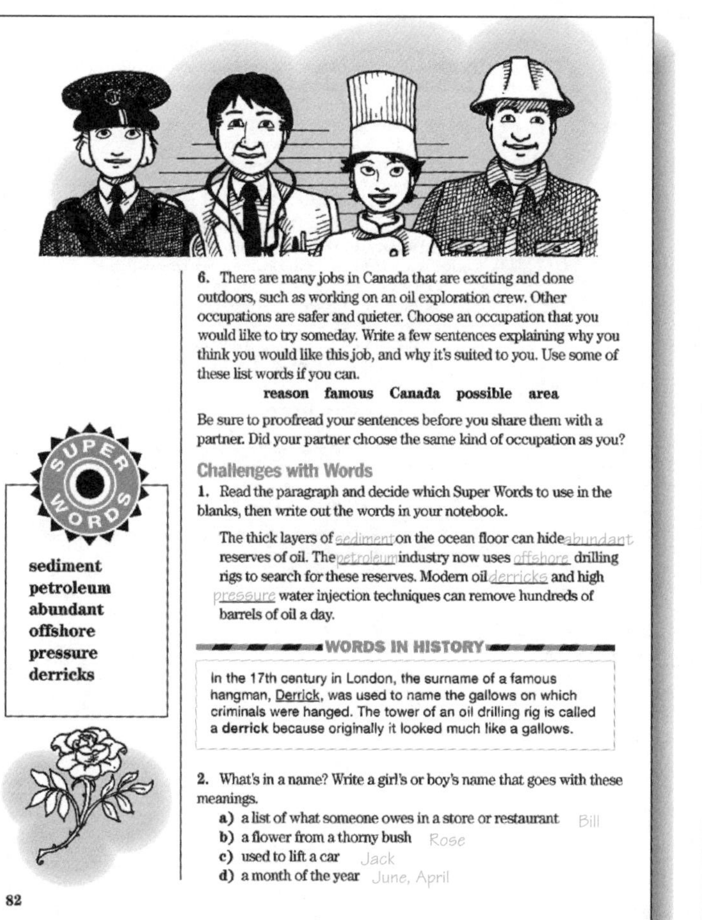

SUPER WORDS

sediment
petroleum
abundant
offshore
pressure
derricks

6. There are many jobs in Canada that are exciting and done outdoors, such as working on an oil exploration crew. Other occupations are safer and quieter. Choose an occupation that you would like to try someday. Write a few sentences explaining why you think you would like this job, and why it's suited to you. Use some of these list words if you can.

reason famous Canada possible area

Be sure to proofread your sentences before you share them with a partner. Did your partner choose the same kind of occupation as you?

Challenges with Words

1. Read the paragraph and decide which Super Words to use in the blanks, then write out the words in your notebook.

The thick layers of sediment on the ocean floor can hide abundant reserves of oil. The petroleum industry now uses offshore drilling rigs to search for these reserves. Modern oil derricks and high pressure water injection techniques can remove hundreds of barrels of oil a day.

WORDS IN HISTORY

In the 17th century in London, the surname of a famous hangman, Derrick, was used to name the gallows on which criminals were hanged. The tower of an oil drilling rig is called a **derrick** because originally it looked much like a gallows.

2. What's in a name? Write a girl's or boy's name that goes with these meanings.

a) a list of what someone owes in a store or restaurant Bill
b) a flower from a thorny bush Rose
c) used to lift a car Jack
d) a month of the year June, April

82

6. Have students survey job expectations and desires in their group. They may wish to categorize occupations under various headings.

occupations			
dangerous	peaceful	indoor	outdoor
oil rig worker	office worker	hairdresser	construction worker
miner	accountant	banker	tree planter
deep sea diver	lawyer	teacher	gardener
lumberjack	sales clerk	plumber	gas meter reader
firefighter	bank teller	doctor	snow plough driver

Challenges with Words

1. Have students substitute the /ə/ symbol for each schwa vowel in the Super Words. Remind them that all the vowels can make the schwa sound. Note that **offshore** has almost equal stress on both syllables.

/ə/ sound		
sédəmənt	pətróleəm	əbúndənt
préssəre	dérrəcks	

Words in History

Have students think of other uses of the word **derrick**. Generally, a derrick is a large machine used to lift and move heavy objects.

2. Encourage students to develop clues to fit other first and last names they can think of. Students could then illustrate these names (or find suitable pictures) and collect them in the form of a booklet. Encourage students from other language backgrounds to talk about the meanings of their names in their languages.

Writing

Editing Conferences

• Many spelling errors by students in the middle grades involve schwa vowels. In editing conferences note if the student is having difficulty with spelling unstressed vowels. Encourage students to work at these words in a positive way, by showing them how much of the word they can spell and by isolating the difficult letters using a cloze procedure. For example, if a student spells **photograph** as phot**a**graph, say "Look, you've got nine out of ten letters correct! Print the word like this: **phot_graph**, and work on remembering the **o**. Remember, it's the **o** from **photo**."

• Stress that proofreading is an important step in communicating through the printed word. Mistakes or words omitted interrupt the flow of communication and make it harder for the reader to get the intended message. On the other hand, if writing is personal and not meant to be shared, mistakes are less important.

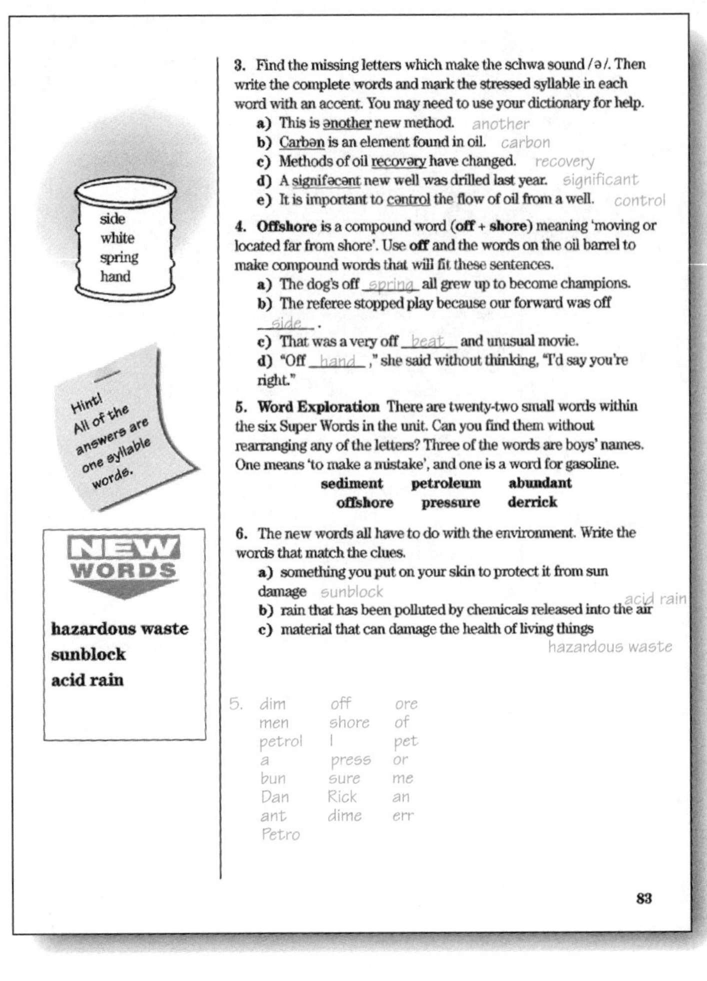

side
white
spring
hand

Hint! All of the answers are one syllable words.

NEW WORDS

hazardous waste
sunblock
acid rain

3. Find the missing letters which make the schwa sound /ə/. Then write the complete words and mark the stressed syllable in each word with an accent. You may need to use your dictionary for help.

a) This is ənother new method. another
b) Carbən is an element found in oil. carbon
c) Methods of oil recovəry have changed. recovery
d) A signifəcənt new well was drilled last year. significant
e) It is important to cəntrol the flow of oil from a well. control

4. **Offshore** is a compound word (**off** + **shore**) meaning 'moving or located far from shore'. Use **off** and the words on the oil barrel to make compound words that will fit these sentences.

a) The dog's off _spring_ all grew up to become champions.
b) The referee stopped play because our forward was off _side_.
c) That was a very off _beat_ and unusual movie.
d) "Off _hand_," she said without thinking, "I'd say you're right."

5. **Word Exploration** There are twenty-two small words within the six Super Words in the unit. Can you find them without rearranging any of the letters? Three of the words are boys' names. One means 'to make a mistake', and one is a word for gasoline.

sediment **petroleum** **abundant**
offshore **pressure** **derrick**

6. The new words all have to do with the environment. Write the words that match the clues.

a) something you put on your skin to protect it from sun damage sunblock
b) rain that has been polluted by chemicals released into the air acid rain
c) material that can damage the health of living things hazardous waste

5. dim, men, petrol, a, bun, Dan, ant, Petro, off, shore, I, press, sure, Rick, dime, ore, of, pet, or, me, an, err

83

3. Note with students that the schwa vowels all occur in unstressed syllables. Have students shift the stress in each word and pronounce it aloud, to hear how the vowel sound changes.

4. Have students do a dictionary search to list other **off** compound words and their meanings.

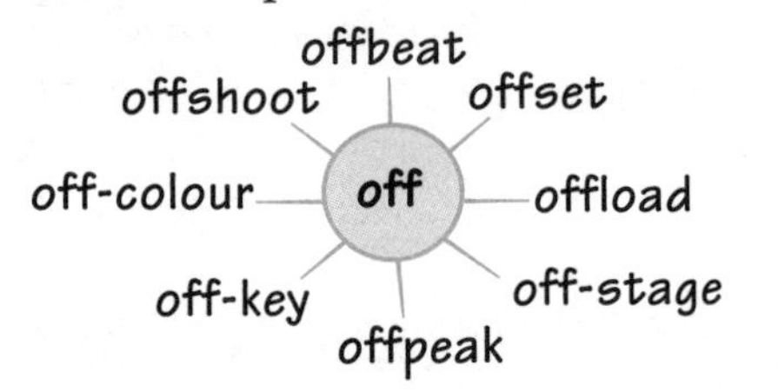

5. You might wish to give students a time limit to find the words. As an extension of the activity, have them write sentences using only the words they found.

New Words

6. Have students examine the new words for schwa vowels (házərdəs, ácəd ráin) and note the stressed syllables in each word, as well as the compound word, **sunblock**. Words such as **hazardous waste** and **acid rain** are also sometimes considered compounds.

Discuss how these new words came into general usage. Your discussion can centre around questions such as the following.

Why were they needed?
What words or phrases did they replace?
What other terms might have been invented instead?

Have students brainstorm other new words and expressions they know that have to do with the environment. They could invent some of their own.

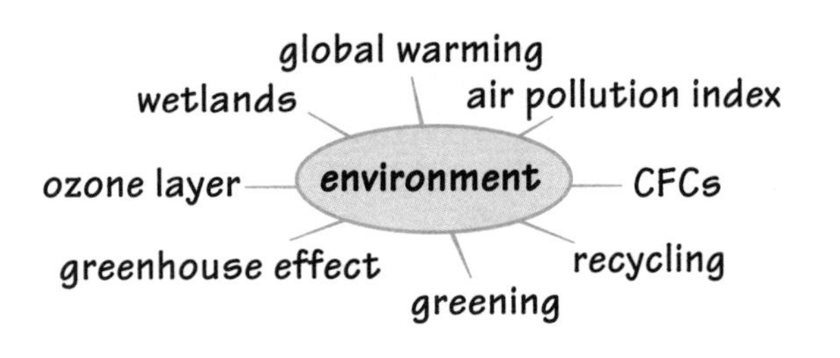

Special Needs

Students need to develop visual and memory strategies to learn the spelling of schwa vowels. Many students who are used to sounding out words will have trouble with those containing unstressed vowels. Help them develop a sense of when the words 'look right' by using activities such as the following.

- highlight the difficult letters

  possIble possible

- sort the words into patterns

  be neath
  be tween

- use cloze

  Man_tob_
  Can_d_

- use a computer keyboard and have students practise spelling the words so that they learn the feel of the sequence of letters.

  c o n t i n e n t

Curriculum Connection

Students will be facing an increasing number of multisyllabic words in their content area subjects at this level. Many of these words will include one or more schwa vowel sounds, and thus pose spelling challenges.

perímeter próvince cápital dívidend
méthod matérials hypóthesis

Assessment

Monitor students' scores on the Unit Test and compare improvement from the Precheck results. Suggest that students share the strategies they used to remember the schwa vowels and other 'tricky parts'. Continue to dictate the words to all students and to include the Super Words for those who completed Challenges with Words. Stress the importance of proofreading before you conduct the self-correction.

Follow-up

Start a class list of words containing schwa vowels for periodic review, adding new words from content areas as they occur. Suggest that students come up with a good title for this list. A special emphasis could be placed on using related words as an aid to spelling longer forms.

related words	
phóto	phótograph
defíne	definítion
compéte	competítion
glóbe	glóbal
decláre	declarátion
infórm	informátion
órigin	oríginal
invíte	invitátion

Teacher's Notes

Looking Back Units 13–17

Patterns to Review

Review the following sound-symbol relationships:

- Long **o** spelled **o** or **ow** as in **hold**, **slowly**
- Plural **-s**, **-es** as in **planets**, **matches**
- Irregular plurals
- Syllables and stress
- Schwa, capital letters

Creating a Personal Review List

Looking Back units should also provide an opportunity for students to review words and concepts which gave them particular difficulty in the preceding units. These personal study lists could involve words from a variety of sources, as suggested below:

- words misspelled in the students' Unit Tests and everyday writing (writing folders, note-books, tests)
- words used throughout the day: current themes, content areas, current events, media, holidays
- lists such as "The 200 Words Most Frequently Misspelled" and "The 200 Words Most Frequently Written" (See Appendix.)

Transfer of Spelling Knowledge

The following suggestions will help students to retain the knowledge and skills they acquire through word study and apply them in their everyday writing:

- Do not treat words on study lists as single entities, but as examples of larger spelling patterns. Build on word patterns to maximize the benefit of word study.
- Reintroduce frequently misspelled words on subsequent lists.
- When errors reoccur in student writing, ask students to recall the strategies they had used for studying these words.
- Discuss the use of spelling strategies for new words as they occur in a variety of classroom contexts.

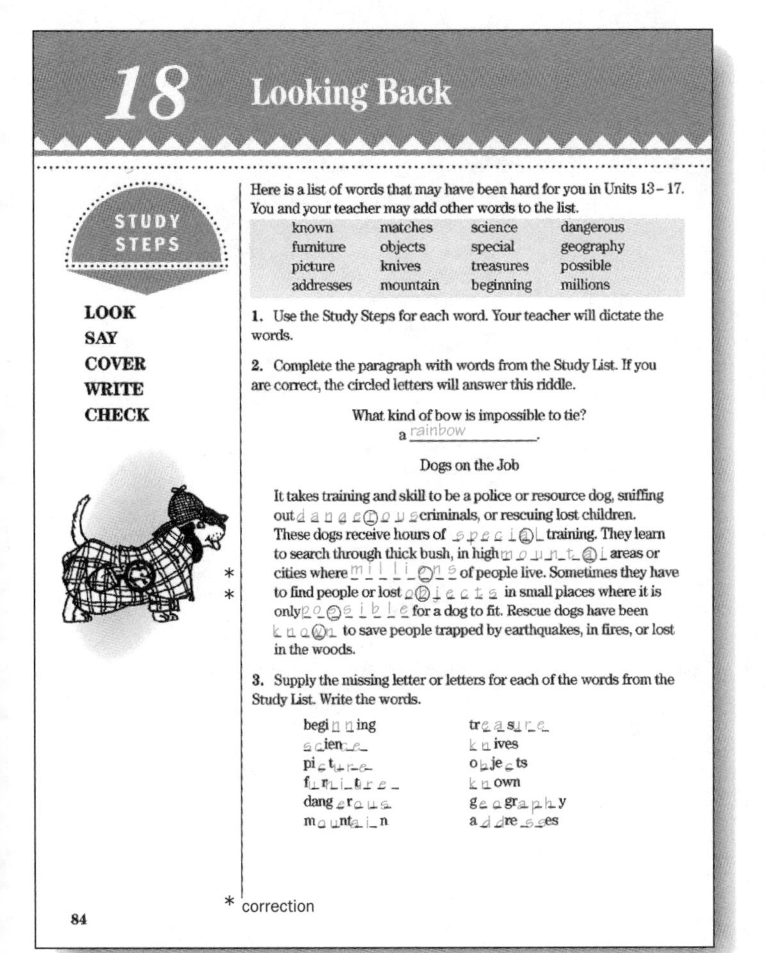

18 Looking Back

STUDY STEPS

LOOK
SAY
COVER
WRITE
CHECK

Here is a list of words that may have been hard for you in Units 13 – 17. You and your teacher may add other words to the list.

known	matches	science	dangerous
furniture	objects	special	geography
picture	knives	treasures	possible
addresses	mountain	beginning	millions

1. Use the Study Steps for each word. Your teacher will dictate the words.

2. Complete the paragraph with words from the Study List. If you are correct, the circled letters will answer this riddle.

What kind of bow is impossible to tie?
a rainbow.

Dogs on the Job

It takes training and skill to be a police or resource dog, sniffing out dangerous criminals, or rescuing lost children. These dogs receive hours of special training. They learn to search through thick bush, in high mountain areas or cities where * millions of people live. Sometimes they have * to find people or lost objects in small places where it is only possible for a dog to fit. Rescue dogs have been known to save people trapped by earthquakes, in fires, or lost in the woods.

3. Supply the missing letter or letters for each of the words from the Study List. Write the words.

beginning — treasure
science — knives
picture — objects
furniture — known
dangerous — geography
mountain — addresses

* correction

84

Dictation

How long have you **known** her?
There was no **furniture** in the room.
My **picture** was hung on the wall.
I have two e-mail **addresses**.
You need **matches** to start a fire.
There were twenty **objects** on the shelf.
Put the **knives** and forks on the table.
Have you ever climbed a **mountain**?
There's a **science** fair next month.
What a **special** day it turned out to be!
Pirates often buried their **treasures**.
I'm **beginning** to get hungry!
A frightened lion can be **dangerous**.
We're studying the **geography** of Canada.
Is it **possible** to ski in summer?
The sun is **millions** of miles away.

2. There may be local stories about the use of specially trained dogs for dangerous missions. Share these with the students, and ask whether their own pets have ever done anything extraordinary.

3. Students could use a different colour of ink or a highlighter pen to emphasize the missing letters. This may help to consolidate their visual memory for these features.

Looking Back

1. In addition to using the Study Steps, students should examine the review words and identify the difficult features of each. Then they can brainstorm strategies to be used in recalling these letter combinations. Some of the 'tricky' parts are:

- double consonants (a**dd**re**ss**es, begi**nn**ing, po**ss**ible, mi**ll**ions)
- silent letters (**k**nown, **k**nives, s**c**ience)
- letters not clearly pronounced (pi**c**ture, ma**t**ches, o**b**jects).

You might wish to have students group words by common spelling patterns.

-ture	-es	-s
furniture picture	addresses matches	objects knives treasures

4. Remind students that, while all three choices will fit the context of the sentence, only one contains the correct number of syllables and/or the desired placement of stress.

5. If students have difficulty with the plural of **knife** or **baby**, review the rules for forming plurals of such words (Unit 15).

6. Students could work in co-operative groups to focus on one pattern. Then all the groups could share their lists and create a class chart for display and reference.

/ō/ spelled			
oa (coat)	o (cold)	o_e (rope)	ow (grow)
boat float oak coal board	patio Mexico potato tomato piano	hole mole compose code shore	throw mow tow blow crow

4. Select the correct word to complete each sentence. Use the number of syllables or the placement of stress to help you select the word.

a) I found a (3 syllables) in the old trunk.

picture photograph knife

b) We ordered (stress on 1st syllable) at the restaurant.

berries spaghetti dessert

c) Science is helping to find answers for the problem of (3 syllables, stress on 2nd syllable).

disease poverty pollution

5. Write the plural form of each picture word.

6. Find at least five words to add to each pattern for spelling the long **o** sound /ō/ as in **go**. You may use words from earlier units, your personal word list, classroom themes, or other subjects.

/ō/ spelled **oa** as in **coat**	/ō/ spelled **o** as in **cold**	/ō/ spelled **o_e** as in **rope**	/ō/ spelled **ow** as in **grow**

85

ESL

Language Snapshot — Spanish

Spanish is a Romance language, related to Italian and Portuguese. It is spoken in Spain, and every country in Central and South America except Brazil and the Guianas, as well as in Puerto Rico and the Dominican Republic.

Language Features

- Spelling is phonetic: that is, spelling and pronunciation have a one-to-one correspondence in Spanish.
- There are 10 vowel sounds, compared to 22 in English. There is no direct correspondence between vowel sounds in the two languages.
- Spanish has a vowel somewhere between long **e** and short **i**, so **beet** and **bit** may be confused.
- The Spanish /a/ can be confused with the English short **a** in **cat**, short **u** in **cut**, or /är/ in **cart**.
- Final consonant clusters such as **st** and **xt** may be omitted as in **fast** and **next**.
- The Spanish sound /ch/ tends to be substituted for the English sounds /sh/, /z/, and /dj/ so that the words **sheep**, **cheep**, and **jeep** all sound, and may be spelled, the same.
- Spanish speakers may pronounce the **y** as in **yes** as a **j**.
- In English, stressed syllables are pronounced more slowly and clearly than unstressed syllables. In Spanish all syllables take the same time to pronounce. Unstressed syllables such as in **dis**/**ap**/point/**ed**, sound 'swallowed' to the Spanish ear.
- Adjectives generally follow nouns (the house **white**; a ball of **tennis**).

Dictionary Skills

1. Pronunciation Key: Each entry word in a dictionary is followed by a pronunciation guide in brackets. When you understand the symbols, you will be able to pronounce a word even if you have never heard it before.

Example: escapade (eś kə pād)

a) Study the pronunciation key below. Notice that each symbol is followed by a key word that tells you the sound.

a	hat	i	it	p	paper	v	very
ā	age	ī	ice	r	run	w	will
ä	far	j	jam	s	say	y	yet
b	bad	k	kind	sh	she	z	zero
ch	child	l	land	t	tel	zh	measure
d	did	m	me	TH	then		
e	let	n	no	th	thin	ə represents	
ē	be	ng	long	u	cup	the sound:	
èr	term	o	hot	ů	ful	**a**	in above
f	fat	ö	go	ü	rule	**e**	in taken
g	go	ô	order			**i**	in pencil
h	he	oi	oil			**o**	in lemon
		ou	out			**u**	in circus

b) Use the pronunciation key to match the pronunciations with these words from Units 13–17.

(nīvz) (griz´lēz) (slō´lē) (bōnz)
knives grizzlies slowly bones

2. Schwa: The symbol /ə/ stands for the schwa sound. Find the schwa symbol in the pronunciation key. Notice that any vowel letter can make this sound. It is found only in unstressed syllables. For example, in the word **pencil**, the **i** makes the schwa sound.

Write the words from Units 13–17 that match these pronunciations. Be careful to spell the schwa sound correctly.

(fō´tə graf´) (fer´nə chə´r) (fa´məs) (kon´tə nənt)
photograph furniture famous continent

Dictionary Skills

1. Remind students that the pronunciation symbols representing a word seldom match the spelling of the word. Homophones, for example, will have identical pronunciation symbols, but will be spelled differently (**rīt**: **right**, **write**, **rite**). Pronunciation symbols are a great help when a reader encounters an unfamiliar word.

Have students examine the pronunciation keys of several dictionaries. Where are the keys located? Are there variations in format? Are different symbols used to represent some sounds?

2. Schwa vowels present difficulties in spelling, particularly as students attempt to use multisyllablic words in their writing. Schwa vowels are a focus in Units 17, 19, and 31.

You might wish to have students work in co-operative groups and identify those review words that contain schwa sounds. Have them create a chart that gives the word and shows the schwa vowel(s). Suggest that students consult a dictionary to check the pronunciation of words.

review word	schwa sound(s)
furniture	fer´ nə chər
picture	pik´ chər
addresses	ə dres´ əz
matches	mach´ əz
mountain	moun´ tən
science	sī´ əns
special	spesh´ əl
treasures	trezh´ ərz
dangerous	dan´ j ərəs
geography	jē og´ rə fē
possible	pos´ ə bəl
millions	mil´ yənz

Exploring Space

1. Encourage students to think of other 'night objects'. A variety of reference sources can be consulted, including encyclopedias (print and CD-ROM), astronomy books and journals, star charts, and software programs.

planets	Pluto, Mars, Venus, Jupiter
stars	Plough, Big Dipper, Pole, Southern Cross
satellites	RADARSAT, NOAA, GOES, EOS
comets	Van Den Bergh, Meier, Herschel, Olbers
other	meteors, asteroids, nebulae, galaxies

2. Students working in groups might want to develop their conversation into a TV or radio interview. It could be a news program, a late-night talk show, or a news documentary. Their program could be presented to the class or recorded on audio or videotape.

3. Since the dialogue is likely to be informal, you might wish to suggest that in their proofreading students pay special attention to the proper formation of contractions.

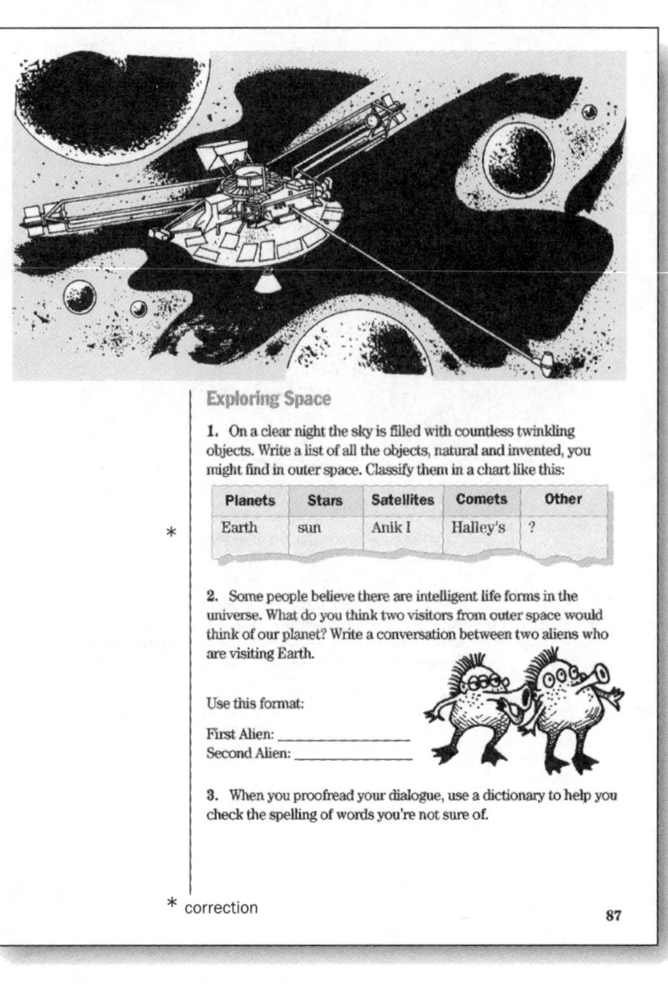

Exploring Space

1. On a clear night the sky is filled with countless twinkling objects. Write a list of all the objects, natural and invented, you might find in outer space. Classify them in a chart like this:

Planets	Stars	Satellites	Comets	Other
Earth	sun	Anik I	Halley's	?

*

2. Some people believe there are intelligent life forms in the universe. What do you think two visitors from outer space would think of our planet? Write a conversation between two aliens who are visiting Earth.

Use this format:

First Alien: ________

Second Alien: ________

3. When you proofread your dialogue, use a dictionary to help you check the spelling of words you're not sure of.

* correction

87

Oral Language and Literature

Students may enjoy creating 'Tom Swifties'. In these sentences, the adverb describes the action taking place.

"Put down those scissors!" he said **sharply**.
"Switch off that light," she said **darkly**.
"Sharpen this knife," she said **bluntly**.

POWERBOOSTERS

13 The long vowel sound /ō/ may be spelled **o** as in **old** or **ow** as in **blow**.
In some words the /cher/ sound follows the pattern **-ture** as in **nature**.

14 In many words the plural is formed by adding **-s** to the singular form.
Singular words that end in the sound /ch/ or /s/ form the plural by adding **-es**.

15 Words that have the pattern **ife** as in **life** form the plural by changing the **f** to **v** and adding **-s**.
Words that end in a consonant plus **y** such as **story** form the plural by changing **y** to **i** and adding **-es**.

16 In words of more than one syllable, stress is placed on only one of the syllables.

17 The spelling of words with the schwa sound /ə/ must be studied carefully as there are many ways of spelling /ə/.

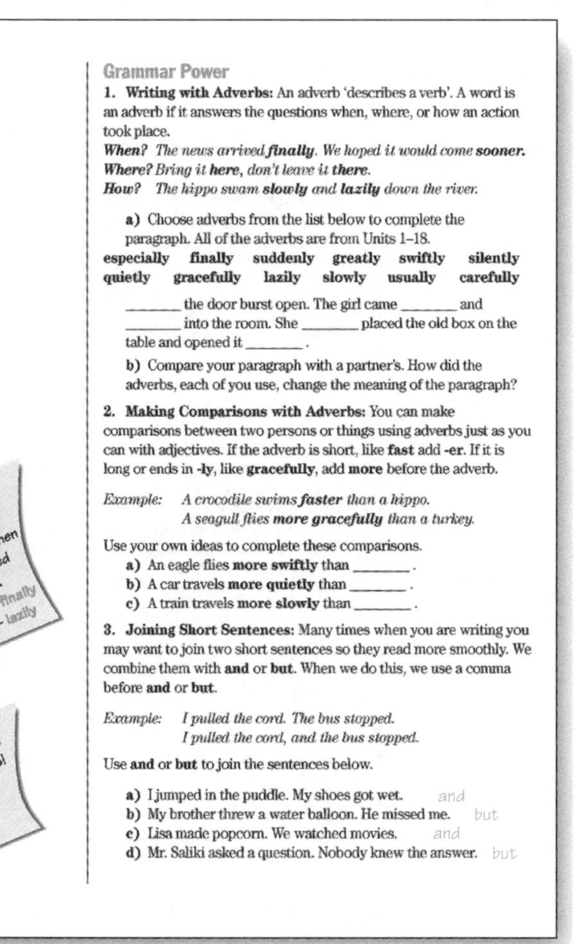

Grammar Power

1. Writing with Adverbs: An adverb 'describes a verb'. A word is an adverb if it answers the questions when, where, or how an action took place.

When? *The news arrived* ***finally****. We hoped it would come* ***sooner.***
Where? *Bring it* ***here****, don't leave it* ***there****.*
How? *The hippo swam* ***slowly*** *and* ***lazily*** *down the river.*

a) Choose adverbs from the list below to complete the paragraph. All of the adverbs are from Units 1–18.

especially finally suddenly greatly swiftly silently
quietly gracefully lazily slowly usually carefully

_______ the door burst open. The girl came _______ and _______ into the room. She _______ placed the old box on the table and opened it _______ .

b) Compare your paragraph with a partner's. How did the adverbs, each of you use, change the meaning of the paragraph?

2. Making Comparisons with Adverbs: You can make comparisons between two persons or things using adverbs just as you can with adjectives. If the adverb is short, like **fast** add **-er**. If it is long or ends in **-ly**, like **gracefully**, add **more** before the adverb.

Example: *A crocodile swims* ***faster*** *than a hippo.*
A seagull flies ***more gracefully*** *than a turkey.*

Use your own ideas to complete these comparisons.

a) An eagle flies **more swiftly** than _______ .
b) A car travels **more quietly** than _______ .
c) A train travels **more slowly** than _______ .

3. Joining Short Sentences: Many times when you are writing you may want to join two short sentences so they read more smoothly. We combine them with **and** or **but**. When we do this, we use a comma before **and** or **but**.

Example: *I pulled the cord. The bus stopped.*
I pulled the cord, and the bus stopped.

Use **and** or **but** to join the sentences below.

a) I jumped in the puddle. My shoes got wet. and
b) My brother threw a water balloon. He missed me. but
c) Lisa made popcorn. We watched movies. and
d) Mr. Saliki asked a question. Nobody knew the answer. but

Watch for changes in spelling, when -ly is added to words.
final — finally
lazy — lazily
Don't forget the commas!

87a

Grammar Power

1. Adverbs are useful words that we 'add' to a verb. Just as an adjective describes a noun, an adverb tells us more about the action of the verb, stating how, when, where, or to what extent the action occurred. Did the hippo swim **quickly** or **slowly** across the river?

Have students note that when **-ly** is added to some base words, there is a change in spelling. Have them examine pairs such as **lazy/lazily** and **lone/lonely** and formulate generalizations such as:

> When adding **-ly** to a base word that ends in **y**, change the **y** to **i**.
> When adding **-ly** to a word that ends in **e**, do not drop the **e**.

You may wish to have students work with a partner to complete a). Stress that other words in the sentence may suggest choices. For example, '**swiftly** or **suddenly** the door **burst** open' makes more sense than '**slowly** or **lazily** the door **burst** open,' since **burst** indicates a quick movement.

2. Discuss with students the generalization for spelling the comparative forms of adverbs: if the adverb is short, add **-er** (**higher**); if it ends in **-ly**, use **more** before the adverb (**more likely**). These structures are useful for comparing two actions.

When students have completed their sentence frames, have them compare their suggestions with a partner, or read them to the class.

3. Talk with students about when to use **and**, and when to use **but**. We use **and** when the sentences being joined generally agree. We use **but** when the meaning contrasts, or disagrees. You may wish to give students more examples and discuss which word should be used.

> It was sunny. The sky was clear.
>
> Alex took off his jacket. He left it hanging on the fence.
>
> He came back to look for it at lunchtime. It wasn't there.
>
> He had to tell his parents. He didn't know how.

Sharing the Secrets with Kids

Be sure to stress that not all sentences should be joined. Too many ***ands*** *and* ***buts*** *are as awkward as too many short sentences. A good writer strives for variety in sentence length, and for a smooth, clear style.*

Writing

- An adverb usually describes a verb. However, it can also modify an adjective (**simply beautiful**) or another adverb (**quite soon**). Students may find the following list of common adverbs useful in their writing. Many of them are also words that are commonly misspelled.

afterward	far	next	today
almost	fast	now	tomorrow
already	here	often	too
also	instead	seldom	usually
away	late	soon	

Proofing Power

1. Explore with students the many kinds of errors the spell check can't catch:

- homophones (**bear/bare**)
- real words that are in the wrong place (**then** for **than**)
- breaks in the wrong place (**though the** instead of **thought he**)
- capitals and periods missing.

2. Some students have particular difficulty spotting spelling errors. To help focus their attention more concisely, you could reproduce the paragraph as a cloze passage, with the incorrect letters left blank.

Proofing Power

1. A spell check is a way to check the spelling of words typed into a computer. It is a program that checks for spelling mistakes and corrects them. Is a spell check the only answer for proofreading? Read the following poem and decide. Then correct any homophone errors you find.

O buoy, I have a spell cheque, *boy/check*
The best theirs ever bean. *there's/been*
I really don't know how two spell, *to*
I just use my machine.
Let's run this poem threw it, *through*
too sea if it is write... *to/see/right*
Hay look! Knot even won mistake, *Hey/not/one*
I'm glad that its so bright. *it's*

2. Read the following paragraph and write the words that are misspelled, giving their correct spelling.

dangerous · *mountain* · *furniture/picture* · *knives* · *treasures* · *objects*

I would love to go on a dangerus journey, wouldn't you? We could go into space and have a whole space mountian to ourselves. We could have furnature and a pitcher of our family on the wall. In our kitchen would be knifes, forks, and spoons. There might even be tresures in the peak of our mountain, or tiny objets to play with.

beginning · *geography/science* · *possible/families* · *millions*

In the begining we might be lonely, but at least we could study geografy and sciense in an interesting place. Maybe it would be possable to invite our familes and friends. The trip would cost milions, but it's worth dreaming about.

87b

Proofreading Strategies

Computer Spell Checks: While a spell check is a useful tool for spotting many spelling and typographical errors, it does not remove the responsibility for proofreading from the writer. In most software programs, the spell checker searches every word in the draft of writing and tries to match it with a word from its built-in dictionary. If it encounters a word not in its dictionary, the spell checker will suggest other words that are closely related in spelling or pronunciation. The writer must then check whether any of the given words is the intended choice.

Much of the effectiveness of a spell check depends on the extent of its dictionary. Many words are highlighted unnecessarily because they are proper nouns or involve technical terms not present in the dictionary. In other cases, spelling errors are not caught because the misspelled word is a homophone (**whether** for **weather**), or matches a different word in the spell check's dictionary (**hopped** for **hoped**). Furthermore, the spell check does not spot grammatical endings such as plurals and tense markers (I **jump** over the fence yesterday). Finally, the student must be able to determine which, if any, of the alternatives offered by the spell check is appropriate.

A spell check may shorten the process of proofreading, but it does not diminish the writer's need for effective proofreading skills. In this sense, a spell check may be compared with a calculator in mathematics. Both devices support the learner but still require a grasp of fundamental concepts.

Hand-held Spell Checks: There are many versions of small spell checks that are roughly the size of a calculator. These devices may be useful for older students who are able to spell well phonetically, but forget visual features of words such as double consonants, silent letters, or schwa vowels. When the student types a word onto the keyboard, the spell check will search its dictionary and try to match the word with one of its entries. If no match is found, it will provide one or more alternatives. Some hand-held spell checks have a built-in dictionary for providing definitions, and a thesaurus. Variations in entry formats should be carefully noted: some units present the letters in alphabetical order, others use a keyboard layout.

There are drawbacks to becoming overly dependent on portable spell checks. Younger students, in particular, would often be better served by learning how to examine words carefully, building on basic spelling patterns, and acquiring a repertoire of spelling strategies.

Homophones
Schwa Vowels
main/mane plains/planes describe

Patterns

Homophones and schwa vowels pose spelling challenges for spellers of all ages. Other spelling features such as short vowels are usually mastered in the early grades, and generally disappear as sources of difficulty.

Since neither homophones nor schwa vowels can be learned through sounding out techniques, a range of spelling strategies needs to be applied to these words.

Preknowledge

Students should have an understanding of the following concepts as they work with the patterns in this unit.

- Syllables. By now, students should be able to determine the number of syllables in a word. Remind them of the technique of placing a hand under their chin and feeling their jaw drop as they articulate each syllable in a word.
- Homophones are words that sound alike but have different meanings and spellings (**hair**/**hare**; **mea**t/**mee**t).
- Stressed and unstressed syllables. In any word of two or more syllables some syllables are stressed more than others (**cláss**/room; re/**céiv**/ing).
- A schwa vowel is the vowel sound contained in an unstressed syllable (óx/ə/gən). Because it is impossible to use sounding out strategies to identify the spelling pattern in such words, students need to develop other ways of remembering the spelling of particular words. You might wish to review some of the material in Unit 17 if students have difficulty with the concept of schwa vowels.

Professional Notebook

Teachers should have no fear whatsoever about the ability of children to make the pattern-to-meaning connection necessary to master homophones. Many fourth graders can identify thirty different automobiles by the most minute features. They want to make the distinction, and no one told them that it is difficult. Problems will arise only when children are asked to make the distinction before they are ready, that is, at a letter-name stage, or when they are systematically taught to attend only to sound rather than to pattern and meaning.

(Henderson 63)

More Patterns

Other patterns you may wish to introduce or review in this unit include the following.

- Base words and derived forms (**scene**/**scenic**; **describe**/**description**; **cells**/**cellular**).

Sharing the Secrets with Kids

*The 'i before **e** except after **c**' rule is useful for learning words such as receive, receipt, perceive.*

Precheck

Because homophones are included in this list, remind students to listen carefully to the sentences and to say the words softly to themselves before writing. Make sure that corrections in Column B of the Student Record Sheet are being done accurately.

Dictation

Plains are large, flat stretches of land.
Describe what he looked like.
A **microscope** is very useful in science class.
Did you **receive** your invitation yet?
The **flower** will bloom any day now.
My **hair** is far too long!
Don't go **without** me please.
Have you heard the **weather** forecast?
The corn **stalk** grew two metres high.
The **main** character was a boy named Ahmed.
The car **passed** us at 150 kilometres an hour.
Have you ever grown a **bean** plant?
I painted a **scene** of a winter playground.
We each have millions of brain **cells.**
Pause for a moment, and think!
Divers breathe **oxygen** under water.

Words in Context

Use the passage as a cloze exercise or have students suggest synonyms for as many list words as possible.

Students could research the topic of grasses and grains. They may wish to talk about the importance of grass in their part of Canada—whether it is grass on a baseball field, hay in a hayfield, wild rice, or carefully-manicured grass on a golf green.

Observing Patterns

1. Challenge students to find other words that fit each of these word families.

2. Ask students to add other words containing the sound /s/ spelled **sc**. A dictionary will be a useful resource for this activity.

3. You might wish to extend this exercise to include stress patterns. (See Critical Thinking, this page.)

4. This activity requires alphabetizing to the fourth letter in the case of **plastic** and **plains**. Check that students have done this rather than just including all the list words beginning with the letter **p**.

Homophones Schwa Vowels

main mane plains planes describe

plains
describe
microscope
receive
flower
hair
without
weather
stalk
main
passed
bean
scene
cells
pause
oxygen

Exploring the World of Grasses

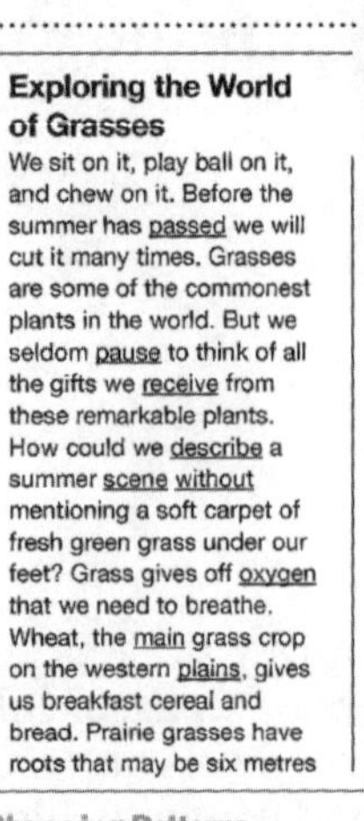

We sit on it, play ball on it, and chew on it. Before the summer has passed we will cut it many times. Grasses are some of the commonest plants in the world. But we seldom pause to think of all the gifts we receive from these remarkable plants. How could we describe a summer scene without mentioning a soft carpet of fresh green grass under our feet? Grass gives off oxygen that we need to breathe. Wheat, the main grass crop on the western plains, gives us breakfast cereal and bread. Prairie grasses have roots that may be six metres deep. Each tiny root hair collects moisture from deep in the soil so the plant can survive dry weather. In high winds, the stalk of grass plants bends but doesn't break. Under the microscope we can see special cells in the stalk. These cells even straighten the grass plant if it is trampled to keep the seed and flower away from the soil. Like the bean plant, grasses such as wheat, rice, and oats are an excellent source of protein for animals and humans.

Observing Patterns

1. Write the list words that have the same spelling pattern and rhyme with the words below.
chair mean gain bells feather cause walk
hair bean main cells weather pause stalk
2. Write the list word that spells the sound /s/ with the same letters as in **scientist**. scene
3. a) Write the five list words that have two syllables. describe receive flower without weather
b) Write the two list words that have three syllables. microscope oxygen
4. Write the three list words that would be found on a dictionary page with these guide words.
parcel / plastic
pains passed pause

88

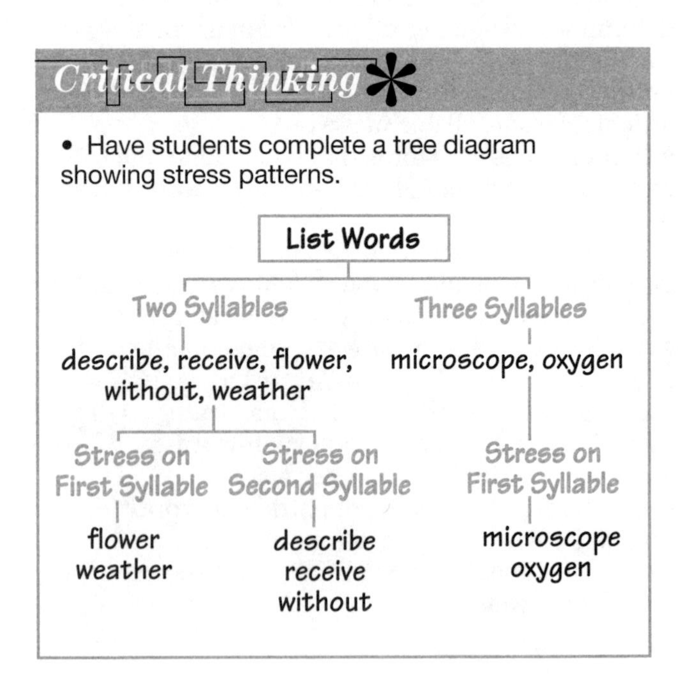

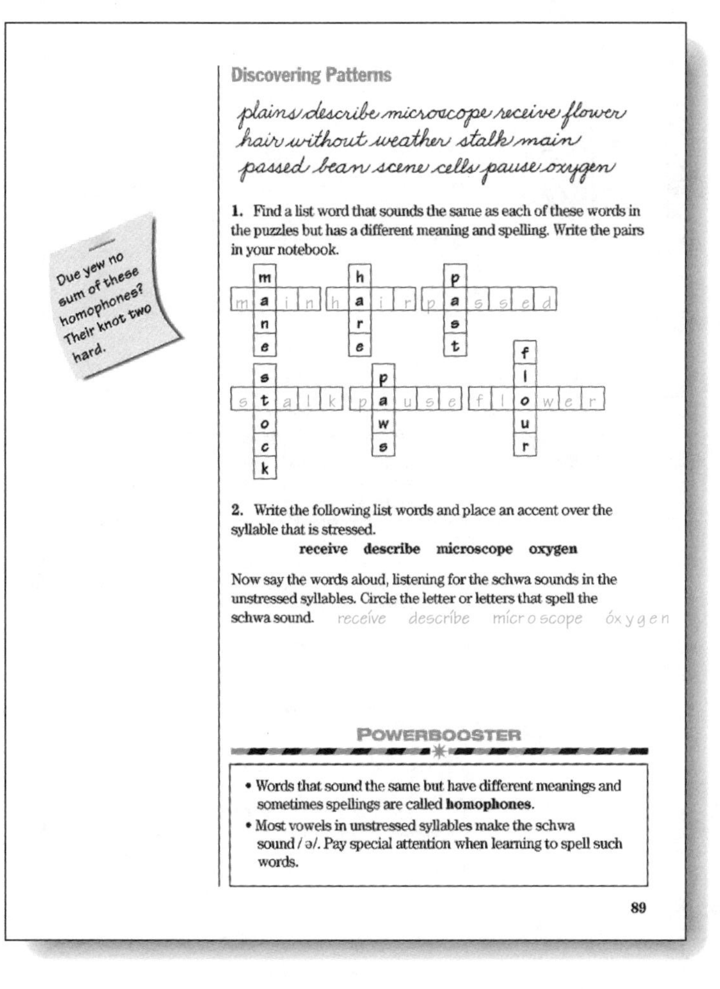

Discovering Patterns

plains describe microscope receive flower hair without weather stalk main passed bean scene cells pause oxygen

1. Find a list word that sounds the same as each of these words in the puzzles but has a different meaning and spelling. Write the pairs in your notebook.

2. Write the following list words and place an accent over the syllable that is stressed.

receive describe microscope oxygen

Now say the words aloud, listening for the schwa sounds in the unstressed syllables. Circle the letter or letters that spell the schwa sound. recéive descríbe mícro scope óx y g e n

POWERBOOSTER

- Words that sound the same but have different meanings and sometimes spellings are called **homophones**.
- Most vowels in unstressed syllables make the schwa sound / ə/. Pay special attention when learning to spell such words.

89

Discovering Patterns

1. Ask students to distinguish the differences in meaning between the words in each homophone pair. They should consult a dictionary to clear up any confusion.

2. The important feature of schwa vowels is that they are not clearly articulated in normal speech, and thus cannot be spelled simply by sounding the word out. Therefore, students must examine such words carefully in order to remember the correct spelling of the schwa sound.

Special Needs

Homophones

Monitor which homophones cause confusion for specific students. Have students help one another develop tricks or strategies for remembering these words. (I like the feel of the **air** on my **hair**.) Have them keep lists of these words along with their meanings for review and dictation.

Schwa vowels

A variety of strategies can be used to help remember schwa vowels:

- highlight the schwa sound in a different colour (a visual strategy)
- illustrate the word (a visual strategy)
- associate the word with another form (cognitive or linguistic strategy).

ox y gen

bal A nce

descr i be / descr i ption

ESL

- Review the concept of homophones with students. In these pairs, the spelling carries the meaning (**passed/past**). The sound is exactly the same. This may be confusing for students whose first languages are spelled phonetically. Make sure the homophones are practised in meaningful sentences. Illustrating the sentences will help students who learn visually to help remember the meaning.

Planes land at the airport.
We grow wheat on the western **plains.**

He has a **flower** in his buttonhole today.
Flour is made from wheat.

We grow **hair** on our heads.
A **hare** is a kind of rabbit.

I **passed** his house on the way to school.
We cannot bring back the **past**.

*Note that in some languages **hair** can be made plural (She has beautiful **hairs**.)

Exploring Patterns

1. Students may benefit from working with a partner on this exercise. Not only must the appropriate word for the sentence context be selected, the correct homophone must also be identified.

Ask students to use some of the remaining homophones from the list (**plains**, **cell,** **been**, **hair**, **flow**, **mane**, **past**, and **stock**) in sentences to illustrate their correct meaning.

2. Suggest that students use a different colour of ink or a highlighter pen to accentuate the letters left blank in the exercise.

3. Generate a list of other words containing the prefixes **micro-** and **tele-**. Ask students to explain the meaning of the word as it relates to the prefix and base word (**microcomputer**: a small computer; **telecommunications**: communication over a great distance).

micro	tele
microcomputer	telephone
microchip	television
microfilm	telemarketing
microwave	telegraph
microphone	telephoto
microdot	telegram
microscope	

4. Ask students to share their word webs. Discuss how the words provided could be clustered into smaller sub-categories. The word web can be used to generate further writing activities such as poems or stories.

Exploring Patterns

1. Select the correct homophones from the word box to write the sentences.

plains	planes	flower	flour	scene	seen
cell	sell	hair	hare	stalk	stock
bean	been	main	mane	past	passed

a) We looked at the beautiful winter scene from the window.
b) Do you stock any bean seeds here?
c) I past by a lovely flower bed at the main entrance to the school.
d) The young hare munched on a stalk of celery.
e) Have you ever seen so many planes in the air?

2. Complete the list words on each plant.

passed weather oxygen scene stalk receive describe

3. The words **microscope** and **telescope** come from Greek. Read these word meanings and use them to write a definition for the above two words. The definitions are started for you.

scope—scientific instrument for helping the eye or ear to make observations
micro—small
tele—far off

a) A microscope is an instrument used to help the eye see things that are small.
b) A telescope is an instrument used to help the eye see things that are far off.

4. Draw word webs for two of the following list words.

hair **weather** **flower** **microscope**

Example:

bean — giant, beanstalk, golden egg, harp; soup, bread, butter; vegetable, garden, carrots, peas; earth, sprout, roots

90

Do you know the rule: i before e except after c? How can it help you spell receive?

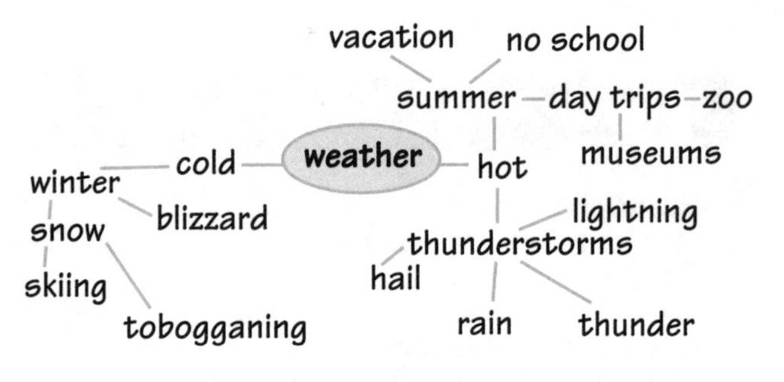

Co-operative Learning

- Have students work in co-operative groups to make up their own homophone games. First have them generate a list of twenty or so homophones. Each group could construct a word search, crossword puzzle, Homophone Concentration game, and so on. The completed puzzles could be shared with other groups and compiled in a booklet for reinforcement activities. Good sources of homophones are *The Student Editor's Guide to Words*, pp.173-174 and *Sharing the Secrets: Teach Your Child to Spell*, p.146.

homophones			
pour	pore	some	sum
course	coarse	bare	bear
fair	fare	fourth	forth
great	grate	board	bored
there	their	steak	stake

5. Before you stretches a beautiful field of soft green grass. List five words that describe the way the grass looks and feels. Then list five words that describe what you like to play or do on grass.

6. Using the word lists you made in exercise 5, write a short paragraph about what you would do if you were the kids in the picture. Be sure to proofread your paragraph for spelling errors with a partner.

SUPER WORDS

whether
prairie
Saskatchewan
slough
pollen
wheat

Challenges with Words

1. Circle the word which doesn't belong in each set of words, and explain why it doesn't belong.

Example:

a) lake, slough, grass, river, creek, pond

Grass is not a body of water.

b) wheat, leaves, rye, barley, oats, rice Leaves are not a grain.
c) field, elevator, prairie, lowland, tundra Elevator is not a land form.
d) Saskatchewan, Prince Albert, Brandon, St. John, Regina Saskatchewan is the only province.
e) buffalo, polar bear, pronghorn, coyote, jack-rabbit A polar bear is not found in warmer climates.
f) hawk, eagle, duck, snake, crow A snake is not a bird.

91

5. and **6.** Encourage students to do their vocabulary building exercise together. Have them discuss the differences between words which are close in meaning, such as **spongy** and **springy**, or **inviting** and **appealing**. Vocabulary enrichment may often be furthered by discussions of this kind.

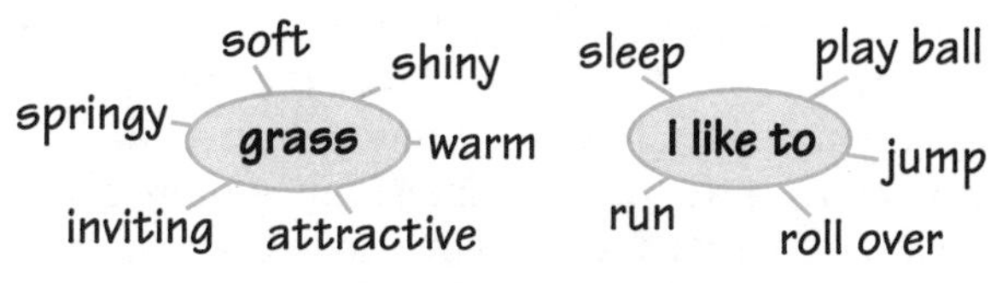

Challenges with Words

1. As a support to the explanations, have students give a title to each set and add more words.

grasses	places grass grows	prairie places	prairie animals	prairie birds
wild rice corn	pampas garden	Winnipeg Calgary	deer prairie dog	vulture

Writing

• What Am I?

As an extension of Exploring Patterns 5 and 6, have students write a vivid description of an insect, plant, bird, or small animal that may be found in the grassy field. The description could be in the form of a paragraph or a poem. The task of classmates is to guess the identity of the living thing being described.

Oral Language and Literature

• Students enjoy homophone and homograph riddles. Two resources we like are *What's a Frank Frank?: Tasty Homograph Riddles* and *Hey, Hay!: A Wagonful of Funny Homonym Riddles.* Challenge students to create their own homograph and homophone riddles.

What's sold at a sail sale? (*sails*)
What's a coarse course? (*an uncut golf green*)
What's a bare bear? (*a bear with no hair*)

• You might want to help students distinguish among the three terms—homograph, homophone, and homonym. Remind them that **homographs** are words that are spelled the same but have different meanings (**mail** carrier; chain **mail**). **Homophones** are words that sound the same but have different meanings and spellings (**pore**/**pour**). **Homonym** is a generic term—an umbrella for all of the above.

2. Students may be interested in discovering the word origins of local community names. They could research by going to their public library or contacting the local historical society. The information could be collected into a booklet or pamphlet for others to read.

3. Challenge students to find as many of the 36 words as they can. When they've identified the homophone of each word that they find, have them use each homophone pair in a single sentence to show the meanings. Since there are 36 pairs of words, partners or trios of students could be given a few to work with.

> Do you know **whether** the **weather** has changed?
> I'll eat my **cereal** while I watch this **serial** on TV.

words in puzzle	homophone(s)	words in puzzle	homophone(s)
serial	cereal	led	lead
red	read	vein	vane
roll	role	rot	wrought
roe	row	moan	mown
him	hymn	mote	moat
some	sum	loot	lute
hi	high	toe	tow
sore	soar	rein	[illegible]
rain	rei[illegible]	[illegible]	[illegible]

4. You might give students a time limit to make this exercise more challenging. It may also help to write each letter of Saskatchewan on a separate card and physically rearrange the letters to form new words.

SASKATCHEWAN	
skate	went
ask	sent
task	seat
new	neat
chew	heat
wane	stew
tack	was
cast	nest
stack	anew
wake	ant
take	sake

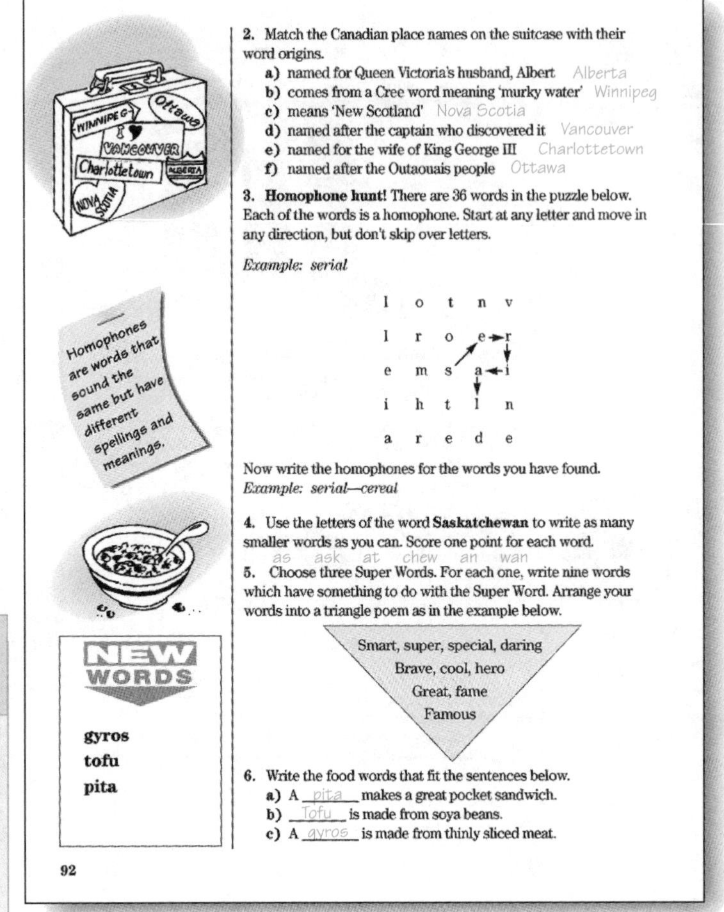

2. Match the Canadian place names on the suitcase with their word origins.
- **a)** named for Queen Victoria's husband, Albert Alberta
- **b)** comes from a Cree word meaning 'murky water' Winnipeg
- **c)** means 'New Scotland' Nova Scotia
- **d)** named after the captain who discovered it Vancouver
- **e)** named for the wife of King George III Charlottetown
- **f)** named after the Outaouais people Ottawa

3. Homophone hunt! There are 36 words in the puzzle below. Each of the words is a homophone. Start at any letter and move in any direction, but don't skip over letters.

Example: serial

l o t n v
l r o e r
e m s a i
i h t l n
a r e d e

Now write the homophones for the words you have found.
Example: serial—cereal

4. Use the letters of the word **Saskatchewan** to write as many smaller words as you can. Score one point for each word.
as ask at chew an wan

5. Choose three Super Words. For each one, write nine words which have something to do with the Super Word. Arrange your words into a triangle poem as in the example below.

Smart, super, special, daring
Brave, cool, hero
Great, fame
Famous

NEW WORDS
gyros
tofu
pita

6. Write the food words that fit the sentences below.
- **a)** A _pita_ makes a great pocket sandwich.
- **b)** _Tofu_ is made from soya beans.
- **c)** A _gyros_ is made from thinly sliced meat.

92

5. Students may enjoy illustrating their poems with drawings or photographs.

New Words

6. Ask students to think of other food words that have entered our language recently. Have these words been borrowed from other languages (**pizza**), named after a person (the Earl of **Sandwich**), or created as new words entirely?

Curriculum Connection

Schwa vowels are often found in the longer words students face in the content areas. Encourage students to apply spelling strategies to the schwas in these words. For example, many students have difficulty with the word **hypothesis**, even though it is used frequently in sciences and mathematics. They could exaggerate the sounds within the word and alter the stress pattern by saying hi/po/**thé**/sis, so that the **e** is a long **e**.

Home Connection

Suggest that parents play the homophone game described in Follow-up with their children. This will help to reinforce common homophone pairs and identify specific challenges.

Dear Parent,

We have been studying homophones in spelling: bar/bear; sore/soar; here/hear, and other words that sound the same but are spelled differently.

You can help your child practise these spellings by writing each homophone on a separate card, then using one of the homophones in a sentence.

-2-

Your child should then hold up the card that has the correct spelling on it. For example, "The accident scene was littered with broken glass."

Some of the homophones you could use are: pour/pore; course/coarse; fair/fare; great/grate; there/their; some/sum; bare/bear; fourth/forth; board/bored; steak/stake.

Assessment

- Are students having difficulty with the actual spelling of homophones (**plians** for **plains**; **sean** for **scene**)? If this is the case, help them to focus on the arrangement of letters within the word.
- Are students confusing homophones one for the other (substituting **stock** for **stalk**)? If this is so, help is needed in the area of meaning.

Follow-up

As a quick check and for reinforcement, have students write each homophone on a separate card. Use one of the homophones in a sentence (The accident **scene** was littered with broken glass.). Each student should hold up the correct spelling of the homophone. Do this for several homophones, and have the students practise among themselves.

Teacher's Notes

20 -ed Ending

grab/grabb**ed**
excite/excit**ed**

Patterns

When students move beyond the early stages of spelling they begin to recognize the structure of words and are aware of smaller word parts such as past tense markers. They will spell **jumped** with an **-ed** ending rather than the **t** that sounding out the word suggests. In **jumped** the past tense is formed simply by adding **-ed** to the base word.

This unit introduces the changes that must be made to some base words when **-ed** is added. In words ending in **vowel** + **consonant**, the final consonant is doubled, thus keeping the short vowel sound of the base word (gra**b**/gra**bb**ed; ma**p**/ma**pp**ed). When the base word ends in a silent **e**, that letter is dropped when **-ed** is added (hop**e**/hop**ed**; excit**e**/excit**ed**). This is probably a matter of avoiding redundancy and pronunciation difficulties. How would we say a word spelled **hopeed**?

Professional Notebook

Children learn to spell pattern by pattern, not word by word. Humans are naturally attuned to perceiving and making use of patterns in all the information they take in and process.... In spite of this, some teachers create spelling lists that are simply collections of random words, usually selected from the story or topic being studied that week. Faced with this kind of random collection of words, children can do little except memorize.

(Gentry/Gillet 89)

Preknowledge

Students should have an understanding of the following concepts as they work with the patterns in this unit.

- Base words. Depending on the base word, changes may need to be made to it when suffixes are added (**step**/step**ped**; **arrive**/arri**ved**).
- -**ed** as a past tense marker. When **-ed** appears at the end of a word it usually indicates the past tense of a verb.
- Schwa vowels. The sound in unstressed syllables is often hard to hear because it is a schwa vowel (remem**ber**ed; **a**ttacked). Students need to develop strategies for recognizing and remembering schwa vowels.
- Proper nouns. Students should remember that proper nouns refer to specific people, places, and things, and are always capitalized (**Earth**; **Captain Cook**).

More Patterns

Other patterns you might wish to introduce or review in this unit include the following.

- Double consonants. As well as the doubling pattern when a suffix is added to a word ending in vowel + consonant, other patterns for double consonants occur in English (a**tt**acked; vi**ll**age; o**ff**icer).
- The capitalization of proper nouns (**Vancouver**; **British**).
- The '**i** before **e** except after **c**' rule (**believed**).
- Schwa vowels (capt**ai**n, offic**e**r, t**o**ward, **a**rrived, **a**ttacked).

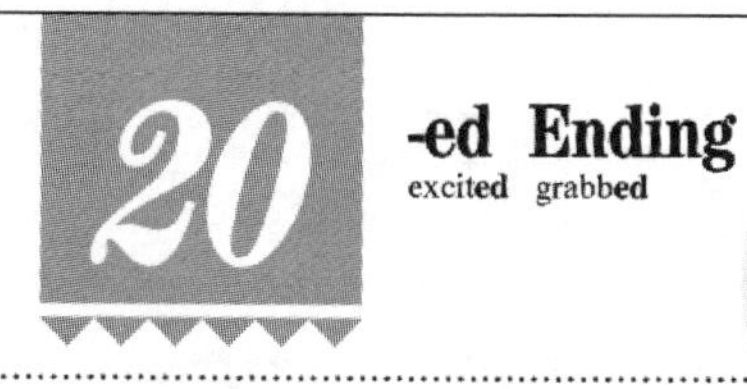

-ed Ending

excited grabbed

excited
watched
captain
believed
mapped
officer
grabbed
stepped
Vancouver
remembered
village
arrived
British
attacked
dropped
toward

Exploring the Routes to Canada

Immigrants have been coming to Canada's west coast for more than 12 000 years! It is believed that the first Canadians arrived on foot. They crossed a land bridge from Asia and began to spread out toward the south and east. Two hundred years ago, British and Spanish newcomers arrived in ships to fight over who would control this land. They grabbed whole islands, attacked each other's settlements, and ignored the fact that the native people had been there for thousands of years. One young officer, who had joined the British navy when he was only thirteen, sailed around the world with the explorer, Captain Cook. His name was George, and he mapped much of the Pacific west coast. He is remembered because he left his name, Vancouver, on the island and the city where his ship dropped anchor and he stepped ashore. It would have excited early Canadians to have watched how the small village of Vancouver turned into the beautiful city it is today.

Observing Patterns

1. Write the two list words that begin with a capital letter.
   Vancouver British
2. Write the eight list words that have double consonants. Then circle the double consonants in each word.
   mapped officer grabbed village arrived attacked dropped
3. Find the correct letter or letters for the schwa sound in these list words, then write the words.
   capt a i n   off i cer   t o ward   a rrived   a ttacked

93

Precheck

Help students deal with any errors they made by assigning activities that use words from Column B of the Student Record Sheet. A student could:

- print the words alphabetically in a list, using a different colour for each letter
- write each word in a sentence that asks a question
- find smaller words inside the list words without rearranging any letters.

Dictation

I'm very **excited** about the party!
They **watched** the game on television.
She's **captain** of the hockey team.
No one **believed** the story.
I **mapped** the route from home to school.
The police **officer** was directing traffic.
We **grabbed** a sandwich for lunch.
You **stepped** on my foot!
Vancouver is on Canada's west coast.
I **remembered** to do my homework.
The **village** grew into a big city.
We **arrived** last at the meeting.
There are many **British** people in Canada.
That dog **attacked** my cat!
I **dropped** the rock on my foot!
We sailed west **toward** the setting sun.

Words in Context

Have students share what they know of other famous explorers. Then have them read the paragraph independently. Ask students to find additional **-ed** words in the paragraph and note the patterns they follow.

Observing Patterns

1. Review the difference between proper and common nouns and the need for proper nouns to be capitalized. You might also point out that **British** is derived from **Britain**.

2. Help students to distinguish between base words in which the double consonants are formed when **-ed** is added, and those in which the double consonants are part of the base. Each of these patterns requires different spelling strategies. With **village**, **officer**, and **attacked**, the double consonants must simply be memorized. The words **mapped**, **dropped**, **stepped**, and **grabbed**, however, reflect a structural rule for adding endings to a base word.

3. Students could highlight these letters with a different colour of ink or print them in larger letters.

ESL

- In many languages, the past tense is marked in ways such as context or word order. In English, the past is indicated by changes to the spelling of the verb. Some irregular verbs make internal changes (**come/came**) or use an entirely new word for the past (**go/went**). However, most verbs indicate the past by adding **-ed**. Point out that pronunciation is not a good guide to spelling, as **-ed** can be pronounced /t/, /d/, or /ed/ (mapp**t**/grabb**d**/excit**ed**), but is always spelled the same.
- For some students, the consonant combinations **gr**, **br**, **dr**, and **st** at the beginning of words are unfamiliar sounds. Students may try to insert an extra vowel in speech and spelling (g**e**rabbed). Help them practise blending the two sounds in:

  grabbed stepped dropped British

Discovering Patterns

1. Have students mark off the **-ed** ending before they underline the base word. This will help them to notice more clearly what has happened to the base (**believ**/ed, **dropp**/ed).

2. Students may work best with a partner to sort the words appropriately. Other words could be added to each list from a variety of sources.

Final Consonant Doubled	Final e Dropped	No Change to Base Word
blurred	advised	adapted
acquitted	revised	edited
conferred	dazed	detected
controlled	raised	adopted
occurred	ignited	designed
preferred	combined	benefited
regretted	confided	limited
omitted	adored	exhibited
scarred	praised	reasoned
knitted	paused	listened

3. and **4.** It may be most efficient to have students work with a partner in a large group to generate these rules. The two rules are restated in the Powerbooster.

4. Complete each sentence with list words.
a) The children were very excited as they watched the circus.
b) Andrew remembered that the money was in the attic but nobody believed him.

Discovering Patterns

excited watched captain believed mapped officer grabbed stepped Vancouver remembered village arrived British attacked dropped toward

1. Write the list words below that have the ending **-ed**, and underline the base word in each. Notice what happens to the base word when the ending **-ed** is added.

watched **mapped** **grabbed** **stepped** **believed**
remembered **arrived** **excited** **attacked** **dropped**

2. Sort the words from exercise 1 into the chart below.

Final Consonant Doubled	Final e Dropped	No change to Base Word
mapped	arrived	watched
grabbed	believed	remembered
stepped	excited	attacked
dropped		

3. Examine the words that double final consonants. What is similar about their base words? Try to state a rule for adding **-ed** to base words like this.

4. Examine the words that drop an **e**. What is similar about their base words? Try to state a rule for adding **-ed** to base words like this.

POWERBOOSTER

- When adding **-ed** to single syllable words ending in vowel-consonant, double the consonant, as in grab—**grabbed**.
- When adding **-ed** to base words ending in silent **e**, drop the **e**, as in excite—**excited**.

94

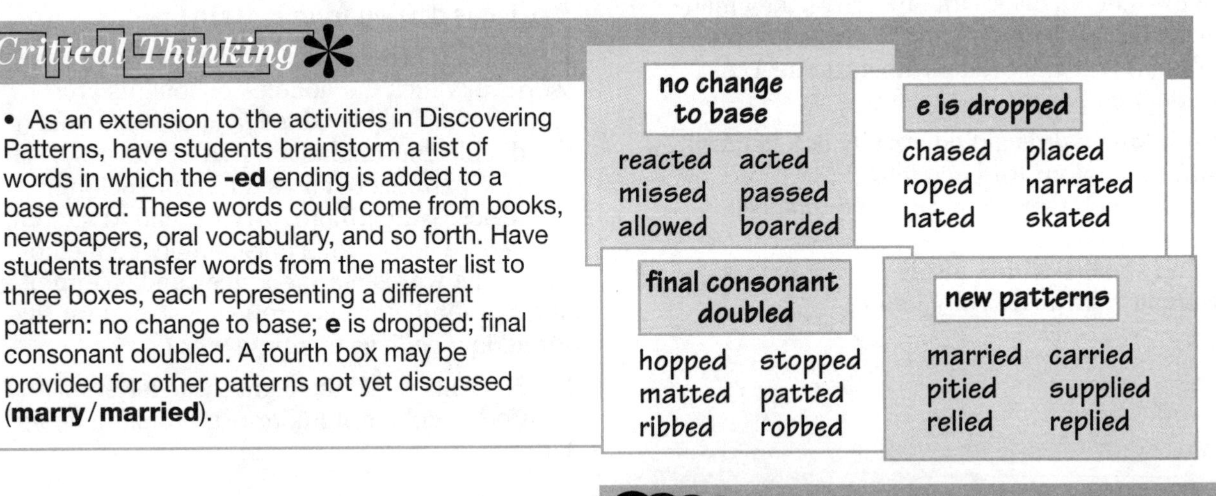

Critical Thinking
no change to base
reacted acted
missed passed
allowed boarded
e is dropped
chased placed
roped narrated
hated skated
final consonant doubled
hopped stopped
matted patted
ribbed robbed
new patterns
married carried
pitied supplied
relied replied

- As an extension to the activities in Discovering Patterns, have students brainstorm a list of words in which the **-ed** ending is added to a base word. These words could come from books, newspapers, oral vocabulary, and so forth. Have students transfer words from the master list to three boxes, each representing a different pattern: no change to base; **e** is dropped; final consonant doubled. A fourth box may be provided for other patterns not yet discussed (**marry/married**).

Oral Language and Literature

- Encourage students to use expressive verbs both in their oral and written language. Consider a number of alternatives for list words such as **watched**, **arrived**, **grabbed**. Be sure students feel comfortable using a thesaurus.
- For a discussion of the use of a thesaurus in the writing process, see *The Student Editor's Guide to Words*, pp.103-108.

Exploring Patterns

1. Add **-ed** to each base word below. Remember, some base words change when **-ed** is added.

battle laugh shop capture slip bump

battled laughed shopped captured slipped bumped

2. The /ch/ sound is sometimes spelled with the consonants **tch** as in **watched**. Combine the letters on the word wheel to spell as many words as you can with the **tch** pattern.

Example:
m + a + tch + ed
= matched

latched latch
matched match
watched watch
hatched hatch
patched patch
scratched scratch
pitched pitch
hitched hitch
ditched ditch
witch

3. Combine each pair of short sentences into a longer sentence.
a) The captain dropped the ship's anchor. Then he stepped into the rowboat. (, and)
b) The British officers attacked the fort. They believed the enemy was hiding inside. (, because)
c) The village people watched the parade. They were very excited. (, and)

4. Complete each analogy with a list word.

An analogy is a comparison between two things or ideas that are alike in some way.

a) Miserable is to **happy** as **bored** is to excited.
b) Airplane is to **pilot** as **ship** is to captain.
c) Doubted is to **believed** as **forgotten** is to remembered

95

Exploring Patterns

1. If students have difficulty with any of the patterns, have them review Discovering Patterns 2 and the Powerbooster on p. 94. Provide additional examples for reinforcement.

2. Develop a master list of words with the **tch** pattern. Ask students to think of other words that spell /ch/ as **tch**. Students may enjoy generating these words in co-operative groups.

stretch batch stitch butcher catch
crutches ketchup clutch Dutch glitch
hitch hatchet sketchbook snatch twitch

3. Discuss the various ways in which each pair of sentences can be combined. Students could indicate which combinations they prefer.

After he dropped the ship's anchor, the captain stepped into the rowboat.
The captain dropped the ship's anchor, and then he stepped into the rowboat.
The captain dropped the ship's anchor, then stepped into the rowboat.

The British officers attacked the fort because they believed the enemy was hiding inside.
They believed the enemy was hiding inside, so the British officers attacked the fort.
The British officers believed the enemy was hiding inside, and so they attacked the fort.

The village people were very excited as they watched the parade.
The village people watched the parade, and they were very excited.
The excited village people watched the parade.

4. Ask students to identify the relationships present in each comparison. For example, **miserable**, **happy**, **excited** and **bored**, are all feelings.

Special Needs

- As further reinforcement for many of the Unit Words, prepare a set of configurations representing several of the words (**village**, **attacked**, **grabbed**, and **watched** have distinctive shapes). Have students match the configurations and list words. This visual approach may help students notice details such as the silent **t** in **watched** as well as double consonants in other words. (See also Multiple Intelligences, p. 157.)

v i l l a g e w a t c h e d g r a b b e d

Co-operative Learning

- Students could work in co-operative groups to add words to each category of the chart in Discovering Patterns 2, and to the word wheel in Exploring Patterns 2.

5. An outline is especially important when writers are describing action, such as in a chase, a game, or an exciting adventure. You may need to discuss ways of achieving variety in describing a sequence of actions. Students should avoid overuse of "Then ...".
(See Writing, below).

first of all	afterward	not long after that
next thing I knew	eventually	next
then	following that	after a while

Challenges with Words

Note with students the double consonants in **commanded** and **possession**, and the spelling of /ėr/ in **skirmish** and **separated**.

Relate the **-ed** patterns in **commanded**, **promoted**, and **separated** to the Powerbooster (p. 94). No change is made to the base word **command**, but the **e** is dropped from **promote** and **separate**.

1. Students could research the life of Captain Cook using library media. They might find excerpts from Captain Cook's own diaries and present this information in various ways, such as interviews, drama, and so on.

2. You might want to explain to students that at one time most, if not all, **-ed** words were pronounced /əd/ (receiv/əd; dream/əd). Some verbs, such as **dream**, have two forms of its past participle: **dreamed** (drēmd) and **dreamt** (dremt).

/əd/	/t/	/d/
started	stopped	failed
detected	locked	tried
investigated	blocked	fried
participated	mopped	peeled
operated	sipped	produced
provided	slipped	reduced
sighted	frisked	severed
alerted	risked	applied
reported	basked	buried

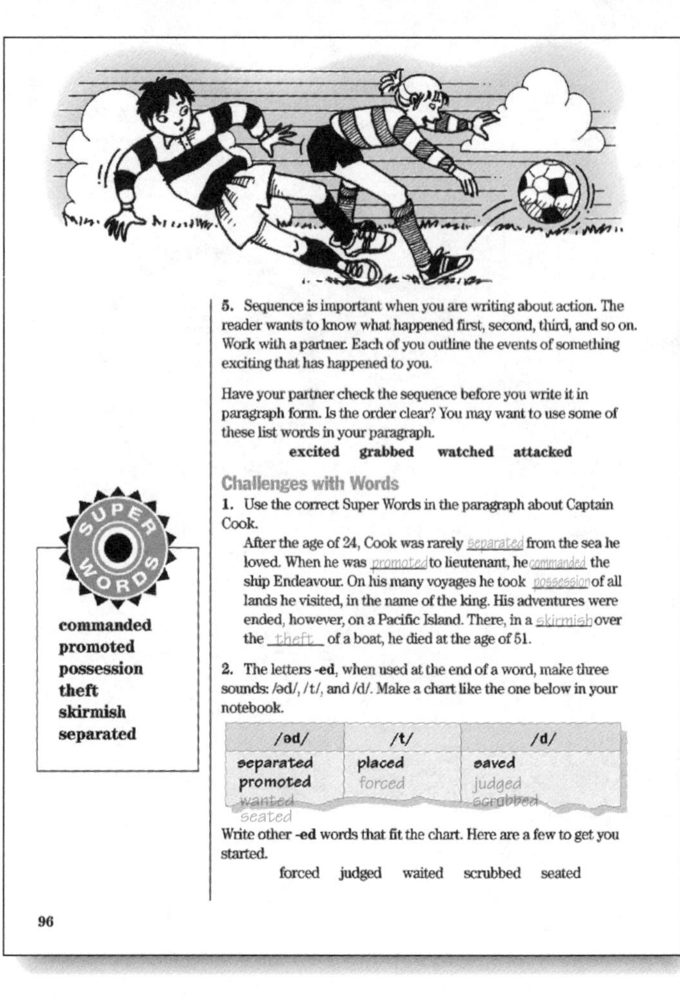

5. Sequence is important when you are writing about action. The reader wants to know what happened first, second, third, and so on. Work with a partner. Each of you outline the events of something exciting that has happened to you.

Have your partner check the sequence before you write it in paragraph form. Is the order clear? You may want to use some of these list words in your paragraph.

excited **grabbed** **watched** **attacked**

Challenges with Words

SUPER WORDS

commanded
promoted
possession
theft
skirmish
separated

1. Use the correct Super Words in the paragraph about Captain Cook.

After the age of 24, Cook was rarely separated from the sea he loved. When he was promoted to lieutenant, he commanded the ship Endeavour. On his many voyages he took possession of all lands he visited, in the name of the king. His adventures were ended, however, on a Pacific Island. There, in a skirmish over the theft of a boat, he died at the age of 51.

2. The letters **-ed**, when used at the end of a word, make three sounds: /əd/, /t/, and /d/. Make a chart like the one below in your notebook.

/əd/	/t/	/d/
separated	placed	saved
promoted	forced	judged
wanted		scrubbed
seated		

Write other **-ed** words that fit the chart. Here are a few to get you started.

forced judged waited scrubbed seated

96

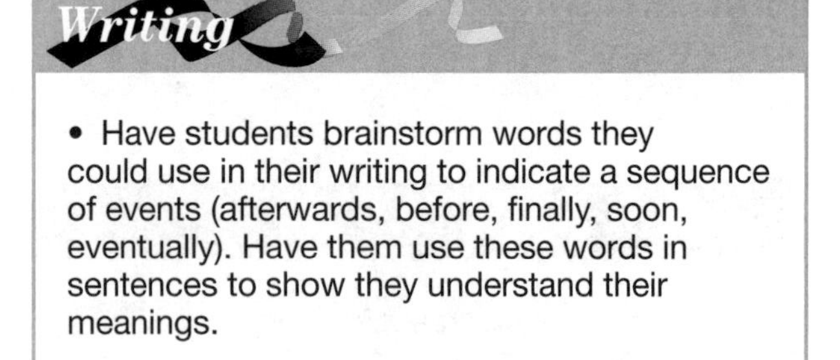

Writing

- Have students brainstorm words they could use in their writing to indicate a sequence of events (afterwards, before, finally, soon, eventually). Have them use these words in sentences to show they understand their meanings.

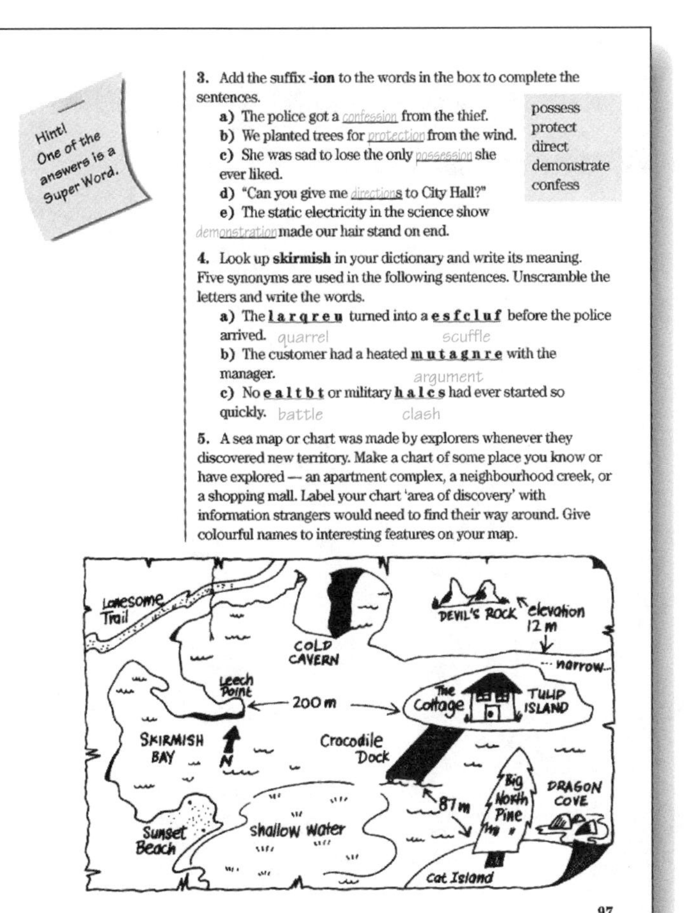

Hint! One of the answers is a Super Word.

3. Add the suffix **-ion** to the words in the box to complete the sentences.

possess
protect
direct
demonstrate
confess

a) The police got a confession from the thief.
b) We planted trees for protection from the wind.
c) She was sad to lose the only possession she ever liked.
d) "Can you give me directions to City Hall?"
e) The static electricity in the science show demonstration made our hair stand on end.

4. Look up **skirmish** in your dictionary and write its meaning. Five synonyms are used in the following sentences. Unscramble the letters and write the words.

a) The **l a r q r e u** turned into a **e s f c l u f** before the police arrived. quarrel scuffle
b) The customer had a heated **m u t a g n r e** with the manager. argument
c) No **e a l t b t** or military **h a l c s** had ever started so quickly. battle clash

5. A sea map or chart was made by explorers whenever they discovered new territory. Make a chart of some place you know or have explored — an apartment complex, a neighbourhood creek, or a shopping mall. Label your chart 'area of discovery' with information strangers would need to find their way around. Give colourful names to interesting features on your map.

97

3. Note that the suffix **-ion** includes the form **-tion** and **-(s)sion**, with or without the preceeding **a** or **i** vowel. The base word, usually of Latin origin, governs the linking vowel and/or consonant, if any, that go with the suffix.

base word	+ -ion
transmit	transmission
relax	relaxation
commit	commission
decide	decision
combine	combination

Have students list ten more **-ion** words along with the correct base word for each. A good source for lists of **-ion** words is *The Student Editor's Guide to Words*, p. 188.

base word	+ -ion
admit	admission
collide	collision
emit	emission
erode	erosion
persuade	persuasion
depress	depression
transfuse	transfusion
decide	decision
fuse	fusion
revise	revision

4. Students may find it easier to unscramble corresponding letter tiles to find the answers.

Students might also try a similar exercise with another Super Word and have a partner unscramble the letters. A thesaurus could be used as a source of synonyms.

5. A useful support to this type of mapping or charting is *The Living Atlas* (Gage). This resource contains sample charts or maps related to the students' immediate community.

Multiple Intelligences

Logical/Mathematical: Use word sort activities involving the three patterns for adding endings (no change to base; double final consonant; drop silent **e**).

Bodily/Kinesthetic: Give students cards with base words (e.g., **step**, **arrive**); have them add an **-ed** card. They must describe any changes to be made to the base, and sort the cards into the patterns described in the Powerbooster.

Visual/Spatial: Use configuration lines or boxes for double consonants; have students match configurations with unit words.

Colour schwa vowels and double consonants so that they stand out visually.

Verbal/Linguistic: Use discussion of spelling patterns (Discovering Patterns), sentence building (Exploring Patterns 3), and word building (Exploring Patterns 2).

Curriculum Connection

Students could research Captain Cook's voyages further and prepare a map illustrating his travels.

Home Connection

This unit contains a number of concepts which could be shared with parents and reinforced at home: double consonants, adding **-ed** endings, sentence combining, word building (**tch** pattern).

Assessment

- If students make errors involving **-ed** endings, notice whether these follow a pattern such as failing to drop the silent **e**, double a final consonant, and so on. In such cases, review the Powerbooster. If the problems relate to double consonants elsewhere in the word (vi**ll**age), discuss strategies for remembering these features.
- Some students may omit letters or syllables in **remembered**. Have students assemble the word using letter tiles, or provide a set of cards, each with one syllable of the word written on it (re/mem/bered). Scramble the syllables and have students rearrange the cards correctly while saying the word aloud.

Follow-up

If students need further work with patterns for adding **-ed**, refer to Units 23, 24, and 25 in *Sharing the Secrets: Teach Your Child to Spell.*

Teacher's Notes

-ed -ing Endings

dried
dream**ing**
hid**ing**

Patterns

This unit introduces the pattern for adding endings to verbs that finish with **consonant** + **y**. Note that when the ending added is **-ed**, the **y** changes to **i** (bur**y**/bur**ied**). However, when **-ing** is added, no change is made to the base word.

The unit also continues the pattern, introduced in Unit 20, of adding **-ed** endings to words that have a final **consonant** + **e**. Here, we look at what happens when **-ed** or **-ing** is added to verbs that end with a **consonant** + **silent e**. In each case, the final **e** is dropped when the suffix is added (**hope/hoped/hoping**).

Preknowledge

Students should have an understanding of the following concepts as they work with the patterns in this unit.

- The present and past tenses of verbs. The **-ed** ending should alert students to the fact that a word is likely a verb in the past tense (**marry/married**). Unfortunately, creating the past tense of every verb is not just a matter of adding **-ed**; there are irregular verbs in English that students simply have to memorize (**I am/I was**).
- Base words and endings. Adding suffixes to a base word sometimes calls for changes to the base word, such as doubling the final consonant or dropping a final **e** (**slam/slammed/slamming; create/created/creating**). Other base words are not changed at all (**wish/wished/wishing**).

More Patterns

Other patterns you may wish to introduce or review in this unit include the following.

- Some base words require no change when **-ed** or **-ing** is added (**dream/dreamed/dreaming**).
- The patterns for spelling the long /ē/ sound (dr**ea**ming, chimn**ey**, bur**y**).

Professional Notebook

English is the most hospitable and democratic language that has ever existed. It has welcomed into its vocabulary words from tens of other languages and dialects, far and near, ancient and modern. As Carl Sandburg once observed, "The English language hasn't gotten where it is by being pure." Purifying our spelling system would obscure our long history of exuberant borrowing.

(Lederer 220)

Sharing the Secrets with Kids

*If **y** were change to **i** before **ing**, there would be words with double **i**. These words are awkward to read and spell. There are a few exceptions, such as **skiing**.*

Precheck

Remind students to listen carefully to how each word sounds and how it is used in the sentence. Some students have difficulty hearing suffixes.

Dictation

A **pioneer** was an early settler in Canada.
The **buried** treasure was never found.
We **carried** our bikes over the stream.
My aunt got **married** last weekend.
He **replied** correctly to the question.
I washed and then **dried** my hands.
Are you **coming** to my party?
Are you **dreaming** of the holidays?
We're **having** a garage sale tomorrow.
I found him **hiding** in the closet.
The **missing** money was soon found.
Her **husband** is a pilot.
Our **teachers** had a meeting on Friday.
My sisters are both medical **doctors.**
The cedar **log** smelled lovely as it burned.
The **chimney** caught fire.

Words in Context

Have students read the paragraph and suggest synonyms for the list words wherever possible. They may also look for other words that follow the unit pattern (**building**, **arrived**). Have students locate the list word that was not used in the paragraph (**replied**) and suggest sentences in which the word could be used.

You might wish to have students brainstorm and list the advantages and disadvantages of pioneer life.

pioneer Life	
advantages	**disadvantages**
new home	have to make new friends
lots of opportunities	needs hard work
chance to own land	soil not always good
no pollution	no indoor plumbing
chance to start over	cold in winter
meet new people	far from home and family
become self-reliant	
an adventure	

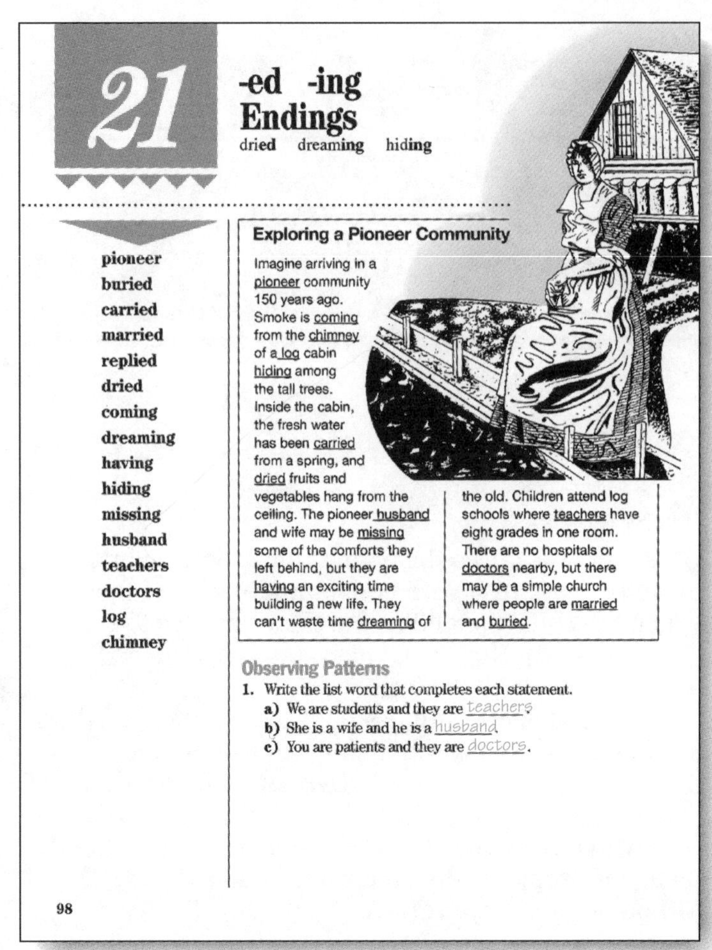

21

-ed -ing Endings

dried dreaming hiding

pioneer
buried
carried
married
replied
dried
coming
dreaming
having
hiding
missing
husband
teachers
doctors
log
chimney

Exploring a Pioneer Community

Imagine arriving in a pioneer community 150 years ago. Smoke is coming from the chimney of a log cabin hiding among the tall trees. Inside the cabin, the fresh water has been carried from a spring, and dried fruits and vegetables hang from the ceiling. The pioneer husband and wife may be missing some of the comforts they left behind, but they are having an exciting time building a new life. They can't waste time dreaming of the old. Children attend log schools where teachers have eight grades in one room. There are no hospitals or doctors nearby, but there may be a simple church where people are married and buried.

Observing Patterns

1. Write the list word that completes each statement.
   a) We are students and they are teachers.
   b) She is a wife and he is a husband.
   c) You are patients and they are doctors.

98

Observing Patterns

1. Advise students that the list word which completes each blank is generally considered the opposite, or antonym, of the noun in the first part of the sentence. Students could suggest antonyms for other list words.

list word	antonym
buried	dug up
carried	dropped
married	divorced
replied	ignored
coming	going

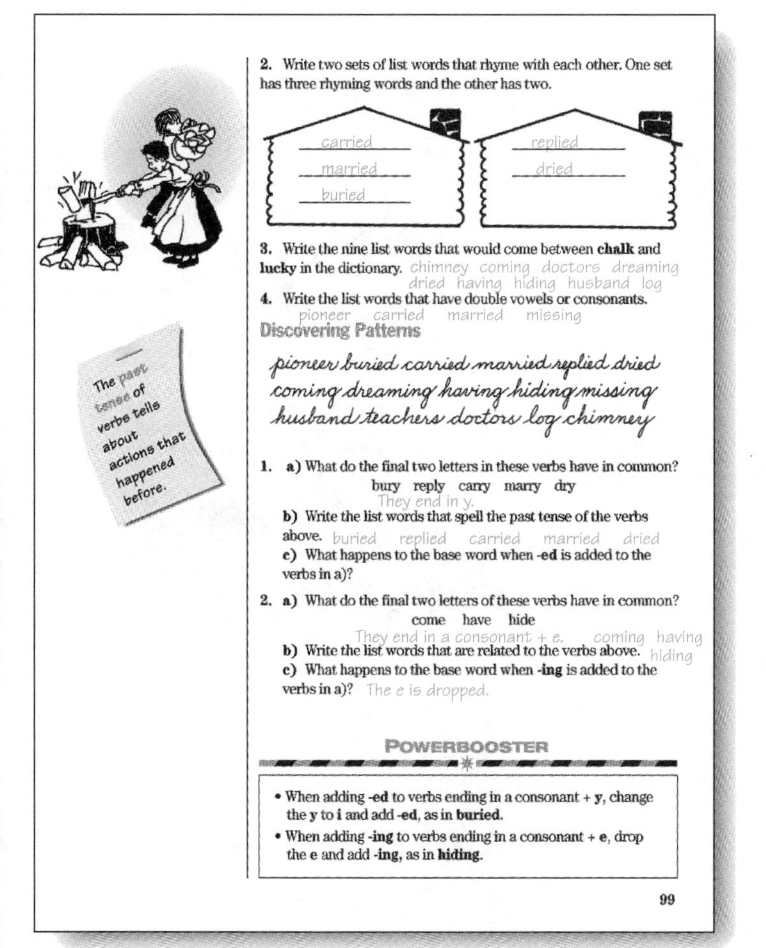

2. Write two sets of list words that rhyme with each other. One set has three rhyming words and the other has two.

carried / married / buried — replied / dried

3. Write the nine list words that would come between **chalk** and **lucky** in the dictionary. chimney coming doctors dreaming dried having hiding husband log

4. Write the list words that have double vowels or consonants. pioneer carried married missing

Discovering Patterns

pioneer buried carried married replied dried coming dreaming having hiding missing husband teachers doctors log chimney

The past tense of verbs tells about actions that happened before.

1. a) What do the final two letters in these verbs have in common? bury reply carry marry dry They end in y.
   b) Write the list words that spell the past tense of the verbs above. buried replied carried married dried
   c) What happens to the base word when **-ed** is added to the verbs in a)?
2. a) What do the final two letters of these verbs have in common? come have hide They end in a consonant + e.
   b) Write the list words that are related to the verbs above. coming having hiding
   c) What happens to the base word when **-ing** is added to the verbs in a)? The e is dropped.

POWERBOOSTER

- When adding **-ed** to verbs ending in a consonant + **y**, change the **y** to **i** and add **-ed**, as in **buried**.
- When adding **-ing** to verbs ending in a consonant + **e**, drop the **e** and add **-ing**, as in **hiding**.

99

2. Note with students that the set of words **buried/carried/married** rhymes even though **buried** has a different spelling pattern from the other two.

3. Students may wish to work in pairs to complete this exercise. In the case of **chimney**, **dreaming**, and **dried** it is necessary to alphabetize to the third letter. It may help some students if you write each list word on a card and have them sort the cards into the correct alphabetical order.

4. Students could highlight these letters in colour or by size of print.

Discovering Patterns

1. Students may need some guidance in noticing that the final two letters in each verb are a **consonant** + **y**. They may focus instead on the fact that four of the words end in the letters **r** and **y**.

2. Note that **come** and **have** are exceptions to the rules of pronunciation in which a silent final **e** usually indicates the preceding vowel is long (**hide**). In these two words the vowels are short. Many of the words that we use on a daily basis are irregular and pose challenges for beginning readers and writers as well as those new to English.

Also point out that each of the verbs in the exercise has an irregular past tense. It may be helpful to begin a list of verbs having irregular past tense forms and add to it as students encounter more over the year.

irregular verbs	
present tense	**past tense**
I am	I was
I hide	I hid
I run	I ran
I come	I came
I have	I had
I give	I gave
I sit	I sat
I eat	I ate

ESL

- Some ESL students may experience difficulty with the **-ing** form of the verb. They may not hear or write the unstressed ending, or the (I) **am**, (she/he) **is** and (they) **are** which are unstressed and quickly passed over in English speech. It may be helpful to explain that the action in progressive tenses is happening 'right now' and to practise with the question form.

  Where are they hiding? They are hiding under the table. They're hiding under the table.

  When is your new bike coming? It is coming on Saturday. It's coming on Saturday.

Exploring Patterns

1. If students have difficulty adding **-ed** or **-ing** correctly, review the rules in the Powerbooster and have them identify the words that fall within each pattern.

3. Remind students that they are looking for list words that have both the sound /ē/ and the spelling patterns indicated. Therefore, they should not include the words **replied** and **dried**, since the letters **ie** do not spell the sound /ē/.

The spelling pattern for /ē/ in **hurried** is actually **y**, from the base word **hurry**. Other examples include **carry/carried** and **marry/married**.

4. Ask students to identify specific Canadians who could be associated with each of these categories.

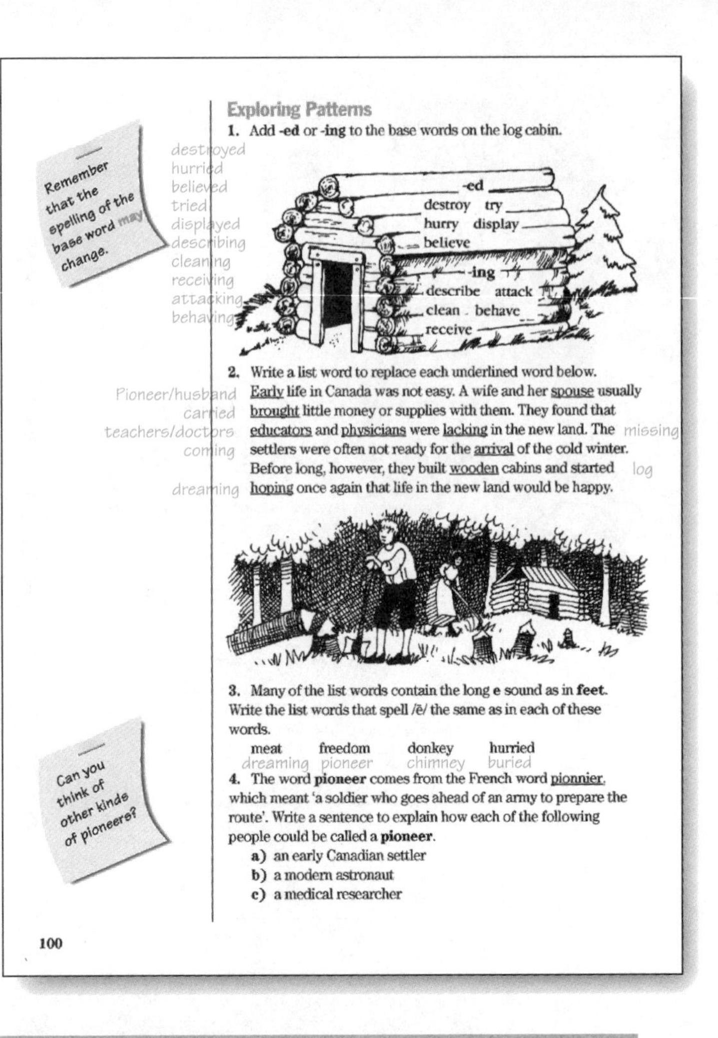

Exploring Patterns

1. Add **-ed** or **-ing** to the base words on the log cabin.

-ed: destroy, try, hurry, display, believe

-ing: describe, attack, clean, behave, receive

destroyed, hurried, believed, tried, displayed, describing, cleaning, receiving, attacking, behaving

Remember that the spelling of the base word may change.

2. Write a list word to replace each underlined word below.

Early life in Canada was not easy. A wife and her spouse usually brought little money or supplies with them. They found that educators and physicians were lacking in the new land. The settlers were often not ready for the arrival of the cold winter. Before long, however, they built wooden cabins and started hoping once again that life in the new land would be happy.

Pioneer/husband, carried, teachers/doctors, missing, coming, log, dreaming

3. Many of the list words contain the long **e** sound as in **feet**. Write the list words that spell /ē/ the same as in each of these words.

meat — dreaming; freedom — pioneer; donkey — chimney; hurried — buried

4. The word **pioneer** comes from the French word pionnier, which meant 'a soldier who goes ahead of an army to prepare the route'. Write a sentence to explain how each of the following people could be called a **pioneer**.

a) an early Canadian settler
b) a modern astronaut
c) a medical researcher

Can you think of other kinds of pioneers?

100

Dr. Maude Abbott (1869–1940) was a world-famous physician and scientist, whose specialty was congenital heart ailments.

Special Needs

- If students have difficulty grasping the rules for adding **-ed** and **-ing**, it may help to construct examples using letter tiles. Form the base word, and have the students remove the silent **e** or change the **y** to **i** while explaining what they are doing. Then have them add the ending. Note that **y** changes to **i** regardless of whether it spells the long **i** (**reply**) or long **e** (**marry**) sound.

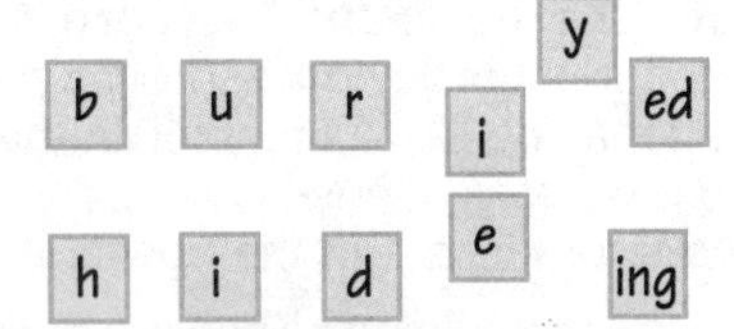

Oral Language and Literature

- Encourage students to use verbs effectively in their oral and written communication. Brainstorm as many alternatives as possible to the verb **replied**. Use a number of these verbs in sentences to show the variations in meaning. Have students read the sentences aloud to show how the verb influences tone and meaning.

replied: answered, retorted, returned, demanded, whispered, begged, pleaded, rejoined, echoed, responded

"I want you to come home," she demanded.
"I want you to come home," she pleaded.
"I want you to come home," she whispered.

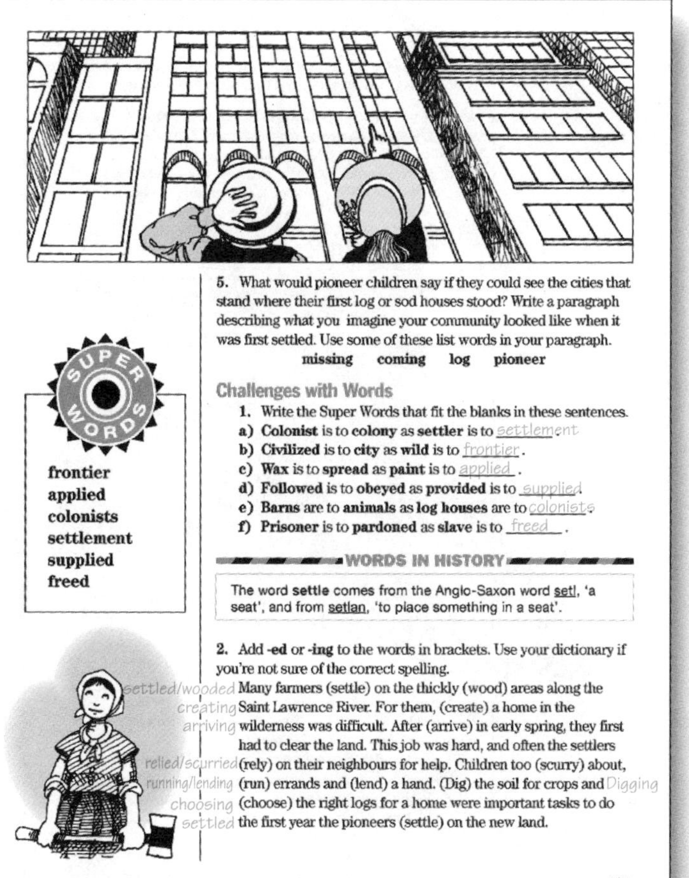

5. What would pioneer children say if they could see the cities that stand where their first log or sod houses stood? Write a paragraph describing what you imagine your community looked like when it was first settled. Use some of these list words in your paragraph.

missing coming log pioneer

SUPER WORDS

frontier
applied
colonists
settlement
supplied
freed

Challenges with Words

1. Write the Super Words that fit the blanks in these sentences.

a) **Colonist** is to **colony** as **settler** is to settlement.
b) **Civilized** is to **city** as **wild** is to frontier.
c) **Wax** is to **spread** as **paint** is to applied.
d) **Followed** is to **obeyed** as **provided** is to supplied.
e) **Barns** are to **animals** as **log houses** are to colonists.
f) **Prisoner** is to **pardoned** as **slave** is to freed.

WORDS IN HISTORY

The word **settle** comes from the Anglo-Saxon word setl, 'a seat', and from setlan, 'to place something in a seat'.

2. Add **-ed** or **-ing** to the words in brackets. Use your dictionary if you're not sure of the correct spelling.

settled/wooded Many farmers (settle) on the thickly (wood) areas along the
creating Saint Lawrence River. For them, (create) a home in the
arriving wilderness was difficult. After (arrive) in early spring, they first had to clear the land. This job was hard, and often the settlers
relied/scurried (rely) on their neighbours for help. Children too (scurry) about,
running/lending (run) errands and (lend) a hand. (Dig) the soil for crops and Digging
choosing (choose) the right logs for a home were important tasks to do
settled the first year the pioneers (settle) on the new land.

101

5. Students may wish to dramatize their description by writing it as a dialogue between the two children in the illustration, or as a radio or television interview with visitors who have 'returned' from the past.

Read excerpts from the writings of Susanna Moodie, an early settler in Canada. They may be available in your local library.

> The early part of the winter of 1837, a year never to be forgotten in the annals of Canadian history, was very severe. During the month of February, the thermometer often ranged from eighteen to twenty-seven degrees below zero. Speaking of the coldness of one particular day, a genuine brother Jonathan remarked, with charming simplicity, that it was thirty degrees below zero that morning, and it would have been much colder if the thermometer had been longer.
>
> (*Roughing It in the Bush*, Chapter 16, "The Fire")

Challenges with Words

1. Discuss the relationships in each analogy. Some, such as e), are straightforward, but others are more abstract in nature.

Words in History

Students might like to investigate other Super Word histories. **Frontier**, for example, comes from the French, *frontiere*, meaning the 'front part of something'. How does this origin relate to the meaning of **frontier** in English?

super word	history
applied	the French *aplier*, to fasten to
colonists	the Latin *colonia*, the plural of *colonus*, a farmer
settlement	the Old English *setl*, a place to sit
supplied	the French *soupleer*, to fill
freed	the Old English *freo*, to love

2. Have students review the Powerbooster (p. 99) before completing this exercise. They should pay special attention to what happens to the base word when an ending is added.

Critical Thinking

• Have students use a Venn diagram to help plan their response to Exploring Patterns 5. The intersection of the two circles represents what would be the same about pioneer times and today, the outside portion of each circle indicates what was unique about each. The points on the diagram will provide comparative details for the paragraph.

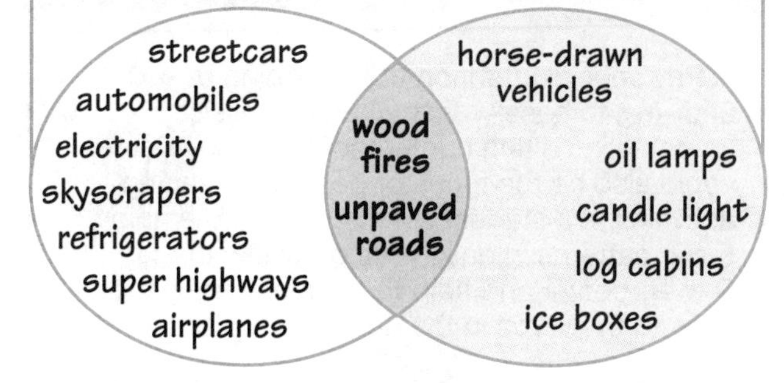

3. Students might like to develop this paragraph into a short history of the settlement of their own or a friend's family in Canada. They might talk with parents and relatives for information.

4. Students might wish to work in groups to complete this activity. They could combine many different facets of pioneer life and extend their newspaper into several pages. The local historical society and library may be helpful as sources of information.

Desktop publishing software would help make the production of the newspaper easy. Suggest that students create an appropriate title for their paper.

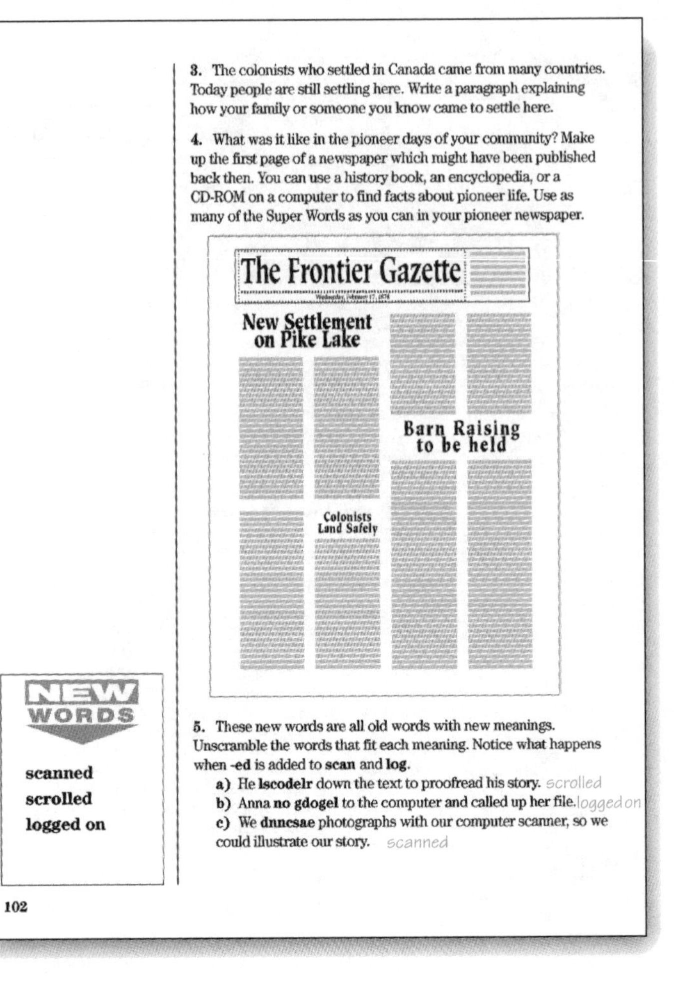

3. The colonists who settled in Canada came from many countries. Today people are still settling here. Write a paragraph explaining how your family or someone you know came to settle here.

4. What was it like in the pioneer days of your community? Make up the first page of a newspaper which might have been published back then. You can use a history book, an encyclopedia, or a CD-ROM on a computer to find facts about pioneer life. Use as many of the Super Words as you can in your pioneer newspaper.

The Frontier Gazette

New Settlement on Pike Lake

Barn Raising to be held

Colonists Land Safely

NEW WORDS

scanned
scrolled
logged on

5. These new words are all old words with new meanings. Unscramble the words that fit each meaning. Notice what happens when **-ed** is added to **scan** and **log**.

a) He **lscodelr** down the text to proofread his story. scrolled

b) Anna **no gdogel** to the computer and called up her file. logged on

c) We **dnnesae** photographs with our computer scanner, so we could illustrate our story. scanned

102

New Words

5. Ask students to brainstorm other basic computer terms that would need to be explained to a novice computer user.

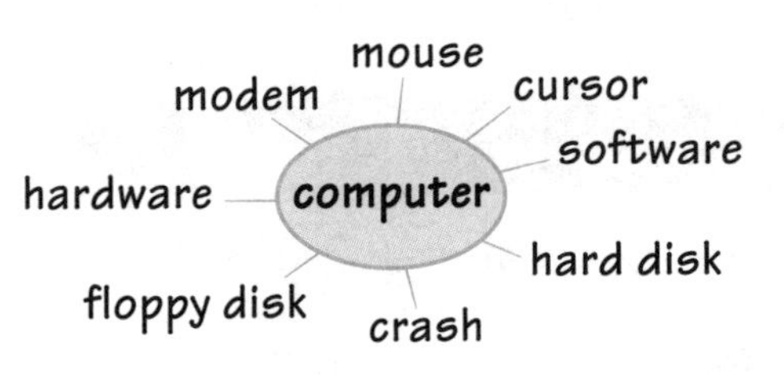

- Co-operative groups can be used effectively in producing the pioneer newspaper described in Challenges with Words 4. Students can contribute to the background research, writing, layout, computer graphics, and so forth.

- Pay special attention to the adding of **-ed** and **-ing** to base words when you assist students in editing conferences. These features could also be the focus of peer proofreading activities. If a student seems unable to employ these patterns in daily writing, review the Powerbooster and help the student apply the rules to the verbs in the draft under discussion.

Curriculum Connection

The theme of pioneers can be integrated into the Social Studies portion of the curriculum, or into themes dealing with Canada's past.

Home Connection

Encourage parents to help their children apply the rules of adding **-ed** and **-ing** to a variety of verbs. They could point out examples of such patterns in the media or in print materials at home, as well as modelling the pattern through notes and written messages that they share with their child.

Assessment

Note whether errors on the Unit Test are related to patterns for adding endings (**comeing** for **coming**) or to problems with visual memory (**comming** for **coming**; **docter** for **doctor**).

Follow-up

- If errors show that the student does not understand the rules for adding endings, review the Powerbooster. These patterns are also dealt with in *Sharing the Secrets: Teach Your Child to Spell*, Units 23-25.
- If the student is making errors because of problems with visual memory, use specific strategies such as colour-coding, configuration, and exaggerating sounds.

Teacher's Notes

Number Words

forty
twice

Patterns

Since number words occur so frequently in our daily lives, it is important to be able to spell them accurately. Some number words, such as **twenty-one**, **twenty-two** and so on follow predictable patterns. Others, such as **eleven** and **twelve** must be memorized separately.

Preknowledge

Students should have an understanding of the following concepts as they work with the patterns in this unit.

• The number of syllables in a word. If students have difficulty identifying the syllables in any word, encourage them either to tap the syllables as they say the word aloud, or to feel how their jaw drops as each syllable is pronounced.

More Patterns

Other patterns you might wish to introduce or review in this unit include the following.

• The capitalization of proper nouns (**Olympic**). Remind students that proper nouns refer to specific places, people, and things, and are always capitalized.
• Compound words are made up of two separate words that together form a new word (**volleyball**).
• The /ôr/ sound can be spelled in several ways:
-or (**sport**, **forty**)
-our (**court**)
-o_e (**score**)

Professional Notebook

Spelling programs should focus on the *logic* of spelling rather than presenting in format and in tone the attitude that most of English spelling is illogical and has to be memorized. (Templeton, *Educational Leadership*, Vol. 43, No. 6:77)

Sharing the Secrets with Kids

One of the hardest words to spell is ***twelfth****. Configuration boxes may help you remember the shape of the word. Or, you can remember the 'elf' in* ***twelfth****.*

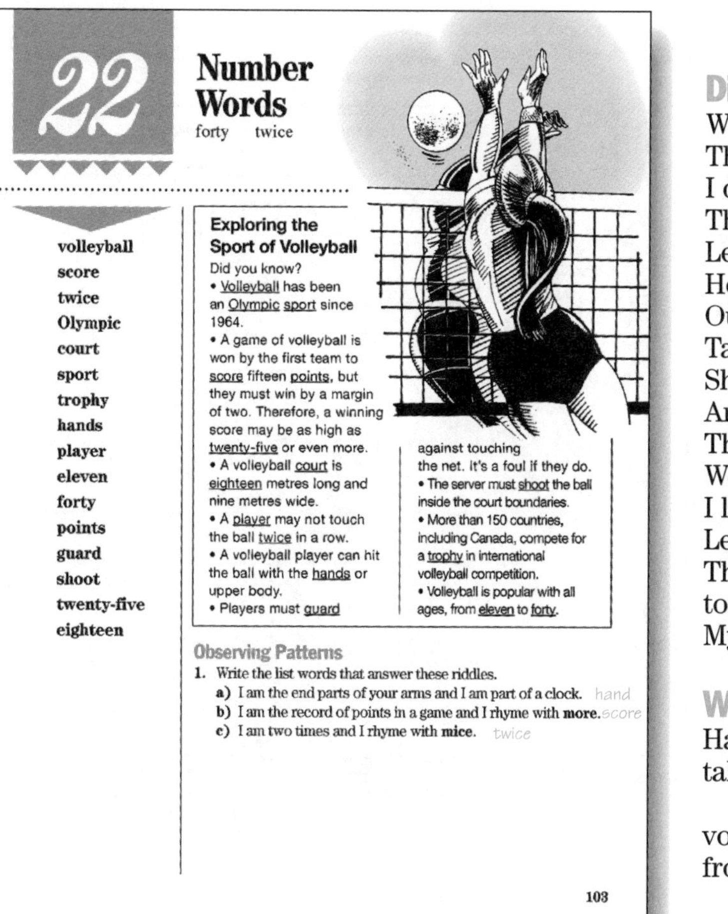

22 Number Words

forty twice

volleyball
score
twice
Olympic
court
sport
trophy
hands
player
eleven
forty
points
guard
shoot
twenty-five
eighteen

Exploring the Sport of Volleyball

Did you know?

- Volleyball has been an Olympic sport since 1964.
- A game of volleyball is won by the first team to score fifteen points, but they must win by a margin of two. Therefore, a winning score may be as high as twenty-five or even more.
- A volleyball court is eighteen metres long and nine metres wide.
- A player may not touch the ball twice in a row.
- A volleyball player can hit the ball with the hands or upper body.
- Players must guard against touching the net. It's a foul if they do.
- The server must shoot the ball inside the court boundaries.
- More than 150 countries, including Canada, compete for a trophy in international volleyball competition.
- Volleyball is popular with all ages, from eleven to forty.

Observing Patterns

1. Write the list words that answer these riddles.
   a) I am the end parts of your arms and I am part of a clock. hand
   b) I am the record of points in a game and I rhyme with **more.** score
   c) I am two times and I rhyme with **mice.** twice

103

Precheck

Remember to pronounce words with normal stress and intonation when you dictate them either on their own or in sentences. Have students make corrections immediately following the dictation.

Dictation

We played **volleyball** on the beach.
The **score** was tied at half-time.
I dropped the ball **twice**!
The **Olympic** games are held every four years.
Let's go to the tennis **court**!
Hockey is my favourite **sport**.
Our team won the baseball **trophy**.
Take your **hands** out of your pockets!
She's the best **player** on the team.
Are there **eleven** players in a hockey team?
They won the game **forty** to six.
We needed three more **points** to win.
I like playing **guard** in basketball.
Let's see you **shoot** a basket.
The game starts at **twenty-five** past eight tonight.
My brother will be **eighteen** tomorrow.

Words in Context

Have students read the paragraph aloud, perhaps taking turns reading the facts.

Students might like to research the rules of volleyball, and list those that have been omitted from the passage.

Observing Patterns

1. Have students create riddles for other list words and share them with the class.

I am one more than ten and one less than twelve (*eleven*).
I am what you will score and I rhyme with joints (*points*).
I try to protect though my job can be hard (*guard*).
I am what you receive when your team wins the game (*trophy*).

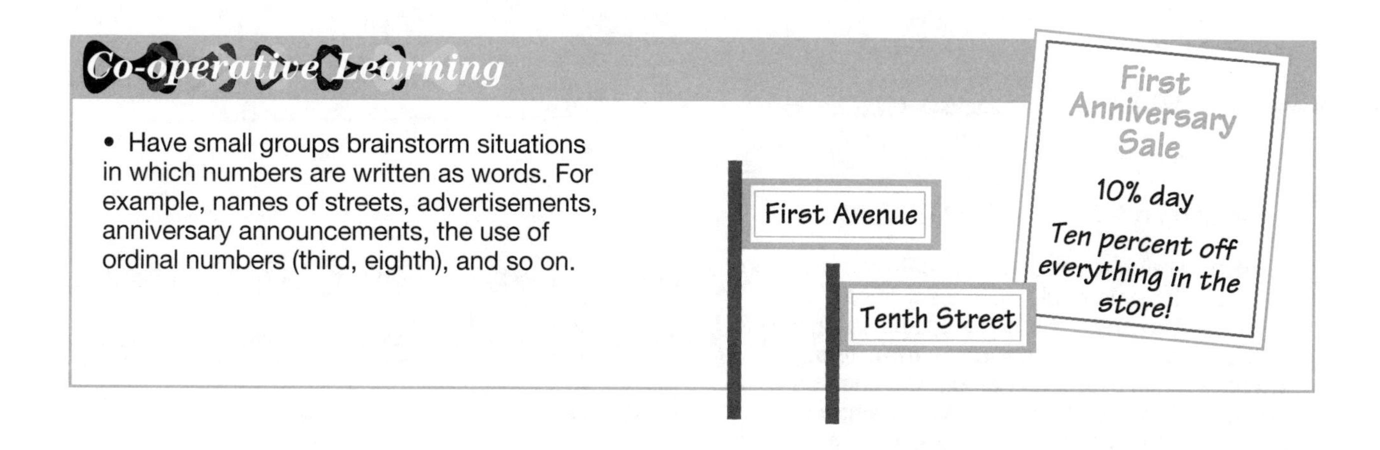

Co-operative Learning

- Have small groups brainstorm situations in which numbers are written as words. For example, names of streets, advertisements, anniversary announcements, the use of ordinal numbers (third, eighth), and so on.

2. If students have difficulty counting the number of syllables, have them say the word aloud and tap each time they hear a distinct syllable.

3. Other list words could be studied through the use of configuration boxes or lines. (See Special Needs, this page.)

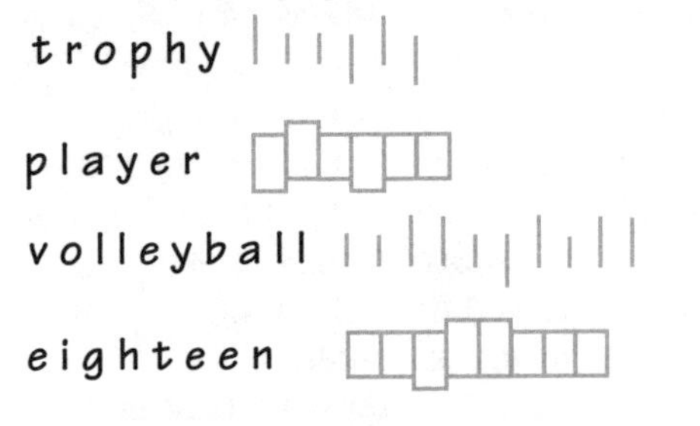

Discovering Patterns

1. Help students to notice that the final **t** is dropped from **eight** when **-teen** is added to make **eighteen**.

2. Contrast the spelling of **forty** in which the **u** is dropped, with the spelling of **fourteen**, in which the letter **u** is retained.

3. Reinforce this pattern with other examples. (See Special Needs, this page.)

4. Point out the fact that a similar pattern occurs with **one/once**, and **three/thrice**, although **thrice** is not commonly used.

two syllables	three syllables
trophy	volleyball
player	Olympic
forty	eleven
eighteen	twenty-five

2. Write the list words that have two syllables and list words that have three syllables.

two syllables **three syllables**

3. Write the list words that fit these shapes.

s p o r t   c o u r t   g u a r d

Discovering Patterns

volleyball score twice Olympic court sport trophy hands player eleven forty points guard shoot twenty-five eighteen

1. Write the number word for 18. Now write the number word that 18 comes from. What happens to the base word when **-teen** is added? eighteen — eight
When -teen is added the t is dropped

2. Write the number word for 40. Now write the number word that 40 comes from. What happens to the base word when **-ty** is added?
forty — four When -ty is added the u is dropped

3. Write the number word for 25. What happens when a single digit (such as 5) is added to a number word such as **twenty**?
twenty-five A hyphen is added

4. Write the number that the word **twice** comes from. two

POWERBOOSTER

• Number words are often based on related numbers as with **eighteen** and **eight**. It is important to notice when a letter has been changed from one number to another, as with **four** and **forty**.

104

Special Needs

• Many of the list words have interesting shapes, with ascending and descending letters. Such words can often be remembered through configuration or line drawings. Prepare a configuration or line drawing for each list word in random order. Have students match the shape with a list word.

twenty-five

score

shoot

twice

points

Olympic

forty

hands

eleven

• Help to reinforce predictable patterns with card games. Students could have a set of cards with the words **twenty**, **thirty**, **forty** and so on in one colour, and single digits such as **one**, **two**, **three**, etc., in a second colour. A hyphen card would be in another shade. Call out a number, and have students form the correct number word by combining the appropriate cards.

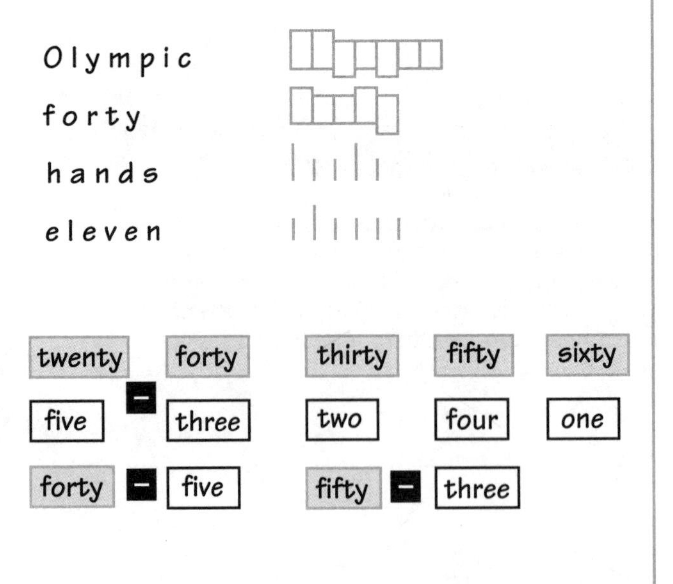

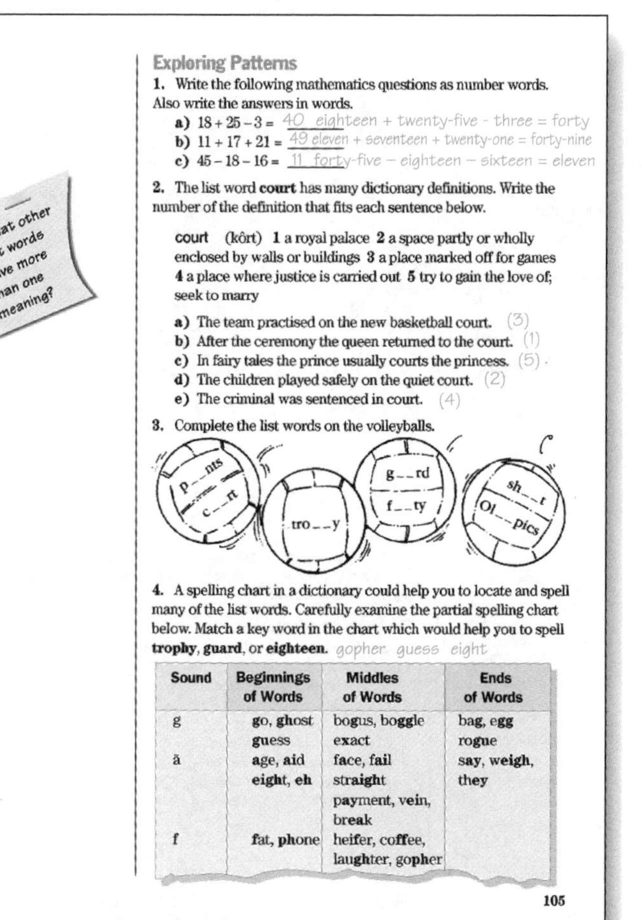

What other list words have more than one meaning?

Exploring Patterns

1. Write the following mathematics questions as number words. Also write the answers in words.

a) 18 + 25 – 3 = 40 eighteen + twenty-five - three = forty
b) 11 + 17 + 21 = 49 eleven + seventeen + twenty-one = forty-nine
c) 45 – 18 – 16 = 11 forty-five – eighteen – sixteen = eleven

2. The list word **court** has many dictionary definitions. Write the number of the definition that fits each sentence below.

court (kôrt) **1** a royal palace **2** a space partly or wholly enclosed by walls or buildings **3** a place marked off for games **4** a place where justice is carried out **5** try to gain the love of; seek to marry

a) The team practised on the new basketball court. (3)
b) After the ceremony the queen returned to the court. (1)
c) In fairy tales the prince usually courts the princess. (5)
d) The children played safely on the quiet court. (2)
e) The criminal was sentenced in court. (4)

3. Complete the list words on the volleyballs.

4. A spelling chart in a dictionary could help you to locate and spell many of the list words. Carefully examine the partial spelling chart below. Match a key word in the chart which would help you to spell **trophy**, **guard**, or **eighteen**. gopher guess eight

Sound	Beginnings of Words	Middles of Words	Ends of Words
g	go, ghost guess	bogus, boggle exact	bag, egg rogue
ā	age, aid eight, eh	face, fail straight payment, vein, break	say, weigh, they
f	fat, phone	heifer, coffee, laughter, gopher	

105

ESL

- Idioms with number words are common in English. Students may enjoy learning some of these.

  The starting rhyme:
  one for the money
  two for the show
  three to get ready
  and **four** to go!

- Other number word idioms include the following.

  Once in a blue moon. (*not very often*)
  Put **two** and **two** together. (*make conclusions from known facts*)
  Three's a crowd. (*one person will feel left out*)
  Forty winks. (*a brief sleep*)

Exploring Patterns

1. Remind the students that both the question and the answer must be written in words.

2. Another list word with a variety of meanings is **hands**. Students could record the different definitions and also the many idioms related to **hand**.

change hands · secondhand · hands down
lend a hand · hands off · hands-on
on the other hand · hand-me-down
hands up

3. Encourage students to use a different colour of ink or a highlighter pen to accentuate the letters replaced by the blanks.

The spelling of **guard** represents one pattern for spelling the sound /g/. Challenge students to find other words fitting this pattern (**guess**, **guest**, **guarantee**, **guitar**, **guilty**, **guide**, **guild**).

4. Students may need guidance in answering this question. Ask them first to identify the letters in **trophy**, **eighteen**, and **guard** which may pose spelling difficulties. Next, determine the sound that these letters produce. For example, the letters **gu** in **guard** spell the sound /g/. Note whether these letters are at the beginning, middle, or end of the word. Then match the sound, position, and spelling pattern with a word from the spelling chart. Thus, the letters **ph** in the middle of **trophy**, make the sound /f/. This combination matches the word **gopher** in the spelling chart.

5. Encourage students to think of other ways of beginning a story about their favourite game or sport. How could they expand on their initial sentences? Suggest they might tell of a special moment, or their personal memories.

Challenges with Words

1. Gymnasium is often shortened to **gym**. This is an example of a 'clipped word', a word created by shortening or clipping an existing form. Ask students to think of other clipped words and their longer original forms. More information about clipped words can be found in *The Student Editor's Guide to Words*, pp.114–115.

long form	clipped word
laboratory	lab
examination	exam
luncheon	lunch
influenza	flu
caravan	van
veterinarian	vet
mathematics	math

Draw attention to the double consonants in **inning** and **offence**, the **tch** pattern in **pitcher**, and the **c** spelling of the sound /s/ in **offence**.

Note also that **uni** in **uniform** usually means one. Explore this meaning with the students and link it with other words containing **uni** (**uni**que, **uni**corn, **uni**versal, **unity**, **uni**on, **uni**cycle, **unify**, **uni**son, **unite**).

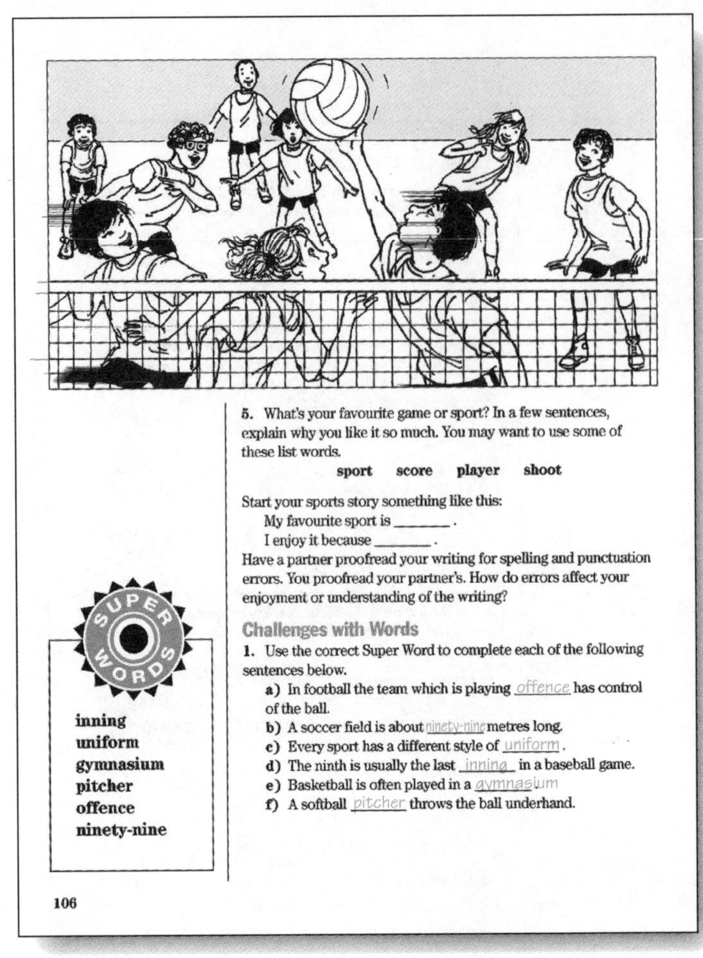

5. What's your favourite game or sport? In a few sentences, explain why you like it so much. You may want to use some of these list words.

sport **score** **player** **shoot**

Start your sports story something like this:

My favourite sport is _______ .

I enjoy it because _______ .

Have a partner proofread your writing for spelling and punctuation errors. You proofread your partner's. How do errors affect your enjoyment or understanding of the writing?

SUPER WORDS

inning
uniform
gymnasium
pitcher
offence
ninety-nine

Challenges with Words

1. Use the correct Super Word to complete each of the following sentences below.

a) In football the team which is playing offence has control of the ball.

b) A soccer field is about ninety-nine metres long.

c) Every sport has a different style of uniform.

d) The ninth is usually the last inning in a baseball game.

e) Basketball is often played in a gymnasium

f) A softball pitcher throws the ball underhand.

106

Writing

- It is important for students to realize that in formal writing numbers are usually written as words. This can be contrasted with forms of writing in which digits are used (e.g., advertisements, sports reports, financial news, weather forecasts). Newspapers and publishers in Canada tend to follow the style of writing the numbers one to ten as words; all numbers above ten are usually written as digits.

2. Number words, such as **ninety-nine**, are used when writing bank cheques. Using the sample bank cheque as a model, write cheques of your own for the amounts listed below.

The cheque is payable to Nanook's Winter Wear

Give the date the cheque is written

CHRIS LEE
123 MAIN STREET
CITY, PROVINCE

Feb. 12 96

Pay to the order of Nanook's Winter Wear $ 123.45

one hundred twenty-three 45/100 DOLLARS

CARA - BANK

0215 42803 010

Write the amount of the cheque in numerals

Write the amount in words

This is Chris's account number

The cheque can't be cashed unless Chris signs it

a) Pay to: Sports Unlimited; for $35.26 thirty-five — 26
b) Pay to: (your town) Midget Hockey League; for $23.48 twenty-three — 48
c) Pay to: Bruno's Pizzeria; for $11.92 eleven — 92
d) Pay to: Town Hardware Ltd.; for $99.37 ninety-nine — 37
e) Pay to: (Your school); for $17.50 seventeen — 50

3. Sports have their own terms or vocabulary. Match up the term in Group A with the sport in Group B.

Group A: spike, home run, blue line, sweep, free throw, love, slalom, first down, penalty kick.

Group B: hockey, football, volleyball, soccer, basketball, baseball, tennis, curling, skiing.

In football, the ball is sometimes called a **pigskin**, because the balls used to be made from pig leather.

4. Choose a team sport you like to play and make a booklet describing how to play it. You might organize your booklet like this:

- Title page
- Table of contents
- A drawing of the playing field or court
- A list of the players on each team and how their position is played
- A description of how the game is played and the method of scoring
- A dictionary or glossary of common terms used in the sport

3. spike – volleyball
home run – baseball
blue line – hockey
sweep – curling
free throw – basketball
love – tennis
slalom – skiing
first down – football
penalty kick – soccer

107

2. Have students also write cheques for amounts over one hundred dollars. (See Home Connection, p. 172 and Co-operative Learning, p. 167.)

3. and 4. Students might wish to work in groups to complete these activities, sharing the knowledge they have of different sports.

Critical Thinking

- Have students work with a partner, each couple having a pair of dice. One person roles the dice and must multiply the two numbers that turn up. The second person must record the product in both digit and number word forms. Person one checks for accuracy of spelling.

$6 \times 5 = 30$ six × five = thirty
$2 \times 4 = 8$ two × four = eight

Oral Language and Literature

- Explore sports metaphors with your students. Try to link each expression with a specific sport. Add other sports metaphors as they come to mind.

metaphor	sport
saved by the bell	boxing
roll with the punches	boxing
go to bat for someone	cricket
touch base with others	baseball
playing the field	baseball
behind the eight ball	pool
not up to par	golf
jumping the gun	sprinting
the ball's in your court	tennis
taking the bait	fishing

Curriculum Connection

Number words are most obviously linked with mathematics and science. Provide students with newspaper reports of basketball or football scores, weather reports containing temperatures, and food ads from flyers. Have students convert the numbers to number words.

Windsor-Essex-Kent

Sarnia-Lambton.

Today..mainly cloudy. High near 6.

Tonight..mainly cloudy. Low near zero.

Wednesday..mainly cloudy.
Wind southeast 30 km/h. High near 13.

Probability of precipitation in percent
20 today, 15 tonight, 10 Wednesday.

Home Connection

Suggest that parents help their children to fill in sample cheques or deposit slips requiring the writing of numbers in words. Have them pay particular attention to words such as **forty** and **eight.** (See Challenges with Words 2.)

Assessment

Note whether errors in the Unit Test indicate a problem with understanding the formation of number words or with the more visual features such as the spelling of the /ôr/ sound, silent letters, letter sequence, and capitalization.

Follow-up

If problems seem to be with the formation of number words, provide additional practice with converting ordinal numbers into number words. Look for number words on signs in the community, in advertisements, around the school, and in the general daily living that students encounter.

Teacher's Notes

Long e
ie as in p**ie**ces
ea as in app**ea**r

Prefix un-
unusual

Patterns

The patterns for spelling long **e** belong to the 'sound' level of English. The prefix **un-** is part of the semantic, or 'meaning' layer of the language. Children tend to concentrate on the sound level of spelling in the early years of school. As they develop both their oral vocabularies and their reading skills, they become increasingly sensitive to elements of meaning. This may begin with the realization that **-ed** at the end of a word often indicates the past tense. Gradually, the meaning connections through prefixes, suffixes, and derived forms of base words help the student with spelling as well as with reading and vocabulary.

Preknowledge

Students should have an understanding of the following concepts as they work with the patterns in this unit.

- Base words and their derived forms become an increasingly important part of the students' spoken and written vocabularies at this level. Help students understand that the spelling pattern of the base word is usually repeated in the derivation (**invite/invitation**).
- Prefixes can be added to many base words for a variety of purposes. The prefix **-un**, for example, usually creates an antonym of the base word (**like/unlike**).
- Word families are made up of words that have the same spelling pattern (**pose/rose/nose**).
- Adding **-ing** and **-ed** to base words sometimes requires changes to that word (**run/running**; **slap/slapped**).
- Words are made up of a number of syllables, some of which are stressed, and some unstressed.

Professional Notebook

Research in vocabulary instruction has underscored the critical importance of students' understanding how prefixes and suffixes combine with base words and root words to create new words. This understanding can help students analyze unknown words they encounter in their reading and lead to a rich expansion and elaboration of their vocabularies.

(Bear et al. 307)

More Patterns

Other patterns you might wish to review or introduce from the list words in this unit include the following.

- Homophones are words that sound alike but are spelled differently (**pair/pear**; **right/write**).
- Some word 'pairs' are not homophones but are similar enough in sound that they are easily confused (**except/accept**; **loose/lose**).

Precheck

You may wish to monitor the self-corrections made in Column B of the Student Record Sheet to ensure that words are indeed being spelled correctly by certain students.

Dictation

Winter **clothing** keeps you warm.
I left my work **unfinished**.
A **suit** has a jacket and pants or skirt.
We ate everything **except** the beans.
Snow in September is **unusual**.
There are two items in a **pair**.
You **appear** to be busy!
Is your suitcase **unpacked** yet?
Pick up those **loose** papers.
There are two **pieces** of cake left.
She **reaches** up to get the book.
The stolen bicycle was **unidentified**.
What **size** of shoes do you wear?
Long **pants** are warmer than shorts!
My dad is **making** dinner tonight.
Hold up your **right** hand.

Words in Context

Have students read the passage as a cloze exercise, perhaps on an overhead. Have them identify the list word that is not used (**except**). Suggest students attempt to add a sentence to the paragraph using **except**.

Observing Patterns

1. Some students may need to say the list words aloud or tap the number of syllables. It may be helpful to consult a dictionary for how these words are divided into syllables and have the students write the words with a dot or slash mark between each syllable. You might find that the base word appears as a dictionary entry, but not the derived form with a prefix. Usually, the prefix is a distinct syllable in the word. (See Special Needs, this page.)

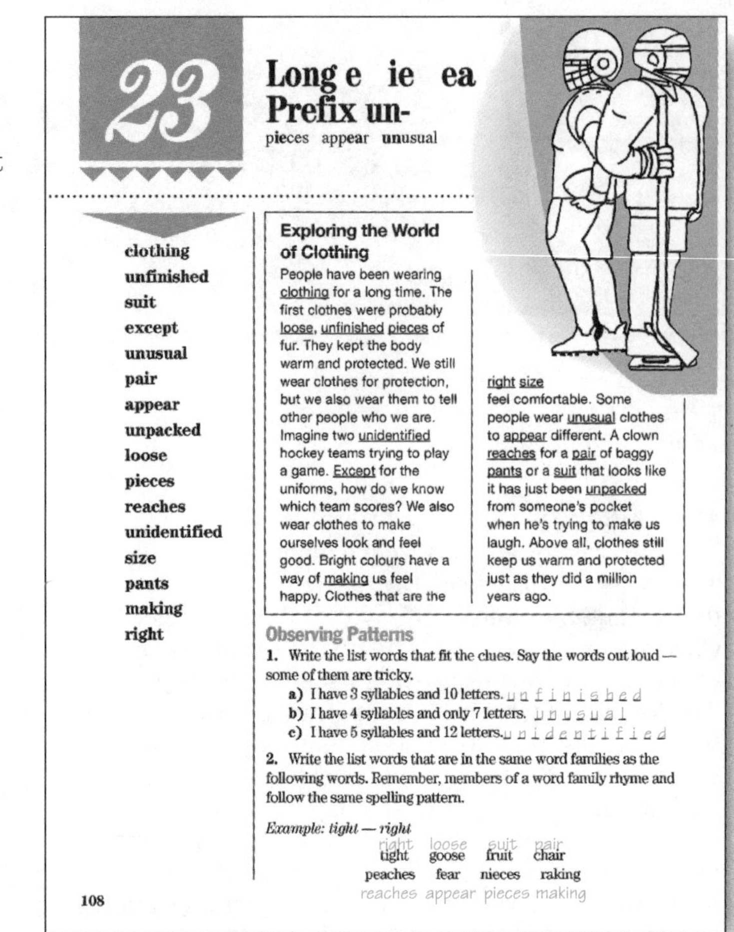

23 Long e ie ea
Prefix un-

pieces appear unusual

clothing
unfinished
suit
except
unusual
pair
appear
unpacked
loose
pieces
reaches
unidentified
size
pants
making
right

Exploring the World of Clothing

People have been wearing clothing for a long time. The first clothes were probably loose, unfinished pieces of fur. They kept the body warm and protected. We still wear clothes for protection, but we also wear them to tell other people who we are. Imagine two unidentified hockey teams trying to play a game. Except for the uniforms, how do we know which team scores? We also wear clothes to make ourselves look and feel good. Bright colours have a way of making us feel happy. Clothes that are the right size feel comfortable. Some people wear unusual clothes to appear different. A clown reaches for a pair of baggy pants or a suit that looks like it has just been unpacked from someone's pocket when he's trying to make us laugh. Above all, clothes still keep us warm and protected just as they did a million years ago.

Observing Patterns

1. Write the list words that fit the clues. Say the words out loud — some of them are tricky.
a) I have 3 syllables and 10 letters. unfinished
b) I have 4 syllables and only 7 letters. unusual
c) I have 5 syllables and 12 letters. unidentified

2. Write the list words that are in the same word families as the following words. Remember, members of a word family rhyme and follow the same spelling pattern.

Example: tight — right

right loose suit pair
tight goose fruit chair
peaches fear nieces raking
reaches appear pieces making

108

2. Ask students to add as many other words as they can to each word family, remembering that the words must rhyme and use the same spelling patterns.

tight	goose	fruit	chair
right fight light	loose moose noose	suit pursuit	pair fair hair

peaches	fear	nieces	raking
reaches beaches impeaches	appear dear gear	pieces	making baking faking

Special Needs

- To help students visualize how derived words have been built, colour code the word parts so that the base is in one colour, prefixes in a second, and suffixes in a third colour.
- Students sometimes omit syllables from longer words because they are relying on visual memory rather than sounding the word out systematically. Provide students with a set of cards containing the following syllables, which, when sorted, will form the list words **unpacked**, **unusual**, **unfinished**, and **unidentified**.

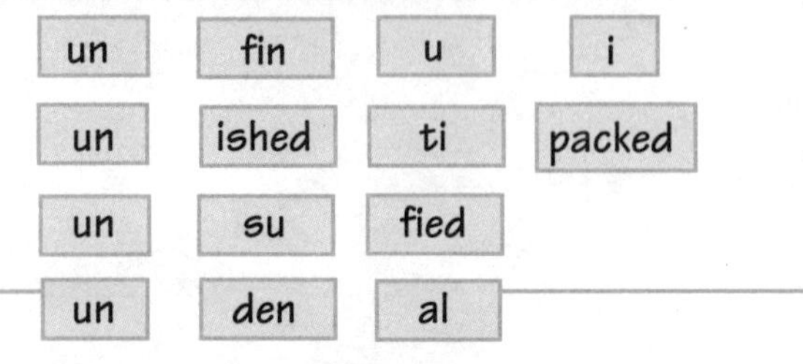

3. Complete these sentences with list words.

I opened my suitcase and unpacked my socks, shirts, and other pieces of clothing. I put everything away except an old shirt and a pair of pants.

Discovering Patterns

clothing unfinished suit except unusual pair appear unpacked loose pieces right reaches unidentified size pants making

1. Write the list words that are related to these base words.
usual finish pack identify
unusual unfinished unpacked unidentified
What does the prefix **un-** do to the meaning of each of the base words?

2. Write three list words that have the sound /ē/ as in **bee.** Underline the letters that spell the /ē/ sound.
appear pieces reaches

POWERBOOSTER

- The prefix **un-** usually means 'not' and changes the meaning of a base word to its opposite.
- The sound /ē/ can be spelled **ie** as in **pieces** or **ea** as in **reaches**.

109

3. Note with students that **clothing** is derived from the base word **cloth**. Even though the pronunciation of the base word changes in the new form, its spelling remains constant. This is an example of the meaning principle in English: *words related in meaning are usually spelled alike even if they are pronounced differently.*

Help students to distinguish the meaning, pronunciation, and spelling differences between **except** and **accept**.

Discovering Patterns

1. The use of the prefix **un-** to change a base word to its opposite is reinforced in Exploring Patterns 1.

2. Review other patterns for spelling /ē/. The **ie** pattern for spelling /ē/ can also be reinforced by the rule 'i before e except after c'. Of course, words such as **weird** are exceptions to this rule!

long /ē/			
ee	**e_consonant_e**	**y**	**e**
need see heel meet agree degree fifteen	theme athlete compete complete these extreme	baby lazy hazy already family hurry steady	me be he

ESL

- Help students build vocabulary for clothing words and practise their use in sentences.
- Note that **pants** and **trousers** may be singular in other languages. (Her pants is green.)

singular	plural	example
	pants	His pants are new.
a pair of pants		A pair of pants is on sale.
	trousers	My trousers are torn.
a pair of trousers		A pair of trousers is in the closet.
	shoes	My shoes are clean.
a pair of shoes		A pair of new shoes is nice.
suit		My dad has a new suit.
clothing		Her clothing is new.
	clothes	Her clothes are new.
size		What size is he?

Exploring Patterns

1. Note that the exercise requires that students also add the suffix **-ed** to all the words except **matched**.

Ask students to think of another scenario, such as a messy bedroom or school desk, and write sentences using words with the prefix **un-**.

My bedroom is **un**tidy.
The bed is **un**made.
The window is **un**latched.
My clothes are **un**pressed.
My books are **un**organized.
My mom is **un**happy!

2. Students might find it helpful to use a highlighter to mark the additions to each word. (See Special Needs, p. 174.)

3. Students could focus on a particular style of clothing (sports, casual, formal) or time of year (summer, winter clothing), and complete the word pole accordingly.

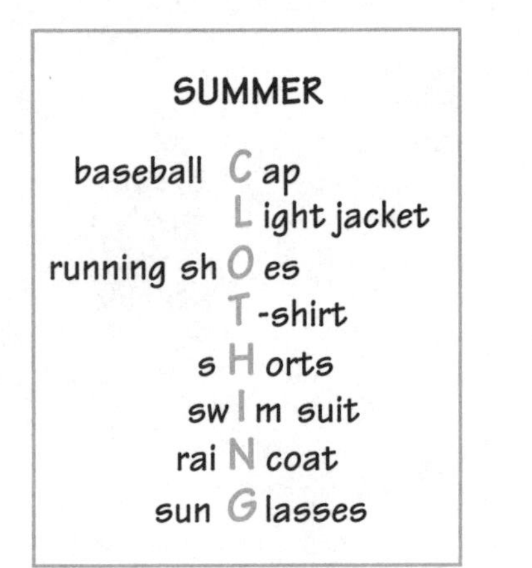

Exploring Patterns

comb
done
button
wash
tie
matched

1. The little girl is very untidy! Describe her by adding the prefix **un-** to words on the mirror.

Her face is unwashed
Her hair is uncombed
Her buttons are undone .
Her shoelaces are untied .
Her socks are unmatched
Her overalls are unbuttoned

2. The words below are built on the list words **except**, **appear**, and **suit**. Complete each sentence with one of the words. Underline the parts that were added.

exception disappear suitcase appearance unsuitable

a) The appearance of the house made us think that it was empty.
b) I'm sorry, but this shirt is unsuitable for the party.
c) We will make an exception to the rule this time.
d) Don't forget your suitcase at the airport.
e) How did you make the rabbit disappear?

3. Make a word pole with the word **clothing**. Add one clothing word for each letter. The pole has been started for you.

C
L
O
BATHING SUIT
H
I
N
G

110

Oral Language and Literature

- Two poems of Shel Silverstein's illustrate the use of suffixes: "Ations" and "Twistable, Turnable Man" in *A Light in the Attic*.

Co-operative Learning

- Give each group a set of cards containing prefixes, base words, and suffixes. Each of the three categories could be coded in a different colour. The task of the group is to combine these parts to form as many words as possible. Cards can be used more than once, but only once for a given word.
- Have students note when a change must be made to the base word (e.g., **unbelievable**).

prefix	base	suffix
un	appear	ance
dis	friend	ed
re	finish	able
	believe	ly

disappear
reappear
appearance
appeared
disappearance
unfriendly
friendly
refinished
refinish
finished
unbelievable
disbelieve
believable

4. Why are these kids wearing special clothing? Write a sentence or two telling the purpose of each outfit.

5. What's the best outfit you've ever worn on a special occasion? Describe your favourite outfit using some of these list words.

pants **pair** **size** **unusual** **pieces**

SUPER WORDS

appearance
expensive
materials
design
unattractive
unfashionable

Challenges with Words

1. Match the correct Super Word to each set of words below. Then add a word of your own to each set.

a)	create	plan	design
b)	old-fashioned	unpopular	unfashionable
c)	valuable	costly	expensive
d)	look	expression	appearance
e)	equipment	supplies	materials
f)	ugly	homely	unattractive

2. The prefix un- means 'not' or 'the opposite'.

a) Choose the correct word in the box to complete the newspaper article.

even
ravel
usual
cover
familiar
folded

POLICE UNCOVERED MISSING JEANS
Today, police un folded the true story of the missing designer jeans. It has been two months since their un usual disappearance. Then a shipment of jeans with un even cuffs and an un familiar logo turned up in a downtown store. When a thread was pulled from one of the logos, it began to un ravel, revealing the famous symbol.

b) If you look in your dictionary under **un-**, you will see there are dozens of words which have this prefix. Choose five of them to write your own sentences.

111

4. Students could choose one of the outfits and elaborate on the nature of the equipment, or describe the clothing needed for their favourite hobby or sport.

5. Remind students of the importance of describing objects in some kind of order or sequence (left to right, top to bottom). Which order is best suited to describing costumes or uniforms?

Challenges with Words

1. Have students write antonyms for the Super Words. Students might have difficulty with **materials** and **design**. Point out to them that not all words have an opposite meaning, while antonyms for words with negative prefixes, such as **un-**, are quite easily found.

super word	antonym
appearance expensive unattractive unfashionable	disappearance cheap attractive fashionable

2. Point out to students that there are other negative prefixes which are often used. For example **dis-**, **in-**, **non-** are three common ones. Have students give examples of words containing these other prefixes and use them in sentences to show the function of the prefix.

negative prefixes		
dis-	in-	non-
disappear disable disadvantage disagree dis	inaccurate inaccessible inactive inadvi	nonsense non-believer nondestructive non-exi nt

Multiple Intelligences

Visual/Spatial: Ask students to complete cloze versions of list words in which difficult letter combinations have been left blank.

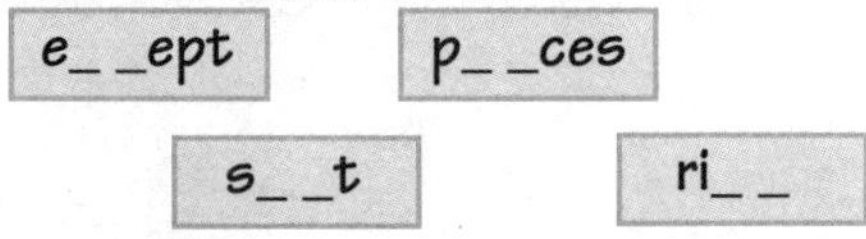

Musical/Rhythmic: The syllables and stress patterns in multisyllabic words can be reinforced through chants or readings which emphasize the stressed syllables.

It's un u su al to find a horn

That's fallen off a uni corn

Logical/Mathematical: Think of mnemonic or memory tricks for remembering similar word pairs or homophones.

The loose moose chased a goose.

Bodily/Kinesthetic: Sort cards representing the spelling patterns for long **e**, or syllables within longer list words. (See Special Needs, p. 174 and Co-operative Learning, p. 176.)

3. Remind students that the **a** in **-ance** is a schwa vowel, and thus difficult to hear. Both **-ance** and **-ence** make the same sound (ə**ns**), as in **clearance** and **presence**.

Have students note that the final **e** is dropped from **insure** when the suffix **-ance** is added (**insurance**).

4. See Critical Thinking, this page.

5. Students could enhance their logos through use of computer graphics, desktop publishing programs, colour printers, or whatever technology is available.

New Words

6. Ask students to suggest words or brand names from fashion that have been introduced in the past few years. If you have access to a catalogue or magazine from a decade ago, it would be interesting to note products or clothing fads that are now out of style.

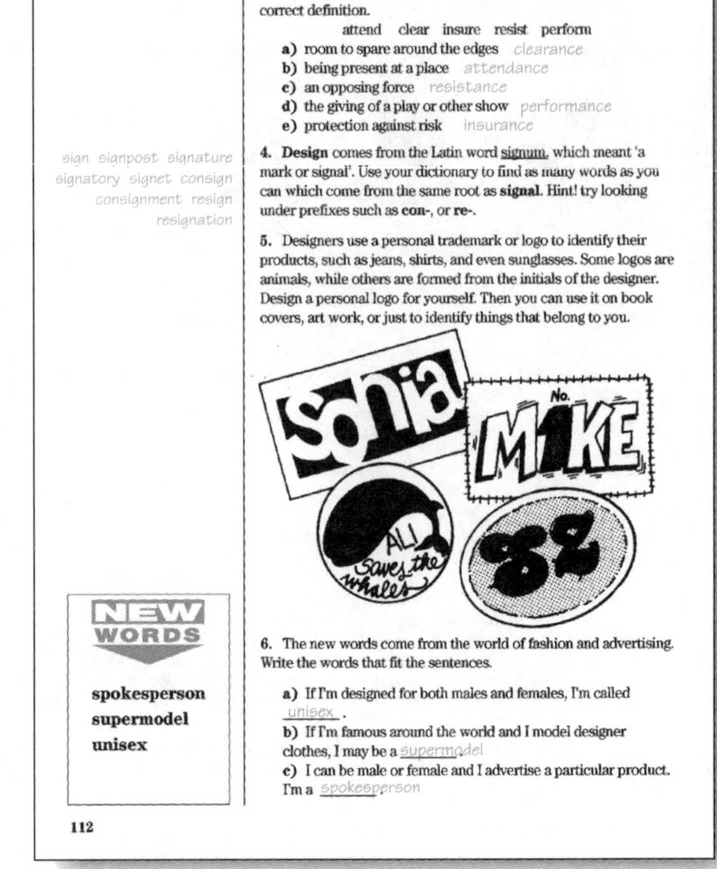

3. Add the suffix **-ance** to the words below and match them to the correct definition.

attend clear insure resist perform

a) room to spare around the edges clearance
b) being present at a place attendance
c) an opposing force resistance
d) the giving of a play or other show performance
e) protection against risk insurance

4. Design comes from the Latin word signum, which meant 'a mark or signal'. Use your dictionary to find as many words as you can which come from the same root as **signal.** Hint! try looking under prefixes such as **con-**, or **re-**.

sign signpost signature signatory signet consign consignment resign resignation

5. Designers use a personal trademark or logo to identify their products, such as jeans, shirts, and even sunglasses. Some logos are animals, while others are formed from the initials of the designer. Design a personal logo for yourself. Then you can use it on book covers, art work, or just to identify things that belong to you.

NEW WORDS

spokesperson
supermodel
unisex

6. The new words come from the world of fashion and advertising. Write the words that fit the sentences.

a) If I'm designed for both males and females, I'm called unisex.
b) If I'm famous around the world and I model designer clothes, I may be a supermodel
c) I can be male or female and I advertise a particular product. I'm a spokesperson

112

Critical Thinking

- Students could use the 'signal' words generated in Challenges with Words 4 to create word games or puzzles. They might construct a word maze or a crossword puzzle, or they might find an idea for an interesting game by looking at a word puzzle book. Puzzles could be shared with the rest of the class.

Curriculum Connection

Have students brainstorm words relevant to a variety of curriculum areas which contain the prefix **un-**.

geography

- un
  - charted
  - explored
  - developed
  - populated

science

- un
  - explained
  - diluted
  - saturated

Assessment

Note possible areas of difficulty with the Unit Test:

- Are students leaving out syllables or letters in longer words? (See Special Needs, p. 174.)
- Is the addition of **-ed** and **-ing** giving problems, especially when this requires a change in the spelling of the base word? (**identify/identified**; **make/making**.)
- Is there confusion between word pairs, such as **loose/lose**; **except/accept**?
- Are students having difficulty with the spelling of long **e** patterns?
- Are students confusing homophone pairs? (**right/write**; **pair/pear**.)
- Do vowel combinations (**sui**t) or consonant combinations (e**xc**ept) create problems?

Teacher's Notes

Looking Back
Units 19–23

Patterns to Review

Review the following sound-symbol relationships and structures:

- Homophones
- Schwa vowels
- **-ed** and **-ing** endings
- Number words
- Long **e** spelled **ie** or **ea** as in **pieces**, **appear**
- **un-** prefix

The following words in the review list are found on the list of "The 200 Words Most Frequently Misspelled."

having, stepped, flower, pieces, receive, without, coming

Creating a Personal Review List

Looking Back units should also provide an opportunity for students to review words and concepts which gave them particular difficulty in the preceding units. These personal study lists could involve words from a variety of sources, as suggested below:

- words misspelled in the students' Unit Tests and everyday writing (writing folders, notebooks, tests)
- words used throughout the day: current themes, content areas, current events, media, holidays
- lists such as "The 200 Words Most Frequently Misspelled" and "The 200 Words Most Frequently Written" (See Appendix.)

Transfer of Spelling Knowledge

The following suggestions will help students to retain the knowledge and skills they acquire through word study and apply them in their everyday writing:

- Do not treat words on study lists as single entities, but as examples of larger spelling patterns. Build on word patterns to maximize the benefit of word study.
- Reintroduce frequently misspelled words on subsequent lists.
- When errors reoccur in student writing, ask students to recall the strategies they had used for studying these words.
- Discuss the use of spelling strategies for new words as they occur in a variety of classroom contexts.

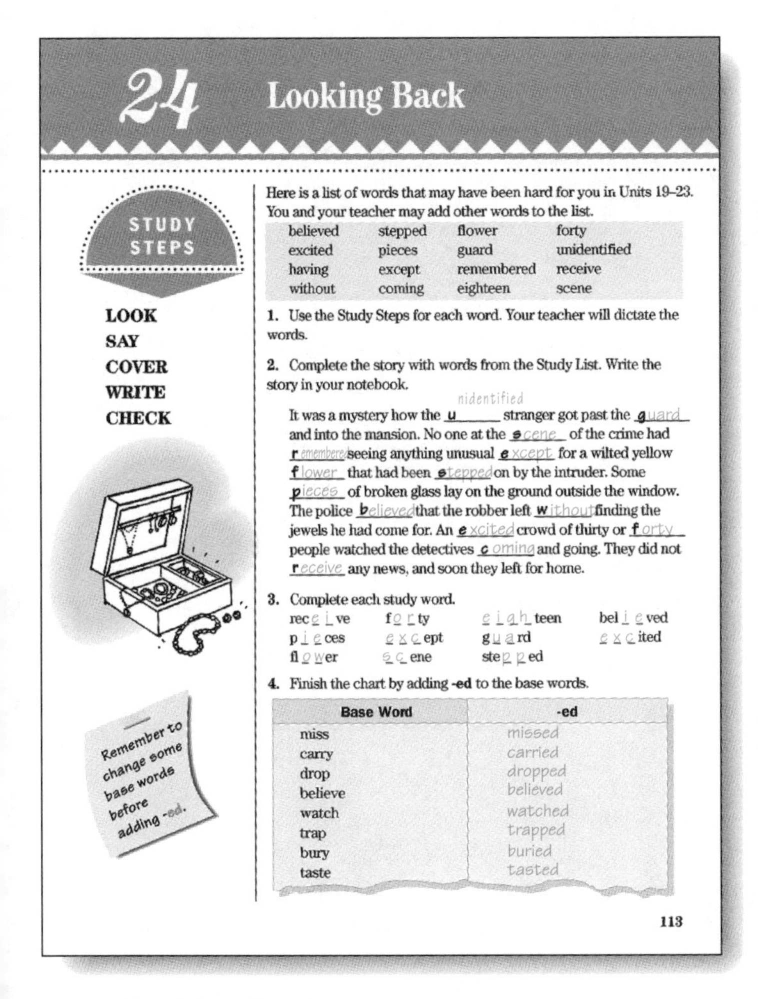

24 Looking Back

STUDY STEPS

LOOK
SAY
COVER
WRITE
CHECK

Here is a list of words that may have been hard for you in Units 19–23. You and your teacher may add other words to the list.

believed	stepped	flower	forty
excited	pieces	guard	unidentified
having	except	remembered	receive
without	coming	eighteen	scene

1. Use the Study Steps for each word. Your teacher will dictate the words.

2. Complete the story with words from the Study List. Write the story in your notebook.

It was a mystery how the u(nidentified) stranger got past the g(uard) and into the mansion. No one at the s(cene) of the crime had r(emembered) seeing anything unusual e(xcept) for a wilted yellow f(lower) that had been s(tepped) on by the intruder. Some p(ieces) of broken glass lay on the ground outside the window. The police b(elieved) that the robber left w(ithout) finding the jewels he had come for. An e(xcited) crowd of thirty or f(orty) people watched the detectives c(oming) and going. They did not r(eceive) any news, and soon they left for home.

3. Complete each study word.

rec e i ve f o r ty e i g h teen bel i e ved
p i e ces e x c ept g u a rd e x c ited
fl o w er s c ene ste p p ed

4. Finish the chart by adding **-ed** to the base words.

Base Word	-ed
miss	missed
carry	carried
drop	dropped
believe	believed
watch	watched
trap	trapped
bury	buried
taste	tasted

Remember to change some base words before adding -ed.

113

Looking Back

1. Draw the students' attention to the following features of the review words:

- four words conform to the rule '**i** before **e** except after **c**, or when it says /ā/ as in neighbour and weigh' (bel**ie**ved, p**ie**ces, rec**ei**ve, **ei**ghteen)
- the consonant combinations in e**xc**ept, e**xc**ited, **sc**ene
- the vowel combination in g**ua**rd
- changes in the base word when an ending is added (**have/having**; **come/coming**; **step/stepped**; **identify/unidentified**)
- number words (**eighteen**, **forty**)
- multisyllabic words (**remembered**, **unidentified**).

Dictation

I **believed** what he said.
She was **excited** about the party.
What are we **having** for lunch?
Don't go **without** me!
I **stepped** on a rock.
The puzzle had a thousand **pieces**.
Everyone's ready **except** me.
Are you **coming** to the movie?
There's a **flower** on the rose bush.
Is your dog a **guard** dog?
Have you **remembered** to bring a pencil?
The town is **eighteen** kilometres away.
I'll be there in **forty** minutes.
The stray dog was **unidentified**.
Did you **receive** the letter?
There was only one **scene** in the play.

2. Ask students to substitute synonyms for as many of the words in blanks as possible without changing the meaning of the story.

word	synonym
unidentified	unknown
scene	location
except	other than
guard	security
remembered	recalled
flower	blossom

3. Students should try to highlight the letters represented by the blanks in some way. They could say the letters aloud while looking at each one, print them in a distinct colour, or they could write them in capitals or in a larger size.

4. If students have difficulty applying the rules for adding **-ed**, review with them the Discovering Patterns sections of Units 20 and 21. Have students add other words to the chart which fit these patterns.

no change	pass/passed match/matched mail/mailed
change y to i	marry/married apply/applied deny/denied
double final consonant	slap/slapped label/labelled hop/hopped
drop silent e	raise/raised approve/approved store/stored

5. Have students write each homophone on a separate card and lay the cards on their desks. Read aloud a sentence containing one of the homophones and ask students to hold up the correct word. This will allow you to see immediately which students are having difficulty. Repeat the activity for the other homophones in the exercise.

6. It may be useful to have students write both the question and answer in words. Students could create other problems in number words, checking in the dictionary for the correct spelling of these words.

25 - 10 + 5 - 10 = ten

20 + 18 - 3 + 15 = fifty

8 - 2 + 11 - 3 = fourteen

7. This puzzle requires students to look at specific review words carefully. Students may enjoy creating other word puzzles using words from the review list. They could make up word searches, crosswords, riddles, and so on.

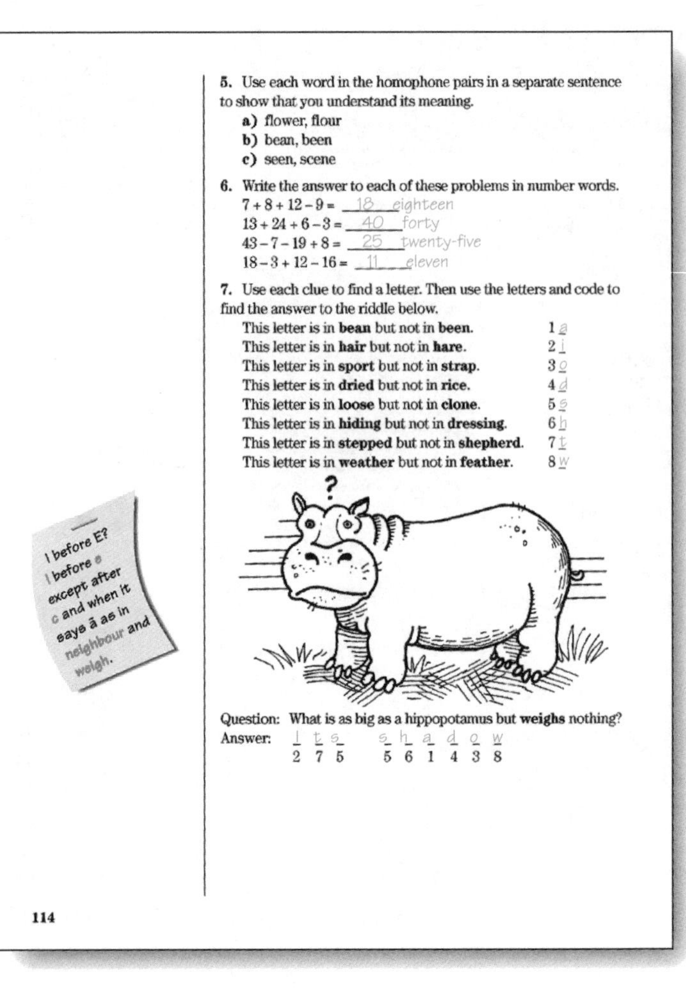

5. Use each word in the homophone pairs in a separate sentence to show that you understand its meaning.

a) flower, flour
b) bean, been
c) seen, scene

6. Write the answer to each of these problems in number words.

7 + 8 + 12 − 9 = 18 eighteen
13 + 24 + 6 − 3 = 40 forty
43 − 7 − 19 + 8 = 25 twenty-five
18 − 3 + 12 − 16 = 11 eleven

7. Use each clue to find a letter. Then use the letters and code to find the answer to the riddle below.

This letter is in **bean** but not in **been**. 1 a
This letter is in **hair** but not in **hare**. 2 i
This letter is in **sport** but not in **strap**. 3 o
This letter is in **dried** but not in **rice**. 4 d
This letter is in **loose** but not in **clone**. 5 s
This letter is in **hiding** but not in **dressing**. 6 h
This letter is in **stepped** but not in **shepherd**. 7 t
This letter is in **weather** but not in **feather**. 8 w

Question: What is as big as a hippopotamus but **weighs** nothing?
Answer: i t s (2 7 5) s h a d o w (5 6 1 4 3 8)

?
I before E?
I before e
except after
c and when it
says ā as in
neighbour and
weigh.

114

ESL

Language Snapshot — Hindi

Hindi is the national language of India. Like other languages of the Indian subcontinent, Hindi is an Indo-Aryan language, derived from Sanskrit. Many students in Indian schools are educated in both English and Hindi.

Language Features

- The Nagari script used to write Hindi is written from left to right as in English.
- The sound system is quite different: English has 22 vowel sounds and 24 consonant sounds. Hindi has 10 vowels, but 40 different consonants.
- English has more consonant clusters at the beginning of words than Hindi. Students may try to insert a short vowel (**istreet** for **street**, **faree** for **free**).
- There are eight distinct sounds in place of English /t/ and /d/.
- Distinctions between English vowels may be difficult. The /a/ in **sad** and the /e/ in **said** are often confused.
- Hindi has only one sound equivalent to the English /v/ and /w/; **vet** and **wet** can be confused in speech and spelling.
- Spelling is phonetic: one sound, one spelling. Some Hindi students, therefore, may pronounce the **h** in **ghost** or **which**.
- Stress is secondary to rhythm. Unstressed syllables may not be heard or spelled. Words such as **con**tent and con**tent** which change meaning according to stress may be difficult.
- There are no capital letters in Hindi script.
- There is no equivalent of the definite article **the**.

Dictionary Skills

1. Idioms: The expression *get out of my hair* means 'go away and stop bothering me'. This expression is called an idiom. An idiom is a phrase or expression whose meaning cannot be understood from the meaning of its individual words.

Most idioms can be found in the dictionary by deciding which word in the expression is the most important. You will usually find the idiom listed at the end of the entry for that word.

Study the idioms listed below for **hand**.

Idioms	Meanings
have one's hands full	be very busy
lend a hand	help or assist
on the other hand	from the opposite point of view

Choose an idiom that fits each sentence below. Write the sentence.

a) Would you please _______ lifting this box? lend a hand
b) My parents _______ with my baby sister. have their hands full
c) I want the bicycle very much; _______, I can't afford it. on the other hand

2. Try to rewrite each sentence below to show that you understand the idiom. Use your dictionary for help.

Example: ***We're in hot water*** *means 'We're in trouble'.*

a) Please drop me a line.
b) Gerry is a fair weather friend.
c) Stop pulling my leg.
d) We're all in the same boat.

115

Dictionary Skills

1. Advise students that it may be necessary to change some words in an idiom to fit the meaning of the sentence. In **b)**, for example, the phrase 'have one's hands full' will become 'have **their** hands full'.

The reference sections of bookstores often contain delightful sources of information about idiomatic expressions. There are books devoted to the idioms of Canada (*Idioms 1 and 2*), as well as more general references such as the *Dictionary of Word and Phrase Origins*. The topic of idioms is also addressed in *The Student Editor's Guide to Words*, pp. 123-124 and *Spelling: Sharing the Secrets*, p. 117.

2. Students who try to locate the meaning of an idiom in the dictionary may need some guidance in determining the key word in the phrase. In each case, ask them to consider both the literal interpretation (as shown by the illustrations) and the underlying meaning. Challenge students to explain each idiom so that someone new to English could understand its meaning.

Students could brainstorm other idiomatic expressions.

How do you do?
Let's hit the books!
It's a dog's life.
I'm in hot water now!

Sharing the Secrets with Kids

Unbiassed language includes everybody, male or female.

biassed	unbiassed
policeman	police officer
crewman	crew member
workman	worker
fireman	firefighter
mankind	human beings

Exploring the World of Sports

1. You could extend this exercise by having students estimate which sports are the most expensive in terms of equipment, fees, etc. Suggest students construct a chart such as the following, containing several criteria for comparison and determine which sports rank most favourably on each feature.

indoor	outdoor	season	danger	players per team
—	baseball	spring/ summer	medium	nine
—	soccer	spring/ summer	medium	eleven
basketball	—	winter	little	five

2. Encourage students to make a simple outline of what they want to mention in their paragraph. Perhaps a common format could be developed by the class and used to compare one sport with another. The various descriptions could be compiled into a booklet for the information of all students.

3. Students may wish to expand on their topic by researching and writing a brief history of the sport. They might want to explore how the modern equipment evolved or how the sport's rules have changed.

In December 1891, Canadian James Naismith invented basketball. At the time he was working in the US. He had been asked to invent a game that could be played inside in winter, and . . .

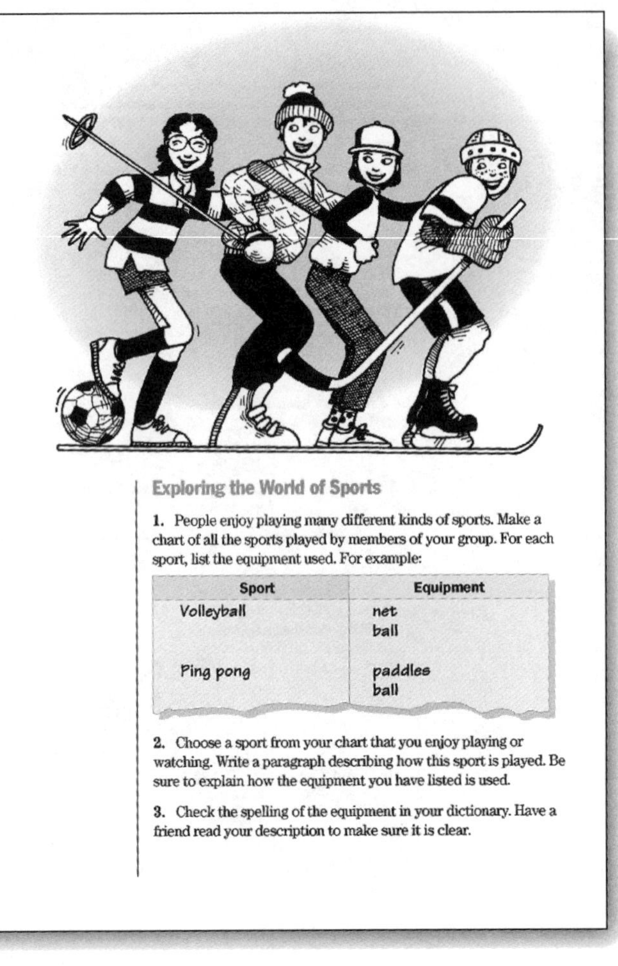

Exploring the World of Sports

1. People enjoy playing many different kinds of sports. Make a chart of all the sports played by members of your group. For each sport, list the equipment used. For example:

Sport	Equipment
Volleyball	net ball
Ping pong	paddles ball

2. Choose a sport from your chart that you enjoy playing or watching. Write a paragraph describing how this sport is played. Be sure to explain how the equipment you have listed is used.

3. Check the spelling of the equipment in your dictionary. Have a friend read your description to make sure it is clear.

116

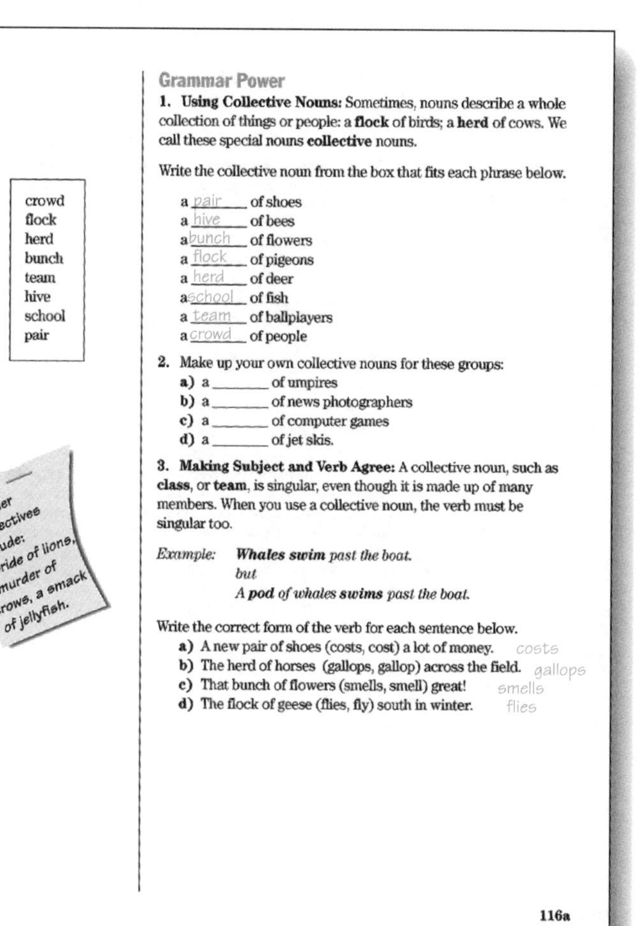
Grammar Power

1. Using Collective Nouns: Sometimes, nouns describe a whole collection of things or people: a **flock** of birds; a **herd** of cows. We call these special nouns **collective** nouns.

Write the collective noun from the box that fits each phrase below.

crowd
flock
herd
bunch
team
hive
school
pair

a pair of shoes
a hive of bees
a bunch of flowers
a flock of pigeons
a herd of deer
a school of fish
a team of ballplayers
a crowd of people

2. Make up your own collective nouns for these groups:
a) a _______ of umpires
b) a _______ of news photographers
c) a _______ of computer games
d) a _______ of jet skis.

3. Making Subject and Verb Agree: A collective noun, such as **class**, or **team**, is singular, even though it is made up of many members. When you use a collective noun, the verb must be singular too.

Example: ***Whales swim*** *past the boat.*
but
A ***pod*** *of whales* ***swims*** *past the boat.*

Write the correct form of the verb for each sentence below.
a) A new pair of shoes (costs, cost) a lot of money. costs
b) The herd of horses (gallops, gallop) across the field. gallops
c) That bunch of flowers (smells, smell) great! smells
d) The flock of geese (flies, fly) south in winter. flies

Other collectives include: a pride of lions, a murder of crows, a smack of jellyfish.

116a

Grammar Power

1. Students may enjoy switching the collective nouns and the objects they match to come up with an interesting word picture. For example:

a team of bees, a flock of flowers, a crowd of shoes

2. Some collective nouns are very interesting or humorous. Suggest that students choose two or three of those given here to illustrate (a pod of whales, a murder of crows, a pride of lions).

3. Stress that when using collective nouns, the verb must remain singular, even though the noun refers to more than one. Give students practice with sentences using the verb **to be**.

A herd of deer (are, **is**) in the woods.

A crowd of people (are, **is**) gathering in front of the City Hall.

A bunch of flowers (are, **is**) a nice present.

POWERBOOSTERS

19 Words that sound the same but have different meanings and sometimes spellings are called **homophones**.
Most vowels in unstressed syllables make the schwa sound /ə/. Pay special attention when learning to spell such words.

20 When adding **-ed** to single syllable words ending in vowel-consonant, double the consonant, as in grab — gra**bb**ed.
When adding **-ed** to base words ending in silent **e**, drop the **e**, as in excite — excit**ed**.

21 When adding **-ed** to verbs ending in a consonant + **y**, change the **y** to **i** and add **-ed**, as in **buried**.
When adding **-ing** to verbs ending in a consonant + **e**, drop the **e** and add **-ing**, as in **hiding**.

22 Number words are often based on related numbers as with **eighteen** and **eight**. It is important to notice when a letter has been changed from one number to another, as with **four** and **forty**.

23 The prefix **un-** usually means 'not' and changes the meaning of a base word to its opposite.
The sound /ē/ can be spelled **ie** as in **pieces** or **ea** as in **reaches**.

4. Adverbs of time tell us when an action is taking place. Have the students discuss which verb tense fits the adverb in each sentence. Suggest other adverbs which would change the time of the action, the verb tense used and, often, the meaning of the sentence. For example:

> **Now,** they get together by e-mail.
>
> **Before,** they got together by __________.

Proofing Power

Have students identify and correct the misspelled words, realizing that the word 'seen' in the clause 'When I seen the ball comeing' is actually a grammatical error.

In addition to correcting spelling, ask students to verbalize what is wrong with each misspelled word:

- letters reversed (**gaurd**, **waer**, **beleive**)
- homophones (**their/there**; **wood/would**)
- improper use of past tense marker (**dreamd**, **kickt**)
- problems with adding endings to base words (**exciteing**, **tryed**, **comeing**, **steped**, **scord**)
- easily confused word pairs (**were/wear**).

If students have difficulty correcting the errors or cannot verbalize the rules, refer to the appropriate Powerbooster from Units 19–23.

---

4. Past, Present, or Future: Every sentence we write tells the reader when the action takes place. It could be in the past, present, or future.

present— I see I am seeing **past**— I saw **future**— I will see

Write the verb in the correct tense in these sentences. Look for adverbs such as **today** or **yesterday**, to tell you if the action is in the past, present, or future.

a) Someday people (*live, will live, lived*) in communities linked by computers. will live

b) Already, some developers (*are planning, planned, will plan*) high-tech neighbourhoods. are planning

c) In the past, people (*visit, will visit, visited*) their neighbours, or (*talk, will talk, talked*) on the telephone. visited talked

d) Now, they (*get together, will get together, got together*) by e-mail. get together

Proofing Power

Read the following paragraph carefully, with a partner. See how many mistakes you can spot. Often proofreaders work as a team.

I beleive that the most exciteing thing in the world is sports. I dreamd of having a career as a professional athlete. Their is just one thing— I'm no good at sports. This year I tryed soccer. When I remembered to were shin pads, I forgot to waer my game socks. When I seen the ball comeing, I steped forward and kickt it with all my might. Usually, it didn't move. But once, when I was playing gaurd, I actually scord—for the other team! My coach said that I wood receive a medal at the end of the season. I did. The "Most Effort" award!

believe/exciting
dreamed
There
tried
wear
wear
saw/coming/stepped
kicked
guard/scored
would

116b

- Some students may need to review the common adverbs of time. Keep a class list that can be added to as new adverbs occur. Suggest that students write a sentence with each one.

sometimes	often	usually
never	soon	afterwards
seldom	always	yesterday

Teacher's Notes

Possessives
father's
cousin's

Patterns

By the middle grades students will have some knowledge of the use of **'s** to show possession. In this unit, students review making a singular noun possessive (the **girl's** book). This involves an understanding of spelling patterns on a deeper level than sound and visual recognition. The possessive and plural forms are identical in sound, so that in speech they can be distinguished only by the way they are used. The possessive is followed by another noun (the **girl's work** was finished); the plural is not (the **girls worked** hard).

In writing, the apostrophe signals the possessive, and the position of the apostrophe tells us whether a possessive is singular or plural (girl's, girls'). Because the letter **s** is also added to form plurals and some contractions (it'**s** a nice day) students need to practise using the apostrophe with singular nouns before moving on to plural possessives and contractions in Units 26 and 27.

Preknowledge

Students should have an understanding of the following concepts as they work with the patterns in this unit.

- Base words and endings. By this stage, students will have a reasonable knowledge of the endings that can be applied to base words. They should be aware that the base word will change in some instances (**clap/clapping**) but not in others (**cover/covered**).
- The concept of singular and plural. The most common way to form a plural in English is to add **-s**. There are of course exceptions to this (**circus/circuses**; **diary/diaries**).
- The idea that the possessive form means 'belonging to' (**Ron's book**/the book belonging to Ron).

More Patterns

Other patterns you might wish to introduce or review in this unit include the following.

- Two and three syllable words with **'s** (**editor's**, **cousin's**).
- The silent letters **w**, **gh** (**writer's**, **though**).
- The sound /f/ spelled **gh** (**laughing**, **enough**).

Professional Notebook

Spelling development...is a process that begins globally, perhaps with a scribble intended to represent a message as a whole, and eventually becomes far more complex, incorporating increasingly elaborated knowledge of the various linguistic levels represented in spelling.

(Wilde 23)

Sharing the Secrets with Kids

Two of the most frequently misspelled words in the English language are ***it's*** *and* ***its****. Many adults have to stop and think before they write either one. The rule is simple: if you can say 'it is', then drop the second* ***i*** *and replace it with an apostrophe.*

Its coat is thick and furry.
It's a bear.

It's my book.
It's fifty pages long.
Its cover is red and blue.

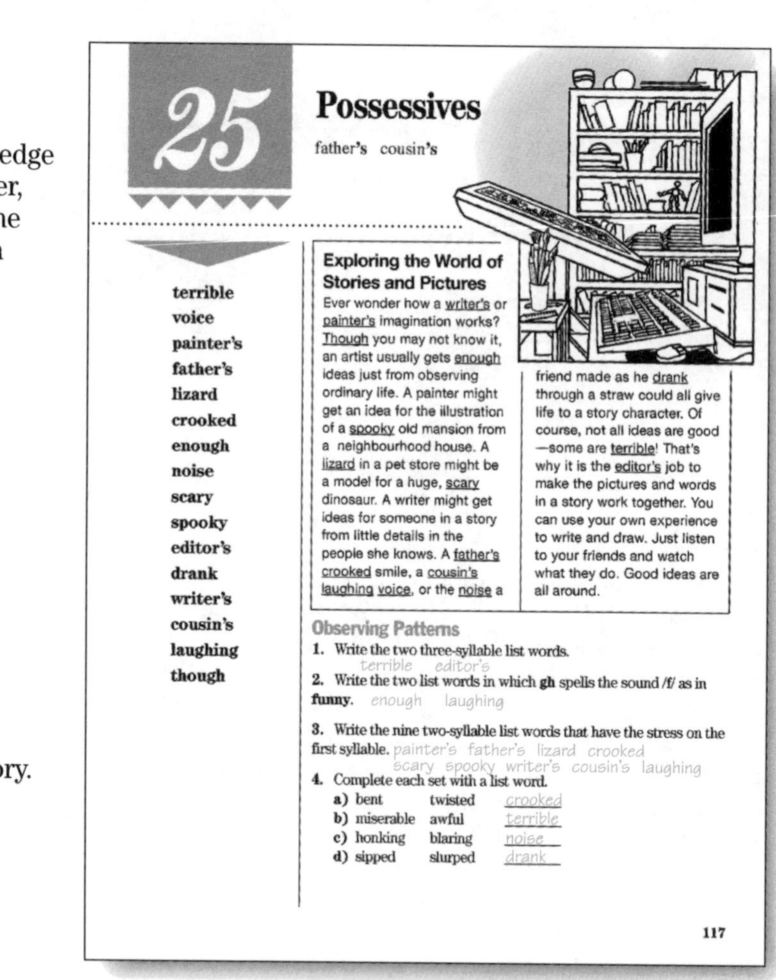

25 Possessives

father's cousin's

terrible
voice
painter's
father's
lizard
crooked
enough
noise
scary
spooky
editor's
drank
writer's
cousin's
laughing
though

Exploring the World of Stories and Pictures

Ever wonder how a writer's or painter's imagination works? Though you may not know it, an artist usually gets enough ideas just from observing ordinary life. A painter might get an idea for the illustration of a spooky old mansion from a neighbourhood house. A lizard in a pet store might be a model for a huge, scary dinosaur. A writer might get ideas for someone in a story from little details in the people she knows. A father's crooked smile, a cousin's laughing voice, or the noise a friend made as he drank through a straw could all give life to a story character. Of course, not all ideas are good—some are terrible! That's why it is the editor's job to make the pictures and words in a story work together. You can use your own experience to write and draw. Just listen to your friends and watch what they do. Good ideas are all around.

Observing Patterns

1. Write the two three-syllable list words. terrible editor's
2. Write the two list words in which **gh** spells the sound /f/ as in **funny**. enough laughing
3. Write the nine two-syllable list words that have the stress on the first syllable. painter's father's lizard crooked scary spooky writer's cousin's laughing
4. Complete each set with a list word.

a)	bent	twisted	crooked
b)	miserable	awful	terrible
c)	honking	blaring	noise
d)	sipped	slurped	drank

117

Precheck

Students should have some previous knowledge of the use of **'s** to show possession. However, for those who do not, illustrate the use of the apostrophe during the self-checking session and remind students that they will have an opportunity to practise this spelling skill during this unit.

Dictation

The tree fell with a **terrible** crash.
The **voice** came from the kitchen.
The **painter's** shirt was filthy.
My **father's** cooking is great!
I bought a **lizard** at the pet store.
A **crooked** path led through the woods.
I had **enough** money to buy popcorn.
The **noise** got louder and louder.
I like **scary** shows on TV.
It was dark and **spooky** in the forest.
The **editor's** job is to help improve your story.
Naz **drank** all his milk.
I've got **writer's** cramp from all this work!
My **cousin's** name is Marta.
They're **laughing** at the joke.
I was scared, **though** it was only a movie.

Words in Context

Have the students read the paragraph, paying particular attention to the words ending in **'s**. You may wish to point out plural words that end in **-s**, such as **ideas** or **friends**, and point out how these are different from the possessive forms. Students could sort the words ending in the /s/ sound into categories.

Observing Patterns

1. Ask students to note the unstressed /ə/ vowels in **terrible** and **editor's**. Have them consult a dictionary to see how the pronunciation is indicated (ter/ə/bəl; ed/ət/ər).

2. Discuss different ways to spell /f/ in English: **f**, **ff**, **ph**, **gh**. Which spellings are never used to spell /f/ at the beginnings of words?

f	ff	ph	gh
free	coffee	photo	cough
life	gaffe	phantom	rough
knife	affair	pharmacy	tough
fiction	stuff	phase	enough
strife	suffer	gopher	laugh
	suffering		

3. If any students include the word **enough** on their list, determine whether they have neglected to read the instructions carefully or whether they have difficulty identifying stressed syllables.

4. Note that **c)** can be completed with either **noise** or **laughing**. Discuss with students which word they think fits the set best, and why. For more work with word sets see Co-operative Learning, p. 189.

Critical Thinking

• Word sorts provide practice in classifying and categorizing. Provide students with word cards with the long and short sounds of **oo** (as in **book** and **spoon**). Give students large hoops or circles drawn on chart paper to sort the cards.

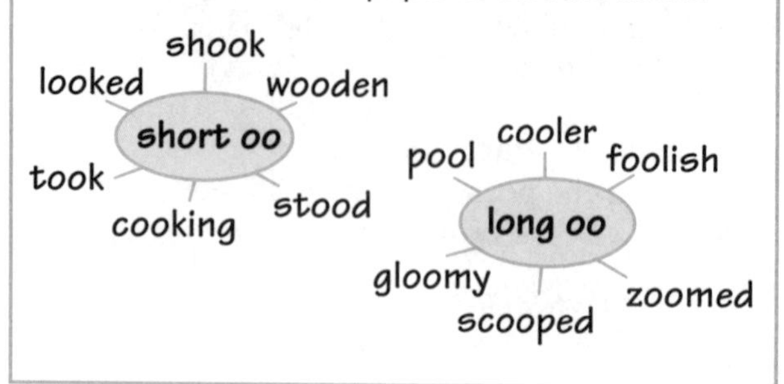

5. Write the list words that would be found in the dictionary between **slippery** and **volcano**. spooky terrible though voice

Discovering Patterns

terrible voice painter's father's lizard
crooked enough noise scary spooky genie's
drank writer's cousin's laughing though

1. Write the list words that end in an apostrophe and **s** ('s). These words mean 'belonging to...' and are called **possessives**. **Possessives** are formed by adding **'s** to a base word. Underline the base word in each possessive list word.

2. Complete each phrase with one of the possessive list words.

the editor's corrections (spelling)

the writer's novel

the painter's canvas and brush

the father's/cousin's footprints

POWERBOOSTER

- We use **'s** to show that something belongs to something or someone, as in **a bird's feather.**

118

5. It may be helpful for some students to jot down the alphabet across the top of the page in their notebook. Help them see that **scary** should not be included since its second letter, **c**, comes before **l**.

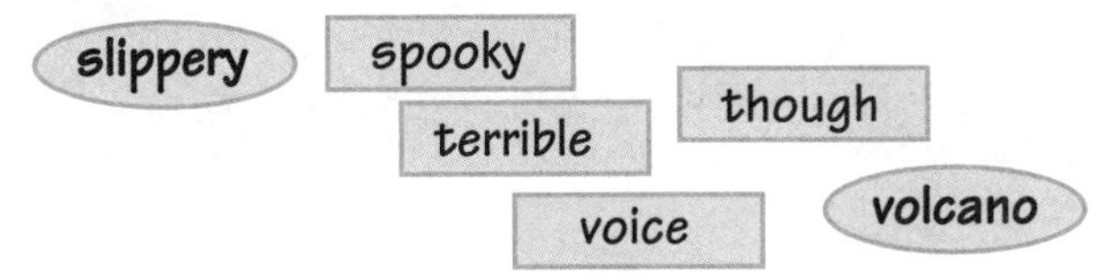

Discovering Patterns

1. Reinforce the generalization for forming possessives by using a number of other examples. Restrict the examples to singular words at this point.

our dog's dish	that cat's paw
their doctor's office	my mom's car
the teacher's pencil	her dad's keys

2. It may help students to know they are looking for a person in each case. Suggest that students substitute other possessive nouns for the list words.

Co-operative Learning

- In Observing Patterns 4, you could divide students into four groups and give each group a set of words from **a)**, **b)**, **c)**, or **d)**. Have each group find at least four more words in a thesaurus or dictionary to go with their set. Then ask students to create a word poem ending in a noun that all the adjectives could describe. Have them share their word poems with other groups.

Honking, blaring
Squealing, shrieking
Squawking, squeaking
HORNS!

Special Needs

- Students may need extra practice with the concept of the possessive. You can use familiar TV shows, as well as illustrations in books, magazines, and newspapers to help students grasp the idea of 'belonging to'. You could make sentence frames such as those shown here. Have students fill in the blank spaces, or match them with answers printed on cards and write the sentences.

Whose hair is blue in *The Simpsons*?
Marge's hair is blue.

What is the dog's name?
The dog's name is Clifford.

Who is the team's new player?
The team's new player is _________.

Exploring Patterns

1. Students who have difficulty with this exercise may need additional practice with other, similar examples. Their problems may lie in converting a phrase to the possessive (the lamp belonging to Aladdin/Aladdin's lamp), or in applying the rules for forming possessives. It may be helpful to use examples from their own classroom.

the wing of the bird/the bird's wing

the book belonging to the teacher/the teacher's book

the birthday of my aunt/my aunt's birthday

2. Creating word webs helps students build vocabulary. Have them share their word webs. Encourage the use of clustering within the word web so that a general term such as **noise** could be broken into sub-units. The word webs will provide an excellent resource for story or poetry writing.

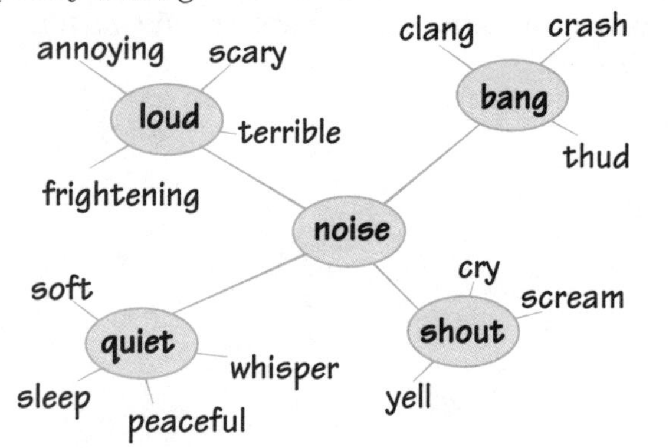

3. Cloze exercises help students focus on the difficult letters in words. Suggest that they create cloze puzzles on word cards with other list words they spelled incorrectly on the Precheck and practise with the cards during the unit.

4. This exercise requires some imaginative thinking. Suggest students work with a partner and remember that the clue to solving the riddles is that the pair of words must rhyme. It may help to work through **a)** as a group.

Exploring Patterns

1. Replace each underlined phrase in the following sentences with a possessive form. Write the sentence.
   - **a)** The toy belonging to the child transformed into a robot. child's toy
   - **b)** The flame of the candle flickered and died out. candle's flame
   - **c)** The voice of my cousin is very strong. cousin's voice

2. Draw a word web for two of these list words: **lizard, noise, scary, crooked.**

Example:

whisper — singing voice — VOICE — children sleeping — yelling loudly

3. Complete the list word on each book page.

te r r ible
ed i t o r 's
la u g h ing
cr o o ked
en o u g h

4. Solve the following riddles with pairs of rhyming words. One word in each pair is a list word.
   - **a)** Has plenty of strength t o u g h e n o u g h
   - **b)** The best singer has a c h o i c e v o i c e
   - **c)** Extremely frightening v e r y s c a r y

119

Oral Language and Literature

- Idioms create special problems for students learning the language for the first time. Provide a selection of idioms that use the possessive. Suggest students supply a name for each and then match the idiom to the same expression in ordinary English.

idiom	meaning
_____'s ears are burning	People are talking about someone
Walk in ________'s shoes	Try to understand how someone feels
Catch ________'s eye	Try to get someone to notice you
Pick _________'s brain	Get ideas from someone
Take ______'s side	Help someone in a disagreement

5. The most important ingredient of a scary story is a spooky setting. You have to make your reader afraid, even before anything has happened.

a) Choose one of the settings below, or your own setting.
b) Describe it in a very spooky way.

an old abandoned house — a dungeon — a lonesome castle

SUPER WORDS

eerie
superstition
hero's
horrible
anxious

Challenges with Words

1. The prefix **super-** means 'above' or 'over'. The Super Word **superstition** literally means a 'belief standing above or over common sense'.

Make a list of the superstitions you know. Divide your list into two columns:

Good Luck Superstitions	Bad Luck Superstitions
a four leaf clover	*walking under a ladder*

2. Match these other 'super-' words below with the correct meaning.

a) superb	above the speed of sound	supersonic
b) supervise	above what is needed	surplus
c) supersonic	above all others; highest in rank	supreme
d) surplus	above ordinary quality; excellent	superb
e) supreme	in charge of others	supervise

120

• **superstition** has four syllables. Which one is stressed?
• **hero's** What might the hero possess? Note that the feminine form **heroine** is no longer widely used. Like **actress**, **waitress**, and **hostess** it is considered by some to be too gender specific.
• **horrible** is derived from the base word **horror**. Note the **-ible** ending. What tactic can you use to remember the **i**? (My eye sees a horrible **i**.)
• **anxious** is an important word, and one of the few to spell the /shus/ ending with **-xious**. Others are **noxious**, **obnoxious**, **overanxious**.

1. Have students write down superstitions they recall, or interview parents and family members to add to the list.

*See a penny, pick it up
And all the day you'll have good luck*

Breaking a mirror brings seven years bad luck

2. Note that not all the words begin with the prefix **super-**. However **surplus** and **supreme** have similar meanings to the other words, in that they suggest the connotation 'above'.

5. Encourage students to look at the opening pages of some of their favourite books or stories to see how the author created the setting. It may also help to use pictures or the illustration on p. 120 as a prompt. Have the students work in groups and describe elements of the setting such as place, time, and weather. Suggest individual students use the setting they have described as the basis for writing a spooky story. Encourage them to add their spooky words to their Personal Review List. (See Writing on this page.)

It was a dark and stormy night ...

The wind whistled through the castle windows ...

Suddenly, an eerie cry rose from the depths of the dungeon ...

Challenges with Words

Have students note the special features of the Super Words:

• **eerie** Double **e** at the beginning of a word is unusual. How many other words in the dictionary begin with **ee**? (**eerier**, **eerily**, **eel**, **eelskin**) **Eerie** sounds like its meaning.

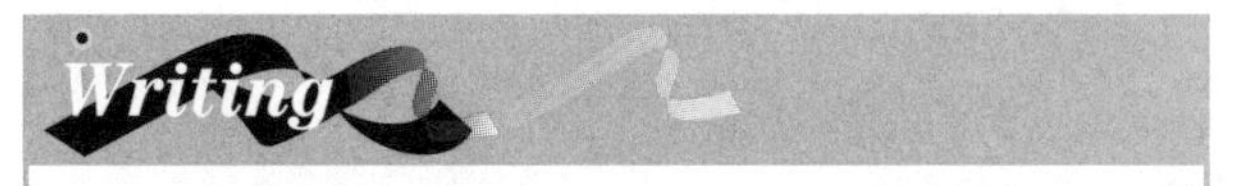

• A small writing group of peers can be an excellent support for helping a young writer develop story settings. Some of the following activities could help students structure the development of their stories.

Once you have a general setting in mind, close your eyes and try to put yourself in that setting.

• Walk through the (house, dungeon, castle) in your mind. See every room and imagine details.
• What's the weather like? Is it hot or cold? Cloudy or sunny? Stormy or calm?
• Use your five senses. What does it smell like? What sounds do you hear? What do you see? How do things feel? Any interesting tastes?

These details can be organized in a flowchart to help the writer bring the setting alive. The writer will not use them all at once, but can return to them whenever a detail of the setting is needed.

3. Both plural and possessive nouns have an **s** at the end. Choose either the plural or possessive form of the word in brackets that fits the sentence.

a) The (winds, wind's) icy breath blew through the old house.
b) The (detectives, detective's) notes were scattered around the desk.
c) For many (days, day's) no one had seen the creature.
e) A strange chest had been discovered in the (castles, castle's) damp dungeon.

4. There are five synonyms for the Super Word **eerie** hidden below. How quickly can you see them in spite of the extra letters? Choose one letter from each pair of letters to find your word. For example, **weird** can be found like this:

b o i s **d**
w e n **r** t

uneasy
a) u e r a s e
t n e o c y

strange
b) h a r u n g m
s t l a c l e

ghostly
c) m h n f i l p
g a o s t u y

fearful
d) f e u r f p l
p i a b v u s

terrifying
e) t o r d e s y u n g
n e l r i f c i t h

5. Brainstorm with a partner to think of some synonyms for the Super Words **anxious** and **horrible**. A thesaurus will be helpful. Write a story using as many of these synonyms as you can. Compare your story with the one your partner wrote. Now trade with another pair of classmates. You may be surprised how many different plots are created with a similar list of words.

NEW WORDS

computer virus
gridlock
freezes

6. New technology has its unexplained mysteries too. People talk about the bugs in their machines that cause weird things to happen.
Write the new words that fit each clue.
a) When everything stops and nothing can move we call it a gridlock.
b) A computer program that causes problems to occur in a computer system is called a computer virus.
c) When the cursor on your computer screen stops moving we say it freezes.

121

3. Remind students that the pronunciation of plurals and possessives is the same and that it is the context that decides how the word should be written. Suggest that students rewrite the exercise using different pairs of words. Have them exchange their sentences with a partner.

4. Give students the clue that they should move their eyes up and down to solve the puzzles. This activity is more challenging if a time limit is given.

Some students may wish to make similar puzzles of their own, using other Super Words or words from their Personal Review List. Have them trade with a partner.

5. Note that both **anxious** and **horrible** are powerful words, full of emotion and thus good for writing. Encourage students to create vocabulary lists on chart paper with the words they discover. Discuss the shades of meaning of each word, or rank them from least worried to most worried. Remind them that professional writers and editors rely on the thesaurus to help them write interesting prose.

anxious	horrible
worried	repulsive
troubled	loathsome
anguished	abominable
careworn	dreadful
concerned	horrid

New Words

6. The New Words can be used and discussed with all students, depending on time and suitability to your class. Students can discuss in a group how the words were brought into the computer world. Which new words do they think are likely to survive, and which might be replaced by others? Can they think of other new words to describe computer problems?

Suggest that students write a computer mystery where things go wrong with technology, using some or all of the new words.

ESL

- Like the plural **s**, the possessive form may give trouble to students whose first language signals possession in other ways (*la plume de ma tante* in French, for example). Also, for speakers of many languages including Chinese, Vietnamese, and Farsi, the final **-s** in both plurals and possessives is difficult to hear and pronounce. This means that care must be taken to help students grasp the sound, structure, and spelling of the possessive form.
- Use a question and answer format to practise the singular possessive. Practise forming the possessive orally before writing.

Whose pen is this? Assim's pen.
Whose hat is this? Ali's hat.
Whose book is this? Carla's book.

- Compare the written form of the plural with the possessive. Have the students highlight or exaggerate the **'s** and **-s** in some way to help them focus on the written form.

The girl**'s** book**s** are in her desk.
The boy**'s** shoe**s** are in the closet.

Home Connection

A recent trend is to use **'s** for plurals as well as possessive forms. Perhaps in a hundred years or so this will become acceptable, but at the moment it is still considered incorrect spelling. Encourage families to reinforce the idea of **'s** for possessive by looking for them in signs (**Eaton's**), in billboard advertisements, and other print in the student's environment. At the same time, they can be looking for the incorrect use of apostrophes (**Fresh Doughnut's**).

Assessment

When checking each student's everyday writing, note those who require extra help, further practice, or reteaching of the use of **'s** to show possession. Provide the necessary small group instruction for all these students. You may also wish to provide proofreading paragraphs with a mixture of plural forms and singular possessives for practice.

Follow-up

Continue to review and revisit the subject of possessives in mini-lessons and in the content areas whenever it arises.

Teacher's Notes

26 Plural Possessives

children's
drivers'

Patterns

Forming plural possessives requires students to move away from phonics-based strategies to using structural principles of the language. They must first determine whether the noun ending in **-s** is singular or plural. If it is plural, the apostrophe signalling possession usually comes after the final **-s** (hunters'). However, with irregular plural forms that do not end in **-s**, an apostrophe **s** is used to show possession (men**'s**, women**'s**, children**'s**). In this unit, both regular and irregular plural nouns are included to provide practice with **'s** and **s'**. Students might need extended practice with many examples of possessive nouns before they master this principle.

Preknowledge

Students should have an understanding of the following concepts as they work with the patterns in this unit.

- Some nouns have irregular plurals (**child/children**).
- Nouns ending in **ch** or **sh** add **-es** to make the plural form (**ranches**).
- Singular nouns add **'s** to show possession (**teacher's**).
- A final **-s** can have the sound /s/ or /z/ (**months**, **drivers'**).
- Many words are made up of base words and endings (**vacate/vacation**; **build/building**).

More Patterns

Other patterns you might wish to review or introduce from the list words in this unit include the following.

- Two- and three-syllable words (**building**, **vacation**).
- The consonant clusters **dr**, **st**, **str** at the beginning of words (**drivers'**, **stock**, **strong**).
- Silent letters (throu**gh**, bu**i**lding, li**gh**tning).
- Irregular plurals (**cattle**, **children**).
- The final **-s** for third person singular forms (**rides**, **goes**)
- Homophones (**stock/stalk**; **through/threw**).

Professional Notebook

In addition to sound and structural patterns, children in the middle years begin paying closer attention to the meaning connections within and among words. Early in this period, they use tense markers and plural forms with greater ease and can explain the logical connections within compound words. These perceptions are gradually extended to more complex elements such as simple prefixes and suffixes.

(Scott, *Spelling: Sharing the Secrets*, 24)

Sharing the Secrets with Kids

Remember—use the **'s** *only for possessive forms and contractions. Students might notice errors on signs and in print (Cooky's and Candy's for Sale), but the* **'s** *is never used when only the plural is needed.*

Plural Possessives

children's drivers'

- vacation
- months
- drivers'
- hunters'
- stock
- rides
- cattle's
- building
- fence
- ranches'
- lightning
- yelling
- children's
- through
- goes
- strong

Exploring the Life of the Cowhands

Although many children's movies, TV shows and books are made about life on the range, the real cowhand life only lasted through the early days of western ranching, from 1870 to 1890. Women as well as men were cowhands and some, like Calamity Jane, became famous. Roundups were held in the spring and fall after the cattle's long months on the open range. Yelling and waving their hats, the cowhands would get the stock ready for the long trip to the rail yard. The cattle drivers' life was no vacation. A cowhand worked hard for low pay, and slept in a building called a 'bunkhouse'. There were many dangers on the trail. A lightning storm or hunters' gunshots could start a dangerous stampede. Nobody rides across the vast western plains on a horse these days, and nobody goes on long cattle drives. These days, most ranches' work is done by truck and a strong fence keeps the cattle in.

Observing Patterns

1. Complete each sentence with a list word. Write the sentences.
   a) The ranches' owners branded their herd.
   b) It was time for the children's story.
   c) The hunters' bright jackets let other hunters see them in the bush.
   d) The drivers' cars were being prepared for the big race.

122

Precheck

Remind students to listen very carefully to the list words used within sentences. It is important that they hear and understand the use of the words before writing possessives. As they self-correct their spelling errors following the Precheck, have them think about why they spelled the words the way they did. Some students at this level hold on to phonics strategies that have served them well in the past.

Dictation

Summer **vacation** begins in June.
I wish summer was six **months** long!
The two **drivers'** cars collided.
The **hunters'** camp was in the woods.
The farmer's **stock** was a hundred cows.
She **rides** her horse every day.
The **cattle's** home was a huge green field.
I'm **building** a cottage at the lake.
There's a **fence** around that field.
The **ranches'** owners held a meeting.
Thunder usually follows **lightning.**
They were **yelling** for our team to win.
The **children's** coats hung in the closet.
Go **through** to the next room.
My family **goes** to the lake in August.
There's a **strong** wind blowing.

Words in Context

As you read through the context paragraph, remind students that plural possessives are not pronounced differently from singular possessives. Exceptions to this rule are words with irregular plural forms, such as **children** and **cattle**.

Observing Patterns

1. Suggest students ask themselves "Who or what did the (story, jackets, cars) belong to?" Discuss the fact that in each case the missing list word is possessive and is plural. Notice other words in the sentences that give clues.

Special Needs

For students who need extra practice with using apostrophes to show possession you might use activities such as the following.

- Cut out magazine pictures showing a variety of singular and plural people and objects. Glue each picture to a card and use them to ask questions orally that require an answer containing the possessive form. Alternatively, you could have a question printed on the card.
- Have students write sentences using possessive forms such as:
  - the girls' hair
  - the women's hands
  - the boys' jeans
  - the children's toys

2. Students could reinforce their memory of these words by drawing configuration boxes for each. Suggest that they can also draw lines representing the height of the letters.

Have them discuss words where shape helps them remember the spelling. Some words, such as **fence** and **goes** are better learned using other strategies because they are relatively 'flat'.

through

building

strong

lightning

yelling

3. Ensure students understand that homophones are words which sound alike but have different spellings and meanings.

You may want to suggest that students work in pairs to develop sentences to show the meanings of the homophone pairs.

I threw the flowerpot through the window.

A farmer's stock is the animals on the farm.

A stalk of corn can be two metres tall.

Discovering Patterns

1. This section of the unit is best addressed as a whole class activity led by the teacher. Most students will need further examples to reinforce the patterns for forming possessive plurals.

2. Write the list words that fit these shapes.

through lightning

building yelling

strong

3. Write the list words that fit these clues.

a) homophone for **stalk** stock
b) surrounds a yard or field fence
c) homophone for **threw** through
d) means the same as **holiday** vacation
e) there are twelve of them in a year months
f) rhymes with **tides** rides

Discovering Patterns

vacation months drivers' hunters' stock rides cattle's building fence ranches' lightning yelling children's through goes strong

s or es is added to make the words plural. Apostrophe is added.

's and s' are tricky. Be careful with these.

1. Write the list words that have an apostrophe at the very end. These words are all plural. Underline the singular form of each word. How has the plural been formed in each word? What has been done to the plural form to make it mean 'belonging to'?

drivers' hunters' ranches'

2. Write the two list words that end in an apostrophe and **s** (**'s**). Beside each word write the singular form. Notice that the plural is not formed by adding **s** or **es** to the base word. What has been added to the plural form to make it possessive, meaning 'belonging to'? cattle's – cow/bull children's – child Apostrophe + s has been added

POWERBOOSTER

- We add an apostrophe (') at the end of the plural form of most words to show possession.
- With irregular plurals, such as **children**, we add an apostrophe and **s** (**'s**) to the plural form.

123

These rules are also applied in Exploring Patterns 1.

2. Explore other irregular plurals with students. Some words are the same in singular and plural forms (**sheep**, **deer**, **moose**, **fish**). You might wish to develop a chart for reference during the unit.

ESL

- Many languages do not form the plural by adding an ending to a noun. In addition, many ESL students have difficulty hearing and pronouncing the final /s/ and /z/. Before students begin their exercises, you might want to practise with some simple school examples.

  The **boys'** coats are on the rack.

  The **students'** books are in their desks.

  The **girls'** bikes are in the bike rack.

- Have the students generate examples from their own experiences, or complete sentence frames using the plural possessive.

  The **dogs'** dishes are in the kitchen.

  The soccer **players'** uniforms are in their lockers.

  The **musicians'** instruments are very beautiful.

- It may also be helpful for ESL students to remember the irregular plural for nouns that name people.

singular	plural
child	children
man	men
woman	women
person	people

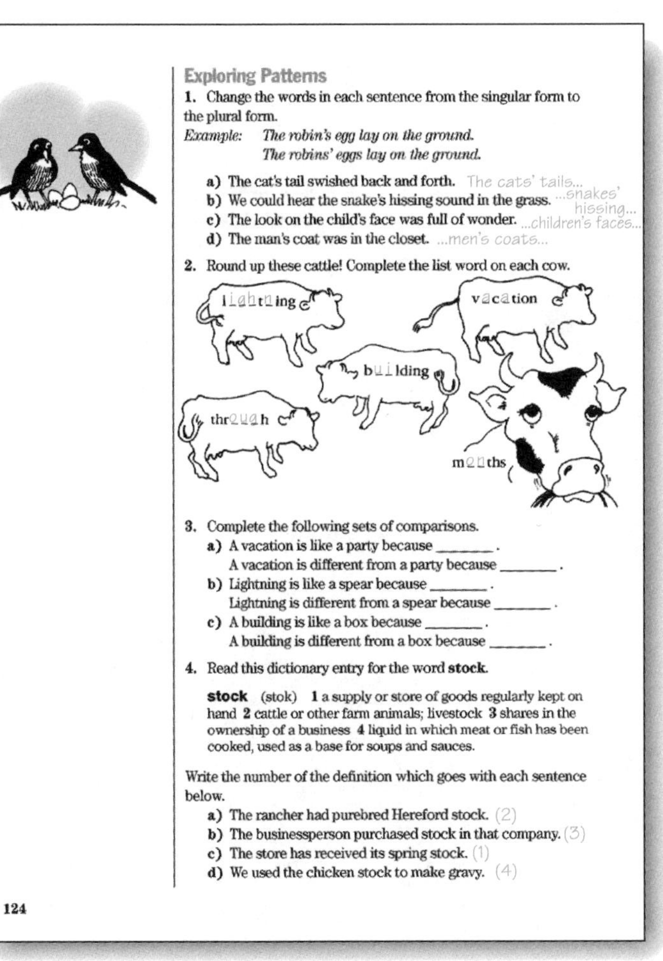

Exploring Patterns

1. Change the words in each sentence from the singular form to the plural form.

Example: *The robin's egg lay on the ground.*
The robins' eggs lay on the ground.

a) The cat's tail swished back and forth. The cats' tails...
b) We could hear the snake's hissing sound in the grass. ...snakes' hissing...
c) The look on the child's face was full of wonder. ...children's faces...
d) The man's coat was in the closet. ...men's coats...

2. Round up these cattle! Complete the list word on each cow.

3. Complete the following sets of comparisons.
a) A vacation is like a party because ______.
A vacation is different from a party because ______.
b) Lightning is like a spear because ______.
Lightning is different from a spear because ______.
c) A building is like a box because ______.
A building is different from a box because ______.

4. Read this dictionary entry for the word **stock**.

stock (stok) **1** a supply or store of goods regularly kept on hand **2** cattle or other farm animals; livestock **3** shares in the ownership of a business **4** liquid in which meat or fish has been cooked, used as a base for soups and sauces.

Write the number of the definition which goes with each sentence below.
a) The rancher had purebred Hereford stock. (2)
b) The businessperson purchased stock in that company. (3)
c) The store has received its spring stock. (1)
d) We used the chicken stock to make gravy. (4)

124

Exploring Patterns

1. Examine the example with students and note that nouns and verbs may also need to be altered in changing the sentence from singular to plural (for example, the irregular verb 'to be' changes from **was** to **were**.) If students have difficulty forming the possessive plural, review the Powerbooster and Discovering Patterns sections.

2. Cloze exercises help students focus on the difficult letter combinations in words such as **building**. Students might like to examine:

- other **ui** words such as **juice**, **cruise**, and **suit**, and note that the sound is different from that in **build** and **building** where the **ui** is pronounced as a short **i**.
- the **n** in **lightning**, which may be omitted. Many students add **e** to create another syllable (**light/en/ing**).
- the **n** in **months**, which is often not pronounced or heard, and contrast it with the word **mouths**, with which it is often confused.
- the **ough** in **through**, pronounced /ew/.

Contrast it with words such as **though**, **enough**, and **cough**. Students need visual and memory strategies to remember how to spell **ough** words.

3. This exercise encourages students to examine the meaning of list words in relation to other words. Provide opportunities for the sharing of ideas and the discussion of features of each key word. (See Critical Thinking, below.)

4. Have students create their own sentences for each of the meanings of **stock**.

Critical Thinking

- Exercises such as Exploring Patterns 3 help students examine the similarities and differences between words. Such classification exercises are useful for developing the concept of spelling as a problem-solving activity. Words are different and alike, not only in their meanings, but also in their origins, and the way they are spelled.

For example:

Building is like **suit** because they are both spelled with **ui**.

Building is different from **suit** because the **ui** makes a different sound in each word.

Through is like **threw** because they both sound the same.

Through is different from **threw** because they spell the /ew/ sound in two different ways.

Hunters' is like **children's** because they both end in the /z/ sound.

Hunters' is different from **children's** because the apostrophe comes in a different place.

5. Students may enjoy working in a small group or with a partner to brainstorm categories of information to include in their ad.

Students can plan the layout and design of their ad, or make a brochure to present to the class. You may want to have some travel ads or brochures on hand to show students the kinds of information included.

Holidays don't always turn out the way we plan. Have students write a story about their dream holiday and how it turned into a nightmare. Remind them to first write their story in rough. They might give their first draft to a partner to proofread. Have them go over and polish this edited version before writing their final draft.

Challenges with Words

1. You might want to point out some of the visual and auditory features of the Super Words. For example:

- **breed** is both a noun and a verb
- **herd** is a homophone of **heard**
- the **ei** in **heifers** is pronounced as a short **e**, unlike the **ei** in **eight** (a long **a**) or **seize** (a long **e**).
- the silent **e** is dropped from the end of **graze** before adding **-ing**
- **dairy** is often confused with **diary**, as only the **a** and **i** are transposed
- **domesticated** has five syllables, with the stress on the second.

Have students write sentences with the Super Words, or use some or all of them in a short paragraph.

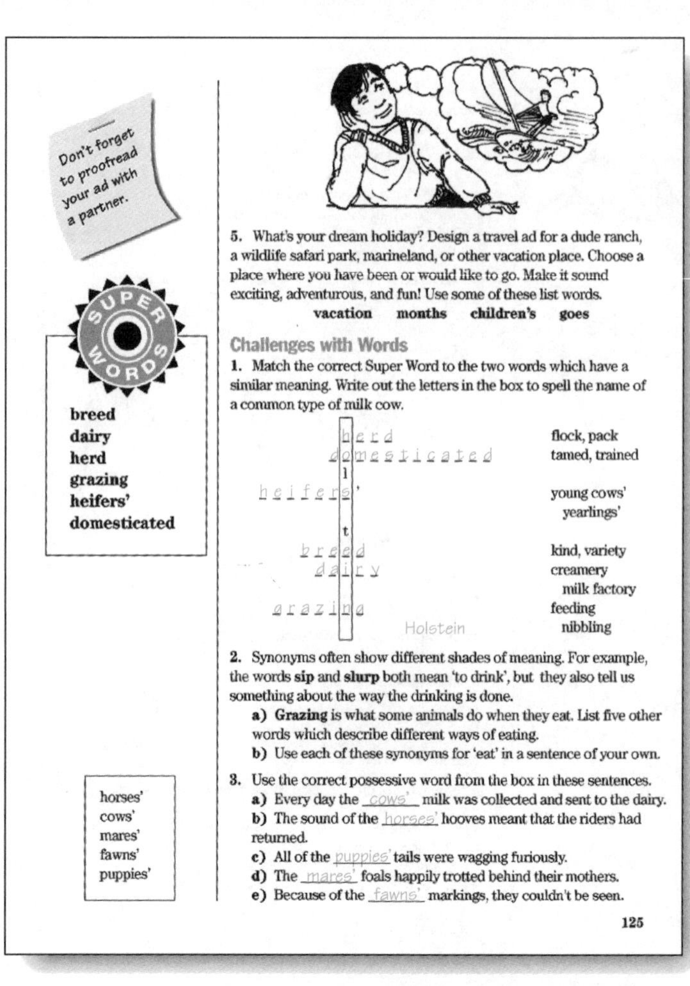

Don't forget to proofread your ad with a partner.

5. What's your dream holiday? Design a travel ad for a dude ranch, a wildlife safari park, marineland, or other vacation place. Choose a place where you have been or would like to go. Make it sound exciting, adventurous, and fun! Use some of these list words.

vacation **months** **children's** **goes**

SUPER WORDS

breed
dairy
herd
grazing
heifers'
domesticated

Challenges with Words

1. Match the correct Super Word to the two words which have a similar meaning. Write out the letters in the box to spell the name of a common type of milk cow.

Answer	Clues
herd	flock, pack
domesticated	tamed, trained
l	
heifers'	young cows' yearlings'
t	
breed	kind, variety
dairy	creamery milk factory
grazing	feeding nibbling

Holstein

2. Synonyms often show different shades of meaning. For example, the words **sip** and **slurp** both mean 'to drink', but they also tell us something about the way the drinking is done.

a) **Grazing** is what some animals do when they eat. List five other words which describe different ways of eating.

b) Use each of these synonyms for 'eat' in a sentence of your own.

horses'
cows'
mares'
fawns'
puppies'

3. Use the correct possessive word from the box in these sentences.

a) Every day the cows' milk was collected and sent to the dairy.

b) The sound of the horses' hooves meant that the riders had returned.

c) All of the puppies' tails were wagging furiously.

d) The mares' foals happily trotted behind their mothers.

e) Because of the fawns' markings, they couldn't be seen.

125

2. There are many words to describe the act of eating. Some of these students will know, others they can find in a thesaurus. Encourage students to use a dictionary to check the meaning of their synonyms. (See Oral Language and Literature, p. 199.)

3. Have students brainstorm other nouns which might go with these plural possessives. Students could then use these possessive noun combinations in written sentences. To make this more challenging, students might only think of nouns with the same initial letter and which end in **-s** (**horses' harness**; **mares' mothers**; **fawns' frowns**; **cows' calves**; **puppies' places**).

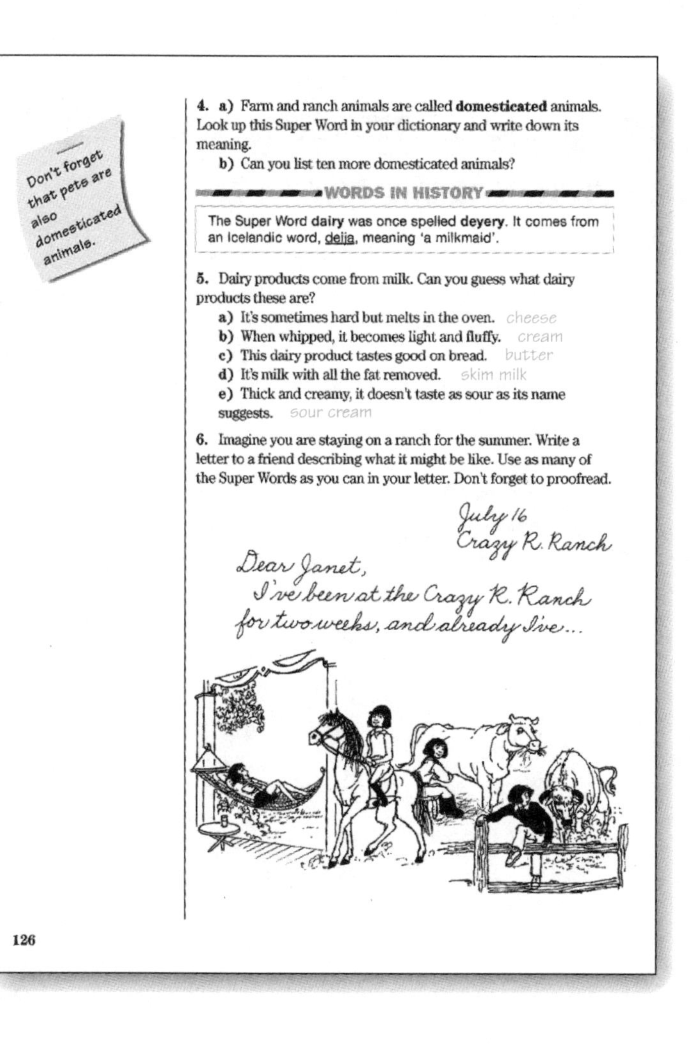

Don't forget that pets are also domesticated animals.

4. a) Farm and ranch animals are called **domesticated** animals. Look up this Super Word in your dictionary and write down its meaning.

b) Can you list ten more domesticated animals?

WORDS IN HISTORY

The Super Word **dairy** was once spelled **deyery**. It comes from an Icelandic word, <u>deija</u>, meaning 'a milkmaid'.

5. Dairy products come from milk. Can you guess what dairy products these are?

a) It's sometimes hard but melts in the oven. cheese
b) When whipped, it becomes light and fluffy. cream
c) This dairy product tastes good on bread. butter
d) It's milk with all the fat removed. skim milk
e) Thick and creamy, it doesn't taste as sour as its name suggests. sour cream

6. Imagine you are staying on a ranch for the summer. Write a letter to a friend describing what it might be like. Use as many of the Super Words as you can in your letter. Don't forget to proofread.

July 16
Crazy R. Ranch

Dear Janet,
I've been at the Crazy R. Ranch for two weeks, and already I've...

126

4. Students might want to research domesticated and wild animals.

5. Students might like to choose another food 'family' such as meat, vegetables, or fruit and make up clues similar to the type in this exercise. They could then exchange clues with a partner and try to guess the foods. Students might also want to add these words to their Personal Review List.

It's round, often red, and has a shiny skin you can eat. (an apple)

You have to take the skin off this orange-coloured fruit. (an orange)

It's long and yellow. (a banana)

Small and round, it can be either green or black and sometimes has seeds. (a grape)

6. The business letter style has changed in recent years, but friendly letters usually retain the form illustrated on page 126. Students might enjoy writing a letter to a real friend, talking about what they have been doing recently. They may also enjoy composing letters on the computer and sending them to other students via e-mail.

Some students, especially if they like drawing, might create picture book stories from their letters for sharing with younger students.

Writing

• Engage students in looking for apostrophes in newspapers, magazines, and other print media. Have them note in each case why the apostrophe was used and whether it was used correctly. It may also be useful to have them go back through writing samples in their own portfolios or writing folders, looking for cases where they used the possessive form.

Oral Language and Literature

• Synonyms not only have different shades of meaning, they often are used to express meaning in different contexts. In other words 'to chow down' also means to eat, but probably would not be used in formal speech. **Slurp** and **gobble** both describe eating in a less than polite manner. It may be interesting for students to sort words according to their connotation.

eating and drinking words		
polite	**rude**	**neutral**
sip	slurp	drink
chew	chomp	munch
swallow	gobble	gulp

Curriculum Connection

Students could research the topic, then write their own paragraph on ranching. A *National Geographic* article, a book on western ranching, or any suitable article would give them more background information.

Linda Granfield's excellent book *Cowboy: A Kid's Album* gives interesting details about the lives of male and female cowhands, with some Canadian examples.

Assessment

Note which students have made the same errors in their Precheck and Unit Tests. If they are having difficulty with the concept and details of making nouns plural and possessive, reassure them that they can develop strategies for learning when and how to use the apostrophe. Make note of those students confusing the use of **'s** and **s'** in order to provide necessary reteaching and further practice with this structure.

Follow-up

• Ongoing editing conferences can help point out where the possessive forms are used (both correctly and incorrectly) in the students' everyday writing.
• Return frequently to short mini-lessons on the plural, possessive, and plural possessive forms throughout the middle years of elementary school.

Teacher's Notes

27 Contractions
doesn't

Patterns

Contractions (is**n't**, ca**n't**) require a strategy beyond just sounding out the word. Visual and memory strategies can help students with spelling contractions once they recognize that two words have been combined, and the missing sounds and letters replaced by an apostrophe. Contractions are an important part of English speech. They are used in informal speech and writing, and in writing dialogue.

Preknowledge

Students should have an understanding of the following concepts as they work with the patterns in this unit.

- Contractions are formed from two base words (they would/**they'd**).
- An apostrophe can replace missing letters in a contraction (does not/**doesn't**).
- The **-ed** ending usually indicates the past tense of a verb (**spotted**).

More Patterns

Other patterns you might wish to introduce or review in this unit include the following.

- Adding **-ing** to base words (**waiting**). In some instances, changes occur in the base word when the ending is added (**lie/lying**).
- When adding **-ed** to a word that ends with a vowel + consonant, the consonant is doubled (**spot/spotted**, **slip/slipped**).
- Some verbs have an irregular past tense (**stand/stood**).
- Compound words are made up of two words that are related in meaning (**groundhog**).
- Homophones are words that sound alike but have different spellings and meanings (**they're/there/their**).

Professional Notebook

I don't necessarily hold with those who consider spelling to be next to godliness, but I do believe that a word's spelling is important in that it is an aspect of that word's personality as surely as its sound, its meaning, and its story. For this reason, throughout my career I have gone out of my way to cultivate in students an interest in words because I believe that if you come to care about them you will pay attention to them, and this in turn will go a long way towards encouraging an interest in their structure as well as their sound and meaning. (Barton/Booth 153)

Sharing the Secrets with Kids

- *All of the homophones* ***their, there,*** *and* ***they're*** *begin with the word* ***the.***
- ***Lying*** *and* ***lay*** *take a bit of practice to use correctly. "I am* ***lying*** *on the couch right now" (present tense of* ***lie****). "I* ***lay*** *here for hours yesterday" (past tense of* ***lie****). So, it's incorrect to say "Go* ***lay*** *on the couch" unless you're a chicken and you're* ***laying*** *an egg.*

Precheck

Remind students to listen for meaning in dictation sentences, especially with contractions. Monitor the results to note which students confuse the placement of the apostrophe.

Dictation

The weekend **doesn't** seem long enough.
We didn't mind **waiting** for supper.
I like **lying** down to watch TV.
Photography is my favourite hobby.
I forgot to put **film** in the camera!
What are McDonald's **golden** arches?
I **spotted** the money on the floor.
I **haven't** heard that group's new song.
The secret **slipped** out by accident!
My parents said **they'd** be here soon.
We **stood** at the front to read our stories.
My dad says **he'll** pick me up if it rains.
The papers **lay** scattered on the lawn.
The **groundhog** is a pest to farmers.
They're sitting on the ground.
The books **weren't** on the right shelf.

Words in Context

The passage provides students with an opportunity to read how the words are used in sentences and to establish their meaning. Discuss words such as **telephoto** and **opportunity** that may be unfamiliar to some students. You might also want to list all the four-syllable words in the paragraph.

Observing Patterns

1. If students do not understand why the consonant is doubled in **spotted** and **slipped**, review the Powerbooster section of Unit 20 (p. 94). Have students think of other words they know which fit this pattern. (See Special Needs, below.)

2. Students could be asked to arrange the words on their selected list in alphabetical order.

Contractions

doesn't

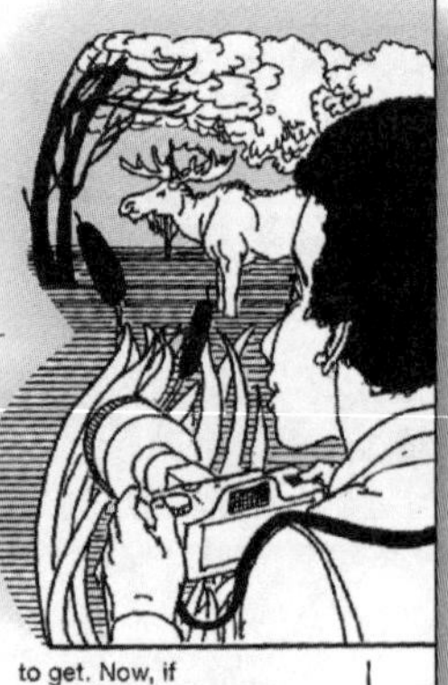

doesn't
waiting
lying
photography
film
golden
spotted
haven't
slipped
they'd
stood
he'll
lay
groundhog
they're
weren't

Exploring the World of Wildlife Photography

Wildlife photography is a fascinating hobby that requires more than just a good camera and lots of film. After all, who ever heard of a moose who stood to pose for a picture? Wildlife photographers are used to lying hidden for hours, waiting for a bird or a groundhog to appear. They're careful to be still and quiet. It doesn't take much to alarm a wild creature, and then a golden opportunity has slipped away. Until quite recently, close-up shots of shy wild animals, such as snow leopards, haven't been easy to get. Now, if photographers spotted such a rare animal in the distance, they would switch to a telephoto lens. With this long-distance lens, they'd be able to get shots that weren't possible before. Very often, the lion that looks like he'll take a bite out of the camera, actually lay a hundred metres away when his picture was taken.

Observing Patterns

1. Write the list words that end in **-ed**. Underline the base word in each. What happens to the base word when **-ed** is added?
spotted slipped — the last consonant is doubled

2. Write the six list words that fall between **debt** and **hotel** in the dictionary. doesn't film golden groundhog haven't he'll

3. Write the list words that rhyme with the following words.
stay buying should dating burnt paid scare
lay lying stood waiting weren't they'd they're

4. Which list word has two /f/ sounds but no letter **f**?
photography

5. Write the list word that can mean either 'telling false stories' or 'resting with the body in a flat position'. lying

127

3. Note that while the pairs rhyme, in most cases they do not share the same spelling patterns for the rhyming sounds (**should**/**stood**).

4. Review with students the different ways of spelling the sound /f/. (See Observing Patterns 2, p. 188.) Students could begin or add to a class list of **ph** words.

5. Encourage students to write their own sentences to show the two meanings of lying.

That man is not telling the truth.
He's ________!
That girl is not feeling well.
She's ___________ down.

Special Needs

- Some students may need additional practice to grasp the concept of doubling the final consonant when **-ed** is added. Point out that the first vowel in each of these words is short, and contrast it with long vowel words.

short vowel	long vowel
stripped	striped
hopped	hoped
tapped	taped

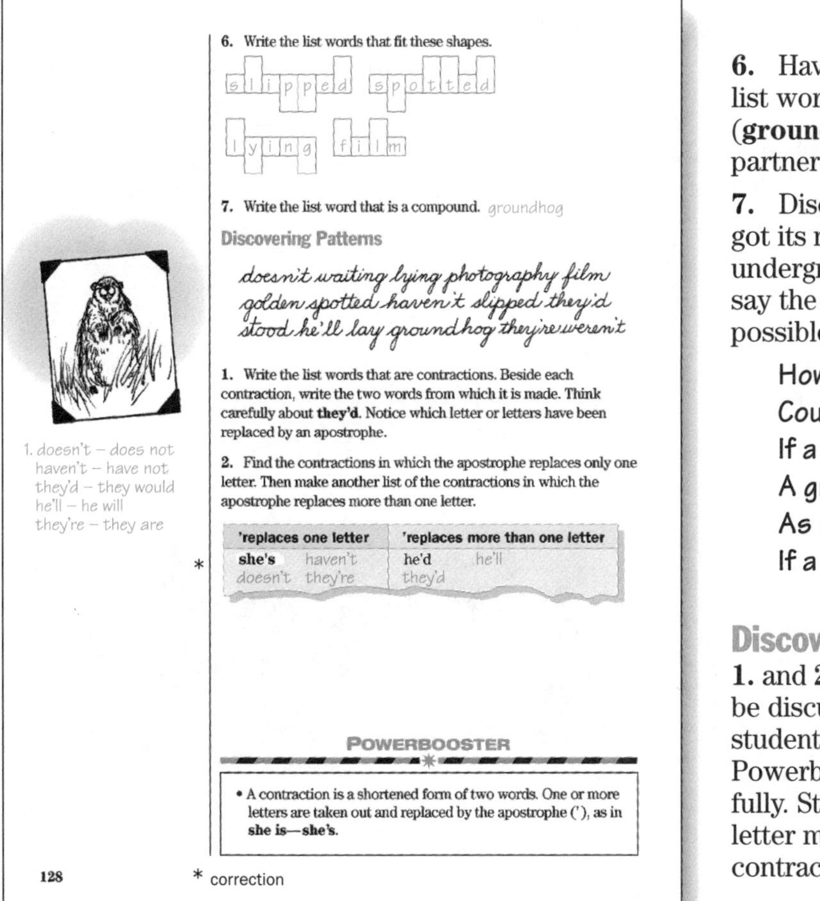
6. Write the list words that fit these shapes.

slipped spotted

lying film

7. Write the list word that is a compound. groundhog

Discovering Patterns

doesn't waiting lying photography film
golden spotted haven't slipped they'd
stood he'll lay groundhog they're weren't

1. Write the list words that are contractions. Beside each contraction, write the two words from which it is made. Think carefully about **they'd**. Notice which letter or letters have been replaced by an apostrophe.

1. doesn't – does not
haven't – have not
they'd – they would
he'll – he will
they're – they are

2. Find the contractions in which the apostrophe replaces only one letter. Then make another list of the contractions in which the apostrophe replaces more than one letter.

'replaces one letter		'replaces more than one letter	
she's	haven't	he'd	he'll
doesn't	they're	they'd	

*

POWERBOOSTER

• A contraction is a shortened form of two words. One or more letters are taken out and replaced by the apostrophe ('), as in **she is—she's**.

128

* correction

6. Have students create word shapes for other list words that have unusual configurations (**groundhog**, **photography**) and challenge a partner to solve the puzzle.

7. Discuss with students how the groundhog got its name because of the way it digs extensive underground tunnels. They might enjoy trying to say the following tongue-twister as rapidly as possible.

How much ground
Could a groundhog grind
If a groundhog could grind ground?
A groundhog could grind
As much ground as a groundhog could grind
If a groundhog could grind ground!

Discovering Patterns

1. and **2.** These two exercises are designed to be discussed by you and the whole group. Help students arrive at the rule stated in the Powerbooster after examining contractions carefully. Students should note that more than one letter may be replaced by the apostrophe in a contraction (they **woul**d/they'd; he **wil**l/he'll).

Multiple Intelligences

• Students who spell **they'd** as **theyd**, or **haven't** as **havent** are probably using a phonetic approach to spelling. It is important to emphasize the structural pattern underlying contractions—two words are combined in such a way that certain sounds are altered and the letters representing these sounds are replaced by an apostrophe.

The concept of contractions can be introduced and reinforced in a number of ways, to appeal to a variety of learning modes.

Visual/Spatial: Use letter tiles to make the two base words. Remove the unused letters and replace with an apostrophe.

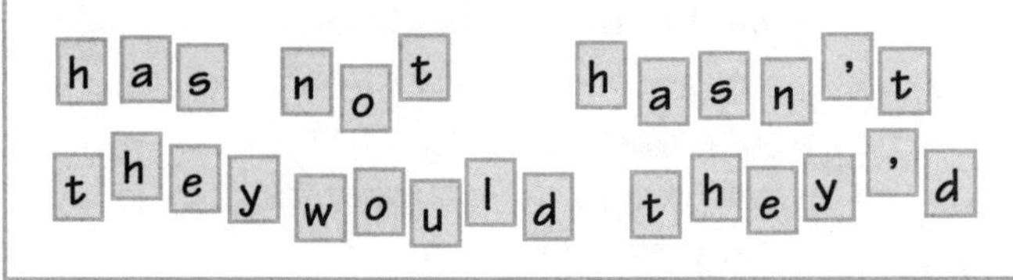

Verbal/Linguistic: Relate contractions to the informal language of speech and dialogue. Change the formal, "they would like to see the puppy" to the informal "they'd like to see the puppy". Talk about the differences in rhythm and tone.

Bodily/kinesthetic: Have students stand holding large letter cards for the words **have not**, **they would**, etc. Have the two groups move closer together, squeezing out the unused letter or letters, and replacing them with a student carrying an apostrophe card.

Logical/Mathematical: Ask students to sort contractions into three groups.

not	would	will
haven't	he'd	he'll
hasn't	she'd	she'll
don't	you'd	you'll

Exploring Patterns

1. Emphasize with students that the apostrophe is inserted in place of the letters which have been removed. If they think of the original two words and the letters replaced, the positioning of the apostrophe should not present a problem.

Ask the students to read the sentences aloud with and without the contractions. What is the difference in tone? (Contractions make the sentences sound more like conversation.)

2. Many adult spellers will scribble a word two or three different ways to see if it looks correct. Students should become comfortable with the idea of checking to see if a word they have written 'looks right'. For many students, particularly those whose visual skills are strong, writing words several ways until they look right is a good way to become a better speller.

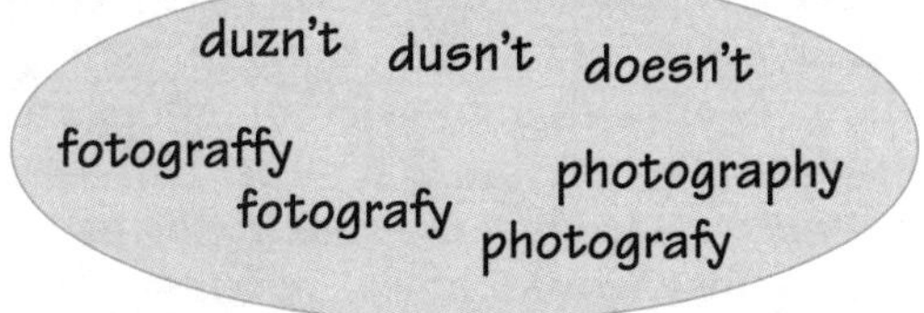

Exploring Patterns

1. Replace each set of underlined words with a contraction.

a) Photography is a hobby that does not always require expensive equipment. doesn't

b) We were not planning to go to the film because we have not got enough money. weren't haven't

c) My grandfather says he will pick us up after the practice. he'll

d) They said they would like to come but they are much too busy. they'd they're

2. Good spellers are like good photographers. They often 'take pictures' of words and store them in their brains, much like photos are stored on film. These 'word pictures' of list words are incomplete. Supply the missing letters and put them back in focus!

d o e sn't w e r e n't h a v e n't p h ot o gr a p h y

3. The verb **lay** means 'put down; place in a certain position'. The verb **lie** means 'have one's body in a flat position along the ground or other surface'. For example, 'We **lay** the blanket on the ground so that we can **lie** on it'. In the following sentences, use the verbs **lay**, **laying**, or **lie**, **lying** correctly.

a) The hens are laying their eggs in the straw.

b) We saw our friends lying on the beach.

c) Be sure to lay your glasses carefully on the shelf.

d) My cat loves to lie on the rug by the fireplace.

129

3. Students may need guidance and additional examples to distinguish clearly between the verbs **lay** and **lie**.

Lying is something you do with your body or when you tell a lie. **Laying** is something you do with another object.

She's **lying** on the bed.

She's **laying** the sheets on the bed.

Would you **lie** to me?

Lay your coat over there.

Tell the dog to **lie** down.

ESL

- Some languages do not have contracted forms. For students from these language backgrounds, words such as **haven't** and **he'll** present certain difficulties. The final **ll** in **he'll**, **she'll**, and **we'll** may not be heard, resulting in sentences such as "she go". Similarly, the final **-s** in **he's**, **she's**, and **it's** may be dropped, resulting in students writing "he going" rather than "he's going". In addition, the final **re** may be difficult to hear and pronounce in **they're**.

- Provide practice with contractions and help students understand the common patterns.

I don't	she doesn't
you don't	he doesn't
they don't	it doesn't
we don't	
I haven't	he hasn't
you haven't	she hasn't
we haven't	it hasn't
they haven't	

4. You're a wildlife photographer who has just found a grizzly bear in your camp. You have two choices—to run, or take pictures. You may never get this close to a grizzly again! Choose what you would do, and explain why you made the choice you did. Compare your choice with a partner's. Did you make the same decision? Use some of these list words in your paragraph.

spotted he'll doesn't they'd film

SUPER WORDS

environment
they've
telephoto
who's
focus
surrounded

Challenges with Words

1. Match the Super Words to the clues below.
   - **a)** When taking pictures of wildlife, you might use a telephoto lens.
   - **b)** The area or location which affects living things is called its environment
   - **c)** They've been gone now for nearly an hour.
   - **d)** Something which is shut in on all sides is surrounded
   - **e)** This contraction has a homophone. who's
   - **f)** When an image is in focus, it's sharp and clear.

2. Here are six words and phrases that have something to do with photography. Write the opposite, or antonym, of each one.

fuzzy clear — dim bright — still life photography action photography
distant near — foreground background — black and white colour

WORDS IN HISTORY

The Super Word **telephoto** was made from two Greek words: tele, meaning 'far off', and photos, meaning 'light'.

130

4. Students might choose to write about their adventure with a grizzly in the first person, as if the action is happening right now. ("I'm standing just outside the clearing of our camp, watching a grizzly bear rip apart our tent. I suppose he's looking for food.") Have students proofread carefully for contractions in their writing.

Challenges with Words

1. Encourage students who experienced no difficulties with the Precheck to study the Super Words. Have them note the following features of the words:

- the **n** in **environment** comes from the base word **environs**
- **they've** is a contraction of **they have**
- **who's** is a homophone for **whose**, the possessive pronoun.

2. Note that there are several possible antonyms for **still life photography**. **Wildlife**, **action**, or **portrait photography** would all be acceptable.

Words in History

You might point out to students that many English words are like **telephoto**, formed by combining two Greek or Latin words. Students might wish to make their own new English words. Have them use a dictionary which explains word histories and choose several Greek and Latin root words. They can then combine them to form new words. For example, **anti** (from Greek meaning 'against') + **photo** (from Greek meaning 'light') = **antiphoto** meaning 'darkness'.

root	Latin	Greek	meaning
pose	ponere		to place
fer	ferre		to bring
tract	trahere		to draw
dict	dicere		to say
contra	contra		against
pro		pro	before
chrome		chroma	colour
therm		therme	heat
phone		phone	sound

Writing

- Some students may wish to develop the writing activity on p. 130 more fully by writing a radio or TV news interview with the photographer (while the grizzly is hanging around!) or with the grizzly bear itself. If they have access to photos of grizzlies, they could write a photo-essay. Or, using a reference source on bears, they could write about what to do and what not to do when meeting a bear.
- Writing partners might research why grizzlies are an endangered species, and what people can do to help them. They could present their report as an interview, news report, or research article.

3. Suggest that students write a paragraph using all four **tele-** words. The Greek word *tele* means 'far, far off'. In English, it is used to mean 'over', 'from', or 'a long way away'.

4. You might want to point out to your students that some modern tele- words, such as **telemarketing** and **telecommunication**, have been created because there were no suitable English words available. Have students suggest other words that have been created for this reason. They might add these to their Personal Review Lists.

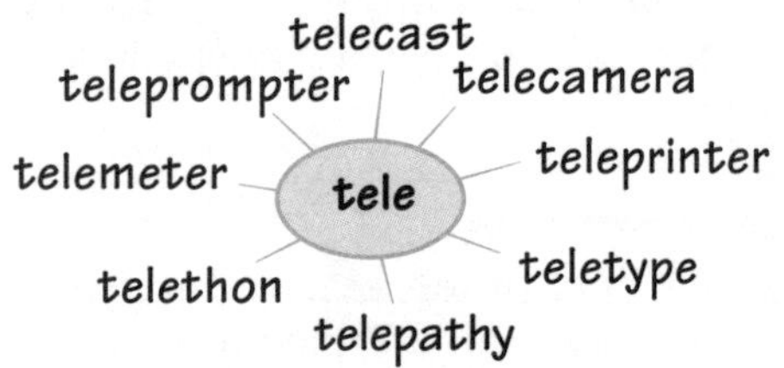

5. Contractions with **-s** are often used more in speech than in writing. We know which words have been contracted by the context of the sentence. Students might want to practise using these contractions in the form of a dialogue or conversation they write.

6. Have students find an interesting photograph of people doing things in a natural environment. Have them write a story about what they think really happened when the photograph was taken.

New Words

7. Have students talk about why the word **mouse** was chosen for the hand-held computer device. Is the plural of computer mouse, mice?

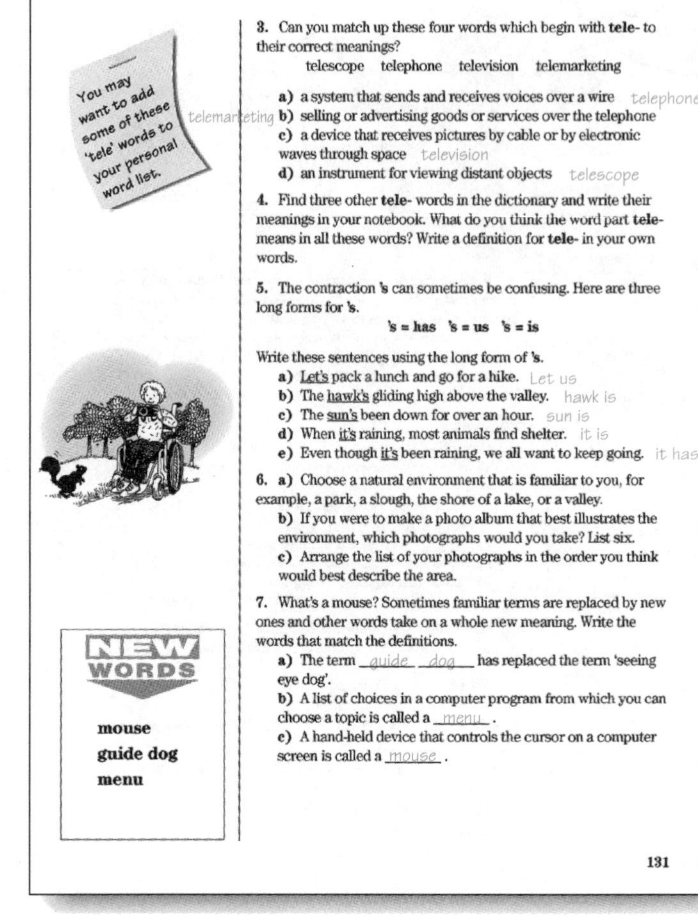

You may want to add some of these 'tele' words to your personal word list.

3. Can you match up these four words which begin with **tele-** to their correct meanings?

telescope telephone television telemarketing

a) a system that sends and receives voices over a wire telephone
telemarketing **b)** selling or advertising goods or services over the telephone
c) a device that receives pictures by cable or by electronic waves through space television
d) an instrument for viewing distant objects telescope

4. Find three other **tele-** words in the dictionary and write their meanings in your notebook. What do you think the word part **tele-** means in all these words? Write a definition for **tele-** in your own words.

5. The contraction **'s** can sometimes be confusing. Here are three long forms for **'s**.

's = has 's = us 's = is

Write these sentences using the long form of **'s**.
a) Let's pack a lunch and go for a hike. Let us
b) The hawk's gliding high above the valley. hawk is
c) The sun's been down for over an hour. sun is
d) When it's raining, most animals find shelter. it is
e) Even though it's been raining, we all want to keep going. it has

6. a) Choose a natural environment that is familiar to you, for example, a park, a slough, the shore of a lake, or a valley.
b) If you were to make a photo album that best illustrates the environment, which photographs would you take? List six.
c) Arrange the list of your photographs in the order you think would best describe the area.

7. What's a mouse? Sometimes familiar terms are replaced by new ones and other words take on a whole new meaning. Write the words that match the definitions.
a) The term guide dog has replaced the term 'seeing eye dog'.
b) A list of choices in a computer program from which you can choose a topic is called a menu.
c) A hand-held device that controls the cursor on a computer screen is called a mouse.

NEW WORDS
mouse
guide dog
menu

131

Encourage students to find other examples of everyday words from the computer world that are used in interesting ways.

crash	freeze	gridlock	surf
scan	import	export	net

Oral Language and Literature

• Many idioms or expressions use the word **lying** or lie.

Lying low (*hiding or not calling attention to oneself*).
Lying in one's teeth (*telling serious lies*).
Has made one's bed and must lie on it (*must accept the consequences of one's actions*).
A white lie (*a harmless lie told to help or comfort someone*).

• Contractions are used in many songs and rhymes. Students can explore their own favourite song lyrics for contractions, or read and copy or underline the contractions in the familiar poem, "I Know an Old Lady".

I know an old lady who swallowed a fly
I **don't** know why
She swallowed that fly
I guess **she'll** die.
And then the old lady she swallowed a spider
That wiggled and tiggled and tickled inside her.
She swallowed the spider to catch the fly
I **don't** know why
She swallowed that fly
I guess **she'll** die
and so on until:
And then the old woman, she swallowed a horse
She's dead, of course!

Curriculum Connection

Students might want to make a collection of interesting wildlife photographs, and could write a short paragraph for some of these. Some possible topics for the paragraph might be: what the animal or animals are thinking; what they are about to do; what emotion the photograph suggests; what person the animal looks like. Magazines such as *National Geographic*, *OWL*, and *Canadian Geographic* are good sources of photos.

Assessment

Have students compare their results on the Unit Test with the Precheck to note improvement. Continue to include Super Words in the Unit Test for those who completed the Challenges with Words exercises. Monitor everyday writing for errors in contractions and the use of the apostrophe.

Follow-up

Have special proofreading sessions for contractions, or develop a stamp or form such as the one shown below.

Date: ____________________

This piece of writing has been checked for:

contractions ....

Teacher's Notes

Suffixes

thank**ful**
kind**ness**

Patterns

Adding prefixes and suffixes to base words greatly expands the written vocabulary of students in the middle grades. At the same time, breaking longer words into base words and endings gives students another strategy for spelling longer words. In this unit, two of the most frequently used suffixes are examined, **-ful** and **-ness**. Students learn that a **y** occurring before either suffix is changed to an **i** (**beauty/beautiful**; **happy/happiness**). They also learn that adding **-ful** transforms nouns into adjectives, while **-ness** turns adjectives into nouns (**wonder/wonderful**; **kind/kindness**).

Preknowledge

Students should have an understanding of the following concepts as they work with the patterns in this unit.

- Base words are the parts of words to which endings can be added (**success/ful**).
- An ending changes the way a word can be used in a sentence, and sometimes also alters its meaning.
- Some base words change the **y** to **i** when endings are added (happ**y**/happ**i**ness).
- Words can be broken down into syllables (**won/der/ful**).
- One syllable in each word receives more stress than the others (**strange**/ness).

More Patterns

Other patterns you might wish to review or introduce from the list words in this unit include the following.

- Compound words (**air/port**).
- The long **o** spelled **o** at the end of words (radi**o**).
- Two- and three-syllable words (**min/ute**, **won/der/ful**).

Professional Notebook

Suffixes, like prefixes, are predictable indicators of pronunciation and sometimes may signal a meaning relationship. The meaning that is signaled by suffixes, however, is not usually a meaning change, but rather, is a change in how and in what position the word can be used in the sentence. Compose is what you do. The composer is the person doing it. A composition is what you have once you have composed. Students need to become aware of how words change when they are signaling different relationships. They also need to realize that there are slight pronunciation changes to root words when suffixes are added.
(Cunningham 177)

Sharing the Secrets with Kids

- *If you can't remember how to spell **beautiful**, remember that **beauty** comes from the French word **beau** meaning 'good-looking'.*
- *If you can't remember how to spell **min**ute, it might help to remember it is spelled the same as min**ute** meaning 'very tiny'.*
- *The double **c** and double **s** in **successful** can be remembered using a rhyme:*
  S-U-C-C-E-S-S
  That's the way you spell success!

Suffixes -ful -ness

thank**ful** kind**ness**

airport
planes
wonderful
crashed
successful
minute
beautiful*
flight
happiness
fairness
thankful
radio
strangeness
faster
landed
kindness

***Beautiful** is one of the 25 most frequently misspelled words.

Exploring the World of Early Flight

When we see planes roar in for a radio controlled landing at an airport, they seem huge and powerful. Yet the first airplane that flew was made of cloth, wires, and wood. Since it couldn't travel faster than a bicycle, it seems a kindness to even call it an airplane! Yet the 'Flyer', as this plane was called, was a wonderful machine. Despite the strangeness of its appearance, it was a beautiful design, and it worked. On December 17, 1903, the Flyer rose into the air, flew for less than a minute under its own power, and landed safely. Imagine the happiness of the inventor when Flyer was successful not once, but several times. In all fairness, the inventor had reason to be thankful. The wind at Kitty Hawk, where the historic flights took place, was strong and gusty. If the Flyer had crashed, the history of flight might have been quite different.

Observing Patterns

1. Unscramble the syllables in each balloon to form list words.

ness i happ — happiness
o di ra — radio
cess ful suc — successful
ti beau ful — beautiful
der won ful — wonderful

132

Precheck

After students have self-checked their Precheck and recorded their misspellings, survey the class to elicit those words which most students found difficult. Highlight these words throughout the unit and challenge the class to eliminate them as errors on the Unit Test.

Dictation

There are lots of planes at the **airport**.
Planes fly to many different places.
We had a **wonderful** vacation.
The cars **crashed** into each other.
She was **successful** in winning the race.
The time is one **minute** to ten o' clock.
What a **beautiful** tree!
Our **flight** was late taking off.
Happiness made me smile.
Fairness means treating people equally.
I'm **thankful** you could come today.
Does everyone own a **radio**?
The **strangeness** of the noise was scary.
Can you run **faster** than me?
The plane **landed** on time.
Thank you for your **kindness** and help.

Words in Context

Have students read the context passage and suggest synonyms for as many list words as possible. Students may be interested in researching the inventors of the 'Flyer', Wilbur and Orville Wright.

You may wish to have students look for other words with suffixes in the paragraph.

list word	synonym
airport	airfield, landing strip
planes	aircraft, airliner, jet
wonderful	amazing, marvelous, awesome
crashed	collided, smashed
successful	winning, triumphant, prosperous
minute	moment, instant, flash
beautiful	attractive, lovely, gorgeous
flight	flying, aviation
happiness	satisfaction, bliss, contentment
fairness	honesty, decency, justice
thankful	pleased, glad, obliged
radio	receiver, tuner,
strangeness	oddness
faster	quicken, swifter
landed	arrived, docked
kindness	good turn, favour, service

Observing Patterns

1. This activity helps students focus on syllables and their sequence within a word. The answers should be written as complete words without syllabic divisions. Have them say the words aloud, noting where the stress falls.

2. a) Students are looking for words within a narrow band of the alphabet. Point out that since there are no words on the list beginning with **e**, all the words they are looking for will begin with **f**.

b) Have students note the difference in the sound of the **-ed** ending (crash**t**, land**ed**). You might have them try to say crash**ed** pronouncing the **-ed** to hear how awkward it sounds (crash/**ed**).

d) Make sure students understand the difference between a compound word, in which two base words are joined, and a word that contains a base and a suffix (**air/port**; **kind/-ness**).

Discovering Patterns

1. These activities are designed to be done with the whole group. Relate changing the **y** to **i** in **beauty/beautiful** to the same pattern in forming plurals (cand**y**/candi**es**) and when adding **-ed** (tr**y**/tri**ed**). Help students see that this is a common pattern in English spelling.

It is important to help students note that the **e** in **care** is not dropped when **-ful** is added (car**eful**).

2. Give students other adjectives that end in **y** and have them add the suffix **-ness**. Ask them to formulate a rule for adding **-ness** to words ending in **y**. Note that there are many more words ending in **y** which students will use at this level than there are words adding **-ful**.

lazy	laziness	ugly	ugliness
crazy	craziness	hazy	haziness
bossy	bossiness	cosy	cosiness
creepy	creepiness	messy	messiness
lonely	loneliness	grumpy	grumpiness

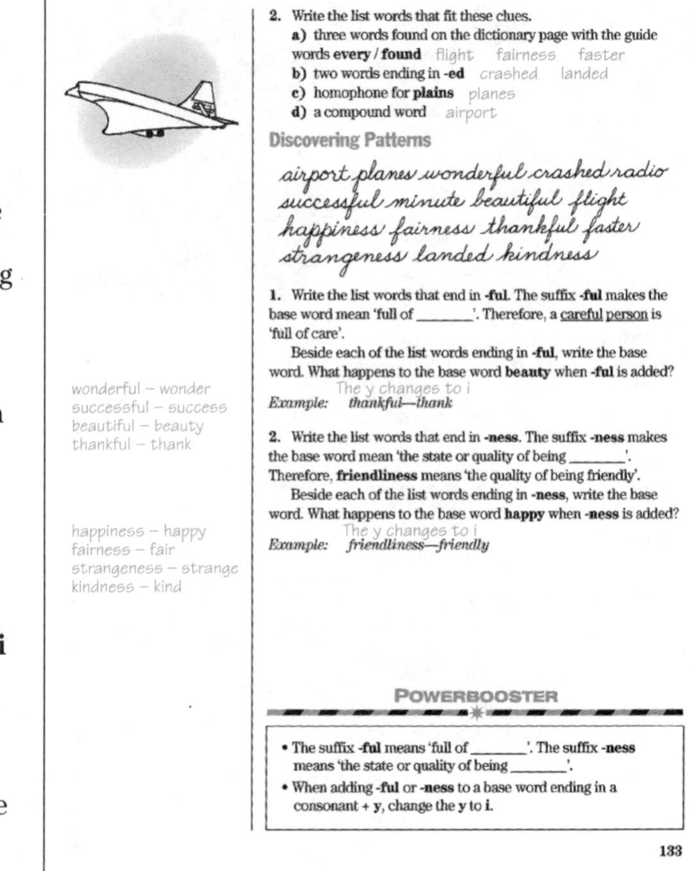

2. Write the list words that fit these clues.
a) three words found on the dictionary page with the guide words **every / found** flight fairness faster
b) two words ending in **-ed** crashed landed
c) homophone for **plains** planes
d) a compound word airport

Discovering Patterns

airport planes wonderful crashed radio successful minute beautiful flight happiness fairness thankful faster strangeness landed kindness

1. Write the list words that end in **-ful**. The suffix **-ful** makes the base word mean 'full of ______'. Therefore, a careful person is 'full of care'.
Beside each of the list words ending in **-ful**, write the base word. What happens to the base word **beauty** when **-ful** is added? The y changes to i
Example: thankful—thank

wonderful – wonder
successful – success
beautiful – beauty
thankful – thank

2. Write the list words that end in **-ness**. The suffix **-ness** makes the base word mean 'the state or quality of being ______'. Therefore, **friendliness** means 'the quality of being friendly'.
Beside each of the list words ending in **-ness**, write the base word. What happens to the base word **happy** when **-ness** is added? The y changes to i
Example: friendliness—friendly

happiness – happy
fairness – fair
strangeness – strange
kindness – kind

POWERBOOSTER

- The suffix **-ful** means 'full of ______'. The suffix **-ness** means 'the state or quality of being ______'.
- When adding **-ful** or **-ness** to a base word ending in a consonant + **y**, change the **y** to **i**.

133

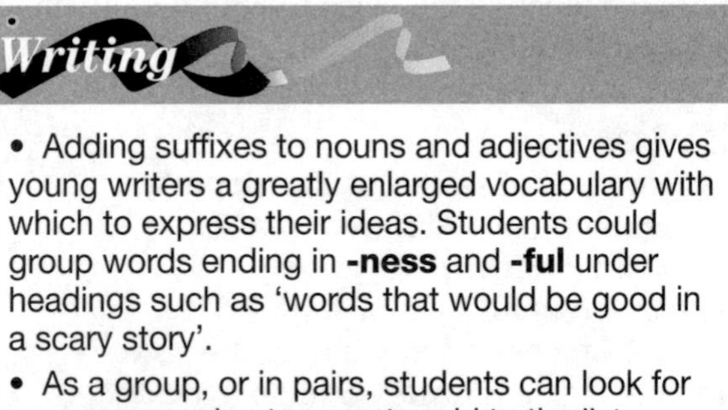

Writing

- Adding suffixes to nouns and adjectives gives young writers a greatly enlarged vocabulary with which to express their ideas. Students could group words ending in **-ness** and **-ful** under headings such as 'words that would be good in a scary story'.
- As a group, or in pairs, students can look for synonyms and antonyms to add to the list.

Special Needs

- Some students may need additional practice with the concept of adding suffixes. A good visual and tactile strategy is to use word cards where the students actually join the suffix to the base word, and then write the word. Create word cards with the base words separate from the suffixes. Have the students join the cards and write the words. A special category of cards ending in **y** and adding **-ness** can be created with a folded section containing an **i** to cover the **y**.

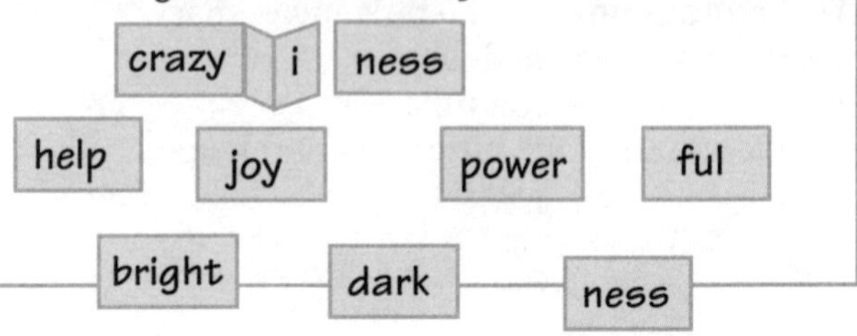

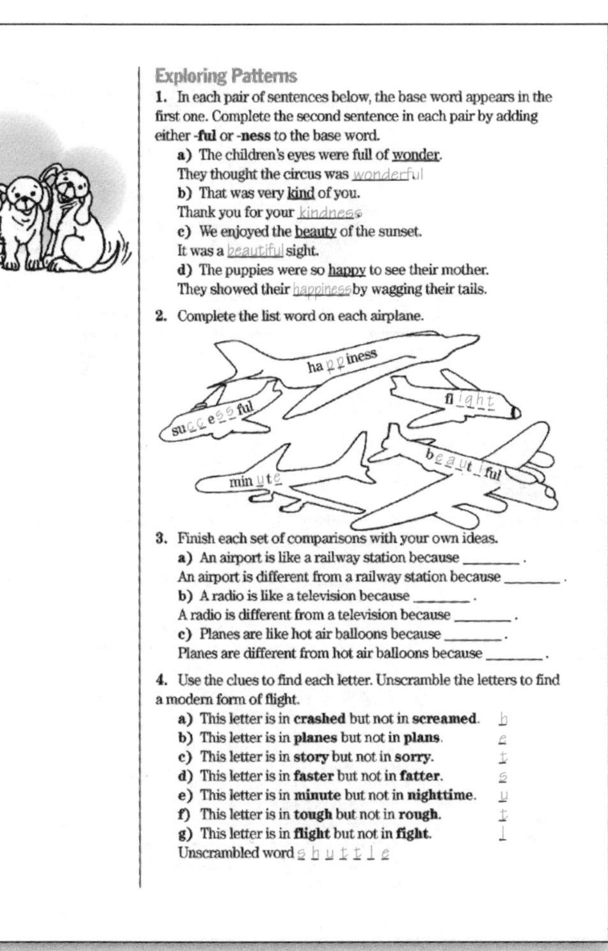
Exploring Patterns

1. In each pair of sentences below, the base word appears in the first one. Complete the second sentence in each pair by adding either -**ful** or -**ness** to the base word.

  a) The children's eyes were full of wonder.
  They thought the circus was wonderful

  b) That was very kind of you.
  Thank you for your kindness.

  c) We enjoyed the beauty of the sunset.
  It was a beautiful sight.

  d) The puppies were so happy to see their mother.
  They showed their happiness by wagging their tails.

2. Complete the list word on each airplane.

happiness
successful
flight
beautiful
minute

3. Finish each set of comparisons with your own ideas.

  a) An airport is like a railway station because _______ .
  An airport is different from a railway station because _______ .

  b) A radio is like a television because _______ .
  A radio is different from a television because _______ .

  c) Planes are like hot air balloons because _______ .
  Planes are different from hot air balloons because _______ .

4. Use the clues to find each letter. Unscramble the letters to find a modern form of flight.

  a) This letter is in **crashed** but not in **screamed**. h
  b) This letter is in **planes** but not in **plans**. e
  c) This letter is in **story** but not in **sorry**. t
  d) This letter is in **faster** but not in **fatter**. s
  e) This letter is in **minute** but not in **nighttime**. u
  f) This letter is in **tough** but not in **rough**. t
  g) This letter is in **flight** but not in **fight**. l
  Unscrambled word shuttle

134

Exploring Patterns

1. If students have difficulty transforming **beauty** and **happy**, review the Discovering Patterns section and the Powerbooster.

2. Suggest that students develop a personal strategy for remembering the difficult letters in the words on the planes. For example:

- relate the double **p** in **happiness** to the base word **happy**
- circle or underline the double consonants in su**cc**e**ss**ful and ha**pp**iness
- relate **flight** to other words with the same **ight** pattern.

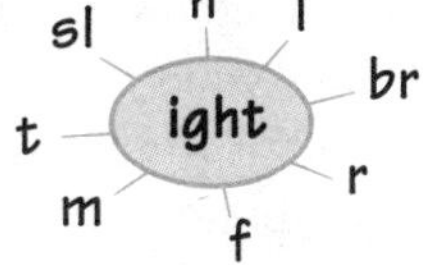

3. Finding the similarities and differences in words helps develop thinking skills. Provide opportunities for students to share their responses to each comparison. At the same time, focus on some of the spelling features of the list words.

- Explode the word **air** and find as many compounds and extensions as possible. (See Co-operative Learning, page 213.)

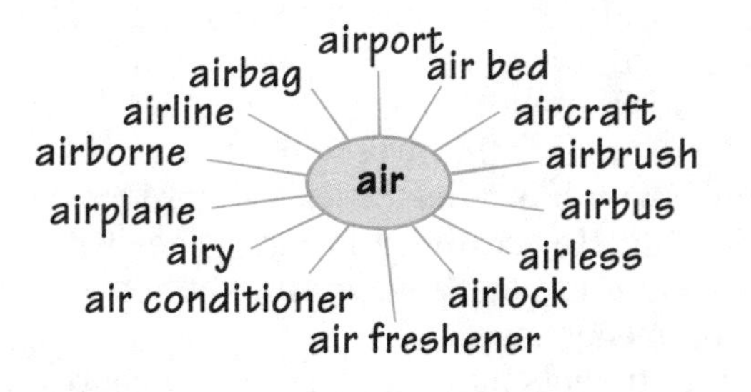

- Use the homophones **planes** and **plains** in sentences which show their meaning.
- Explore the family of words that end in the sound /ēo/ (**io** as in **radio**, **audio**, **cheerio**, **Ontario**, **patio**, **polio**, **ratio**, **studio**, **trio**, **portfolio**). Have the students invent riddles for a partner to solve (What famous cereal ends in **ios**? Cheer**ios**.)

4. Word transformation activities develop the thinking skills of comparing and sorting. In order to complete the activity students need to read carefully, compare words letter by letter, and finally unscramble a word to fit a meaning clue. You may wish to have students work with a partner if they find the activity challenging. Other students could create their own word puzzle using the same format and different list words.

Oral Language and Literature

- A long time ago Charles Schultz, the creator of the *Peanuts* cartoon, wrote a book called *Happiness is a Warm Puppy*. It was a pattern book, which provided definitions of happiness, depending on the character's point of view. To become acquainted with the use of nouns ending in **-ness**, students could work in small groups to develop their own definitions for happiness and other words.

  Friendliness is...asking someone to your party.

  Creepiness is...going into a dark room alone.

  Cosiness is...snuggling up with a pillow and blanket in front of the TV.

  Messiness is...my sister's bedroom.

  Bossiness is...my brother when he tells me to clean up my room!

- Students may want to illustrate their definitions and combine them in booklets.

5. Encourage students to use their imaginations. Would they like to invent a device to provide clean water? create a pollution-free form of transportation? Suggest that they consider their audience when they write. For example, when writing to share with a partner, they should try to write about a topic that would interest or amuse a peer. Ask them to consider how their writing might be different if they were writing on this topic for a school essay contest.

Challenges with Words

1. Before completing the paragraph with the Super Words, have students look at the special spelling features of the words:

- **constructed** adds **-ed** to the base word **construct**, meaning 'to build'.
- **rudder** has a double **d**; contrast it with **ruder**. (That was a **ruder** remark than the last one!)
- **swiftness** adds the suffix **-ness** to make the noun.
- **eventful** adds the suffix **-ful** to mean 'full of action'.
- **propeller** has three syllables with the stress on the second and **-er** at the end, not **-or**.
- **biplane** uses the prefix **bi-**, meaning two, as in **bi**cycle.

2. Have students list as many words as possible that start with **bi-** and **tri-**. Suggest they add these words to their Personal Review List. Under **bi** in the dictionary they will find many words beginning with **bio**, from the Greek word *bios*, meaning 'life' (**biography**, **biology**). They will need to sort these out from words where the prefix **bi-** means 'two'.

3. Some students may wish to create a chart showing the types of aircraft used by airlines. Most airlines have brochures and booklets describing their fleet.

type of aircraft	seating capacity	cargo capacity	cruising speed
Airbus A340	284	14 861 kg	869 km/h
Boeing 747-433	299	38 695 kg	917 km/h
Boeing 767-233	195	9 059 kg	853 km/h
DC9-32	92	1 546 kg	821 km/h

4. Remind students that the **y** in **weary** changes to an **i** when adding **-ness**.

Have students list more words ending in **-ful** and **-ness**. Remind them that **-ful** words are adjectives and **-ness** words are nouns (**dirtiness**, **bagginess**, **fairness**, **strangeness**, **armful**, **colourful**, **successful**, **wonderful**).

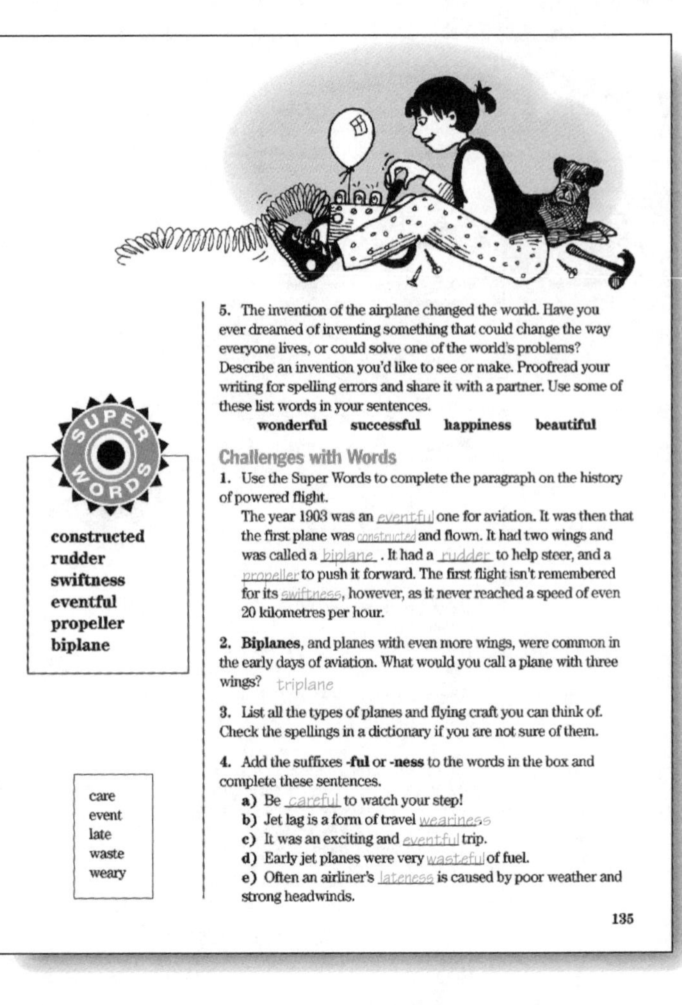

5. The invention of the airplane changed the world. Have you ever dreamed of inventing something that could change the way everyone lives, or could solve one of the world's problems? Describe an invention you'd like to see or make. Proofread your writing for spelling errors and share it with a partner. Use some of these list words in your sentences.

wonderful **successful** **happiness** **beautiful**

SUPER WORDS

constructed
rudder
swiftness
eventful
propeller
biplane

Challenges with Words

1. Use the Super Words to complete the paragraph on the history of powered flight.

The year 1903 was an eventful one for aviation. It was then that the first plane was constructed and flown. It had two wings and was called a biplane . It had a rudder to help steer, and a propeller to push it forward. The first flight isn't remembered for its swiftness, however, as it never reached a speed of even 20 kilometres per hour.

2. **Biplanes**, and planes with even more wings, were common in the early days of aviation. What would you call a plane with three wings? triplane

3. List all the types of planes and flying craft you can think of. Check the spellings in a dictionary if you are not sure of them.

care
event
late
waste
weary

4. Add the suffixes **-ful** or **-ness** to the words in the box and complete these sentences.

a) Be careful to watch your step!
b) Jet lag is a form of travel weariness
c) It was an exciting and eventful trip.
d) Early jet planes were very wasteful of fuel.
e) Often an airliner's lateness is caused by poor weather and strong headwinds.

135

Critical Thinking

- Categorizing is a good way to practise a key thinking skill while paying close attention to words. This may be particularly useful for ESL students who are learning English stress patterns.
- Have students make a word tree diagram with the list words, categorizing the words according to whether they have one, two, or three syllables. Break this down further by asking them to sort the words by stress patterns.

one syllable
- crashed
- flight

two syllables
- stress on 1st
  - airport
  - minute
  - fairness
  - thankful
  - strangeness
  - faster
  - landed
  - kindness

three syllables
- stress on 1st
  - wonderful
  - beautiful
  - happiness
  - radio
- stress on 2nd
  - successful

5. Both a **rudder** and a **propeller** are parts of a small aircraft. Use a dictionary, an encyclopedia, or a CD-ROM on a computer, to help you match up the airplane parts to the diagram of a plane. Then write the meaning of each word you match up.

wing	fuselage	rudder	cabin
propeller	airleron	elevator	flap

rudder
elevator
cabin
fuselage
wing
flap
propeller
aileron

6. How many words with 3, 4, or 5 letters can you make from the Super Word **constructed**? You can rearrange the letters in any order, but do not include words with capital letters. Score one point for each word you make and find out what type of plane you have constructed.

Plane	Score
single engine plane	0 – 20
private jet	21 – 30
commercial transport plane	31 – 40
supersonic jet airliner	41 +

Why not add some of these words to your personal list?

136

5. Have students list other important parts of a plane (or jet). They might classify their list into categories such as electronic controls and meters, engine parts, flight controls, design and structural parts, and so on.

6. This exercise can be made more challenging if students are given a time limit.

Students may want to design a crossword or a word search puzzle using the words they have **constructed** and exchange their puzzle with a partner. (See Co-operative Learning, this page.)

Co-operative Learning

- Word explosions are a graphic way of showing how adding endings to base words increases vocabulary, while keeping a grip on spelling. Have students work in small groups to create word explosions on chart paper to share with the whole group.

successfully
successful
success
unsuccessful
unsuccessfully

- Students who have researched the names of aircraft or aircraft parts may enjoy creating a word search with the words they have found. The word searches can be exchanged with a spelling partner or another small group.

ESL

Some students from language backgrounds such as Farsi, Spanish, and Arabic have difficulty with the way in which some words in English change meaning when the stress is shifted from one syllable to another, even though the spelling remains the same. Provide oral practice with these words in context to strengthen the meaning/stress connection.

- Many languages do not have the same stress patterns as English. Students may find unstressed suffixes difficult to hear and thus spell in such words as for**get**ful and **strange**ness. To help with the spelling of these final unstressed syllables, have students practise saying the words with extra care at first, tapping or clapping the syllables, and pronouncing the final /əs/ in **-ness** and /əl/ in **-ful**.

stress changes	
minute (60 seconds)	mi**nute** (tiny)
present (a gift/to be there)	pre**sent** (to give formally)
content (what is written or said)	con**tent** (happy/satisfied)
record (a written account)	re**cord** (the act of making a record)
convict (a prisoner)	con**vict** (prove guilty)

Curriculum Connection

• Although inventors in many other countries including France were very close to inventing an airplane, the American Wright brothers, Wilbur and Orville, were the first actually to fly their aircraft. Students may be interested in researching the invention of flight, and the race to see which inventors could get their creations into the history books.
• Students might wish to do further research about aviation. Have them brainstorm ideas for their topic, then select and research two or three important ideas they identified. They could use print and/or computer media, or interview someone from an airline company. Students might prefer to work in groups to complete this activity.

Assessment

Did the class eliminate highlighted words from the Precheck? Have the students self-correct their Unit Test and record errors on the Student Record Sheet. Words that they find particularly challenging could go on their Personal Review List.

Follow-up

Continue to monitor writing portfolios and everyday writing to see if structural rather than sounding out strategies are used for longer words. For example, if students still write **wonderfull** they need more practice with the structural pattern of adding the suffix **-ful**.

Teacher's Notes

Compound Words

backyard

Patterns

Longer words are easier to spell and read when we understand the logic behind them. This is especially important for poor spellers, who may feel they have to memorize every letter in a long word. Students need to distinguish base words they probably already know within compounds and understand that they are related by meaning. A **boathouse** is a house for a boat; a **houseboat** is a boat that is like a house. In compounds, the last base word usually names the object, the first word describes it. The stress almost always falls on the first syllable in compounds.

Preknowledge

Students should have an understanding of the following concepts as they work with the patterns in this unit.

- Longer words can be made of base words and endings (**straight/straighten**) or of two distinct words (**back/yard**).
- In compounds, the two base words are related in meaning (**air/port**).

More Patterns

Other patterns you might wish to introduce or review in this unit include the following.

- The modal, or helping, verb **should** + other verbs (I **should** write a letter).
- Homophones (**paws/pause**; **straight/strait**).
- Initial consonant combinations **br**, **pr**, **tr**, **str**.

Professional Notebook

Since the dawn of English, speakers and writers of the mother tongue, true to the Germanic roots of their language, have created words by joining together two or more independent meaning-bearing elements, called morphemes, to form compounds. As any page of Anglo-Saxon literature illustrates, compound words are abundant in Old English, a language that sought to express new ideas, not by borrowing from foreign tongues but by combining whole words already in the vocabulary.
(Lederer 237)

Sharing the Secrets with Kids

*Many students need a personal strategy to remember the spelling of **because,** one of the top fifty frequently misspelled words. In some lists, it is the first two-syllable most often misspelled word, and is probably misspelled in more ways than any other word (**beccause, becuase, becuzz**). See which students can come up with the most interesting and effective mnemonic for **because.***

Precheck

Remind students to say the words softly to themselves before writing. Repeat the list after dictation to encourage proofreading before the self-correction. Pay particular attention to the spelling of **because**.

Dictation

There's **someone** at the door.
I had pancakes for **breakfast**.
You're **probably** right!
I like ice cream **because** it's delicious.
Our **backyard** is huge.
I **should** do my homework.
She's **training** for the Olympics.
Can you solve the **problem**?
Our dog has a **doghouse**.
Has **anyone** got a pencil?
It's going to rain on the **weekend**.
The dog's **paws** were muddy.
There's a **reward** for finding the money.
Can your dog perform **tricks**?
Are you **calling** my name?
Go **straight** home from school.

Words in Context

You may wish to use the paragraph as a cloze passage, with students supplying list words for the blanks.

Observing Patterns

1. The shape of each word could be reinforced by drawing configuration lines after writing the word. Have students note how word shape is not particularly helpful in words such as **someone** because all the blocks are the same height. It is a more useful strategy for words such as **should** and **problem**.

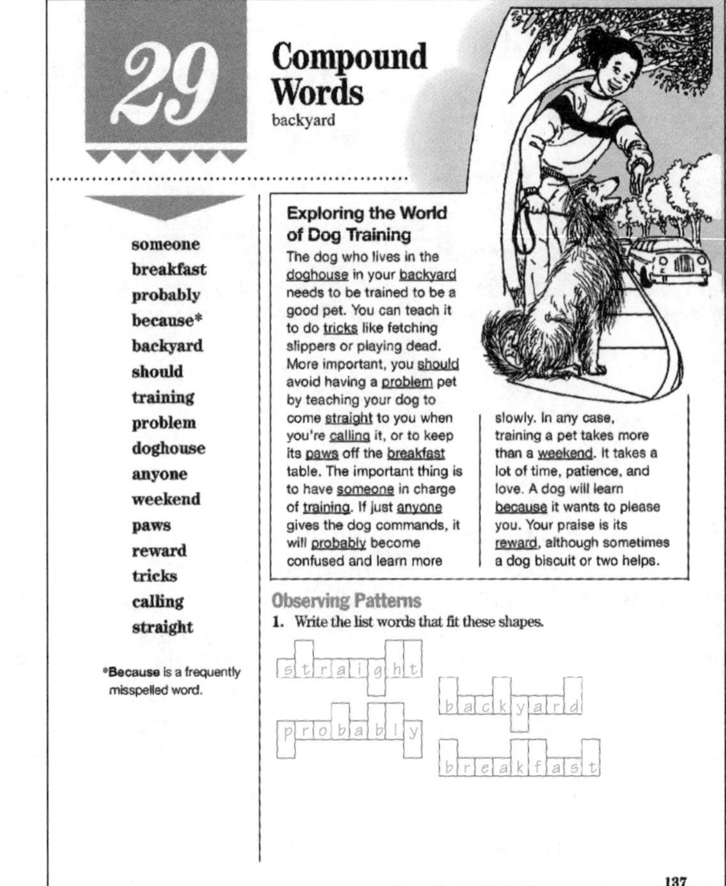

29

Compound Words

backyard

someone
breakfast
probably
because*
backyard
should
training
problem
doghouse
anyone
weekend
paws
reward
tricks
calling
straight

*Because is a frequently misspelled word.

Exploring the World of Dog Training

The dog who lives in the doghouse in your backyard needs to be trained to be a good pet. You can teach it to do tricks like fetching slippers or playing dead. More important, you should avoid having a problem pet by teaching your dog to come straight to you when you're calling it, or to keep its paws off the breakfast table. The important thing is to have someone in charge of training. If just anyone gives the dog commands, it will probably become confused and learn more slowly. In any case, training a pet takes more than a weekend. It takes a lot of time, patience, and love. A dog will learn because it wants to please you. Your praise is its reward, although sometimes a dog biscuit or two helps.

Observing Patterns

1. Write the list words that fit these shapes.

s t r a i g h t
b a c k y a r d
p r o b a b l y
b r e a k f a s t

137

Special Needs

- Students who find the spelling of longer words challenging can be helped by breaking compound words into their two base words, and realizing that the spelling of the base words *does not change*. For example, to spell **earring**, you write **ear** and **ring** together, not omitting an **r**.
- Write the base words of each compound on a separate card. Have the students match the cards and write the words. New cards can be added as new compounds are learned. Focus this activity on compounds which have double letters in the middle.

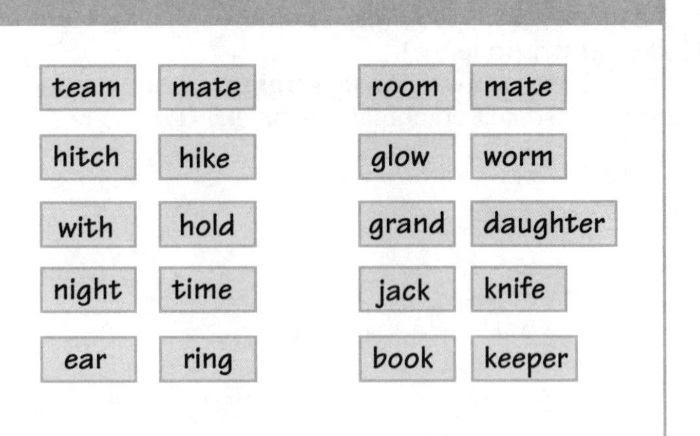

team
mate
room
mate
hitch
hike
glow
worm
with
hold
grand
daughter
night
time
jack
knife
ear
ring
book
keeper

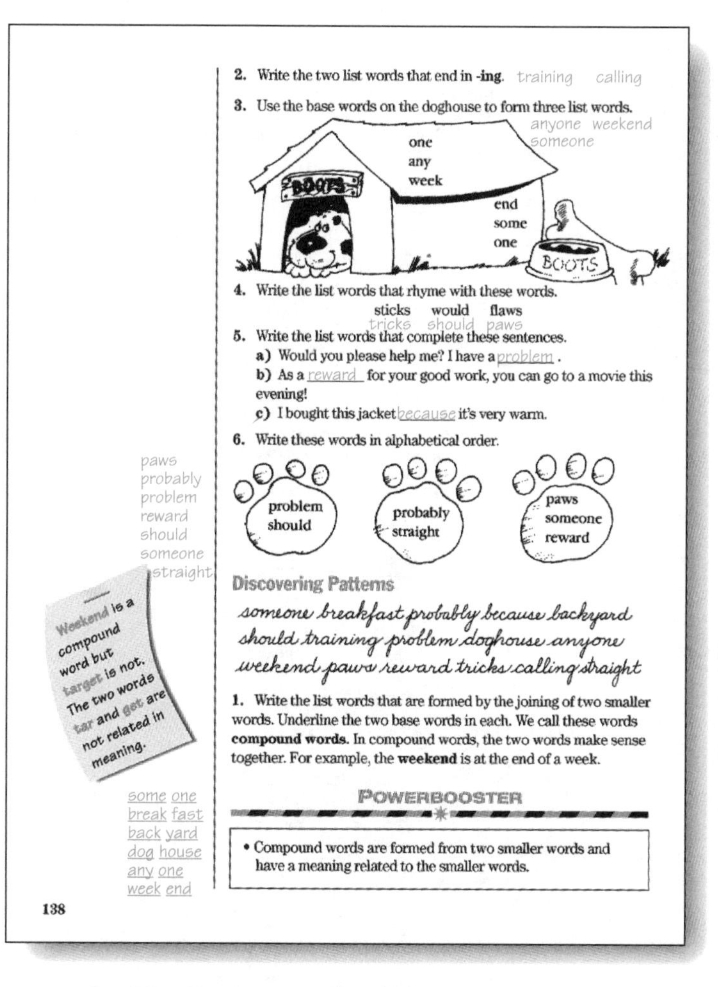

2. Write the two list words that end in **-ing**. training calling

3. Use the base words on the doghouse to form three list words. anyone weekend someone

one any week / end some one

BOOTS

4. Write the list words that rhyme with these words.
sticks would flaws
tricks should paws

5. Write the list words that complete these sentences.
a) Would you please help me? I have a problem.
b) As a reward for your good work, you can go to a movie this evening!
c) I bought this jacket because it's very warm.

6. Write these words in alphabetical order.
problem should | probably straight | paws someone reward

paws probably problem reward should someone straight

Discovering Patterns

someone breakfast probably because backyard should training problem doghouse anyone weekend paws reward tricks calling straight

1. Write the list words that are formed by the joining of two smaller words. Underline the two base words in each. We call these words **compound words.** In compound words, the two words make sense together. For example, the **weekend** is at the end of a week.

Weekend is a compound word but target is not. The two words tar and get are not related in meaning.

some one
break fast
back yard
dog house
any one
week end

POWERBOOSTER

• Compound words are formed from two smaller words and have a meaning related to the smaller words.

138

2. Note how the word **training** is often used as a noun (your dog's **training** is important). Give other examples of **-ing** words that are often used as nouns.

Swimming is fun.
Adding big numbers is easy.
Hitting is an important skill in baseball.
Clothing is expensive here.
Coughing can keep you awake all night.

3. Have students brainstorm a list of as many other compounds as they can think of using **some**, **any**, **one**. (See Special Needs, p. 216.)

some	any	one
somewhere	anywhere	no one
somebody	anybody	one-liner
someday	anyhow	one-piece
somehow	anyplace	one-time
something	anything	everyone

4. Note that the rhyming words have the same spelling patterns (**flaws/paws**). Develop word wheels with as many rhyming words as possible using the same patterns.

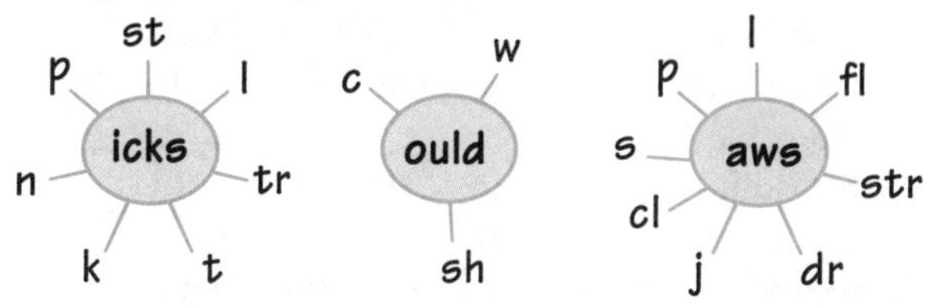

5. When students have identified the list words that fit the blanks, have them think of synonyms that would also fit the meaning of the sentences.

problem	reward	because
difficulty question	payment recompense	since as

6. The list word **probably** is often misspelled because it is mis-pronounced as two syllables (**prob/bly**) or the last two syllables are not heard clearly (**prol/ab/ly** or **prob/al/ly**). Practice with saying the word carefully and exaggerating the unstressed syllable as they write will help students master this difficult word.

Note that with **probably** and **problem**, students will need to look at the fifth letter of the words in order to alphabetize them.

Discovering Patterns

1. Remind students that a compound word must contain two smaller words and that the meaning of the compound is logically connected to the two words. As the note in the margin explains, words such as **carpet** and **carnation** are not compounds because the two words are not related in meaning.

Brainstorm with students a list of compound words on a topic such as sports, and discuss with them how the two words are related in each.

football, basketball, volleyball, baseball, skateboard, sailboard, snowboard, rollerblade

It's interesting to note that 'rollerblade' is a trademark, and not simply a generic term for inline skates. Perhaps it is one of those trade-marks (as was 'linoleum') that will eventually lose its protected status because it becomes part of the language.

Exploring Patterns

1. c) Note that **mad** could be substituted for **hot**. Have students discuss the difference between the meanings of **madhouse** and **hothouse**. (Because 'madhouse' might be an offensive term to some, it was not included in the exercise.)

Students could brainstorm compound words beginning with the word **house** (**housewarming**, **houseboat**, **housetop**, **housefly**, **housework**, **housecoat**, **household**, **houseware**).

2. Ask students to explore the relationships within each set of comparisons, and suggest other words that would fit the first pair. (See Critical Thinking, p. 219.)

> **Evening** is to **morning** as **sunset** is to **sunrise.**
>
> **No** is to **yes** as **goodbye** is to **hello.**

3. Students may enjoy drawing picture clues for other compound words and solving one another's puzzles.

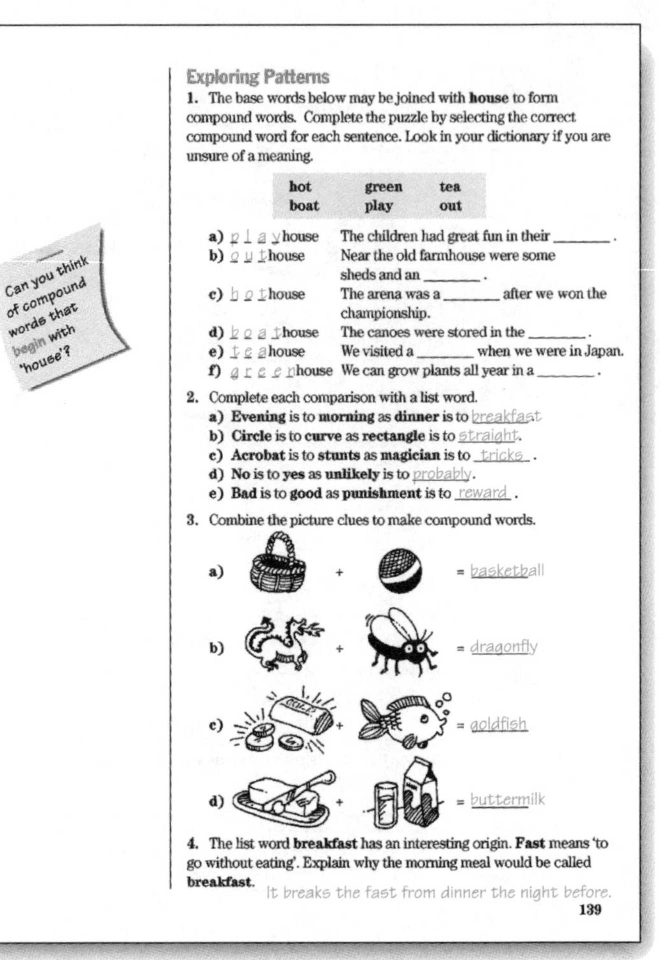

Can you think of compound words that begin with 'house'?

Exploring Patterns

1. The base words below may be joined with **house** to form compound words. Complete the puzzle by selecting the correct compound word for each sentence. Look in your dictionary if you are unsure of a meaning.

hot	**green**	**tea**
boat	**play**	**out**

a) p l a y house The children had great fun in their ______ .
b) o u t house Near the old farmhouse were some sheds and an ______ .
c) h o t house The arena was a ______ after we won the championship.
d) b o a t house The canoes were stored in the ______ .
e) t e a house We visited a ______ when we were in Japan.
f) g r e e n house We can grow plants all year in a ______ .

2. Complete each comparison with a list word.
a) **Evening** is to **morning** as **dinner** is to breakfast
b) **Circle** is to **curve** as **rectangle** is to straight.
c) **Acrobat** is to **stunts** as **magician** is to tricks .
d) **No** is to **yes** as **unlikely** is to probably.
e) **Bad** is to **good** as **punishment** is to reward .

3. Combine the picture clues to make compound words.
a) + = basketball
b) + = dragonfly
c) + = goldfish
d) + = buttermilk

4. The list word **breakfast** has an interesting origin. **Fast** means 'to go without eating'. Explain why the morning meal would be called **breakfast**. It breaks the fast from dinner the night before.

139

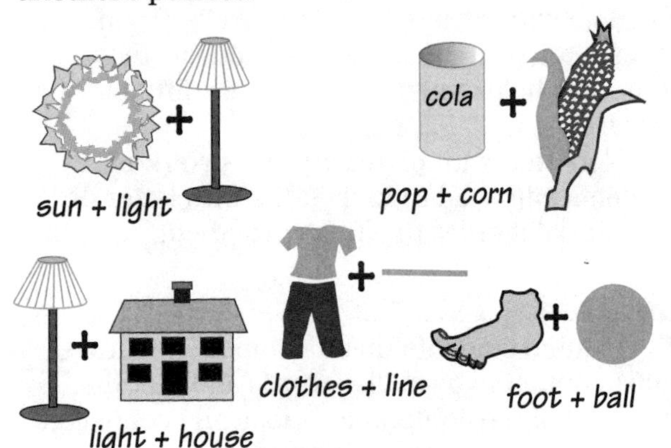

4. Explain to any students who are unfamiliar with the term that a **fast** is a period when people go without eating. **Breakfast** then means to **break** a **fast** by eating. Point out the change in pronunciation from the short **e** sound in **breakfast** to the long **a** sound in **break**.

ESL

- Compound words can cause problems for ESL students. Some students may have trouble distinguishing between:

  a **blackbird** (a kind of bird)
  a **black bird** (a bird that is black in colour).

  a **greenhouse** (where plants are grown)
  a **green house** (a house that is painted green)

  English speakers recognize the difference because of the stress. We stress the first syllable when the word is a compound. For example, we know that a **race**horse is a horse that runs fast and a **horse**race is a race for horses. Provide ESL students with many opportunities to listen to, pronounce, and spell compound words, grouping them into patterns. For example, there are many compound words made with weather words such as **rain** and **sun**.

raincoat	sunrise	snowflake
rainbow	sunburn	snowstorm
raindrop	sunset	snowsuit
	sunflower	snowball
	sunlight	

PUPPIES FOR SALE

You may want to use words from your personal word list in your dialogue.

SUPER WORDS

greyhound
kennel
purebred
veterinarian
checkup
championship

5. "I want a dog!" Most kids have said this to their parents at one time or another. Imagine the conversation this girl is having with her dad. What arguments will each of them use to convince the other? Work with a partner to write a short dialogue between the girl and her father. Use some of these list words.

should **because** **probably** **breakfast** **someone**

Challenges with Words

1. Choose the Super Word that best fits the crazy clues below. Be careful! Some of these are tricky.

a) A pet doc. veterinarian
b) Ken'll do. kennel
c) "In the first place," she said. championship
d) 100% natural ingredients used in this dough. purebred
e) Its dim colour chases after you. greyhound
f) "Say aah," a doctor might say. checkup

2. A compound word like **purebred** is made of up two real words, **pure** and **bred** (the past tense of **breed**). Make as many compound words as you can with these words. For example, **cross** and **roads** make **crossroads**. Answers will vary

cross town over hand

crossword crosswalk township townhouse handbook handball handcuff overboard overcome overall

3. The **greyhound** is a type of dog well known for its speed and ability to hunt. Many other dog breeds are also noted for special abilities. Use your dictionary to find out what these breeds are famous for: collie, Saint Bernard, bloodhound, Newfoundland dog, Doberman pinscher.

140

5. Before writing, students can co-operatively generate a list of pros and cons for having a dog. Encourage students to role play their dialogues with the class. They may wish to vote on whether the child or parent wins the argument in each case.

Many students will have personal pet stories to share. Invite them to write on this topic, and present their work in any format that appeals to them (cartoons, skits, and so on).

Critical Thinking

- Demonstrate strategies for completing analogies as in Exploring Patterns 2. Give some examples of common categories used in comparing words. Have students give more examples for each type of comparison, and then try to write their own analogy puzzles.

time of day	evening/morning
opposites	no/yes
whole to part	hand/finger
occupation to work	acrobat/stunts

Challenges with Words

Have students who have experienced little or no difficulty with the words on the Precheck study the Super Words using the Five Study Steps (Look, Say, Cover, Write, Check). Have them consider the special spelling features of the words:

- **greyhound** is a compound word. Note where the stress falls. How would this be said differently from a hound that happened to be grey—a **grey** hound?
- note the double consonant in ke**nn**el.
- **purebred** is another compound. Note the difference from **thoroughbred**, generally used only for horses.
- **veterinarian** has six syllables, but is commonly pronounced with five. Divide the word into syllables and mark the stress (**vet/er/in/ár/i/an**).
- **checkup** is a compound made from a verb—to **check up** on someone or something.
- **championship** is not a compound word because the two words are not related.

1. Students might want to make up their own set of crazy word clues for some words in their Personal Review List or the list words in this unit. (What's a home with a woof? A **doghouse**.)

2. You may wish to point out to students that some common compound words such as **near-sighted** and **baby-sitter** have a hyphen. Others can be written as one word or two. **Backyard** can be written either way and **lookout** changes depending on how it is used (**look out** [v.], **lookout** [n]).

Students might want to use their compound words in a word search puzzle, crossword puzzle, or word game similar to those in Challenges with Words 1 and 3, Unit 25. Students might exchange their puzzle with a partner.

3. Have students identify the compound words given (**bloodhound**, **Newfoundland**). Ask them to list other dog breeds and identify the compound words. They may wish to add these compounds to their Personal Review List.

breeds of dogs		
basset hound	bulldog	bullmastiff
dachshund	dalmation	deerhound
great dane	Irish wolfhound	Jack Russell
poodle	scottie	shepherd

Words in History

Students may want to investigate word histories of other Super Words and record these in a Words in History notebook.

4. Have students make a chart listing types of animal houses and the animals which might live in them. Students may wish to work in small groups.

stable/horses	hive/bees
kennel/dogs	sty/pigs

5. a) You may wish to remind students that **faithful** is not a compound word as **-ful** is a suffix, spelled with one **l**.

b) Have students use some or all of these descriptive words to describe a dog they have known. They may want to exchange their descriptions with a partner and try to guess the type of dog.

6. Remind students of the **five W** words used in any news report, whether it is in a newspaper, radio, or TV news broadcast.

Who What When Where Why

New Words

7. The English language adds new words constantly. Many are new compounds, used to describe objects from the world of technology, sports, and science. Discuss with students how words may begin as two separate words, advance to a hyphenated word, and are often finally written as one word.

Have them note that **monorail** is not a true compound, as **mono-** is a prefix, meaning 'one'. Suggest that they look for other words, new or old, that use the prefix **mono-** (monochrome, monocle, monopoly).

WORDS IN HISTORY

Kennel comes from the Latin word canile, 'a house for dogs', which came from the Latin word canis, meaning 'dog'.

4. a) Do you know these other animal houses? Unscramble the animal house names in the box and match them to the animals listed below.

e t n s	**a)** a house for farm animals barn
o c p o	**b)** a home for wolves den
r b n a	**c)** a house for young birds nest
n d e	**d)** a chicken's house coop

b) Choose three animals and write a sentence or two explaining what kind of home they live in.

5. a) Here are four words about dogs. Write a synonym for each one.

yapping shaggy faithful domesticated

b) Write four 'dog' words of your own. Challenge a partner to find a synonym for each one.

6. Imagine you are a reporter at a dog show. Write a newspaper article describing the show. Try to use as many Super Words as you can in your article. You might begin like this.

LOCAL DOG CLUB RUNS OFF WITH CUP

The Kempville Kennel Club has once again run off with most of the ribbons at this year's local dog show. The 'best in show' championship cup went to Midget, a sleek greyhound owned by...

NEW WORDS

camcorder
user-friendly
monorail

7. The words that are combined to make the new words help make the meaning clear. **Camcorder** sounds like camera and recorder. **User-friendly** clearly means easy to use and **monorail** is a railway car that runs on one track. Mono means 'one'. Unscramble the new words in the sentences below.

a) My aunt's computer is very **srue-rlyfidne.** user-friendly
b) We rode the **airlnomo** at the zoo. monorail
c) We took our **dermacroe** with us on our vacation to make a video of our trip. camcorder

141

Writing

- Review the rules for writing dialogue with students, and have them use these as a basis for writing a short dialogue.

Rules for Writing Dialogue

1. Change the paragraph each time you change speakers.
2. Put the words actually spoken between quotation marks.
3. Put the punctuation—commas, periods, question marks—inside the closing quotation marks.

Oral Language and Literature

- Suggest that students work with a partner to invent oral riddles to present to the group. Provide them with lists of compounds as a resource. Students can illustrate their riddles and make a Compound Riddle Book for the classroom.

groundhog, rattlesnake, hummingbird, mockingbird, woodpecker, skyscraper, windshield, glowworm, butterfly, horsefly, dragonfly

What kind of bird makes fun of you?	A **mockingbird!**
What kind of tool can you use to clean the sky?	A **skyscraper!**
What kind of insect says 'neigh, neigh'?	A **horsefly**

Home Connection

Students and their parents can find compound words everywhere in the home and community—in restaurants, flyers and newspaper ads, sports articles, and computer information. Suggest that they collect a list of compounds they have seen and bring it to class.

> We found the following computer compounds: desktop, hardware, software, keyboard

Assessment

Monitor everyday writing and portfolios for the spelling of compounds. Watch for missing syllables, especially at the end of the first word in compounds. This may indicate those students who need extra practice proofreading or sounding words as they write.

Follow-up

Have students keep a list of compounds they often misspell, and remind them to refer to it when the need arises.

Teacher's Notes

Looking Back Units 25–29

Patterns to Review

Review the following structures:

- Possessives
- Plural possessives
- Contractions
- Suffixes **-ful** and **-ness**
- Compound words

The following words in the review list are found on the list of "The 200 Words Most Frequently Misspelled."

beautiful, minute, probably, they're, because, months

Creating a Personal Review List

Looking Back units should also provide an opportunity for students to review words and concepts which gave them particular difficulty in the preceding units. These personal study lists could involve words from a variety of sources, as suggested below:

- words misspelled in the students' Unit Tests and everyday writing (writing folders, notebooks, tests)
- words used throughout the day: current themes, content areas, current events, media, holidays
- lists such as "The 200 Words Most Frequently Misspelled" and "The 200 Words Most Frequently Written" (See Appendix.)

Transfer of Spelling Knowledge

The following suggestions will help students to retain the knowledge and skills they acquire through word study and apply them in their everyday writing:

- Do not treat words on study lists as single entities, but as examples of larger spelling patterns. Build on word patterns to maximize the benefit of word study.
- Reintroduce frequently misspelled words on subsequent lists.
- When errors reoccur in student writing, ask students to recall the strategies they had used for studying these words.
- Discuss the use of spelling strategies for new words as they occur in a variety of classroom contexts.

30 Looking Back

STUDY STEPS

LOOK
SAY
COVER
WRITE
CHECK

Here is a list of words that may have been hard for you in Units 25–29. You and your teacher may add other words to the list.

enough	through	happiness	straight
laughing	photography	minute	they're
building	beautiful	probably	because
lightning	successful	should	months

1. Use the Study Steps for each word. Your teacher will dictate the words.

2. Complete each sentence with words from the Study List. Write the sentences in your notebook.

a) A minute later a bolt of lightning hit the barn.

b) To be successful in the hobby of photography you will probably need months of practice.

c) The happiness of the children could be seen through their beautiful smiles and laughing voices.

d) You should go straight home today because there isn't enough time to play before dinner.

142

They could then further classify the words according to whether **gh** makes the sound /f/ or is silent.

gh	/f/	silent
enough laughing lightning through straight	enough laughing	lightning straight through

Looking Back

1. In addition to using the Study Steps, ask students to suggest ways to group the review words for study purposes, and then to apply appropriate spelling strategies to deal with the challenges. Students could, for example, use a visual approach to group together the words that contain **gh** and highlight those letters.

Dictation

Do you have **enough** money to buy candy?
What are you **laughing** at?
It was hot inside the **building**.
There was **lightning** during the storm.
Go **through** to the other room.
My favourite hobby is **photography**.
What a **beautiful** day it is!
Were you **successful** in the contest?
She smiled with **happiness**.
Wait a **minute**!
He'll **probably** win first prize.
What **should** we do next?
Go **straight** home from school.
Do you know where **they're** going?
I'm happy **because** it's the weekend.
It's only three **months** till my birthday.

2. Students should realize that the correct choice in each case must fit the shape of the configuration and also the context of the sentence.

The shapes of all the study words could be reinforced through the use of configuration lines.

should | | | | | |

POWERBOOSTERS

25 We use **'s** to show that something belongs to something or someone, as in **a bird's feather.**

26 We add an apostrophe (') at the end of the plural form of most words to show possession, as in **the boys' fathers**.
With irregular plurals, such as **children**, we add an apostrophe and **s** (**'s**) to the plural form, as in **the children's books**.

27 A contraction is a shortened form of two words. One or more letters are taken out and replaced by the apostrophe ('), as in **she is** — **she's**.

28 The suffix **-ful** means 'full of ________'. The suffix **-ness** means 'the state or quality of being ________'.
When adding **-ful** or **-ness** to a base word ending in a consonant +**y**, change the **y** to **i**.

29 Compound words are formed from two smaller words and have a meaning related to the smaller words.

3. Remind students that words are broken into syllables according to the rules of syllabication, not necessarily as they are broken in normal speech. Therefore, **happiness** is divided as **hap/pi/ness** rather than **ha/ppi/ness**.

Some students may learn the sequencing of syllables more effectively through a tactile approach. Have them print each syllable on a separate card, scramble the syllables, and sort them into the target words. You might wish to have them do the same with other review words.

cess	ful	suc
suc	cess	ful

a	prob	bly
prob	a	bly

4. The word **minute** could be accented on either the first or second syllable depending on the meaning (**min'ute**, a unit of time; **minute'**, something that is very small).

Encourage students to say the words aloud to help determine stress. Suggest they use a dictionary to confirm their choices.

5. If students have difficulty forming possessives correctly, review the Powerboosters in Units 25 and 26. The concept of possessive forms is hard for many students to grasp, and practice with additional sentences may be needed. (See *Teach Your Child*, Unit 29.)

6. Review the Powerbooster in Unit 28 with students who do not change y to **i** in **beautiful.** Note with students the progression from **use** to **useful**, to **usefulness**. A similar pattern can be shown with **help**, **thank**, and **joy**.

Ask students to fill in the blank squares with other words which may take the suffixes **-ful** or **-ness**.

7. Provide additional sentences for students who still find it difficult to form contractions. Review the Discovering Patterns and Powerbooster sections in Unit 27, or reinforce the concept with *Teach Your Child*, Unit 30.

successful photography
probably beautiful
happiness

enough lightning
laughing minute
building because

3. Unscramble the syllables to make words from the Study List.

cess ful suc   a prob bly   ness pi hap
tog phy pho ra   ti beau ful

4. Write the two-syllable words from the Study List. Put an accent (´) over the syllable that is stressed.

5. Use the possessive form to complete each of the following statements. The first one has been done for you.

a) The bicycle belonging to the girl is the girl's bicycle.
The bicycles belonging to the girls are the girls' bicycles
b) The coat belonging to the man is the man's coat
The coats belonging to the men are the men's coats
c) The toy belonging to the child is the child's toy
The toys belonging to the children are the children's toys

6. Add the suffix **-ful** or **-ness** to the words on each square.

beauty	beautiful	force
useful	-ful	forceful
use	plentiful	plenty

happy	happiness	useful
strangeness	-ness	usefulness
strange	friendliness	friendly

Don't forget to make your own review list of difficult words.

7. Substitute a contraction for the underlined phrase in each sentence.

a) The dog does not want to obey its owner. doesn't
b) Are you sure you have not forgotten something? haven't
c) We were not successful in finding the snake's hiding place. weren't
d) They are very thankful for their wonderful friends. They're

143

Have students form contractions by combining words from columns A and B, or B and C. Ask them to select four of the words from their list, and use them in sentences.

A	B		C
they	has	should	not
she	is	could	
I	have	would	
he	are	does	
you	am		

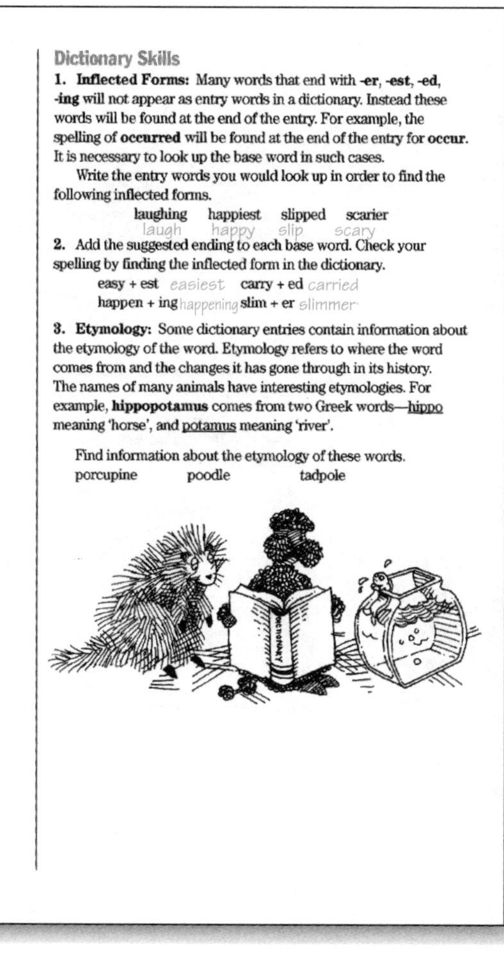

Dictionary Skills

1. Inflected Forms: Many words that end with **-er**, **-est**, **-ed**, **-ing** will not appear as entry words in a dictionary. Instead these words will be found at the end of the entry. For example, the spelling of **occurred** will be found at the end of the entry for **occur**. It is necessary to look up the base word in such cases.

Write the entry words you would look up in order to find the following inflected forms.

laughing happiest slipped scarier
laugh happy slip scary

2. Add the suggested ending to each base word. Check your spelling by finding the inflected form in the dictionary.

easy + est easiest carry + ed carried
happen + ing happening slim + er slimmer

3. Etymology: Some dictionary entries contain information about the etymology of the word. Etymology refers to where the word comes from and the changes it has gone through in its history. The names of many animals have interesting etymologies. For example, **hippopotamus** comes from two Greek words—hippo meaning 'horse', and potamus meaning 'river'.

Find information about the etymology of these words.

porcupine poodle tadpole

144

Dictionary Skills

1. It is important for students to realize that the word they are seeking in a dictionary may not be an entry on its own. Students must be able to identify the base word to find the words in the list.

It may be necessary to practise identifying the relevant base word with words from themes, other subject areas, personal spelling lists, etc.

base word	pilot	measure	map
inflected form	piloted	measuring	mapping

2. You may wish to double-check that students have used the guide words on the dictionary page to help locate each base word.

3. Many dictionaries have symbols indicating the etymology of the word. The *Gage Intermediate Dictionary*, for example, uses ☞ to signal etymology.

Students should be aware that etymological information comes at the end of the dictionary entry. They may also need to refer to the key which explains the abbreviations for languages of origins (e.g., ME — Middle English). Ask students to indicate the language of origin and the way in which the meaning was derived for each word. It may be interesting to compare etymological information from more than one source.

poo·dle

☛ *Etym.* From German *Pudel*, short for *Pudelhund* 'splash dog' made up of *pudeln* 'to splash in water' + *Hund* 'dog', so-called because it was used by hunters to bring game from water.

(*Gage Canadian Dictionary Intermediate*)

Exploring the World of Urban Animals

1. Have students share the results of their brainstorming sessions. Students may be surprised to discover how many wild animals live in their region. The list could be divided into animals the students have/have not seen.

2. Students may enjoy examining reference books such as *A Field Guide to Mammals*, or *A Field Guide to Animal Tracks* to see how information on animals is organized.

An organizer that students may find useful is a 'P.B.E.' chart that outlines physical characteristics, behavioural traits, and environment.

physical characteristics	behavioural traits	environment
rabbit: furry, small, four-footed, ...	avoids people, shy ...	woods, gardens, my backyard!

Students could use their research to create animal 'Who am I?' puzzles.

my scientific name:	peromyscus maniculatus
my habitat:	forests and grasslands
my appearance:	pale grey to reddish-brown fur; my tail is dark above and light below; I weigh 18–35 g.
my main habits:	I nest in burrows in the ground, in trees, stumps, or buildings. I eat seeds, nuts, and acorns; I store my food in my cheek pouches.
who am I?:	a deer mouse

3. For schools with access to the Internet, the World Wide Web may be an excellent source of information for students.

Exploring the World of Urban Animals

Animal Report Sheet

NAME: Raccoon

SCIENTIFIC NAME: Procyon lotor

HABITAT: Any wooded area in a city, town, or country location.

DESCRIPTION: The raccoon has dark bands across its eyes...

1. Brainstorm with a partner to list wild animals that live in your region. Remember, many small wild animals live in cities and towns near people.

2. Choose one urban animal and list all of its characteristics. For example: habitat, colour, size, diet, etc. Use this list to help you write a brief report describing your animal. Use the Report Sheet at the top of the page as your model.

3. Make a list of sources you could use to find information for your report. For example: encyclopedias, magazines, newspapers, television programs, or CD-ROMs. Use some of these sources to help you write your report.

145

Proofreading Strategies

1. The first time you proofread a draft, put a mark beside any word you think may be spelled incorrectly. Trust your feelings. If you think a word 'doesn't look right', there is a good chance it is misspelled.

2. When you find a word you think is misspelled, try writing it a different way. Does this version 'look better'?

3. Be aware of the type of errors you most often make. Go through your work looking for each of these errors in turn.

4. Keep a dictionary beside you as you proofread.

5. Record the words you misspelled in your Personal Dictionary. Identify strategies that will help you remember the spelling of these words.

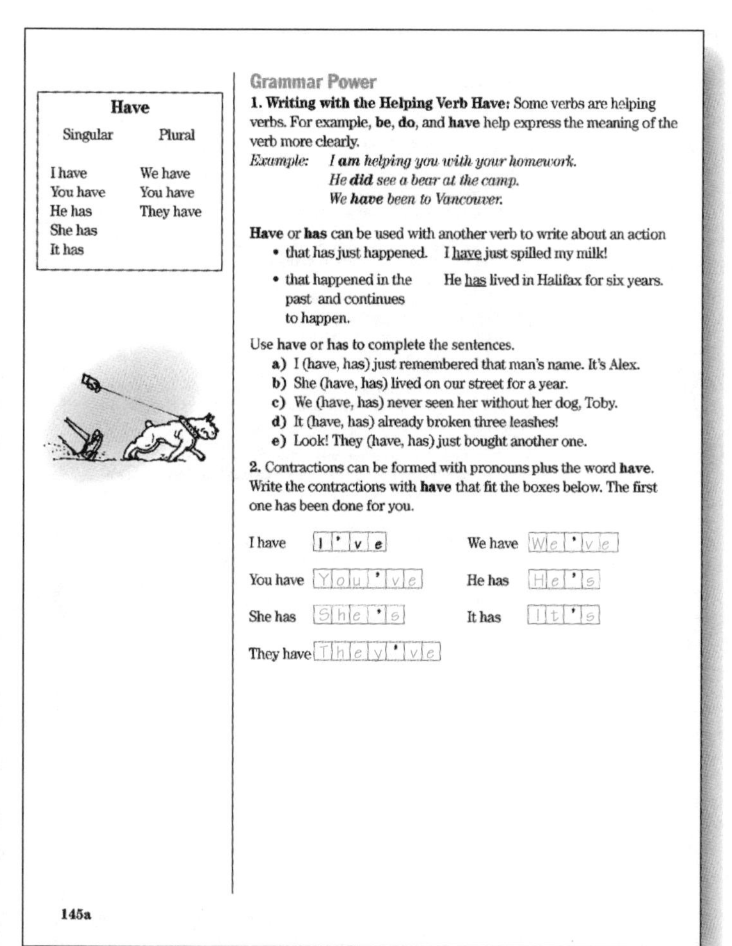

Have	
Singular	Plural
I have	We have
You have	You have
He has	They have
She has	
It has	

Grammar Power

1. Writing with the Helping Verb Have: Some verbs are helping verbs. For example, **be, do,** and **have** help express the meaning of the verb more clearly.

Example: ***I am** helping you with your homework.*
*He **did** see a bear at the camp.*
*We **have** been to Vancouver.*

Have or **has** can be used with another verb to write about an action

- that has just happened. — I have just spilled my milk!
- that happened in the past and continues to happen. — He has lived in Halifax for six years.

Use **have** or **has** to complete the sentences.

a) I (have, has) just remembered that man's name. It's Alex.
b) She (have, has) lived on our street for a year.
c) We (have, has) never seen her without her dog, Toby.
d) It (have, has) already broken three leashes!
e) Look! They (have, has) just bought another one.

2. Contractions can be formed with pronouns plus the word **have**. Write the contractions with **have** that fit the boxes below. The first one has been done for you.

I have	I've	We have	We've
You have	You've	He has	He's
She has	She's	It has	It's
They have	They've		

145a

Grammar Power

1. Note that in the example 'he did see a bear at the camp', the verb **did** is used to express emphasis. The helping verb **do** is most often used to ask questions such as:

Did he go to his friend's house after school?
Do you live on Baker Street?
Does she have a little sister?

The present perfect tense to express action which has just happened, happened in the past and continues to happen, or happens habitually, will be familiar to students from their reading and in speech.

She has written six sentences.
We have watched that TV show.
They have lived in Canada for five years.

Students from some language backgrounds may not use **have/has** or **is/are** in the standard pattern. One way to approach this is to explain that in school we write and say it this way, at least at the present time. It's important to help students see English as a dynamic language that is in constant development. Today's slang may be tomorrow's standard English.

2. Suggest that students use the contractions to write their own sentences. Note that **she's**, **he's**, and **it's** can also mean **she is**, **he is**, and **it is**. Contrast the two uses:

She's going to her grandmother's (she is).
She's been there before (she has).

He's a great hockey player (he is). He's played for that team for six years (he has).

It's cold (it is). It's been cold all day (it has).

ESL

Language Snapshot — Cantonese

The Chinese language is a collection of many dialects. One of the most important of these is Cantonese. All Chinese speakers share a common written language with similar basic features which may cause difficulties for some students learning English as a second language.

Language Features

- Our alphabetic, left to right English script seems very spread out to Chinese readers and writers, since they write in ideograms and pictograms. This may make it difficult to identify and write individual words.
- The lack of consistent spelling rules may lead to difficulties such as writing **docter** for **doctor**, or **anser** for **answer**.
- Students may have difficulty hearing and spelling the English sounds or syllables which are not clearly articulated.

  around may be spelled **aroud**
  horror may be spelled **horro**
  studying may be spelled **studing**
- Some students may confuse base words and their functions in sentences with the derived forms as in **difficult** and **difficulty**.

  She likes **walk**.
  It is very **difficulty** to hear him.

3. Quotation marks are like little baskets to hang the words we actually speak. Explain to students that they signal the reader that these are the actual words of the character, or **direct speech**.

Some points of punctuation to share with students are given below.

"I can't help it if my feet are too big," *James shouted.* Use a comma at the end of the direct speech, and a period at the end of the sentence.

"Give me those shoes," Nina said, "or I'll tell Dad." Use a comma after **said** and a lower case letter if the character finishes a sentence.

"You'll never get these shoes," James said. "I'm going to keep them." Use a period if the character keeps talking, but starts a new sentence after **said**.

"Stop!" shouted James. "What do you think you're doing?" Exclamation marks and question marks also go inside the quotation marks.

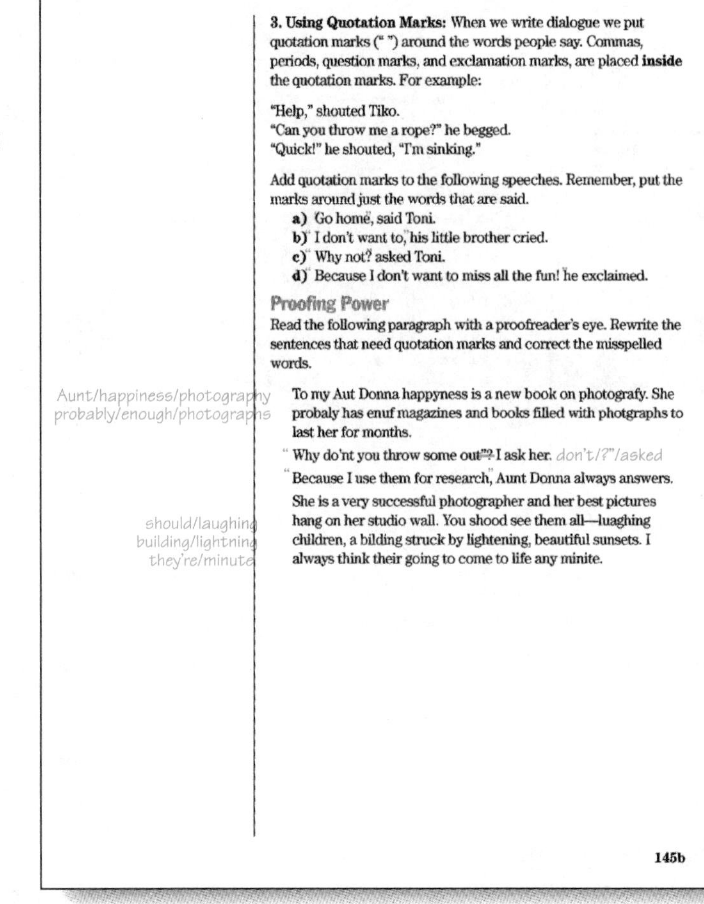

3. Using Quotation Marks: When we write dialogue we put quotation marks (" ") around the words people say. Commas, periods, question marks, and exclamation marks, are placed **inside** the quotation marks. For example:

"Help," shouted Tiko.
"Can you throw me a rope?" he begged.
"Quick!" he shouted, "I'm sinking."

Add quotation marks to the following speeches. Remember, put the marks around just the words that are said.

a) "Go home," said Toni.
b) "I don't want to," his little brother cried.
c) "Why not?" asked Toni.
d) "Because I don't want to miss all the fun!" he exclaimed.

Proofing Power

Read the following paragraph with a proofreader's eye. Rewrite the sentences that need quotation marks and correct the misspelled words.

Aunt/happiness/photography
probably/enough/photographs

To my Aut Donna happyness is a new book on photografy. She probaly has enuf magazines and books filled with photgraphs to last her for months.

"Why do'nt you throw some out"? I ask her. don't/?"/asked

"Because I use them for research," Aunt Donna always answers.

She is a very successful photographer and her best pictures hang on her studio wall. You shood see them all—luaghing children, a bilding struck by lightening, beautiful sunsets. I always think their going to come to life any minite.

should/laughing
building/lightning
they're/minute

145b

Proofing Power

You may wish to ask students to express their feelings when proofreading a passage containing so many spelling errors. Does it make it difficult to understand the meaning of the piece? Is it annoying or frustrating? Does it take away from the writer's attempt to communicate with the reader?

Teacher's Notes

31 Schwa Vowels

/ə/ as in enorməs
/əl/ as in naturəl

Patterns

The unit reinforces the schwa vowel that was introduced in Unit 17 and extended in Unit 19. Because schwa vowels occur in unstressed syllables and are not pronounced clearly, they pose a spelling challenge. This is especially true for students who rely on the strategy of sounding words out.

Preknowledge

Students should have an understanding of the following concepts as they work with the patterns in this unit.

• The number of syllables in a word. At this level students increasingly use multisyllabic words in their oral and written vocabularies.
• Stressed and unstressed syllables. Students should feel comfortable in distinguishing between the two.
• Pronunciation symbols. Helps students recognize and understand such symbols as those used in **thrü** (through), **stôrm** (storm), **mezhər** (measure).

More Patterns

Other patterns you might wish to introduce or review in this unit include the following.

• Homophones, words which sound alike but are spelled differently, can pose challenges for unwary spellers. Students might keep their personal homophone list, and add to it as they encounter new pairs (**their/there**).
• Base words and derived forms (**history/prehistoric**). Knowing the base from which another word is derived can often help with the spelling of the second word.
• Prefixes (**dis-**, **pre-**) Adding a prefix seldom changes a base word; adding a suffix to the same word might well require changes (**history/prehistory**; **history/historic**).
• /ər/ spelled **ur** (**natural**; **turtle**) and **er** (**longer**; **eaters**).
• /ôr/ spelled **or** (**enormous**; **prehistoric**).

Professional Notebook

One reason English has accumulated such a vast word hoard is that it is the most hospitable and democratic language that has ever existed. English has never rejected a word because of its race, creed, or national origin. Having welcomed into its vocabulary words from a multitude of other languages and dialects, ancient and modern, far and near, English is unique in the number and variety of its borrowed words.

(Lederer 25)

Sharing the Secrets with Kids

As students discover more complex homophones, suggest that they keep a personal list.

allowed–aloud
chilly–chili
hanger–hangar

Precheck

Remind students to write their words in a column in their notebooks or in section A of the Student Record Sheet. The correction of any errors should be written beside the misspelled word. It is sometimes helpful for tricky parts to be underlined or boxed to draw students' attention to that part of the word.

Dictation

Dinosaurs are **prehistoric** animals.
A magician can make things **disappear**.
Dinosaurs were **enormous** creatures.
Mammals are warm-blooded animals.
Water is a fish's **natural** habitat.
Don't walk in the **middle** of the road!
The 1990s are the **age** of computers.
Their mother is a veterinarian.
There were two vets in the office.
Where are you going?
Which line is **longer**?
Have you **reached** the end of the book?
It's my brother who **fights**, not me!
Some animals are meat **eaters**.
A dinosaur's **brain** was small.
A sea **turtle** can be one metre long.

Words in Context

Have students read the paragraph and identify the list word which does not appear (**middle**). Ask them to use this word in a sentence, either about dinosaurs or on a topic of their choice.

Observing Patterns

1. Be sure students understand the term **homophone**. The meaning of each homophone is dealt with in Exploring Patterns 2.

2. Note that the first syllable is stressed in each word. The stress patterns and syllable breaks can be confirmed by consulting the dictionary entries.

3. Explore the logic of word building by beginning with the base word **history**, then adding the prefix **pre-** (**prehistory**). Finally, drop the **y** from the base and add the suffix **-ic** (**prehistoric**).

Students could also apply the meaning of the prefix **pre-** (before) to other words (**preview**, **prevent**, **prenatal**, **preschool**, **premature**, **prearrange**, **preassigned**, **precede**, and **precondition**).

4. The pairs of rhyming words in each case are from the same word families and therefore have

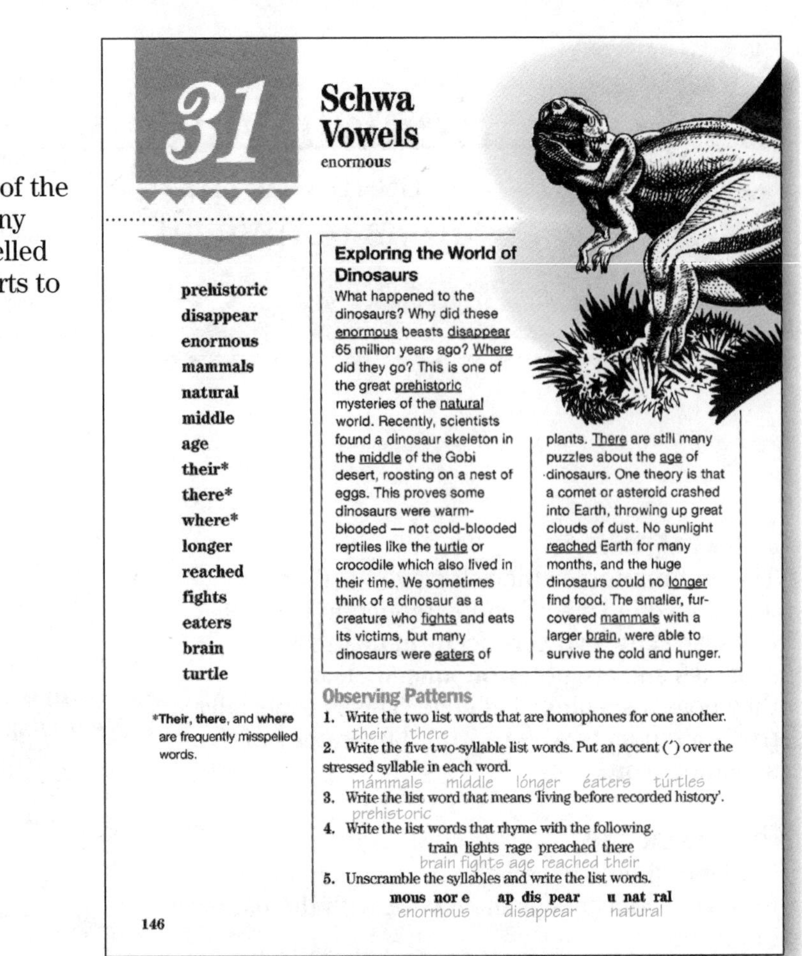

31 Schwa Vowels
enormous

prehistoric
disappear
enormous
mammals
natural
middle
age
their*
there*
where*
longer
reached
fights
eaters
brain
turtle

*Their, there, and where are frequently misspelled words.

Exploring the World of Dinosaurs

What happened to the dinosaurs? Why did these enormous beasts disappear 65 million years ago? Where did they go? This is one of the great prehistoric mysteries of the natural world. Recently, scientists found a dinosaur skeleton in the middle of the Gobi desert, roosting on a nest of eggs. This proves some dinosaurs were warm-blooded — not cold-blooded reptiles like the turtle or crocodile which also lived in their time. We sometimes think of a dinosaur as a creature who fights and eats its victims, but many dinosaurs were eaters of plants. There are still many puzzles about the age of dinosaurs. One theory is that a comet or asteroid crashed into Earth, throwing up great clouds of dust. No sunlight reached Earth for many months, and the huge dinosaurs could no longer find food. The smaller, fur-covered mammals with a larger brain, were able to survive the cold and hunger.

Observing Patterns

1. Write the two list words that are homophones for one another.
their there
2. Write the five two-syllable list words. Put an accent (´) over the stressed syllable in each word.
mámmals míddle lónger éaters túrtles
3. Write the list word that means 'living before recorded history'.
prehistoric
4. Write the list words that rhyme with the following.
train lights rage preached there
brain fights age reached their
5. Unscramble the syllables and write the list words.
mous nor e ap dis pear u nat ral
enormous disappear natural

146

the same spelling patterns (**train/brain**). Ask students to add other words to each of the five word families.

train	lights	rage	preached	there
brain	fights	age	reached	where
refrain	nights	cage	beached	
drain	rights	page	leached	
grain	sights	sage	impeached	
rain	tights	stage		
stain				
vain				

5. To extend this activity, write each syllable of the three words on a separate card, as well as the syllables of **pre/his/tor/ic**. Shuffle all the cards into a deck and have students unscramble the deck to form each of the four target words.

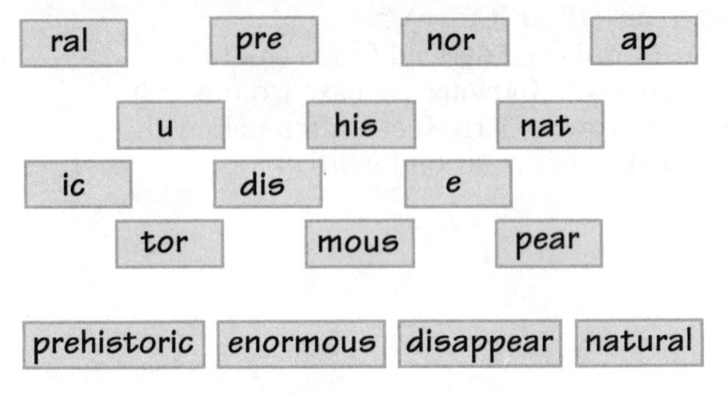

6. Write the words that fit these shapes.

turtle fights

disappear

prehistoric

7. Write the three list words that have double consonants.

disappear mammals middle

Discovering Patterns

prehistoric disappear enormous mammals natural middle age their there where longer reached fights eaters brain turtle

1. In Unit 17 we studied the schwa sound /ə/. This is the vowel sound in unstressed syllables such as in **accident** /ak´sə dənt/, **about** /ə boút/, **bottom** /bót əm/. Say the list words and look carefully at those that have the schwa sound.

2. The sound /əl/ is often found at the end of words, and can be spelled a number of ways, as **handle**, **animal**, **pencil**, and **angel**. Write the list words that end in the sound /əl/ in two columns.

/əl/ spelled **le** as in **handle**	/əl/ spelled **al** as in **animal**
middle	natural
turtle	mammals

POWERBOOSTER

- The sound /əl/ may be spelled in a number of ways including **le** as in **handle**, and **al** as in **animal**.

147

6. Configuration shapes help some students to remember visual features of words. A variation on configuration boxes is to draw the word using lines: fights

An effective reinforcement activity is to draw a series of line configurations for the list words and have students link the shapes with the appropriate list words.

7. Students could circle, underline, or highlight the double consonants.

Discovering Patterns

1. It may be difficult for some students to identify schwa sounds since, by definition, they are not well-articulated. You may wish to direct their attention to the schwa sounds in the list words **disappear** and **natural**. In both cases, the correct schwa vowel can be remembered by returning to the base word (**appear**, **nature**), assuming that students can spell the base words.

2. The sound /əl/ presents a challenge to many spellers since they must somehow remember whether it is spelled **le**, **al**, **el**, or **il**. Students who previously have relied on sounding out words will find such a strategy ineffective for this particular pattern.

Students may wish to include extra columns for /əl/ spelled **il** (pencil) and **el** (ang**el**).

le	al	el	il
handle	accidental	fuel	gerbil
candle	actual	funnel	civil
bundle	bridal	hazel	council
swindle	burial	jewel	lentil
double	carnival	mongrel	tendril
chuckle	casual	model	nostril

ESL

- In some languages, each syllable of a word receives the same stress, or is given equal time in speech. Students from these language backgrounds may find English speakers 'swallow' half their words, because of the unstressed syllables. It may be helpful to clap or tap the rhythm of longer words, giving extra force to the stressed syllable. Students can also compare how stress patterns change/don't change as prefixes and suffixes are added (ap péar/dis ap pear´; his´ tor y/his tór i cal).

- Another useful strategy would be to create word circles or lists of words ending in the unstressed /əl/ syllable spelled with different patterns (mammal, middle, turtle, bottle).

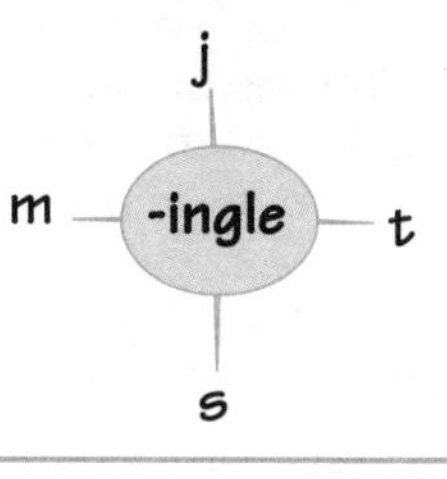

Exploring Patterns

1. If students have difficulty using pronunciation keys, review the Dictionary Skills section of Looking Back, Unit 18 (p. 141).

2. Some students may need additional examples to reinforce the correct spelling of the homophones. Ask students to justify their choices on the basis of meaning.

bear/bare	The grizzly is a huge _______.
	The cupboard was _______.
fair/fare	The _______ had a big roller coaster.
	The bus _______ was 95 cents.
great/grate	That's a _______ idea!
	The fire's _______ was full of ashes.
hole/whole	There's a _______ in my sock.
	He ate the _______ pie!

3. Students will need to 'shrink' the word **prehistoric** down to **history**.

Ask students to expand the base word **appear** using prefixes and suffixes, and list as many related words as possible.

prefix	disappear reappear
suffix	appearance appeared appearing
both	disappearance reappearance disappearing reappearing disappeared reappeared non-appearance

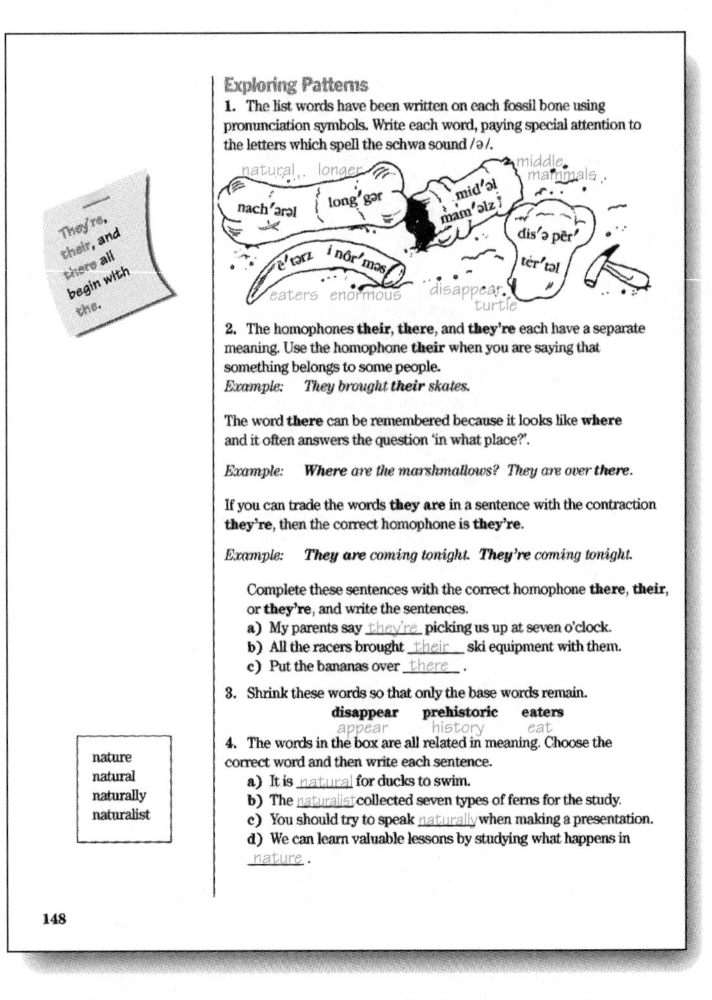
Exploring Patterns

1. The list words have been written on each fossil bone using pronunciation symbols. Write each word, paying special attention to the letters which spell the schwa sound /ə/.

2. The homophones **their**, **there**, and **they're** each have a separate meaning. Use the homophone **their** when you are saying that something belongs to some people.

*Example: They brought **their** skates.*

The word **there** can be remembered because it looks like **where** and it often answers the question 'in what place?'.

*Example: **Where** are the marshmallows? They are over **there**.*

If you can trade the words **they are** in a sentence with the contraction **they're**, then the correct homophone is **they're**.

*Example: **They are** coming tonight. **They're** coming tonight.*

Complete these sentences with the correct homophone **there**, **their**, or **they're**, and write the sentences.

a) My parents say they're picking us up at seven o'clock.
b) All the racers brought their ski equipment with them.
c) Put the bananas over there.

3. Shrink these words so that only the base words remain.

disappear **prehistoric** **eaters**
appear history eat

nature
natural
naturally
naturalist

4. The words in the box are all related in meaning. Choose the correct word and then write each sentence.

a) It is natural for ducks to swim.
b) The naturalist collected seven types of ferns for the study.
c) You should try to speak naturally when making a presentation.
d) We can learn valuable lessons by studying what happens in nature.

148

4. This activity shows the logic behind building derived forms from base words. Note that the double **l** in **naturally** is easily remembered when it is recognized that the suffix **-ly** is added to **natural.** Students could practise the systematic building of words by adding letter tiles to base words and making the necessary changes to the base.

science, scientific, scientifically, scientist
hope, hopeful, hopefully, hopeless
love, loving, lovingly, lovely
equip, equipped, equipping, equipment

Critical Thinking

- There are a number of prefixes which can mean 'not'. Have students link one of these prefixes **(dis-, il-, un-, im-, ir-)** to each word in the chart and write the derived form, as in **dis** + **appear** = **disappear.**
- Ask students to use each word in a sentence, either orally or in writing.

proper/improper	mature/immature
educated/uneducated	continue/discontinue
respect/disrespect	obey/disobey
responsible/irresponsible	certain/uncertain

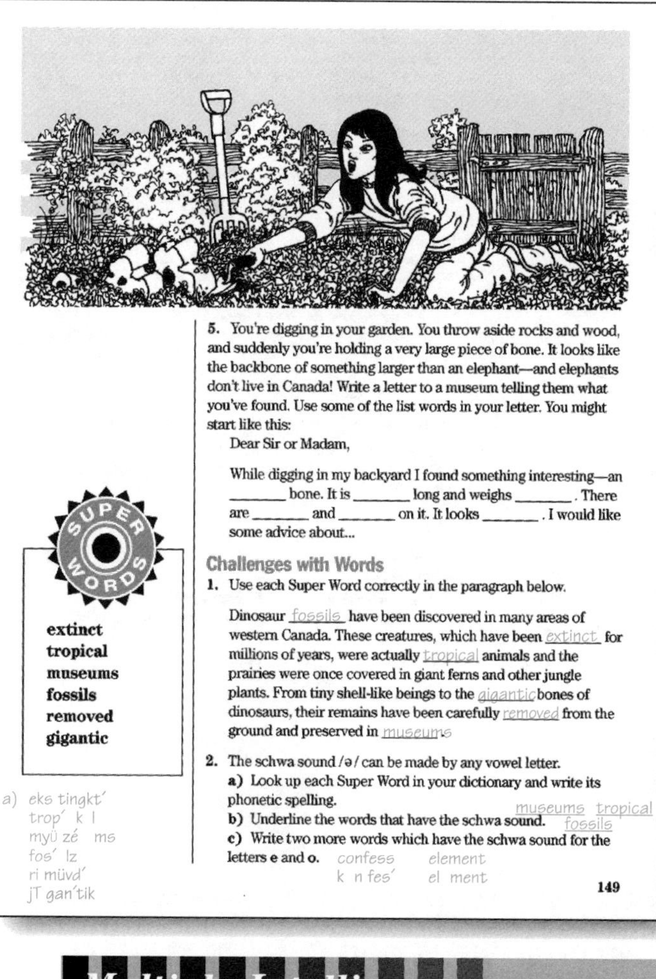

SUPER WORDS

extinct
tropical
museums
fossils
removed
gigantic

5. You're digging in your garden. You throw aside rocks and wood, and suddenly you're holding a very large piece of bone. It looks like the backbone of something larger than an elephant—and elephants don't live in Canada! Write a letter to a museum telling them what you've found. Use some of the list words in your letter. You might start like this:

Dear Sir or Madam,

While digging in my backyard I found something interesting—an _______ bone. It is _______ long and weighs _______. There are _______ and _______ on it. It looks _______. I would like some advice about...

Challenges with Words

1. Use each Super Word correctly in the paragraph below.

Dinosaur fossils have been discovered in many areas of western Canada. These creatures, which have been extinct for millions of years, were actually tropical animals and the prairies were once covered in giant ferns and other jungle plants. From tiny shell-like beings to the gigantic bones of dinosaurs, their remains have been carefully removed from the ground and preserved in museums.

2. The schwa sound /ə/ can be made by any vowel letter.
a) Look up each Super Word in your dictionary and write its phonetic spelling.
b) Underline the words that have the schwa sound.
c) Write two more words which have the schwa sound for the letters **e** and **o**.

a) eks tingkt′
trop′ k l
myü zé ms
fos′ lz
ri müvd′
jT gan′tik

b) museums tropical fossils

c) confess element
k n fes′ el ment

149

Multiple Intelligences

- Schwa vowels and multisyllabic words require the use of a variety of strategies other than sound.

Visual/Spatial: Students could use different forms of visualization.
- configuration boxes and lines. (See Observing Patterns 6.)
- colour code the difficult features of words
- cloze procedure for isolating specific letters (nat _ r _ l)

Bodily/Kinesthetic: Have students unscramble letters or syllables using cards or letter tiles. (See Observing Patterns 5.)

Verbal/Linguistic: Students may enjoy grouping words by word families or rhyming patterns. (See Observing Patterns 4.)

Logical/Mathematical: Have students systematically build multisyllabic words using base words, prefixes, and suffixes. (See Exploring Patterns 4.)

5. You may wish to have students use a formal style for writing letters (as in a letter to a museum). Suggest a format for the letter, and stress the importance of supplying complete information concerning how to contact the writer.

Some students may prefer to write a story about locating dinosaur or fossil remains.

Challenges with Words

1. Have students note the following consonant sounds in the Super Words:

- **ex**tinct (**x** and **c** are not clearly articulated)
- **gig**antic (the letter **g** spells two sounds, /j/ and /g/)
- fo**ss**ils (double **s**)

2. It is important to emphasize that all vowels can make the /ə/ sound. Have students make a chart with the vowels as headings. Ask them to list five or so words with the /ə/ sound in the appropriate column. Students may want to use a dictionary to help them.

a	e	i
general	comedy	admiration
moral	competition	obligation
normal	excellent	credit
appear	licence	orbit
alive	blister	spirit
disappear	eager	deposit

o	u
composition	memorandum
ecological	column
information	columnist
traitor	autumn
alligator	forum
scissors	quorum

3. Suggest that students write the list of words formed by adding **ex-** and **re-** to each base before answering the questions. Ask them to write a sentence for each word that is not used in the question (**repress**, **excite**, **repose**, **export**, **exclaim**). A dictionary would help clarify meanings.

4. Have students list at least three specific places that can be found in each region. Ask them to select one of these locations and do further research on its geography. They might find it helpful to develop a series of questions to assist in organizing their research. (What is the average temperature in January? What are common types of wild animals found there?) CD-ROMs on world geography, desktop publishing software, and spreadsheet or graphing programs could be useful to students in presenting their findings.

forest	arctic	prairie
BC rainforest	Ellesmere Island	Saskatchewan
Sherwood Forest	Greenland	South African Veld
Petrified Forest National Park	North Pole	Mongolia
alpine	**desert**	**coastal**
the Alps	Painted Desert	Halifax, NS
Rocky Mountains	Sahara	Vancouver, BC
Aidirondacks	Mojave	Key West, FL

5. Point out to students that the metric prefix **giga-** is used to mean a value of 1 000 000 000 (one billion).

dinosaur	fierce, heavy, huge, extinct, scary, frightening, reptile, wild, movie star, colossal
CN tower	high, graceful, useful, huge, massive, enormous, striking, eye-catching, unique, famous
cruise ship	elegant, fast, big, fun, safe, luxurious, relaxing, busy, crowded, beautiful

Have students share the ten words they have chosen to describe something **gigantic** and try to guess what the object is.

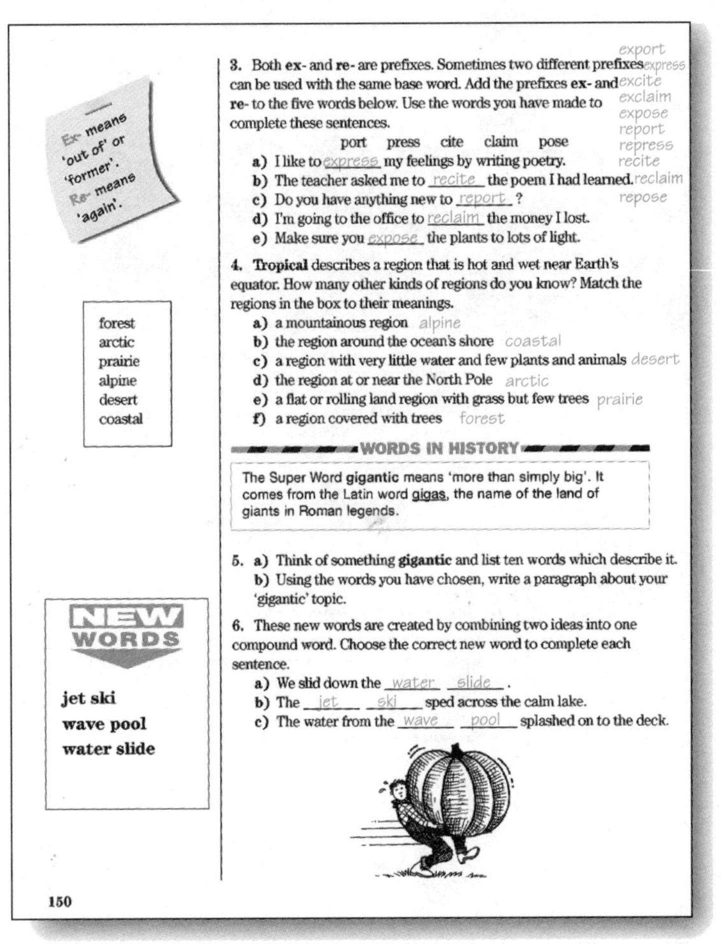

Ex- means 'out of' or 'former'. Re- means 'again'.

3. Both **ex-** and **re-** are prefixes. Sometimes two different prefixes can be used with the same base word. Add the prefixes **ex-** and **re-** to the five words below. Use the words you have made to complete these sentences.

port press cite claim pose

a) I like to express my feelings by writing poetry.
b) The teacher asked me to recite the poem I had learned.
c) Do you have anything new to report?
d) I'm going to the office to reclaim the money I lost.
e) Make sure you expose the plants to lots of light.

export, express, excite, exclaim, expose, report, repress, recite, reclaim, repose

forest
arctic
prairie
alpine
desert
coastal

4. **Tropical** describes a region that is hot and wet near Earth's equator. How many other kinds of regions do you know? Match the regions in the box to their meanings.

a) a mountainous region alpine
b) the region around the ocean's shore coastal
c) a region with very little water and few plants and animals desert
d) the region at or near the North Pole arctic
e) a flat or rolling land region with grass but few trees prairie
f) a region covered with trees forest

WORDS IN HISTORY

The Super Word **gigantic** means 'more than simply big'. It comes from the Latin word gigas, the name of the land of giants in Roman legends.

5. **a)** Think of something **gigantic** and list ten words which describe it.
b) Using the words you have chosen, write a paragraph about your 'gigantic' topic.

NEW WORDS

jet ski
wave pool
water slide

6. These new words are created by combining two ideas into one compound word. Choose the correct new word to complete each sentence.

a) We slid down the water slide.
b) The jet ski sped across the calm lake.
c) The water from the wave pool splashed on to the deck.

150

6. Ask students to think of other words related to water sports.

sailboard, surfboard, boardsailing, parasailing, windsurfing, water ski, surfing, ski boat

Oral Language and Literature

- Dennis Lee's anthology of poems, *Jelly Belly*, contains three dinosaur poems "Dopey the Dinosaur" (p. 43), "The Dinosaur Dinner" (p. 44), and "Torontosaurus Rex" (p. 44).
- Challenge students to write their own dinosaur poems and share them with others.

Writing

- As students use more multisyllabic words in their writing, they are bound to face increasing challenges with schwa vowels. Have them go over the early drafts of various pieces of writing and note their spelling errors. How many of these errors reflected problems with schwa vowels?

Curriculum Connection

The theme of dinosaurs lends itself to investigations of Greek and Latin prefixes and suffixes. Have students combine various word parts to create their own imaginary dinosaurs and other prehistoric beasts. Draw the creatures to match the characteristics indicated by the prefixes, base words, or suffixes.

For example, a slimy 3-footed fish could be an **ichthymyxotriped**.

prefix/suffix	meaning	from
itchy	fish	Greek
tri	three	Latin
ped	foot	Latin
myxo	slimy	Greek

Home Connection

Suggest that parents use letter tiles or syllables written on cards to help their child deal with the multisyllabic words. Colour-coding of schwa vowels can provide visual reminders of these letters.

Assessment

• Note the patterns of errors on the Unit Test. Are students having difficulty with:
- homophones (**there**/**their**)
- multisyllabic words (**prehistoric**)
- schwa vowels (dis**a**ppear)
- double consonants (mi**dd**le; disa**pp**ear)?

• It will also be useful to examine the students' writing in other areas such as their portfolios and notebooks to note whether these patterns of spelling errors are persistent.

Follow-up

Have students use strategies from a variety of intelligences to study words that continue to give them difficulty. (See Multiple Intelligences, p. 233.) Suggest that they work with others who have similar errors, or pair up with someone who can help them with these words.

Teacher's Notes

Capital Letters
Thursday

Patterns

In Unit 17, students looked at capital letters, mainly as they occur in geographical locations, and considered the difference between common and proper nouns. Distinguishing between the two may be a difficult concept for students at this level, and they will need help to remember that proper nouns—the names of *specific* places, people, and things—are always capitalized; common nouns are not (**D**octor Ahmed; the **d**octor). In this unit, students take the concept one step further, and see that the days of the week and months of the year are also proper nouns. They have the opportunity to explore the history and origins of these words, and so continue to expand their vocabularies.

Preknowledge

Students should have an understanding of the following concepts as they work with the patterns in this unit.

- Upper and lower case letters. As their written and spoken vocabularies increase, students will become better able to identify instances when a capital letter is required. Continue to give them practice in differentiating between common and proper nouns.
- Syllables. Students will encounter more and more multisyllabic words as they progress through the middle grades. Spelling, and understanding, will be much easier for them if they are adept at hearing and counting the syllables in words.
- Stressed and unstressed syllables. Identifying stressed and unstressed syllables in a word helps students with meaning and with spelling. Knowing which syllable has the main stress can go a long way to unravelling some of the mysteries of certain English words (min**úte**/**mín**ute).

More Patterns

Other patterns you might wish to introduce or review in this unit include the following.

- Multisyllabic words (**Wednesday**, **November**).
- Common and proper nouns (**calendar**, **August**).

Professional Notebook

It is unfortunate, in a way, that we learn words when we are so very young, for as we become adult we often take these strange symbols for granted. By then there is little of mystery in them for us. We are apt to think vaguely that words just happened and were always so. We have no sharp feeling that they were born much as babies are born. That they are vibrant with life and are always changing. That they grow up and often, like us, take on the greater responsibilities that go with maturity. And that, by the end of their days, for die they often do, they will frequently have life histories as long and distinguished as human biographies in a copy of *Who's Who*.

(Funk 1–2)

Sharing the Secrets with Kids

*It may be helpful when trying to spell the second syllable in **Wednesday** to remember it's a day named after the Norse god, **Woden**.*

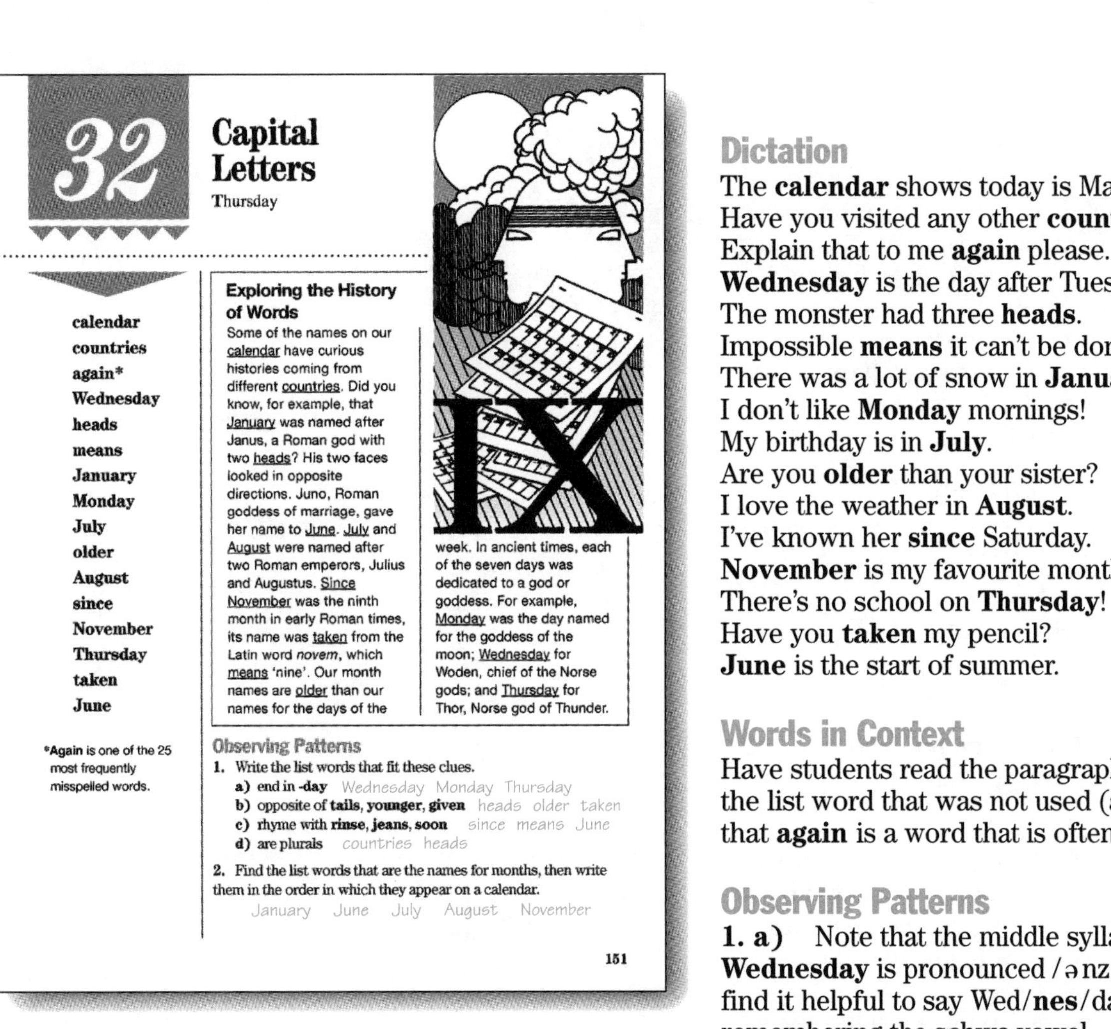

32 Capital Letters

Thursday

calendar
countries
again*
Wednesday
heads
means
January
Monday
July
older
August
since
November
Thursday
taken
June

*Again is one of the 25 most frequently misspelled words.

Exploring the History of Words

Some of the names on our calendar have curious histories coming from different countries. Did you know, for example, that January was named after Janus, a Roman god with two heads? His two faces looked in opposite directions. Juno, Roman goddess of marriage, gave her name to June. July and August were named after two Roman emperors, Julius and Augustus. Since November was the ninth month in early Roman times, its name was taken from the Latin word *novem*, which means 'nine'. Our month names are older than our names for the days of the week. In ancient times, each of the seven days was dedicated to a god or goddess. For example, Monday was the day named for the goddess of the moon; Wednesday for Woden, chief of the Norse gods; and Thursday for Thor, Norse god of Thunder.

Observing Patterns

1. Write the list words that fit these clues.
   a) end in **-day** Wednesday Monday Thursday
   b) opposite of **tails, younger, given** heads older taken
   c) rhyme with **rinse, jeans, soon** since means June
   d) are plurals countries heads
2. Find the list words that are the names for months, then write them in the order in which they appear on a calendar.
   January June July August November

151

Precheck

To help students who had several errors on this dictation, assign one of the following exercises to be completed either at school or at home.

- Design a chart to classify words by the number of syllables they contain. Fill in the chart with words from Unit 32.
- Write all your list words in a column in alphabetical order but print the words you had difficulty with on the Precheck.

Special Needs

- Students might benefit from visual strategies such as colour-coding or writing difficult letters of a word in a larger size. Help them to recognize and deal with the following features of list words:

  calendar calənder
  again often misspelled as 'agen'
  Thursday /ėr/ spelled **ur**
  countries /u/ spelled **ou**; changing **y** to **i** to form plural
  Wednesday /ənz/ spelled **nes**

Dictation

The **calendar** shows today is March 4th.
Have you visited any other **countries**?
Explain that to me **again** please.
Wednesday is the day after Tuesday.
The monster had three **heads**.
Impossible **means** it can't be done!
There was a lot of snow in **January**.
I don't like **Monday** mornings!
My birthday is in **July**.
Are you **older** than your sister?
I love the weather in **August**.
I've known her **since** Saturday.
November is my favourite month.
There's no school on **Thursday**!
Have you **taken** my pencil?
June is the start of summer.

Words in Context

Have students read the paragraph and identify the list word that was not used (**again**). Stress that **again** is a word that is often misspelled.

Observing Patterns

1. a) Note that the middle syllable in **Wednesday** is pronounced /ənz/. Students may find it helpful to say Wed/**nes**/day as a way of remembering the schwa vowel.

Students may also need to think of a strategy for remembering the spelling of /ėr/ in **Thursday**. They could circle the letters that make the sound, or write them in an exaggerated size.

Th(ur)sday ThURsday

c) Point out that in two of the three rhymes, the words are from the same word family, but in the third (**soon/June**), the spelling patterns are different. Students could suggest other words that fit the same rhyming patterns.

d) Notice that the plural is formed in **countries** by changing **y** to **i** and adding **-es**.

The word **means** is most often used as a verb rather than as a plural noun (this **means** you are the winner). **Means** as a plural noun usually occurs in the context of money or a method of doing something (I don't have the **means** to repay my debts; he has no **means** of getting there).

2. Remind students that the names of months and days of the week are proper nouns and are therefore capitalized.

3. As a reinforcement activity, write the individual syllables from all the other list words of two or more syllables on cards or randomly on a large single sheet of paper. Have students unscramble the cards or cut up the paper and arrange the syllables correctly to form the various words. This tactile approach is particularly useful for students who have difficulty sequencing syllables, or who learn best in a bodily/kinesthetic mode.

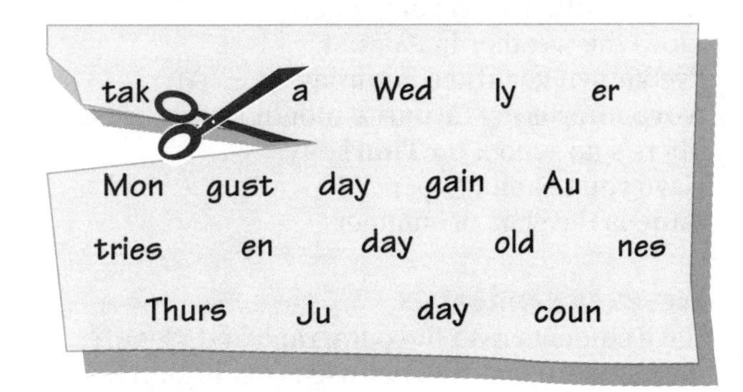

tak
a
Wed
ly
er
Mon
gust
day
gain
Au
tries
en
day
old
nes
Thurs
Ju
day
coun

4. Students might find it interesting that when **August** is pronounced with the stress on the last syllable, **augúst**, it means 'inspiring reverence and admiration' (people were silent in the **august** presence of the queen). You might also wish to point out that when the word is used in this way it is an adjective, not a proper noun, and is therefore not capitalized.

5. As well as considering the shape of **Wednesday**, students must also focus on the **nes** syllable since in normal speech we often say **wenz/dā**. It may help if students exaggerate the pronunciation (**Wed/nes/day**) or highlight the letters when they write the word.

3. Unscramble the syllables to find these list words.

vem ber No November **dar cal en** calendar **ar Jan y u** January

4. Write these words and place an accent (´) over the syllable that is stressed.

August **July** **again** **countries**

5. Write the list words that fit these shapes.

Wednesday countries Thursday taken

6. Write the list word with four syllables. January

Discovering Patterns

calendar countries again Wednesday heads means January Monday July older June August since November Thursday taken

1. Look at the words and notice which ones have capital letters. Divide the list words that begin with capital letters into the following categories.

Days of the Week	Months of the Year	
Wednesday	January	August
Monday	July	November
Thursday	June	

POWERBOOSTER

• Days of the week and months of the year are always written with a capital letter.

152

Discovering Patterns

1. Students could complete each column with the remaining days of the week and months of the year. They should check the spelling of these words in a dictionary. You might wish to have them rearrange the chart in either chronological or alphabetical order, or both. For example, the days of the week in alphabetical order: **Friday**, **Monday**, **Saturday**, **Sunday**, **Thursday**, **Tuesday**, and **Wednesday**.

Writing

• We often use the days of the week and months of the year in notes and memos. In such contexts, the abbreviated form is usually acceptable. Students could determine the abbreviations used for days of the week and months of the year. The dictionary is one source, although the abbreviations are usually given a separate entry apart from the longer version.

days	months	
Mon.	Jan.	Aug.
Tues.	Feb.	Sept.
Wed.	Mar.	Oct.
Thurs.	Apr.	Nov.
Fri.	May	Dec.
Sat.	Jun.	
Sun.	Jul.	

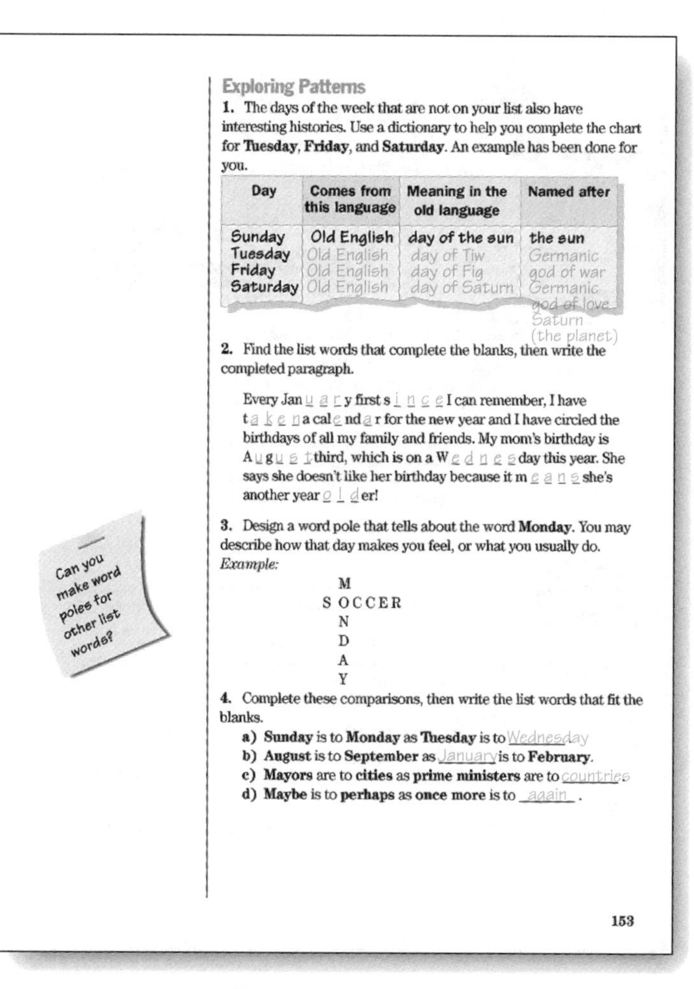

Exploring Patterns

1. The days of the week that are not on your list also have interesting histories. Use a dictionary to help you complete the chart for **Tuesday**, **Friday**, and **Saturday**. An example has been done for you.

Day	Comes from this language	Meaning in the old language	Named after
Sunday	Old English	day of the sun	the sun
Tuesday	Old English	day of Tiw	Germanic god of war
Friday	Old English	day of Fig	Germanic god of love
Saturday	Old English	day of Saturn	Saturn (the planet)

2. Find the list words that complete the blanks, then write the completed paragraph.

Every Jan u a r y first s i n c e I can remember, I have t a k e n a cal e nd a r for the new year and I have circled the birthdays of all my family and friends. My mom's birthday is A u g u s t third, which is on a W e d n e s day this year. She says she doesn't like her birthday because it m e a n s she's another year o l d er!

3. Design a word pole that tells about the word **Monday**. You may describe how that day makes you feel, or what you usually do.
Example:

M
S OCCER
N
D
A
Y

4. Complete these comparisons, then write the list words that fit the blanks.

a) **Sunday** is to **Monday** as **Tuesday** is to Wednesday
b) **August** is to **September** as January is to **February**.
c) **Mayors** are to **cities** as **prime ministers** are to countries
d) **Maybe** is to **perhaps** as **once more** is to again.

Can you make word poles for other list words?

Exploring Patterns

1. Students might wish to work in pairs or small groups. An etymological dictionary is a useful reference source for the classroom. (See Critical Thinking.) Remind students that information on etymology is usually found at the end of a dictionary entry.

April. The Roman name 'Aprilis' is based on the Latin word *aperio*, meaning 'open'. Thus, the name of the month refers to the opening of spring buds in April.
September. The Latin word *septem* means 'seven'. The Roman year started in March, so September was the seventh month. When the calendar changed, September became the ninth month, but the name remained the same.

2. Students should pay special attention to the letters omitted in **calendar**, since they represent schwa vowels (**kal/ən/dər**).

3. Students should be given an opportunity to share their word poles. They could be illustrated and displayed in the classroom. It would be interesting to contrast word poles based on **Monday** with others based on **Saturday**!

Saturday makes me feel

S leepy
h A ppy
a T rest
U nreal
p R etty good
gla D
f A ntastic
merr Y

4. Ask students to identify the nature of the relationships in each set of comparisons. **Maybe** is a synonym for **perhaps**; **once more** is a synonym for **again**.

ESL

- Days of the week and months of the year do not require capital letters in some languages, such as French. In other languages, such as Farsi and Hindi, there are no capital letters. Students may benefit from a review of proper nouns and some of the common examples of their use. Invite them to suggest examples based on their own experiences.

  I come from ______, a city in __________.
  My birthday is in the month of __________.
  My favourite day of the week is __________.
  The languages I speak are __________, and English.
  My favourite holiday is ______________.

Critical Thinking

- Books on word origins can be valuable additions to your classroom reference materials. Three we like are *The Concise Oxford Dictionary of English Etymology*, *Word Origins: An Exploration and History of Words and Language*, and *An Avalanche of Anoraks*.
- Have students work in groups to explore the origins of words that belong to a particular category. One group might brainstorm a list of words related to food; another could explore sports words, and so on.

5. This exercise lends itself to brainstorming with partners or in small groups. Have the students list the old and new names and suggest a reason for each choice.

You could suggest a 'name the months' contest, with each group trying to come up with the most interesting and original set of names.

Here is a set of new names based on the weather (January to December).

January - **Snower**; February - **Tireder**;
March - **Windy**; April - **Wetter**;
May - **Warmer**; June - **Nicer**; July **Hotter**;
August - **Greatest**; September - **Cooler**;
October - **Gorgeous**; November - **Colder**;
December - **Freezer**.

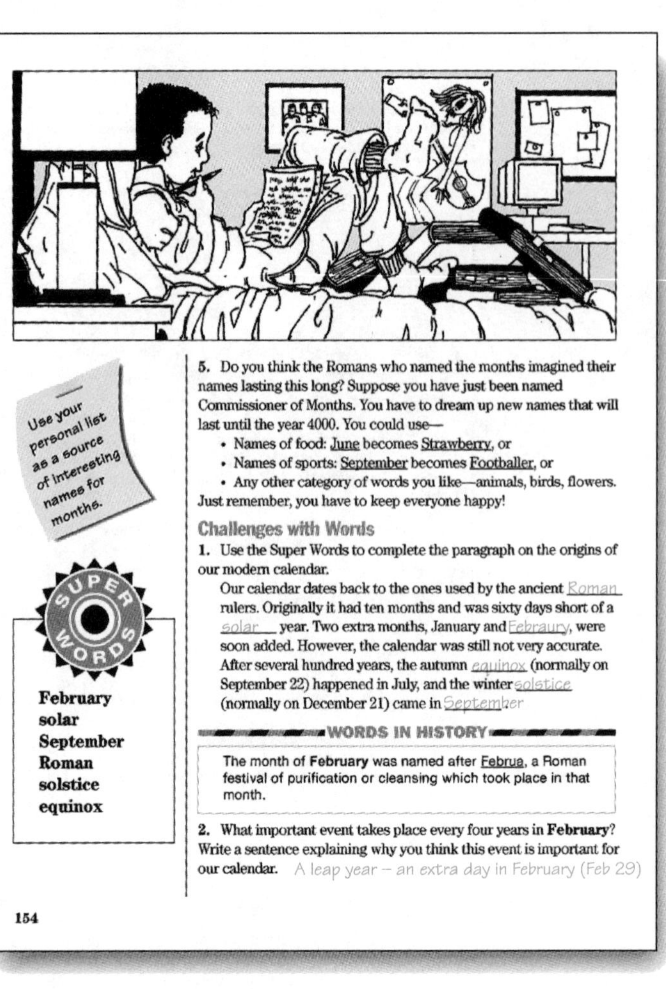

Use your personal list as a source of interesting names for months.

5. Do you think the Romans who named the months imagined their names lasting this long? Suppose you have just been named Commissioner of Months. You have to dream up new names that will last until the year 4000. You could use—

- Names of food: June becomes Strawberry, or
- Names of sports: September becomes Footballer, or
- Any other category of words you like—animals, birds, flowers.

Just remember, you have to keep everyone happy!

Challenges with Words

1. Use the Super Words to complete the paragraph on the origins of our modern calendar.

Our calendar dates back to the ones used by the ancient Roman rulers. Originally it had ten months and was sixty days short of a solar year. Two extra months, January and Febraury, were soon added. However, the calendar was still not very accurate. After several hundred years, the autumn equinox (normally on September 22) happened in July, and the winter solstice (normally on December 21) came in September

SUPER WORDS

February
solar
September
Roman
solstice
equinox

WORDS IN HISTORY

The month of **February** was named after Februa, a Roman festival of purification or cleansing which took place in that month.

2. What important event takes place every four years in **February**? Write a sentence explaining why you think this event is important for our calendar. A leap year – an extra day in February (Feb 29)

154

Co-operative Learning

- Exploring Patterns 5 is well-suited to a co-operative learning format. Inform the students that even the Romans had difficulty naming the days of the week and months of the year. In some cases, they paid tribute to the gods; in others, they honoured local politicians.

month	origin
January	Janus, the Roman god of gates and beginnings, shown with faces on front and back
February	*februa*, a Roman feast of purification, held in this month
March	Mars, the Roman god of war
April	*aperio*, Latin for 'open'
May	Maia, one of the seven daughters of Atlas
June	Juno, the queen of the gods in Roman mythology
July	Julius Caesar, who was born in this month
August	Augustus Caesar, the first Roman emperor

Challenges with Words

1. If students are not familiar with the terms **solstice** or **equinox**, draw their attention to 'Words in History' and the marginal note on p. 155 of the student text.

Point out that often **February** is not pronounced correctly because the first **r** is left out (**Febuary**). By pronouncing the word correctly, they can remember to include the **r**.

2. Have students, either individually or in small groups, brainstorm the problems that might result from being born on February 29. Using these problems as ideas, students might then write a story about someone who was born on leap year day. They could write their story in the form of a newspaper article, an interview, fiction, or whatever they felt appropriate.

It's hard only having a birthday once every four years. It means all my friends are older than I am even though we're the same age ...

3. Many other English words have come from Latin, the language of the ancient Romans. For example, the Latin word hortus meant 'a small garden'. Our English word **horticulture** means 'the science of growing plants'.

a) Match up these other Latin words to the English words they are related to:

Latin	English
domus	culinary
aqua	aquarium
culina	cubicle
tabula	domestic
cubiculum	table

b) Now see if you can match the original Roman meanings to the Latin words above.

a kitchen culina
a house domus
a small bedroom cubiculum
an office area tabula
a channel for transporting water aqua

WORDS IN HISTORY

The word **equinox** comes from two Latin words aequus, meaning 'equal', and nox, meaning 'night'. At the equinoxes (March 21 and September 22), all places on Earth have days and nights of exactly twelve hours each.

There are two solstices each year. One in June, the longest day of the year, and one in December, the shortest day of the year.

4. The **solstices** and **equinoxes** are special times of the year. In most cultures, many holidays and festivals occur on or around these dates. In Roman times, the religious festival of **Saturnalia** was celebrated from December 17 to 23, during the time of the winter **solstice**.

a) What special holidays can you think of which take place around the **solstices** or **equinoxes**? Write down one or two events for each time of year.

b) Choose one of these special festivals and write a paragraph describing what this holiday is like.

155

3. Have students write other words which are related to these Latin words. They might organize their list in chart form or collaborate with a partner to make a booklet of these words.

domus	domicile, domain, domesticate
aqua	aqueduct, aquamarine, aquaplane
culina	culinary
tabula	tabular, tabulate, tabled
cubiculum	cube, cubist, cubic

4. Have students complete a chart such as 'How We Know the Seasons.' Students might want to add their own categories. It would be interesting for all your students to compare the different traditions belonging to the various cultural backgrounds present within your classroom.

	special foods	sports	type of clothing	holidays	what I do
Spring Equinox				Easter	celebrate
Summer Solstice		baseball			
Fall Equinox			light jacket		
Winter Solstice	turkey				

Oral Language and Literature

• Compare the days of the week and months of the year in a variety of languages. The students in your class may come from a variety of language backgrounds and will be able to contribute information. Record the results on charts. Are there similarities in the written form of these words? In their pronunciation? Note that in the case of **Wednesday**, the English and French versions appear quite different (Mercredi), yet both are named after the same god in mythology. They simply use different sources for the god's name—English uses **Woden**, the Norse name; French uses **Mercury**, the Roman name.

English	French	German	Italian
Monday	lundi	Montag	lunedi
Tuesday	mardi	Dienstag	martedi
Wednesday	mercredi	Mittwoch	mercoledi
Thursday	jeudi	Donnerstag	Giovedi
Friday	vendredi	Freitag	venerdi
Saturday	samedi	Samstag	sabato
Sunday	Dimanche	Sonntag	Domenica

Curriculum Connection

Many foods we eat are named after the part of the world where they originated. Have students try to identify the foods associated with these geographic locations. Ask students to suggest other examples.

Lima, Peru	lima beans
Parma, Italy	parmesan cheese
Brussels, Belgium	brussels sprouts
Bologna, Italy	baloney
Sardinia	sardines

Home Connection

Encourage parents to extend the list words to include all the days of the week and months of the year. Parents can discuss the 'tricky spots' in these words and help their child devise strategies for recalling them. (**U** love Sat**ur**day.)

Assessment

Note the challenging features of the list words as described in Special Needs. Also inspect student errors on the Precheck and Unit Test for frequent misspellings. Have students discuss these difficult features and suggest strategies for handling them.

Follow-up

Monitor the spelling of days of the week and months of the year as students record dates in their notebooks. It may help to insist that they write the words in full for a time rather than use abbreviations.

Teacher's Notes

33 Related Words
sign—signal

Patterns
The concept of related words formed from a common base word is a major principle in written English. This feature of written English facilitates reading, since the reader can often relate a new word to a previously learned related word (e.g., **musician** to **music**).

The meaning principle can, however, pose spelling challenges. Unless the writer understands the connection in meaning between **music** and **musician**, it may be tempting to spell the derived form as **musition** or **musishun**. On the other hand, related words can provide vital spelling clues. By relating **sign** to **signal**, the silent **g** can be remembered. Similarly, the schwa vowels in words such as opp**o**sition and def**i**nition can be determined by returning to the spelling of the base word, where these vowels are clearly sounded (opp**o**se, def**i**ne).

Preknowledge
Students should have an understanding of the following concepts as they work with the patterns in this unit.

- The concept of base words and related forms. Students should remember that most base words and words derived from them share a common spelling pattern (**sign/signal/signpost/signaller /signalled**).
- The number of syllables in a word. If some students still have difficulty identifying the number of syllables in a word, encourage them to tap or clap the syllables as they say the word.
- Stressed syllables. If a word contains two or more syllables, one syllable usually receives more stress than the others (**de/cíde**, **réc/tangle**).
- The plural form changing **f** to **v** and adding **-es** (**thieves**).

More Patterns
Other patterns you might wish to introduce or review in this unit include the following.

- Homographs. Words that have the same spelling but different meanings can be challenging for students.
- Idiomatic expressions (**sign up**, **sign on**).
- Silent letters (bu**s**iness, la**y**er, si**g**n). Students should develop strategies for remembering the silent letters in words.

Professional Notebook
The English language is a fascinating object of study. Particularly for students in the intermediate grades and above, a thematic unit on language could be an enjoyable topic of learning that is also bound to have positive effects on spelling. Such a unit could explore questions such as Germanic and Romance language words in English, the source of loan words in our vocabulary, changes in spelling over time, and the etymology of silent letters. (Wilde 235)

Sharing the Secrets with Kids
*The 'meaning principle' states that words related in meaning are usually related in spelling, even if they are pronounced differently. Thus, **sign** and **signal** are spelled in a similar fashion, even though the **g** in the base word is silent.*

Precheck

Students must listen extra carefully to the use of the list words in context for this unit. Stress the importance of waiting until after the dictation sentence before writing the words.

Dictation

A **pyramid** is a huge monument built of stones.
Decide what you want to do now!
Wait for the **signal** to cross the road.
It's none of your **business**!
A **rectangle** has four straight sides and four angles.
The **sign** in the window said 'closed'.
Our **decision** was to go to the mall.
What's the most **southern** part of Canada?
Go away, I'm **busy**!
Seattle is **south** of Vancouver.
The **young** chipmunk sat on my foot.
The river flooded over its **bank**.
Small children play with building **blocks**.
Today's **youth** listen to some pretty loud music.
The **thieves** were caught by the police.
Put another **layer** of paper on your model.

Words in Context

Have students suggest synonyms for the list words. Discuss how synonyms have different shades of meaning (**blocks/chunks**). You may also wish to discuss why it is difficult to find synonyms for words such as **south** and **southern**.

Students might wish to research some aspect of life in ancient Egypt. Encourage them to use folk tales and other fiction books on the subject, as well as non-fiction books, filmstrips, picture and vertical files, and electronic media. Have them choose a topic before they begin (e.g., clothing, work, daily life).

list word	synonym(s)
pyramid	pillar, tower, monument
decide	conclude, determine
signal	motion, gesture, sign
business	affair, matter
rectangle	box, quadrilateral
sign	hint, indication
decision	resolution, conclusion
busy	engaged, occupied, absorbed
young	youthful, juvenile
bank	edge, rim, border
blocks	cubes, sections
youth	adolescence
thieves	robbers, looters
layer	thickness, coating

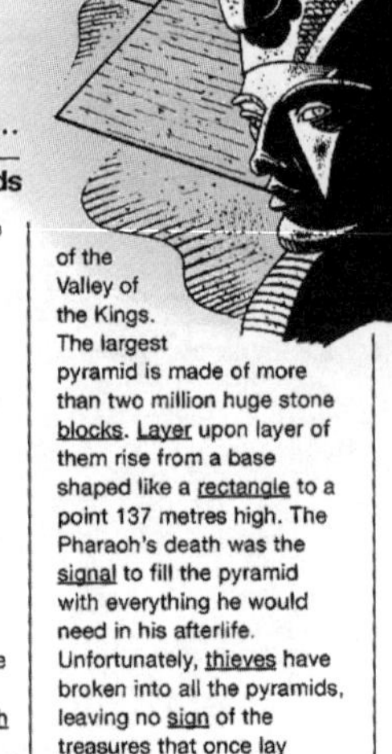

pyramid
decide
signal
business
rectangle
sign
decision
southern
busy
south
young
bank
blocks
youth
thieves
layer

decíde
sóuthern
búsy
sígnal
búsiness
láyer

Exploring the Pyramids

The pyramids of Egypt were built as tombs for the Pharaohs, or kings of ancient Egypt. The young Pharaoh would decide where he wanted his pyramid to stand. He made the decision in his youth because the business of building a pyramid was a lifetime task. Egyptian farmers built the huge tombs on the west bank of the Nile River when they weren't busy in the fields. All of the great pyramids are near Cairo. There are none in southern Egypt, but south of Cairo, at Luxor, are the fabulous underground tombs of the Valley of the Kings. The largest pyramid is made of more than two million huge stone blocks. Layer upon layer of them rise from a base shaped like a rectangle to a point 137 metres high. The Pharaoh's death was the signal to fill the pyramid with everything he would need in his afterlife. Unfortunately, thieves have broken into all the pyramids, leaving no sign of the treasures that once lay within.

Observing Patterns

1. Write the six list words that have two syllables. Place an accent (´) over the syllable that is stressed.

2. Write the list word that is the plural of **thief**. thieves

3. Write the list words that match these pictures.

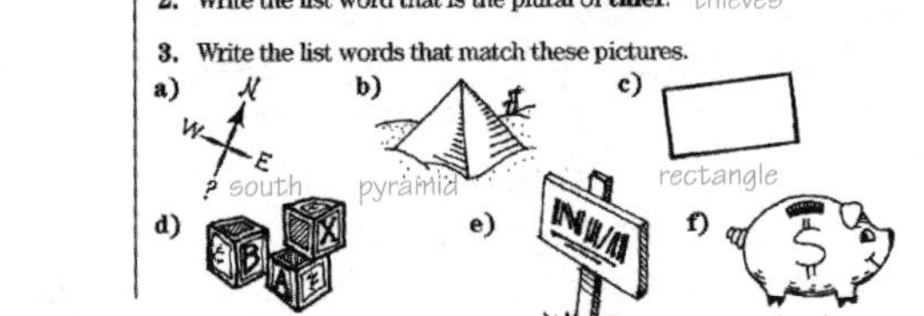

156

Observing Patterns

1. Two list words may pose difficulties for students. **Pyramid** has three syllables, although some students may think it has two as the letter **a** spells a schwa sound and is not clearly articulated (pyrəmid). Similarly, **layer** has a schwa ending (layər) which is not clearly sounded and some students may identify the word as having one syllable rather than two. Help students to notice these features, both by saying the words and by looking at them.

2. Have students provide other plurals that follow the pattern in **thieves** (leaf/**leaves**; calf/**calves**; half/**halves**; knife/**knives**; elf/**elves**; shelf/**shelves**; loaf/**loaves**; wolf/**wolves**).

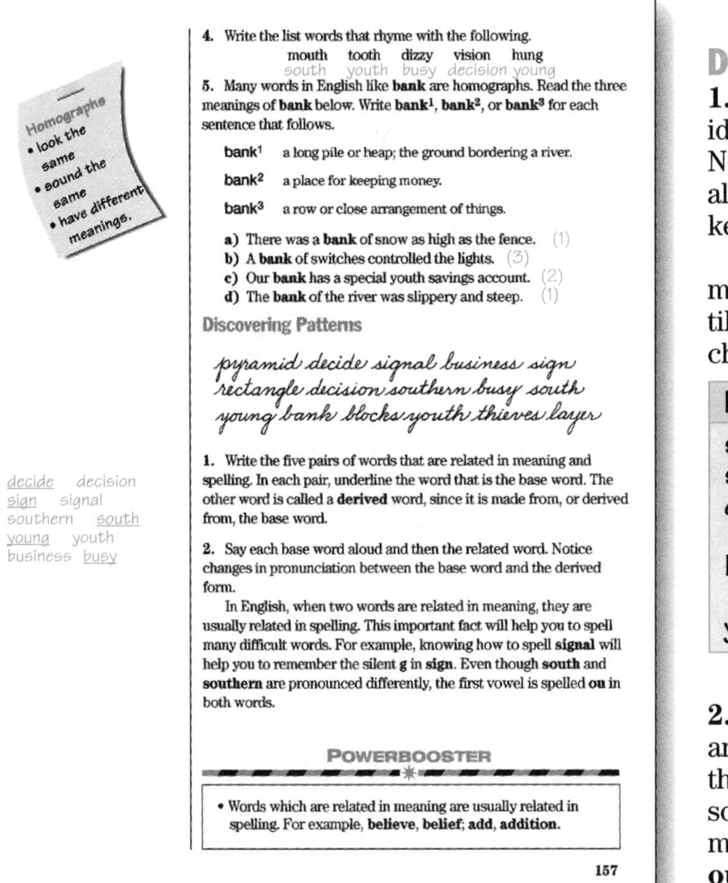

4. Write the list words that rhyme with the following.

mouth tooth dizzy vision hung
south youth busy decision young

5. Many words in English like **bank** are homographs. Read the three meanings of **bank** below. Write **bank¹**, **bank²**, or **bank³** for each sentence that follows.

bank¹ a long pile or heap; the ground bordering a river.

bank² a place for keeping money.

bank³ a row or close arrangement of things.

a) There was a **bank** of snow as high as the fence. (1)
b) A **bank** of switches controlled the lights. (3)
c) Our **bank** has a special youth savings account. (2)
d) The **bank** of the river was slippery and steep. (1)

Discovering Patterns

pyramid decide signal business sign rectangle decision southern busy south young bank blocks youth thieves layer

1. Write the five pairs of words that are related in meaning and spelling. In each pair, underline the word that is the base word. The other word is called a **derived** word, since it is made from, or derived from, the base word.

decide decision
sign signal
southern south
young youth
business busy

2. Say each base word aloud and then the related word. Notice changes in pronunciation between the base word and the derived form.

In English, when two words are related in meaning, they are usually related in spelling. This important fact will help you to spell many difficult words. For example, knowing how to spell **signal** will help you to remember the silent **g** in **sign**. Even though **south** and **southern** are pronounced differently, the first vowel is spelled **ou** in both words.

POWERBOOSTER

• Words which are related in meaning are usually related in spelling. For example, **believe**, **belief**; **add**, **addition**.

157

4. Note with students that in most of the rhyming pairs, different spelling patterns are used to produce the same sounds (**tooth/youth**; **dizzy/busy**; **hung/young**). Have students provide other rhyming words for each of these sound patterns.

tooth	bung, clung, flung, rung
dizzy	fizzy, frizzy, tizzy
hung	booth, eyetooth, uncouth

5. Note with students that a homograph is different from a word that has multiple meanings. The different forms of a homograph usually come from different word origins, and each is given a separate entry in the dictionary. **Shade**, for example, has several meanings that are not homographs and therefore share the same entry word in the dictionary; **bank** has three entry words that are homographs. (See Oral Language and Literature, p. 247.)

Discovering Patterns

1. Some students may need assistance in identifying the base word in some of the pairs. Note that there is a word, **busyness**, which is also derived from **busy**. (Your **busyness** is keeping you from enjoying yourself.)

Have students examine the various changes made to the base words. It may help to use letter tiles and have students make the necessary changes.

base word	derived form	changes
south	southern	add **-ern**
sign	signal	add **-al**
decide	decision	drop **de** and add **-sion**
busy	business	change **y** to **i** and add **-ness**
young	youth	change **ng** to **th**

2. It is vitally important that students develop an awareness of the basic principle in spelling that meaning usually takes precedence over sound. Thus, **young** and **youth**, related in meaning, both contain the vowel combination **ou**, even though the words are pronounced differently. Students must gradually move from a reliance on the sound/symbol level of spelling to an awareness that meaning relationships may also provide vital clues to the spelling of a word.

Ask students to suggest other base words and their derived forms. You might wish to have students categorize the words according to the changes required in the base word.

/t/ to /sh/		long vowel to short	
detect	detection	athlete	athletic
duplicate	duplication	extreme	extremity
recollect	recollection	grateful	gratitude
exhibit	exhibition	nation	national
violate	violation	severe	severity
long or short vowel to schwa /ə/		**silent consonant to sounded**	
admire	admiration	bomb	bombard
oblige	obligation	column	columnist
compose	composition	muscle	muscular
install	installation	resign	resignation
specific	specify	condemn	condemnation

For other patterns of base words and their derived forms see *A Student Editor's Guide to Words* pp. 55–58 and 170–173.

Exploring Patterns

1. Note with students the changes in spelling from base word to derived form in the pairs **busy/business** and **decide/decision**.

Explore other derived forms for each of the base words used in the exercise. Students may find the dictionary a helpful resource.

2. Use the same prepositions (**off**, **up**, **in**, **out**) with other verbs. Have students work in co-operative groups to generate as many idioms as possible, and be prepared to explain the meaning of each phrase. What's the difference, for example, between 'hang up', 'hang in', and 'hang out'?

back off, cut off, get off
back up, cut up, get up, hang up
back in, cut in, get in, hang in
back out, cut out, get out, hang out

3. Give students an opportunity to share their drawings and display them in the classroom. Students might like to illustrate other list words.

4. It is important that students focus on the missing letters in each word. Discuss the challenges posed by the various features and brainstorm strategies for addressing these difficulties.

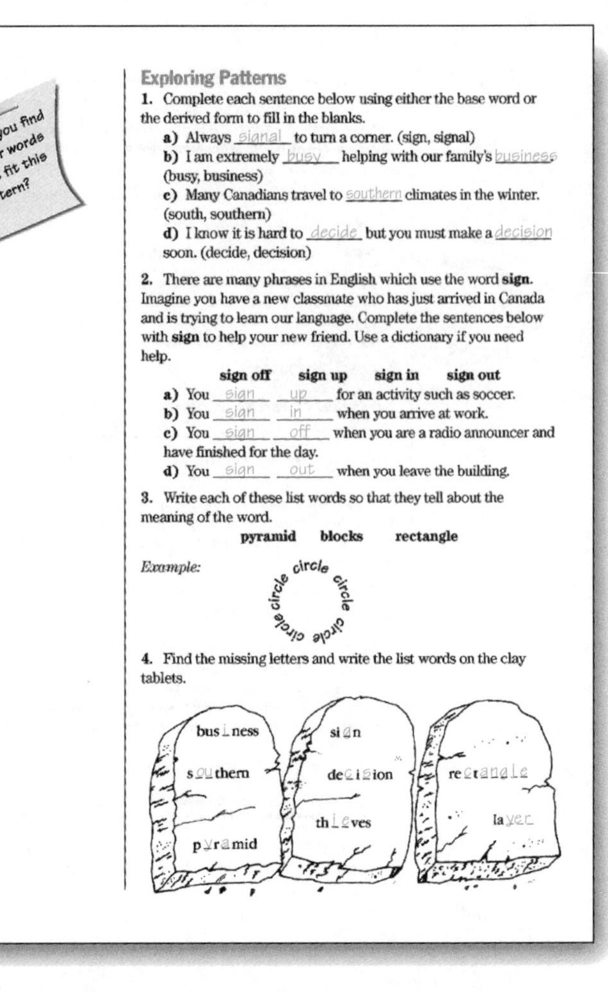

Can you find other words that fit this pattern?

Exploring Patterns

1. Complete each sentence below using either the base word or the derived form to fill in the blanks.

a) Always _signal_ to turn a corner. (sign, signal)
b) I am extremely _busy_ helping with our family's _business_. (busy, business)
c) Many Canadians travel to _southern_ climates in the winter. (south, southern)
d) I know it is hard to _decide_ but you must make a _decision_ soon. (decide, decision)

2. There are many phrases in English which use the word **sign**. Imagine you have a new classmate who has just arrived in Canada and is trying to learn our language. Complete the sentences below with **sign** to help your new friend. Use a dictionary if you need help.

sign off **sign up** **sign in** **sign out**

a) You _sign_ _up_ for an activity such as soccer.
b) You _sign_ _in_ when you arrive at work.
c) You _sign_ _off_ when you are a radio announcer and have finished for the day.
d) You _sign_ _out_ when you leave the building.

3. Write each of these list words so that they tell about the meaning of the word.

pyramid **blocks** **rectangle**

Example: circle circle circle circle circle circle

4. Find the missing letters and write the list words on the clay tablets.

158

Special Needs

- Students who find spelling difficult often miss the logic of how words are built, and see longer words simply as more letters to memorize. Helping students to build words systematically will lessen the need for memorization and build their confidence in attacking words. Begin with simple compound words, then move to the formation of plurals, tense changes, and adding **-ed** and **-ing**. Reinforce the concept of base words whenever possible. Adding prefixes and suffixes will increase the written vocabulary of students dramatically.
- Word building can be conducted with individuals or in a group setting.

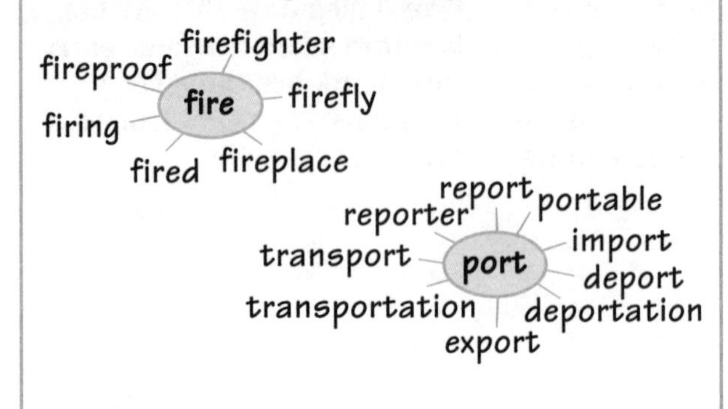

ESL

- Have students watch for shifts in the stressed syllable in related words.

sign, síg nal, síg na ture, as sígn ment
búsy, bús i ness
decíde, dec í sion
réc tang le, rec táng u lar
spéc tac le, spec tác u lar

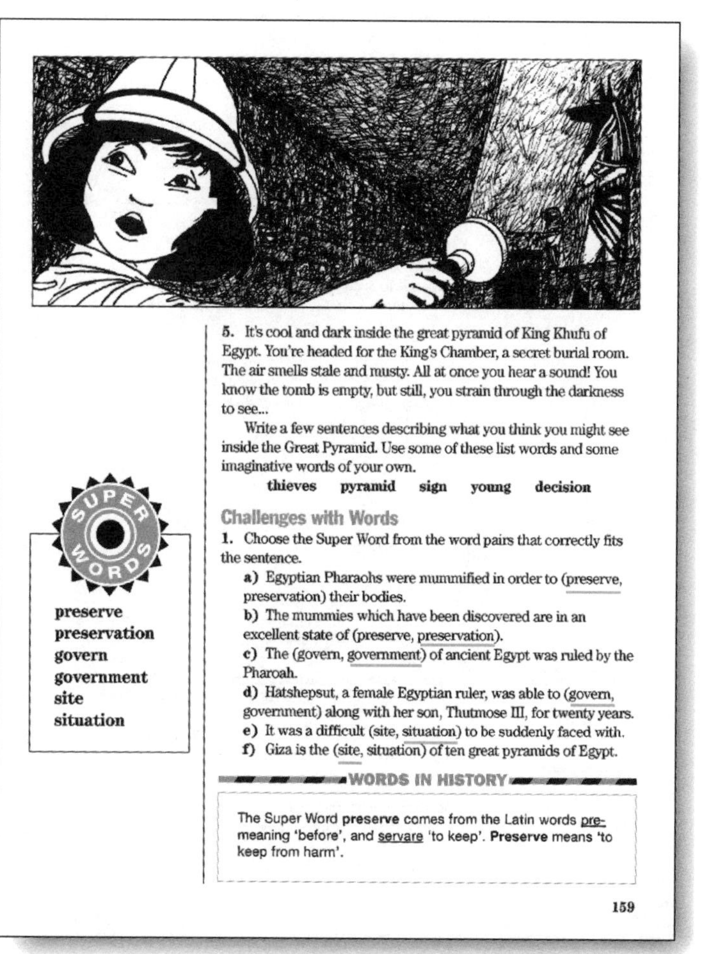

5. It's cool and dark inside the great pyramid of King Khufu of Egypt. You're headed for the King's Chamber, a secret burial room. The air smells stale and musty. All at once you hear a sound! You know the tomb is empty, but still, you strain through the darkness to see...

Write a few sentences describing what you think you might see inside the Great Pyramid. Use some of these list words and some imaginative words of your own.

thieves pyramid sign young decision

SUPER WORDS

preserve
preservation
govern
government
site
situation

Challenges with Words

1. Choose the Super Word from the word pairs that correctly fits the sentence.

a) Egyptian Pharaohs were mummified in order to (preserve, preservation) their bodies.
b) The mummies which have been discovered are in an excellent state of (preserve, preservation).
c) The (govern, government) of ancient Egypt was ruled by the Pharoah.
d) Hatshepsut, a female Egyptian ruler, was able to (govern, government) along with her son, Thutmose III, for twenty years.
e) It was a difficult (site, situation) to be suddenly faced with.
f) Giza is the (site, situation) of ten great pyramids of Egypt.

WORDS IN HISTORY

The Super Word **preserve** comes from the Latin words pre- meaning 'before', and servare 'to keep'. **Preserve** means 'to keep from harm'.

159

5. Have students discuss the topic before writing. They may wish to summarize their discussion in a web such as the following.

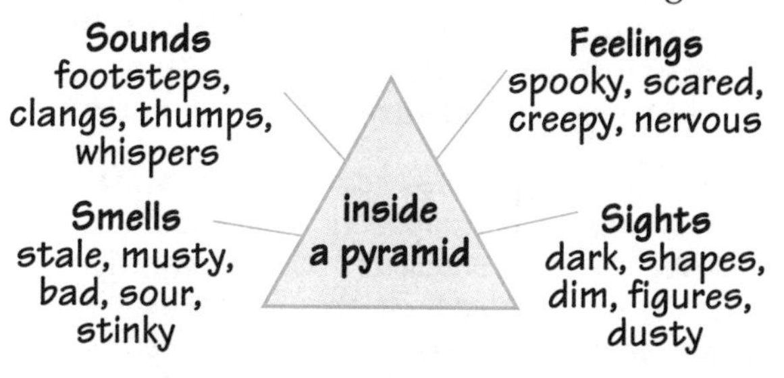

Challenges with Words

More advanced spellers may enjoy the treatment of related words in *Sharing the Secrets*, Unit 34 (pp. 112-114; 146). Some of the base words and related forms you might wish students to consider are given in the following chart.

confer/conference	major/majority
divide/dividend	politics/political
fatal/fatality	regular/regularity
harmony/harmonious	reside/resident

1. Have students write other related words for each pair of Super Words.

preservation
preservative
preserves
preserve
preserving
preserved

Oral Language and Literature

• Heteronyms, like homographs, are two or more words that are spelled the same but have different meanings and origins. The difference between homographs (as used in Observing Patterns 5) and heteronyms is that heteronyms also have different pronunciations. Therefore, **cóntent** (Have you read the content of the report?) and **contént** (Are you content with its contents?) are heteronyms.

bass (fish)/bass (drum)
wind (turn)/wind (blowing)
dove (bird)/dove (past tense of dive)
minute (time)/minute (tiny)

• Have students suggest other heteronyms and use each pair in a single sentence to show the meanings (The wind caused the sheet to wind round the pole.). The sentences should be read aloud so that the differences in pronunciation can be heard.

Writing

• Students could explore the concept of homographs further through reading some *Amelia Bedelia* books. The humour in this series is based on confusion created when Amelia misinterprets the meaning of a homograph. For example, when she plays baseball and is told to run home, she does just that!

• Students could create their own stories based on a confusion of homographs, and present them in a number of ways, including scripts, interviews, storybooks, and cartoons.

2. Have students list other **pre-** words. To make this more challenging, a time limit could be given.

Ensure that students distinguish the prefix **pre-** (**preview**, **precaution**) from the simple letter cluster **pre** (**pressure**, **pretzel**, **pretty**).

predates	predestined	predictable
predetermine	predisposed	precise
preclude	precocious	precognition
preconceive	precondition	precook
preadolescence	preamble	preadvertise
prearrange	preassemble	precedent
preceding	precheck	

You may wish to have students select words from this list and find the dictionary definition, explaining how the prefix **pre-** influences the meaning.

3. Have students work through one of the puzzles together so that the format is clear. They might try forming words with the letters of some other Super Words (**preservation** or **government** would make good choices). These words might be used in word search puzzles, crossword puzzles, word poems, or a puzzle similar to this one.

preservation	government
vat rate sat vote note sate not rote riot server pert rave	govern overt rot over mover term vote note rent germ gent never

New Words

4. *Words that Count Women In* is a useful guide to inclusive language that is not gender specific. It is available from the Ontario Women's Directorate, 2 Carleton St., 12th Floor, Toronto, ON M5B 2M9 (416) 314-0300.

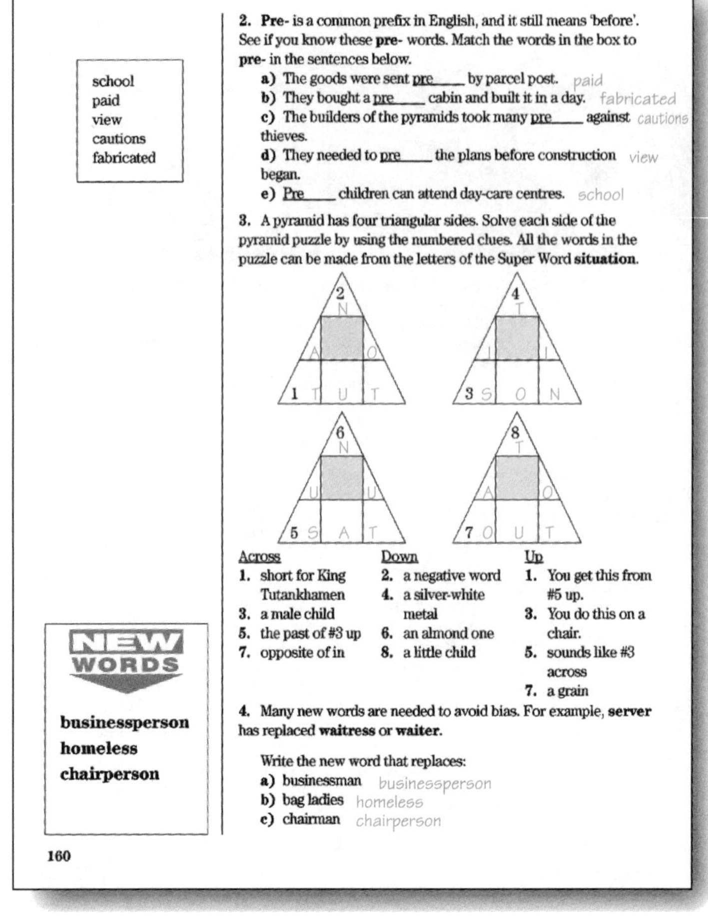

school
paid
view
cautions
fabricated

2. Pre- is a common prefix in English, and it still means 'before'. See if you know these **pre-** words. Match the words in the box to **pre-** in the sentences below.

a) The goods were sent pre____ by parcel post. paid
b) They bought a pre____ cabin and built it in a day. fabricated
c) The builders of the pyramids took many pre____ against thieves. cautions
d) They needed to pre____ the plans before construction began. view
e) Pre____ children can attend day-care centres. school

3. A pyramid has four triangular sides. Solve each side of the pyramid puzzle by using the numbered clues. All the words in the puzzle can be made from the letters of the Super Word **situation**.

Across
1. short for King Tutankhamen
3. a male child
5. the past of #3 up
7. opposite of in

Down
2. a negative word
4. a silver-white metal
6. an almond one
8. a little child

Up
1. You get this from #5 up.
3. You do this on a chair.
5. sounds like #3 across
7. a grain

NEW WORDS

businessperson
homeless
chairperson

4. Many new words are needed to avoid bias. For example, **server** has replaced **waitress or waiter**.

Write the new word that replaces:
a) businessman businessperson
b) bag ladies homeless
c) chairman chairperson

160

Critical Thinking

- Provide students with a series of words either on cards or written randomly on a sheet of paper. Have them sort the words into categories according to the base. Include a 'distractor' for each series of words — a word which contains some of the letters of the set, but which does not share the same base word.

base word:	nation	compete	edit
	national nationality international multinational	competition competitor competitive competitively	editor editorial edition editorship
distractor:	carnation	computer	edible

Curriculum Connection

Students will encounter multisyllabic words in various subject areas. Examine these words for base words and prefixes or suffixes. For example, **multinational** = **multi** + **nation** + **al.** Create a class list of the words, and add new words as students find them.

Home Connection

Encourage parents and students to watch for words that use prefixes, bases, and suffixes. Have a contest for the longest word students actually find in a print source such as a magazine or newspaper.

Families could also try to build new words and supply a logical definition for them. 'Sniglets' are words created to describe a modern condition. In *The Miracle of Language* (p.62) Richard Lederer provides an example of a sniglet: **hozone** — the place where one sock in every laundry load goes to.

Assessment

The list words present a variety of spelling challenges. Have students examine both their Precheck and Unit Test errors to determine the nature of spelling problems. Some likely areas of difficulty include:

- silent letters (si**g**n, bus**i**ness)
- letters or syllables not pronounced clearly (lay**er**)
- schwa vowels (pyr**a**mid)
- plural patterns (thie**ves**)
- **i** before **e** rule (th**ie**ves)
- consonant patterns
- /s/ (de**c**ide)
- /z/ (bu**s**y)
- base words and related forms (**decide/decision**)

Follow-up

Help students to determine effective strategies for learning the spelling of words which continue to give them difficulty. Share these approaches with others in the form of class discussions, partners, or co-operative small groups.

Teacher's Notes

-ought Words
brought

Patterns

Words using the **ought** structure are challenging because of the unusual vowel/consonant combination. Using a sounding out strategy, such words would seem to be logically spelled **ot** (**brot**). Students therefore need to bring alternative strategies into use when dealing with this spelling pattern.

Preknowledge

- Students should have an understanding of the following concepts as they work with the patterns in this unit.
- Base words. Recognizing the base word in a longer word will help students both with spelling and understanding the meaning of words.
- Multisyllabic words. Identifying the number of syllables in a word, and isolating the base word are important skills for successful spellers.
- Rhyme. Often, words that rhyme share a common spelling pattern (**brought/bought**), though this is not always the case (**thought/not**).

More Patterns

Other patterns you might wish to introduce or review in this unit include the following.

- The suffix **-ment** (move**ment**, entertain**ment**).
- Inflected forms: An inflected form is a variation in the form of a word to show case, number, gender, person, tense, mood, or comparison.

write/writing
start/started
battle/battles
special/specially

Professional Notebook

Altogether, then, the core vocabulary from which modern spelling lists are made has a direct relation to language development. These lists have a high utility for the learner in their own right, and are suitably representative of the underlying word-knowledge principles that require mastery. On these grounds it may be held that properly derived spelling lists today are not at all artificial but a true sample of natural language.

(Henderson 86)

Sharing the Secrets with Kids

*Grouping **ough** words by rhyming patterns helps to remember their spelling.*

brought	*rough*	*through*	*cough*	*bough*
thought	*tough*	*slough*	*trough*	
fought	*enough*			
bought				
ought				

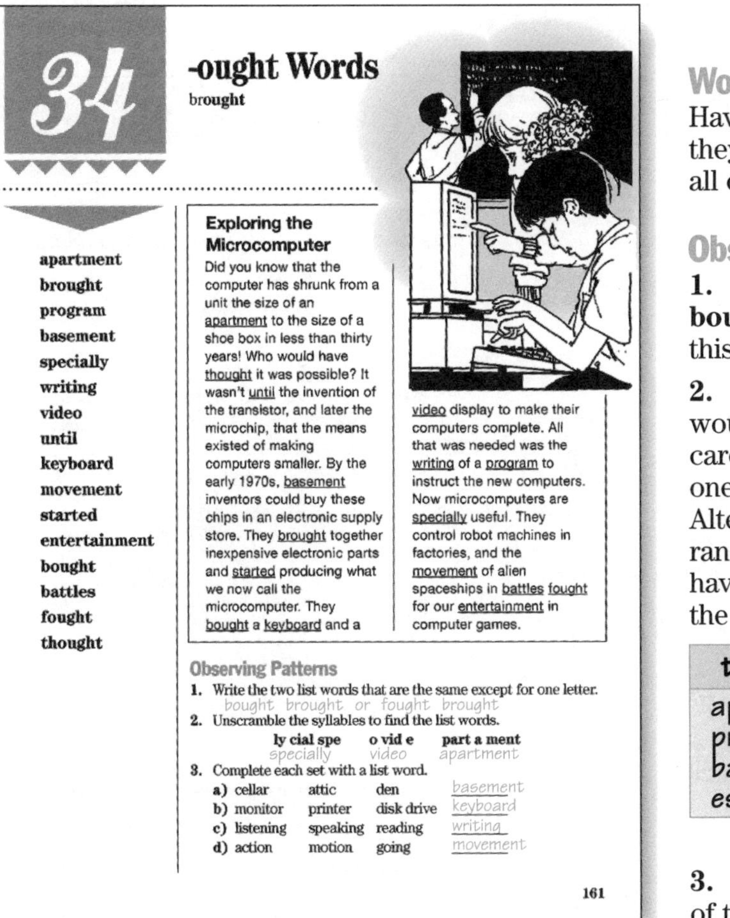

34 -ought Words

brought

apartment
brought
program
basement
specially
writing
video
until
keyboard
movement
started
entertainment
bought
battles
fought
thought

Exploring the Microcomputer

Did you know that the computer has shrunk from a unit the size of an apartment to the size of a shoe box in less than thirty years! Who would have thought it was possible? It wasn't until the invention of the transistor, and later the microchip, that the means existed of making computers smaller. By the early 1970s, basement inventors could buy these chips in an electronic supply store. They brought together inexpensive electronic parts and started producing what we now call the microcomputer. They bought a keyboard and a video display to make their computers complete. All that was needed was the writing of a program to instruct the new computers. Now microcomputers are specially useful. They control robot machines in factories, and the movement of alien spaceships in battles fought for our entertainment in computer games.

Observing Patterns

1. Write the two list words that are the same except for one letter.
   bought brought or fought brought
2. Unscramble the syllables to find the list words.
   ly cial spe — specially; o vid e — video; part a ment — apartment
3. Complete each set with a list word.
   a) cellar attic den — basement
   b) monitor printer disk drive — keyboard
   c) listening speaking reading — writing
   d) action motion going — movement

161

Words in Context

Have students read the paragraph. Suggest that they write their own paragraphs, using some or all of the list words.

Observing Patterns

1. Either of the pairs **bought/brought** or **bought/fought** would be acceptable answers to this question.

2. A more challenging version of this exercise would be to give students a scrambled set of cards, each card having a single syllable from one of the two-, three-, or four-syllable list words. Alternatively, you could write the syllables randomly on a single large sheet of paper then have students cut out the syllables and assemble the words.

two-, three-, and four-syllable words		
apartment	writing	movement
program	video	started
basement	until	entertainment
especially	keyboard	battles

3. Have students identify the subject of each of these sets. Students could work in small groups to create word webs for a specific set, brainstorming to add appropriate words.

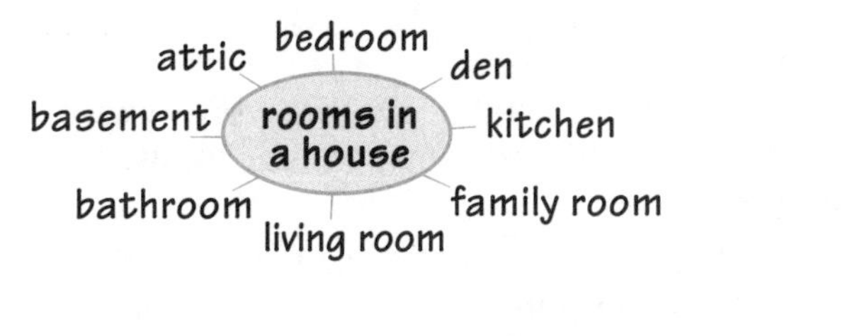

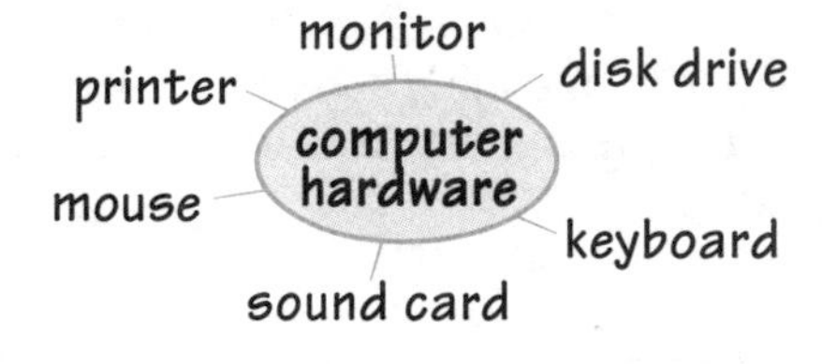

Precheck

Have a final 'elimination' game with any errors appearing in Column B of the Student Record Sheet. After students have self-checked their Precheck and recorded their misspellings, survey the class to elicit those words which most students found difficult. Highlight these words throughout the unit and challenge the class to eliminate them as errors on the Unit Test.

Dictation

We're moving to a new **apartment** soon.
I've **brought** you a cookie.
The TV **program** was interesting to watch.
Our **basement** was flooded last week.
The cake was made **specially** for our class.
Your **writing** is easy to read!
Video games are great fun!
Wait here **until** ten o' clock.
A computer needs a **keyboard**.
There was a **movement** behind the bushes.
The game ended when it **started** to rain.
The **entertainment** night was a great success.
I **bought** a computer with my savings.
Some video games contain space **battles**.
The two brothers **fought** all the time.
They **thought** it was time to go home.

4. Note that **keyboard** is a compound word. Many words created to describe new technology are compound words. The elements of compounds may be joined, as in **keyboard**, or separate, as in **hot dog**. Ask students to brainstorm compound words related to technology.

bar code, couch potato, database, desktop, hard disk, hardware, joystick, keypad, laptop, notebook, software, spreadsheet, word processing

5. Note that with **program** it is necessary to alphabetize to the fourth letter.

6. You might wish to have students use scrambled syllables as described in Observing Patterns 2.

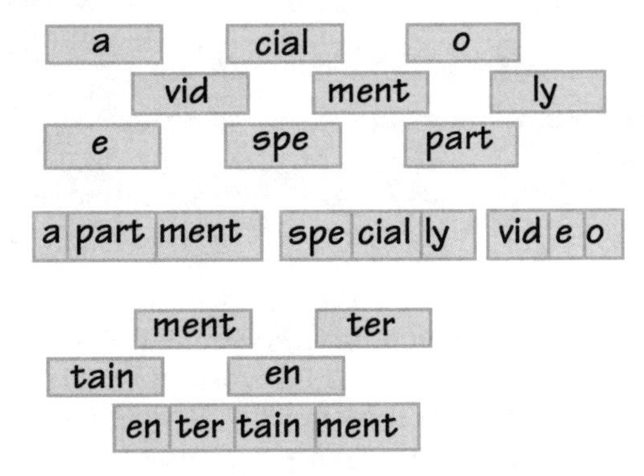

ment ter
tain en
en ter tain ment

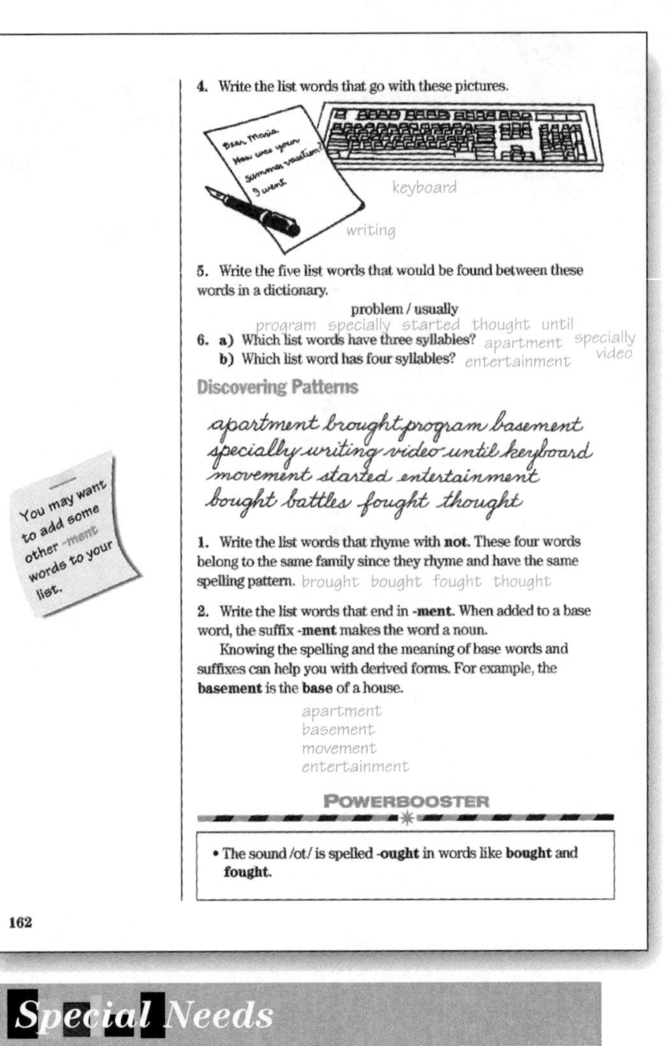

4. Write the list words that go with these pictures.

5. Write the five list words that would be found between these words in a dictionary.

problem / usually

program specially started thought until

6. a) Which list words have three syllables? apartment specially video

b) Which list word has four syllables? entertainment

Discovering Patterns

apartment brought program basement specially writing video until keyboard movement started entertainment bought battles fought thought

You may want to add some other -ment words to your list.

1. Write the list words that rhyme with **not**. These four words belong to the same family since they rhyme and have the same spelling pattern. brought bought fought thought

2. Write the list words that end in **-ment**. When added to a base word, the suffix **-ment** makes the word a noun.

Knowing the spelling and the meaning of base words and suffixes can help you with derived forms. For example, the **basement** is the **base** of a house.

apartment
basement
movement
entertainment

POWERBOOSTER

- The sound /ot/ is spelled **-ought** in words like **bought** and **fought**.

162

Discovering Patterns

1. Ask students to think of other words which contain the **-ought** spelling pattern (**ought**, **sought**).

2. Students might speculate on the meaning of 'apartment', considering the base word is **apart**. 'Apartment' comes from the Latin verb *appartare*, meaning separate. Therefore, an **apartment** is a separate dwelling in a larger building.

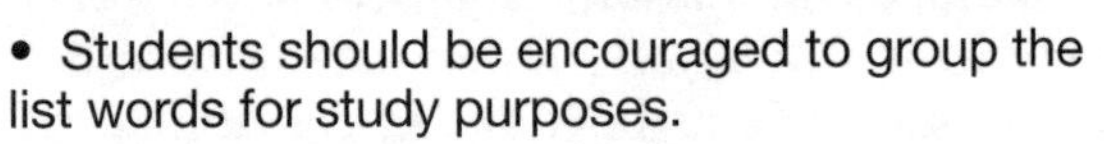

- Students should be encouraged to group the list words for study purposes.

  /ot/ pattern: brought, bought, fought, thought

  suffix **-ment**: apartment, entertainment, movement

- Other words will need to be examined individually.

  specially: spelling of the /sh/ sound; adding **ly** to base

  until: only one **l** at the end

  writing: silent **w**; drop the **silent e** when adding **-ing**

- Have students examine their Precheck responses to identify problem areas in specific list words. Compare Precheck and Unit Test errors to detect any persistent difficulties.

ESL

- Silent letters are difficult to remember, especially for students who are used to a one-to-one sound/letter relationship in their first language. Help them practise grouping words with silent **ought** into patterns.

bring/brought	think/thought
buy/bought	fight/fought

- Give students practice using sentences that establish the context for the **ought** forms of various words.

I have ________ about it for a long time. (think)
I ________ about it all day yesterday. (think)
I have ________ enough food for a week. (buy)
I ________ it this morning. (buy)
They ________ all the way home. (fight)
He has ________ with his cousin before. (fight)

Exploring Patterns

1. Complete the list words displayed on the computer monitor.

b a s e ment	vid e o	unt i l
th o u g h t	w r iting	a part m e n t
m o v e ment	br o u g h t	k e y b o a rd

2. Add the suffix **-ment** to each base word on the printout to make a noun. Then use your new words to write the complete sentences.

- **amuse** amusement
- **enjoy** enjoyment
- **pay** payment
- **punish** punishment
- **announce** announcement

a) The convicted thief wondered what his punishment would be.
b) The students were eager to hear the announcement about the basketball game.
c) You may make your payment at the cashier's desk.
d) We visited a wonderful amusement park on our vacation.
e) The children got so much enjoyment from the magic show.

3. Use the list words ending in **-ought** in sentences. You may use more than one of the words in the same sentence.

4. Use the letters of the word **entertainment** to compute as many small words as you can. Score 2 points for every two-letter word, 3 for every three-letter word, and so on. Calculate your score to see what kind of word computer you are.

Microcomputer	=	0 – 40
Minicomputer	=	41 – 80
Electronic Brain. All systems go!	=	81 +

5. Design word webs for the list words below. You may use any word that is connected in some way with the centre word.

video writing apartment

163

2. Note with students that the silent **e** in **amuse** and **announce** is retained when adding a suffix that starts with a consonant as in **-ment**. If the suffix begins with a vowel, as in **-ing**, the final **e** is dropped (**amusing**).

3. Ensure that students sequence the final letters in these words correctly. Drawing configuration boxes or lines for each will help students to see the basic shape pattern and discriminate among words. Note that **fought** and **bought** share identical configurations.

bought/fought thought brought

4. Compile a master list of the words generated and calculate the total score for the group.

5. Encourage students to subdivide their webs into smaller webs branching out from the central word. Have them share their word webs with a partner to see the number of associations possible. You might wish to compile a master web for each of the three words and display them in the classroom.

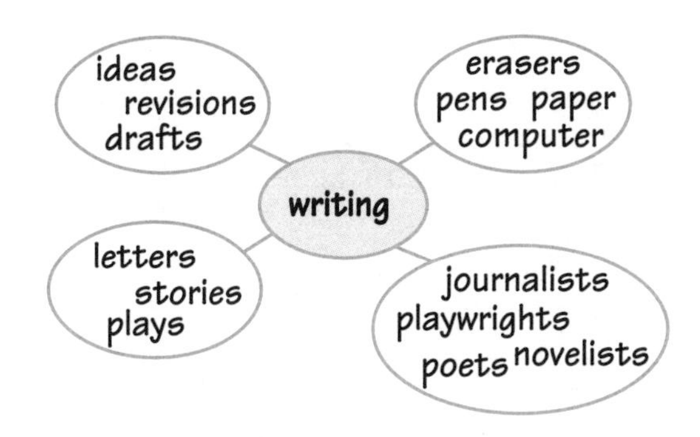

Exploring Patterns

1. Have students discuss the features of each word that may present a spelling challenge. For example, **until** is often misspelled as **untill**; the silent **w** at the beginning of **writing** is sometimes forgotten by students, so that the word becomes **riting**. Ask students to suggest strategies that will help them remember the 'tricky' features of these words.

Writing

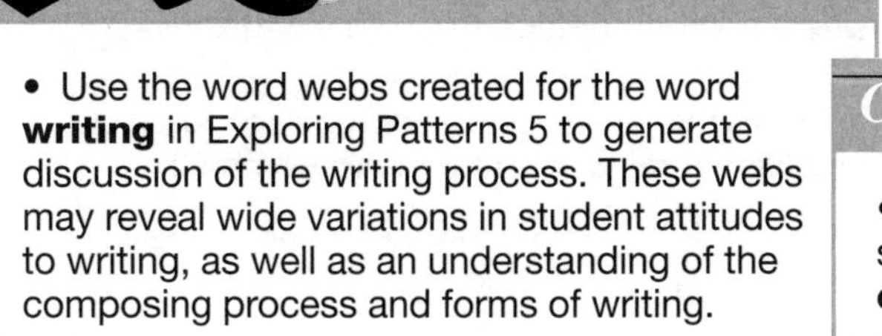

- Use the word webs created for the word **writing** in Exploring Patterns 5 to generate discussion of the writing process. These webs may reveal wide variations in student attitudes to writing, as well as an understanding of the composing process and forms of writing.

Critical Thinking

- Ask students to determine how common the spelling pattern **eo** is at the end of words (**video**, **cameo**, **stereo**).
- What other spelling pattern spells the sound /eo/? Is this a more common pattern?

  portfolio, patio, polio, pistachio, scorpio, radio studio, scenario, trio

6. Invite students to see that in directing a machine to do a job, no essential information can be omitted. Have students role-play the robot carrying out instructions.

1. Exit closet.
2. Climb stairs to bedroom.
3. Enter bedroom
4. Step over clothes lying on floor.
5. Walk to bed.
6. Straighten duvet.
7. Shake duvet.
8. Straighten duvet.
9. Shake pillows.
10. Step over clothes lying on floor.
11. Exit bedroom.
12. Descend stairs.
13. Return to closet.

Challenges with Words

Help students to examine each Super Word carefully, noting the following features:

- schwa vowels in monit**o**r and experim**e**nt
- suffix **-ful** in **thoughtful**. When /ful/ is a suffix it is spelled with only one **l**
- the base words for **processing** (process), **electronic** (electric), and **thoughtful** (thought)
- **software** is a compound word (see Observing Patterns 4).

1. Ask students to create sentences of their own that contain one or more of the Super Words. Have them share their sentences with a partner.

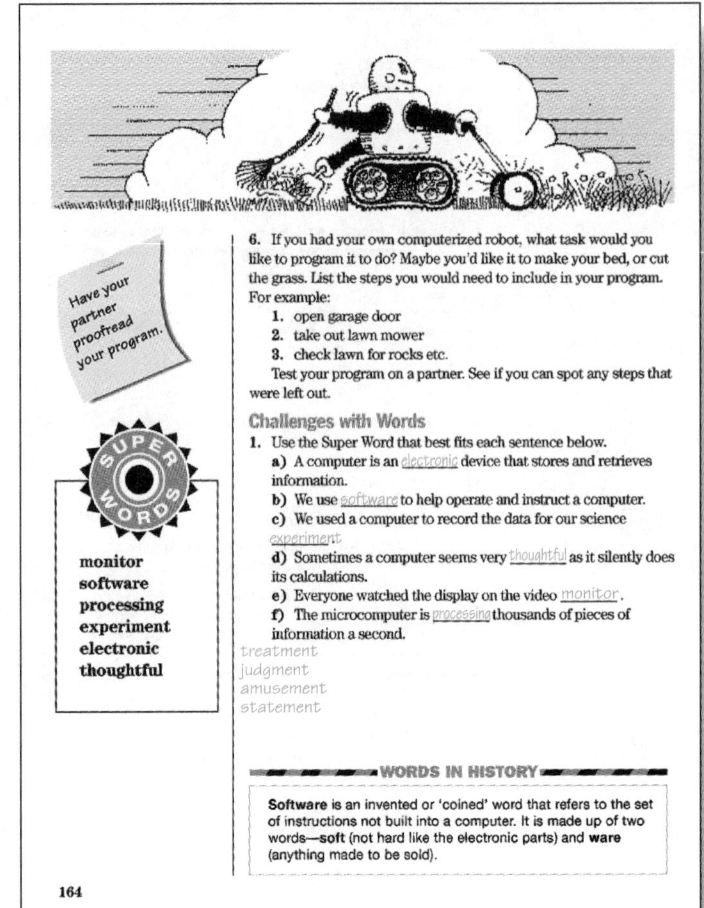

Have your partner proofread your program.

6. If you had your own computerized robot, what task would you like to program it to do? Maybe you'd like it to make your bed, or cut the grass. List the steps you would need to include in your program. For example:

1. open garage door
2. take out lawn mower
3. check lawn for rocks etc.

Test your program on a partner. See if you can spot any steps that were left out.

SUPER WORDS

monitor
software
processing
experiment
electronic
thoughtful

Challenges with Words

1. Use the Super Word that best fits each sentence below.

a) A computer is an electronic device that stores and retrieves information.

b) We use software to help operate and instruct a computer.

c) We used a computer to record the data for our science experiment

d) Sometimes a computer seems very thoughtful as it silently does its calculations.

e) Everyone watched the display on the video monitor.

f) The microcomputer is processing thousands of pieces of information a second.

treatment
judgment
amusement
statement

WORDS IN HISTORY

Software is an invented or 'coined' word that refers to the set of instructions not built into a computer. It is made up of two words—**soft** (not hard like the electronic parts) and **ware** (anything made to be sold).

164

Co-operative Learning

The following activities could be done effectively in a co-operative group setting.

- Constructing word webs (See Exploring Patterns 5 and Observing Patterns 3.)
- Generating compound words that have been 'coined' for technolog. (See Observing Patterns 4.)
- Using the letters of **entertainment** to produce smaller words (See Exploring Patterns 4.)

2. When you combine the following letters, you can spell 4 five-letter words. Add the suffix **-ment** to every word and they will fit the definitions below.

a a a d e e e g j m r s s t t t t u u

a) (trick or ?) + **ment** = a way of curing a disease treatment
b) (starts with **j**) + **ment** = a decision from a judge judgment
c) (starts with **a**) + **ment** = pleasure or fun amusement
d) (starts with **st**) + **ment** = an account or report statement

3. See if you know these other 'coined' words. Combine two words from the following list and match them to their meanings.

tray chip copy hard ash
up micro photo ware pick

a) A kind of printed reproduction is a photocopy
b) A small truck with an open back is a pick up.
c) A container for ashes is an ashtray.
d) A tiny electronic wafer is called a microchip
e) The mechanical or electronic parts of a computer are called its hardware.

4. Here are some more computer words. Look them up in your dictionary and write their meanings in your notebook.

program monitor bit byte RAM floppy disk

5. **a)** Computers use special number codes when processing information. They are called **ASCII** codes. ASCII stands for **American Standard Code for Information Interchange**. Use the

ASCII Code	46	65	66	67	68	69	70	71	72	73	74	75	76	77
Character	.	A	B	C	D	E	F	G	H	I	J	K	L	M
ASCII Code	78	79	80	81	82	83	84	85	86	87	88	89	90	
Character	N	O	P	Q	R	S	T	U	V	W	X	Y	Z	

ASCII codes below to decode this sentence about computers.

84 72 69 70 73 82 83 84 70 85 76 76 89
69 76 69 67 84 82 79 78 73 67 67 79 77 80 85 84 69 82
87 65 83 67 65 76 76 69 68 69 78 73 65 67 46

b) Now try writing a few sentences using some of the Super Words. Put your sentences into ASCII code and see if a partner can decode them.

THE FIRST FULLY ELECTRONIC COMPUTER WAS CALLED ENIAC.

165

2. Note that **judgment** is sometimes spelled without dropping the **e** from the base word (**judgement**). This exercise uses the form **judgment**. Should students use the spelling **judgement** they will be short an **e** for the other base words. Explain that both spellings are correct, although **judgment** is generally preferred.

3. Observing Patterns 4 includes a list of compound words that have been 'coined' in recent years to describe new technology. Students might add their own new words to the list, scanning newspapers and computer magazines as sources. Have students write a short definition for each new word they create.

4. There are, of course, many more computer words. Students might like to do further research into computer technology and how a computer works. They may wish to specialize in areas such as the Internet or multimedia technology.

5. ASCII is pronounced 'askey'. Point out that the code numbers given here are for capital letters only. Lower case letters have different codes.

Students may want to investigate ASCII further. Most computer manuals list the code. Have students write ASCII code messages using upper case letters, as well as punctuation. They can then exchange with a partner and solve each other's messages.

73 67 79 78 68 85 67 84 69 68 65 78
69 88 80 69 82 73 77 69 78 84, 85 83 73 78 71
69 76 69 67 84 82 79 78 73 67 ...

I conducted an experiment, using electronic equipment, ...

Multiple Intelligences

• The word list lends itself to a variety of intelligences.

Visual/Spatial: Use configuration boxes or lines for the **ought** pattern. (See Exploring Patterns 3.) Use cloze activities such as that in Exploring Patterns 1

Bodily/Kinesthetic: Have students work with scrambled syllables. (See Observing Patterns 2.)

Verbal/Linguistic: Explore word formation and word meaning through word webs, semantic sets, and 'coined' words.

Logical/Mathematical: Have students determine base words, suffixes, numbers of syllables, and word families.

Interpersonal: Use the suggestions given throughout the unit for co-operative learning activities.

Curriculum Connection

Since the theme of the unit is the microcomputer it may be fruitful to explore the pros and cons of using a spell checker as an aid to spelling. How can it help learning to spell? What are its drawbacks? Students may be able to contribute examples of the spell check's failure to spot errors due to word substitution or homophones.

A discussion of the use of computer software in spelling instruction is found in *Spelling: Sharing the Secrets*, pp. 177-179.

Home Connection

• Let parents know of the specific spelling challenges posed by the list words (see Special Needs, p. 252) and encourage them to work with their child to develop strategies to recall these features. Special attention should be paid to errors made on the child's Precheck.

• Families may also enjoy writing and deciphering messages using ASCII codes. (See Challenges With Words 5.)

Assessment

Look for patterns of errors in both Precheck and Unit Test responses. Students should be encouraged to identify their own areas of need. A checklist similar to the one given here may help to isolate difficulties.

Error in spelling...	Ask yourself...
fought, bought	Did I write the letters in the correct order?
brought, thought	Did I use the correct number of letters?
apartment, entertainment	Did I include each syllable?
movement	Did I leave the base word the same?
specially	Did I spell **cial** correctly? Did I add **ly** to **special**, and keep both **l**s?
until	Did I spell **until** with one **l** or two?
writing	Did I remember the silent **w**? Did I drop the **e** when adding **-ing**?

Follow-up

Students could work alone or in pairs to devise strategies to overcome their identified problems. See Multiple Intelligences, p. 255, for a variety of strategies.

Teacher's Notes

35 Looking Back
Units 31–34

Patterns to Review

Review the following sound-symbol relationship and structures:

- Schwa vowels as in **enormous** (ənorməs)
- Capital letters
- Related words as in **sign/signal**
- **-ought** words as in **brought**

The following words from the review list appear on the list of "The 200 Words Most Frequently Misspelled":

again, where, there, thought, until, brought, middle, writing

Creating a Personal Review List

Looking Back units should also provide an opportunity for students to review words and concepts which gave them particular difficulty in the preceding units. These personal study lists could involve words from a variety of sources, as suggested below:

- words misspelled in the students' Unit Tests and everyday writing (writing folders, notebooks, tests)
- words used throughout the day: current themes, content areas, current events, media, holidays
- lists such as "The 200 Words Most Frequently Misspelled" and "The 200 Words Most Frequently Written" (See Appendix.)

Transfer of Spelling Knowledge

The following suggestions will help students to retain the knowledge and skills they acquire through word study and apply them in their everyday writing:

- Do not treat words on study lists as single entities, but as examples of larger spelling patterns. Build on word patterns to maximize the benefit of word study.
- Reintroduce frequently misspelled words on subsequent lists.
- When errors reoccur in student writing, ask students to recall the strategies they had used for studying these words.
- Discuss the use of spelling strategies for new words as they occur in a variety of classroom contexts.

Looking Back

1. In addition to having students follow the Study Steps, encourage them to share strategies for recalling specific features of words:

- exaggerating sounds: Wed/**nes**/day, bus/**i**/ness
- grouping by spelling pattern: **thought**, **brought**
- double consonants: disa**pp**ear, mi**dd**le
- homophones: **there/their**

Dictation

You're late for school **again**!
Do you know **where** Australia is?
The magician made the rabbit **disappear**.
Soccer practice is on **Wednesday**.
The students cleared **their** desks.
Put the book over **there**.
How many **countries** are in Africa?
What is your **decision** on the matter?
My mom runs her own **business**.
There's a fresh **layer** of paint on the wall.
What's all the **excitement** about?
We **thought** it would be easy to leave.
My birthday is not **until** September.
Have you **brought** your notebook?
Never walk in the **middle** of the road!
I've been **writing** a letter to you.

2. Challenge students to create new sentences using the words from the Study List. Can they link the sentences together in a meaningful paragraph?

3. The shapes of these words could be reinforced further by having students draw configuration lines after each word.

A set of configurations could be drawn for the entire Study List, and students could link the shapes with each word. This strategy reinforces an overall visual image of the word, and draws attention to ascending and descending letters.

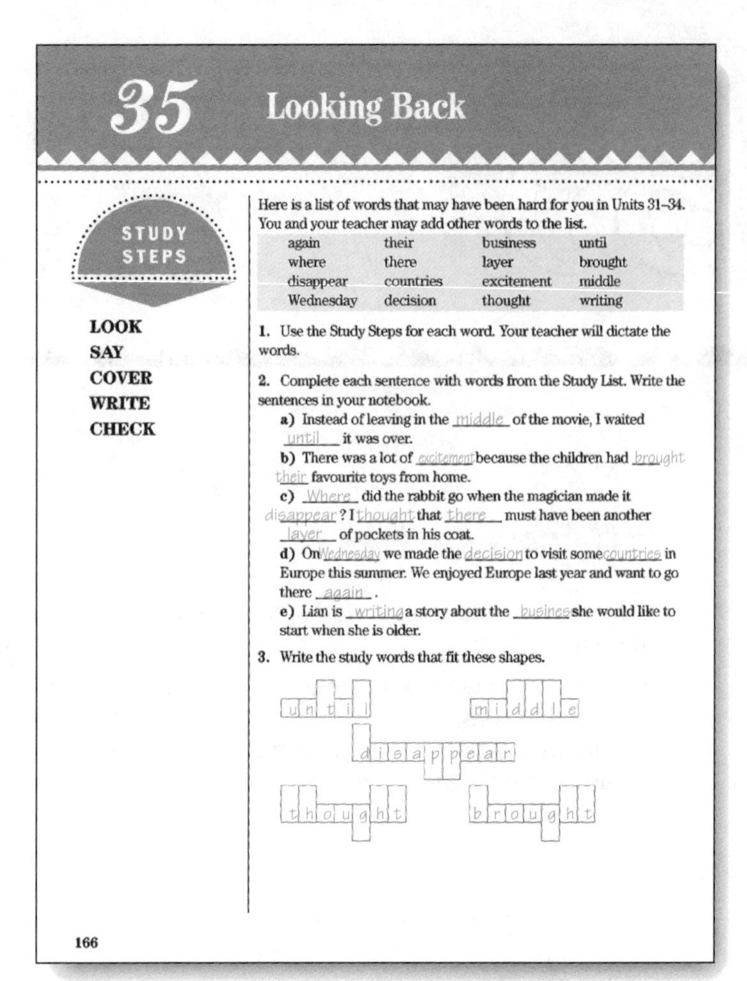

35 Looking Back

STUDY STEPS

LOOK
SAY
COVER
WRITE
CHECK

Here is a list of words that may have been hard for you in Units 31–34. You and your teacher may add other words to the list.

again	their	business	until
where	there	layer	brought
disappear	countries	excitement	middle
Wednesday	decision	thought	writing

1. Use the Study Steps for each word. Your teacher will dictate the words.

2. Complete each sentence with words from the Study List. Write the sentences in your notebook.

a) Instead of leaving in the middle of the movie, I waited until it was over.

b) There was a lot of excitement because the children had brought their favourite toys from home.

c) Where did the rabbit go when the magician made it disappear? I thought that there must have been another layer of pockets in his coat.

d) On Wednesday we made the decision to visit some countries in Europe this summer. We enjoyed Europe last year and want to go there again.

e) Lian is writing a story about the busines she would like to start when she is older.

3. Write the study words that fit these shapes.

until middle disappear thought brought

166

POWERBOOSTERS

31 The sound /əl/ may be spelled in a number of ways including **le** as in **handle**, and **al** as in **animal**.

32 Days of the week and months of the year are always written with a capital letter.

33 Words which are related in meaning are usually related in spelling. For example, **believe**, **belief**; **add**, **addition**.

34 The sound /ot/ is spelled **-ought** in words like **bought** and **fought**.

agáin Wédnesday
coúntries búsiness
láyer untíl
míddle wríting

4. Write the study words that have two syllables. Put an accent (´) over the syllable that is stressed.

5. Write the base word for each of these study words.

disappear	**excitement**	**writing**	**countries**	**business**
appear	excite	write	country	busy

6. Complete each word on the wheel with the letters that spell the sound /əl/ as in coup**le**.

batt, sign, mamm, rectang, natur, terrib, midd, trav — /əl/

7. Explode these words by adding prefixes, suffixes, plural endings, and so on.

appear sign excite

Example: *natural* *unnatural*
nature
naturalist *naturally*

Add any interesting words to your personal list.

8. Find the missing letters that would complete these review words. Pay special attention to the schwa /ə/ vowels in the unstressed syllables.

enorm o u s	dis a pp e a r	f ou ght
cal e nd a r	bus i ness	u nt i l
e x c it e ment	Wed n e s day	nat u r a l

167

4. Each of the two-syllable words also contains a spelling challenge. Draw attention to these features as well as the stress patterns.
For example:

again	schwa vowel in first syllable (əgain)
until	only one **l** at the end
middle	double consonant; /əl/ spelled **le** at the end

5. Draw students' attention to cases in which the base word is altered when an ending is added (**writing**, **countries**, **business**). Contrast these words with **excitement**, in which no change is made to the base when the suffix is added (**-ment** begins with a consonant, not a vowel). For further reinforcement of these patterns, review the Powerboosters for Units 20, 21, and 28.

6. Have students group the words according to the patterns for the /əl/ ending. Ask students to work in groups to add other examples to each of these patterns.

al	el	le
national	nickel	double
vital	barrel	wrinkle
vertical	channel	chuckle
horizontal	easel	struggle

7. Students could work with partners to generate as many words as possible for each set. The whole group could then share their word explosions. Dictionaries should be made available for checking the spelling of the derivatives formed.

Reinforce the 'meaning principle' underlying these constructions: words that are connected in meaning are usually linked in spelling even if they are not pronounced the same. Therefore, **sign** and **signal** both contain the letter **g** even though in the base word the **g** is silent. Although this principle creates some spelling challenges, it is a benefit for reading new words, since an unfamiliar word can be associated with a word the reader already knows.

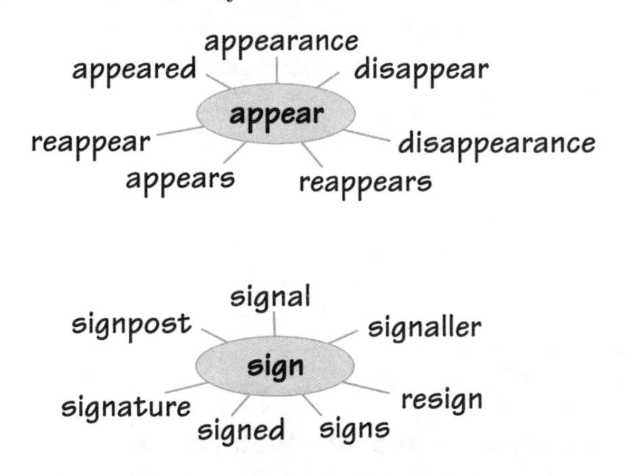

8. Students could fill in the missing letters with a different colour of ink to help retain the visual image for these features.

Dictionary Skills

1. Ask students to brainstorm idioms for other parts of the body.

foot	foot loose and fancy free; put your foot in your mouth
shoulder	a shoulder to cry on; shoulder the blame

Dictionaries devoted to idioms and expressions help provoke students' interest in the origins of words and phrases. Three we like are the *Oxford Pocket English Idioms*, the *Oxford Learner's Dictionary of English Idioms*, and *Go For It: Canadian Idioms.*

2. Some of the idioms that students may generate are: after my own heart, at heart, break someone's heart, by heart, have a heart of gold, have one's heart in the right place, a heart-to-heart talk, and lose heart.

Students may enjoy drawing the literal interpretation of some of these idioms such as 'my heart was in my mouth!'

Dictionary Skills

1. Idioms: Dictionary entries often include idioms or expressions. The following idioms all involve the word **head**.

Idiom	Meaning
go to one's head	make one conceited
hang one's head	be ashamed and show it
heads up	be careful, watch out
keep one' s head	stay calm

Complete each sentence with one of the expressions. You will need to adjust the words to fit the sentence.

hung their heads
Heads up
go to one's head
keep one's head

a) They ______ in shame when they were caught cheating.
b) ______ ! The principal's coming.
c) Don't let three wins ______ .
d) It's important to ______ when the game begins.

2. a) Brainstorm idioms or expressions related to the word **heart**. Check the dictionary when you run out of ideas.
b) Use four of these expressions in sentences.

168

ESL

Language Snapshot – Vietnamese

Vietnamese is spoken in Vietnam, as well as by some people living in Cambodia, Laos, and Thailand. Although many words are borrowed from Chinese, the grammatical structure of the language is different. Vietnamese is a tonal language, expressing meaning by using one of six tones.

Language Features

- Vietnamese has a complex vowel system, and words all have one syllable. In English, students meet words with more than one syllable, which may change in form depending on grammar (**go/went**).
- The consonant system is very different, and some students may have difficulty with /f/, /th/, /dj/, /sh/, and /ch/.
- The final /s/ and /z/ in plural nouns may be omitted in speech and spelling.
- Vietnamese spelling is completely phonetic—sounds are always spelled the way they are pronounced.
- There is no verb 'to be'. Time is often expressed through context using expressions such as **yesterday**, **today**, **last year**.
- Adjectives follow nouns and pronouns.

Exploring the Wilderness

1. Without electricity and running water, life would certainly be different. Make a list of all the things you might need if you were to live in a world without these modern conveniences. For example: wood stoves, fuel (wood or coal), a well or spring, hand tools, candles, etc.

2. Imagine you are living in the wilderness, far from hydro and telephone lines. Write a letter describing your life to a friend living in a modern city or town.

3. Proofread your letter. Check carefully to make sure your spelling and punctuation are correct.

169

Exploring the Wilderness

1. Have students create an idea web to explore the equipment and supplies they might need to live in the wilderness.

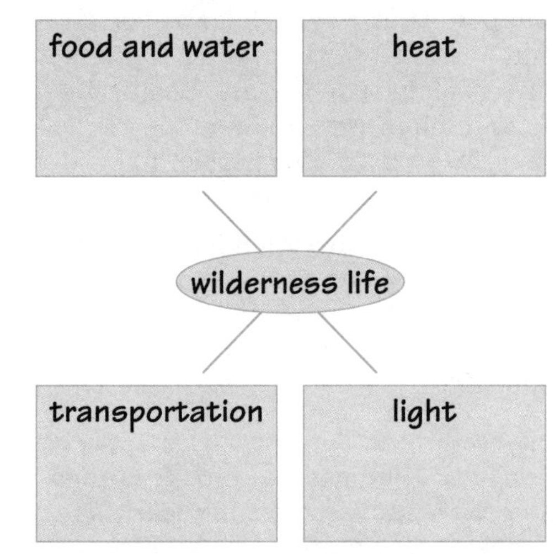

2. Encourage students to use the information they have collected in their idea web to write the letter. They may also wish to write a wilderness adventure story with the information.

Students might enjoy reading stories such as *Frozen Fire*, by James Huston.

3. Review proofreading strategies with students. Encourage them to exchange their draft with a partner and proofread each other's work carefully.

Proofreading Strategies

Editing a piece of writing involves much more than correcting spelling. When students are focussing on spelling errors, however, they should be helped to develop efficient proofreading skills. Your own experiences will probably confirm that proofreading your own work is difficult. There is a tendency to focus on meaning and to miss obvious spelling mistakes. It is useful, therefore, to have students regularly serve as peer editors for one another.

If you find that peer editors are missing too many errors, you might help them focus by using a peer editing form or rubber stamp. The categories chosen could reflect spelling patterns you have addressed in class. Having the editor sign the form also stresses accountability for the proofreading.

Grammar Power

1. and **2.** Many important verbs in English are irregular. Instead of adding **-ed** to make the past tense and the past perfect (I jump / I jump**ed** / I have jump**ed**), these verbs have a special form. Add to the list of verbs whenever a new irregular verb comes up in class. Challenge students to think of ways to organize the irregular verbs to make them easier to remember.

3. Remind students that each time a speaker changes, we need a new paragraph. Give them passages such as the following to punctuate with quotation marks, and then put in paragraphs.

> The police officer tipped back her cap. Are you on holiday here she asked. Yes, Anne answered. We've been here for nearly a week now. It was a great holiday, Sam sniffled, until this happened! Don't worry, said the police officer. I'm sure we'll get it straightened out, before your parents return.

Ugh!
I have just
eaten a bug!

Grammar Power

1. Special Verb Forms: Some verbs use a special form with the helping verb **have.**

Example: *They* ***eat*** *lunch everyday at 12 o'clock.*
They ***have*** *eaten all the apples.*

Match the verbs with their special forms.

fly	flown	written
be	been	gone
write	written	flown
go	gone	sung
speak	spoken	been
drive	driven	spoken
sing	sung	driven

2. Use some of the verbs above to complete these sentences.

a) She has _gone_ to Japan for the summer.
b) They have _spoken_ English all their lives.
c) We have already _been_ to that movie twice!
d) My sister has just _driven_ her new car around the block.
e) You have _sung_ that song so many times my head aches.

3. Writing Paragraphs: A paragraph is a signal to the reader. It means a change in speaker, or a new thought. Indent the first line of a new paragraph to show this change.

In the following piece of writing there are no paragraphs, and it is hard to tell who is speaking. Rewrite the piece, beginning a new paragraph each time the speaker changes.

> "Can you come to my house tonight?" José asked his friend, Fernando. "I don't think so," Fernando sighed. "Why not?" José wanted to know. "I have to look after my little brother." "That's too bad," José said. "I have a new video game I wanted to show you."

169a

Oral Language and Literature

- Challenge students to think of silly rhyming verses and poems to help them remember irregular verbs.

> I write, I wrote, and have written
> Then why
> Do I
> Bite, bit and have bitten?
>
> I shake, shook, and have shaken
> When I take, took, and have taken.
> So why
> Don't I
> Bake, book, and was baken?

4. Making Comparisons: Some adjectives have special comparative and superlative forms.

Word	Comparative	Superlative
good	better	best
bad	worse	worst
far	farther	furthest
little	less	least

Use these special forms and your own ideas to state your opinions.

a) I think tomato soup is _______ food, a chicken sandwich is _______ , and pizza is the _______.

b) I think rainy weather is _______ , a thunderstorm is _______ , and a hurricane is the _______ .

c) I have _______ interest in skiing, _______ in tennis, and the _______ in golf.

Proofing Power

Proofread the following paragraph and correct all the errors you can find.

On Wednesday, my friend Alycia and I went to her mom's office in the midle of the city. We pretended we had our own buisness and had fun riting letters to our clients in many countrys. We stayed untill lunchtime and then went to a nearby restrant. In all the excitement, I forgot to bring my wallet. I thoght I had bruoght it with me, but I must have left it at home. When the bill came, I wanted to diappeare! I made the decission right then and there that I'd never forget it agen.

middle/business
writing/countries
until/restaurant
thought
brought
disappear/decision
again

169b

4. In Unit 12, students studied making comparisons with adjectives, and in Unit 18, comparing with adverbs. In this unit, some irregular comparisons are studied.

Remind students that these comparative forms are commonly used and give many oral examples. Also remind them that **the** must be used before the superlative.

Have students work with a partner, using the adjectives in the box to state their own opinions.

Proofing Power

Suggest that students use the cloze procedure to isolate the spelling errors in the paragraph. This technique involves rewriting the correct letters and leaving a blank space for each incorrect one.

mid_le   bu_ _ness   _riting
countr_ _s   rest_ _rant

The advantage of the cloze procedure is that credit is given for what the writer knows, and the incorrect portions are pointed out for correction. Students can use this technique when editing a peer's work or marking a dictation, and teachers can make use of it in editing conferences.

Note that this approach is less effective when extra letters are added to the word, as in **untill** and **diappeare**.

Sharing the Secrets with Kids

Good, better, the best are adjectives, used with nouns.

*I'm a **good** runner, Jeri is **better**, but Sami is **the best** runner in our class.*

*If we are modifying a verb, we must use the adverb **well**, but **better** and **the best** remain the same.*

*I run **well**, Jeri runs **better**, but Sami runs **the best**.*

Teacher's Notes

Appendix

The 200 Words Most Frequently Misspelled

(based on a random sample of 3540 compositions written by adults as well as children in Canada)

about
accident
actually
afraid
again
all
almost
always
and
animals
another
are
around
away
awhile

back
bear
beautiful
because
been
before
began
behind
believe
better
bird
birthday
brought
built
buys
bye

came
can't
catch
caught
certainly
chases
children
climbed
come
coming
could
couldn't
cousins

decided
didn't
different
doctor
does
doesn't
dollars
don't

engine
equipment
especially
ever
every
everybody
everyday
everything
exciting

family
fell
few
field
finally
finished
fired
first
flowers
for
found
funny
friend

girls
going
government

happened
happily
having
heard
here
him
his
hole
home
horses
hospital
house

I'm
into
its
it's

just

knew
know

let's
like
lived
looked

met
middle
might
minute
months
mountains
myself

names
necessary
neighbour
next
no
nothing
now

o'clock
off
once
one
opportunity
others
our
out
outside

parents
parliament
people
picked
pictures
piece
place
pollution
practicing
pretty
probably

quiet
quite

really
receive
responsible
right

said
saw
scared
school
screamed
second
shoot
shot
situation
slept
so
society
some
something
sometimes
spotted
started
stepped
stopped
strange
summer
surely
surprise
swimming

take
than
that's
the
their
them
then
there
there's
they
they're
things
thought
threw
throw
to
too
tried
turned
two

until
upon

very

wanted
wasn't
went
we're
were
weren't
what's
when
where
without
wouldn't
writing

you're

The 200 Words Most Frequently Written

(in descending order of frequency)

the	go	after	started	made	thought
and	like	house	put	never	always
I	day	dog	old	here	bear
a	were	little	night	didn't	tree
to	out	from	has	want	wanted
was	up	could	your	right	place
in	his	mother	off	horse	yes
it	at	people	us	don't	really
he	him	into	around	car	eat
my	her	just	next	heard	last
we	be	over	other	called	left
of	get	see	well	why	oh
is	would	now	away	door	it's
you	home	or	fun	something	thing
they	not	school	three	take	another
on	some	their	cat	water	through
that	came	play	where	only	find
went	saw	an	Mom	long	say
when	if	by	told	morning	black
for	as	come	boy	five	run
so	because	big	Dad	make	gave
one	going	did	again	things	even
then	what	no	found	I'm	should
she	time	man	more	girl	best
said	will	am	nice	much	
but	very	good	friends	years	
there	do	too	way	bed	
had	down	once	think	lot	
me	them	ran	asked	look	
have	about	name	friend	four	
with	back	know	father	lived	
are	our	took	looked	many	
all	can	how	summer	fish	
got	two	who	first	new	

Bibliography

Avis, W. S., *et al. Gage Intermediate Dictionary*. Toronto: Gage Educational Publishing Limited, 1991.

Barton, Bob. "A Storyteller Comments: Highway Relish," in *Spelling Links* edited by David Booth. Markham, Ontario: Pembroke Publishers Limited, 1990.

Bear, Donald, Shane Templeton, Marcia Invernizzi, and Francine Johnston. *Words Their Way: Word Study for Phonics, Vocabulary, and Spelling Instruction*. Upper Saddle River, NJ: Prentice-Hall Inc., 1996.

Bradford, Karleen. *The Other Elizabeth*. Toronto: Gage Educational Publishing Limited, 1982.

Bradley, Lynette. "Organizing Sound and Letter Patterns for Spelling," in *Handbook of Spelling: Theory, Process and Intervention* by Gordon Brown and Nick Ellis. Chichester, England: John Wiley & Sons, 1994.

Burt, William Henry. *A Field Guide to the Mammals: Field Marks of all North American Species Found North of Mexico*. 3rd ed. Boston: Houghton Mifflin, 1976.

Calkins, Lucy. *The Art of Teaching Writing*. Portsmouth, NH: Heinemann, 1986.

The Concise Oxford Dictionary of English Etymology. New York: Oxford University Press, 1993.

Crooker, William S. *Oak Island Gold*. Boisbriand, Québec: Nimbus Publishing, 1993.

Cunningham, P. *Classrooms That Work: They Can All Read & Write*. Scarborough, Ontario: Harper Collins, 1994.

Funk, Wilfred. *Word Origins: An Exploration and History of Words and Language*. New York: Wings Books, 1950.

Gentry, Richard, and Jean Wallace Gillet. *Teaching Kids to Spell*. Portsmouth, NH: Heinemann Educational Books, Inc., 1993.

Granfield, Linda. *Cowboy: A Kid's Album*. Toronto: Douglas & McIntyre, 1993.

Henderson, Edmund. *Teaching Spelling*. Boston: Houghton Mifflin, 1985.

Houston, James. *Frozen Fire: A Tale of Courage*. Toronto: McClelland and Stewart, 1977.

Lederer, Richard. *Adventures of a Verbivore*. New York: Pocket Books, 1994.

——. *Crazy English: The Ultimate Joy Ride Through Our Language*. New York: Pocket Books, 1989.

——. *The Miracle of Language*. New York: Pocket Books, 1991.

——. *The Play of Words*. New York: Pocket Books, 1990.

Lee, Dennis. *Jelly Belly*. Toronto: Macmillan, 1989.

Lunn, Janet. *The Root Cellar*. Toronto: Penguin Books Canada Limited, 1983.

Maestro, Guillio. *What's a Frank Frank? Tasty Homograph Riddles*. New York: Houghton Mifflin Co., 1984.

McLay, Vera. *Idioms 1*. Hull, Québec: Public Service Commission of Canada, 1991.

——. *Idioms 2*. Hull, Québec: Public Service Commission of Canada, 1979.

McPartland, P. *Go For It: Canadian Idioms*. Scarborough, Ontario: Prentice Hall, 1994.

Moodie, Susanna. *Roughing it in the Bush*. The New Canadian Library, Malcolm Ross gen. ed. Toronto: McClelland and Stewart Ltd., 1962 (first pub. 1852).

Murie, Olaus Johan. *A Field Guide to Animal Tracks*. 2nd ed. Boston: Houghton Mifflin, 1974.

Oxford Learner's Dictionary of English Idioms. London: Oxford University Press, 1993.

Oxford Pocket English Idioms. London: Oxford University Press, 1993.

Parish, Peggy. *Amelia Bedelia*. 1st Harper Trophy ed. New York: Harper Trophy, 1992.

Phythian, B. A. *A Concise Dictionary of English Idioms*. Rydalmere, NSW: Hodder and Stoughton, 1986.

Rees, Nigel. *Dictionary of Word and Phrase Origins*. London: Cassell, 1994.

Schultz, Charles. *Happiness is a Warm Puppy*. San Francisco: Determined Productions, Inc., 1962.

Scott, Ruth. *Spelling: Sharing the Secrets*. Toronto: Gage Educational Publishing, 1993.

——. *The Student Editor's Guide to Words*. Toronto: Gage Educational Publishing Company, 1991.

Scott, Ruth, and Sharon Siamon. *Sharing the Secrets: Teach Your Child to Spell*. Toronto: Macmillan Canada, 1994.

Silverstein, Shel. *A Light in the Attic*. New York: Harper Row, 1981.

Swan, Michael, and Bernard Smith. *Learner English: A Teacher's Guide to Interference and Other Problems*. Cambridge, England: Cambridge University Press, 1987.

Tarasoff, Mary. *Spelling Strategies You Can Teach*. Victoria, BC: Active Learning Institute Inc., 1990.

Templeton, Shane. "Synthesis of Research on the Learning and Teaching of Spelling." *Educational Leadership*. Vol. 43, No. 6 (March, 1986).

Terban, M. *Hey, Hay!: A Wagonful of Funny Homonym Riddles*. New York: Houghton Mifflin Co., 1991.

Thorn, Elizabeth A., and Joan M. Irwin. *Handshakings. Expressways II*. Toronto: Gage Educational Publishing Company, 1988.

White, Robert J. *An Avalanche of Anoraks*. New York: Crown Trade Paperbacks, 1994.

Wilde, Sandra. "Understanding Spelling Strategies: A Kidwatcher's Guide to Spelling. Part 2," in *The Whole Language Evaluation Book* edited by Ken Goodman, Yetta Goodman, and Wendy Hood. Portsmouth, NH: Heinemann Educational Books Inc., 1989.

——. *You Kan Red This: Spelling and Punctuation for Whole Language Classrooms, K–6*. Portsmouth, NH: Heinemann Educational Books Inc., 1992.

Words that Count Women In. Toronto: Ontario Women's Directorate, 1992.

Teacher's Notes